T0213051

Lecture Notes in Computer Science　　10690

Commenced Publication in 1973
Founding and Former Series Editors:
Gerhard Goos, Juris Hartmanis, and Jan van Leeuwen

More information about this series at http://www.springer.com/series/7409

Nuno Nunes · Ian Oakley
Valentina Nisi (Eds.)

Interactive Storytelling

10th International Conference
on Interactive Digital Storytelling, ICIDS 2017
Funchal, Madeira, Portugal, November 14–17, 2017
Proceedings

 Springer

Editors
Nuno Nunes (iD)
Instituto Superior Técnico
Lisbon
Portugal

Valentina Nisi (iD)
University of Madeira
Funchal
Portugal

Ian Oakley (iD)
Ulsan National Institute of Science
 and Technology
Ulsan
Korea (Republic of)

ISSN 0302-9743   ISSN 1611-3349 (electronic)
Lecture Notes in Computer Science
ISBN 978-3-319-71026-6   ISBN 978-3-319-71027-3 (eBook)
https://doi.org/10.1007/978-3-319-71027-3

Library of Congress Control Number: 2017959623

LNCS Sublibrary: SL3 – Information Systems and Applications, incl. Internet/Web, and HCI

Printed on acid-free paper

This Springer imprint is published by Springer Nature
The registered company is Springer International Publishing AG
The registered company address is: Gewerbestrasse 11, 6330 Cham, Switzerland

Preface

This volume contains the proceedings of ICIDS 2017: the 9th International Conference on Interactive Digital Storytelling. ICIDS 2017 took place at the Madeira Interactive Technologies Institute (Madeira-ITI), Funchal, Madeira Island, Portugal. This year the conference included several categories and tracks such as workshops, demos, posters, a doctoral consortium, and an international art exhibition.

ICIDS is the premier annual venue that gathers researchers, developers, practitioners, and theorists to present and share the latest innovations, insights, and techniques in the expanding field of interactive storytelling and the technologies that support it. The field regroups a highly dynamic and interdisciplinary community, in which narrative studies, computer science, interactive and immersive technologies, the arts, and creativity converge to develop new expressive forms in a myriad domains that include artistic projects, interactive documentaries, cinematic games, serious games, assistive technologies, edutainment, museum science, and advertising, to mention a few.

The ICIDS conference has a long-standing tradition of bringing together academia, industry, designers, developers, and artists into an interdisciplinary dialogue through a mix of keynote lectures, panels, long and short article presentations, posters, workshops, lively demo sessions, and the art exhibition. Additionally, since 2010, ICIDS has been hosting an international art exhibition open to the general public. This year we inaugurated a new entry, the doctoral consortia, enabling PhD students to receive feedback on their ongoing research.

The review process was extremely selective and many good papers could not be accepted for the final program. Altogether, we received 88 submissions in all the categories. Out of the 65 submitted full and short papers, the Program Committee selected only 16 long papers and four short paper submissions for presentation and publication, which corresponds to an acceptance rate of 31%. In addition, we accepted 13 submissions as posters, and five submissions as demonstrations, including some long and short papers that were offered the opportunity to participate in another category. The ICIDS 2017 program featured contributions from 47 different institutions in 18 different countries worldwide.

The conference program also hosted three invited speakers:

Jay Bushman an award-winning producer and writer of transmedia and platform-independent entertainment. He was the Transmedia producer and a writer for "The Lizzie Bennet Diaries" and a groundbreaking video and social media modernization of "Pride and Prejudice" – the show won an Emmy Award for Outstanding Original Interactive Program and had over 70 million views on YouTube. He was the cocreator and co-showrunner of the sequel interactive series "Welcome to Sanditon." As a writer and producer at Fourth Wall Studios, Jay helped to create the Emmy-winning series "Dirty Work," and wrote and created the show "Airship Dracula." Jay has worked on interactive campaigns for properties including "Game of Thrones," "Silicon Valley," "Terminator: Genisys," and "Arrival." He has also worked as a writer and consultant for major studios and networks, including Google, HBO, Disney, Paramount, Bad Robot, and Lucasfilm. An innovator and leader in the transmedia community, he pushes the boundaries of next-generation entertainment. Jay was one of the original founders of the professional organization Transmedia Los Angeles (now StoryforwardLA), and one publication even named him "The Epic Poet of Twitter." Jay's keynote was on "Transmedia Storytelling: No, Really, What Is It?" The joke goes like this: "Put two transmedia creators in a room together, and pretty quickly you'll have three definitions of transmedia." Everybody who uses the terms means something a little different. With stories from the trenches of making transmedia projects over the last ten years, this talk delved into what people mean when they say "transmedia" and why nobody can agree.

The second keynote speaker was Pia Tikka, Adjunct Professor of New Narrative Media and a professional filmmaker. She is the principal investigator of the NeuroCine research project and has held a position as a director at Crucible Studio, Department of Media, Aalto University. In the field of naturalistic neurosciences, she has acted as a core member of the directory group of the neuroscience research project aivoAALTO at Aalto University. Her research in neurocinematics focuses on studying the neural basis of storytelling and creative imagination. She has contributed to neuroeconomics as a member of the advisory board of the NeuroService research project at the Laurea University of Applied Sciences, funded by Tekes, the Finnish Funding Agency for Innovation. She is a Fellow of Life in the Society for Cognitive Studies of the Moving Image. Currently, her research team NeuroCine applies neuroimaging methods to study the neural basis of narrative cognition. Pia's keynote was on "Systemic Second Order Authorship for Creating Complex Narratives – A Neurophenomenological Approach." In the beginning of the twenty-first century, the theoreticians of interactive narrative celebrated the birth of the creative audience at the corpse of the author, echoing Roland Barthes's words in *La mort de l'auteur* (1967). But this may have been premature. The notion of second-order authorship allows for the reformulation of creative authorship in a manner inspired by the neurophenomenology and systemic enactive mind theory by Francisco Varela and colleagues (1991). This was exemplified by describing the authorship of enactive co-presence between a virtual screen character and the viewer.

The third keynote speaker was Suzanne Scott, an assistant professor of Media Studies in the Department of Radio-Television-Film at the University of Texas at Austin. Her work has appeared in *Critical Studies in Media Communication*, *Transformative Works and Cultures*, *Cinema Journal*, and *New Media & Society*, as well as numerous anthologies, including *How to Watch Television* and *The Participatory Cultures Handbook*. Together with Melissa Click, she has co-edited *The Routledge Companion to Media Fandom* (2018), and her current book project considers the gendered tensions underpinning the media industry's embrace of fans within convergence culture. Suzanne's keynote was "Choose Your Own Adventure: Fandom and the Future of Interactive Storytelling." Fan culture has, from its inception, treated media objects as inherently interactive, playing in the textual gaps and margins and, in some cases, radically reimagining a storyworld's fictive limits. Tracing both the history of transformative fan texts (e.g., fanfiction, fan vids) from analog to digital participatory cultures, as well as the politics of these industrially unauthorized interactions, this keynote suggested that the barriers to embracing a more expansive conception of "interactive digital storytelling" lie in lingering anxieties surrounding authorial and commercial control. Just as scholarly work on interactive storytelling must acknowledge programmatic or structural limitations on user agency, even as we celebrate the participatory and collaborative capacity of the form, this talk explored how media industries, creators, and technologies alternately curtail and foster fan culture's interactive impulses.

In addition to paper and poster presentations, ICIDS 2017 featured a preconference workshop day with five workshops:

WS1: History of Expressive Systems, organized by Mark J. Nelson and James Ryan

WS2: Transmedia Journalism and Interactive Documentary in Dialogue, by Renira Rampazzo Gambarato and Alessandro Nanì

WS3: Authoring for Interactive Storytelling, organized by Charlie Hargood, Alex Mitchell, David Millard, and Uli Spierling

WS4: Bringing Together Interactive Digital Storytelling with Tangible Interaction: Challenges and Opportunities, organized by Alejandro Catala, Mariët Theune, Cristina Sylla, and Pedro Ribeiro

WS5: Film-Live: An Innovative Immersive and Interactive Cinema Experience, organized by Mattia Costa, Chiara Ligi and Francesca Piredda

In conjunction with the academic conference, the Art Exhibition of the 9th International Conference on Interactive Digital Storytelling was held at the conference venue, Vidamar Resorts, during November 14–15, 2017. The 2017 ICIDS Art Exhibition featured a variety of art pieces of interactive storytelling in various media including Web-documentaries, VR film, narrative games, augmented reality mobile applications, and Transmedia projects produced by over 30 artists of national and international origin. The exhibition's theme of "Time & Tempo" encouraged artists to explore the intrinsic qualities of interactive narrative as a time-based medium, user rhythms, and storytelling themes that incorporate history, time-travel, or other playful engagements.

Each submission was reviewed independently by three members of the selection jury, after which each submission received a meta-review analysis from the curators. Submissions were scored on a graded scale, which was averaged across all reviewers for the meta-review and final decision. The exhibition artwork is featured in the ICIDS 2017 ISBN numbered catalogue published by ETC Press.

We would like to express our gratitude and sincere appreciation to all the authors included in this volume for their effort in preparing their submissions and for their participation in the conference. Equally we want to heartily thank all the members of the Organizing Committee and the Program Committee. Thanks as well to our art exhibition jurors for their accuracy and diligence in the review process, our invited speakers for their insightful and inspirational talks, and the workshop organizers for the dynamism and creativity that they brought to the conference. A special thank goes to the ICIDS Steering Committee for granting us the opportunity to host ICIDS 2017 at Madeira-ITI in Funchal, Portugal. Thanks to you all!

November 2017

Valentina Nisi
Nuno Nunes
Ian Oakley

Organization

General Chair

Valentina Nisi   Madeira-Interactive Technologies Institute,
University of Madeira, Portugal

Program Chairs

Nuno Nunes   Instituto Superior Técnico, Lisbon, Portugal
Ian Oakley   Ulsan National Institute of Science and Technology,
Ulsan, Republic of Korea

Local and Communication Chairs

Deborah Castro   Madeira-Interactive Technologies Institute, Portugal
Cláudia Silva   Madeira-Interactive Technologies Institute, Portugal
Marko Radeta   Tigerwhale, PL, RS; Madeira-Interactive Technologies
Institute, Portugal

Doctoral Consortia Chair

Nuno Correia   Universidade Nova de Lisboa, Portugal

Demo Chairs

Paulo Bala   Madeira-Interactive Technologies Institute, Portugal
James Ryan   University of California, Santa Cruz, USA

Art Exhibition Chairs

Mara Dionisio   Madeira-Interactive Technologies Institute, Portugal
Rebecca Rouse   Rensselaer Polytechnic Institute, Troy, USA

Workshop and Tutorial Chairs

Nuno N. Correia   Madeira-Interactive Technologies Institute,
University of Madeira, Portugal
Sonia Matos   Madeira-Interactive Technologies Institute, Portugal;
University of Edinburgh, UK

Student Volunteers Chair

Vanessa Cesario   Madeira-Interactive Technologies Institute, Portugal

Steering Committee

Luis Emilie Bruni   Aalborg University, Denmark
Gabriele Ferri   Amsterdam University of Applied Sciences, The Netherlands
Andrew Gordon   University of Southern California, USA
Hartmut Koenitz   HKU University of the Arts, Utrecht, The Netherlands
Alex Mitchell   National University of Singapore, Singapore
Frank Nack   University of Amsterdam, The Netherlands
David Thue   Reykjavik University, Iceland

Program Committee

Elisabeth André   Augsburg University, Germany
Ruth Aylett   Heriot-Watt University, UK
Julio Bahamon   University of North Carolina at Charlotte, USA
Alok Baikadi   University of Pittsburgh, USA
Udi Ben-Arie   Tel Aviv University, Israel
Rafael Bidarra   Delft University of Technology, The Netherlands
Anne-Gwenn Bosser   Ecole Nationale d'Ingénieurs de Brest, France
Luis Emilio Bruni   Aalborg University, Denmark
Daniel Buzzo   University of the West of England, UK
Beth Cardier   Sirius-Beta.com
Marc Cavazza   University of Kent, UK
Fred Charles   Bournemouth University, UK
Fanfan Chen   National Dong Hwa University, Taiwan
Teun Dubbelman   Hogeschool voor de Kunsten Utrecht, The Netherlands
Gabriele Ferri   Amsterdam University of Applied Sciences, The Netherlands
Mark Finlayson   Florida International University, USA
Henrik Fog   Aalborg University, Denmark
Andrew Gordon   University of Southern California, USA
Dave Green   Newcastle University, UK
Charlie Hargood   University of Southampton, UK
Sarah Harmon   Bowdoin College, Brunswick, USA
Ian Horswill   Northwestern University, USA
Ichiro Ide   Nagoya University, Japan
Noam Knoller   Utrecht University, The Netherlands
Hartmut Koenitz   HKU University of the Arts, Utrecht, The Netherlands
James Lester   North Carolina State University, USA
Boyang Li   Disney Research, USA
Vincenzo Lombardo   Università di Torino, Italy
Sandy Louchart   Glasgow School of Art, UK
Stephanie Lukin   Army Research Laboratory, USA

Brian Magerko	Georgia Institute of Technology, USA
Peter A. Mawhorter	Massachusetts Institute of Technology, USA
Gonzalo Méndez	Universidad Complutense de Madrid, Spain
David Millard	University of Southampton, UK
Alex Mitchell	National University of Singapore, Singapore
Paul Mulholland	The Open University, UK
John Murray	University of California, Santa Cruz, USA
Frank Nack	University of Amsterdam, The Netherlands
Michael Nitsche	Georgia Institute of Technology, USA
Federico Peinado	Universidad Complutense de Madrid, Spain
Paolo Petta	Austrian Research Institute for Artificial Intelligence, Austria
Rikki Prince	Southampton University, UK
Justus Robertson	North Carolina State University, USA
Remi Ronfard	Inria, France
Christian Roth	Hogeschool voor de Kunsten Utrecht, The Netherlands
Rebecca Kane Rouse	Rensselaer Polytechnic Institute, USA
Jonathan Rowe	North Carolina State University, USA
James Ryan	University of California, Santa Cruz, USA
Emily Short	Spirit AI, UK
Mei Si	Rensselaer Polytechnic Institute, USA
Marcin Skowron	Austrian Research Institute for Artificial Intelligence, Austria
Kaoru Sumi	Future University Hakodate, Japan
Nicolas Szilas	University of Geneva, Switzerland
Mariët Theune	University of Twente, The Netherlands
David Thue	Reykjavik University, Iceland
Emmett Tomai	University of Texas – Rio Grande Valley, USA
Martin Trapp	Austrian Research Institute for Artificial Intelligence, Austria
Mirjam Vosmeer	Hogeschool van Amsterdam, The Netherlands
Stephen G. Ware	University of New Orleans, USA
Nelson Zagalo	University of Minho, Portugal
Jichen Zhu	Drexel University, USA

Demo and Poster Committee

Morteza Behrooz	University of California, USA
Melanie Dickinson	University of California, USA
David Elson	Google, USA
Max Kreminski	University of California, USA
Ben Kybartas	McGill University, Canada
Jo Mazeika	University of California, USA
Mark J. Nelson	Falmouth University, UK
Melissa Roemmele	University of Southern California, USA

Art Exhibition Jurors

Alex Mitchell	National University of Singapore, Singapore
Arnau Gifreu	University of Girona and University of Barcelona, Spain
Ben Samuel	UC Santa Cruz, USA
Hartmut Koenitz	University of the Arts Utrecht, The Netherlands
Maria Engberg	Malmö University, Sweden
Suzanne Scott	University of Texas at Austin, USA

Contents

Story Design

RheijnLand.Xperiences – A Storytelling Framework
for Cross-Museum Experiences   3
   Timo Kahl, Ido Iurgel, Frank Zimmer, René Bakker,
   and Koen van Turnhout

Effective Scenario Designs for Free-Text Interactive Fiction   12
   Margaret Cychosz, Andrew S. Gordon, Obiageli Odimegwu,
   Olivia Connolly, Jenna Bellassai, and Melissa Roemmele

Dynamic Syuzhets: Writing and Design Methods for Playable Stories   24
   Hannah Wood

Plans Versus Situated Actions in Immersive Storytelling Practices   38
   Sarah Lugthart, Michel van Dartel, and Annemarie Quispel

Location and Generation

Experiencing the Presence of Historical Stories with Location-Based
Augmented Reality   49
   Ulrike Spierling, Peter Winzer, and Erik Massarczyk

Developing a Writer's Toolkit for Interactive Locative Storytelling   63
   Heather S. Packer, Charlie Hargood, Yvonne Howard,
   Petros Papadopoulos, and David E. Millard

Level of Detail Event Generation   75
   Luis Flores and David Thue

History and Learning

Grimes' Fairy Tales: A 1960s Story Generator   89
   James Ryan

The Narrative Logic of Rube Goldberg Machines 104
   David Olsen and Mark J. Nelson

Cinelabyrinth: The Pavilion of Forking Paths 117
   Chris Hales

Verb+s Is Looking for Love: Towards a Meaningful Narrativization
of Abstract Content.   126
  Serena Zampolli

Games

Wordless Games: Gameplay as Narrative Technique   137
  Yuin Theng Sim and Alex Mitchell

A Framework for Multi-participant Narratives Based on Multiplayer
Game Interactions.   150
  Callum Spawforth and David E. Millard

Gaming Versus Storytelling: Understanding Children's Interactive
Experiences in a Museum Setting   163
  Marko Radeta, Vanessa Cesario, Sónia Matos, and Valentina Nisi

Emotion and Personality

Using Interactive Storytelling to Identify Personality Traits.   181
  Raul Paradeda, Maria José Ferreira, Carlos Martinho,
  and Ana Paiva

How Knowledge of the Player Character's Alignment Affect Decision
Making in an Interactive Narrative   193
  Mette Jakobsen, Daniel Svejstrup Christensen,
  and Luis Emilio Bruni

Thinning the Fourth Wall with Intelligent Prompt   206
  Rossana Damiano, Vincenzo Lombardo, and Antonio Pizzo

Virtual, Mixed and Augmented Reality

Who Are You? Voice-Over Perspective in Surround Video   221
  Mirjam Vosmeer, Christian Roth, and Hartmut Koenitz

Empathic Actualities: Toward a Taxonomy of Empathy
in Virtual Reality   233
  Joshua A. Fisher

Design for Emerging Media: How MR Designers Think About
Storytelling, Process, and Defining the Field.   245
  Rebecca Rouse and Evan Barba

Posters

An Interactive Installation for Dynamic Visualization
of Multi-author Narratives 261
  Caterina Antonopoulou

Factors of Immersion in Interactive Digital Storytelling 265
  Sebastian Arndt, Martin Ervik, and Andrew Perkis

Evaluating User Experience in 360° Storytelling Through Analytics 270
  Paulo Bala, Valentina Nisi, and Nuno Nunes

Towards an Interaction Model for Interactive Narratives 274
  Elin Carstensdottir, Erica Kleinman, and Magy Seif El-Nasr

Using Interactive Fiction to Teach Pediatricians-in-Training
About Child Abuse 278
  Grant P. Christman, Sheree M. Schrager, and Kelly Callahan

Interactive Imagining in Interactive Digital Narrative.................. 282
  Colette Daiute and Robert O. Duncan

Repetition, Reward and Mastery: The Value of Game Design Patterns
for the Analysis of Narrative Game Mechanics...................... 286
  Teun Dubbelman

Towards a Narrative-Based Game Environment for Simulating
Business Decisions 290
  Stanley Yu Galan, Michael Joshua Ramos, Aakov Dy, Yusin Kim,
  and Ethel Ong

What is a Convention in Interactive Narrative Design? 295
  Hartmut Koenitz, Christian Roth, Teun Dubbelman,
  and Noam Knoller

Interactive Storytelling for the Maintenance of Cultural Identity:
The Potential of Affinity Spaces for the Exchange and Continuity
of Intergenerational Cultural Knowledge 299
  Juliana Monteiro, Carla Morais, and Miguel Carvalhais

Applying Interactive Documentary as a Pedagogical Tool in High
School Level 303
  Valentina Moreno and Arnau Gifreu-Castells

Interactive Storytelling System for Enhancing Children's Creativity........ 308
  Kaoru Sumi and Nozomu Yahata

Open World Story Generation for Increased Expressive Range   313
  David Thue, Stephan Schiffel, Tryggvi Þór Guðmundsson,
  Guðni Fannar Kristjánsson, Kári Eiríksson,
  and Magnús Vilhelm Björnsson

Demos

Collisions and Constellations: On the Possible Intersection
of Psychoethnography and Digital Storytelling   319
  Justin Armstrong

Evaluating Visual Perceptive Media   323
  Anna Frew and Ian Forrester

Biennale 4D – Exploring the Archives of the Swiss Pavilion
at the «Biennale di Venezia» Art Exhibition.   327
  Kathrin Koebel, Doris Agotai, Stefan Arisona, and Matthias Oberli

Subject and Subjectivity: A Conversational Game Using Possible Worlds.   332
  Ben Kybartas, Clark Verbrugge, and Jonathan Lessard

The *AntWriter* Improvisational Writing System: Visualizing
and Coordinating Upcoming Actions   336
  Alex Mitchell, Jude Yew, Lonce Wyse, Dennis Ang,
  and Prashanth Thattai

Doctoral Consortium

How Interactivity Is Changing in Immersive Performances:
An Approach of Understanding the Use of Interactive Technologies
in Performance Art   343
  Ágnes Karolina Bakk

Interactive Storytelling to Teach News Literacy to Children   347
  Ioli Campos

Enhancing Museums' Experiences Through Games and Stories
for Young Audiences.   351
  Vanessa Cesário, António Coelho, and Valentina Nisi

That's not How It Should End: The Effect of Reader/Player Response
on the Development of Narrative   355
  Lynda Clark

Leveraging on Transmedia Entertainment-Education to Offer Tourists
a Meaningful Experience   359
  Mara Dionisio, Valentina Nisi, and Nuno Correia

Embodied and Disembodied Voice: Characterizing Nonfiction
Discourse in Cinematic-VR   363
    Phillip Doyle

Learning and Teaching Biodiversity Through a Storyteller Robot   367
    Maria José Ferreira, Valentina Nisi, Francisco Melo, and Ana Paiva

Authoring Concepts and Tools for Interactive Digital Storytelling
in the Field of Mobile Augmented Reality   372
    Antonia Kampa

NOOA: Maintaining Cultural Identity Through Intergenerational
Storytelling and Digital Affinity Spaces   376
    Juliana Monteiro, Carla Morais, and Miguel Carvalhais

An Epistemological Approach to the Creation of Interactive
VR Fiction Films   380
    María Cecilia Reyes

User and Player Engagement in Local News
and/as Interactive Narratives   384
    Torbjörn Svensson

Grammar Stories: A Proposal for the Narrativization
of Abstract Contents   388
    Serena Zampolli

Workshops

Bringing Together Interactive Digital Storytelling with Tangible
Interaction: Challenges and Opportunities   395
    Alejandro Catala, Mariët Theune, Cristina Sylla, and Pedro Ribeiro

Film-Live: An Innovative Immersive and Interactive Cinema Experience   399
    Mattia Costa, Chiara Ligi, and Francesca Piredda

Workshop Transmedia Journalism and Interactive Documentary
in Dialogue   403
    Renira Rampazzo Gambarato and Alessandro Nani

Authoring for Interactive Storytelling Workshop   405
    Charlie Hargood, Alex Mitchell, David E. Millard,
    and Ulrike Spierling

1st Workshop on the History of Expressive Systems   409
    James Ryan and Mark J. Nelson

Author Index   413

Story Design

RheijnLand.Xperiences – A Storytelling Framework for Cross-Museum Experiences

Timo Kahl[1]([✉]), Ido Iurgel[1], Frank Zimmer[1], René Bakker[2], and Koen van Turnhout[2]

[1] Rhine-Waal University of Applied Sciences, Friedrich-Heinrich-Allee 25,
47475 Kamp-Lintfort, Germany
{timo.kahl,ido.iurgel,frank.zimmer}@hochschule-rhein-waal.de
[2] Hogeschool van Arnhem en Nijmegen, Ruitenberglaan 26, 6826CC Arnhem, The Netherlands
{Rene.Bakker,Koen.vanTurnhout}@han.nl

Abstract. In the Rhine-Waal region of Germany and the Netherlands eight, museums would like to engage adolescents and youngsters in museum visits. Using digital media, visitors should be warmed up, thrilled and get involved in storytelling deeply connected to these museums. Therefore, the project partners of RheijnLand.Xperiences (RLX) are developing a framework and several implementations that allow employing storylines for cross-organizational museum experiences. The key aspect of innovation is the creation of a "continuation network" of partner locations, where the visit to one location leads to the desire to continue the experience at a next location of the network. Therefore, it is mandatory to have junctures between the museums in order to facilitate the continuation. Apart from storytelling methods, several other concepts are being examined, such as "hyperportals", "culture caching", using good practices like persuasive technology and theoretic notions like "blended experience", and "mixed reality". In order to achieve that goal, RLX makes heavily use of innovation and user centered development methods, such as design thinking, idea generation, co-creation, early prototypes, aiming at setting exemplary methodological steps.

Keywords: Museum visit · Cross-organizational · Continuation network · Interactive digital storytelling · Culture caching · Hyperportals · Co-creation · Design thinking

1 Introduction

The application of digital media technologies in cultural institutions is being discussed for several years. In the Rhine-Waal region of Germany and the Netherlands, eight museums will foster the engagement of adolescents and youngsters in museum visits. Using digital media, the visitors should be warmed up, thrilled and get involved in storytelling deeply connected to these museums and to the region. This is quite a challenge as the focus of the eight museums vary from modern art (for example Museum Arnhem) to archeology (like Xanten), with some in between (e.g. Schloss Moyland).

From 2017–2019, the museums will bring to life this ambitious goal, together with the universities of applied sciences Hochschule Rhein-Waal and Hogeschool van

© Springer International Publishing AG 2017
N. Nunes et al. (Eds.): ICIDS 2017, LNCS 10690, pp. 3–11, 2017.
https://doi.org/10.1007/978-3-319-71027-3_1

Arnhem en Nijmegen, regional tourist offices and Erfgoed Gelderland. The project is funded by the European Union in the framework of the Interreg programme, by public administrations and other participating partners.

The overall goal of the project is to develop a framework that allows creating story-lines for cross-organizational museum experiences. This requires a high grade of flexibility, e.g. with respect to integration of changing exhibitions in the story line and to different partner constellations (see Fig. 1).

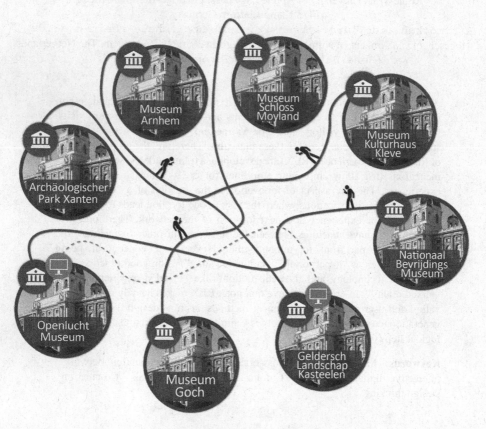

Fig. 1. RLX at a glance.

The key aspect of RLX' innovation is the creation of a "continuation network". A "continuation network" is a network of partner locations – here, museums, where the visit to one location leads to the desire to continue the experience at a next location of the network. This shall be achieved by creating a sense of completion by the follow up visit, and of corresponding incompleteness without the continuation visit.

Therefore, it is mandatory to have junctures between the museums in order to facilitate the continuation of activities. Apart from storytelling methods, several other concepts are being examined, such as "hyperportals", "culture caching", using good practices like persuasive technology and theoretic notions like "blended experience", and "mixed reality". A "hyperportal" is a short, meaningful integration of a glance into museum B, e.g. with Augmented Reality (AR), while visiting museum A, to promote curiosity and the awareness of the possibility to visit the other museum of the network. "Culture caching" is the activity of collecting (mainly virtual) cultural objects as part of the storyline and as additional motivation within a visit to a cultural institution, inspired by activities as geocaching, treasure hunting, and collectionism in general. Engaging and committing humans to particular actions is the core of persuasive technology [1, 2]. Maintaining the identity of the museums, and even strengthening it, is a main concern of the project. Blended experience is thus a strong requirement. A guideline to explore various mixtures of real and virtual experiences can be described in the Pine and Korn Multiverse with time, space and matter dimensions [3].

RLX also makes heavily use of innovation and user centered development approaches, such as design thinking, idea generation, co-creation, early prototypes, aiming at setting exemplary methodological steps. With this, we want to contribute to the development of methods in Interactive Digital Storytelling (IDS) that focus on the final user experience (UX).

2 State of the Art

Museums provide a favourite playground for IDS experiments due to the various facets of storytelling that occur in museums, such as "history", artist's "biography", the inherently personal approach to art, which can be transmitted through "personal stories", or the joy of "reporting" to friends and family of a museum experience. The CHESS project has studied several aspects of mobile technology, storytelling and AR for museum visits. Of particular interest are their experiments to promote social interaction in spite of individual devices, without making communication mandatory for the experience – an approach of high relevance to RLX, since we assume that many young visitors will come in small groups [4]. Kuflik et al. have researched the pre and post visit phase to a museum [5], in addition to the core visit; for RLX, the in-between visit phase is of particular relevance, which implies similar challenges. Zancanaro et al. reports on innovative uses of tangible devices to structure the museum visit [6] – for RLX, those insights will become important when we decide, for the experience in the inside of a particular museum, on how much shall happen on a mobile device, and on what shall be presented through dedicated, locally fixed interaction systems. In SPIRIT, following the lines of the older GEIST-project [7], Spierling et al. [8] have created a linear story experience based on georeferenced movies for a historical site; the notion of narrative, time and location dependent adaptation, employed GEIST (similar to [13]), is of high relevance to RLX, because the visitor retains much of his freedom to choose individual pace and path. But the authorial burden will probably be too heavy to adopt such a strategy directly in RLX. In SPIRIT, filmed sequences are employed (similar to [13], which uses rendered videos); RLX will rely on real time graphics, because of the advantages of real time behavior generation, the communication design opportunities of using more abstract virtual characters, and the easier authoring and adaptation to changes in the museums. Apps are already in regular use by many museums; top quality examples include the

Städel Museum in Frankfurt, where inspiring questions are part of the audiovisual guide [9], or the app of the Rijksmuseum [10] in Amsterdam, which already integrates presentations from different perspectives and a family oriented game, but no IDS.

Our work differs from the previous work through the concept of a continuation network, i.e. we are creating concepts, techniques and software to integrate several museums within a narrative and experience framework, where a satisfactory UX within a museum leads to the desire to continue the experience within another museum. Furthermore, we are systematically and extensively developing and employing user centred innovation methods, with design thinking as a core approach, to devise the most appropriate UX.

3   Requirements Analysis

As one of the first steps in the project a requirements analysis was performed and is still ongoing. The analysis is based on expert interviews with professionals of the participating museums and surveys of museum visitors. This leads to a set of business requirements which focuses on the overall goals of the solution. In addition, in its initial stage the project focusses on gathering user (stakeholder) requirements. The user requirements mainly apply to the storyline and are the basis for the implementation described in Sect. 5. In a next phase of the project we will specify these requirements in order to derive solution specific functional and non-functional requirements.

3.1   Business Requirements

In general, the framework should take into account the requirements of a heterogeneous audience. This might also lead to various implementations and can range from interactive games (or a set of games) for a younger target audience to interactive storylines based e.g. on a hero's journey story pattern for experienced museum visitors. In any case the storyline has to be adaptable in order to facilitate the integration of exchange exhibitions and different partner constellations. Further on, the access to the story and games should be possible from any participating museum. One of the most important business requirement deals with the integration of museum visitors. From the very beginning of the project, museum visitors will be invited to co-create the story and the concepts, following participatory design methods.

3.2   User Requirements

In addition to these generic business requirements we gathered a set of user specific requirements for museum visitors and the technical roles (e.g. system administrators). For the **museum visitors**, it was very important that the stories are context-sensitive and adaptable to the visitor's tempo and different routes within the museum. The UX shall be intensified by the integration of AR technologies. Especially in a cross-organizational scenario this offers a wide range of possibilities to interlink different museums, e.g. with hyperportals (cf. above). Tangible offers such as information kiosks and exhibits will foster UX and immersion, and the fusion of digital and tangible content. Further on, a navigation functionality should be included to find the most exciting and informative path through the museum. However, it should not be given too much information in order not to constrain the tension arc of the game or the story. Based on the interviews we assume that story and game play would function both with and without virtual characters; however, a fictional character will facilitate the realisation of flexible storylines.

Concerning the **technical roles** the key players of the participating museums highlighted that the editing of the storyline should be performed easily. Most interview participants mentioned that the application will be further maintained by professional users without extensive programming skills.

4 Framework Design

According to the requirements described in the previous chapter the technical framework supports different user groups. In order to accommodate completely different stories and flexible storylines (e.g. along a route which interlinks several museums), the framework must be flexible and modular, and it consists at least of the following fundamental components.

The **main component** ("story engine" in a wide sense) enables users, e.g. a director of a museum, to implement stories and to create storylines for different routes (see Sect. 5), e.g. inside a museum and also along several museums which are interlinked on a route. Using the main component authors can develop different objects, such as interactive games, quizzes, heroic journeys, "hyperportals" and integrate them into a story etc. They are able to create objects also for various target groups such as children and elderly people.

Visitors can interact with objects in museums, e.g. they can touch info-kiosks, exhibits, and sculptures. To include such tangibles in the stories and story lines, i.e. objects which visitors interact with along several stations inside a museum or on a route including different museums, a **tangibles component** will be provided.

Another basic component allows the **communication** with other points along the routes and enables visitors to **navigate** inside and outside the museums. Here, the technical communication e.g. of the "hyperportals", which are implemented in the main component and which lead visitors to the next location or supply information about the next point, could be realized.

The **administrative component** allows login mechanisms and realizes the technical link of the other components.

The framework allows the implementation of very different applications that encourage visitors to visit different locations 'along a story'. Due to its flexible and modular architecture it can also be used in other application areas where several locations are to be "interlinked".

5   Implementation of the Storyline

Methodologically, we currently follow a double top-down and bottom-up strategy of (i) employing innovation methods to devise desirable examples of story usage, with a strong emphasis on creativity and UX; and of (ii) structuring the conceptual design space, informed by narratology theory, in order to understand, on a higher abstraction level, the field of possibilities. I.e., on the one hand, we are using innovation methods, oriented by Design Thinking, for the methodic creation and testing of ideas; on the other hand, we are systematically devising the field of possible types of stories that could be employed for the task of creating a continuation network, and working on viable examples for each possible type, in order to find out the best possible narrative approach. Both directions, top down from a design space organization and bottom up from creativity and innovation techniques, nurture each other and shall lead to an excellent UX solution (cf. [12] on this method).

Among the many possible variations of story usage that we are systematically analyzing are a "motivation story" that motivates the collecting and the other activities, while the development of the storyline is only loosely coupled – the story of the extra-terrestrial curator, cf. below, is an example; a linear "unfolding story", where each activity step of the visitor unfolds another story beat of a linear or slightly bifurcating story, with a focus on suspense and identification with story persons; a "hidden story", where fabula and syuzhet[1] are separated and the visitor will discover "what happens". On different axis of the design space, we will find the possibility to break the story into pieces or perspectives and present only partial views that visitors could talk about to connect their experiences (cf. e.g. [12]); stressing on combining non-linearity and a computed story arc, thus focusing on individual adaptation and the potential of revisiting in order to experience variations.

As a first approach to employ stories to create a continuation network, Stefan Mann, director of museum Goch, has developed the narrative of a smuggler from planet Satorius, who travels to Earth with the task of smuggling works of art for a museum of his planet on the history of mankind in the last 20 centuries. The visitor plays the role of this smuggler and has the mission to collect works of art, which he can "dematerialize" with his/her device and send to the Satorius museum. In order to accomplish the mission, the visitor has to visit a series of the museums of the network. We employ this story as an initial frame for our test developments. The storyline itself, its conceptual perspective on IDS, and alternatives and variations are being examined independently.

We focus currently on scenarios with kids and young adults as individual experiencers. In future steps, collaboration within families and joint experiences will be examined as well. We assume that two different approaches might become necessary to accommodate the different needs of individual users of different age groups.

Our first test scenario assumes a persona of 12 years of age. Nic is the only child and visiting the art museum Goch with his parents. He enjoys the activities with his family, and is open and curious about the exposition; but playing smartphone games is more of

---

[1] The story events (fabula) and the way they are told (syuzhet).

his passion, and passive art contemplation will easily bore him. His parents want to introduce Nic to art, but also enjoy the visit by their own rights.

For the Nic persona, we have first to understand specific issues: (1) How much distraction is appropriate, and how does it influence the appreciation of the artworks? (2) How much does the "culture caching" task of collecting objects contribute to the motivation? (3) How is the family experience affected by the RLX-app?

We have developed the Elevator Man app to approach these questions (see Fig. 2), and to have a starting point for co-creation, active design participation sessions with kids visiting museums.

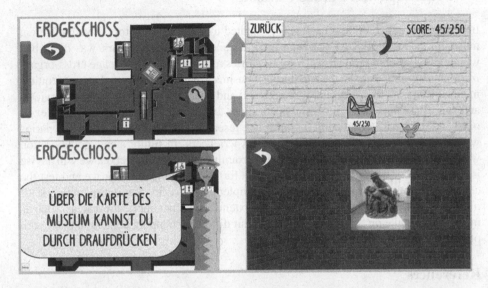

Fig. 2. Elevator Man. Counter clockwise: use of a talking virtual character in an assistance role (E-Man), of an orientation map, of mini-games, and of an exposition room for reward images.

This test app does not yet implement the full Satorius story, but employs its strategy of motivating the visitor to collect art items and curate (while avoiding the unattractive term) his/her own exposition with them. As a means of collecting an item, the user has to answer a question that requires discovery of the museum space and observation of the artwork, and has to finish a mini-game that is related to the artwork. The deployment of the software shall start in summer 2017, and interviews with visitors and co-creation gatherings shall occur latest in autumn.

Assuming a persona of 12 years, it seems appropriate to place emphasis on the entertainment aspects of the RLX-app, switching forth and back from a setting where the experience of the artwork is essential, to moments where the kid can play, communicate and move around, even if this means distraction, to a certain extent.

For young adults – 21 y/o, say, alone in the art museum, with genuine interest in the visit, self-motivated, but more used to digital media and lacking background knowledge – a quite different approach might be necessary. In this case, for an art museum, we expect that the RLX mediated experience will be more artistic by itself, in order to induce an appropriate state of mind that helps focussing on the museum experience, with the least amount of distraction from it, while at the same time conveying important background information. Thus, the function of storytelling becomes different and much more demanding in this second case. Several concepts are currently being discussed. For instance, we are examining how to employ a polyphonic approach for young adults who visit Beuys' Museum Schloss Moyland, where a story Beuys would enter into a dialogue with a hare, commenting on the museum visit and reproducing some of Beuys' art theories.

6   Conclusion and Future Outlook

In the present paper, an approach was presented to encourage visitors to visit different museums 'along stories'. For this, a modular and flexible framework was described which allows users to implement various stories and storylines to manage cross-organizational museum visits. In the RLX project business requirements and also user requirements concerning the storyline were gathered and analyzed based on expert interviews and surveys of museum visitors. First storylines and the app Elevator Man were developed and will be a starting point for our future research. Currently we focus on scenarios with kids and young adults as individual experiencers. In future steps, collaboration within families and joint experiences will be examined as well. Further on, we will devise innovative narrative concepts and implement further storylines to improve and test the cross-organizational framework and its implementation in the entire network of museums. Finally, the framework could be extended to other application areas, such as motivating people on "shopping tours" to visit different shopping centers in a network of cities.

References

1. Cialdini, R.B., Goldstein, N.J.: Social influence: compliance and conformity. Annu. Rev. Psychol. **55**, 591–621 (2004). https://doi.org/10.1146/annurev.psych.55.090902.142015
2. Fogg, B.J.: Persuasive technology: using computers to change what we think and do. Ubiquity (2002). https://doi.org/10.1145/764008.763957. Article No. 5
3. Pine, J., Korn, K.C.: Infinite possibility – Creating Customer Value on the Digital Frontier. Berrett-Koehler Publishers, Oakland (2011)
4. Katifori, A., Perry, S., Vayanou, M., Pujol, L., Chrysanthi, A., Ioannidis, Y.: Cultivating mobile-mediated social interaction in the museum: towards group-based digital storytelling experiences. In: Museums and the Web 2016, MW 2016, Los Angeles, USA (2016). http://mw2016.museumsandtheweb.com/paper/cultivating-mobile-mediated-social-interaction-in-the-museum-towards-group-based-digital-storytelling-experiences/. Accessed 15 June 2017
5. Kuflik, T., Wecker, A.J., Lanir, J., Stock, O.: An integrative framework for extending the boundaries of the museum visit experience: linking the pre, during and post visit phases. Inf. Technol. Tour. **15**(1), 17–47 (2015). https://doi.org/10.1007/s40558-014-0018-4. Springer
6. http://mw2015.museumsandtheweb.com/paper/recipes-for-tangible-and-embodied-visit-experiences/. Accessed 15 June 2017

7. Spierling, U., Grasbon, D., Braun, N., Iurgel, I.: Setting the scene: playing digital director in interactive storytelling and creation. Comput. Graph. **26**, 31–44 (2002). https://doi.org/10.1016/S0097-8493(01)00176-5. Elsevier

8. Spierling, U., Kampa, A., Stöbener, K.: Magic equipment: integrating digital narrative and interaction design in an augmented reality quest. In: Proceedings of International Conference on Culture and Computer Science, ICCCS 2016, Windhoek, Namibia, 25–28 October 2016, pp. 56–61 (2016)

9. http://www.staedelmuseum.de/de/angebote/staedel-app. Accessed 14 June 2017

10. https://www.rijksmuseum.nl/en/guided-tours/multimediatour. Accessed 13 June 2017

11. Ribeiro, P., Sylla, C., Iurgel, I., Müller, W.: STREEN – designing smart environments for story reading with children. In: Interaction Design & Architecture(s), ID&A, pp. 86–106. Springer, Heidelberg (2017, to appear)

12. Callaway, C., Stock, O., Dekoven, E.: Experiments with mobile drama in an instrumented museum for inducing conversation in small groups. ACM Trans. Intell. Inf. Syst. **4**(1), 1–39 (2014). https://doi.org/10.1145/2584250

13. Lombardo, V., Damiano, R.: Storytelling on mobile devices for cultural heritage. New Rev. Hypermedia Multimedia **18**(1–2), 11–35 (2012)

Effective Scenario Designs for Free-Text Interactive Fiction

Margaret Cychosz[1], Andrew S. Gordon[2(✉)], Obiageli Odimegwu[2],
Olivia Connolly[2], Jenna Bellassai[3], and Melissa Roemmele[2]

[1] University of California, Berkeley, CA, USA
mcychosz@berkeley.edu
[2] University of Southern California, Los Angeles, CA, USA
{gordon,roemmele}@ict.usc.edu, {odimegwu,oconnoll}@usc.edu
[3] Oberlin College, Oberlin, OH, USA
jbellass@oberlin.edu

Abstract. Free-text interactive fiction allows players to narrate the
actions of protagonists via natural language input, which are automatically directed to appropriate storyline outcomes using natural language processing techniques. We describe an authoring platform called
the Data-driven Interactive Narrative Engine (DINE), which supports
free-text interactive fiction by connecting player input to authored outcomes using unsupervised text classification techniques based on text
corpus statistics. We hypothesize that the coherence of the interaction,
as judged by the players of a DINE scenario, is dependent on specific
design choices made by the author. We describe three empirical experiments with crowdsourced subjects to investigate how authoring choices
impacted the coherence of the interaction, finding that scenario design
and writing style can predict significant differences.

1 Free-Text Interactive Fiction

Among the various benchmarking evaluations used in Artificial Intelligence
research, the Choice Of Plausible Alternatives (COPA) evaluation [9] is particularly interesting in its relationship to interactive digital storytelling. In each
item of this 1000-question evaluation, software systems are presented with an
English-language *premise* and two *alternatives*, and asked to select which of
the two is more plausibly the causal consequence of the premise (or in some
questions, its antecedent). In all questions, both alternatives are possibly the
next event in the narrative context of the premise, but only one is unanimously
judged as more plausible by multiple human raters. An example question from
the COPA development set is as follows:

Premise: I knocked on my neighbor's door. What happened as a RESULT?
Alternative 1: My neighbor invited me in.
Alternative 2: My neighbor left his house.

© Springer International Publishing AG 2017
N. Nunes et al. (Eds.): ICIDS 2017, LNCS 10690, pp. 12–23, 2017.
https://doi.org/10.1007/978-3-319-71027-3_2

Despite its simplicity, success on the COPA evaluation has been a challenge for researchers in both commonsense reasoning and natural language processing. For commonsense reasoning researchers, the broad-domain of the situations presented in the questions has proved to be difficult to tackle with formal modeling methods, as has the use of natural language representations. For natural language processing researchers, the problem is that COPA includes no training data for use with familiar supervised machine learning approaches. Indeed, the systems that have achieved success on the COPA evaluation have all employed unsupervised approaches that gather statistical information about how words co-occur in very large, broad-domain text corpora [1,3,4,9].

The struggles of researchers working on the COPA evaluation have much in common with those seen in interactive digital storytelling. Here, researchers continually strive to increase the agency and free-will of players, and provide authors with the technical tools to create interactive experiences across an increasingly broad range of narrative domains. As with COPA questions, the central concern is algorithmically determining *what happens next* as a consequence of a player's action. In addition, the goal to support rich agency in increasing open domains will be difficult to meet using formal models of fictional story worlds and their causal mechanisms. Noting the parallels between COPA and interactive digital storytelling, we began to explore whether approaches that performed well on the COPA evaluation could be used *directly* as an engine for interactive fiction.

To test this idea, we built the Data-driven Interactive Narrative Engine (DINE), a web-based platform for authoring and deploying textual interactive fiction. DINE scenarios are structured as an interconnected set of *pages*, each of which is a variant of a COPA question consisting of a *setup* and an arbitrary number of alternatives *(outcomes)*, which are automatically selected and shown as the causal consequences of the player's own free-text narration of their actions (the *premise*). For example, the previous COPA question might be transformed into a DINE page in the following manner:

(setup)	On his porch, I heard the football game on my neighbor's television.
(input)	>
(outcome)	My neighbor invited me in. We sat down to watch the game [...]
(outcome)	Through the window I could see him on his couch. [...]
(outcome)	With my ear to the door, I heard him cheering for his team. [...]
(outcome)	Returning home, I found myself locked out of my house. [...]

In this example DINE page, the player reads the page setup and types what they would do in the situation, e.g., I knocked on my neighbor's door. The system then processes the input as the premise of a COPA question, selecting and displaying the outcome that is most plausibly the causal consequence of the player's action. Authors can link these outcomes to subsequent DINE pages or to endings, allowing for arbitrarily complex branching storylines [7]. Alternatively, an outcome can be displayed without advancing the storyline, prompting the player to narrate another action in the same context. In these cases, DINE will select the next most plausible outcome that has not already been shown to the player. When the player feels that the shown outcome is incoherent, DINE provides a *huh?* button that replaces the outcome with the next one in the ranked list.

To automatically rank the authored outcomes, we used a top-performing COPA system that computes the average Pointwise Mutual Information (PMI) between words in the player's input and the first six words of each outcome, where the pairwise PMI statistics are computed by processing a corpus of millions of nonfiction personal stories from Internet weblogs [3]. Although other systems have demonstrated improvements on the COPA evaluation that are statistically significant [4], the differences are marginal, and not likely large enough to be apparent to players of a DINE interactive scenario. Instead, we believe that more substantive differences in the coherence of player interactions are going to stem from how the scenarios are written. Well-crafted DINE scenarios will have compelling setups that establish expectations about the space of possible outcomes, and compelling outcomes that adequately cover this space while advancing rich storylines. Coherence may furthermore be affected by how outcomes relate to each other on a page, or even by stylistic choices of the author in presenting the voice of the narrator and storyline characters. Rather than focus on technology, this paper explores how choices made by the authors of DINE scenarios can promote coherent interactive storytelling experiences.

We hypothesize that the coherence of the interaction, as judged by the players of a DINE scenario, is dependent on specific design choices that the author makes. In this paper, we describe our efforts to empirically investigate this hypothesis through a series of three large-scale experiments with crowdsourced subjects.

2   Scenario Design Patterns

We employed two full-time writers for ten weeks, tasked with authoring a collection of DINE scenarios for use in our experiments. During this period, these writers authored 100 new DINE scenarios, consisting of a total of 210 pages. Roughly half of these scenarios were single-page interactions, with the remainder consisting of four or fewer pages. The topics and genres of these fictional scenarios were left up to the authors, and included science-fiction adventures, psychological thrillers, romantic comedies, and skills-training situations. We encouraged the authors to explore the space of possible interaction styles afforded by the DINE approach, and conducted daily discussions of the merits of design decisions.

Several surprising design patterns emerged from the authors' creative efforts. We organized the design space along two dimensions, namely how the page outcomes were related to each other and how the page setup prompted players to type certain actions. With respect to the page outcomes, our writers made them either *order-dependent* or *order-independent*. Our initial intuition was that DINE writers should prefer order-independent outcomes, where the coherence of each outcome's text would be high regardless of which of the other outcomes had already been shown to the player. In this model, players might try a number of actions to move the story forward before transitioning to a new page. Crucially, none of these actions would change the current context enough to invalidate the coherence of other outcomes. An example of this design was seen in a page where the player is trying to stay awake while driving a cargo truck on the highway at night, as follows:

(input)   > I rolled down the window

(outcome)   As I rolled down the windows to usher in the night air, I felt disheartened. It was muggy out. Lukewarm and goopy like soup left untended and allowed to congeal. It settled around me, heavy, making me even more drowsy than before. The road swam, slow and sluggish, before my eyes.

(input)   > I drank my energy drink

(outcome)   As I gulped the energy drink down in long, greedy pulls, I felt hopeless. I had tried this before. Coffee. Five-hour Energy. Even caffeine pills once. It would work but only for an hour or two. [...]

(input)   > I finished my sandwich

(outcome)   Eating the sandwich only made me more drowsy. I felt it sitting heavy at the bottom of my belly. [...]

(input)   > I turned on the radio

(outcome)   The radio blared country music into the silence of the car. [...] It was all just a dull ringing in the air around me. My eyes kept easing shut and before snapping open again.

The interactive experience was much different on pages with order-dependent outcomes, i.e. where outcomes would only be coherent to the player if they had already seen one or more of the other outcomes on the page. This design pattern was frequently used by our writers to lead players through a specific sequence of behaviors, with each new outcome suggesting the behavior that the author expected next from the player. In this model, the text would often only make sense if the player was a willing participant — any creative deviations on their part would derail the writer's narrative. An example of this design was seen in a page where the player is exploring an empty house while dog-sitting for a neighbor, as follows:

(setup)   The dogs immediately rushed upstairs. I didn't want them to get into trouble or break anything else. I followed them up to the third floor. On the ground of the hallway was a shattered picture frame.

(input)   > I looked at the picture

(outcome)   Picking the frame up, I looked at the faded black and white photo of a family in front of the farmhouse. Mr. Larson had shown me the photo before. Henry sat on the porch with his two brothers and two sisters while their parents stood behind them. Sammy the dog began licking water off the hardwood floor.

(input)   > I wondered why the floor was wet

(outcome)   The hardwood floor hallway was wet, as if someone dripping in water had walked along the hall. The water stopped at the fourth room down the hall.

(input)   `> I went down the hall`

The strong order-dependence of the outcomes produces an interactive narrative that is essentially linear — the player's textual input only serves to advance the storyline to the next passage of written text. This model questions the role of (perceived) free-will in interactive storytelling, emphasizing instead a cooperation between author and player. The player's job is to figure out what text the author expects the player to type, and the writer's responsibility is to make it possible to do so given the storyline.

The second dimension in the space of page design patterns was how the page setup was written, specifically how it prompted the player to take certain actions. We observed three main types of setups in the pages written by our authors:

1. A **mystery** setup presents the player with some problem or puzzle that needs to be solved. The author expects the player to type actions that they believe will solve the mystery. Examples: *How do I get out of this locked room? How do I keep my teenage friends from starting a forest fire?*
2. A **decision** setup presents the player with a forced choice. The author expects the player to either choose one of the options, or gather more information to make the decision. Examples: *Should I tell my friend that she looks ridiculous in her new dress? Should I intervene when I see a parent harming a child?*
3. A **task** setup informs the player of exactly what they are expected to do. Examples: *I am in front of the queen and I am expected to bow. I just woke up and I am expected to do my morning stretches.*

The actual length of the setups written by our authors varied widely, from a single paragraph to the length of a chapter in a novel. Often the very long setups would include backstory and character development that was largely unrelated to the player's interaction. For example, the player may read the long, depressing tale of the protagonist's failed attempt to become a professional concert pianist, as setup for an interaction about a mysterious noise in the middle of the night. These DINE scenarios blurred the genre boundary between interactive fiction and traditional short stories, with the interactive component serving as an intermission in a linear text, rather than as a central focus of the work.

3   Authoring Experiments

Observing a broad range of scenario design patterns from the two writers, we sought to better understand the impact of these design decisions through a series of human-subject experiments. As a web-deployed application, the DINE platform affords the easy collection of player interaction data from crowdsourced workers on the Internet. We recruited crowdsourced workers to participate in three controlled experiments, each targeting a different set of scenario characteristics. In the first experiment, we investigated the effect of the type of setup (*mystery*, *decision*, or *task*), using 25 scenarios across these three categories as stimuli. In the second experiment, we explored the role of setup length and outcome structure (*order-dependent* or *order-independent*) with stimuli that manipulated these characteristics in multiple versions of the same scenario. In the third experiment, we manipulated the tense (*past* or *present*) and dialogue style (*narrated* or *quoted*), and further investigated whether these factors affected the player's own writing style, and whether this in turn affected the accuracy of the underlying model for selecting outcomes.

3.1   Experiment 1: Setup Type

We observed three types of setups in the scenarios authored by the two writers (*mystery*, *decision*, or *task*). Each type creates different expectations about what sort of text is likely to be entered by the player, and may respond differently to unanticipated or creative player input. Mystery-type setups place the fewest expectations on the player's actions, and require the author to anticipate a broad variety of potential actions when crafting the scenario. In decision-type setups, the player is expected to take actions that correspond to implicit or explicit options, and the author must at least provide appropriate outcomes for the range of choices. In task-type setups, the player is expected to do one thing only, and the author focuses on appropriately responding to this action. We hypothesized that the coherence of the player experience, indicated by the dependent variables of huh-rate and coherence ratings, is determined by the degree to which the author was required to anticipate player creativity, i.e. that mystery-type setups would yield the most coherent scenarios, and task-type setups the least.

For this first experiment, N = 393 participants were recruited from an online crowdsourcing service (http://www.crowdflower.com). All participants were self-reported American English speakers living in the United States at the time of the experiment. Each participant completed one interactive DINE scenario and was compensated $1.00 USD. Total participation time was no more than 8 min. A total of 2368 user inputs were collected. No demographic information was collected from participants in this first experiment. Participants were redirected from the crowdsourcing website to the online website that hosts DINE scenarios. Participants were told that they would be interacting with a computer to tell a story and were also told how to generate alternative responses via the *huh?* button when presented with incoherent outcomes. The interactive scenario ended when the player had reached a terminal outcome, or when all available outcomes had been presented. Data from all unfinished scenarios were discarded from analysis. At the end of the experiment, participants completed a post-questionnaire where they rated the coherence of the interaction on a five-point Likert scale, answering the question "How coherent was your story?"

As experimental stimuli, we selected 25 DINE scenarios from the pool of 100 scenarios authored by the two writers, distributed across three categories of setup-type. Mystery-type setups, where the player is presented with some

Table 1. Summary statistics for Experiment 1

Setup type	Coherence rating		Huh-rate
	Median	Mean (SD)	Mean (SD)
Mystery	4	3.66 (1.17)	0.19 (0.07)
Decision	4	3.59 (1.26)	0.20 (0.06)
Task	3	3.18 (1.20)	0.25 (0.11)

problem or puzzle to solve, were the most prevalent in these scenarios (N = 14). Decision-type setups (N = 5) presented players with a forced choice, and task-type setups (N = 6) told the player exactly what they were supposed to do.

Table 1 summarizes the differences observed in coherence ratings and huh-rate across the three setup types. As per our hypothesis, mystery-type setups produced the highest coherence ratings and lowest huh-rate, whereas task-type setups produced the lowest coherence ratings and highest huh-rate. We found that setup-type (mystery, decision, task) was a significant predictor for coherence ratings ($\beta = -0.61811$, p = 0.038), fitting a cumulative link mixed model (ideal for ordinal dependent variables). However, setup-type was not a significant predictor of huh-rate, analyzed using a generalized linear mixed effects model. Furthermore, we observed that our two dependent measures were not directly correlated in these 25 scenarios (cor = 0.05). To better control the individual factors that may determine these two measures in our subsequent experiments, we changed our approach to use multiple variations of a single DINE scenario as our experimental stimuli.

3.2 Experiment 2: Setup Length and Order Dependence in Outcomes

In Experiment 2 we examined the role of two additional structural characteristics that varied in the writers' scenarios, namely length of the setup and order dependencies in the outcomes. Our hypothesis was that longer setups would lead to more coherent interactions, as more text would afford more opportunities for the author to establish the goals and disposition of the protagonist; knowing who they were should help players know what they should do. We also hypothesized that DINE scenarios with order-dependent outcomes would be less robust to player creativity and more susceptible to failures due to classification errors, resulting in lower coherence ratings and higher huh-rates. Our approach in Experiment 2 was to experimentally manipulate these factors as independent variables, namely by having our writers craft four versions of a single scenario for use as stimuli in a 2×2 experimental design.

For the second experiment, N = 200 additional English-speaking America-residing participants were recruited from the same online crowdsourcing service. Mean participant age was 32.08 (SD = 10.66). Each participant completed one interactive DINE scenario and was compensated $1.00 USD. Total participation time was no more than 8 min. A total of 711 user inputs were collected. Participants were eliminated from the analysis for the following reasons: performed the experiment twice (second performance deleted) or completed demographic information but did not perform experiment. This left the analysis with N = 190 participants. Only N = 135 participants provided the post-hoc Likert-scale coherence rating. Participants who did not complete the post-questionnaire were not eliminated from the analysis in Experiment 2. Participants interacted with the DINE system as instructed in Experiment 1.

For stimuli, we selected a single DINE scenario, an absurdist psychological-horror story about a home invasion, as the basis for creating four experimental variations. Each of these four variations was created by the original writer of the scenario, with instructions about two dimensions of variation. First, we varied the length of the setup. Two variants were given very long setups of approximately 1,000 words, providing the player with a rich backstory about the scenario protagonist that details the difficult life events that preceded the night when a mysterious noise in her bedroom wakes her up. The other two variants provide only a brief setup of approximately 50 words, describing awakening to the sound of a mysterious noise. Likewise, we varied the order-dependence of the scenario outcomes. Two variants were written with high order-dependence, where each outcome was suggestive of the next action expected of the player. The other two variants were written with order-independent outcomes, where the outcomes would be coherent regardless of the order they were read by the player.

Table 2 summarizes the differences observed in coherence ratings and huh-rate across each of the two sets of variables. The results show higher coherence ratings for scenarios with a long setup and order-independent outcomes, and lower huh-rates for scenarios with a short setup and order-independent outcomes. The order dependence of outcomes was a significant predictor of coherence ratings ($\beta = -0.9530$, $p = 0.020$), fitting a cumulative link mixed model, but setup length was not a significant predictor. Neither setup length nor outcome order-dependence had a significant effect on huh-rate, as determined by a two-way ANOVA. Our analyses of huh-rate statistics suggests that it may be too coarse of a dependent measure for evaluating the impact of author design choices. We addressed this issue in Experiment 3 by conducting a more thorough analysis of the coherence of individual interactions.

Table 2. Summary statistics for Experiment 2

Variable	Coherence rating		Huh-rate
	Median	Mean (SD)	Mean (SD)
Long setup	3	3.43 (1.10)	0.25 (0.35)
Short setup	3	3.32 (1.23)	0.21 (0.32)
Order-dependent	3	3.14 (1.17)	0.20 (0.32)
Order-independent	4	3.55 (1.24)	0.26 (0.35)

3.3   Experiment 3: Setup Tense and Dialogue Style

In Experiment 3 we investigated how the author's writing style affected the coherence of DINE scenarios, specifically looking at the variables of tense (present or past) and the way that dialogue is written (quoted or narrated) in the setup and outcomes of a scenario. In traditional interactive fiction it is common to author scenario text in the present tense second-person voice, e.g. *You are in a maze of twisty little passages, all alike* [6]. In contrast, we observed that our two writers wrote DINE scenarios exclusively in the first-person past tense. Likewise, our writers freely mixed the use of quoted dialogue (direct speech) and narrated dialogue (indirect speech) when describing conversations between storyline characters. We hypothesized that these stylistic variations would be factors in the coherence of DINE scenarios, reasoning that players would adapt their own writing style to match that of the authors, and that these differences might affect the performance of the unsupervised text classifier that underlies the DINE software.

We investigated tense and dialogue style as independent variables in a 2×2 experimental design, using four variations of a single DINE scenario as our experimental stimuli. An additional $N = 200$ English-speaking America-residing participants were recruited from the same online crowdsourcing service. Mean participant age was 32.1 ($SD = 11.50$). Each participant completed one interactive DINE scenario and was compensated $1.00 USD. Total participation time was no more than 8 min. A total of 2536 user inputs were collected. All participants were required to complete the post-questionnaire in Experiment 3. Participants interacted with the DINE system as instructed in Experiments 1 and 2.

As stimuli, we selected a single DINE scenario as the basis for creating four experimental variations. In this story, the player is a school teacher struggling to deal with a male student who is both abusive and abused, written as a mystery-type setup with order-independent outcomes. Each of these four variations was crafted by the two writers, with instructions about two dimensions of variation. First, we varied the tense, writing two variations entirely in the first-person past tense (*"I stood nervously outside the principal's office*) and two in the first-person present tense (*I stand nervously outside of the principal's office*). Second, we varied the style of dialogue, with two variants with quoted dialogue (*"We do need to do something."*) and two with narrated dialogue (*He agrees with me that we do need to do something*).

Table 3 summarizes the differences observed in coherence ratings and huh-rate across each of the two sets of variables. The results show higher coherence ratings for past tense scenarios and narrated dialogue, and lower huh-rates for present tense scenarios and narrated dialogue. Fitting a cumulative link model we found that neither variable was a significant predictor of coherence ratings ($p > 0.05$), but observed a tendency for the variable of dialogue ($\beta = -0.4455$, $p = 0.0781$). Specifically, a negative beta coefficient for quoted dialogue indicates that as quoted dialogue is used, the coherency ratings decrease. Analysis of variance (two-way ANOVA) showed a significant effect for the dialogue variable on huh-rate ($F(1,211) = 11.1375$, $p < 0.001$) but not for tense.

Table 3. Summary statistics for Experiment 3

Variable	Coherence rating		Huh-rate
	Median	Mean (SD)	Mean (SD)
Past tense	3	3.36 (1.15)	0.27 (0.20)
Present tense	3	3.22 (1.29)	0.25 (0.26)
Quoted dialogue	3	3.16 (1.21)	0.32 (0.29)
Narrated dialogue	4	3.45 (1.20)	0.20 (0.23)

Effect of Writing Style on Player's Language Use. Given the significant effect of dialogue type on huh-rate and a tendency in that direction for coherence rating, we conducted two additional analyses to determine (1) if the type of dialogue the authors used affected user dialogue choice and (2) if story tense affected the tense that users chose. To conduct this analysis, user inputs from Experiment 3 were hand-annotated by a single annotator with formal training as a linguist. This set was first filtered to remove user inputs that were unintelligible or not narrative text (N = 200), as well as inputs for which there was no possible coherent outcome in the stimuli scenarios (N = 588). The remaining inputs were annotated for tense (present or past) and dialogue style (narrated or quoted). Some player inputs had ambiguous tense (N = 1,087) or did not contain dialogue (N = 246) and were discarded from analysis. This resulted in N = 1,500 examples of user input for dialogue analysis and N = 661 for tense analysis.

Analyzing this data by fitting binary logistic regression models, we found that the writer's choice of tense was a strong predictor of the user's choice of tense ($\beta = 0.5590$, p < 0.0001), and that the writer's choice of dialogue style was a strong predictor of the user's choice of dialogue style ($\beta = 2.1508$, p < 0.0001).

Effect of Player's Language Use on Classification Accuracy. Given the effect of scenario tense and dialogue style on the player's language use, we next investigated whether these language characteristics affected the performance of the underlying model that is used to select outcomes, described in Sect. 1. To conduct this analysis, Experiment 3 user inputs were hand-annotated with the scenario outcome that constituted the most coherent response, as judged by a single annotator trained as a linguist, and compared with the outcome actually selected by the underlying DINE text classifier. All user inputs from the previous analysis were annotated, with the addition of those interactions labeled as having no dialogue or ambiguous tense (these were eliminated in the previous analysis). This resulted in a total of N = 1,742 user inputs, each assigned to one of three dialogue style classes (no dialogue, narrated dialogue, or quoted dialogue), one of three tense classes (ambiguous tense, present tense, or past tense), and the correctness of its classification.

A binary logistic regression was fit to predict the classification (correct or incorrect) with the predictors of tense and dialogue style. Dialogue style was a significant predictor ($\beta = 0.6240$, p = 0.0217), where an incorrect classification is more likely for user input of the no dialogue class. Tense showed an insignificant effect ($\beta = 0.5863$, p $= 0.0847$) with a tendency for present-tense input to predict incorrect classifications.

In summary, Experiment 3 identified a significant effect of the author's dialogue style on huh-rate and a tendency in that direction for coherence rating. Together, the two subsequent analyses hint at the causal mechanisms involved. We see that players are likely to match the author's dialogue style and tense when typing their intentions into DINE scenarios, and that players' choice of dialogue style has a significant effect on the ability of the underlying model to select the most appropriate outcome (bias against no dialogue), and a tendency for tense, as well (bias against present tense).

4   Discussion

From the player's perspective, interactions with DINE are not markedly different from previous free-text interactive digital storytelling prototypes. From the author's perspective, however, DINE greatly reduces the amount of development effort required to successfully process natural language player input. Previously, language processing pipelines have required knowledge-based parsers backed by rich domain models [5,8], or the collection and annotation of copious amounts of player input for use as training data [2,12]. In many ways, DINE resembles recent attempts at case-based interactive digital storytelling [10,11], where large corpora of narrative texts are used to make predictions about what happens as a result of the player's actions. DINE differs from these systems in the way that text corpora are exploited; instead of assembling new stories from multitudes of contributing authors, DINE uses corpus statistics to select its contributions from those written by a single author. DINE removes the technical aspects of language processing from the authoring process, shifting the focus toward the more familiar task of telling good stories.

From a research perspective, the ability to rapidly author new scenarios affords new opportunities for empirical evaluations, where variations in the scenario are the experimental manipulation. Experimental manipulations with large subject pools are uncommon in interactive storytelling research precisely because of high scenario development costs, in both time and expertise. By reducing these costs, we made a number of new findings concerning free-text interactive fiction. We found setup type, outcome order-dependence, and (possibly) dialogue style were predictors of the coherence of player's interactions. We found that players match the writing style of authors with respect to tense and dialogue style, and that these changes were predictive of the performance of the underlying model for selecting outcomes. These findings provide guidance to future authors of DINE scenarios, and encourage future exploration of novel designs and algorithms that further support free-text interaction in interactive digital storytelling.

Acknowledgments. This material is based upon work supported by the National Science Foundation under Grant No. 1560426. The projects or efforts depicted were or are sponsored by the U.S. Army. The content or information presented does not necessarily reflect the position or the policy of the Government, and no official endorsement should be inferred.

References

1. Goodwin, T., Rink, B., Roberts, K., Harabagiu, S.: UTDHLT: COPACETIC system for choosing plausible alternatives. In: Proceedings of the 6th International Workshop on Semantic Evaluation (SemEval 2012), Montreal, Canada (2012)
2. Gordon, A., van Lent, M., van Velsen, M., Carpenter, P., Jhala, A.: Branching storylines in virtual reality environments for leadership development. In: Proceedings of the Sixteenth Innovative Applications of Artificial Intelligence Conference (IAAI-2004), San Jose, CA (2004)
3. Gordon, A.S., Bejan, C., Sagae, K.: Commonsense causal reasoning using millions of personal stories. In: Proceedings of the Twenty-Fifth Conference on Artificial Intelligence (AAAI-2011), San Francisco, CA (2011)
4. Luo, Z., Sha, Y., Zhu, K.Q., Hwang, S.W., Wang, Z.: Commonsense causal reasoning between short texts. In: 15th International Conference on Principles of Knowledge Representation and Reasoning (KR-2016), Cape Town, South Africa (2016)
5. Mateas, M., Stern, A.: Integrating plot, character and natural language processing in the interactive drama facade. In: Proceedings of Technologies for Interactive Digital Storytelling and Entertainment (TIDSE), Darmstadt, Germany (2003)
6. Montfort, N.: Twisty Little Passages: An Approach to Interactive Fiction. MIT Press, Cambridge (2003)
7. Packard, E.: The Cave of Time. Bantum Books, New York (1979)
8. Rickel, J., Marsella, S., Gratch, J., Hill, R., Traum, D.R., Swartout, W.: Toward a new generation of virtual humans for interactive experiences. IEEE Intell. Syst. **17**, 32–38 (2002)
9. Roemmele, M., Bejan, C., Gordon, A.: Choice of plausible alternatives: an evaluation of commonsense causal reasoning. In: Proceedings of the AAAI Spring Symposium on Logical Formalizations of Commonsense Reasoning, Stanford University (2011)
10. Roemmele, M., Gordon, A.S.: Creative help: a story writing assistant. In: Schoenau-Fog, H., Bruni, L.E., Louchart, S., Baceviciute, S. (eds.) ICIDS 2015. LNCS, vol. 9445, pp. 81–92. Springer, Cham (2015). https://doi.org/10.1007/978-3-319-27036-4_8
11. Swanson, R., Gordon, A.S.: Say anything: using textual case-based reasoning to enable open-domain interactive storytelling. ACM Trans. Interact. Intell. Syst. **2**(3), 16:1–16:35 (2012)
12. Traum, D., et al.: New dimensions in testimony: digitally preserving a holocaust survivor's interactive storytelling. In: Schoenau-Fog, H., Bruni, L.E., Louchart, S., Baceviciute, S. (eds.) ICIDS 2015. LNCS, vol. 9445, pp. 269–281. Springer, Cham (2015). https://doi.org/10.1007/978-3-319-27036-4_26

Dynamic Syuzhets: Writing and Design Methods for Playable Stories

Hannah Wood[(✉)]

School of Writing, Falmouth University, Penryn, UK
hannah.wood@falmouth.ac.uk

Abstract. The holodeck vision of the future of Interactive Digital Storytelling (IDS) assumes a world that reacts around players as *story protagonists*; but, we have seen how this approach faces challenges in negotiating the delivery of narrative affect and player agency within current technological and Artificial Intelligence (AI) realities. By approaching the field through creative writing practice, this paper argues that casting players as *experience*—rather than *story*—*protagonists*, has proved an effective alternate means of writing and designing for Playable Stories. Through close analysis of the growing Story Exploration Game genre and comparison with interactive theatre, four new terms—the *dynamic syuzhet*, *authored fabula*, *fixed syuzhet* and *improvised fabula*—are introduced to show how writing and designing for players as *experience protagonists* can negotiate the needs of narrative and player agency, provide means to combine *mimetic* and *diegetic* player experiences, pair *self-directed* and *empathic* engagement, and offer opportunities to use *dramatic irony*—a cornerstone of narrative drive in other storytelling forms that is unexploited in interactive storytelling. The study that formed the basis of this paper was driven by the question of how writers can develop practice within the current constraints of the form and informed the development of my own indie video game *Underland*.

Keywords: Playable stories · Creative writing · Video games · Story Exploration Games · Interactive theatre · Immersive theatre · Dynamic syuzhet · Fixed syuzhet · Improvised fabula · Authored fabula · Dramatic irony · Experience protagonists · Experiential narratives · Interactive narrative design · Interactive storytelling · Players · Player agency · Player roles · Mimetic · Diegetic · Narratology

1 Introduction

Interactive Digital Storytelling (IDS) has long struggled with the issue of how to negotiate narrative and player agency. In *Hamlet on the Holodeck* [1], Murray proposed one future as the *holodeck*, a digital simulation players can enter and have adapt around them as *story protagonists*. The science fiction thriller TV series *Westworld* [2] represents that futuristic 'idyll' in its Western-themed amusement park populated by robots indistinguishable from real humans. Though IDS is a wide-ranging field, the vision of the holodeck has been adopted as the form's holy grail. This is evident in the predominant characterization of players as *story protagonists* in video games, the volume of research into how AI can shape worlds around players, and Chris Crawford's citation of AI-based,

N. Nunes et al. (Eds.): ICIDS 2017, LNCS 10690, pp. 24–37, 2017.
https://doi.org/10.1007/978-3-319-71027-3_3

one-act, interactive drama *Façade* [3] as the "one piece of software that we can all agree comprises genuine interactive storytelling" [4]. There is cutting edge work being done to find the future of computer-generated narrative experiences;[1] but this paper takes an alternate approach through the lens of creative writing in a bid to ask how writers can create a sustainable practice within current technological realities? In this it argues that casting players as protagonists of the *experience*, rather than of the *story*—an approach that is becoming increasingly sophisticated in the growing Story Exploration Game genre—can deliver interactive experiences that respond to calls for more complex emotional experiences and difficult themes, whilst also overcoming criticisms of railroading, shoot-first-talk-later, real-time storytelling, entitlement simulators and cutscenes in video games. This conclusion was arrived at through close analysis of the Story Exploration Game form, interviews with video game creators, my own writing practice and the development of a script for video game *Underland* [5]. After outlining some of the current challenges and limitations, this paper will explore the opportunities that arise out of constraints and why an approach with players at the centre of the experience, rather than the story, can be a powerful way to negotiate the delivery of narrative affect and player agency.

2   Chasing the AI Dragon

2.1   Processing Emotional Complexity

Crawford's famous 1992 'Dragon Speech' [6] called for video games that express the breadth of human emotion and experience, and combine interactivity and narrative affect. At ICIDS 2015, he claimed the dragon had still had not been slain because those chasing a holodeck dream have focused on putting human reality inside a machine, endowing computers with the human capabilities of processing the complex emotional responses that give stories their power [4]. Current AI has difficulty modelling complex human experiences—like love, friendship, jealousy or betrayal—in numbers and systems without being necessarily reductive, and so struggles to cope with unexpected player input. It is much easier for computers to simulate the physics of objects hitting each other. As a result, there is a prevalence of video games with physics-based structures, like shooters and puzzle games, rather than those which focus on the more intimate details of life. As game designer, AI researcher and neuroscientist, Demis Hassabis, argues:

> There's a reason why games have evolved in the direction of shooters. You're not going to have a conversation. You're not going to show any emotions. You just have to shoot them [...] I promised myself I would come back to games once I had done something with AI. What would it really be like to have characters who understand emotions and motivation? That's when games will come into their own [7].

Hassabis's bid to uncover the neural coding, or 'algorithms,' that process memory and imagination in the brain is part of a drive to create digital characters with realistic

---

[1] At the Institute for Creative Technologies at USC and The Centre for Games and Playable Media at UC Santa Cruz to name a couple of places.

emotions. AI characters who can remember what has happened and project future possibilities have the potential to realize the ambition of the holodeck: a virtual world we can enter as players and will react authentically to whatever we do without the need for content to be pre-scripted. *The Sims* [8] is the oft-cited example of an effective *emergent narrative* experience but studies have found that it does not produce "consistently interesting" or "well formed" stories [9]. As has also been noted, rules systems author experiences and inculcate narrative affects and *The Sims* can be "understood as a subtle system for spreading the ideology of corporative late capitalism" [10]. Solving AI-complete may realize the holodeck in the future, but we are not there yet and must remain cognizant of the narrative affects algorithms encode.

2.2 Entitlement Simulators

The AI approach to designing playable stories is linked to casting players as *story protagonists* in a world that shapes around their choices. Early rhetoric in the field of interactivity was triumphalist about its potential to deliver player freedom, to kick back at the 'hegemony of narrative' and let players author and control their own stories. This concept of player freedom and control is contentious since it is questionable how 'free' of constraint one can be when operating within any system, and is perhaps why many games reflect on this theme. As Murray argues:

> Players can only act within the possibilities that have been established by the writing and programming […] unless the imaginary world is nothing more than a costume trunk of empty avatars, all of the interactor's possible performances will have been called into being by the originating author […] The interactor is not the author of the digital narrative, although the interactor can experience one of the most exciting aspects of artistic creation—the thrill of exerting power over enticing and plastic materials. This is not authorship but agency [1].

Interactivity is the interplay between agency and responsiveness, rather than an offer of complete power or 'freedom,' and video games have been fairly critiqued as "entitlement simulators" repeatedly offering players the ability to dominate and win the game [11]. Convincing players they are powerful, and that by playing right they will win, obscures the fact they are not in control of the narrative. The prevalence of heroic player roles is—as Jayanth argues—a limited use of agency and player subjectivity that restricts the development of the form [11]. The call to design worlds around players as *story protagonists* plays into power fantasies rare in other art forms where characters do not get what they want all the time [11]. Exploring other forms of player-protagonism, rather than recycling heroic protagonism, is a means of diversifying what games offer.

2.3 Real-Time, Railroading and Cutscenes

Technological obstacles in the form have also borne other well-known problems for digital games when players are the nexus on which the story, plot and narrative turns. Real-time storytelling and immersion in continuous 3D space, to maintain an illusion that players are present and in control of what unfolds, can lead to undramatic sequences with players wandering around space trying to work out what to do next. Jumps cuts, as used in *Virginia* [12], are one answer that can maintain drama but raise another associated problem of player presence as story protagonist: 'railroading,' forcing players to jump through narrative hoops to create dramatic tension and achieve game goals. *The Stanley Parable* [13] turned this critique into an existential, in-game joke that comments on how players are always defined by the game system, rather than their own free will. Another stalwart, the cutscene, forces players to put down their controllers to watch expositional sequences that cannot be achieved in gameplay because Player Characters cannot yet converse freely with Non-Player Characters (NPCs). These techniques—real-time, railroading and cutscenes—all receive complaints of breaking player immersion in both narrative and gameplay and are directly related to the assumption of players as *story protagonists*.

3   Player Engagement

3.1   Goal-Directed and Empathic

I am taking the time to outline known challenges IDS faces because they are obstacles contemporary writers and creators must traverse. This background also helps make sense of why Story Exploration Games use other devices to negotiate narrative and player agency. Lankoski's research identifies two types of engagement with characters in computer games—*goal-related* and *empathic* [14], which is analogous to Ryan's distinction between *self-directed* and *empathetic* engagement [15]. Lankoski categorizes goal-related engagement as an 'I' experience, where players act to reach their own goals; and empathic engagement as being about identification with 'Others,' through *recognition*, *alignment* and *allegiance* with characters. He then argues that cognitive overload from the constant stimulation of goal-related demands can reduce empathic engagement. When players are *story protagonists* they have a self-directed 'I' experience, where demands for action can stress motor skills and limit the emotional palette of expression and engagement. Meretzky [16] has also expressed reservations that a character can reveal an inner self when controlled by a player and Frasca [17] argued "the more freedom the player is given, the less personality the character will have." The danger is a reduction in empathic engagement, one of the cornerstones of narrative affect in other storytelling forms. If a playable story lacks the ability to generate empathy it follows that it might suffer in its attempts to deliver an emotionally complex narrative experience. This is not to argue you can never have empathic engagement in 'I' experiences (*Tomb Raider* [18] and *Life Is Strange* [19] are examples of it happening), but it does suggest that it is often diminished: (1) by the goal-related, high cognitive load in these types of games and demand for action; (2) by the difficulty of expressing a recognizable self outside of the player via a character constructed through the decisions of players; and (3) because current AI cannot yet power a virtual world that responds with the emotional complexity and authenticity of the real world.

3.2   Mimetic and Diegetic Player Experiences

Useful terms to distinguish between 'I' and 'Other' engagement are *mimetic* and *diegetic player experiences*, using them to classify how the story is experienced—the *experiential narrative*—rather than how it is presented [20]. When players are story protagonists they have a *mimetic experience*; and when they are not at the narrative centre but a story is uncovered as they play, it is a *diegetic experience*. Video games do not, however, limit themselves to these poles and also blend the *mimetic* and *diegetic*.[2] In the Story Exploration Game *Firewatch* [22], for example, players enact the role of Hank, escaping marriage responsibilities by manning a firewatch tower. This *mimetic experience* is mechanic lite and avoids stressing players with goal-directed demands that might shut down the ability to process other characters' stories. The game plays on what Jenkins terms the *evoked narrative* [23] of 'man alone in vast wilderness' to tap into players' collective narrative unconscious and suggest danger is imminent. It then intensifies that through shadowy figures watching from precipices, disappearing teenagers, ransacked towers and a strange surveillance station monitoring his radio communications. Relying on video games' propensity for science fiction conspiracy plots, a story of abducted or murdered teens and a nefarious government organization researching UFOs and aliens gets implied. This is all subverted by the *diegetic experience* where players (as Hank) uncover the tragedy of previous firewatch Ned, a war veteran with PTSD, whose 12-year-old son died in a climbing accident, causing him to abandon his post and hide in the forest for three years. The *mimetic* and *diegetic* intersect as players discover how, after accidently bumping into Hank, Ned feared he would be discovered, so weaved a threatening conspiracy around him to distract him from finding the truth. Hank readily embraced the conspiracy narrative in a bid to escape his own problems, including abandoning his ill wife. In *Firewatch*, there is no grand conspiracy or Boss to defeat, just inescapable human mistakes and realities. The stories of Hank and Ned, the *mimetic* and *diegetic experiences*, echo each other to reinforce themes around how people cope with tragedy and the futility of running from reality. The paralleling of stories, and use of form, can also be interpreted as a critique of video games' focus on escapism, rather than more intimate human relationships and realities.

Combining *mimetic* and *diegetic experience* is not new to video games, it happened in *Portal* [24], and AAA FPS *Bioshock* [25] was particularly praised for its use of environmental storytelling to uncover what happened in the underwater city of Rapture; but, it is a trope that Story Exploration Games have built on. *What Remains of Edith Finch* [26], released this year, also blended *mimetic* and *diegetic* elements, but in a different way by using poetic mechanics that enable players to enter the perspective of another character and access how it might feel to be them. For example, in the vignette related to Lewis, who worked in a cannery, players start by chopping off fish heads with the right thumbstick; then when Lewis's fantasy world starts to emerge in the lefthand side of the screen, they navigate through it simultaneously with the left side thumbstick. Players are split in the same way Lewis is, embodying his emotions and subjectivity through play. Further dramatic tension is added through voice-over of a psychiatrist describing her diagnosis of him. Throughout the game, players experience Finch family

---

[2] Ryan's [21] distinctions between Internal-Ontological, Internal-Exploratory, External-Exploratory and External-Ontological interactive modes help show how that happens through player positioning in relation to the narrative.

stories through a *diegetic experience* and *mimetic embodiment*, coupling *self-directed* and *empathic* engagement in a way Playable Stories are uniquely able.

4 Story Exploration Games

4.1 Deep Gaming

Story Exploration Games (SEGs) often separate players in time and space from story events, casting them as investigators or archeologists choosing how they uncover story. This can produce a variety of potential *experiential narratives* and is a means of generating empathy, as gameplay causes players to configure cause and effect in someone else's story. This is a different means of generating empathy from when a player, who is mimetically enacting a character, empathizes with the trials and tribulations of their NPC side- kick because they witness them in real-time, as with Alyx Vance in *Half-Life 2* [27], for example. Some argue spatiotemporal distance reduces empathy, but that does not happen in the SEGs discussed so far. Two distinct benefits are: (1) conversations can have more authenticity because they do not have the technological barrier of being generated by a system in real-time; (2) players are not cognitively overloaded with goal-directed mechanical tasks, so can take time to enter another character's perspective or experience. Significantly, the SEG genre emerged out of *Dear Esther* [28] and *The Stanley Parable*, both Mods of *Half-Life 2*, itself a watershed moment in game narrative, the absence of cutscenes being one of its innovations. These games removed shooter mechanics and reduced the goal-directed mechanical tasks to open up other storytelling possibilities, exploring human realities other than the hero quest narrative. What has so far been less explored, however, is how separating players from the time of narrative events provides the opportunity for video games to use *dramatic irony*, a temporal manipulation that generates narrative drive and which I have explored in my own practice and will discuss in Sect. 6. SEGs have built on video game traditions, and implemented *mimetic* and *diegetic* elements in new ways, to offer interactive storytelling experiences where narrative and player agency merge to support meaning and where innovation and commercial potential are matched.[3] This genre is an effective response to Crawford's dragon slaying ambition for games that express deeper and more complex emotions and empathy, which has been echoed in the call by industry practitioners and commentators for "deep gaming" [34]. One of the ways they do that is by making players the centre of the experience rather than the story.

4.2 The Beginner's Guide

The Beginner's Guide [35] illustrates how games can move away from player centrality and presence in the narrative to achieve powerful narrative affects. Game creator, Davey Wreden, invites players to experience a series of short games made by his friend, Coda,

---

[3] Many SEGs have been critical and commercial successes. *Gone Home* [29] sold 250,000 copies in six months [30]; *Her Story* [31] sold 100,000 in a month [32]; *Firewatch* has sold nearly 800,000 on Steam alone [33].

to understand what was going on in Coda's head at the time of making them. In the opening address, Wreden says: "I want us to see past the games themselves. I want us to get to know who this human being really is." The explicit aim is not to enable players to achieve a goal but to access someone else's experience and generate empathy. In this it tackles difficult themes, including loneliness, isolation, fear, identity, and artistic creation versus the seduction of external validation and approval.

The game's recurring 'puzzle door' motif is described as a means Coda uses to close off an idea or chapter in his life. One chapter takes on this symbol in a short action sequence set on a space ship where players see a puzzle door hurtling towards them; their job is to stop it or it will crash into the ship and restart the level. On the ship are crew members with boxes for heads that have the words "Blind" and "Research" emblazoned across them. The "Blind" ones are asking what is going on and bemoaning why they cannot see. "Research" is propped against the window saying: "I can't die like this" and "am I going to be killed by a giant door." These are metaphors for how Coda feels making a game. The solution is to take a lift to the next level where players find another crew member with "Truth" for a head. To progress players must trigger dialogue options that conclude there is no easy 'puzzle door' solution and the only way to survive is to speak the truth. The form and content of the demo work together to express a complexity of emotion that is relatable and offers a 'deep gaming' experience.

The mini-games in *The Beginner's Guide* are poetic metaphors for Coda's psychology and through navigational agency players experience his perspective and come to empathize with his struggle, which in turn offers them a chance to recognize themselves. As McKee argues, empathy is not selfless, it is an emotional process through which audience members experience a story 'as if' it has happened to them and learn about themselves "vicariously" [36]. SEGs offer a narrative world outside of players as *story protagonists*, but agency over how they experience it, to deliver stories that explore complex themes.

4.3 Everybody's Gone to the Rapture

In *Everybody's Gone To The Rapture* [37], players do not know who or what they are when they arrive in a deserted Shropshire village. As they move around the space, the apocalyptic happenings are recounted to them through remembered scenes and environmental storytelling. This *diegetic player experience* delivers both narrative impact, as players empathize with the stories of characters in their moments before death, and agency as they assemble the larger narrative through non-linear exploration of the open world space. Creator Dan Pinchbeck said The Chinese Room studio wanted "to make something that was very much about the idea of agency, about choice, about discovering a story rather than being told a story, and you feeling very much at the centre of that" [38]. In this, Pinchbeck makes a distinction between putting players at the centre of the story and putting them at the centre of the experience, distanced a step from the fiction itself. The discovery of story as a primary focus of play can be traced back to early adventure games, and the player agency offered in the assemblage of story draws on the heritage of experimental literature, including the Dennis Wheatley and J G Links crime dossier books [39]; but, SEGs continue to push forward, and popularize, non-linear structures, and narrative depth via diegetic experience, which helps overcome obstacles encountered when players are story protagonists. The separation of the shape of the material and the shape of the experience is a useful way to understand how SEGs combine narrative and player agency effectively.

5 Dynamic Syuzhets

5.1 Live and Digital Comparisons

Narratologist Viktor Shklovsky made a famous distinction between the *fabula*, the raw material of a story, and *syuzhet*, the way a story is organized [40]. Traditionally this has been considered in relation to timeline, the fabula being events in chronological order, the syuzhet being the selection of those same events in an order conceived for narrative affect. In Story Exploration Games, player agency often enables different ways of experiencing the fabula (story)—through non-linearity or branching pathways, for example—making the syuzhet (plot and narrative) dynamic (playable) [20]. Story content is often authored and then handed to players to play, which in turn produces its own story (hence the suitability of the term Playable Story). At other times, players are entered into a situation where the narrative structure (syuzhet) is fixed—over time and space, for example—and the story that happens within it (the fabula) is open to variation as a result of players' actions and improvisations in dialogue with the set system. An authored syuzhet framework is handed to players who then author the stories (fabula) within it—they are the story's 'raw material' and 'result' as a consequence of play (again, a Playable Story) [20]. This second configuration (a *fixed syuzhet* and *improvised fabula*) is often found in interactive theatre where actors are able to improvise around unpredictable player behaviour in order to maintain immersion, something currently trickier to achieve in digital work [20]. *The Money* [41] is an example where players are put in a civic setting with a pot of money they have contributed to and a time limit to unanimously decide how its spent. The rules and narrative architecture provide a *fixed syuzhet* but what emerges inside that is down to the characters in the room, creating an *improvised fabula*. Equally, digital playable stories have benefits when compared to live work. *Press Go* [42] a multilocational interactive murder mystery I wrote for the Almeida Theatre had a branching pathway structure, but that was constrained by the physical limits of space, time and number of actors in a way that it would not be using digital technology.

An evolving means by which SEGs balance narrative and player agency in digital work is by combining an *authored fabula* and a *dynamic syuzhet*, which then offers a personalized *experiential narrative* based on how players choose to explore [20]. This format has taken some cues from the immersive theatre of Punchdrunk where the story material—linear character arcs and settings—do not change and form the *authored fabula*. Layered over this is an exploratory mechanic where masked players pick and choose where they go and what they see, providing agency over their experience of story. This allows for multiple configurations and perception changes. Players come away with a personalized *experiential narrative* because they have been given the power to play it via a *dynamic syuzhet* [20].

5.2 Gone Home

Punchdrunk has acknowledged the influence of video games on its work [43] and developers Fullbright have discussed the influence of Punchdrunk on their work [44], demonstrating how the forms inspire and inform one another.[4] In *Gone Home* [29] players play Katie who has returned home from a year abroad to find her new family home empty. Katie is not the protagonist of the story but at the heart of the experience that uncovers the story. That experience is structured via a *dynamic syuzhet* which offers players agency over how they jigsaw the story together, as framed by the *evoked narrative* of a survival horror—an abandoned gothic house on a dark and stormy night. The *evoked narrative* provides suspense that gives *self-directed* emotional stakes to the navigational choices being made by players. As players explore the space, they uncover the *authored fabula* through *embedded* and *environmental narrative* (also Jenkins' [23] classifications) that subvert the expectations of the *evoked narrative* to reveal the central story of Katie's sister Sam, a teenager struggling to settle at a new school, falling in love and coming out as a lesbian to disapproval from parents, Jan and Terry. Jan and Terry's complicated lives are also revealed in exploration that uncovers affairs, failed careers and childhood sexual abuse. *Gone Home*'s *authored fabula* is loosely structured in three acts corresponding to zones of the house, but the *dynamic syuzhet* offers non-linear exploration of the space. It is possible to get into the attic and reach the climax of the story from the opening foyer, for example. By embodying Katie, players enter Turner's *liminoid* space where they leave behind their own identities but are also not completely the character in the fiction [46]. This space is one where empathy can be created, especially when players are not cognitively stressed with self-directed, mechanical game tasks. As *experience protagonists*, players operate as detectives trying to decipher the story. The central mechanics (or player verbs) of 'searching' and 'exploring' enable decisions on how the story is pieced together and parallel the search for meaning and identity central to the stories of Sam, Jan and Terry. Similarly, the fear players feel in the haunted house setting echoes the central protagonist's fear of expressing her true self. *Gone Home*'s construction of players as protagonists of the experience creates the conditions for this coupling of *self-directed* and *empathic* engagement where players parallel and embody the emotions of other characters through play. This doubling up of engagement, that brings form and content together to express meaning, is something playable stories can do that other narrative forms cannot.

Gone Home was a watershed moment for video games that showed a way forward for players outside of 'fight or flight' experiences of mastery, winning and triumph; where the process was not about dominating fantasy worlds but understanding human worlds by interacting with character fears and motivations. This continues to evolve as the popularity of SEGs grows and more gain critical and commercial success. Fullbright's recently released game *Tacoma* [47] is set in space but about personal relationships, future workplace politics and commercial exploitation rather than space marine battles. It also uses an *authored fabula/dynamic syuzhet* structure and is a fuller realization of the Punchdrunk model where you can follow multiple actors to witness the

---

[4] Fullbright was founded by artists who had worked on the *Bioshock* series with Ken Levine, who took all his employees to see a Punchdrunk show while they were making it [45].

same event from different perspectives, but it also does something new. Players are salvager, Amy, on a space ship in 2088, able to explore a multi-threaded plot and witness exchanges between crew members to work out why they have disappeared. Unlike a Punchdrunk show, the digital form enables players to rewind, pause and fast forward the exchanges, and therefore time, for closer analysis of detail and to switch between characters. In this game, the narrative arc of the Player Character also becomes a means to pair *self-directed* and *empathic* emotion in relation to the themes exploring the impact of AI and automation on human lives.

5.3 Her Story

The coupling of *self-directed* and *empathic* engagement is also at work in *Her Story* [31], where players access a 1990s police database with archive video clips of twins answering questions relating to a murder.[5] The game mechanic is a simple emulation of Googling; to uncover what happened players enter keywords into a search field and return tagged clips. The *dynamic syuzhet* provides multiple non-linear ways of accessing the content so each player's *experiential narrative* can be different. Traditional dramatic tension that builds towards climax is replaced by dramatic tension in the event of play as the picture builds out. In the detective work of searching the police database to uncover what this murder case is all about, your *self-directed* emotions as a player wanting to crack the case are incited: how good are your detective skills? Can you solve it faster than everyone else? What are the keywords that will unlock the mystery? In selecting search terms, you are also asked to examine your own assumptions and, potentially, prejudices. This is still in play when watching the video clips that result from your searches, but via these players also gain *empathic* engagement as Hannah and Eve explain what happened and why. An extra layer is added when a reflection on the screen reveals that you are playing from the point-of-view of the murder victim's child, trying to find out who your parents are. Your *self-directed* emotions as a player are subsumed into *empathic* engagement with the character of Sarah as you imagine her motivation as your own. In the act of searching you embody the emotions Sarah feels as she searches for knowledge about her parents.

In contrast to the other SEGs discussed, *Her Story* departs from the familiar model of the immersive sim and illusion of player presence in 3D space. This introduces narrative tension through omission which—unlike jump cuts in a linear narrative—aids, rather than limits, agency. Sid Meier famously asserted that games are "a series of interesting decisions" for players [49] but *Her Story* makes the case for them also being considered a series of interesting gaps. Players in the *mimetic* mode tend to live through cause-and-effect in real time, which can negate the narrative drive generated in the gaps as players are encouraged to work it out. In the *diegetic* mode of *Her Story*, players are actively engaged in working out the chains of cause-and-effect. Non-linearity, omissions, reliability of testimony and the operation of the game mechanic combine to

---

[5] The creation of this game saw Sam Barlow step outside the studio system because he felt it was something no publisher would want to make [48], reflecting a trend for SEGs to emerge out of indie developers or academia.

complicate the resolution of the mystery, leaving no comfortable objective truth and interpretation that requires consideration of deeper themes around family and relationships.

6 Dramatic Irony

6.1 Underland

A close analysis of the structures of Story Exploration Games was a means to inform my own practice as a writer of Playable Stories. A research question within this was: how can writers use the form, within current technological realities, to create effective experiences that negotiate narrative and player agency? This creative practice research impacted the creation of a script for crime drama video game, *Underland*. In *Underland* the story protagonist is a journalist arrested for murder. In early iterations, where the Player Character was the journalist, I encountered frustrations with railroading, real-time and cutscenes. Applying a different structure, where players were the protagonist of the *experience*, rather than of the *story*, opened up other writing possibilities and solutions. In the final version, you play an investigative psychologist analyzing evidence to find the killer's motive. In the non-linear investigation, you can choose any path you like through environments, scenes and character correspondence to solve two murders. At the climax, there is then a flip in interactive mode where you become the *story protagonist* and impact the outcome. Using an *authored fabula* and *dynamic syuzhet* enabled me to balance the needs of narrative and player agency and pair *self-directed* and *empathic* engagement, but another discovery emerged out of the writing process, which was the ability to use *dramatic irony*. McKee [36] identifies three main tools writers use to create narrative drive and hold the interest of their audience: mystery, suspense and dramatic irony. Mystery occurs when players know less than characters; suspense when they can foresee outcomes but do not know exactly what will unfold; and dramatic irony when they know more than characters and are motivated to find out how they will reach a conclusion they already know but can do nothing to stop. For instance, when *Sunset Boulevard* [50] opens with a dead protagonist, audience attention is held by wanting to find out how and why it happened, and then in observing the progress of a character who cannot see how things will end up. Mystery and suspense are often used in video games but dramatic irony is notably absent because it works on the basis of the player knowing more than the protagonist and not being able to intervene in their fate. Casting players as *story protagonists* does not allow them to know their own fate and do nothing about it without being dramatically dissatisfying; but, an alternate viewpoint as *experience protagonists* provides the opportunity to manipulate time and allow players to see the fate of story protagonists, a hook which can generate narrative drive and motivate them to actively uncover why it ended that way. In *Underland*, dramatic irony works on a macro level by opening with a journalist arrested on suspicion of murder, generating drive for players to analyze the evidence and find out why; but the *authored fabula/dynamic syuzhet* combination also enables it to work on the micro level of scenes, with *environmental* and *embedded narrative* playing off one another. For example, a player entering a space and triggering scenes from the past can have more freedom to explore the environment than the characters did in that scene. This raises the possibility of seeing something the characters at the time did not, thereby activating dramatic irony. The ability to generate tension and narrative drive in *Underland* through dramatic irony is founded on players being protagonists of the game experience rather than the game story. This shows how digital Playable Stories can extend and alter the operations of an established narrative device in a new way [20].

7 Conclusion

This paper has approached the field of IDS from the perspective of creative writing in a bid to understand how writers can make work now. After identifying some of the current technological challenges that impact on the delivery of narrative and player agency in interactive works, it departs from the vision of the holodeck and explores the techniques at work in the growing Story Exploration Game genre. The new terms *improvised fabula, dynamic syuzhet, fixed syuzhet* and *authored fabula* were introduced to show how Story Exploration Games have offered a way forward that balances narrative and player agency, combines *mimetic* and *diegetic player* experiences, couples *self-directed* and *empathic* engagement and provides the opportunity to use *dramatic irony*. These findings were all based on analysis of the consequences of making players experience, rather than story, protagonists. In this configuration, the operational mechanisms of narrative drive can be achieved without limiting agency because players are not steering the story but the experience. In this, the paper has aimed to add to the multifaceted topic of writing for games.

References

1. Murray, J.H.: Hamlet on the Holodeck: The Future of Narrative in Cyberspace. Free Press, New York (1997)
2. HBO: Westworld (2016)
3. Mateas, M., Stern, A.: Façade. http://www.interactivestory.net
4. Crawford, C.: The Siren Song of Interactive Storytelling. In: [keynote] ICIDS 2015, Copenhagen, Denmark (2015)
5. Wood, H.: Underland
6. Crawford, C.: The dragon speech. In: CGDC 1992, Santa Clara, California (1992)
7. Rose, F. (ed.): The Art of Immersion: How the Digital Generation is Remaking Hollywood, Madison Avenue, and the Way We Tell Stories, pp. 284–287. W.W. Norton & Co., New York (2011)
8. Maxis: The Sims. Electronic Arts (2000)
9. Ryan, J.O., Mateas, M., Wardrip-Fruin, N.: Open design challenges for interactive emergent narrative. In: Schoenau-Fog, H., Bruni, L.E., Louchart, S., Baceviciute, S. (eds.) ICIDS 2015. LNCS, vol. 9445, pp. 14–26. Springer, Cham (2015). https://doi.org/10.1007/978-3-319-27036-4_2
10. Sicart, M.: Family values: ideology, computer games & The Sims. In: DIGRA 2003, Utrecht, The Netherlands (2003)
11. Jayanth, M.: Forget protagonists: writing NPCs with agency for '80 days' and beyond. In: GDC Game Narrative Summit 2016, San Francisco, California (2016)

12. 505 Games: Virginia (2016)
13. Galactic Café: The Stanley Parable (2013)
14. Lankoski, P.: Player character engagement in computer games. Games Cult. **6**(4), 291–311 (2011)
15. Ryan, M.-L.: From narrative games to playable stories: towards a poetics of interactive narrative. Story Worlds J. Narrative Stud. **1**, 43–59 (2009)
16. Meretzky, S.: Building character: an analysis of character creation. Gamasutra. http://www.gamasutra.com/resource_guide/20011119/meretzsky_01.htm. Accessed 07 June 2016
17. Frasca, G.: Rethinking agency and immersion: playing with video game characters. In: ACM SIGGRAPH 2001, Los Angeles, California (2001)
18. Square Enix: Tomb Raider (2013)
19. Square Enix: Life is Strange (2015)
20. Wood, H.: Playable stories: writing and design methods that negotiate narrative and player agency. Ph.D. thesis, University of Exeter, UK (2016). http://hdl.handle.net/10871/29281
21. Ryan, M.-L.: Narrative as Virtual Reality 2: Revisiting Immersion and Interactivity in Literature and Electronic Media, pp. 162–165. John Hopkins University Press (2015)
22. Campo Santo: Firewatch (2016)
23. Jenkins, H.: Game design as narrative architecture. In: Harrigan, P., Wardrip-Fruin, N. (eds.) First Person: New Media as Story, Performance, and Game, pp. 118–130. MIT Press, Cambridge (2004)
24. Valve: Portal (2007)
25. 2K Games, Inc.: Bioshock (2007)
26. Annapurna Interactive: What Remains of Edith Finch (2017)
27. Valve: Half-Life 2 (2004)
28. The Chinese Room: Dear Esther (2012)
29. The Fullbright Company: Gone Home (2013)
30. Conditt, J.: Gone home finds 250k sales, most on steam. http://www.engadget.com/2014/02/06/gone-home-finds-250k-sales-most-on-steam/?ncid=rss_truncated. Accessed 27 Oct 2016
31. Barlow, S.: Her Story (2015)
32. Porter, M.: Her Story hits 100,000 sales. http://uk.ign.com/articles/2015/08/11/her-story-hits-100000-sales. Accessed 27 Oct 2016
33. Steam Spy: Firewatch. https://steamspy.com/app/383870. Accessed 23 Aug 2017
34. Bluestein, A.: Video games for grown-ups: with gamer demographics changing fast, "deep games" offer cerebral, creative—and often offbeat—content. http://www.fastcompany.com/3038466/wideo-games-for-grown-ups. Accessed 21 Oct 2015
35. Everything Unlimited: The Beginner's Guide. (2015)
36. McKee, R.: Story Seminar. Regent's University, London (2014)
37. The Chinese Room: Everybody's Gone To the Rapture. Sony Santa Monica (2015)
38. Pinchbeck, D.: Everybody's gone to the rapture: games showcase. BAFTA Guru Talk. Piccadilly, London (2015)
39. https://www.denniswheatley.info/crimedossiers. Accessed 24 Aug 2017
40. Cobley, P.: Narratology. In: Groden, M., Kreiswirth, M., Szeman, I. (eds.) The John Hopkins Guide to Literary Theory and Criticism. John Hopkins University Press, Baltimore (2005)
41. Honnor, S.: The Money (2013)
42. Wood, H.: Press Go (2017)
43. McMullan, T.: The immersed audience: how theatre is taking its cue from video games. https://theguardian.com/technology/2014/may/20/how-theatre-is-taking-its-cue-from-video-games. Accessed 20 May 2014

44. Gaynor, S.: Why is gone home a game? In: GDC 2014, San Francisco, California (2014)
45. Suellentrop, C., Sutherland, J.J.: Shall We Show Tacoma [podcast], August 2017
46. Turner, V.: The Anthropology of Performance. PAJ Publications, New York (1988)
47. Fullbright: Tacoma (2017)
48. Wood, H.: Could there be a speculative script industry for narrative games? https://www.gamesindustry.biz/articles/2017-07-11-could-there-be-a-speculative-script-industry-for-narrative-games. Accessed 24 Aug 2017
49. Alexander, L.: Sid Meier on how to see games as sets of interesting decisions. In: GDC 2012. http://www.gamasutra.com/view/news/164869/GDC_2012_Sid_Meier_on_how_to_see_games_as_sets_of_interesting_decisions.php. Accessed 06 Apr 2016
50. Paramount Pictures: Sunset Boulevard (1950)

Plans Versus Situated Actions in Immersive Storytelling Practices

Sarah Lugthart[✉], Michel van Dartel, and Annemarie Quispel

Centre of Expertise for Art, Design and Technology, Avans University of Applied Sciences,
Breda, The Netherlands
{sm.lugthart,mf.vandartel,a.quispel}@avans.nl

Abstract. While much research on immersive storytelling practices is focused on outcomes and audience experiences, much less attention has hitherto been given to research on the relationship of such outcomes and experiences to the design process. In this paper, we introduce the distinction between two modes of design to the domain of immersive storytelling: 'plans' and 'situated actions'. In a small comparative case study, we investigate how these two modes of design affect the creative outcomes of the design process of immersive stories and their reception. The case study reveals important relations between the method chosen to design an immersive story and aspects of the outcomes of such design processes, which emphasizes the importance of the mode of design in creating immersive stories.

Keywords: Immersive storytelling · Situated action · Design methods

1 Introduction

In recent years, a wide range of novel narrative media practices developed alongside more traditional storytelling practices. These novel practices, often referred to as 'immersive storytelling', generally deploy new media technologies to absorb audiences more, suspend disbelief further, and allow for multisensorial experiences [1, 2]. Consequently, creating immersive stories is nowadays key to domains such as transmedia and Virtual Reality (VR). These novel narrative media practices bring new challenges as well as possibilities to the domain of storytelling. For instance, they expand the diversity of media through which narratives can be communicated to an audience and increase the control that can be given to an audience over how a narrative unfolds [2]. Although much has been researched on these challenges and possibilities in relation to the outcomes and audience experiences [1, 2, 3], the design processes that give rise to them have received relatively little attention. In many design domains, where recent technological development brought along new challenges and opportunities in creating user experiences, such as in gaming, novel design methods that take the actions of users and audiences as crucially informative to the design process, such as playtesting or testing with prototypes [3], have been distinguished from more traditional methods that are based on preconceived plans, such as blueprints or scripts. In the domain of computer science, for instance, Suchman [4] makes a distinction between 'plans' and 'situated

© Springer International Publishing AG 2017
N. Nunes et al. (Eds.): ICIDS 2017, LNCS 10690, pp. 38–45, 2017.
https://doi.org/10.1007/978-3-319-71027-3_4

actions' to emphasize the importance of context in the cognitive processes of users. Suchman defines plans as "an attempt to prescribe the sequence of actions that will accomplish some preconceived end" and as "prerequisite to the action" ([4]: p. 22). The course of situated actions, however, "depends in essential ways upon the action's circumstances" (ibid.: p. 38). Contrary to plans, situated actions are not based on rules or procedures, as "we walk into a situation, [...] identify its features, and match our actions to it" (ibid.: p. 43). So, when a design process is based on situated actions, then changes happen in the moment of execution of actions, that in turn may trigger new actions. In contrast, when a design process is based on plans, then changes happen when actions derived from a predetermined plan are evaluated against the criteria set by that plan, after which the next action in the plan may be executed. While Suchman's distinction between plans and situated actions has led to a vast body of research in computer science, it has also had a significant impact on design methodologies in domains far beyond the realm of computer science (see, e.g., [5]). Although an overview of research and design methods inspired by Suchman's distinction falls beyond the scope of this paper, a particularly illustrative example of the novel design methods that it gave rise to is the 'Aulaia method' for the design of alternative reality games. This method, in short, successfully tackles the issue that designing such games are typically large and complicated undertakings by developing them in-situ and on the basis of situated actions taken during the execution of a game [6]. Although design methods such as the 'Aulaia method' clearly indicate a relevance for situated actions in the design of interactive and immersive stories, it is still to be investigated, however, how such novel methods impact the immersive stories they result in.

As immersive storytelling practices are currently expanding to many new domains and are gaining attention from other disciplines [2, 7], a better understanding of the relationship between the mode of design and the immersive stories they result in is urgently needed to help designers make better informed decisions. In this paper, we present a case study to explore this relation and to address the research question: *How does the decision for plans or situated actions in the design process of immersive stories affect its creative outcomes?* Below, in Sect. 2, we will first introduce our case study. Subsequently, we will present our results in Sect. 3 and discuss our findings in Sect. 4, before concluding with some directions for future research in Sect. 5.

2 The Case Study

In the context of a minor program titled *Research in Immersive Storytelling*, 26 students each produced an immersive storytelling project over the course of 10 weeks. These projects were subsequently presented in an exhibition titled '*It is _____ After All*' on January 27th 2017, as part of the annual *Cultuurnacht Breda*, in which cultural institutions in the city of Breda open their doors to the public from 7 pm until 11 pm.[1] For reasons of manageability, only 15 of the 26 minor students participated in this case study. For these 15 students and their immersive storytelling projects, we analyzed the relationship between the mode of design (plans or situated actions) chosen by the student

---

[1] https://www.cultuurnachtbreda.nl.

(participant) and the outcomes exhibited (creative outcomes). The 15 students that participated in the case study majored in a variety of domains related to immersive storytelling, such as film (FI, 5 students), animation (AN, 5 students), illustration (IL, 1 student), spatial design (SD, 1 student), fine art (FA, 1 student) and multimedia design (MD, 2 students). All of the participating students studied at Avans University of Applied Sciences (NL), and had recently entered their third year of a four-year Bachelor's degree program. At the start of the minor program, participants were assigned to develop an immersive story to be presented at the *Cultuurnacht Breda*. They were free to use any (mix of) media and instructed that the presentation should demonstrate their storytelling skills as well as their ability to make creative use of technology. For our case study, we distinguished projects whose designs were based on plans from projects whose designs were based on situated actions, by determining whether or not some form of storyboard or script was used in the design process. When a storyboard or script was used to design a project, it was categorized as 'plans'; all other projects were categorized as 'situated actions'.

The outcomes of an immersive story design process can be analyzed on the level of the story itself as well as on the level of the experience of that story by an audience, which we will below refer to as the 'immersive story' and 'reception', respectively. To gain deeper insight into how the participants' decision to design on the basis of plans or situated actions affected their creative outcomes, we evaluated its impact on both the 'immersive story' as well as the 'reception'. An audience survey was conducted at the Cultuurnacht Breda to gain insight into the reception of the immersive stories produced as part of the case study. During the event, participants handed out surveys to visitors that had just experienced one of the 15 immersive stories. A total of 81 visitors completed a survey, which asked them to respond to three statements ('I felt I was watching the story', 'I felt I was within the story', and 'I felt I was an actor in the story') inspired by a categorization of immersive stories developed by Dolan and Bye [8]. Although developed to measure how much 'agency'(i.e. possibility to create meaningful interaction) an audience has in VR experiences, their categorization is also useful in the broader context of immersive storytelling, as it distinguishes between types of storytelling that put the audience in the role of 'Ghost'(i.e., an omniscient ghost who is observing his or her surroundings) or 'Character' (i.e., a character integrated within the plot of the story),

Character Presence

		Ghost	Character
Impact on Story	No Impact	I felt I was **watching** the story	I felt I was **within** the story.
	Impact	I felt I was **within** the story.	I felt I was an **actor** in the story

Fig. 1. The three statements used in the survey in the categorization adapted from [8].

and between types of storytelling in which the audience has an impact on the story and those in which it does not. Figure 1 positions these three statements within the quadrant that Dolan and Bye developed to categorize different types of storytelling. Visitors were asked to rate how well each of these three statements applied to their experience on a seven-point scale (1. Completely disagree, 2. Disagree, 3. Somewhat disagree, 4. Neither agree nor disagree, 5. Somewhat agree, 6. Agree, 7. Completely agree). For the sake of our statistical analysis below, we will take this scale to be uniformly distributed.

3   Results

Our case study yielded 15 immersive stories (creative outcomes) and 81 completed surveys. Below, we will first present and discuss the creative outcomes (Subsect. 3.1), to subsequently focus on their reception (Subsect. 3.2).

3.1   Creative Outcomes

Table 1 displays the titles of the 15 immersive stories that our case study yielded, together with the major topic of the student who conceived it, the mode of design chosen for the design process, whether or not the creative outcome was interactive in nature, and which type of media was used to communicate the story to its audience. As Table 1 shows, seven of the 15 creative outcomes were categorized as 'plans', while eight were categorized as 'situated actions'. It also shows that all participants majoring in film (FI) opted for a mode of design based on plans. Eleven of the creative outcomes were not interactive in nature, whereas four outcomes were interactive. The type of interaction varied greatly between the four interactive projects, however. In *Sound of Space*, for example, the audience had to walk around through the exhibition space holding a radio while tuning into the 'sounds of different planets'. Another immersive story, *Finger Logic*, consisted of a performance in which the participant took a role as the lead actor of the story and invited the audience to participate in a 'finger reading' session. Remarkably, only one outcome that resulted from a mode of design based on plans was interactive, whereas three outcomes that resulted from a design process based on situated actions were interactive in nature. Eight creative outcomes were screen-based, of which three involved VR that was based on either film or animation. One of the creative outcomes used radio as its medium, whereas another used a book. Four of the outcomes combined multiple media to communicate their story and were categorized as 'Mixed Media'. Such projects typically integrated various media into one coherent experience, without favoring one medium over another. The project *Monolith*, for example, consisted of a door with light and audio peeking through at the bottom. Another example of a mixed media story, *Presence and Absence*, consisted of an audiovisual space that the audience would walk into.

Table 1. Creative outcomes and their properties

Title	Major	Mode of design	Interaction	Media
Adapt to Change	AN	Situated actions	Non-interactive	VR/Animation
Audio Memories	CMD	Situated actions	Non-interactive	Audio
The Cat	IL	Situated actions	Non-interactive	Video
Depth Perception	FI	Plans	Non-interactive	Video
Escape	FI	Plans	Non-interactive	Video
Finger Logic	AN	Plans	Interactive	Performance
In Schaapskleding	FI	Plans	Non-interactive	Video
Mechanical Emotions	SD	Situated actions	Interactive	Mixed Media
Monolith	FI	Plans	Non-interactive	Mixed Media
Presence and Absence	FA	Situated actions	Non-interactive	Mixed Media
Rupsje Nooit Erkend	AN	Plans	Non-interactive	Book
Simulife	AN	Situated actions	Non-interactive	VR/Animation
Somewhere in the Void	FI	Plans	Non-interactive	VR/Film
Sound of Space	CMD	Situated actions	Interactive	Radio
We Create Worlds	AN	Situated actions	Interactive	Mixed Media

3.2 Reception of the Creative Outcomes

During the exhibition, 38 surveys were completed in response to experiences of stories designed on the basis of plans, while 43 surveys were completed in response to experiences of stories designed on the basis of situated actions. As the major topics of the students and the media they used, yielded categories too small for statistical analysis of those factors, we will limit our analysis below to the effects of the mode of design and (non-)interactive nature of the stories on their reception.

Figure 2 (left) illustrates the effect of the mode of design on reception by showing the mean responses to the three statements for stories designed on the basis of plans and for those designed on the basis of situated actions. An independent-samples t-test showed no significant differences between scores on statement 1 ("I felt I was watching the story") for plans (M = 5.50, SD = 1.31) and situated actions (M = 5.28, SD = 1.68), $t(79) = .65$, $p = .515$. Neither did we find significant differences between scores on statement 2 ("I felt I was within the story") for plans (M = 5.58, SD = 1.06) and situated actions (M = 5.70, SD = 1.28), $t(79) = .45$, $p = .653$. For statement 3 ("I felt I was an actor in the story"), however, an independent-samples t-test indicated that scores were significantly higher for creative outcomes based on situated actions (M = 4.77, SD = 1.84) than for those based on plans (M = 3.74, SD = 1.88), $t(79) = 2.49$, $p = .015$.

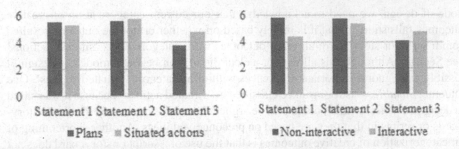

Fig. 2. Mean response per statement, differentiated between designs based on plans and situated actions (left) and differentiated between interactive and non-interactive stories (right).

Figure 2 (right) shows the mean responses to the three statements for stories that were interactive in nature and those that were not. An independent-samples t-test indicated that scores on statement 1 ("I felt I was watching the story") were significantly higher for non-interactive stories (M = 5.84, SD = 1.04) than for interactive stories (M = 4.36, SD = 1.89), t(79) = 4.54, p < .001. We found no significant differences for scores on statement 2 between interactive (M = 5.40, SD = 1.32) and non-interactive designs (M = 5.75, SD = 1.32), t(79) = 1.24, p = .218, or for scores on statement 3 between interactive (M = 4.80, SD = 1.92) and non-interactive stories (M = 4.05, SD = 4.80), t(79) = 1.63, p = .106.

4 Discussion

Although their statistical significance could not be demonstrated, it is interesting to observe that in our case study: (i) participants majoring in film prefer to design stories on the basis of a script or storyboard (i.e., 'plans') and (ii) plans lead to non-interactive creative outcomes more often than situated actions do. The first observation, can be explained by two important differences between the practices of filmmakers and those of other designers and artists. First, producing film is a relatively costly endeavor, as it typically involves the hiring of external staff to assist in the production, while other design and art practices more often rely on the labor of the individual artist or designer, if not in collaboration with relatively permanent team [9]. Therefore, filmmakers may be more inclined than artists or designers to plan ahead in detail before entering production. Secondly, other artists and designers are also less inclined than filmmakers to plan ahead in detail because their results benefit from more iterative design processes. For instance, the quality of a multimedia design is often argued to depend on how well user-feedback was incorporated in the design [10]. The second observation, that plans seem to lead to non-interactive creative outcomes more often than situated actions do, might suggest a causal relationship between the two. However, it could also be explained by the professional profile of the maker, since we also observed that film majors are more likely to adopt such a mode of design. To fully understand the relationship between creative outcomes and mode of design, these relations between professional profile, mode of design and (non-)interactive nature of the outcome need to be explored in more detail in future research. Regarding the relationship between creative outcomes and mode of design, we need to acknowledge that our current categorization of creative outcomes falls short in that it is merely based on whether or not the outcome resulted from a script or storyboard; all other outcomes were categorized as 'situated actions' (see Sect. 2). Although this allows for a clear distinction between modes of design, it possibly also ignores important differences within the category 'situated actions'. One outcome, *Simulife*, was for instance classified as 'situated actions' because it was based on design sketches, while it could also be argued that such sketches are similar to storyboards or scripts in that they are based on preconceived ideas. Another shortcoming of our categorization of creative outcomes is that the use of a script or storyboard does not exclude the potential incorporation of situated actions in later stages of development. One of the creative outcomes, *Finger Logic*, was for instance based on a script that was adapted according to audience-responses during the performance of the story. These shortcomings lead us to conclude that future research on the relationship between creative outcomes and modes of design will be difficult without a better way to categorize these modes, which in turn requires a better definition of 'situated actions'.

Our analysis of the reception of the creative outcomes revealed two significant effects: (i) visitors identified with the statement 'I felt I was an actor in the story' significantly more when the story that they experienced was designed on the basis of situated actions then when it was designed on the basis of plans, and (ii) visitors who experienced a non-interactive immersive story identified with the statement 'I felt I was watching the story' more than visitors who had experienced an interactive story. These effects suggest that stories designed on the basis of situated actions are likely to result in the bottom-right category of Fig. 1, indicating a high level of agency according to Dolan and Bye [8], while audiences typically experience a low level of agency in non-interactive immersive stories. Although only the latter can be explained as the direct effect of the presence or absence of interaction, also the first effect could be indirectly caused by it, as projects designed on the basis of situated actions are more likely to result in outcomes that are interactive in nature. It remains to be investigated whether the agency experienced by the audience can be entirely attributed to the interaction provided, or if the mode of design chosen to develop the story also has a more direct impact on it. Investigating interactions between these factors, however, requires a larger, and preferably more controlled, set of stimuli. Finally, it should be noted that two other factors may have influenced the reception of the creative outcomes. First, the three statements leave some room for interpretation: Being 'within' a story, for example, could refer to both a mental or a physical state. Second, our survey data may have been affected by a social desirability bias amongst its respondents, as several participants in our case study invited their friends and family to the Cultuurnacht Breda and some of the surveys may therefore have been completed by visitors that were in one way or another acquainted to the participant that developed the creative outcome they experienced. Although it was in no way suggested that the surveys were an instrument to evaluate a participant's achievement, the possibility that respondents interpreted the request to complete a survey as such cannot be completely excluded.

5   Conclusions and Future Research

Our case study revealed that interaction seems key in explaining why creative outcomes designed on the basis of situated actions make visitors feel like an actor more than creative outcomes designed on the basis of plans. Based on this finding, we draw the following conclusion regarding the research question introduced in Sect. 1: *How does the decision for plans or situated actions in the design process of immersive stories affect its creative outcomes?* As situated actions lead to interactive outcomes more often than plans do, they provide an audience with a relatively high level of agency. Whether or not situated actions also more directly impact creative outcomes and their reception remains to be investigated. As we already pointed out, however, these conclusions should be considered as preliminary findings. In our future research, we hope to more deeply explore the relationship between the design processes involved in immersive storytelling and their creative outcomes, by addressing more specifically whether designers and artists that make interactive work benefit from a mode of design based on situated action over one based on plans. As mentioned before, such research first and foremost requires a better way to categorize these modes of design, based on a more refined definition of 'situated actions'.

References   •

1. Ryan, M.: Narrative as Virtual Reality 2: Revisiting Immersion and Interactivity. John Hopkins University Press, Baltimore (2015)
2. Rose, F.: The Art of Immersion. How the Digital Generation is Remaking Hollywood, Madison Avenue and the Way we tell Stories. W.W. Norton & Company, New York (2011)
3. Newton, K.: The storyteller's guide to the Virtual Reality audience. https://medium.com/stanford-d-school/the-storyteller-s-guide-to-the-virtual-reality-audience-19e92da57497. Accessed 22 Jul 2017
4. Suchman, L.: Plans and Situated Actions: The Problem of Human-Machine Interaction. Xerox Corporation, Palo Alto (1987)
5. Simonsen, J., Svabo, C., Strandvad, S., Samson, K., Hertzum, M., Hansen, O. (eds.): Situated Design Methods. MIT Press, Cambridge (2014)
6. Kristiansen, E.: Alternate reality games. In: Simonsen, J., Svabo, C., Strandvad, S., Samson, K., Hertzum, M., Hansen, O. (eds.) Situated Design Methods, pp. 241–258. MIT Press, Cambridge (2014)
7. Machon, J.: Immersive Theater: Intimacy and Immediacy in Contemporary Performance. Palgrave Macmillan, Basingstoke (2013)
8. Dolan, D., Bye, K.: Four different types of stories in VR. http://voicesofvr.com/292-the-four-different-types-of-stories-in-vr/. Accessed 22 Jul 2017
9. Long, B., Schenk, S.: The Digital Filmmaking Handbook, 4th edn. Cengage Learning, Boston (2012)
10. Koskinen, I., Zimmerman, J., Binder, T., Redstrom, J., Wensveen, S.: Design Research Through Practice: From the Lab, Field and Showroom. Elsevier, Waltham (2011)

Location and Generation

Experiencing the Presence of Historical Stories with Location-Based Augmented Reality

Ulrike Spierling[✉], Peter Winzer, and Erik Massarczyk

Hochschule RheinMain, Unter den Eichen 5, 65195 Wiesbaden, Germany
{ulrike.spierling,peter.winzer,erik.massarczyk}@hs-rm.de

Abstract. In the SPIRIT research project, a location-based Augmented Reality (AR) storytelling application has been developed with the goal to support the imagination of lively historical events at places of cultural significance. We describe a showcase scenario and report on its quantitative and qualitative evaluation, conducted at the Saalburg Roman fort, an outdoor museum site near Bad Homburg in Germany. 107 random voluntary visitors were observed using the app, before filling questionnaires that were then analyzed with SPSS. Specifics of the app include a novel interaction pattern that uses positioning sensors of mobile devices and image recognition to trigger content, featuring transparent videos as ghost-like overlays on the camera image of the environment. Results presented in this paper show that in general, the app was effective and fun to use. Further, there have been differences in the experience of presence concerning the AR representation, as well as in the comprehension and appreciation of the story's content. Concluding, we discuss influencing parameters on the results and draft hypotheses for future work.

Keywords: Interactive storytelling · User experience evaluation · Location-based storytelling · Augmented Reality · Interaction design

1 Introduction

Augmented Reality (AR) systems enable the seamless integration of 'made-up' digital impressions in the perception of everyday real environments. Therefore, since their first appearance, tourism [9] and cultural heritage [24] have been considered as application areas. Ranging from simple information to gaming and storytelling, varying philosophies for interaction have been explored [3, 13, 14]. Differences still lie in the degree to which a concept is readily applicable. Thus, AR systems often introduce unfamiliar user interaction styles due to hardware developments [4]. Within the last three to five years, personal handheld devices have been getting ubiquitous as platforms for gaming and entertainment, including mainstream concepts for museums or tourism. With reasonable screen sizes, a variety of sensors and increased computational power, hopes and expectations are now also raised for storytelling with mobile AR.

We report on a user evaluation of a complex prototype enabling location-based AR storytelling. It has been developed within the applied research project SPIRIT, with the goal to explore the applicability of location-based AR on off-the-shelf hardware for a

© Springer International Publishing AG 2017
N. Nunes et al. (Eds.): ICIDS 2017, LNCS 10690, pp. 49–62, 2017.
https://doi.org/10.1007/978-3-319-71027-3_5

museum environment, as well as boundaries for storytelling and design. In this project, in order to develop a full experience, several aspects had to be tackled by an interdisciplinary team. These include (i) the development of a new location-based AR player app (running on Android tablets and smart phones), (ii) a formalized content structure as XML dialect to be authored by storytellers or game designers, (iii) a plot engine parsing the content structure, managing the presentation in time and in relation to contexts and variables, (iv) the conception of sensor-based interaction patterns, tested with users in formative evaluation cycles, and (v) a case study production for an outdoor museum site, integrating the experience of a historic drama on the spot with factual information to be acquired in context. During development, iterative formative evaluations with preliminary content have supported design hypotheses concerning interaction with and staging of the story content. Many of these test persons in about 20 design cycles were media-savvy. However, we expected to achieve different results within the real environment.

We evaluated the resulting prototype within regular operations of the museum. 107 visitors filled questionnaires after using our tablets during a tour of about 30 to 40 min, being accompanied and observed by two researchers. In the following, we report on the insights gained by this evaluation. First, we describe our intended interactive story experience, as well as design hypotheses and constraints. We also relate our approach to the state of the art. After explaining the setup of the empirical investigation, we report on the most significant results relating to design parameters for interactive dramatic experiences with AR.

2   Interactive Storytelling with the SPIRIT Prototype

One of the first visions of this project, which was inspired by possibilities of location-based AR, was to realize the metaphor of 'meeting the spirits of history' right at the place where they lived their lives – ideally, with no profane GUI elements that remind at a technical operation system. Consequently, several aspects of interaction design and storytelling had to be combined during conception: location scouting including local facts and visual perspectives as backdrops for action, suitable ideas for fictional characters and drama with connections to historical facts, and finally, interaction design that caters to the functional constraints, which are intricately interwoven with the achievement of the novel enabling technology. The result is a novel interaction pattern that new users need to learn at the start location of their first walk with the app. After that, the interaction pattern repeats at all further locations. For simplicity and to avoid over-complex interactions in the first instance, the prototype tested here works with a linear story, although a developed plot engine would enable the management of non-linear and conditional content.

2.1   Content Description of the Evaluated Experience

Visitors (as subjects) at the outdoor museum site of the Saalburg Roman Fort [22] started with a tutorial that explains the interaction with the SPIRIT app. The goal is to find spirits that appear at specific historical places. The spirit 'Aurelia' is introduced. She provides us with memory images that we can use as visual stencils (Fig. 1, center) to find views of places that had been meaningful for her. Step-by-step, the tutorial guides us to visualize spirits, holding the tablet vertically in front of these backdrops. Users can also follow lateral arrows to turn the tablet to the left or to the right, visualizing further spirits in the space around (Fig. 2). The menu is pointed out as well, consisting of buttons for listing met 'spirits', 'facts', 'progress' and a 'map' (Fig. 1, left).

Fig. 1. Searching methods 'map' and 'memory stencil' for finding active areas and triggering spirits.

Fig. 2. One active area with three viewing directions. After triggering the house of the spirit 'Titus' in the central view, he urges us to go into the fort. Turning about 90° to the left points into our walking direction, where we see Aurelia and Aliquander leave after their discussion with Titus. Turning back to the right reminds us that some strange guys follow us.

After the tutorial, Aurelia's memories begin in her former village – now only visible as low-rise mural remains – outside the main gate of the Roman fort (Fig. 1, center). We witness her parents, who try to rescue villagers into the fort, because of an announced attack of Germanic tribes. She also remembers that after the attack, two girls show her a piece of wood, which expresses a call for help from a kidnapped carriage. Together with her friend Aliquander, with whom she seems to share neighborly friendship as well as a beginning romance, she follows the cart to the eastern gate. Figure 2 shows the second location of the tour, at which their friend Titus gives them hints that the cart might contain stolen weapons, together with a kidnapped armorer. Titus urges Aurelia to warn her father, the Centurion of the fort.

Following Aurelia's memories, the visitor then has to pass the eastern gate to get into the fort. After these two meetings with other spirits, we learn that a Germanic ruler uses corrupt auxiliary soldiers to get hold of Roman weapons, only to beat the Romans with their own means. Following Aurelia's warning, the Romans try to stop the cart, thereby getting into another attack. Aurelia fears that Aliquander's life gets jeopardized, when she realizes that she cannot think of a life without him. Back at the main gate, her memories reveal to the visitor that after this incident, they had married and started a family. With the feeling of a happy end, they died in their old age, long after the fort had been abandoned by the Roman Empire as a consequence of the attacks.

In summary, two fictional threads are contained in the story – a tentative romantic love story of young adults in the village, and the complex political plot of Germanic assaults and corruptibility of auxiliary cohorts. Some story events trigger notifications in the facts menu (see Fig. 1, right), indicating that there is some brief factual information related to the situation. Users can read this at their convenience in between fictional scenes. For example, the village was indeed attacked in the year AD 233, and we learn details about the situation of women and auxiliaries during the Roman occupation.

2.2   Technical Constraints Influencing the User Experience

The functionality underlying the SPIRIT player has been described elsewhere [8, 12] and is not in the focus of this contribution. However, in order to use the system, some knowledge of it has proven useful, in order to develop a suitable conceptual image of successful interaction. The visual recognition is based on the ORB algorithm [21], searching camera images for matching pixel patterns in a set of reference images. These reference images are photographed backdrops for spirit scenes, prepared during authoring. The 'memory stencil' images have no direct function in the process, only indirectly, as mere support devices for users to find places with backdrops and point at these with low speed. The recognition works sufficiently reliable, especially as the system supports ad-hoc adding of current photographs in advance of a tour. However, on days with frequent changes in lighting conditions, the system might still have difficulties, resulting in recognition failure as well as in false positives.

The triggering of new video content, after the tablet is turned to the left or to the right, is accomplished by the gyroscope sensor, which works incrementally. Apparently, for novice users, the proper momentum and degree of turning is hard to guess, unless the movement is demonstrated by someone. Therefore, the tutorial, which shows an animated modelled action, has been considered as necessary by most novice users. After adopting the movement, this interaction works reliably.

The augmented content consists of prepared video sequences with live-acting characters. Bluescreen production and chroma-key postproduction let them look like floating in thin air on top of the device's camera image of real surroundings. After their appearance, characters seem to stay at their 'place' within the image of the real environment – as expected for AR content. This is a crucial feature for the user experience of presence, but nevertheless, it can lead novice users, who are inexperienced in AR, to missing the visualization when they move the tablet too fast, while the audio continues.

Concluding, issues due to the technicalities of the prototype did partially influence the assessed user experience in our test.

2.3 Goals for the Interactive Story Experience

Through dramatic staging in front of the ruins and reconstructed historical buildings, the actors stay 'in character', re-enacting fictional personal memories with emotional content. Associated facts exist, however, our design demanded to avoid situations, in which characters also adopt the role of modern museum guides. Therefore, brief text summaries of factual knowledge can only be consulted separately on demand of the user, anytime in between.

The goals we wanted to achieve with the specific design have been (i) the experience of 'presence' of the spirits in the real environment, which is associated with a sense of 'genius loci', (ii) motivation and interest to learn more about the Roman world through an emotional story, and (iii) the freedom to use the menu at the individual user's convenience for appreciating the connection of the story to historical facts. One important design parameter, which distinguishes our prototype from other solutions, is the inclusion of the 90° turns. With this interaction pattern, we can stage different characters surrounding the user, and can prompt the user to look into specific physical directions. Our hypothesis is that this aspect supports a sense of place, together with the appreciation of the presence of the events within the real locality.

3 Related Work

Location-based Augmented Reality is an emerging topic, especially in application areas in the realm of storytelling, education, and historical information connected to geographic places. Blurry lines exist between location-based gaming and storytelling, and between serious applications and entertainment [3, 13, 20, 25]. Recent evaluations addressed learning outcomes and experiential qualities [7, 15]. The results of these support our design goal to not focus on stories for the acquisition of knowledge, but for motivational aspects, such as gaining empathy with the past. Additionally, AR does not yet rely on standardized user interaction styles, as different hardware approaches lead to unfamiliar systems that have to be learned by novice users in the first place. There is still a lack of evaluation with non-technical target groups, as a majority of subjects used to be recruited within the academic field [2] or higher education settings [1]. In our project, we created a novel and unique interaction style that we have not found elsewhere yet. We evaluated it with regular museum visitors, spanning a great diversity of people including families. Besides testing the usability, the experience aspired by design relates most to the feeling of presence [16, 19], sense of place [6] or aura [17]. In other projects, these factors have been evaluated with applications that so far do not resemble our integration of the search for places, turning around and rendering through video-based storytelling. Still, there are outcomes in line with those of our study, concerning the necessary distribution of attention focus between media and the environment.

4   Empirical Analysis

4.1   Survey

The empirical survey was carried out by students of Hochschule RheinMain on 5 days in May/June 2017 at the Saalburg Roman Fort [22]. The interviewers randomly invited regular museum visitors to participate in the testing and survey. Single and pair visitors, as well as small groups and families constituted subjects to participate most likely. That way, a total of 70 groups of visitors could be acquired to walk the tour with the app. 2 researchers accompanied each tour, one for support and one observer taking notes of situational reactions and remarks. 107 subjects from these test groups completed the post-tour questionnaire and answered additional qualitative questions. The form included 26 groups of questions with 40 single questions, of which – besides the topics of demographics, usability and learning – 20 items were related to 'storytelling' in the broader sense. For answering most questions, a 5-step Likert scale was used.

In this paper, we focus on these 20 storytelling-related questions. Further, we take into account 3 questions addressing potential disturbing or interference factors. In the following, we analyze the results in terms of their reliability and validity. Based on this, various correlation and regression analyses are carried out [10, 11]. Before detailing the statistical analyses, we summarize basic facts:

- Out of the 107 subjects, 62 were female and 45 male. The numbers per age groups are as follows: <20 (34), 21–29 (16), 30–39 (13), 40–49 (19), 50–59 (18), >60 (7). The average experience with similar apps (e.g., Pokémon GO, Ingress, Geocaching, AR) is "low" (2.1 on the Likert scale, with 1 for "not at all" and 5 for "very much" experienced).
- The users rated the experience mainly positive (average grades of 4.0–3.8, where 5 is highest degree of approval), based on the questions "I had fun using the app", "I wish the app would be available also in other museums with fitting content", "I recommend the app".
- 88.8% of the users confirmed that there have been 'any' disturbing factors while using the app. Grades for single causes fell between 2 (low influence) and 3 (medium influence). Thus, most troublesome was "Holding the tablet" (2.8), "Technical problems" (2.7), "Long dialogs" (2.7) and "90 degree turns" (2.6).
- Regarding the questions (a) "Through the app, I could immerse myself into the Saalburg's history" and (b) "I got the impression that the characters were present like ghosts in the environment", the users responded between rather positive and neutral, i.e. average grades of 3.5 for (a), and 3.1 for (b).
- Out of factors for a potential perception of historic 'aura', the aspects "Scenes relating to locations", "Historical characters", "Search for locations" and "Map" received the highest degrees of approval (average grades of 3.7–3.6).
- Concerning parameters for the "Motivation to continue", all items were ranked rather positive ("Search for locations" 3.8, "Novelty of the app usage" 3.7, "Suspense of the story" 3.2).

4.2 Reliability and Validity

Reliability is a measure of the formal accuracy of surveys. It is that part of the variance that can be explained by differences in the characteristic to be measured, and not by (measurement) errors. Reliable results must mainly be free of random errors (i.e. reproducibility of results under the same conditions). We use Cronbach's Alpha to measure the reliability, where values higher than 0.7 represent a good reliability. Accordingly, the concepts and data collected are to be considered as reliable (see Table 1).

Table 1. Cronbach's alpha and validity analysis

Questions related to the concepts of ...	Cronbach's Alpha	KMO	Bartlett-Test	Cumulative Variance
Fun / Recommendation (a)	0.887	0.799	p < 0.000	74.832%
Interference Factors (b)	0.711	0.712	p < 0.000	41.680%
Presence (c)	0.878	0.849	p < 0.000	64.374%
Appraisal of the Story (d)	0.836	0.770	p < 0.000	61.527%

Validity refers to the consistency of an empirical measurement with a logical measurement concept. Based on literature, a significant Bartlett test ($p < 0.050$) indicates a valid data collection. This is supported by the Kaiser-Meyer-Olkin test (KMO), which indicates good validity by a value higher than 0.7. For a good explanation rate, the cumulative variance has to be higher than 50%, i.e. if a large part of the variances of the collected data can be explained, the collected data are valid. Thus, nearly all presented results in Table 1 support validity, but the cumulative variance for the questions related to interference factors, which is lower than 50%. This means in this case that 41.680% of the variances of the collected data can be explained.

Examples for questions of each concept are: (a) "I enjoyed using the app" (3 items), (b) "The following factors bothered me while using the app" (6 items), (c) "I got the impression that the characters were present as ghosts in the real environment" (9 items), (d) "I liked the story" (5 items).

4.3 General Correlation Analysis

The correlation coefficient analysis determines the degree of linear relationship between two individual variables (however, not the degree of dependence). A correlation of 1.000 shows a 'perfect' relationship, and a value higher than 0.500 is classified as a 'good' relation [5]. Between all our relevant 23 variables/questions, 253 correlation coefficients exist. We identified 65 correlation coefficients that are significant ($p < 0.050$) and have a value over 0.500. For the sake of brevity, we list here only relationships with correlation coefficients higher than 0.700:

- Relation between variables "I wish the app would be available also in other museums with fitting content" and "I recommend the app" (coefficient 0.765).

- Relation between the variables "I was motivated to continue by the suspense of the story" and "I liked the story" (coefficient 0.755), which supports strongly the results of the regression analysis.
- Relation between the variables "I had fun using the app" and "All in all, I rate the app concept …" (coefficient 0.718), which shows that the overall rating of the app is mostly related to the 'fun factor'.
- Relation between the variables "I gained knowledge of the Saalburg through using the app" and "I liked the story" (coefficient 0.708), which shows that the gaining of knowledge is strongly related to the level of appraisal of the story.

4.4   Regression Analysis on Presence Factors

Regression analysis explains relationships between a dependent variable and one or more independent variables. Beyond general correlations suggested by the collected data, we are especially interested in criteria to achieve the perception of 'presence' of the historical scenes in the environment through AR. Therefore, we performed regression analysis for the dependent variables "Through the app, I could immerse myself into the Saalburg's history" (Table 2) and "I got the impression that the characters were present as ghosts in the real environment" (Table 3).

Table 2. Regression analysis – dependent variable "Through the app, I could immerse myself into the Saalburg's history"

Independent Variables/Questions	Regression Coefficient	Significance (p)
"Characters were present as ghosts"	**0.203**	**0.009**
"Perception of historic aura fostered by …"		
Image overlay	0.083	0.342
90 degree turns	0.129	0.116
Historical characters	0.195	0.073
Scenes relating to locations	**0.218**	**0.047**
Search for locations	0.189	0.055
Map	**-0.203**	**0.046**
Audio	0.112	0.168

Table 3. Regression analysis – dependent variable "Characters were present as ghosts"

Independent Variables/Questions	Regression Coefficient	Significance (p)
"Perception of historic aura fostered by … "		
Image overlay	0.177	0.181
90 degree turns	0.152	0.218
Historical characters	0.208	0.202
Scenes relating to locations	0.031	0.850
Search for locations	0.062	0.678
Map	0.038	0.805
Audio	**0.257**	**0.036**

The dependent variable "Through the app, I could immerse myself into the Saalburg's history" is

- significantly positive ($p < 0.050$) influenced by the variable "Impression that the characters were present as ghosts in the real environment" (coefficient 0.203),
- significantly positive ($p < 0.050$) influenced by the variable "Perception of historic aura fostered by scenes relating to locations" (coefficient 0.218),
- significantly negative ($p < 0.050$) influenced by the variable "Perception of historic aura fostered by the map" (coefficient −0.203).

Although all the regression coefficients do not exceed the desired 0.500, based on Brosius [5] the values (higher than 0.200) can be classified as sufficient. In the particular case in question, where the change of the dependent variable is explained by only one or a few independent variables, explanatory rates (=regression coefficients) higher than 0.2 can already be regarded as worthwhile to be considered as indications. (The R-square of 61.9% shows, that descriptive variables reach a good explanation rate, i.e. dependent variables can be explained to a high degree with the independent variables.)

This means that if a user gets stronger impressions by the named variables ("Characters were present as ghosts" and "Perception of historic aura fostered by scenes relating to locations"), he or she will feel more strongly immersed into the history of the Saalburg. Remarkably, the variable "Perception of historic aura fostered by the map" influences the immersion negatively, i.e. the search actions with the map seem to tend to hinder rather than to promote the immersion into the history of the Saalburg.

The dependent variable "Characters were present as ghosts" is significantly positive ($p < 0.050$) influenced only by the variable "Perception of historic aura fostered by Audio". The coefficient 0.257 is higher than 0.200 and can be classified as sufficient [5]. (The R-square of 34.1% shows that descriptive variables reach a good explanation rate.) Due to the fact that only one significant independent variable could be identified, a stepwise regression analysis is performed to analyse each of independent variables more specifically. The stepwise regression leads again to a significantly positive ($p < 0.050$) influence of the variable "Perception of historic aura fostered by Audio" (coefficient 0.393), as well as to a significantly positive ($p < 0.050$) influence of the variable "Perception of historic aura fostered by 90 degree turns" (coefficient 0.293). Again, the regression coefficients (higher than 0.200) can be classified as sufficient [5]. (However, the R-square of 19.1% shows that descriptive variables reach only a poor explanation rate.)

From the quantitative data, "Audio" has the strongest influence on the extent to which users of the app feel the 'presence of ghosts'. Also the aspect of "90 degree turns" seems to support the 'ghost feeling'. However, due to the low explanatory rate of the stepwise regression, it is recommendable to look into the qualitative analyses for other indicators to the aspects of presence.

4.5   Regression Analysis on Story Appraisal

As shown in Table 4, the dependent variable "I liked the story" is

- significantly positive ($p < 0.050$) influenced by the variable "Motivated to continue by the suspense of the story" (coefficient 0.634),
- significantly positive ($p < 0.050$) influenced by the variable "Motivated to continue by the search of locations" (coefficient 0.328),
- significantly positive ($p < 0.050$) influenced by the subject's age (coefficient 0.129).

Table 4. Regression analysis – dependent variable "I liked the story"

Independent Variables/Questions	Regression Coefficient	Significance (p)
"Age"	0.129	0.005
"Motivated to continue by ..."		
Suspense of the story	0.634	0.000
Novelty of the app usage	0.073	0.317
Search of locations	0.328	0.000

The coefficients higher than 0.200 can again be classified as sufficient. The R-square of 68.3% shows that the descriptive variables reach a good explanation rate. All in all, the factor "Suspense of the story" has a very strong influence (coefficient 0.634) on the extent to which users liked the story.

4.6 Qualitative Analysis

Next to the quantitative data collection, we acquired qualitative data, in order to also get input on open aspects that the questionnaire did not cover. The accompanying researchers in each tour filled an observation form, to mainly note spontaneous remarks or reactions of users to situations. The observer also registered who (of a group) used the tablet, an own account of the subjects' initial motivation, how much support was required, and what different parts of the interface were used. Further, after their tour, subjects were asked a last open question concerning the story contents they remember, and how they liked certain aspects of it. If they agreed, this short conversation was audio-recorded. Afterwards, all filled forms and audio tapes were transcribed verbatim, and then sorted by the method of structural content analysis [18], building categories, and developing hypotheses from these. Thus, for some aspects that can hardly be explained with the statistical data at hand, we got further insights, as users partly provided explicit verbal explanations. Here, we only briefly summarize selected key insights to complement our statistical results, especially regarding the concept of presence and interactive story appreciation. Any quotes are translated from German.

Most comments of users or peculiarities in their interaction that were noted down concerned the finding of locations (115 notes in this category), the story content (91 notes) and the 90° turning (66 notes).

Although in principle, our interaction concept has proven to be learnable, many users needed some time to grasp the 90° turns, before they managed after a while. Apparently, several users did not experience the AR overlay, i.e., (to try or manage) to perceive the video characters as floating 'in reality' at a location, visible through a magic window ("Where is he gone?"/"The head is cut off"). Thus it is comprehensible that those did not get the point of having to turn around at all. ("I don't understand why turning around should be good"). Positive examples include a father managing it immediately, after the daughter demonstrated the movement to him, or "Now it's OK, I just needed to get used to the turning", or a family pointing to the direction of where the cart might be now in reality (after the video characters had pointed there). There were also many positive reactions to the first appearances of Augmented Reality ("Oh how cool", a girl trying to 'feel' the ghosts) and awareness that the real environment is seen through (friends/partners try to join the spirits in the camera image, "I can see you").

When asked to reproduce details of the experienced story content after the tour, given answers were very diverse. Some claimed not to remember anything ("I mainly paid attention to the app, that's the problem"). Only few presented a comprehensive account of almost all events. In these cases, the story elements were mixed in with the user's own journey report and attached to places.

Many reported at first to remember love story elements. However, although the majority thought of the romantic aspect as positive or neutral, about a quarter of the interview partners expressed negative remarks about it ("Amusing, but unnecessary"/"I was rather bothered by it, because it is [...] not so much related to the Saalburg, rather a private story, appeared inappropriate to me.") Others indeed realized its relationship to the Saalburg ("Why not! I mean, when I just want to present how life was here in general, then it's probably just necessary"). Several people claimed their desire and expectation to learn "more facts" when they visit a museum. Very few users made use of the "Facts" button in the menu, though.

On the other hand, some mentioned having been influenced by the test situation ("If I would be here alone and would have time, I would probably sit down and read every fact"). The group aspect also influenced other interactions, such as the 90° turns. As a matter of fact, it is easily possible to watch the content on a tablet-size device as a group of three. However, 90° turns then require the bystanders to jump around in order to follow (a father giving commands "Now everybody turn back!").

The observers also noted several remarks of users who were bothered by having to walk back to an already visited location ("We want to see more of the Saalburg!"), although according to the story, it made sense to return. Actually, reducing the experience to a limited number of places was not part of our ideal concept, but due to prototype and evaluation practicality. However, the remarks also point to characteristics of designing progress structures in location-based AR, as its concepts of moving around differ from adventure games played at a computer. Especially museum visitors might expect a 'guided tour'.

5 Conclusion

With the SPIRIT project, we developed a system and prototypical content for a specialized form of location-based interactive storytelling with Augmented Reality. The prototype has been evaluated with end-users concerning some special design goals connected to the Augmented Reality experience, namely to feel a connection to a place and presence of spirits, as well as the appreciation of the form of storytelling. While the interaction design and the presence have been pre-tested in iterative cycles with media-savvy subjects, showing promising results, this was the first evaluation with random museum visitors.

Based on the quantitative evaluation we found that overall, users liked the app and would recommend it. However, many users reported also disturbing factors interfering with their usage. Our mentioned goals, particularly the feeling of a connection to the place and the presence of spirits, have not yet been fully achieved; on average, the users rated these aspects only slightly positive to neutral. It is still interesting to look at the correlating items. For the "Perception of historic aura", the items "Scenes relating to locations" and "Historical characters" are the strongest supporting factors. The factor "90 degree turns", however, is interesting, as the majority of people had problems with it, due to usability issues with this unfamiliar interaction. Looking into the qualitative evaluation results suggests that those participants who did not report problems with the 90° turns, expressed indeed a connection of the story to the place. This aspect needs further investigation.

The statistical analysis shows that the majority of the survey's results are reliable and valid. The regression analysis suggests that the "Perceived presence of ghosts" has the strongest influence on the extent to which users of the app could immerse themselves into the history, "Audio" has the strongest influence on the extent to which users of the app feel ghosts present and the variable "Suspense of the story" has a very strong influence on the extent to which users like the story.

For future work, the results point out that the introduction of unfamiliar interaction patterns (together with technical insufficiencies of the prototype) influenced the experience of presence, however with prospects that further development can reduce the disturbing factors.

Acknowledgements. This work has been funded (in part) by the Federal Ministry of Education and Research (BMBF) in Germany (03FH035PA3). We thank all project members for their support (see [23] for videos and personal credits). Special thanks go to students in Media Management at the RheinMain University of Applied Sciences, who conducted the inquiries.

References

1. Bacca, J., Baldiris, S., Fabregat, R., Graf, S., Kinshuk: Augmented reality trends in education: a systematic review of research and applications. Educ. Technol. Soc. **17**(4), 133–149 (2014)
2. Bai, Z., Blackwell, A.F.: Analytic review of usability evaluation in ISMAR. Interact. Comput. **24**(6), 450–460 (2012)
3. Ballagas, R., Kuntze, A., Walz, S.P.: Gaming tourism: lessons from evaluating rexplorer, a pervasive game for tourists. In: 6th International Conference, Pervasive 2008, Sydney, Australia, pp. 244–262 (2008)
4. Brancati, N., Caggianese, G., De Pietro, G., Frucci, M., Gallo, L., Neroni, P.: Usability evaluation of a wearable augmented reality system for the enjoyment of the cultural heritage. In: Proceedings of the 11th International Conference on Signal-Image Technology and Internet-Based Systems (SITIS). IEEE (2015)
5. Brosius, F.: SPSS 8 Professionelle Statistik unter Windows, Kapitel 21 Korrelation, pp. 497–509. International Thomson Publishing (1998)

6. Chang, Y.-L., Hou, H.-T., Pan, C.-Y., Sung, Y.-T., Chang, K.-E.: Apply an augmented reality in a mobile guidance to increase sense of place for heritage places. Educ. Technol. Soc. **18**(2), 166–178 (2015)
7. Chen, P., Liu, X., Cheng, W., Huang, R.: A review of using Augmented Reality in education from 2011 to 2016. In: Popescu, E., et al. (eds.) Innovations in Smart Learning, pp. 13–18. Springer, Singapore (2017). https://doi.org/10.1007/978-981-10-2419-1_2
8. Dastageeri, H., Storz, M., Coors, V.: SPIRIT – Videobasierte mobile Augmented Reality Lösung zur interaktiven Informationsvermittlung. In: Proceedings of DGPF 2015, Band 24, pp. 288–295. Deutsche Gesellschaft für Photogrammetrie, Fernerkundung und Geoinformation e.V., Köln (2015)
9. Feiner, S., MacIntyre, B., Höllerer, T., Webster, A.: A touring machine: prototyping 3D mobile augmented reality systems for exploring the urban environment. In: Proceedings of the First International Symposium on Wearable Computers (ISWC 1997), Cambridge, MA, pp. 74–81 (1997)
10. Field, A.: Discovering Statistics Using SPSS, 4th edn. Sage Publications Ltd., London (2013)
11. Hair, J.F.J., Anderson, R.E., Tatham, R.L., Black, W.C.: Multivariate Data Analysis, 3rd edn. Macmillan, New York (1995)
12. Kampa, A., Spierling, U.: Requirements and solutions for location-based augmented reality storytelling in an outdoor museum. In: Culture and Computer Science – Augmented Reality, Proceedings of KUI 2016, pp. 105–117. VWH-Verlag, Glückstadt (2016)
13. Keil, J., Pujol, L., Roussou, M., Engelke, T., Schmitt, M., Bockholt, U., Eleftheratou, S.: A digital look at physical museum exhibits. In: Proceedings of Digital Heritage 2013, Marseille. IEEE (2013)
14. Kretschmer, U., Coors, V., Spierling, U., Grasbon, D., Schneider, K., Rojas, I., Malaka, R.: Meeting the spirit of history. In: Proceedings of the International Symposium on Virtual Reality, Archaeology and Cultural Heritage, VAST 2001, Glyfada, Greece, pp. 161–172 (2001)
15. Li, R., Zhang, B., Sundar, S.S., Duh, H.B.-L.: Interacting with augmented reality: how does location-based AR enhance learning? In: Kotzé, P., Marsden, G., Lindgaard, G., Wesson, J., Winckler, M. (eds.) INTERACT 2013. LNCS, vol. 8118, pp. 616–623. Springer, Heidelberg (2013). https://doi.org/10.1007/978-3-642-40480-1_43
16. Lombard, M., Ditton, T.: At the heart of it all: the concept of presence. Comput. Mediat. Commun. **3**(2) (1997)
17. MacIntyre, B., Bolter, J.D., Gandy, M.: Presence and the aura of meaningful places. Presence Teleop. Virtual Environ. **6**(2), 197–206 (2004)
18. Mayring, P.: Qualitative Inhaltsanalyse: Grundlagen und Techniken. Beltz, Weinheim (2010)
19. McCall, R., Braun, A.K.: Experiences of evaluating presence in augmented realities. PsychNol. J. **6**, 157–172 (2008)
20. Rodrigo, M.M., Caluya, N.R., Diy, W.D., Vidal, E.C.E.: Igpaw: intramuros—design of an augmented reality game for philippine history. In: Proceedings of the 23rd International Conference on Computers in Education (2015)
21. Rublee, E., Rabaud, V., Konolige, K., Bradski, G.R.: ORB: an efficient alternative to SIFT or SURF. In: Proceedings of IEEE International Conference on Computer Vision (ICCV 2011), Barcelona, pp. 2564–2571 (2011)
22. Saalburg Roman Fort, Archaeological Park. Homepage. http://www.saalburgmuseum.de/. Accessed 25 Aug 2017
23. Spirit Homepage. http://spirit.interactive-storytelling.de/. Accessed 25 Aug 2017

24. Vlahakis, V., Karigiannis, J., Tsotros, M., Gounaris, M., Almeida, L., Stricker, D., Gleue, T., Christou, I.T., Carlucci, R., Ioannidis, N.: Archeoguide: first results of an augmented reality mobile computing system in cultural heritage sites. In: Proceedings of the International Symposium on Virtual Reality, Archaeology and Cultural Heritage, VAST 2001, Glyfada, Greece, pp. 131–139 (2001)
25. Weber, J.: Designing engaging experiences with location-based augmented reality games for urban tourism environments. Doctorate thesis, Bournemouth University (2017)

Developing a Writer's Toolkit for Interactive Locative Storytelling

Heather S. Packer[1], Charlie Hargood[2], Yvonne Howard[1],
Petros Papadopoulos[1], and David E. Millard[1(✉)]

[1] University of Southampton, Southampton, UK
{hp3,ymh,pp1v15,dem}@ecs.soton.ac.uk
[2] University of Bournemouth, Bournemouth, UK
chargood@bournemouth.ac.uk

Abstract. Despite the increasing popularity of locative interactive stories their poetics are poorly understood, meaning that there is little advice or support for locative authors, and few frameworks for critical analysis. The StoryPlaces project has spent two years working with over sixty authors creating locative stories. Through analyzing the stories themselves, and interviewing readers, we have developed a simple writer's toolkit that highlights the challenges and opportunities offered by locative fiction. In this paper, we describe our approach and outline twelve key pragmatic and aesthetic considerations that we have derived from our experience and analyses. Together these reveal that the main challenge in locative literature lies in aligning the narrative text, the structural logic, and the demands and affordances of the landscape.

Keywords: Locative literature · Interactive narratives · Authoring

1 Introduction

Locative Stories are narratives read on mobile devices where the reader interacts with the story by physically moving between locations. They were initially used for applications such as tour guides [6], but in recent years there has been a focus on interactive fiction [9], and the incorporation of new technologies (such as augmented reality [20]). Despite this interest, there has been relatively little work on the poetics of locative stories - how they function to produce an effect in the reader. Such a poetics is needed to understand how authors can use the landscape to help tell their story.

StoryPlaces is a research project to explore these poetics, by working with writers in a number of different *Story Projects*. We have then analyzed their stories to understand the sorts of structures and methods they use [11], and have interviewed readers to understand how the interaction between narrative and landscape affected their experience. We have also developed our own location-based story using co-operative inquiry, and have used this experience to reflect on the decisions taken during the authoring process [17].

© Springer International Publishing AG 2017
N. Nunes et al. (Eds.): ICIDS 2017, LNCS 10690, pp. 63–74, 2017.
https://doi.org/10.1007/978-3-319-71027-3_6

In this paper, we draw on our story analyses and reader interviews from the first two Story Projects (Southampton and Bournemouth) and our co-operative inquiry to present an authoring toolkit in the shape of twelve pragmatic and aesthetic recommendations to authors. We have used this toolkit with our third story project (Crystal Palace Park), and present here one of these stories as a case study to show how those recommendations can be used in practice. Our hope is that they will help authors directly in shaping and creating their work, but also that they will inform future authoring and analytic tools.

2   Background

Locative literature, or location-based storytelling, has its routes in the digital tour guides created in the 1990s [6]. But over the last twenty years, alongside an improvement in location sensing and device capability, there has been a far broader range of applications. For example:

Tour Guides: There are a number of frameworks authors can use to publish tour guides, including HIPS which was used for the Louvre tour [6] and REXplorer [2]. There are also location aware tour guides that use factual stories to paint a picture of a place [19].

Educational Tools: Educational tools focus on the process of learning about a place, and might therefore, be considered a natural extension of a guide. Examples include interactive educational tools such as Gaius' Day in Egnathia [11] and 'edutainment' systems such as Geist [14]. There are also location aware systems that use the same sculptural model as StoryPlaces, including the Ambient Wood project [22], and the Chawton House project [24].

Location Aware Games: This category includes systems with game mechanics connected to player context as well as augmented reality experiences, such as Viking Ghost Hunt [20] or University of Death [8]. The work of [1] begins to describe two considerations when designing location aware games. Specifically, 1.5 Consider the social conventions of the place (e.g. not loud speaking in a church) and 1.7 Consider to include activities/events that are not part of the game but happen in the real world.

Location Aware Fiction: Focuses on delivering an engaging story within a place. There are many examples of locative fiction including The iLand of Madeira [9], San Servolo, travel into the memory of an island [21], and a collection of stories around Dublin [18].

It has been argued that these kinds of locative systems are better termed *Ambient Literature* as a challenge to the primacy of location and in an effort to foreground a more human and less sensory dimension [10]. Others have looked at the area from a more experiential perspective, for example modeling interaction as a trajectory that the user takes through complex spaces [3]. These perspectives do consider the wider context of locative interactions, but their complexity is also a barrier to their use by authors.

As a reaction to this complexity, we have deliberately pared down the experience to focus on narrative and place, primarily working on the domain of locative fiction, although our findings can be applied to the other categories. Our locative narratives are derived from a sculptural hypertext approach [4,25], which imagines the narrative as a collection of pages with constraints and behaviors (allowing location to be modeled as just another constraint). Pages can contain any combination of text, images, and audio.

There are many papers which provide recommendations for structuring hypertext narratives, which may be drawn upon when writing for place [5,7,13]. Specifically, the work presented in [12] provides a practical approach to structuring a branching story, using four stages: paper, prototype, production, and testing. There are also approaches for character development from different perspectives [23]. But otherwise, there is limited advice for authors. Most of the papers describing locative literature focus on a single framework, without discussing overarching practices. In fact, most papers which present digital locative narratives offer little practical advice on their creation.

3   Methodology

We have undertaken exploratory research using a novel framework of sequential story projects, developing our understanding at each stage and feeding it into the next [15]. The first two story projects were:

1. **Southampton Old Town** where we worked with forty creative writing students to write locative stories within the old city. We took a paper prototyping approach to keep the process open, so that we could understand the authoring process and develop authoring tools [11]. Five stories were chosen to be implemented for reader evaluation, and we also commissioned a professional writer to create a tent-pole story for a public launch.
2. **Bournemouth Natural Science Society** where we worked with local authoring groups and colleges to create interactive locative stories based on the collections of the Bournemouth Natural Science Society. Five authors got to the point of having complete stories, and again we commissioned a professional author to create a more substantial story alongside them.

For both projects, we hosted a public launch. If they were willing we recorded semi-structured interviews with readers immediately after they had completed the story to understand their experience. These typically took between 15 and 30 min. In total, we recorded 25 interviews in Southampton, and 9 in Bournemouth.

Alongside these we also undertook the creation of our own locative story, taking advantage of a three day workshop and makespace on the Island of Tiree to create a longer experience called *The Isle of Brine* that could explore more complex and interactive structures [16]. We recorded and analyzed our experience as a co-operative inquiry, a qualitative method based on experiential reflection, focusing on the design decisions around narrative structure and location [17].

We then drew on these 13 stories, 34 interviews, and co-operative inquiry to establish a toolkit for authors in the form of twelve recommendations. We then used these in our third story project, based at Crystal Palace Park in London, once more commissioning a professional author to undertake a more substantial piece of work. As a form of validation we present that story, *Fallen Branches* by Katie Lyons, and critically analyze it against the toolkit in order to see the impact of the recommendations.

4   The Toolkit

The toolkit we have created is a set of advice for location-authors, divided into Dealbreakers, Pragmatics, and Aesthetics. In each case, we have described the entry in the toolkit and provided an example of the evidence behind it.

4.1   Dealbreakers

The first three entries in the toolkit may appear to be self-evident, but we were surprised exactly how many of the authors and stories overlooked them. In our experience, if the story did not adhere to these qualities than most readers would choose not to read, or would abandon the reading when this became clear.

Points of Arrival/Departure: Think about where readers will start and end your story (which may be in more than one place), and how well these match the normal ways that they arrive in or depart from a place. For example, think about starting near a standard point of entrance, and finishing near to the same place (as people often leave by the same route they arrive).

Participant: I guess we did makes some decisions about what routes to walk. But, I think that was mainly about, like, to do with where we want to finish, rather than what would be a good walk to do this story to.

Isle of Brine used three distinct areas of the island (one for each Act) so this was especially important, as readers are likely to drive between areas, so each Act of the story starts and ends in a car park, with the assumption that the reader will explore the pages of the Act on foot before returning to their car.

Be Mindful of the Reader's Effort to Move: Readers are more likely to choose a page that is nearer to them than one that is further away, and may ignore optional pages at a distance altogether. Avoid sending them on zig-zagging routes, or making them double-back too much.

Writers commonly underestimated how much effort it was for readers to move long distances, and how frustrating it was to be forced to retread their steps.

Participant: one location is quite near another location, but, actually, I can see how the toing and froing, for some people, wouldn't be what they wanted to do.

Participant: I feel like people would become tired and then would be, like, less inclined to be open to what you've got to say in the Act, by the end of it, anyway.

The Southampton story *The Destitute and the Alien* is a linear historical story. The writer wanted to locate scenes in appropriate locations, but many were along the old waterfront and the focus moved between them as logically required, without consideration of the spatial layout. In one case this made the reader walk 500 m to read 200 words before being asked to walk back again.

Less criticism was directed at stories that used revisiting if they were mindful to maintain a continuous progression. For example, the story *The Titanic Criminal in Southampton* was well received despite revisiting areas and this might be attributed to its looping structure as opposed to a more zig zagging path.

Consider Total Time to Read: Consider the total time it will take to experience the narrative and whether it fits with the normal time constraints for people visiting that location. For example, one story could be designed to be read during a lunch break, or another story could be a more committed multi-hour experience.

Participant: I'd have probably chosen that one, but when we looked and it takes that long to do it - if we'd have come earlier in the day, maybe we would have...

In the Bournemouth story *Seeker of Secrets* the author created his story based on existing knowledge, using a virtual map to choose locations. He was later surprised to realize that it took four hours to read on location, which was inappropriate for most of the audience: tourists with around an hour to spare.

This is not a limit on absolute length, for example *Isle of Brine* takes a similar time, but is designed as a larger experience, more akin to an afternoon exploring the island. Furthermore, it is broken into three sections, each at a separate location, and may be split into separate reading experiences over multiple days.

There are other solutions too. The Bournemouth story *The Pathways of Destiny* is a children's story focused on choice. Here the author created optional paths that allowed an early exit. By keeping required content to a minimum the author created an experience that the reader was able to control while still having a 'complete' story experience.

4.2 Pragmatic Considerations

Use Landscape to Control Navigation: For example, laying pages along paths so that they are typically read in a particular order, looking for loops in the landscape that could be used to help readers revisit pages, or placing key choices at junctions and crossroads.

Isle of Brine uses paths to create an illusion of choice, for example, in the first Act the story opens in the car park with a single path running the 200 m to the beach, the path nodes do not have preconditions, meaning that they all appear in the reader at once as potential destinations, but in practice they will always be read in order, as the reader moves along the path to the beach.

In *The Pathways of Destiny* a question is posed in a plaza, which opens two potential answers to the north and south of the reader. Symbolically the northern answer, in the direction of the town, leads to adventure, but the southern one, in the direction of the sea, leads to an earlier conclusion.

Identify and Use Bottlenecks in the Landscape: Bottlenecks such as gates, lone paths, or passes, are good places to put important narrative information, as most of your readers will pass through them and read any pages placed there.

In *Isle of Brine* there are key pages associated with the car parks, as the entrance and exit of each Act, key narrative information (for example, important background information on secondary characters) is deliberately placed in these pages to guarantee that all readers would encounter them.

Identify High Cost Locations: Certain locations are difficult to reach (they may be far away, up a steep hill or steps, or be otherwise inaccessible), these should only be used as optional pages, and might be considered as rewards.

Participant: I want a way to not just finish early but to say "I can't get there but I still want to read the rest of the story" or something

Participant: It was quite a long old walk up there to St Mary's and back again... It's, like, I don't know. I mean, you can't change the geography of Southampton, obviously, but if there was maybe something else along the way

One story (not selected for publication) was for practical purposes unreadable; it followed the story of a shipping container, with non-optional pages in New York and Southampton - authors used to the flexible time and space of their storyworlds seem slow to adapt to the practicalities of locative literature.

Consider Accessibility and the Reader's Safety: On their walk will the reader be alone? Are the locations visible and well-populated? Are there access issues, e.g. for wheelchair users, or a family with a buggy? While using place to set the tone it is important that you do not put your readers at risk.

Participant: So, there's a bit of a risk ... you're looking about you, but you're also looking at your screen, and, you know, you feel you're slightly aware of [being] this person going around following a screen and not looking round about you

One Southampton story (not selected for publication) used time of day as a condition for some of its pages, requiring readers to visit isolated areas of the city in the middle of the night - effective for setting a mood, but not very practical.

4.3   Aesthetics

Narrative Areas: Consider how to use the landscape to create narrative areas, e.g.: stages of a journey, or areas with different themes or tones. It will help readers if important transitions in your narrative match transitions in physical space (from one area to another).

For example, *Pathways of Destiny* uses the plaza at the foot of Bournemouth Pier as a setup area, where the reader meets the protagonists and makes choices about what role to take in the rest of the story, moving to the Lower Garden for the main quest where that role is assumed. *Isle of Brine* uses three different areas of the island for its three Acts, each of which has a different tone.

Identify Points of Interest in the Landscape: Consider how to use points of interest within your story. An important landmark demands attention within the narrative. These landmarks naturally draw readers to particular points. However, ignoring points of interest creates a disconnect between the story and the landscape - which may also be useful.

Points of interest can be overused, resulting in something more like a guide.

Participant: The story we've done today was based on history and the one that we almost did and aborted partway through because the kids were bored was much more like a historical tour guide than a story.

So there is a need to balance the focus between the fictional and real worlds, this can be done by using points of interest for narrative effect rather than explaining them. For example, *Notes on an Illegible City*, an eclectic collection of poems and prose on Southampton's past, future, and present, uses a key location outside an ancient church and in view of the medieval Bargate. However, the poem is about neither. Rather they are a fulcrum around which the poem can transport the reader into the past, the two acting as points of constancy that contrast with the shifting human life that is the poem's subject.

Consider the Theme/Tone of the Space: Consider the theme and tone of the space and its relationship to the theme and tone of the narrative. The space may change over time, depending on time, season, year, or weather.

In one reading a key change in access could have damaged the experience, as the page was read outside rather than inside a church, but was saved by the atmosphere of the environment.

Participant: The church didn't work so well because it was locked so we couldn't get in and see the font. But then it was quite nice because they were playing – doing some organ rehearsal, and it just, kind of, made an atmosphere ...

Use Diegetic References Carefully: Diegetic references are mentions of the real world environment within the story. They can create a strong connection between the story and the place, but be mindful of how the landscape might change, and consider how the story would be affected.

In *The Pathways of Destiny* the author uses an area near a tethered balloon, where tourists could take rides, the story refers to the balloon explicitly. But in the months between the story being written and published the balloon was removed for maintenance, creating confusion for readers at that point of the story. Diegetic references can be powerful, and circumstances such as the balloon above cannot really be planned for, but using them sparingly and avoiding more obvious problems (such as weather or seasonal changes) should limit the risk.

Participant: it made it almost a little more real ... You almost feel like a sort of special part of it. It was saying, it was here and it was this, and you might be sheltering under a bus stop, which is exactly what I was doing at the time.

Write to Hold Attention: Write to hold the attention of the reader, both the device and events in the landscape are likely to be a distraction to your story. Therefore, it is important to consider ways in which you can hold attention (e.g. using style and pacing, or engaging subject matter), and/or write in such a way that less attention is required to be successful (e.g. using a poetic form, multimedia, or brevity - punchy installments of around 150 words fit on a single screen of most phones and are very effective).

Participant: ...there's just a lot of things going on round about you, other people walking around who are completely outside the story. So, it's kind of an interesting experience for, yeah, both the things that link to the story, but also the things that are challenging you and distracting you.

Participant: I really liked the pictures. And, being there, having the pictures there, and then the building in front of you, I think that was really good. And, definitely added to the experience of reading.

5   Discussion and Example

From our experiences in StoryPlaces it is clear that the more effective locative stories work in tandem with their locations and landscapes.

Aesthetically our authors created new fictional layers on top of the real landscape, or revealed layers that had been lost. For example, drawing attention to appearance and disappearance, contrasting now/then and revealing connections between different perspectives of place. Harmony between narrative and place will create a sense of connection in a reader and increase their feeling of presence. Discord will be jarring, and draws attention to the dual nature of their experience, although that might be appropriate for some stories. On a practical level authors have three ways of influencing their reader's navigation through the story. They can use narrative logic (such as unlocking a node) to restrict reader choices, they can use the landscape to encourage readers to move through particular routes and visit nodes in a particular order, and they can use the writing itself to influence reader decisions – using titles, hints and the content of pages to encourage readers to follow certain paths.

In general, being more open (using writing or landscape to control reader movement through the story) will result in more interactive stories with the reader feeling greater agency. On the other hand, a linear story will probably use narrative logic as the main way to control reader progress, but must make sure that this matches the way landscape influences navigation. Many of the practical recommendations are concerned with aligning the requirements of the narrative and landscape. If they are at odds (linear pages that are scattered too far, or which require constant doubling back) it will be frustrating for the reader.

Figure 1 shows the sculptural structure of the Crystal Palace Park story authored by Katie Lyons for our final story project. During development, Katie had access to our past projects, as well as the toolkit, and in two design meetings with the project team explained the structure (which we then translated into constraints and behaviors) and also explained the rationale behind her decisions.

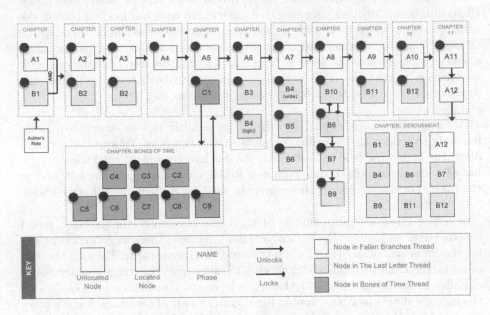

Fig. 1. The Sculptural Structure of Fallen Branches by Katie Lyons

Fallen Branches is constructed of three threads. The first, Fallen Branches (the A nodes), is a contemporary story, and describes a young women returning to Crystal Palace Park to fulfill the dying wishes of her Father. The second, The Last Letter (the B nodes), takes the form of a series of letters and letter fragments, and describes the story of two young lovers in the shadow of World War 1. The third, the Bone of Time (the C nodes), is an historical account of an incident in 1900 when an elephant killed its keeper and escaped from the palace.

Fallen Branches is the main thread that follows a circular route through the park. As the reader progresses, the nodes of the Last Letter appear and disappear in the landscape around them, these are optional and provide insight into the characters. At a certain point (Chap. 5) the reader can move away from the main story into a separate garden to experience the Bones of Time. This is effectively an historical sub-story that provides background on the heirlooms, once completed it rejoins the main thread. Once Fallen Branches ends the key letters from the Last Letter become available with no location constraints, so that the reader can return to them later even if they leave the park.

In writing Fallen Branches Katie took key decisions in line with the toolkit.

Dealbreakers: Katie was mindful of the advice to consider points of arrival and departure (the story starts and ends at Crystal Palace Station), and also of the physical effort it takes readers to move, which is minimized by following a circular route around the park. Twice (node B4, and nodes B6/B10) Katie explicitly changes the structure to avoid double backs. In node B4 she makes the hotspot larger so that it can be activated from further away, and nodes B6/B10 lock one another, meaning that once the reader has made a choice, the other (which would then be out of their way) is no longer available. Making the Bones of Time an optional part of the story was also an effort to create a viable one hour story, as was the decision to open up all the key letters at the end with no location restrictions. This is explained in the author's note, and takes the pressure off the reader to collect every single node as they go.

Other Pragmatics: Although Fallen Branches is fairly tightly structured, Katie felt able to reduce the logical constraints in the Bones of Time sub-story, and allow the landscape (the path through the garden) to control navigation. Katie has also clearly identified some high cost locations at the top of the hill, and at the far end of the terrace, as these are only used for optional Last Letter nodes.

Aesthetics: The story uses a number of key points of interest (the sphinxes, grand central steps, and bust of the Palace's creator), but uses these as gathering points for reminiscence, rather than feeling the need to explain them. There is also use of narrative areas, as if the reader chooses to move from the contemporary nodes of Fallen Branches to the historical story in Bones of Time, this corresponds with the movement to a new area unused for any other part of the story. Katie's story also captures the themes of the park itself, which are of absence, loss, and past grandeur (the Crystal Palace burned down in 1936 and became derelict), while her story sets these in more human terms there is clearly an alignment between the theme of the place and the theme of the story.

6   Conclusions

In this paper we have described how we have used three locative story projects, part of the StoryPlaces project, to explore the poetics of locative literature. By engaging with over sixty authors in Southampton, Bournemouth, and London we have helped to develop and publish thirteen different locative stories, and conducted and analyzed 34 semi-structured interviews with their readers. We have also developed our own locative story through a co-operative inquiry process on the island of Tiree, reflecting on the design and narrative decisions we had to make throughout the process.

Based on these experiences we have developed a simple toolkit for locative authors in the shape of twelve recommendations. Three Dealbreakers, pragmatic considerations that must be observed to produce a readable story; four additional Pragmatic aspects, opportunities to use landscape to control agency and solve interactive narrative problems; and five Aesthetic aspects, ways in which landscape and narrative can work together to increase their impact on the reader.

We have used this toolkit in our third and final story project in Crystal Palace Park, and as a validation, we have presented the story we commissioned as part of this project, *Fallen Branches*, and have explained how the author has followed the recommendations during the creation process.

Our work is the first significant attempt to capture the emerging craft of writing locative narratives, and to turn this into applicable design theory.

We are now exploring how the toolkit might inform the design of digital writing tools (for example, authoring tools that embed some of the recommendations, or analytical tools that look for some of the known problems). Our hope is that our work will refocus attention on the narrative potential of interactive locative storytelling, and lead to more sophisticated examples that use landscape and narrative together to manage agency, improve the reader experience, and reinforce the themes and emotional impact of the story.

References

1. Ardito, C., Sintoris, C., Raptis, D., Yiannoutsou, N., Avouris, N., Costabile, M.F.: Design guidelines for location-based mobile games for learning. In: International Conference on Social Applications for Lifelong Learning, pp. 96–100 (2010)
2. Ballagas, R., Kuntze, A., Walz, S.P.: Gaming tourism: lessons from evaluating REXplorer, a pervasive game for tourists. In: Indulska, J., Patterson, D.J., Rodden, T., Ott, M. (eds.) Pervasive 2008. LNCS, vol. 5013, pp. 244–261. Springer, Heidelberg (2008). https://doi.org/10.1007/978-3-540-79576-6_15
3. Benford, S., Giannachi, G., Koleva, B., Rodden, T.: From interaction to trajectories: designing coherent journeys through user experiences. In: ACM CHI2009, vols. 1–4, pp. 709–718. ACM Press, New York (2009). <Go to ISI>://000265679300083 http://dl.acm.org/citation.cfm?doid=1518701.1518812
4. Bernstein, M.: Card shark and thespis: exotic tools for hypertext narrative. In: ACM Hypertext 2001, pp. 41–50. ACM (2001)
5. Bizzocchi, J., Woodbury, R.F.: A case study in the design of interactive narrative: subversion of the interface. Simul. Gaming 34(4), 550–568 (2003)
6. Broadbent, J., Marti, P.: Location aware mobile interactive guides: usability issues. In: ICHIM, vol. 97, pp. 88–98 (1997)
7. Buckley, J.: "The play's the thing"-computer simulations and digital storytelling: a review of hamlet on the holodeck: the future of narrative in cyberspace. In: Murray, J.H. (ed.) The Free Press, New York, 324 p (1998)
8. Bunting, B.S., Hughes, J., Hetland, T.: The player as author: exploring the effects of mobile gaming and the location-aware interface on storytelling. Future Internet 4(1), 142–160 (2012)

9. Dionisio, M., Nisi, V., van Leeuwen, J.P.: The iLand of Madeira location aware multimedia stories. In: Aylett, R., Lim, M.Y., Louchart, S., Petta, P., Riedl, M. (eds.) ICIDS 2010. LNCS, vol. 6432, pp. 147–152. Springer, Heidelberg (2010). https://doi.org/10.1007/978-3-642-16638-9_19

10. Dovey, J.: Ambient literature: writing probability. In: Ubiquitous Computing, Complexity and Culture, pp. 141–154 (2016)

11. Hargood, C., Hunt, V., Weal, M.J., Millard, D.E.: Patterns of sculptural hypertext in location based narratives. In: ACM Hypertext 2016, pp. 61–70. ACM (2016)

12. Koenitz, H.: Design approaches for interactive digital narrative. In: Schoenau-Fog, H., Bruni, L.E., Louchart, S., Baceviciute, S. (eds.) ICIDS 2015. LNCS, vol. 9445, pp. 50–57. Springer, Cham (2015). https://doi.org/10.1007/978-3-319-27036-4_5

13. Koenitz, H.: Towards a specific theory of interactive digital narrative. In: Interactive Digital Narrative, pp. 91–105 (2015)

14. Malaka, R., Schneider, K., Kretschmer, U.: Stage-based augmented edutainment. In: Butz, A., Krüger, A., Olivier, P. (eds.) SG 2004. LNCS, vol. 3031, pp. 54–65. Springer, Heidelberg (2004). https://doi.org/10.1007/978-3-540-24678-7_6

15. Millard, D., Hargood, C.: A research framework for engineering location-based poetics. In: NHT 2015, held in Conjunction with ACM Hypertext 2016 (2015). https://eprints.soton.ac.uk/388165/

16. Millard, D., Hargood, C.: Location location location: experiences of authoring an interactive location-based narrative. In: ICIDS 2016, August 2016. https://eprints.soton.ac.uk/399628/ https://eprints.soton.ac.uk/399628

17. Millard, D., Hargood, C.: Tiree tales: a co-operative inquiry into the poetics of location-based narratives. In: ACM Hypertext 2017, July 2017. https://eprints.soton.ac.uk/408310/

18. Nisi, V., Oakley, I., Haahr, M.: Inner city locative media: design and experience of a location-aware mobile narrative for the dublin liberties neighborhood. In: Intelligent Agent, vol. 6 (2006)

19. Nisi, V., Oakley, I., Haahr, M.: Location-aware multimedia stories: turning spaces into places. Universidade Cátolica Portuguesa, pp. 72–93 (2008)

20. Paterson, N., Kearney, G., Naliuka, K., Carrigy, T., Haahr, M., Conway, F.: Viking ghost hunt: creating engaging sound design for location-aware applications. Int. J. Arts Technol. **6**(1), 61–82 (2012)

21. Pittarello, F.: Designing a context-aware architecture for emotionally engaging mobile storytelling. In: Campos, P., Graham, N., Jorge, J., Nunes, N., Palanque, P., Winckler, M. (eds.) INTERACT 2011. LNCS, vol. 6946, pp. 144–151. Springer, Heidelberg (2011). https://doi.org/10.1007/978-3-642-23774-4_14

22. Rogers, Y., Price, S., Fitzpatrick, G., Fleck, R., Harris, E., Smith, H., Randell, C., Muller, H., O'Malley, C., Stanton, D., et al.: Ambient wood: designing new forms of digital augmentation for learning outdoors. In: Conference on Interaction Design and Children, pp. 3–10. ACM (2004)

23. Strohecker, C.: A case study in interactive narrative design. In: 2nd Conference on Designing Interactive Systems, pp. 377–380. ACM (1997)

24. Weal, M.J., Cruickshank, D., Michaelides, D.T., Millard, D.E., De Roure, D.C., Howland, K., Fitzpatrick, G.: A card based metaphor for organising pervasive educational experiences. In: PerCom Workshops 2007, pp. 165–170. IEEE (2007)

25. Weal, M.J., Millard, D.E., Michaelides, D.T., De Roure, D.C.: Building narrative structures using context based linking. In: ACM Hypertext 2001, pp. 37–38. ACM, New York (2001). http://doi.acm.org/10.1145/504216.504231

Level of Detail Event Generation

Luis Flores and David Thue[✉]

Center for Analysis and Design of Intelligent Agents, School of Computer Science,
Reykjavik University, Menntavegur 1, Reykjavik 101, Iceland
{luis12,davidthue}@ru.is

Abstract. Level of detail is a method that involves optimizing the amount of detail that is simulated for some entity. We introduce an event generation method to optimize the level of detail of upcoming events in a simulation. Our method implements a cognitive model, which uses an estimate of the player's knowledge to estimate their interest in different aspects of the world. Our method predicts the salience of upcoming events, and uses this salience value to define the level of detail of potential new events. An evaluation of our method's predictive capacity shows generally higher accuracy than a baseline predictor.

1 Introduction

Level of detail (LOD) is a method that involves reducing the complexity of a simulation when doing so would be transparent to one or more players. It can decrease the complexity of geometry [3], artificial intelligence [3,10], or physics computations [7]. Since simulating everything at a high level of detail could be very expensive, LOD is very important in video games, as it allows a larger game world to be simulated while still maintaining believability. Simulations can take advantage of this method by reducing the detail in which different aspects of the simulation are run, ideally producing and maintaining just enough data to serve the player's current interests.

In the context of Interactive Storytelling, conveying a rich simulation (or at least a convincing illusion thereof) can improve the believability of the story's world, and particularly with respect to its scale and feeling of being "alive" [11]. While distance and visibility are commonly used metrics when deciding the LOD of simulated *objects* (e.g., to speed up graphics rendering), these metrics seem unlikely to work for every aspect of a simulation, and particularly for the *events* that occur therein. For example, if an upcoming event is critical to the player's pursuit of a given goal, the simulation should ensure that event is generated with a high enough LOD to allow the player to achieve their goals, regardless of how distant or visible the event currently is.

In this work, we propose a method to optimize the level of detail with which events in a simulated world are generated, using a given estimate of the player's knowledge to then estimate their interest in different aspects of the world. By estimating a potential event's level of interest for the current player (i.e., its *salience*) we can avoid generating unnecessary details for that event.

© Springer International Publishing AG 2017
N. Nunes et al. (Eds.): ICIDS 2017, LNCS 10690, pp. 75–86, 2017.
https://doi.org/10.1007/978-3-319-71027-3_7

1.1   Background

Our model of salience draws inspiration from Cardona-Rivera et al.'s *Indexter model* [1], which predicts the salience of previous events in the user's memory based on the current world state. Contrary to their work, the model that we propose uses salience as a metric when generating *future* events; a lack of salience for a potential new event means that we can reduce the amount of detail that gets generated for the properties of that event.

The Indexter model is based on the Event-Indexing Situation Model (EISM) by Zwaan et al. [12,13], which is a cognitive model of online narrative comprehension. The EISM categorizes a narrative into events with important details, and each event is categorized by different key factors (called *indices*). The EISM represents each event by indexing the following elements: *Time, Space, Protagonist, Causation,* and *Intention*. Using the EISM, the Indexter model computes the salience of a past event with respect to a current event, and this computation is initially made with respect to each of the five indices. Two events have a value of 1 for a given index when they both "share" that index (i.e., they both occur in the same time frame or place, they both involve the story's protagonist, they are causally related, or they both serve a single intention). For example, two events that occur in the same location share the space index, and thus have a value of 1 for space salience. The Indexter model attaches a weight w_* to each index such that the weighted sum of all of the indices is bound to $[0, 1]$. Given this constraint, the equation to calculate the salience of event e_i w.r.t. e_n is:

$$salience(e_i, e_n) = w_t t_{e_n} + w_s s_{e_n} + w_p p_{e_n} + w_c c_{e_n} + w_i i_{e_n} \qquad (1)$$

where $t_{e_n}, s_{e_n}, p_{e_n}, c_{e_n},$ and i_{e_n} represent the time, space, protagonist, causality, and intention indices, respectively. The authors of the Indexter model set the same weight to every index, that is $\forall *, w_* = 0.2$.

Some limitations arise when considering applying the Indexter model to LOD-based generation. First, it estimates salience as a relationship between two events (one past, one current), while we aim to estimate the salience of a *future* event with respect to the player's current knowledge. Second, it computes only binary salience values for each index, which is too coarse too allow for any more than two levels of detail, and also risks producing an unbelievable simulation when LOD-based generation is used. For example, if the player's current event was not at the location of a candidate event, the Indexter model would compute its space salience as 0 – the lowest possible value. In LOD-based generation, however, a minimum salience value must be reserved for "no detail" to enable large-scale simulations. By setting every non-local event to minimum salience, the Indexter model (as-is) would prevent the details of any such events from ever being generated, leading to an unbelievable simulation.

In this paper, we present an extension to the Indexter model that allows the salience of a potential future event to be estimated with respect to an estimate of the player's knowledge. To enable LOD-based event generation using this model, we expand the value range of three of the five indices and generate event details on a per-index basis.

2   Problem Formulation

We aim to generate events at varying levels of detail (LODs), based on a model of the player's expected interest in the events that could be generated. We use the term *salience* to describe this player interest, and *generator* to describe the system that produces the events. An LOD-based event generator that uses salience must meet several requirements.

First, to balance the simulation's computation with its believability, the level of detail that the generator uses must vary with the expected salience of each candidate event. Second, since salience must be used during the generation process, each event's salience must be given or estimated before generation occurs, and such an estimate can only be made *after* some properties of the candidate event are already known (such as its time, location, the agents involved, etc.). We assume that the salience of each event will not be given, and therefore must be estimated. Third, since judgments of salience are influenced by memory [1], salience should be estimated based on both the current state of the simulation and the player's knowledge of what has been simulated thus far. Fourth, each output of the generator must be a description of an event whose content was determined using the level of detail that the generator selected.

Intuitively, a good solution to this task can be identified by its production of events that players find to be salient, given their knowledge of the simulation and its current state. We will judge our solution by using it to predict the salience of different events (with respect to their properties) and comparing the results to ground truth values obtained from a survey.

3   Related Work

One popular approach to applying level of detail is to use distance-based metrics (e.g., between an object's position and the player's position [3]). The closer the object to the player, the higher the level of detail rendered. As we argued in Sect. 1, distance-based metrics can be insufficient for the generation of events.

Sunshine-Hill's *LOD Trader* [10] aims to optimize the perceptual quality of a simulation by estimating the realism of every agent within each scene. *LOD Trader* lacks or ignores the influence of the current player's knowledge of the given world, contrary to our approach.

In physical simulations, LOD techniques focus on adapting the type of physical model used for different objects by understanding the importance of the object and the efficiency of different models at reacting to the current simulation state [7]. Our method aims to simulate the events of a world; not its physics.

Estimating salience is an important part of information retrieval [6], social network analysis [6], and text summarization [8]. Typically, a graph-based ranking algorithm is used to estimate the importance of each node in a graph by considering the global information of the graph. The algorithm checks the number and the quality of the links connected through the graph to determine how important each node is. We employ similar graph-based techniques to estimate the salience of some event properties, including space and time (Sect. 4.1).

4   Proposed Approach

We propose a method to optimize the generation of upcoming events in a simulation using a level of detail approach. By using an estimate of the player's knowledge about both the simulation and the current world state, this method allows us to estimate the salience of different event properties during generation, which then determine the level of detail of the generated events. We define the properties of an event based on the indices in Zwaan et al.'s EISM model [12,13], as described in Sect. 4.1. In general, events with many salient properties are created with a high level of detail, meaning that each event's properties are described in full detail. Events with few salient properties are created with a low level of detail, meaning that their properties are lightly detailed or omitted completely. Figure 1 gives an overview of how our generator produces descriptions of new events.

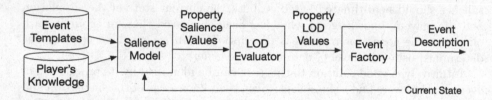

Fig. 1. Our process for level of detail event generation.

Our generator makes use of event templates, which constrain the values that each event's properties can take on during the generation process. Given an event template and an estimate of the player's knowledge, our generator first estimates a separate salience value for each property in the given event template (Salience Model in Fig. 1). Given these values, it then decides a level of detail independently for each property (LOD Evaluator). Finally, our generator creates a description of the event based on the chosen LOD values (Event Factory).

4.1   Salience Model

Our generator's salience model estimates the salience of potential upcoming events with respect to the current world state and the player's knowledge. Specifically, we extend the Event Indexing Situation Model (EISM) [12] to define the salience of an potential future event. To give our generator a variety of levels of detail to choose from, the salience model estimates the salience of each event property independently. Properties are evaluated differently depending on how they affect the player or the current state of the world. The evaluated properties are protagonist (renamed "social"), time, space, causation, and intention. While the EISM protagonist index represents whether the player is involved in the event, we chose to expand the range of this value by additionally representing how socially close the player is to the agents involved in such event.

The **social salience** of an event depends on how closely the agents in the event are related to the player in a social sense. When the player is involved in the event, a salience of 1 is set. Otherwise, we create a social graph (Fig. 2: right) to represent relations between agents and determine the social salience. To compute social salience for event e, we use the following equation:

$$social\_salience(e) = \begin{cases} 1 & \text{if player is involved} \\ 1 - \frac{social\_distance_e + 1}{n} & \text{otherwise} \end{cases} \quad (2)$$

where n is the total number of agents and $social\_distance_e$ represents the minimum number of edges between any agent that the player knows and any agent that is involved in the event e.

The **space salience** of an event is calculated by checking how close the event location is to the player. A salience of 1 occurs when the event is held in the same location as the player. Otherwise, a location graph is constructed where nodes are locations and edges represent traversable paths between locations (Fig. 2: left). To compute space salience for event e, we use the following equation:

$$space\_salience(e) = \begin{cases} 1 & \text{if player is involved} \\ 1 - \frac{space\_distance_e + 1}{n} & \text{otherwise} \end{cases} \quad (3)$$

where $space\_distance_e$ is the minimum distance from event e's location to any location that the player knows and n is the total number of locations.

The **time salience** of an event depends on both the event time (when it occurs) and its propagation rate (how quickly its effects spread across the world). A low time salience means the event time is not salient to the player, or the event's effects will take too much time to reach the player. This model prefers events that reach the player sooner. To compute time salience for event e, we use the following equations:

$$time\_salience(e) = \begin{cases} 0 & \text{if } reach\_time(e) > limit \\ \frac{limit - reach\_time(e)}{limit} & \text{otherwise} \end{cases} \quad (4)$$

$$reach\_time(e) = \frac{player\_distance_e}{propagation_e} \quad (5)$$

where $reach\_time(e)$ represents the time that the effects of the event e will take to reach the player, $player\_distance_e$ represents the distance between the player and event e's location, $propagation_e$ represents the propagation rate of event e, and $limit$ is the longest time that the player will stay interested in an event.

The **causation salience** of an event was used in the EISM to represent whether or not two events were causally related. Since our model evaluates a single event in isolation, we adapted the causation index to indicate whether the player can potentially acquire a new goal (thus triggering a new causal chain of actions) by attending the event. We define causation salience $c_e = 1$ when the event e offers a new goal to the player and $c_e = 0$ otherwise.

The **intention salience** of an event was used in the Indexter model to represent whether or not two events were part of the same intentional plan.

Since our model evaluates only one event, we adapted this index to indicate whether the player can achieve a current goal by attending the event. We define intention salience $i_e = 1$ when the event e shares the same goal as the player, and $i_e = 0$ otherwise.

Once it has computed the salience of every property, the generator calculates the **total salience** for a given event. Similar to the Indexter model [1], we compute this total as a weighted sum of individual salience values with equal weights ($\forall *, w_* = 0.2$). We compute the total salience of event e as follows:

$$event\_salience(e, p) = 0.2s_e + 0.2p_e + 0.2t_e + 0.2c_e + 0.2i_e \qquad (6)$$

where p is the player and s_e, p_e, t_e, c_e, and i_e are the property salience values for social, space, time, causation, and intention respectively.

The total salience is used to select the most salient event after all the event templates have been considered. Before generation can begin, our method must first determine a viable level of detail for each property in the selected event.

4.2 The Level of Detail Evaluator

The level of detail evaluator converts each event property salience value to a high, medium, or low LOD. The event factory avoids generating any details when a low LOD is used.

The **social property** has three levels of detail. *High* LOD: the player is involved; the event factory creates a full detail description of the agents involved. *Medium* LOD: a known agent is involved, or the agent involved is very close to a known agent; the event factory creates details of the known/close agents involved. *Low* LOD: the agents involved are unknown.

The **space property** has three levels of detail. *High* LOD: the event is happening in the same location as the player; the event factory creates a full description of the event location. *Medium* LOD: the event location is known to the player; the event factory only creates the location name. *Low* LOD: the location is not known to the player.

The **time property** has three levels of detail. *High* LOD: the event's effects will reach the player quickly; the event factory creates full details of the event's time. *Medium* LOD: the event's effects reach the player late, but it is still salient to the player based on the value of *limit* (Eq. 4); the event factory creates the event date without the exact time frame. *Low* LOD: the event's effects reach the player late, and it is not salient to the player.

The **causation property** has two levels of detail. *High* LOD: the event allows the player to acquire a new goal; the event factory creates a description of the new goal that could be acquired. *Low* LOD: the event does not allow the player to acquire a new goal.

The **intention property** has two levels of detail. *High* LOD: the event satisfies one of the player's goals. The event factory creates the description of the event goal. *Low* LOD: the event does not satisfy one of the player's goals.

Table 1. Sample event templates.

	Event 1	Event 2	Event 3
Title	The orcs are gathering	A wild dragon appeared	A troll has kidnapped the wizard
Player	No	Yes	No
Agents	Traveler	Wizard	King, Sage
Locations	Valley	Fire Cave	Castle
Propagation	1	2	4
Goal	Spy on the orcs	Kill the dragon	Talk to the king
Cause	Talk to the king	Recover the treasure	Rescue the wizard

4.3 The Event Factory

Once we have the level of detail for each property in a given event template, the event factory creates an event description according to the given levels of detail. The event factory uses *Tracery* [2] to create event descriptions. *Tracery* is a grammar-based generation library and uses grammar rules to generate content. The event factory specifies one grammar rule per index, and each grammar rule is more or less detailed depending on the given level of detail. Finally, the event factory combines the grammar for each event property to create a full event description. Sample outputs are given in Sect. 4.4.

4.4 Event Generator in Action

Our generator begins by instantiating an event template, each of which is specified as a set of high level event properties as shown in Table 1. Overall, the generator estimates the total salience of each template and generates an event description from the template that has the highest total salience. For the sake of simplicity, consider the world shown in Fig. 2. Assume that all the events would occur at the same time, and that the player's location is the *castle*.

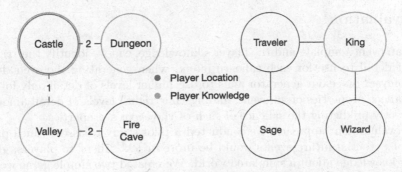

Fig. 2. Locations and social graphs. The player's knowledge is shown in orange. Numbered edges show distances between locations. (Color figure online)

Table 2. Events salience and level of detail (L = Low, M = Medium, H = High).

Property	Event 1		Event 2		Event 3	
	Salience	LOD	Salience	LOD	Salience	LOD
Social	0.50	L	1.0	H	0.75	M
Space	0.75	M	0.5	L	1.0	H
Time	0.66	M	0.5	L	1.0	H
Intention	0.0	L	0.0	L	1.0	H
Causation	0.0	L	1.0	H	1.0	H
Total	0.38	N/A	0.6	N/A	0.95	N/A

The player's goals are to *talk to the king* and *recover the treasure*. The player has knowledge of the following locations: *castle*, *dungeon*, and *valley*. The only agent the player knows is the *king*. To compute the time salience, we set the *limit* time to 3 time units.

Table 2 shows the property salience values that would be computed for the event templates in Table 1, given the player's knowledge and the world state. The event factory would then create the following event descriptions for the levels of detail given in Table 2. Annotations appear as emphasized text.

Event 1: The orcs are gathering *(event title)*. It will take place at the valley *(space, medium LOD)*. It is happening today *(time, medium LOD)*.

Event 2: A wild dragon appeared *(event title)*. You are involved in this, and the hunter is attending as well *(social, high LOD)*. You will be offered the chance recover the treasure if you attend *(causation, high LOD)*.

Event 3: A troll has kidnapped the wizard *(event title)*. It is taking place at castle, it is happening outside the gates *(space, high LOD)*. The king is attending *(social, medium LOD)*. It will take place today at noon *(time, high LOD)*. Get ready to talk to the king *(intention, high LOD)*. You will be offered the chance to rescue the wizard if you attend *(causation, high LOD)*.

5   Evaluation

Given an event template and the player's knowledge, can we identify the "right" level of detail to use for each salience index, when generating the event for a given player? Since our generator aims to use higher levels of detail only for the more salient properties of an event, finding the "right" levels of detail amounts to correctly predicting the salience of each of the event's properties.

To evaluate our approach, we conducted a pilot study to assess which properties of potential future events would be more or less salient to players, given certain knowledge about a simulated world. We created two simple game worlds as testbeds, defining the world state and the player's knowledge of the agents, locations, and goals as shown in Table 3. To reduce bias in our experiment, the worlds have the same structure but different contexts: the location and social graphs in both worlds will result the same graph structure, but the characters

Table 3. Game worlds used to test our approach.

	World 1	World 2
Player location	Castle	Husavik
Player's goal	Talk to the king	Capture an elf
Known locations	Castle, Dungeon, and Valley	Husavik, Keflavik, and Borganes
Known agents	King	President

and locations are different. Figure 2 shows the location and social graphs for World 1; World 2 had four locations based on the real world and four agents named "tourist", "president", "bellman", and "dentist". The player's knowledge and world state were shown via text during the study.

For each event property and for each level of detail that our method would consider for that property, we proposed an event to each participant such that our generator would use the given level of detail for the given property. Then, we asked the players to rate how interesting the event seemed with respect to that event property. We asked one such question per property's level of detail, for each of our testbed world states. We asked questions related to the current world state and player's knowledge such as: *"will you be interested in a new event if it is located at the castle?"*, *"will you be interested in the new event if the king is involved?"*, and *"will you be interested in the new event if it is happening today?"* Participants could respond to each question by selecting "Very much interested", "Somewhat interested" (for social, space, and time), or "Not at all interested". We collected data for each event property at each of the levels of detail that our method considers for that property (recall Sect. 4.2).

For **social salience**, we asked the players how interested they would be in three new events, where each event involved one of the three different agents that would cause our method to use a high, medium, or low LOD, respectively. The high LOD is used when the social salience is between 1.0 and 0.75. The medium LOD is used when the social salience is between 0.75 and 0.5, meaning an agent involved is known to the player. A low LOD is used when the social salience is less than 0.5, meaning that agent unknown agents are involved.

For **space salience**, we asked the players how interested they would be in a new event for each of the three levels of detail for the space property. A high LOD is used when the space salience is between 1.0 and 0.75. A medium LOD is used when the space salience is between 0.75 and 0.5, meaning the event location is known to the player. A low LOD is used when the space salience is less than 0.5, meaning the event location is unknown.

For **time salience**, we asked the participants how interested they would be in new events involving three different levels of detail: when the event is about to happen, when the event is happening in a few days, and when the event will only happen after a long time.

For **causation salience**, we asked the participants how interested they would be in the new event if it would motivate them to achieve new goals.

For **intention salience**, we asked the participants how interested they would be in a new event if they could achieve their current goals by attending the event.

Table 4. Summary of results for the user study, using the worlds shown in Table 3.

Salience	World	Accuracy	Precision		
			High	Med	Low
Social	1	46.5%	77.0%	18.7%	43.7%
	2	54.8%	77.0%	25.0%	62.5%
Space	1	43.1%	66.7%	35.4%	27.1%
	2	50.0%	56.3%	54.2%	40.0%
Time	1	52.1%	60.4%	64.5%	31.2%
	2	49.3%	62.5%	54.1%	31.2%
Causation	1	65.6%	79.1%	N/A	52.1%
	2	58.3%	72.9%	N/A	43.7%
Intention	1	60.4%	79.1%	N/A	41.6%
	2	68.7%	89.5%	N/A	47.9%

5.1   Data and Results

Our model is trying to solve a prediction problem: given a particular event property, we predicted how much interest a property can produce in players. Our system effectively classifies each property as *very interesting, somewhat interesting,* or *not interesting* and then maps each of those values to the appropriate level of detail (*High, Medium,* or *Low,* respectively). In our pilot study, we gathered a total of 48 responses from participants recruited via social media. We computed accuracy and precision for each of the five event properties (social, time, space, intention, causation), for each world set. Accuracy measures how often our generator's predictions are correct overall. Precision measures how often our generator predicts a level of detail correctly. As we were unable to find a similar solution to compare against our method, we decided to compare our generator against a uniform random predictor. Table 4 shows our results.

6   Discussion and Future Work

The results for the five saliences values showed accuracies much better than what a uniform random predictor would produce (33.3% and 50.0% when using as two or three levels of detail, respectively). However, if we compare against a random predictor that considers the bias observed in the data, the results for social and space are disappointing. For example, a predictor that always predicted high detail would obtain accuracies near 50% for social salience, using the data from our study. That said, our results for social salience may have been biased by the agent names we used. Specifically, having an important agent or someone with a high authority (e.g., "king" or "president") may have raised levels of interest among players, even though they did not know those agents. We suspect that places with inherently interesting names can also influence the player's interests.

We used a compelling name ("fire cave") in World 1 and a random real place name in World 2, and players were more interested in an event whose location had the more interesting name.

Players seemed to be somewhat interested even when our method predicted a low level of detail, suggesting that a generator should always display something at this LOD, rather than omitting all details. Given these results, we are interested in changing our approach to better distinguish between low detail and no detail.

The event factory used in our approach generates a simple text description of an event, which is not computationally expensive. We thus do not gain much computational savings from our approach. The gains for a more complicated factory could be larger, and testing this hypothesis remains as future work.

A few limitations arise when using our event generator's model. This model focused on a single player, and so we used the EISM's notion of a "protagonist" as the current player of the simulation. We would like to determine if extending this model is needed to handle more players, since important agents in the simulation seem to influence the interest of players.

Space and social saliences can be computed in a better way. For instance, we use the total number of nodes in the graph when creating the space or social graphs. This might be overkill if the simulation has a large number of locations and agents. A possible way to improve it is to use the width of the graph (the "longest shortest distance") instead of the total number of nodes. Finding good values for the parameters of our model, such as the time index's *limit* value, the thresholds for mapping property salience values to levels of detail, and the weights for computing total salience, remains an open problem.

Although we aim to support more than two levels of detail for each type of salience, we have currently done so for only three of the five types. We are interested in finding a way to compute causation and intention salience across a wider range of values; the Indexter model's use of a plan-based representation seems promising in this regard [1]. Finally, our method relies on having a reasonable estimate of the player's knowledge of the simulated world. While tracking what information a player has been exposed to is conceptually straightforward, knowing which information they have retained is a difficult problem [5]. It would be interesting to integrate our work with an active model of player knowledge [9].

7   Conclusion

Level of detail is a method that involves reducing the amount of detail that is generated for some entity. Using level of detail in a simulation has the potential to help improve performance, reducing computational load, as creating new events in a simulation can be resource intensive.

In this paper, we proposed an event generator that works to optimize the level of detail with which events in the world are generated, based on estimates of the salience of individual properties in each event. Our salience model is an extension of the Event-Indexing Situation Model (EISM) [12] and inspired by the Indexter model [1], offering the new capability of estimating the salience of a future event with respect to the current world state and an estimate of the player's knowledge. We presented this model in the context of a novel event generator, which uses the model to produce event descriptions at various levels of detail. By estimating salience values and generating event descriptions on a per-property basis, our generator is capable of producing a wide range of descriptions for each generated event. We validated the accuracy and precision of our salience model in a pilot user study, finding that our model outperforms a uniform random predictor.

Acknowledgements. Some parts of this text appear in the first author's M.Sc. dissertation [4].

References

1. Cardona-Rivera, R.E., Cassell, B.A., Ware, S.G., Young, R.M.: Indexter: a computational model of the event-indexing situation model for characterizing narratives. In: Proceedings of the 3rd Workshop on Computational Models of Narrative, pp. 34–43 (2012)
2. Compton, K., Mateas, M.: Casual creators. In: Proceedings of the International Conference on Computational Creativity, ICCC (2015)
3. Cournoyer, F., Fortier, A.: Massive crowd on assassin's creed unity: AI recycling. In: Presentation at the Game Developer's Conference (GDC 2015). GDC Vault, UBM Tech. (2015)
4. Flores, L.: Level of detail event generation. M.Sc. dissertation. School of Computer Science, Reykjavik University (2017)
5. Magerko, B.: Evaluating preemptive story direction in the interactive drama architecture. J. Game Dev. **2**(3), 25–52 (2007)
6. Mihalcea, R., Tarau, P.: Textrank: bringing order into texts. In: Conference on Empirical Methods in Natural Language Processing, pp. 404–411. Association for Computational Linguistics (2004)
7. Paris, S., Gerdelan, A., O'Sullivan, C.: CA-LOD: collision avoidance level of detail for scalable, controllable crowds. In: Egges, A., Geraerts, R., Overmars, M. (eds.) MIG 2009. LNCS, vol. 5884, pp. 13–28. Springer, Heidelberg (2009). https://doi.org/10.1007/978-3-642-10347-6_2
8. Roth, M., Ben-David, A., Deutscher, D., Flysher, G., Horn, I., Leichtberg, A., Leiser, N., Matias, Y., Merom, R.: Suggesting friends using the implicit social graph. In: Proceedings of the 16th ACM SIGKDD International Conference on Knowledge Discovery and Data Mining, pp. 233–242. ACM (2010)
9. Rowe, J.P., Lester, J.C.: Modeling user knowledge with dynamic Bayesian networks in interactive narrative environments. In: 6th AAAI Conference on Artificial Intelligence and Interactive Digital Entertainment, pp. 57–62. AAAI Press (2010)
10. Sunshine-Hill, B.: Perceptually driven simulation. Ph.D. thesis, University of Pennsylvania (2011)
11. Sunshine-Hill, B.: Managing simulation level-of-detail with the LOD trader. In: 6th International Conference on Motion in Games, pp. 13–18. ACM (2013)
12. Zwaan, R.A., Langston, M.C., Graesser, A.C.: The construction of situation models in narrative comprehension: an event-indexing model. Psychol. Sci. **6**(5), 292–297 (1995). JSTOR
13. Zwaan, R.A., Radvansky, G.A.: Situation models in language comprehension and memory. Psychol. Bull. **123**(2), 162–185 (1998). APA

History and Learning

Grimes' Fairy Tales: A 1960s Story Generator

James Ryan[✉]

Expressive Intelligence Studio, University of California, Santa Cruz, USA
jor@soe.ucsc.edu

Abstract. We provide the first extensive account of an unknown story generator that was developed by linguist Joseph E. Grimes in the early 1960s. A pioneering system, it was the first to take a grammar-based approach and the first to operationalize Propp's famous model. This is the opening paper in a series that will aim to reformulate the prevailing history of story generation in light of new findings we have made pertaining to several forgotten early projects. Our study here has been made possible by personal communication with the system's creator, Grimes, and excavation of three obscure contemporaneous sources. While the accepted knowledge in our field is that the earliest story generator was Sheldon Klein's automatic novel writer, first reported in 1971, we show that Grimes's system and two others preceded it. In doing this, we reveal a new earliest known system. With this paper, and follow-ups to it that are in progress, we aim to provide a new account of the area of story generation that lends our community insight as to where it came from and where it should go next. We hope others will join us in this mission.

Keywords: Story generation · History of the field · Computational narrative

1 Introduction

We are digging up the dead: systems, documents, and other intellectual contributions from the early period of story generation that our community has, in the intervening decades, forgotten. Our project is to dismantle the prevailing history of this area, which we now know is inaccurate in several ways, to furnish a new account that tells us more about where we came from and where we should go next.[1] To carry out this project, we are scouring archives, translating documents, and engaging in personal correspondences with the scholars and system builders who were active in this period. Our discoveries include three systems that precede what is widely believed to be the earliest story generator; we are poised in a follow-up paper to nearly triple the number of known systems from before 1990. In many cases, these exhumed systems anticipate approaches that, decades later, appeared to be novel. Our scholarly process follows Wardrip-Fruin's method for

---

[1] This larger project is being conducted in collaboration with Michael Mateas and Noah Wardrip-Fruin, so I use plural pronouns in this paper.

© Springer International Publishing AG 2017
N. Nunes et al. (Eds.): ICIDS 2017, LNCS 10690, pp. 89–103, 2017.
https://doi.org/10.1007/978-3-319-71027-3_8

digital media archaeology [48]: we are as interested in intellectual contexts as technical ones, and we treat systems holistically, with special attention to their underlying processes. In addition to unearthing forgotten story generators, we are also excavating historically important documents that have not been discussed or cited in decades (or ever, in some cases). Here, we present some of our findings for the first time by providing an extensive account of an essentially unknown pioneering system from the early 1960s.

But why should we care about old, forgotten work? If we view story generation as a vast design space, we can think of each implemented system as an exploratory vessel that ventures into a previously uncharted sector. If these exploratory missions are successful, they signal directions that future systems may move further into to find greater success. When success is not had, the failed projects tell us which areas to avoid. In this way, we learn about spaces that incrementalist research may push further into, dead sectors that we should not return to, and all the other still uncharted areas that we do not know much about at all. Thus, both good and bad systems generate new knowledge that is useful to contemporary and future practitioners. But when we forget about past systems—novel explorations in design space—we lose the knowledge that was generated by those systems: we forget what has been explored and what has not, and which areas are worth exploring further. As we discuss below, more than fifty years ago, the system we profile here anticipated, and then abandoned, an approach to story generation that is currently in vogue.

Beyond these fundamental practical reasons lies one of principle: as a field and as a community, we owe it to ourselves—and our forebears and our successors—to record an accurate historical record. How would you like your work to be forgotten? We, moreover, owe it to ourselves to maintain a record that encompasses not just a series of names and dates, not just a series of system architectures, but also the intellectual through lines that trace our history. Story generation is an applied technical area, but all human endeavor, especially in the area of research, has intellectual underpinnings and emerges out of intellectual contexts. Even in technical areas, there is a history of ideas that undergirds the evolution of systems over time. Returning to practical concerns, good ideas for systems can lead to bad implementations of them, and so we should track ideas too so that we might have another stab at carrying them out well.

In this paper, we provide the first extensive account of an essentially unknown story generator that was developed by linguist Joseph E. Grimes in the early 1960s. Grimes's pioneering system was the first to take a grammar-based approach and the first to operationalize Propp's famous model [40]. Is it the first ever story generator? The prevailing belief in our field is that Sheldon Klein's automatic novel writer, first reported in 1971 [28], is the earliest known system. In this paper, we show that at least three systems preceded Klein's. Thus, beyond presenting the first extensive account of Grimes's pioneering system, a broad contribution of this work is to proclaim a new earliest system. With this paper, and follow-ups to it that are in progress, we aim to provide a new account of the area of story generation that tells our community more about where we came from and where we should go next. We hope others will join us in this mission.

2 Grimes' Fairy Tales

Joseph E. Grimes earned his PhD from Cornell University in 1960, where soon after he became a professor of linguistics.[2] Since 1952, he had been a member of the Summer Institute of Linguistics (SIL), an organization based at the University of Oklahoma whose mission includes the documenting of unwritten human languages. Grimes's wife, Barbara F. Grimes, was also an SIL member and an accomplished linguist.[3] The two made their home in Mexico City, where they were documenting the Huichol language, which is spoken among indigenous peoples in the Sierra Madre Occidental. Though a field linguist, Joe Grimes had a curious interest in computers, having encountered machines—and the "statisticians and computer people" who operated them—at both Cornell and Oklahoma.

2.1 An Invitation

Upon returning to his home in Mexico City in 1960, Grimes learned of an invitation for social scientists to make use of the IBM 650 computer at the Universidad Nacional Autónoma de México there. His interest was piqued, and he took up the offer. Because he was assisting indigenous peoples in the area, the director of the university's computer lab assigned an assistant to teach Grimes how to program the machine, which used drum memory ("I had to specify where on the drum the next instruction would be") and punch cards. "My first program was a concordance maker to show the context of every morpheme in text collections of Mexican Indian languages," Grimes told us. Concordance studies typified the early history of humanities computing,[4] and the method was popular among linguists and folklorists of that time [12,32]. It is Grimes's "fifth or sixth" computer program, however, that is of special intrigue to us.

2.2 An Idea

"There was a Russian scholar, I think the name was Vladimir Propp, who had laid out an interesting hypothesis about how folk tales are put together," Grimes recalled recently. Propp's *Morphology of the Folktale*, first published in Russian in 1928, was translated into English for the first time in 1958, by Laurence Scott [13]. While this preceded the more seminal 1968 translation,[5] the work had an immediate impact among western scholars in a variety of disciplines,

---

[2] Unless otherwise noted, information and quotes provided in this section originate from personal communications with Joe Grimes (email correspondences dated June 1, 2017; June 19, 2017; June 27, 2017; and August 19, 2017).

[3] For almost thirty years, she was editor of *Ethnologue*, the preeminent catalogue of human languages.

[4] Father Busa's exhaustive indexing of all the words in the works of Thomas Aquinas [9], begun in 1949, is considered the birth of the digital humanities [25].

[5] And George Lakoff's influential 1964 reformulation using recent developments from Chomskyan linguistics [31].

Fig. 1. In the early 1960s, linguist Joseph E. Grimes programmed an IBM computer, at the Universidad Nacional Autónoma de México, to generate stories. His system used Vladimir Propp's narrative elements and sequences and told stories in natural language prose, using simple English or Spanish. (Courtesy IBM Corporate Archives)

```
A LION HAS BEEN IN TROUBLE FOR A LONG TIME. A DOG STEALS SOMETHING THAT
BELONGS TO THE LION. THE HERO, LION, KILLS THE VILLAIN, DOG, WITHOUT A
FIGHT. THE HERO, LION, THUS IS ABLE TO GET HIS POSSESSION BACK.
```

Fig. 2. One of the first computer-generated stories. This example tale produced by Grimes's system appeared in the IBM *Business Machines* article about the project [1]; it appears to be the only system output that survives today. The intelligent use of referring expressions and of the discourse marker 'thus' position this system at the cutting edge of natural language generation in the early 1960s.

notably influencing the legendary structuralist Lévi-Strauss [13,34]. Around this time, Grimes also encountered work on narrative structure by the sociolinguist William Labov: "[Labov was] looking at the structure of nearly-got-killed stories, which he observed people would tell time after time and settle into a pattern not very different from what other people used for similar stories." With these ideas converging on him, and with his knowledge of computer programming increasing, Grimes had an idea.

Fig. 3. Remarkably, Grimes used his generated tales as instruments in the linguistics field task of documenting the Huichol language: "I present the simulated stories to a native user of a language such as Senor Diaz [pictured] and observe his reactions to them, looking especially for places where he bogs down in trying to follow the plot. Such observations on a number of stories, and a number of different native speakers, lead to a picture of the linguistic process at work." (Courtesy IBM Corporate Archives)

2.3   A Computer Storyteller

In the summer of 1960 or 1961, Joe Grimes began programming an IBM 650 computer to tell stories. As noted above, for a decade or so linguists and folklorists had been producing machine concordances of stories, but the notion of encoding stories at a higher-level representation (*i.e.*, higher than an index of lexical items) was just beginning to emerge [10]. The notion of generating stories with a computer was especially obscure; Klein's automatic novel writer would not appear for a decade [28].[6] "I hadn't heard of anybody else trying to do what I was trying to do," Grimes told us recently.

Somebody at IBM Mexico eventually caught wind of the project and saw an opportunity: a Huichol speaker was visiting Grimes in the city, but would be leaving soon, and a Life Magazine photographer—the distinguished Cornell Capa—was available. A meeting was arranged at IBM headquarters, where Capa took photos (see Figs. 1 and 3) and another individual interviewed Grimes and his Huichol associate, who had never seen a computer before. The result of all this was a written account of Grimes's project that appeared in the May 1963

---

[6] A notable exception here is SAGA II, a 1960 system that we discuss in Sect. 3.

issue of *Business Machines*, IBM's employee journal. Its author wrote this about the system's processes [1, p. 11]:

> Dr. Grimes uses a basic fairy tale pattern and then programs the computer using a Monte Carlo approach so it will print out stories in a completely random manner. This involves selecting at random the path from episode to episode within the story, the action by which each episode is accomplished, and the characters which will assume the various roles. The computer can produce about 10^{20} plausible variations on a single fairy tale theme, according to Dr. Grimes.

We asked Grimes what the generated outputs looked like, and his recollection was that the stories were rendered in "simple English or Spanish." An example story is included in the IBM article (see Fig. 2), but unfortunately it appears to be the only output of the system that survives today. Grimes had a remarkable use case for his synthetic tales, as the article explains [1, p. 11]:

> "These stories are an experimental tool," says Dr. Grimes. "I present the simulated stories to a native user of a language [...] and observe his reactions to them, looking especially for places where he bogs down in trying to follow the plot. Such observations on a number of stories, and a number of different native speakers, lead to a picture of the linguistic process at work. From these observations it is possible to proceed to a hypothesis about the underlying linguistic system."

The usage of generated stories as physical field instruments is peculiar, and intriguingly anticipates current projects that are exploring the use of generated stories for practical applications [24, 41].[7] In the mid-1970s, Grimes would further pioneer the incorporation of computers in linguistics fieldwork by innovating, with a student, the use of portable computers in the field [46].

The system itself was produced multiple times, first on the IBM 650 and later on an IBM 1401 at the Universidad Nacional Autónoma de México, and in between on an IBM 1401 at the University of Oklahoma. Grimes programmed the 650 version in machine language and probably used Fortran for the 1401 versions. He recalls that it took a few minutes to generate a single tale, with considerable speed-up on the faster 1401.

It initially appeared to us that Grimes had not himself reported the system in any publication (and this was his recollection as well), but after scouring for some time we discovered two original sources. A 1965 volume called "The Use of Computers in Anthropology" includes an appendix with brief notes from researchers about ongoing projects, to which Grimes contributed a short write-up called "Linguistic and anthropological projects using the computer" [22].

---

[7] There are also interesting connections to one of the all-time major story generators, MEXICA [39]: both were developed in Mexico City, and while Grimes's system aided his field study of the Huichol people, MEXICA's generated stories are about the Mexica people, who are also indigenous to modern-day Mexico.

In it, he notes a series of projects that had utilized the University of Oklahoma's IBM 1401 computer (emphasis ours) [22, p. 516]:

> the calculation of the Grimes-Agard index of linguistic divergence from sets of phonological correspondences, automatic positional analysis of affix systems, *Monte Carlo simulation of folk tale plots*, Program Evaluation and Review Technique analysis of field work projects, preparation and updating of bibliographies, and research into a string manipulation approach to mechanical translation

This single phrase was Grimes's only reporting of the system in an English-language publication. The other original source, which provides a more extensive description of the system, appeared as a section in a 1965 paper published in a Spanish-language linguistics journal [21]. We arranged for this section, titled 'La Simulación,' to be translated into English [23].[8] In the text, Grimes cites the specific influence of Propp and motivates the project [23, p. 1]:

> the fairy tale is a globally diffused literary genre with a very simple architecture. Several prior investigations over this topic have limited themselves to cataloguing the elements of the tale; but Propp suggests that, in addition, the global structure of the tale should be discussed, which manifests itself in each one, and which is what allows the development of new tales made according to the same global structure. I have simulated the structure that Propp defines in a computer, by way of a process that selects elements at random and orders them in the due sequence, resulting in elements for tales that have never been told, but are recognized as tales nonetheless.

He also references the more practical use of the generated tales, with additional implications for testing Propp's theory: "If the result of this process is a series of sentences or texts that the speakers of the language judge acceptable, the underlying description must be good" [23, p. 2]. Grimes recently confirmed this notion to us: "In a way it was a test of Propp's hypothesis, that certain story elements could be recognized in any story."

As for how exactly the system worked, Grimes does not have a strong recollection, but the contemporaneous sources that we have discovered provide some clues. In [23, p. 1], we find this his system operationalizes Propp's model by "a process that selects elements at random and orders them in the due sequence." This would suggest that a subset of Propp's 31 functions [40] are randomly selected and then ordered properly (Propp's list of functions is partially ordered). The example story shown in Fig. 2 initially appears to include four narrative beats, and the latter three coincide nicely with specific Proppian functions: respectively, *villainy*, *victory*, and *liquidation*. Proppian tales also include expression of an initial situation, but the opening sentence "A lion has been in trouble for a long time" corresponds better to one of the initial functions than to a

---

[8] Quotes here have been translated into English by Rogelio E. Cardona-Rivera.

generic initial situation. In the IBM article [1], Grimes notes that his system can generate 10^{20} unique tales, but choosing four randomly from a set of 31 would yield 31^4 combinations, a much smaller number.[9] While the example story in Fig. 2 only includes the *hero* and *villain* Proppian archetypes, there are five more. Additionally, the IBM article notes that "the action by which each episode is accomplished" is also randomly selected [1, p. 11], so each episode must have had multiple candidate actions. Still, these additional combinatorics probably do not get us to 10^{20} possibilities. Given this, we surmise that the system could generate tales with more than four elements.

A remaining issue is how the system rendered the selected elements in natural language. Our best guess is that each action was associated with a realization template, with gaps that corresponded to character archetypes being filled in with character references. Two subtle features of the generated story shown in Fig. 2 merit more explanation, however. First, the prose makes intelligent use of referring expressions: for example, 'a lion' is used the first time the character is introduced, and thereafter 'the lion' or 'the hero, lion.' Second, the discourse marker 'thus' is used to express a discourse relation between the final segment and the earlier ones. These are striking features for the time. Below, we argue that this project may have represented the state of the art of natural language generation in the early 1960s.

2.4   Aftermath

The 1963 IBM article noted this about the future of the project [1, p. 11]:

> Dr. Grimes has laid out plans for a volume of computer-produced folk tales that linguists anywhere can use as an experimental tool in their studies of language. Dr. Grimes' colleagues have suggested that an appropriate title for the book might be *Grimes' Fairy Tales*.

This book never appeared for the same reason that Grimes did not write more about the project—the generated outputs were not good: "The thing I never put my finger on was that my computer's stories had Propp's elements and sequences, but they were all boring." By the mid-1960s, Grimes had abandoned the project: "I had too much going on successfully in other areas, so I decided to leave this one for somebody else." Others did come along.

In 1968, Robert I. Binnick was a research assistant in Victor Yngve's lab at the University of Chicago who was working alone on a curious side project.[10] Inspired by his mentor's pioneering work in natural language generation [50], as well as George Lakoff's recent revision to Propp's model [31], Binnick was developing a Proppian story generator of his own. The system, as he recalls, was a "COMIT program instantiating a (probably) context-free phrase-structure

---

[9] And ordering constraints would further reduce the size of this space.

[10] Unless otherwise noted, information and quotes about this project originate from personal communications with Bob Binnick (email correspondences dated June 23, 2017, and August 9, 2017).

grammar." It could generate "plot outlines or at best a series of statements of events," but the results were "nothing like a real story that a story-teller would tell." Like Grimes, Binnick did not think his results merited publication, and the system was only reported offhandedly: in a sentence-and-a-half aside of a 1969 paper, he noted that his generated stories were "partly abominable and partly amusing" [7, p. 27]. Until now, Binnick's system was also forgotten.

A few years later, in 1971, Sheldon Klein introduced his system for generating murder mysteries [28], the first widely reported effort in story generation. Klein and Grimes were friends who were "tuned to the same frequencies" and ran into each other at (computational) linguistics meetings, but they never worked together. Grimes recalls them discussing stories, but he was not aware of Klein's system and assumes Klein was not aware of his ("I didn't think of it as anything to brag about"). Klein never mentioned Grimes in his work, instead citing Roald Dahl's short story "The Great Automatic Grammatizator" as his primary influence [28, p. 2].

Grimes's system would likely not be known today had the notable folklorist Alan Dundes not mentioned it in his 1965 paper "On Computers and Folk Tales" [12, p. 188].[11] The paper is about computer *encoding* of stories, but in a footnote Dundes says this about Grimes's project before pointing to the IBM article:

> It should be realized that there are other possible uses for computers in the study of folk tales. For example, computers can be used to generate folk tales. Linguist Joseph E. Grimes has succeeded in programming the essence of Vladimir Propp's morphological pattern of folk tales and he has been able to generate tales. Grimes plans to use these artificial [sic] tales for "planting" experiments in "the field."

Before abandoning the project, Grimes demonstrated his system in a seminar at Kansas State University that was held in December 1965 [2–6]. In the week leading up to it, a local newspaper described the event in this way [6]: "Grimes will run a simulation of folk-tale plots by random process, enabling a 1620 computer to compose folk tales, one after the other." Intriguingly, reports also stated that the demonstration would be filmed for later use as training materials [4,6]. We contacted the Kansas State University archives to ask whether any footage survives today,[12] but none could be found—an archivist there suspected that the film would have been stored in a building that was burned down in 1968. It is still possible that other materials related to Grimes's project exist today—code listings, punch cards, or printouts, perhaps—but everything that has turned up so far has been reported in this paper.

3 The First Story Generator?

Essentially all publications in the area of story generation cite Klein's automatic novel writer [28] as the earliest known system (*e.g.*, [19]), and a few make

---

[11] Grimes's own brief accounts in English and Spanish have never been cited.

[12] Email correspondence dated July 13, 2017.

Fig. 4. The earliest known story generator is a 1960 MIT system called SAGA II, which generated scenes from television screenplays in the western genre. CBS showcased the system on a program called "The Thinking Machine," which featured discussion of its architecture (left) and live-action renditions of three generated scenes (right); actual system output is also shown here (middle). (Courtesy Computer History Museum)

the worse mistake of attributing this to TALE-SPIN, which was introduced even later, in 1975 [36] (*e.g.*, [14]). That being said, a handful of scholars *have* become aware of Grimes's project, through the footnote in Dundes's paper [12, p. 188].[13] Unfortunately, every one of these scholars has misattributed the system to Dundes [15,33,43,45] or to a collaboration between Dundes and Grimes [16,17,29]. Thus, beyond providing the first extensive account of this project, this paper is also the first to correctly attribute the system to its true author, Grimes.

While Grimes's 1963 story generator predates Klein's 1971 effort,[14] it is not the earliest known story generator. In October 1960, CBS honored the upcoming 1961 centennial of the Massachusetts Institute of Technology (MIT) by producing a television series called *Tomorrow*. One episode, called "The Thinking Machine," profiled uses at MIT of the TX-0 digital computer, including a program named SAGA II that generated screenplays in the TV western genre (see Fig. 4).[15] Mark Sample rediscovered this material in 2013 and wrote about SAGA II in the context of randomness in expressive systems [44], but until now no one has articulated its place as the earliest known story generator; this is another contribution of this paper. In the CBS program, the SAGA II architecture is discussed and three generated scenes are acted out, including a degenerate one in the style of Meehan's 'mis-spun tales' [37]. A technical memorandum between the system programmer and the project lead also survives [38], which gives some insight into the system's processes: scenes are broken into narrative beats, each of which is defined as a branching action structure that is traversed probabilistically according to the story state. The system's operation is illustrated in the CBS program using a tidy flow chart. Intriguingly, this architecture anticipates

---

[13] In our field, Lee's 1994 master's thesis is the earliest such work [33].

[14] And indeed Binnick's 1969 system does too.

[15] The episode is available online at http://techtv.mit.edu/videos/10268-the-thinking-machine-1961---mit-centennial-film; the segment of interest begins around the 32-min mark.

Klein's murder-mystery generator, which Marie-Laure Ryan characterizes using a probabilistic flow chart in an unknown (but very good) 1987 paper [42].

If Grimes began developing his system in the summer of 1960—a possibility that he has stated to us—then perhaps his system existed in some form before SAGA II did. The safest bet, though, is to rely on the publication dates of extant materials, and in that regard SAGA II precedes his system by at least one and a half years.[16] Curiously, in the 1963 IBM article, Grimes references the rigid narrative structure of TV westerns [1, p. 11]:

> "All fairy tales contain a number of segments," says Dr. Grimes, "and there are definite constraints on the order in which these segments can be placed. In a rather cramped subtype of the fairy tale known as the TV western, for example, the gunslinger in the black hat can be done in only after he has perpetrated some kind of villainy. To arrest him for vagrancy at the outset and keep him in jail until the final commercial, would violate the esthetic sense of every third grader in the land."

We asked Grimes if he recalled ever seeing the CBS program, and specifically whether SAGA II could have been an influence on his project, but he was sure that he had not been aware of the work.

4   Conclusion

Grimes's system is incredibly important to our field. If it is not the first story generator, since SAGA II was reported first, it is still the earliest known system to generate complete stories (SAGA II only generated scenes). More specifically, it is the earliest known Proppian system, preceding even the seminal second translation of Propp into English in 1968 and Lakoff's influential 1964 reformulation of the model [31]. Now, in the present day, we are experiencing a revival in Proppian story generation (e.g., [20]), which could be considered curious given that Grimes (and also Binnick) found the approach to be unworthy more than fifty years ago. More broadly, Grimes's system is the first to use *story grammars*, a major 1970s approach that until recently had been largely abandoned in light of Black and Wilensky's famous 1979 skewering [8].[17] As the present repeats the (until now) forgotten past, we wonder how the history of story generation (and narrative modeling more broadly) would be altered had Grimes reported, as early as the mid-1960s, the negative result of his Proppian system that could generate 10^{20} "boring" tales.[18]

---

[16] Another consideration is how 'story generation' is defined, but we will leave that discussion for a different paper.

[17] Story grammars did not go down without a fight [35], and their appeal in contemporary contexts is evidenced by Kate Compton's Tracery [11].

[18] To be clear, we are not calling for the abandonment of Proppian story generation. Rather, we mean to shed light on the origins of this approach, and in this light we find that the earliest attempts were curiously aborted. In any event, even successful entrants in this tradition should acknowledge their forebears: Grimes and Binnick.

Finally, there is another aspect of Grimes's project that merits discussion. While the generated prose of the example story shown in Fig. 2 may not impress readers today, it has features that suggest the need to reappraise the early history of natural language generation. First, let us summarize the prevailing historical account of this area. In 1961, Victor Yngve produced a seminal paper reporting a system that could produce grammatically correct nonsense sentences, *e.g.*, "A proud, little, proud and heated headlight is little and shiny" [50, p. 77]. AUTO-BEATNIK, one of the earliest computer poetry generators, used a similar technique to produce sentences of comparable quality: "All blows have glue, few toothpicks have wood" [49, p. 97]. This was the state of the art of natural language generation in 1962 [18], and the following year Sheldon Klein and Robert F. Simmons pushed the cutting edge a bit farther by maintaining dependency structure within generated sentences [27]. The first reported system to generate discourse comprising multiple sentences appeared in Klein's follow-up work of 1965 [26]. Grimes's system, we now know, did this as early as 1963. Moreover, as the generated story in Fig. 2 demonstrates, the system made intelligent use of referring expressions—'a lion' is used the first time the character is introduced, and thereafter 'the lion' or 'the hero, lion'—and also a discourse marker, 'thus'. Given these novel features, and what we know about the state of the art in the early 1960s, it would seem that Grimes's system was among the most advanced natural language generation projects of its time.

This paper is the first in a series on the forgotten early history of computer story generation. Until now, Grimes's pioneering system had been known to only a handful of scholars, each of whom misattributed it to another creator. We have provided here the first extensive account of the project, made possible by personal communication with its true creator and excavation of three obscure contemporaneous sources [1,22,23]. In addition to profiling Grimes's 1963 story generator, we have also introduced another early Proppian system—Binnick's 1969 one—and have been the first to declare that the 1960 SAGA II system [38] is now the earliest known story generator.[19] Thus, while the prevailing belief in our field has been that Klein's automatic novel writer [28] was the first story generator, we have shown that it has at least three antecedents. We stated at the beginning of this paper that our larger project is to dismantle the prevailing history of this area, which, as we have begun to show here, is inaccurate in several ways. Eventually, we will furnish a comprehensive account that integrates all of our findings. While others have conducted technical reviews of the field [19,30] and deep dives into specific systems [47], our larger project is the first attempt at an extensive intellectual history. We aim specifically for a rich account that tells us more about where we came from and where we should go next, and we hope that others will join us in this mission.

Acknowledgments. We are deeply indebted to Joseph E. Grimes, who, over the span of two months, graciously answered numerous questions about his project. Likewise, we thank Robert I. Binnick for taking the time to respond to inquiries regarding his own

---

[19] Again, we note that Mark Sample rediscovered this system in 2013 [44].

pioneering system. Rogelio E. Cardona-Rivera pitched in to translate Grimes's Spanish-language account of his system—this translation proved to be a critical source. L.J. Strumpf, of the IBM Corporate Archives, furnished another major source, the *Business Machines* article. He also provided high-quality scans of the archival images included in this paper—these have not been seen since the photographs were taken in 1963. Finally, we would like to thank Cliff Hight, archivist at Kansas State University, who also provided assistance on the project.

References

1. Exploring the fascinating world of language. Bus. Mach. **XLVI**(3), 10–11 (1963). Courtesy IBM Corporate Archives
2. Language to be discussed. Kansas State Collegian **72**(60), 6, 14 December 1965
3. Linguist demonstrates shortcut to translating. Kansas State Collegian **72**(60), 1, 14 December 1965
4. Linguist to explain methods. Kansas State Collegian **72**(53), 4, 7 December 1965
5. Linguistics expert to give demonstration of methods. Kansas State Collegian **72**(59), 1, 13 December 1965
6. Linguists demonstration Monday at Kansas State. The Manhattan (Kansas) Mercury, 1, 7 December 1965
7. Binnick, R.I.: An application of an extended generative semantic model of language to man-machine interaction. In: Proceedings of the Conference on Computational Linguistics, pp. 1–34 (1969)
8. Black, J.B., Wilensky, R.: An evaluation of story grammars. Cogn. Sci. **3**(3), 213–229 (1979)
9. Busa, R.: The annals of humanities computing: the index thomisticus. Comput. Humanit. **14**(2), 83–90 (1980)
10. Colby, B.N., Collier, G.A., Postal, S.K.: Comparison of themes in folktales by the general inquirer system. J. Am. Folklore **76**(302), 318–323 (1963)
11. Compton, K., Kybartas, B., Mateas, M.: Tracery: an author-focused generative text tool. In: Schoenau-Fog, H., Bruni, L.E., Louchart, S., Baceviciute, S. (eds.) ICIDS 2015. LNCS, vol. 9445, pp. 154–161. Springer, Cham (2015). https://doi.org/10.1007/978-3-319-27036-4_14
12. Dundes, A.: On computers and folk tales. Western Folklore **24**(3), 185–189 (1965)
13. Dundes, A.: Binary opposition in myth: the Propp/Lévi-Strauss debate in retrospect. Western Folklore **56**(1), 39–50 (1997)
14. Eger, M., Potts, C.M., Barot, C., Young, R.M.: Plotter: operationalizing the master book of all plots. In: Proceedings of the Intelligent Narrative Technologies and Social Believability in Games, pp. 30–33 (2015)
15. Fairclough, C.: Story games and the OPIATE system. Ph.D. thesis, University of Dublin, Trinity College (2004)
16. Ferri, G.: Between procedures and computer games: semiotics of practices as a unifying perspective. In: Proceedings of the International Association for Semiotic Studies, pp. 291–302. Universidade da Coruña (2012)
17. Ferri, G.: Narrative structures in IDN authoring and analysis. In: Koenitz, H., Ferri, G., Haahr, M., Sezen, D., Sezen, T.İ. (eds.) Interactive Digital Narrative: History, Theory and Practice, pp. 77–90. Routledge (2015)
18. Garvin, P.L.: Computer participation in linguistic research. Language **38**(4), 385–389 (1962)

19. Gervas, P.: Computational approaches to storytelling and creativity. AI Mag. **30**(3), 49 (2009)
20. Gervás, P.: Propp's morphology of the folk tale as a grammar for generation. In: Proceedings of the Computational Models of Narrative, pp. 106–122 (2013)
21. Grimes, J.E.: La computadora en las investigaciones humanísticas. Anuario de Letras. Lingüística y Filología **5**, 163–174 (1965)
22. Grimes, J.E.: Linguistic and anthropological projects using the computer. In: The Use of Computers in Anthropology, pp. 515–516 (1965)
23. Grimes, J.E., Cardona-Rivera, R.E., Ryan, J.: Translation of "La Simulación" (2017). Available upon request
24. Harrison, B., Riedl, M.O.: Learning from stories: using crowdsourced narratives to train virtual agents. In: Proceedings of the Artificial Intelligence and Interactive Digital Entertainment, pp. 183–189 (2016)
25. Hockey, S.: The history of humanities computing. In: A Companion to Digital Humanities, pp. 3–19 (2004)
26. Klein, S.: Automatic paraphrasing in essay format. Mech. Transl. Comput. Linguist. **8**(3–4), 68–83 (1965)
27. Klein, S., Simmons, R.F.: Syntactic dependence and the computer generation of coherent discourse. Mech. Transl. **7**(2), 50–61 (1963)
28. Klein, S., et al.: A program for generating reports on the status and history of stochastically modifiable semantic models of arbitrary universes. University of Wisconsin Tech. Rep. TR142 (1971)
29. Koenitz, H., Ferri, G., Haahr, M., Sezen, D., Sezen, T.İ.: Introduction: the evolution of interactive digital narrative theory. In: Koenitz, H., Ferri, G., Haahr, M., Sezen, D., Sezen, T.İ. (eds.) Interactive Digital Narrative: History, Theory and Practice, pp. 69–76. Routledge (2015)
30. Kybartas, B., Bidarra, R.: A survey on story generation techniques for authoring computational narratives. Trans. Comput. Intell. AI Games (2016)
31. Lakoff, G.: Structural complexity in fairy tales. The Study of Man **1**, 128–150 (1972)
32. Lamb, S.M., Gould, L.: Concordances from computers (1964)
33. Lee, M.: A model of story generation. Master's thesis, University of Manchester, Manchester (1994)
34. Lévi-Strauss, C., Weightman, J., Weightman, D.: The Raw and the Cooked: Introduction to a Science of Mythology. Pimlico New York, NY (1994)
35. Mandler, J.M., Johnson, N.S.: On throwing out the baby with the bathwater: a reply to Black and Wilensky's evaluation of story grammars. Cogn. Sci. **4**(3), 305–312 (1980)
36. Meehan, J.R.: Using planning structures to generate stories. Am. J. Comput. Linguist. **33**, 78–94 (1975)
37. Meehan, J.R.: The metanovel: Writing stories by computer. Ph.D. thesis, Yale University (1976)
38. Morse, H.R.: Preliminary operating notes for SAGA II. MIT Technical Memorandum 8436-M-29 (1960)
39. Pérez ý Pérez, R., Sharples, M.: Mexica: a computer model of a cognitive account of creative writing. J. Exp. Theoret. Artif. Intell. **13**(2), 119–139 (2001)
40. Propp, V.: Morphology of the Folktale. University of Texas Press (2010)
41. Riedl, M.O., Harrison, B.: Using stories to teach human values to artificial agents. In: Proceedings of the AI, Ethics, and Society, pp. 105–112 (2016)
42. Ryan, M.L.: The heuristics of automatic story generation. Poetics **16**(6), 505–534 (1987)

43. Sack, W.: Une machine à raconter des histoires: propp et les software studies. Les Temps Modernes **5**, 216–243 (2013)
44. Sample, M.: An account of randomness in literary computing (2013). Presented at Modern Language Association
45. Smith, J.B.: Thematic structure and complexity. Style **9**, 32–54 (1975)
46. Summer Institute of Linguistics: First portable computer for linguistic fieldwork. https://www.sil.org/history-event/first-portable-computer-linguistic-fieldwork. Accessed 22 Jun 2017
47. Wardrip-Fruin, N.: Expressive Processing: Digital fictions, Computer Games, and Software Studies. MIT Press, Cambridge (2009)
48. Wardrip-Fruin, N.: Digital media archaeology: interpreting computational processes. In: Media Archaeology: Approaches, Applications, and Implications, pp. 302–322 (2011)
49. Worthy, R.M.: A new American poet speaks: the works of A.B. Horizon. A Magazine of the Arts **IV**(5), 96–99 (1962)
50. Yngve, V.H.: Random generation of English sentences. In: Proceedings of the Machine Translation of Languages and Applied Language Analysis, pp. 66–80 (1961)

The Narrative Logic of Rube Goldberg Machines

David Olsen[1]([✉]) and Mark J. Nelson[2]([✉])

[1] Aeiouy Computer Media and Entertainment, Hollister, CA, USA
dolsen@aeiouy.org
[2] The MetaMakers Institute, Falmouth University, Cornwall, UK
mjn@anadrome.org

Abstract. Rube Goldberg's cartoons famously depict absurd, unreasonably complex machines invented by Professor Lucifer G. Butts to carry out simple tasks. *Rube Goldberg machine* has now become a byword for overly complicated machinery or bureaucracy of any kind. The specific structure of Goldberg's original cartoons, however, is quite interesting. Beyond simply being complex, his machines are based on a particular repertoire of objects used in stereotypical, coincidental, and comical ways, exhibiting almost as much of a narrative logic as a mechanical logic. In this paper, we analyze the structure of these cartoon machines' construction, with a view towards being able to generate them using a planning formalization of this analysis.

Keywords: Rube Goldberg machine · Computational humor · Narrative generation · Planning

1 Introduction

One of the signature gags of cartoonist Rube Goldberg (1883–1970) was to "invent" fantastical, complex machines that, through a series of absurdly unnecessary intermediary operations, would eventually succeed in performing a simple task. This genre is now termed the *Rube Goldberg machine* [3,5,10], and a few examples are shown in Figs. 1, 2 and 3.

We put "invent" here in scare quotes not only because of the machines' obvious lack of practical utility for accomplishing their stated goals, but because the original machines as conceived by Goldberg himself exist only in a cartoon world, not as physical machines. The concept has since inspired people to build complex real-world contraptions that capture some of these machines' spirit, and which are also termed Rube Goldberg machines. The real-world machines, however, exhibit a quite different logic, one more akin to an extended version of a domino show than to the absurdist logic of Goldberg's cartoons (as we will discuss further).

This paper's main aim is to structurally analyze the logic followed by Rube Goldberg machines in their original cartoon-world formulation. Goldberg intended these impractical inventions in part as "symbols of man's capacity for

© Springer International Publishing AG 2017
N. Nunes et al. (Eds.): ICIDS 2017, LNCS 10690, pp. 104–116, 2017.
https://doi.org/10.1007/978-3-319-71027-3_9

A Simple Way to Take Your Own Picture

PROFESSOR BUTTS GOES OVER NIAGARA FALLS IN A COLLAPSIBLE ASH-CAN AND HITS UPON AN IDEA FOR A SIMPLE WAY TO TAKE YOUR OWN PICTURE.

WIGGLE BIG TOE (A), PULLING STRING (B) AND RAISING HOOK (C), WHICH RELEASES SPRING (D) AND CAUSES HAMMER (E) TO STRIKE PLATFORM (F) AND CATAPULT ARABIAN MIDGET (G) TO TRAPEZE (H). WEIGHT OF ARAB CAUSES BAR (I) TO TILT AND PULL CORD (J), WHICH UPSETS PITCHER OF SYRUP (K). SYRUP DRIPS ON CAMERA-BULB (L) ATTRACTING HUNGRY FLY (M) WHICH SWOOPS DOWN, ALLOWING WEIGHTED END OF BAR (N) TO LIFT SCREEN (O) WHICH HAS BEEN SHUTTING OFF VISION OF MOUSE (P). MOUSE SEES CHEESE (Q) AND JUMPS. TRAP (R) SNAPS, CAUSING SWATTER (S) TO SWAT FLY THEREBY SQUEEZING BULB & TAKING PICTURE. IF PICTURE IS NO GOOD DON'T BLAME IT ON INVENTION. IT'S THE WAY YOU LOOK.

Fig. 1. A simple way to take your own picture

exerting maximum effort to accomplish minimum results" [10, p. 53]. But beyond the unnecessary mechanical complexity, the machines gain additional absurdity and impracticality by incorporating components that would be unlikely to work reliably (or at all) in a real machine, such as the actions and reactions of animal characters. In addition, many of the machines exhibit violence in their operation, towards both animals and humans, that makes them uncomfortable to contemplate—and unethical to build—as real machines.

Based on our analysis of the logic of Rube Goldberg machines, we have implemented a preliminary generator, in a planning formalism, to produce novel machines in this style. This implementation is intended in part as a generative test of our analysis, and in part as our actual practical medium-term goal. Besides being interesting to analyze, our focus on Rube Goldberg machines comes from a desire to procedurally generate interactive videogame puzzles in this style. Videogame puzzles have previously been generated using a simple backwards-chaining planner [1], which is an approach we also adopt here. But here our goal is to set up the planning problem so that the resulting puzzles have the characteristically comical Rube-Goldberg-machine feel.

2 Cartoon and Physical Machines

The general concept of a Rube Goldberg machine is culturally widespread, to the point where it has become a byword for any overly complicated apparatus or process, from physical devices to bureaucratic procedures. Goldberg's machines themselves, however, have a much more specific character beyond the basic starting point of being unnecessarily complicated, which it is our goal to model.

Goldberg's machines are always in cartoon form, and almost none could actually be built, for reasons ranging from their dependence on coincidence to their incorporation of animal cruelty (as will become apparent from the explanation of a few machines in the following section). In this absurd form of mechanization they bear some similarity to roughly contemporaneous depictions of machines in avant-garde art, especially by the Dadaists, who appear to have been aware of Goldberg's work, although he himself was uninterested in "high art" and didn't comment on theirs [4].

People have however built physical machines often described as Rube Goldberg machines, and it is worth briefly looking at how they differ. To focus on an example that also has a significant narrative running through it (rather than being purely a complex machine), the Japanese television show *Pythagora Switch* has built a series of strongly narrative-driven domino-like machines described as Rube Goldberg machines [9]. These have also become popular in the west after being uploaded to YouTube with English subtitles.[1] In these machines, a character, Biisuke, engages in adventures, as he is captured at one point, rescued by friends, etc., all through the operation of an intricate series of chained mechanical reactions.

These mechanical reactions essentially form a large domino show, but with more diverse objects than simply falling dominoes. The logic of operation is that each movement hits the next device, triggering it to move and continue the sequence. Therefore the design is largely based around space: the machine components must all physically chain with each other, and there are generally recurring elements, such as in the case of the Biisuke machines a track for rolling balls, that are re-used to connect parts together.

In cartoon Rube Goldberg machines, by contrast, space is not really the primary concern. In a sense they are actually much simpler. There is a goal state, and the intervening steps are mostly there to be funny, not to contribute to an impressive feat of virtuosic machine-building, as in the physical examples. The only real requirement on the components in a cartoon machine is that each plausibly connects the chain, leaning heavily on the reader being able to implicitly read what its role in the machine is.

It is usually conceptually clear to the reader what role each of the components play in the cartoon machines, but their actual function depends on coincidence, luck, and suspension of disbelief. The overall machine does thus exhibit a kind of mechanical logic in which the apparatus achieves an end goal through a sequence of internal events chained together in a logically consistent manner. But it is an absurdist mechanical logic, which incorporates characters—in most cases characters whose presence is not even really necessary in the first place—who react to events and to other characters.

Therefore in some respects the logic of (cartoon) Rube Goldberg machines is more similar to the internal logic of narrative structures, which require some degree of coherence but not strict fidelity to physics, than it is to the strictly mechanistic logic of real-world machines. Our attempt here to discern a kind of coherent narrative logic in Rube Goldberg machines is therefore related to the (relatively sparse) existing work on investigating the internal logic of cartoons, such as the Road Runner and Coyote scenarios of *Looney Tunes* [6,8].

---

[1] https://www.youtube.com/watch?v=trDnp3dWlXk.

Taking the Shirt off the Taxpayer's Back

TRUMAN (A) PLAYS PIANO, KNOCKING OVER BOWL
CONTAINING AMERASIA SECRET PAPERS (B) — FUMES (C)
OVERCOME REPUBLICAN SENATOR (D), WHO FALLS BACK,
CAUSING SPOON (E) TO TOSS SURPLUS POTATO (F) —
JOE DI MAGGIO (G) SWINGS, CAUSING REVOLVING
MECHANISM (H) TO SET OFF LEFTOVER 4TH OF JULY
ROCKET (I) WHICH HITS DICE BOX (J), CAUSING IT TO
THROW A NATURAL — DISTRICT ATTORNEY (K) RUNS TO
INVESTIGATE GAMBLING, CAUSING ROPE (L) TO PULL
SHIRT (M) OFF TAXPAYER'S BACK!

Fig. 2. Taking the shirt off the Taxpayer's back

3   Principles of Rube Goldberg Machines

A single Rube Goldberg *invention* is a comic with three separate parts: the
title, the cartoon, and the description. The title could be considered the most
important part for interpretation, as it provides a framework for the action in the
world, explaining the practical goal that the invention is trying to accomplish.
The cartoon depicts the placement of objects in the world, each labeled. Finally
the text describes what is going on, i.e. the potential moves that link the objects
labeled together to achieve the stated goal.

The machines themselves are invariably complex, often ridiculous and while
always providing a path to the end goal described in the title, the end goal is
something often beyond expectation. Besides being large and overly complex,
they tend to twist the meaning behind what they do, subverting expectations
either through the outcome, the components, or the reader-assumed motivations for the machine. What makes them more ridiculous is that despite having
required apparent feats of ingenuity to invent such a complex machine, they can
only be used once without rebuilding. The machines' initial condition is almost
always a precarious arrangement of components, some even in mid-motion or in
rather unlikely scenarios. If the machine were actually set in motion—which is
never shown explicitly, only implied by the arrangement of components—all this
careful design would come crashing down, with most components ending up out
of place and some destroyed. Running the machine a second time would involve
carefully setting up these unlikely scenarios that got the machine to work in the
first place (after possibly sourcing new components).

Marzio [5, p. 145] reports that Goldberg drew at least one of these machines
per week between 1909 and 1935, amounting to over 1,000 examples, although
to our knowledge there is no comprehensive archive available, and only a

small subset are collected in anthologies. In this section we break down the common types of components of Rube Goldberg machines, as well as what role those components play in the overall machines' operation and narrative, based primarily on analyzing the subset of machines collected in an anthology published in 2000 [10].

3.1   Chaining Components

Despite all the complexity when the viewer looks at the machines, with steps that are numerous, ridiculous, and unlikely, it should nonetheless be immediately apparent that the machines have a potential to work. Each thing placed in the world provides the necessary conditions for that particular component to work, forming a chain of coincidental action that produces a result, even if not exactly the one advertised. The machines can be made of humans, animals, or inanimate objects, most often some sort of mixture.

Each step may seem contrived or even random, but it fits with its context: the item earlier in the chain must cause an action that this item uses, in a sense, to complete its own action, which then leads to the next item down the chain. In some of Goldberg's own discussions, this can sound like a machine constructed through backwards-chaining planning:

> "For instance, when I have a goat crying in one of my cartoons, I have to give a satisfactory reason for having him cry. So I have someone take a tin can away from him." —Rube Goldberg [7]

The steps are thus pairs of objects with actions gluing them together; the state of one object and action must fit with what the next object needs.

3.2   Beginning, Middle, and End

Objects can be roughly divided into three regions of the machine: The initial object, the final object, and the ones in between. The initial object uses a pre-determined state of the world to start the action. This object itself may even be reasonable by the standards of the objects relating to the goal; for example, a mouse may simply be standing in the area (because it is later needed for shooting into space). This is not always the case though, and sometimes the initial choice may also seem whimsical or random.

The final object is the final step achieving the goal. It illustrates the purpose of the machine, but as with the rest of the machine, there may be twist expectations of what is supposed to be done to achieve the nominal goal of the machine. A machine to get rid of a mouse, for example, ends by shooting it into space. While this is legitimate way of removing a mouse, it is not the end goal—a dead mouse on earth—that we might expect.

The objects that make up the bulk of the machine, in the middle, are much less constrained, and often seem almost random in how they are picked. They can vary in type, but don't necessarily need to. They can vary in placement, but again that isn't necessary. The only real rule seems to be that when viewed through the lens of a single step, the action must seem somewhat reasonable (a very relative term in this case), as well as—and this is a hard requirement—look overly complex and ridiculous from a wider perspective.

3.3   Types and Roles of Objects

The types of objects commonly found in Rube Goldberg machines can be grouped based on certain attributes of the objects, or of actions that the objects can perform. Table 1 summarizes three primary types of objects: humans, animals, and (inanimate) items. Each type of object can be further categorized by which of the object's characteristics the machine wants to use, as follows.

Humans. The sub-categories that humans can be split into are: humans as a motive force, humans representing an occupation or other noteworthy characteristic, generic humans, and humans as actors in a coincidence. Humans as a motive force put people into the role of a human-looking machine; they can be attached to other inanimate components and provide the force needed to run those components. For example, a human can push a lever down, the same work that could have done by a rock. Humans with an obvious occupation or

Table 1. Types of objects commonly found in Rube Goldberg machines

Category	Subcategory	Description	Example
Human	Generic	Person who does things a stereotypical human would likely do in a situation	A person at a lunch table will probably eat their sandwich
	Object	Hybrid person/object subsystem. Human is the motive force, but only as engine for movement	Person sitting on a chair falling over
	Coincidence	Human as an engine for coincidence to occur	Person slips on banana peel
	Attribute	Person with a characteristic that causes them to act in a stereotypical way	Baseball player will hit baseball thrown at them in any situation
Animal	Attribute	Attribute that is viewed to be inherent in an animal	Mice are attracted to cheese
Item	Subsystem	Multiple items that combine to create a single action	A pulley and rope for lifting things
	Physics	Item with a physical characteristic that allows it to move in the world	A feather floats up in a puff of air
	Attribute	Item with a characteristic affecting animate objects	A piece of cheese attracts a mouse

other noteworthy characteristic can be used by the machine to imply an obvious action; these sometimes include characters with specifically identified names or titles. Joe DiMaggio in Fig. 2 shows up swinging a bat, because when a baseball player sees a baseball and they have a bat, of course they will swing at it. When humans are used to act like generic humans, they act in stereotypical (though perhaps exaggerated) ways and often poke fun at some aspect of human nature. They do "normal" things: they answer phones, they pick interesting things off the ground, and all manner of other activities. Finally, humans can be a object taking part in a coincidence. They again are a motive force in this case, but an entity with movement whose sole reason for existence is because *someone* had to be there to slip on that banana peel.

Animals. Animals have no subcategories. In every case we have found, the role of an animal in a Rube Goldberg machine is the same: to embody a stereotypical attribute perceived to be inherent in that type of animal (similar to the subcategory of humans who are used to represent an occupation). Implied animal attributes usually result in particular actions that the animal is obviously supposed to take. Mice like cheese, so they will try to eat it; goats eat anything so they will chew on that tin can; bulls are ornery so they will charge at people, etc. These characteristics don't have to be particularly accurate, just something that popular conception has this type of animal doing that would be immediately apparent to most readers.

Items. Inanimate items can be split into one of several subcategories: multiple items that form a sort of subsystem, items with physical properties, or items with some sort of attribute that has an affect on a human or animal. The subsystem might be a pulley attached to the trigger of a gun on one end and a weight on the other. This whole apparatus is a single conceptual step in the process and therefore we consider it as one item. Objects used for their physical characteristics might be a shape, like a wedge, or some other more active characteristic, like being magnetic. This is generally related to movement of the object or other inanimate objects. Items with attributes that affect animate objects typically cause the human or animal to do something, but don't necessarily do anything themselves. A mouse is attracted to cheese, but all the cheese has to do is be in sight of the mouse; the action is on the part of the mouse.

The same object can serve, and often does, in more than one of the subcategories at different points during the machine's operation; each step may use a different characteristic of an object. For example, oranges have the physical characteristic of being round, so they can roll, but they also attract birds who want to eat them. So there might be a sequence such as: 1. A bird flies to the orange to eat it, but instead pushes it down, 2. The orange rolls off the bench and hits something.

3.4   Example

To illustrate the principles of Rube Goldberg machines outlined in the previous section, we'll walk through an analysis of the example shown in Fig. 3. The basic

Fig. 3. Automatic suicide device for unlucky stock speculators

characteristic of the comic is typical of a Goldberg *invention*. Here the textual description on the left side gives context to the comic on the right side, and the title states the overall goal. The point of the machine in this comic is rather morbid: it is a suicide machine for people who have received bad news about their stock portfolio.

The outside factor that starts the action is receiving a phone call (presumably from a stock broker). The action sequence from that point on is: the telephone wakes a sleeping office manager, who pushes a lever, which knocks over a glider, which lands on a dwarf, who jacks up a jack, which pushes up a pig, who eats a potato, which bothers a bookkeeper, who moves down, pulling a string, which pulls the trigger on a gun. Unpacking these events in detail:

1. Initial state. The telephone is ringing because it received a call (presumably from the stock broker). This is a physical characteristic of phones.
2. The telephone ringing wakes up the sleeping office manager. An attribute of phone ringing is that it can awaken sleeping people (or perhaps animals). Generic people are awakened by loud noises.
3. The office manager stretches when awakened, and in doing so hits a lever. This is a human providing motive force for an item. The item has the physical characteristic of being able to be pushed.
4. The lever drops the glider that was on the other side of the lever. This is a physical characteristic of one object causing the physical characteristic of another object to be activated.
5. The glider hits the dwarf in the head. The physical characteristic of the glider matches with human coincidence of happening to be under the falling glider.
6. The dwarf jumps up and down, causing the jack lever to move, pushing up the jack. The dwarf is acting as a generic human, jumping up and down while angry (as angry people are stereotypically depicted in cartoons). The jack has a physical characteristic that causes it to rise when used.
7. A pig who is on the jack eats the potato, because it is now within range. Pigs are animals who like to eat things—such as potatoes, which have an attribute of attracting pigs to eat them.

8. However the potato is attached to the bookkeeper, so it causes annoyance when eaten, which causes the bookkeeper to move. In this case it is a human/item system, and is caused by generic human characteristics (being annoyed, moving in response to annoyance) with the same human involved on both sides.
9. The bookkeeper is also attached to a string, which is part of a string/pulley system. The bookkeeper is part of another human/item system which is attached to an item subsystem.
10. The string is furthermore attached to a trigger on a gun, which is pulled, thereby shooting the gun. This is the item subsystem using physical characteristics of an object.
11. Final state. A dead person, shot.

The first thing to note is that the machine does set out what is supposed to do: the person is dead in the end. It twists expectations by causing the death not just because of a bad call from the stock broker, but if any call is received on this particular telephone.

The next thing to note is that one can see the biggest characteristics of Rube Goldberg machines: it is long and complicated to do something that would be quite easy to do otherwise. The only required items for this machine are the telephone, gun and person getting shot.

Given that it is a Rube Goldberg machine, we can see that actions of objects do have reasonable, if unlikely, reasons for happening. Why a bookkeeper has a potato on his collar, the viewer may never know. But it is reasonable to expect that a pig might eat the potato if it saw it there to be eaten, and this would understandably cause distress to a person who would then move, all reasonable given the circumstances.

The choice of objects placed for this particular machine are a mixed bag, some random and some suited to the setting. Most of the people don't seem out of place. Some of the items are also reasonable; having a telephone in an office is normal and would likely to be there even in a more realistic scenario, and the gun in an office is not too unreasonable—this is America, after all.

The rest is less clearly there for a reason. Why is there a pig? Why was there a potato attached to a collar? Could the pig have been replaced by a goat, and the potato with a tin can, and produced a similar result? How could a system be designed to generate this kind of scenario?

4   Generating Rube Goldberg Machines

From our analysis of Rube Goldberg machines' structure, the basic operation of a generator becomes clear. We represent object/action pairings as plan operators, and their various possible roles in a machine and relationships to other objects (stereotypical, physical, etc.) are encoded as operator preconditions and postconditions. The actual planning is quite straightforward, simply chaining together actions so that pre- and post-conditions match; the bulk of the logic that captures the nature of Rube Goldberg machines is in the design of the operators.

4.1   Designing Operators

Consider the following four-step machine to turn on a light:

1. The cat chases the mouse.
2. The mouse runs towards the hole.
3. The mouse presses button (by running over it).
4. The button turns on the light.

Each of these steps must have a reason for it to occur, e.g. the mouse is running because a cat is chasing it. The objects that are causing the action to occur must then in turn be present and similarly motivated. Table 2 shows these four steps analyzed into precondition and postcondition pairs that relate an action done by one object to another.

Table 2. Actions redesigned as pre-conditions and post-conditions

	Precondition	Postcondition
1	Cat sees mouse	Cat chases mouse
2	Cat is chasing mouse	Mouse runs away
3	Mouse runs over a button	A button is pressed
4	A button is pressed	A light turns on

We turn each precondition and postcondition pair here into a plan operator that matches actions and objects, and use a STRIPS-style planner [2] to chain them together in a coherent way. World state, and the pre/post-conditions that change it, generally represents either the presence of objects, or the recent occurrence of an action that might motivate another action. In contrast to standard STRIPS planning world state therefore does not stay constant until explicitly changed; state representing recent actions that might motivate a subsequent action "times out" if not used.

One big advantage when planning in Rube Goldberg machines is that we can always assume coincidence will help us achieve the outcome that is most advantageous to us, when multiple outcomes are possible. This allows us to define a minimal list of preconditions and postconditions, since we can always take the desired outcome, the one that might happen if we want it to.

In addition to regular state, there are a few pseudo-states that can be asserted and checked to influence the behavior of the planner. From our analysis of Rube Goldberg machines, there are often certain constraints on object reuse, or on placement of objects with similar postconditions. For example, a reason for the mouse running is the important part, and having more than one mouse will just confuse matters and make the machine's logic less apparent. To capture these constraints, `no_repeat` tells the system to not re-use an operator even if the preconditions match, and `single_matched_state` tells the system to not use a operator that has a postcondition which was already used elsewhere. This allows operators to influence some of the higher-level structure of the machines, limiting confounding elements that would confuse the main line of the action.

4.2   Example Generated Plan

A simple planning problem using the operators abstracted from the four-step machine discussed above is shown in Table 3. Each of the operators shows a causal link between actions where the preconditions match the postconditions. We can use the fact that in a Rube Goldberg machine we don't have to worry about what *could* happen but rather what we want to happen. So the fact that the mouse runs over the button when it potentially could have run anywhere is the system's choice and not the result of any kind of "honest" simulation.

Table 3. Example plan

Plan conditions	single_matched_state	
Initial state	mouse_exists, cat_exists, mouse_seen, cheese_exists	
Operator	Preconditions	Postconditions
cat_chasing	cat_exists, mouse_exists, mouse_seen, no_repeat	cat_chasing
mouse_running	cat_exists, mouse_exists, cat_chasing, no_repeat	mouse_running
cheese_seen	cheese_exists, mouse_exists, no_repeat	mouse_running
button_pressed	mouse_running	button_pressed, no_repeat
light_on	button_pressed	light_on
Goal state	light_on	

The group of actions shown here can produce two possible plans: cat_chasing, mouse_running, button_pressed; or, similar but with a different initial action, cheese_seen, mouse_running, button_pressed. These two plans just show the basic variety that can be generated from a few operators; longer, more complicated plans come naturally given more operators—although whether that alone is enough to make them sufficiently Rube Goldbergesque remains an open question, discussed below.

5   Conclusions and Future Work

This paper presents a structural analysis of Rube Goldberg machines, specifically of the narrative logic used in the machines depicted in Rube Goldberg's own cartoons. Besides the well-known unnecessary complexity of these machines—"maximum effort to accomplish minimum results"—the cartoon machines usually include human or animal characters as machine components, and their implied operation heavily relies on readers being able to recognize stereotypical actions suited to, for example, mice or goats or stockbrokers. Often these machines would not actually work, based as they are on coincidences, but each component sufficiently matches those that come before and after it in the sequence that the reader can read what is supposed to happen. In that sense they have an internal narrative consistency.

We further extracted some of the more concrete principles used by Professor Lucifer G. Butts in designing his inventions. The inventions' most iconic feature is found in the types of components and how they are suggestively arranged without ever showing the machine explicitly operating. Machines can include human, animal, and inanimate objects, each of which is used in a specific set of ways, summarized in Table 1, that both effect the machine's operation and provide motivations for the existence and operation of the machines' other other components. Using this analysis, we built a planning engine that takes potential Rube Goldberg machine elements defined as plan operators, and chains them into plausible, coherent machines that follow the logic as we've analyzed it in this paper.

Future work involves fully realizing the generation of machines. We currently generate only half of a typical Rube Goldberg cartoon: the textual half that explains the chain of actions comprising the machine's operation. The other half, of course, is the drawn cartoon machines themselves. To generate that requires laying out the components spatially, with a suitable visual style and setting. The constraints for layout in a cartoon world based on coincidence are fairly loose, but nonetheless not entirely absent, and constraints on layout might even be able to drive aspects of the generation process. In addition, the title is often important, and we do not currently generate a title for the machine; or, what might be even better, generate a machine for a given title.

In addition, we have only a small number of operators in our current proto-type, so cannot generate nearly the range of machines seen in Goldberg's works. We have slowly added to this by analyzing more original cartoons and identifying actions in them. However our current approach of individually handwritten operators representing specific object/action combinations does not scale very well; we would like to move towards a more factored representation, based on a dictionary of items with defined attributes from which actions fitting several types of schema can be generated. This would allow for automatically generated operators with preconditions and postconditions that still fit the typology of Rube Goldberg machine actions as we've analyzed it here.

Finally, our analysis here is structural, while many of the adjectives we've used to describe Rube Goldberg machines—"absurd", "comical", "ridiculous"— seem to have a clearly stylistic component. It may be that some of these arise naturally by virtue of the structure, since a complex machine that depends on animal components and coincidence has a certain amount of built-in absurdity. But to produce interesting, coherent cartoons along the lines of those drawn by Goldberg, we may need a more explicit model of style, and/or an explicit model of narrative features such as absurdity. An explicit reader model may also be needed in order to generate machines where the narrative logic is, while absurd, still apparent; the "pseudo-states" used in Sect. 4.1 to ensure that the main line of action in the machine isn't obscured are an ad-hoc step in that direction.

References

1. Dart, I., Nelson, M.J.: Smart terrain causality chains for adventure-game puzzle generation. In: Proceedings of the IEEE Conference on Computational Intelligence and Games, pp. 328–334 (2012)
2. Fikes, R., Nilsson, N.: STRIPS: a new approach to the application of theorem proving to problem solving. Artif. Intell. **2**(3–4), 189–208 (1971)
3. Goldberg, R., Keller, C.: The Best of Rube Goldberg. Prentice Hall, Englewood Cliffs (1979)
4. Marzio, P.C.: Art, technology and satire: the legacy of Rube Goldberg. Leonardo **5**(4), 315–324 (1972)
5. Marzio, P.C.: Rube Goldberg: His Life and Work. Harper & Row, New York (1973)
6. McCartney, R., Anderson, M.: The believability of Road Runner cartoons: logical consistency conquers unreality. In: Proceedings of the AAAI Workshop on Entertainment and AI/A-Life, pp. 6–11 (1996)
7. O'Connor, B.: Inside the whimsical but surprisingly dark world of Rube Goldberg machines. The Verge, April 2015. https://www.theverge.com/2015/4/22/8381963
8. Olsen, D., Mateas, M.: Beep! Beep! Boom!: towards a planning model of Coyote and Road Runner cartoons. In: Proceedings of the 4th International Conference on Foundations of Digital Games, pp. 145–152 (2009)
9. Plante, C.: This adorable Rube Goldberg machine tells the story of brotherly love. The Verge, April 2017. https://www.theverge.com/2017/4/21/15382804
10. Wolfe, M.F., Goldberg, R.: Rube Goldberg: Inventions. Simon & Schuster, New York (2000)

Cinelabyrinth: The Pavilion of Forking Paths

Chris Hales[(⊠)]

University of Liepāja, Liepāja, Latvia
chris.hales.interactive@gmail.com

Abstract. An important and technologically innovative interactive cinema experience, Cinelabyrinth was a large-scale architectural pavilion built in the form of maze-like interconnecting screening rooms, affording its visitors a navigable, yet carefully structured, narrative environment. It was created in 1990 for the Osaka World Expo and was one of the last major projects of Radúz Činčera, whose most well-known work was the Kinoautomat of 1967. Despite the originality of Cinelabyrinth and the individual role it offered its users—audience members could physically navigate the branching structure without depending on any majority decision—the project has left little imprint on the academic literature. An analysis of the Cinelabyrinth's design and function is presented so as to enable interactive filmmakers now benefitting from digital technology to better understand the potential of large-scale multiscreen non-linear narratives.

Keywords: Interactive cinema · Branching structure · Non-linear narrative · Cinelabyrinth · World Expo · Radúz Činčera · Kinoautomat

1 Introduction

Constructing a non-linear branching narrative is a process frequently associated with developing coherent story pathways, often with the help of specialised software such as *Twine*[1]. Unusually, in the case of the Cinelabyrinth pavilion at the 1990 Osaka World Expo, the construction was not metaphoric but real and solid, as the pathways offered to the visiting audience were interconnections between a maze-like series of screening rooms in which filmed sections of the fictional story could be viewed. Although as Psarra makes clear, "narrative enters architecture in many ways," [1] it is certainly unusual for audience members to be quite literally walking through the branching structure of a cinematic story, and an analysis of this ambitious project is of benefit to those designing the digital non-linear narrative experiences of today.

Cinelabyrinth was one of the last major projects of Radúz Činčera (1923–1999), who emerged from behind the Iron Curtain onto the world stage with Kinoautomat, a prototype of interactive cinema that captured the imagination of the public at Expo'67 in Montreal. Recognised as the world's first interactive film, Kinoautomat has deservedly received a significant amount of academic research and analysis [2, 3]. Much of the material presented in this article was gathered collaterally during the author's visits to

---

[1] Available from http://www.twinery.org.

N. Nunes et al. (Eds.): ICIDS 2017, LNCS 10690, pp. 117–125, 2017.
https://doi.org/10.1007/978-3-319-71027-3_10

Činčera's daughter Alena in relation to Kinoautomat research—this material included Činčera's personally compiled list of all his major projects. In Kinoautomat, audience groups sitting in a custom-built cinema were given several opportunities to vote on binary choices during a fictional film narrative, the successful option being that with the majority vote. There was nothing digital or computerised about Kinoautomat, the technology was electromagnetic (using relays similar to those found in the telephone exchanges of the time) and multiple 35 mm film projectors were used to show the film. Realised 23 years later, the Cinelabyrinth was fundamentally different in its concept, function and technology and marked a turning point for Činčera (then aged 67) from the restrictions of the analogue era to the potential of the digital age.

Činčera, with a background in both theatre and film, was part of a creative generation producing large-scale and technologically innovative projects for World Expo exhibitions: during the Cold War these high-profile events were used by many Communist states as propaganda and a chance to showcase their cultural and technological prowess. Budgets were generous and "although these inventors lived under a totalitarian regime, they enjoyed more freedom of experimentation than they would have in some Western countries." [4] Such was his reputation that the rock musician Peter Gabriel, known for his technically innovative stage shows, met Činčera in the late seventies but nothing concrete resulted from the discussions [5]. After a meeting in Prague in 1998 Michael Naimark reported that Činčera "acknowledged his ambiguous stance between art and commerce" [6]. Cinelabyrinth in fact represented part of the Japan Gas Association's Gas Pavilion at the Osaka "Flower Expo" (April to September 1990) with the involvement of Dentsu Inc. of Japan. The year of 1990 has additional significance because the first democratic elections took place in Czechoslovakia that year after the Velvet (or Gentle) Revolution had taken place late in 1989 (the separate Czech and Slovak republics did not come into being until 1992). Despite this, a major project such as Cinelabyrinth with a budget of five million dollars must have been planned and prepared under the old regimes and could not have arisen as a direct consequence of (but would have benefitted from) the dramatic changes taking place in the country of its creation. The film shown in the pavilion takes a clear ecological theme rather than making any expression of freedom, although each visitor is indeed empowered with freedom of choice rather than suffering the so-called 'tyranny of the majority' associated with group voting—the leaflet advertising Cinelabyrinth stated "Make your choice and then proceed. Enjoyment at your will".

2   From Kinoautomat to Cinelabyrinth

Činčera's initial proposal for something resembling Cinelabyrinth is connected closely to Kinoautomat at Expo'67. A Montreal newspaper (Dimanche Dernière Heure; the journalist was Jean-Louis Laporte) reported in 1970 that Činčera was to bring Kinoautomat back to the Expo fairground for the year 1971 in a new format: a real architectural labyrinth with many projection rooms in which "the audience must walk around to follow the development of the story. Sometimes the protagonists will be lost, but will later be found again. Turning left gives a different story than turning right. If by chance one turns left again, the audience can continue their story but it will have branched for a second time". The fact that this news was announced in a press release suggests the project was well on the way to becoming a reality (filming locations were specified) but ultimately it was not made and references to any similar project disappear until Osaka in 1990. Činčera remained productive with Kinoautomat reprised at Expos in 1968 and 1974 and in Prague in 1971, as well as a version shown at Expo'81 in Kobe in connection with Osaka Gas. A collaborative project *Vertical Cinemascope* gave him a first trip to Osaka for Expo'70 and *The Scroll* was shown at Expos in 1986, 1988 and 1992— Činčera's primary interest was large-scale spectacle, and branching narrative was only one of his methods for achieving this.

Given that at least one 35 mm film projector would have been necessary per room, it can be reasonably assumed that expense and technical difficulties were the reason why the ambitious labyrinth project was shelved in 1971. One might argue that the project was ahead of its time and Činčera's regular technical experts Jaroslav Frič and Bohumil Mika belonged to a pre-digital generation that did not embrace rapidly developing computer technologies, preferring bulky and antiquated electromagnetic systems. Fortunately two technical solutions emerged in the 1980s, both with a connection to Japan, which would have brought the project back on the agenda. Firstly the development of the LaserDisc, a true non-linear audiovisual delivery system of reasonable quality with the Japanese company Pioneer Corporation as the majority stakeholder in the format. Secondly, as Hornbeck reports, the "first LCD color video projector was introduced to the market in 1989 by the Sharp Corporation," [7] with another Japanese company Epson also an early manufacturer. Although these remained analogue technologies the functionality and affordances were closer to the digital tools of today.

In terms of non-linear narrative, the fiction-based branching structure which had been such a novel aspect of Kinoautomat was no longer unusual—it had been popularised worldwide since 1979 by the *Choose Your Own Adventure* (CYOA) series of paperback books (which went on to sell 250,000 copies). Činčera nonetheless felt his projects were technology independent, reflecting towards the end of his career that:

> "Unlike the recent interactive computer games and CDROMs, the Kinoautomat was presented in a group audience situation: it was not designed for just one man sitting in front of a computer monitor… Kinoautomat in 1967 represented a "stone-age" of interactivity as to the technology, but is a very original and advanced presentation form, still attractive and impressive until today. And it is easy to improve (which we do) its technology by recent computerized components." [8].

It is hard to say whether the CYOA books might have influenced the genre of film eventually designed for Cinelabyrinth, which was basically a children's fantasy adventure, but presumably a branching narrative was now no longer enough to ensure sufficient novelty for such a prestigious event as a World Expo—but adding physical walkability of the narrative through decorated rooms provided the standout feature. The Cinelabyrinth therefore represents a change in thinking about the role of the user (the project might usefully be analysed through the emerging discipline of 'experience design') by allowing a personalised journey and outcome whilst retaining the benefits of a shared group experience. Činčera was clearly well aware from his experiences with Kinoautomat that a majority vote system did not necessarily permit viewers to see what they had made the effort to vote for and this could lead to dissatisfaction.

3   The Cinelabyrinth

The Cinelabyrinth pavilion, which had an external aspect resembling multiple green pyramids, held within it a control room of 22 LaserDisc players (with corresponding monitors) feeding into eleven rooms (so-called 'show spaces') which were equipped with a total of 22 video projection screens. Each of the choice-enabled rooms had a main 4 m × 3 m projection screen, a live presenter, and two smaller side screens, making them similar to the Kinoautomat theatre but without the vote tally system. Traversing the Cinelabyrinth each audience member would have three opportunities to physically move to a screening room of their choice, thus guaranteeing they would view the sequences that they wanted. Since each room was devoted to a particular sequence played from its own LaserDisc, there was no need for any complex logic—it was a case of coordination and timing of when each LaserDisc was restarted (whether this was done automatically to a clock, or manually by an operator, is unclear). An astonishing audience throughput of up to 15,000 a day was possible in Cinelabyrinth, an impressive figure when compared to the Kinoautomat of Expo'67 which totalled 67,000 visitors in six months, this being possible by allowing a group of up to 200 (at busiest times) to enter the pavilion every ten minutes. Room sizes became progressively smaller with each choice made, since statistically smaller and smaller numbers would be expected to visit them, and each was ornately designed and decorated (including a background soundscape such as the chirping of jungle insects) to suit the theme so as to immerse audiences into the changing narrative locations.

The art- and stage design of the Cinelabyrinth show spaces was credited to R. Máca and J. Frič with the SCARS production team. Činčera was listed as director, and credited with the script alongside M. Macourek and H. Franková. A diagram of the architectural layout and the narrative structure it afforded is presented as Fig. 1: the diagram makes it clear how certain rooms had multiple entry points so as to limit the extent of the branching possibilities and rooms were sized to reflect the average amount of visitors they might attract. A brief description of each show space is given in the Appendix. Since audience members would traverse four show spaces a total of about forty minutes of filmic content would be seen (at ten minutes per room). A live host introduced each room to its incoming audience and offered humanising guidance to visitors at the moment of choice. The narrative of the film, whose title translates roughly as *The Flying House*, was described in its contemporary publicity (reproduced on p. 100 of Bielicky [4]) as follows:

> "The story is an adventure fantasy about four children and their quest to save an oak tree. Cinelabyrinth lets you participate in a fantastic adventure. The story starts in the garden of a beautiful castle where an old oak tree is about to be cut down. The children Honza, Kuba, Suzanne and Fanda are asked by the spirit of the tree to save it. With the aid of magic acorns, the four children start on their fantastic adventure beyond spatial and temporal bounds. The story develops in different ways according to the visitor's choices. Every story consists of exciting and humorous scenes. Travelling with the children, the audience can experience adventures as they attempt to save the tree." [9].

As the pavilion doors open to start the experience, a new group of audience are led into one large room ('The Castle and Park'), a concealed screen is revealed and all watch the opening sequence together under the guidance of a stage presenter. The first scene ends with the on-screen oak tree being halted in mid-fall, the action transferring to two smaller side screens to represent the two potential story paths. Each room, apart from the four rooms used for the finale which required just the one projection, had this three-screen arrangement (hence 22 LaserDisc projections were required). The screens were not revealed until the audience had been greeted into the room by its resident presenter and the exit doors remained hidden until the moment of choice.

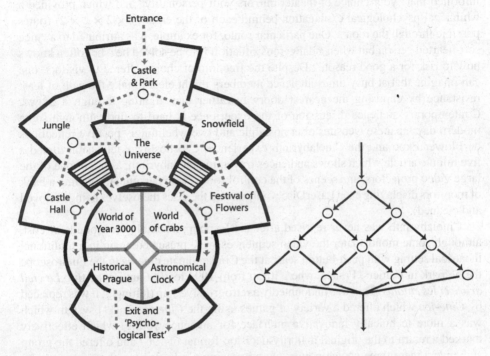

Fig. 1. The layout of the Cinelabyrinth and a diagram of its narrative structure.

These choices represent the travelling locations of the magical flying house in which the children pursue their quest to save the oak tree: for example after the first sequence, two previously hidden doors are revealed offering the choice to fly to a hot place ('The Jungle') or a cold place ('The Snowfield'). Several show spaces were unsurprisingly themed on Prague. Whereas the plot of the original Kinoautomat film was based on realism and sequential plot continuity, Cinelabyrinth used magic and fantasy to allow the protagonists to explore a variety of exotic locations and also to travel in time (for example, two competing room choices were 'The World of the Year 3000' or 'Historical Prague'). The film's final sequence was the same for all audience members: the rescue of the tree. Michael Naimark describes it as follows:

"At the moment when the kids [in the film] shout "we did it!" the screen in front raises up to reveal a full-size replica of the tree used in the film. Simultaneously, three other screens on the other three sides of the tree rise up, revealing four theaters with everyone who began in the first room, now all facing each other. The gag was that no matter which options were chosen, the kids successfully saved the tree. It was as manipulative as the first Czech piece made 23 years earlier [Kinoautomat], but this time they made it transparent. The effect of realizing everyone 'won' and now were all in the same room together was really very powerful." [10].

The implication here is that the dramatic revelation of the shared ending was an effective ploy that overcame the potential disappointment of realising that personal choices had not led to a variety of endings—Kinoautomat also had only one end scene but was deliberately coy about which alternative pathways actually existed.

Visitors exiting the Cinelabyrinth could examine the leaflet they were given which informed that "your choice of theater mirrors your personality" and which provided a whimsical psychological explanation behind each of the eight ($1 \times 2 \times 2 \times 2$) routes possible through the rooms. One particular route, for example, was attributed to a "nice soft-hearted person but when a dangerous situation is to be solved he (she) often knows how to risk for a good reason". Despite the freedom of choice offered to visitors, one can imagine that at busy times audience members might elect to take the path of least resistance by choosing the nearest doorway rather than fighting through a crowd. Contemporary audience discussion of the experience is hard to find, although some modern day Japanese websites offer nostalgic and overwhelmingly positive reflections on Flower Expo and the Cinelabyrinth experience. Czechoslovak television filmed a five minute article which shows audiences traversing the labyrinth, a shot of one of the large video projectors. and scenes of the control room (with personnel watching a bank of monitors displaying each LaserDisc's output, and the discs themselves being removed and cleaned).

Cinelabyrinth was never reprised after the Expo, presumably on grounds of cost, although some months later the video sequences were presented again in a traditional theatrical setting with push-button seats at the Cinéautomate cinema in the Futuroscope theme park in Poitiers, France, where it ran from 1991 to 1996 under the title *Le vieil arbre et les enfants*. This was undoubtedly a retrogressive step (tellingly, it was replaced by *Ciné-jeu* which offered a variety of games using the *Cinematrix* [11] system which was a more technically innovative interface for audience voting) which effectively marked a return to the original majority-decision format of 1967 and offered the group audience a mere three choice points. On witnessing *Cinéautomate*, the media scholar Erkki Huhtamo reported the voting to be "over-determined by multiple forms of direct address: stopping the film, projecting graphic signs on the screen, turning on the lights and even having a live hostess appear on the stage to direct the voting!" [12] With interactive technologies rapidly developing, the traditional staging of the show must have seemed an anachronism at a time when Huhtamo was calling for a greater sophistication in interactive artworks: "It is difficult to introduce intelligent multi-person interactivity into a situation in which a traditional audience sits in an auditorium... The problem with multi-person interactive cinema is related to the very fact of combining it with a 19th century idea of public spectacle and the audience." [12]. In contrast, writing just a couple of years later than Huhtamo, Naimark [10] claimed that two of just four interactive art projects to have genuinely moved him were Kinoautomat and Cinelabyrinth, although his judgement may have been influenced by the engaging qualities of the filmic narratives and the high (filmic) production values which at the time were rare in the field of interactive creativity.

4   Conclusion

In terms of building a physical construction as a non-linear audiovisual narrative, nothing of the scale or ambition of Cinelabyrinth seems to have been attempted before or since, and the project remains a unique example of an architectural interpretation of branching narrative. It is doubtful that Cinelabyrinth directly influenced any subsequent works of physically constructed narrative since it was not extensively documented. One might vaguely compare the overall design with certain aspects of later projects including theme park rides, handheld museum/exhibition guides (which tell related information as rooms are visited), theatre pieces which require audiences to move from room to room, or installations by video artists using multiple rooms in which to project interrelated video material. Nevertheless, examples of *interactive* non-linear film interface through significant audience displacement are notably rare.

From a contemporary perspective, with the inherent non-linearity of digital files and with inexpensive flat screens and video projection so commonplace, one cannot underestimate the 'digital' thinking behind Cinelabyrinth, which owes its primacy to its awareness of the potential of the then-new technologies of LaserDisc and LCD projection. The project made little or no use of computer technology, but replacing the LaserDisc players with today's low cost computers (such as the Raspberry Pi) loaded with the relevant digital video files would be the only change required to stage it today. Choreographing the video screening times could be controlled simply by means of preset chronological times (e.g. all video sequences repeat every ten or fifteen minutes) or a more centralised control system could be implemented by wireless communication. The army of hardworking live presenters could now be replaced by 3D animated characters or pre-recorded actors projected onto human-shaped screens, and these flawless digital presenters would never suffer from boredom or fatigue.

Taking things a step further, these digital presenters might become algorithmically intelligent, and the decreasing cost of hardware would enable the underlying narrative structure to be more complex—taking inspiration, for example, from Umberto Eco's labyrinthine library at the heart of The Name of The Rose [13]. With digital technology there would be no need to have each room permanently dedicated to a particular projected film sequence, doors to other rooms could be activated or hidden depending on the narrative being shown, and finding an exit route might itself be part of the goal in the manner of the popular 'Escape Room' paradigm (although this would inevitably make the experience more gamelike). Sophisticated geolocation could keep an eye on visitors and flat display screens and ubiquitous computer technology could be embedded in the rooms to replace the static and passive décor used in Cinelabyrinth. Each user's experience could be personalised by means of a handheld device such as a smartphone using earphones to deliver varying soundtracks and voiceovers and enabling augmented reality to permit the discovery of virtual content within the labyrinth. Suitable stories for a future labyrinth might well be those that link closely to the physical activity of exploring rooms/spaces in the manner of several of the *Choose Your Own Adventure* plots, bearing in mind that the concept of *The Flying House* enabled visitors to move through space and time by means of the show spaces—there was no unified metaphor such as exploring all the rooms of a haunted house or a cave system.

The communal aspect of exploring Cinelabyrinth with others, whilst retaining freedom to wander, and the fundamental premise of experiencing a non-linear film, are key characteristics that could easily be retained in a digital reinterpretation (the discussion here is of course based on retaining the dedicated physical space rather than reinterpreting the labyrinth as a virtual entity). It is worth bearing in mind that only eight discrete pathways were possible through Cinelabyrinth so that outcomes were not unique to each individual—an audience member would inevitably be accompanied by others, most probably strangers, on their narrative trajectory. A future labyrinth might be configured with a roster of non-linear films of different genres in the manner that this is currently done with digital cinema technology so as to provide a varied programme of daily screenings/stagings. Experience designers might inform on the optimum size of groups admitted to the digital labyrinth and how these audience members interact with each other—bearing in mind that cinemas can accept hundreds of passive viewers per screening whereas Escape Rooms take up to a dozen active participants who work as a team. Designing and overseeing the entire endeavour would be a far greater challenge than it was for Radúz Činčera but fortunately today's digital creatives already have experience in complex transmedia storytelling projects and have the required tools and gadgets at their disposal to expand the Cinelabyrinth concept to a new, exciting, and potentially profitable, level.

Appendix

The show spaces of Cinelabyrinth as described in the leaflet handed out to visitors:

1. **Castle & Park:** A world of harmony – full of elaborate tapestries.
2A. **Jungle:** A wild world of animals – all made of beautiful glasswork.
2B. **Snowfield:** An open space of pure, white snow.
3A. **Castle Hall:** A large and mystifying hall of mirrors.
3B. **The Universe:** The eternity of space.
3C. **Festival of Flowers:** A brilliant fete of flowers.
4A. **World of The Year 3000:** He world of the future – made only of metal.
4B. **World of Crabs:** The watery world of the sea.
4C. **Historical Prague:** A simulation of that city in its glorious age of culture and art.
4D. **Astronomical Clock:** A Gothic-style grandfather clock.

References

1. Psarra, S.: Architecture and Narrative: The Formation of Space and Cultural Meaning. Routledge, Abingdon (2009)
2. Carpentier, N.: Media and Participation: A Site of Ideological-Democratic Struggle. Intellect, Bristol/Chicago (2011)
3. Hales, C.: Spatial and narrative constructions for interactive cinema, with particular reference to the work of Radúz Činčera. In: Hales, C., Kelomees, R. (eds.) Expanding Practices in Audiovisual Narrative, pp. 143–170. Cambridge Scholars, Newcastle (2014)

4. Bielicky, M.: Prague – A place of illusionists. In: Weibel, P., Shaw, J. (eds.) Future Cinema, the Cinematic Imaginary after Film, pp. 96–100. MIT Press, Cambridge/London (2003)
5. Bright, S.: Peter Gabriel – An Authorised Biography. Sidgewick & Jackson, London (1988)
6. Naimark, M.: Interval trip report on world's first interactive filmmaker, Prague (1998). http://www.naimark.net/writing/trips/praguetrip.html
7. Hornbeck, L.J.: From cathode rays to digital micromirrors: A history of electronic projection display technology. Texas Instrum. Tech. J. (special DLP issue) 15(3), 7–46 (1998)
8. Činčera, R.: Kinoautomat. The historically undoubtfully first interactive multimedia programme implemented at EXPO 1967 in Montreal in 1967. Unpublished manuscript (1996)
9. Japan Gas Association: Poster for Cinelabyrinth (1990)
10. Naimark, M.: Interactive art – Maybe it's a bad idea. In: Leopoldseder, H., Schopf, C. (eds.) Cyberarts, International Compendium Prix Ars Electronica, pp. 28–33. Springer Press, Vienna (1997)
11. Carpenter, L.: Cinematrix, Video imaging method and apparatus for audience participation. U.S. Patents 5210604 (1993) and 5365266 (1994)
12. Huhtamo, E.: Seeking deeper contact: interactive art as metacommentary. Convergence 1(2), 81–104 (1995)
13. Eco, U.: Il Nome Della Rosa. Bompiani, Milan (1980)

Verb+s Is Looking for Love: Towards a Meaningful Narrativization of Abstract Content

Serena Zampolli[✉]

Università degli Studi di Genova, Genoa, Italy
serena.zampolli@edu.unige.it

Abstract. This paper discusses the development of a process to narrativize abstract content in the context of English taught as a foreign language, focusing on the teaching of grammar rules which are problematic for Italian learners. It argues that content in story-form is better processed by the human brain compared to non-narrative content, and highlights how the discussion on narrativization of abstract content is still open. Then it describes the challenges to the development of such process, explains a narrativization proposal, and illustrates its development, structure and application. Finally, it presents preliminary results of a first exploratory application in a school context, showing that the process is clear and direct enough to be applied successfully by secondary school students. This process could be the first step towards a new representation of abstract knowledge and the automated creation of metaphorical stories.

Keywords: Language learning · Narrative learning · Storytelling · Narrativization · Grammar

1 Introduction

This paper discusses the development of a process to narrativize abstract content in order to facilitate its understanding and memorization. It was developed and it is now being studied in the context of foreign language teaching. The target abstract concepts chosen for the experimentation are grammar rules often misused by Italian learners who speak English as a Foreign Language[1] [22]. However, this process is not intended to be applied only to foreign grammar rules, but to other fields as well: it wants to be a first step towards a new representation of any abstract content. Once accomplished and widely tested, this process could constitute the basis for the creation of automated procedures to narrativize abstract content.

The proposed process can generate stories that can be presented in various forms (written, oral, multimedia). The form chosen for this project is that of short narrative videos, which means stories with both a verbal and a visual component. Section 2 of this paper explains the reason behind this choice, providing evidences supporting the

---

[1] "Speaking English as a Foreign Language" in the definition of Paolo Balboni [1]: they study and practice English living in their home-country, Italy, or anyway in a non-English speaking country.

© Springer International Publishing AG 2017
N. Nunes et al. (Eds.): ICIDS 2017, LNCS 10690, pp. 126–134, 2017.
https://doi.org/10.1007/978-3-319-71027-3_11

idea that visualization and narrativization can ease understanding and memorization of abstract concepts. Section 3 is dedicated to the challenges faced while developing the proposed process, which is then described in Sect. 4. Section 5 presents preliminary results of a first exploratory application in a school context, and reflects on needed future research.

2 Theoretical Framework

Our memories can be of two different types: episodic/autobiographical and semantic. [16] The first can be recalled willingly as narrative scenes, while the latter are "embedded not in narrative scenes but in a web of associations" [5]. Abstract concepts are filed as semantic memories, not framed into story-form, and they need to be constantly reinforced in order not to be lost [11, 12]. Grammar rules belonging to a foreign language are abstract concepts and therefore need constant reinforcement [6] but there might not be opportunities for this to happen. This might be the reason why Italians who speak English as a Foreign Language struggle with the retrieval of many English grammar rules (even if they know them) and fail to apply them correctly while speaking.

The struggle might be overcame if the form of the information is changed: if the grammar rules are presented not as abstract concepts but as stories, they are no longer stored in the semantic memory but in the episodic memory. This makes it possible to consciously retrieve them, independently of the amount of reinforcement.

This is not the only reason favouring a narrative input over a non-narrative one. Our brain is hardwired to rely on stories and stories have played a crucial role in the development of our species [9]. The structure of story is innate in our minds to the point that we automatically use story elements, story relationships, story architecture to understand and to make sense of real-world events [3]. Furthermore, we also organize, sort, understand, relate and file experience into memory in story-form [15]. It seems therefore logical that providing the brain with a narrative input means providing it with the information shaped into the form that is the easiest for it to process.

Narrative is not the only key element in terms of memorization: our brain also strongly relies on visuals. Professional mnemonists enhance their memory by using an ancient technique called "method of *loci*" (the most ancient form of "memory palace" or "memory theatre"): they consciously convert the information they are asked to memorize into images, and distribute those images along familiar spatial journeys. This technique takes advantage of human visual and spatial memories, and can be learned by everybody. It makes abstract concepts concrete, and therefore memorable. It allows us to create any kind of image: the more unique they are, the more memorable. They also do not need to be still: if they are animated they are more effective [8].

Stories have a strong link with visualization: even in a basic textual form, they have the power to create mental images. Their sensory details create images that allow trans-domain neural mapping within the mind of the story receiver [9]. This result can be argued to be even more at hand if the story is told not only via words, but using multimedia artifacts. For all these reasons, narrative videos were selected as the final artifacts to embody the stories created with the proposed process.

Despite the consistent amount of research studies about the advantages of the narrative form, stories are still not used much in education when it comes to the teaching of abstract concepts. They are used to frame information and make it more appealing, but a process to narrativize abstract content effectively is still needed. Several attempts have been made (see, e.g., [4, 17] for mathematics; [18] for biosciences), but the question is still open, especially in relation with grammar learning. This paper is an attempt towards that result.

3 Challenges

The first challenge is the lack of a shared definition of "story" all scholars agree on. However, there are features they all identify as structural [7]: the presence of events [14], and the presence of characters. Just to cite a well-known and relevant example, Bruner [2] defines narrative as "a unique sequence of events, mental states, happenings involving human beings as characters or actors". Characters can be human, but they can also be animals or objects who are given agency by being enabled to behave human-like.

In a story, the visible part is made of characters and settings, and here lies the second challenge: if we want the story to translate the grammar rules, it means we need to make the abstract concepts visible. The best way to achieve this is by using metaphors. Metaphors allow the coding from an abstract domain (feelings, like love) to a concrete domain (e.g., a beautiful rose, a thorny rose). Moreover, they allow us to get acquainted with a new concept through one that is already known [10]. This translates into the process as the task of identifying the defining characteristics of the abstract elements involved and then find a human creature, an animal, an object, which can embody them. We will see this in detail in the next section. We will also see how insights from narratology and performative storytelling play a relevant role in defining this process.

The last challenge was that of finding a process which could be applied to any grammar rule. The investigation related to this point is still ongoing

4 A Proposal for Narrativizing Abstract Concepts

The subject matter of this study is the group of common mistakes Italians make when speaking English as a foreign language [19]. The rules related to those mistakes seem hard to retrieve and apply, and it can be argued that the traditional textual form used to present them might not be effective. Memorization and learning might be facilitated by transforming them in a form that is easier for the brain to process: visual story-form. Grammar rules, however, are abstract concepts and can not be easily turned into stories. Herein lies the main challenge of this research.

At this stage, the proposed narrativization technique aims at being used by learners as a tool to help them memorize, retain, retrieve and then apply grammar rules, until the linguistic process is automatized by the brain and no longer needs memory aids.

Section 4.1 explains the development of the proposed narrativization process so far, and Sect. 4.2 illustrates its structure and application.

4.1 Development of the Narrativization Process

The first grammar rule transformed into a story was the addition of the suffix -s to verbs whose subject is a third person singular, as in the construction "She walks to the store". The developed story is titled "Speed Dating"[2] and tells of a guy, Verb+s, who takes part in a speed date event, meeting several possible partners (the pronouns). Things are not going well, until he meets She, a girl with whom he amiably converses. When the date event is over, Verb+s decides to ask She if they can see each other again. She agrees enthusiastically and introduces Verb+s to her friends: a guy, He, holding a stuffed animal named 'It'. The story ends with the four happily together.

This first attempt envisaged a process made of two phases. In the first phase, knowing that a story needs characters, the linguistic elements involved in the rule were made visual: they were identified and characterized in accord with their meaning as language items, which means they were shaped into human characters that behave consistently with the personality features. For example, the pronoun "I" was characterized as egocentric and constantly taking selfies. The second step, knowing that at least one event is needed, was identifying a key action able to encode the relation among characters according to the considered grammar rule. In our example, Verb+s fits only with third singular pronouns, so it was necessary to find an action or situation where one person selects one other person by choosing among many. The situation chosen was a speed date, but many others are possible This means that different stories can be created for the same rule, allowing for this process to be creative.

This first version of the process aimed at creating a core (made of characters and one key action), and developed the story around it. When it was tested on other rules, it proved not to always be productive: it created characters and put them in relation through a key action, but the result was a static image where nothing really happened. Something was not working, and it was necessary to reconsider it. In order to do so, we went back to narratology.

According to Narratology, a story is made of one or more Events, and each Event is the transition between two States-of-things, differentiated by at least one of their features [20]. The problem with this first version of the process was that it created only one State-of-things, and a second one was that something needed to happen between states.

The narratological concept of State-of-things can be difficult to grasp for non specialists, while our aim was to design a process that everybody could easily learn and apply. Performative storytelling provided inspiration on how to overcome this obstacle. Contemporary performative storytellers active in the cultural movement called "Storytelling Revival" have several, sometimes hundreds, of stories in their repertoire and tell them improvising the words when they perform in front of an audience [13]. They memorize stories not as words, but as images: each tale corresponds to a small amount of very detailed canvas, which serve as memory anchors. The storyteller can recall the sequence of images related to a specific story and weave the narration out of it on the spot, making every performance unique.

---

[2] To see the video of the story visit https://youtu.be/_PK86pWaEJY.

Inspired by this, the idea of the State-of-things was kept as a reference but it was decided to focus on the creation of images, not States, and call them scenes.

So far, the process had proved fit to create one Scene: one image which was a visualization of the rule. This image needed to be at the end of the story, the final image that sticks with the learner.

In order to have a story, a second Scene was needed, and this image would constitute the beginning. Every story needs a conflict (i.e., an issue to be resolved), hence the beginning Scene needed to be different from the final one and somehow include the germ of a conflict. In the next section we see how all these elements have been included in the proposed narrativization process.

4.2 Scheme of the Narrativization Process

The first version of the narrativization process is maintained, but it does not constitute the whole process, only its first step. Therefore, the first thing that needs to be done is to visualize the grammar rule and turn it into an image. We do so by identifying the linguistic elements which are part of the rule because they will become our characters. For example, in "Speed Dating", the linguistic elements involved are Verb + s and the pronouns I, You singular, He, She, It, We, You plural, and They.

Second, we must identify what traits those elements have, so that we can shape the appearance and the personality of the correspondent characters. To do so, it is useful to brainstorm and write a list of adjectives for each element, then choose two or three and use them to characterize a character which can embody that element. We need also to identify one key action that puts the characters in relation with each other and tis apt to embody the grammar rule we are working on (see Sect. 4.1).

The characters do not need to be human, but can be animals, objects, or anything else. However, they need to be granted agency, a fundamental trait of story characters.

We can characterize our elements in many ways. For example, if there are linguistic elements which share the same category, so can do their characters. In "Speed Dating" all pronouns are female (with the exception of You, genderless), while Verb+s is male.

The result is a static image we call landing image, encompassing how many details we want (as long as they are functional to the delivering of the rule), and which is a visual metaphor of the rule. In the "Speed Dating" example, the final image shows Verb+s in the sole company of She, He, It.

The second phase consists of creating another scene which will serve as beginning of the story, what we call starting image. We have two options.

A first option is that of starting the story with an empty space, the chaos at the beginning of creation stories: all the elements are present but not in the correct order, and not yet connected. In this case, the starting image and the landing image differ because in the latter the characters are acting according to the grammar rule, which means performing the key action (in the case of "Speed Dating", Verb+s selecting only She, He, It to be with him), whilst in the initial one they have yet to meet and/or find the right thing to do. A second option is explained below.

The third phase consists in connecting the two images. In order to go from the starting image to the landing one, something needs to happen. This implies that the characters are to be involved into actions. The process is represented in the scheme (Fig. 1).

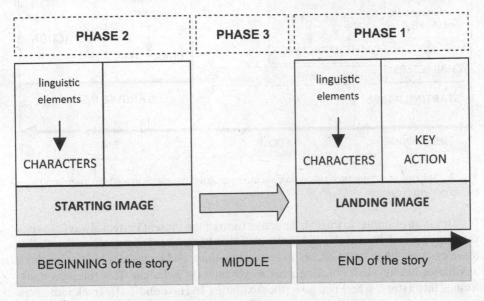

Fig. 1. A scheme of the proposed narrativization process

It is important not to introduce characters which are not related to the rule, in order to avoid distraction and confusion. These stories do not need to be very long: the sharper they are, the more effective. The best choice is to make them ironic or to present unusual situations, providing the learners with a memorable input.

As mentioned before, conflict and unexpected situations are essential elements of stories, that contribute to make them meaningful and interesting [3]. If the grammar rule we are working on is associated with a mistake commonly made by foreign learners, this gives us the opportunity to address the issue by incorporating the mistake into our story. This is the second option we mentioned before; it consists in starting the story with the same image of the landing, creating a conflict, and then solving the problem. In order to do so, we need to apply the same visualization process to the elements of the mistake, also turning it into a character. Then, we need to identify which disruptive action such character/mistake performs, causing some problem, and turn that into the conflict of the story. In this case, we use the word "conflict" not necessarily as a synonym of "battle", but as it is used in Narratology, that is, in the sense of "competition": a competition which can have only one winner (Fig. 2).

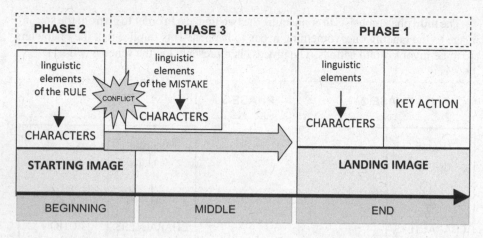

Fig. 2. Scheme of the narrativization process incorporating the common mistake associated with the target grammar rule

This is an example. In English the active form of the Present Perfect always requires the auxiliary verb "to have" combined with a Past Participle. The corresponding Italian tense can use either "to have" or "to be" as auxiliary, and so Italians tend to use both auxiliaries in English, mimicking what they would do in Italian. This rule was transformed into a story[3] where two guys (the auxiliaries To Have and To Be) make advances to two girls (Past Participles), but only one of them, To Have, succeeds while the other, To Be, is left alone at a cafe.

The character(s) embodying the mistake can be part of the starting image or they can come into action later in the story. This means the conflict can be hinted from the beginning or it can appear only in the middle of the story, then becoming the center of the action.

5   Future Research

A first exploratory experimentation was run in June 2017: 25 students in their second year of high school (15–16 years old) were taught the proposed process and asked to apply it to produce a short video. The experience aimed to verify if this narrativization process was clear and sound enough to be understood and correctly implemented by people with an average cultural level yet not particularly expert in narrativization. The results were encouraging: all students were able to apply the process and to create a story version of an assigned grammar rule. In a final questionnaire administered to check their opinion on the activity, 92% of the students said they understood the process of visualizing the rule to create the landing image, and 84% reported that they understood well how the narrativization process worked and was to be applied. These answers appear particularly satisfactory

---

[3] To see this story, visit the link https://youtu.be/y5sF2wQywB8 .

if we consider that creating a story embodying abstract knowledge is neither a straightforward nor an intuitive task but one that requires abstraction skills and metalinguistic reflection.

The results of this preliminary experiment mark a point in favour of the possibility to effectively implement the proposed process in a variety of learning environments and situations, and also possibly use it as the starting point for the construction of automated procedures. However, these initial results are not sufficient and further testing in diverse learning situations is needed to verify the process' soundness, and also to evaluate its impact on a cognitive level. Since the proposed process is intended as a first step towards a meaningful narrativization of any abstract content, if it will prove valid to work on grammar rules its application could be extended and adapted to other knowledge areas dealing with abstraction.

The proposed process is a first step towards a representation of knowledge that could lead to a wider application of a narrative approach in diverse subjects and fields, and might constitute a basis for automating the representation of abstract content in narrative form. This would constitute a much needed addition to make the delivery of any types of information more satisfactory, since narrative has been proven to be beneficial for learning on both the cognitive and motivational/emotional levels [21, 22].

Acknowledgments. I would like to show my gratitude to Giuliana Dettori for her mentorship and help during the writing of this paper. I would also like to thank the three anonymous reviewers for their precious insights. I am also grateful to Daniel Levin who took the time to correct the text.

References

1. Balboni, P.: Le sfide di Babele. Utet, Torino (2002)
2. Bruner, J.: Acts of Meaning. Harvard University Press, Cambridge (1990)
3. Bruner, J.: Making Stories: Law, Literature, Life. Harvard University Press, Cambridge (2003)
4. Burton, L.: The implications of a narrative approach to the learning of mathematics. In: Burton, L. (ed.) Learning Mathematics: From Hierarchies to Networks, pp. 21–35. Garland Inc, New York (1999)
5. Carey, B.: How we Learn: The Surprising Truth about When, Where and Why it Happens, p. 9. Random House, New York (2015)
6. Daloiso, M.: I fondamenti neuropsicologici dell'educazione linguistica. Libreria Editrice Cafoscarina, Venezia (2009)
7. Dettori, G., Paiva, A.: Narrative learning in technology-enhanced environments. In: Ludvigsen, S., Balacheff, N., De Jong, T., Lazonder, A., Barnes, S. (eds.) Technology-Enhanced Learning: Principles and Products, pp. 55–69. Springer, Berlin (2009)
8. Foer, J.: Moonwalking with Einstein: The Art and Science of Remembering Everything. The Penguin Press, New York (2011)
9. Haven, K.: Story Proof: The Science Behind the Startling Power of Story. Libraries Unlimited, Westport (2007)
10. Hoorn, J.F.: Metaphor and the brain: behavioral and psychological research into literary metaphor processing. Thesis Vrije Universitet (1997)

11. Mandler, J., Johnson, N.: Remembrance of things parsed: story structure and recall. Cognit. Psychol. **9**, 111–151 (1977)
12. Mandler, J.: Stories, Scripts, and Senses: Aspects of Schema Theory. Lawrence Erlbaum, Hillsdale (1984)
13. Odangiu, F.: The actor in the storytelling school. In: Dramatica: Studia Universitatis Babes-Bolyai. Thematic issue: Narrative Structures in Contemporary Performing Arts, vol. 62 (LXII), pp. 23–34, 1 March 2017. http://studia.ubbcluj.ro/download/pdf/1078.pdf
14. Abbott, H.P.: The Cambridge Introduction to Narrative. Cambridge University Press, Cambridge (2002)
15. Schank, R.: Tell me a Story: Narrative and Intelligence. Northwestern University Press, Evanston (1990)
16. Schumann, J., Crowell, S., Jones, N., Lee, N., Schucter, S.A., Wood, L.A.: The Neurobiology of Learning: Perspectives from Second Language Acquisition. Lawrence Erlbaum Associates, Mahwah (2004)
17. Solomon, Y., O'Neill, J.: Mathematics and narrative. In: Language and Education, vol 12, no. 3, pp. 210–221 (1998)
18. Spinozzi, P., Hurwitz, B. (eds.): Discourses and Narrations in the Biosciences. V&R Unipress, Gottingen (2011)
19. Swan, M., Smith, B. (eds.): Learner English (2nd Edition) A Teacher's Guide to Interference and Other Problems (Cambridge Handbooks for Language Teachers). Cambridge University Press, Cambridge (2001)
20. Tornitore, T.: Della Narratologia. Genova University Press, Genova (2014)
21. Dettori, G., Giannetti, T., Paiva, A., Vaz, A. (eds.): Technology-Mediated Narrative Environments for Learning. Sense Publishers, Rotterdam (2006)
22. Dettori, G., Morselli, F.: Accessing knowledge through narrative context. In: Kendall, M., Samways, B. (eds.) Learning to Live in the Knowledge Society. ITIFIP, vol. 281, pp. 253–260. Springer, Boston (2008). https://doi.org/10.1007/978-0-387-09729-9_39

Games

Wordless Games: Gameplay as Narrative Technique

Yuin Theng Sim[✉] and Alex Mitchell

Department of Communications and New Media, National University of Singapore,
Singapore, Singapore
e0013224@u.nus.edu, alexm@nus.edu.sg

Abstract. In this paper, we look at how gameplay can be used to tell stories in a game without the help of words. Through close readings of three wordless games with a strong narrative focus, *Journey, Brothers: A Tale of Two Sons* and *A Bird Story*, we explore how gameplay within wordless games can help to convey a narrative. We have identified four techniques by which gameplay is used for storytelling: gameplay as enacting narrative, manipulating player controls for narrative effect, gameplay for exploring narrative setting, and gameplay as time progression. We discuss these techniques in relation to existing concepts of player experience, and suggest ways gameplay can help to circumvent issues of ambiguity in wordless narrative in games.

Keywords: Close reading · Player experience · Game design · Wordless games

1 Introduction

The idea that games can tell stories has long been a point of contention, resulting in many debates between two camps, each contending that games can or cannot tell stories. The debate on *whether* games can tell stories has moved on to *how* exactly games tell stories. As games remediate other forms of media and add the dimension of interactivity, the role of interactivity in games becomes crucial when looking at the potential of games as a storytelling medium. Researchers have begun to consider the relationship between game mechanics and narratives [1–3]. In this paper, we are interested in the role that interactivity plays in conveying the narrative, particularly in wordless games.

Before delving into why we are looking specifically at wordless games, we must first look at the role that language plays in conveying narratives. When thinking about narratives, verbal or textual storytelling would probably come to mind. The literal meaning of narrating presupposes that there is a narrator telling the story, and also implies that narration is done through verbal or written language. Traditionally, a narrative can be loosely defined as causal relationships of a sequence of events [4] consisting of the discourse—the act of narrating by a narrator and the form in which it is conveyed —and the story [5]. As this traditional definition requires the presence of a narrator, classical narratology has largely been limited to literary studies, with much focus put on the linguistic component of narrative discourse [6]. Classical narratology however is unable to accommodate other storytelling mediums when solely defined by linguistic discourse. Ryan proposes to rethink narrative as a mental construct formed in the minds

© Springer International Publishing AG 2017
N. Nunes et al. (Eds.): ICIDS 2017, LNCS 10690, pp. 137–149, 2017.
https://doi.org/10.1007/978-3-319-71027-3_12

of the audience when they interpret and experience the narrative text. Ryan identifies five dimensions to narrative: spatial, temporal, mental, formal and pragmatic. She defines narrative as "a sequence of events involving thinking individuals, linked by causal relations, motivated by a conflict, and aiming at its resolution" [7: p. 43].

Redefining narratives cognitively allows for a wider range of mediums to be included. However, much emphasis is still placed on language. Since language is able to effectively represent and convey ideas that are intangible and abstract, language naturally affords storytelling [8]. Language continues to be the most commonly used mode of storytelling, although not necessarily the most predominant [5]. Ryan [9] further points out that only language can express propositions and explicitly indicate the causal events in a narrative. Despite this, she does not discount the capability of other mediums to convey narratives. In fact, she argues that visual and aural modes are indeed able to represent temporal changes, and may even surpass language in terms of representation.

Given that most narratives rely heavily on language to convey causality and abstract ideas, narratives that are conveyed without the medium of language risk being ambiguous and frustrating to understand [10], and may require more effort on the reader's part to make sense of the narrative. This is possibly the case with storytelling in wordless games. However, this is also precisely why wordless games are an interesting case study to look at when examining the narrativity of games. Without using words to make explicit the events and meanings in the game, the game has to compensate for wordless ambiguity by relying more on the aural and visual modes as well as interactivity to help the player form meaning without language. Thus, in the absence of language, interactivity and gameplay will arguably need to take on a bigger role in conveying the narrative than in narrative games with words. The narrative experience of wordless games also differs from other games as such games potentially provide players with the ability to use their own experiences to create a meaning and a narrative unique to the player themselves. The act of inferring the narrative can add another dimension of difficulty to games, requiring players to figure out the game narrative on top of the gameplay. Solving the ambiguous narrative can possibly allow players to achieve a sense of satisfaction in figuring out the narrative, but on the other hand, the additional difficulty may act as an obstruction to the gameplay, making it crucial for the game mechanics to support the game narrative. By looking at such games, we can further understand the roles that interactivity and game mechanics play in supporting the game narrative.

The term "wordless" in this paper is defined as games with no in-game dialogue, in-game text or paratext relating to the narrative within the game. Paratext, as defined by Genette, is "a zone between text and off-text, a zone not only of transition but also of transaction" [11: p. 2]. In this paper, the "text" in wordless games refers to the main game, and off-text refers to text outside of the main game; paratext here refers to the text that is out of the game narrative context but still part of the game, such as the instructions and user interface. Thus, instructional and menu paratext that are not associated with or hint at the game narrative are not taken into consideration when looking at whether a game is "wordless". In addition, although the title of the game is simultaneously a paratext and can possibly reference the narrative of the game, game titles will not be taken into consideration as it is unlikely for a game to be released without a title.

The paper will first begin by briefly reviewing related literature on the relationship between the ludic and narrative elements in games, not to revisit the debate on whether games can tell stories but instead to examine how research has moved beyond the original debate. Next, the paper will identify and address the research problem and the methodological approach taken in the paper. Subsequently, we will introduce the techniques identified and discuss the potential impacts on the player's experience. Lastly, we conclude with suggestions for future work.

2 Related Work

The question of the narrativity of games has sparked fierce academic debates in the past [12–14], with each side advocating for emphasis to be placed on either narrative or ludic elements when studying games. However, the debate has since shifted to looking at the different ways a game can allow both elements to work together.

Moving past the ludology vs narratology debate, a concept that has garnered much attention in the field of game studies, ludonarrative dissonance, comes from looking at how in certain instances gameplay and narrative serve to work against each other. Ludonarrative dissonance was first mentioned by Hocking [15] in his critique of how the narrative objectives of Bioshock contradict with the ludic objectives. Hocking discusses how the game mechanic of harvesting or saving Little Sisters acts in direct opposition to the narrative objective of helping Atlas. The game mechanic makes it easier to progress by harvesting Little Sisters, which advocates for rational decision making in the players, while at the same time the game narrative encourages the player to help Atlas, which is inconsistent with the gameplay of harvesting sisters. Hocking points out that this "dissonance", the inconsistency between game and narrative objectives, hinders the player from becoming immersed in both the narrative and gaming experience.

With the term ludonarrative dissonance being used to critique the inconsistencies between narrative and gaming objectives, the term ludonarrative resonance was introduced to describe the direct opposite: the idea that game mechanics and narrative can work together in tandem. The term, first coined by Brice [16], is defined as "the successful use of game mechanics to communicate a narrative experience" [17]. Giving an example of how the hand-holding mechanic in *ICO* could tell a typical narrative of "boy-saves-girl" through the mechanic, she goes further to declare that "narrative [actually] is a game mechanic, as much as game mechanics can also be narrative elements".

Taking the idea of ludonarrative resonance a step further, Pynenburg introduces the notion of ludonarrative harmony, wherein there is a "positive symbiotic relationship between the narrative and gameplay of an interactive narrative" [18: p. 24]. He distinguishes ludonarrative harmony from ludonarrative resonance by highlighting how the game mechanic and narrative should "enhance" each other instead of just merely being complementary. He added that a game with narrative and mechanics working in harmony will allow players to better sustain the flow state and immersion.

While the concept of ludonarrative resonance and dissonance are increasingly advocated for a more cohesive gaming and narrative experience, the concepts have not been further developed, and are mainly used as a means for critiquing games. However, several researchers have recently further explored and developed the notion that a narrative can be conveyed through game mechanics. Dubbelman proposes the idea of narrative game mechanics, which he defines to be "game mechanics [that] invite agents, including the player, to perform actions that support the construction of engaging stories and fictional worlds in the embodied mind of the player" [2: p. 43]. His notion of narrative game mechanics stems from the theories of cognitive narratology and the concept of "mental constructs" as mentioned in the introduction. Through case studies of three games, he identified how the same basic game mechanic of a shooter game can build tension, enhance characterisation and evoke empathy just from recontextualising the core mechanics. At the same time, the use of a unique game mechanic can serve to confront players with serious moral dilemmas.

Similarly, Larsen and Schoenau-Fog [3] introduce a Narrative Quality of Game Mechanics Model for analysing the relationship between the ludic and narrative elements in a game by adopting concepts from ludology and narratology to form a cohesive model. Both Dubbelman and Larsen and Schoenau-Fog emphasise that the contextualisation of the game mechanic is able to evoke emotional and aesthetic responses to the narrative. However, this implies the contextualisation is heavily dependent on other narrative elements to set the scene. In fact, Dubbelman was careful to point out that narrative game mechanics do not exist in isolation but will often be supported by other narrative devices such as dialogue and in-game text.

3   Research Problem

Previous works considering the narrative capability of game mechanics address the question of *whether* gameplay can tell stories, but do not answer the question of *how* gameplay conveys or supports the narrative. In this paper, we are focusing on the different ways that gameplay can convey a narrative in the *absence* of words. This allows us to focus on the gameplay techniques used to convey the narrative. We define gameplay as the set of actions a player can perform and the resulting actions taken by characters, objects or elements as feedback to player actions [19]. In addition, we will explore whether gameplay can solve the problem of causality that is likely to arise in the absence of language, and identify several techniques that wordless games use to do so.

4   Method

Through close readings of *Journey* [20], *Brothers: A Tale of Two Sons* [21] and *A Bird Story* [22], we identify different ways in which each game uses gameplay to help convey the narrative wordlessly. As proposed by Bizzocchi and Tanenbaum [23], close reading is a method of analysing and deciphering a text adapted from the field of literary studies. A close reading of a game involves deconstructing its features and elements to understand what contributes to a cohesive gameplay experience. The method requires repeated playthroughs of a game, with each playthrough seeking to surface new understandings of the game system. Focusing on particular aspects of the game acts as an "analytical lenses", which helps to narrow down an otherwise overly broad scope of a piece of game text. In this paper, we will use the player actions in the game as lenses to look at how the gameplay within each game helps to convey or reinforce the narrative.

5 Results: Techniques

We will now discuss the four gameplay techniques we identified from *Brothers: A Tale of Two Sons*, *Journey* and *A Bird Story*: gameplay as enacting narrative, manipulating player controls for narrative effect, gameplay for narrative exploration, and gameplay as time progression.

5.1 Close Reading: Brothers: A Tale of Two Sons

Brothers: A Tale of Two Sons is an adventure puzzle game that tells the story of two brothers setting off on a journey to find a cure for their ailing father. Throughout their journey, they encounter creatures and people who may aid or hinder them in their quest. The game contains no written narrative text, and only uses spoken fictional nonsense dialogue that cannot be deciphered. In *Brothers: A Tale of Two Sons*, the gameplay works to convey the narrative by having the players enact the sequence of events.

Gameplay as Enacting Narrative. *Brothers: A Tale of Two Sons* was released on the PlayStation, Xbox and PC platforms, but requires a controller to play the game. The main game mechanic requires both brothers to work together to solve environmental puzzles. The player simultaneously controls both brothers on the same controller, the elder brother controlled using the left joystick and triggers and the younger brother using the right joystick and triggers. Each brother has different traits: the older brother can move heavy levers and boost the younger brother up to higher places, whereas the younger brother is able to squeeze through the bars of locked gates. Most of the time the game requires simultaneous control of both brothers to solve puzzles. For example, when climbing cliffs, the player must hold down the left and right triggers so that the brothers hang on to the rocks. In another instance, when the brothers must cross a bridge, the player must keep the younger brother running in a wheel to keep the bridge lowered by continuously circling the right joystick while moving the older brother to cross the bridge and catch a sheep to replace the younger brother in the running wheel.

The narrative of the game is about how the brothers go on a journey, overcoming obstacles together. The mechanics of having both brothers work together to solve environmental puzzles lets the player enact the bulk of the narrative of the game. By solving the puzzles, the player can progress the narrative. Letting the player's actions play out the narrative itself reduces any ambiguity that the player might feel about the narrative as the player would know for certain that their actions within the game had a direct impact on the narrative events, making the causality of the events within the game unambiguous. The mechanics of *Brothers: A Tale of Two Sons* not only convey the narrative of the game perfectly, but also embody and communicate the relationship between the brothers. The game mechanics requires the brothers to work together to solve the puzzles. The coordination of the brothers at the gameplay level implies trust and a connection between them, and is representative of the relationship between the brothers. The puzzles become progressively more difficult as the player progresses in the game. To clear all the obstacles the player must get used to or improve on their coordination of the brothers. This also represents the development of the relationship between the brothers as they overcome various challenges. Thus, the gameplay not only creates the narrative, it also drives the narrative forward and mirrors the narrative progression.

In addition to supporting the overall narrative of the brothers going on a journey, the gameplay also helps to create meaningful narrative events by adding a new objective or context to the mechanic. There are mini events at points of the game where the brothers must work together to save other creatures or people in danger, such as freeing a trapped troll from an ogre or a trapped griffin in a cage, with both creatures eventually returning the favour by helping the brothers. In one example, the brothers chance upon a man trying to commit suicide. The brothers can save the man if the player acts fast enough, letting the little brother climb up the tree to cut the noose while the older brother supports the suicidal man from the bottom. If the player is unable to save the man, a short cut scene of the brothers looking sadly at the body of the man is then shown. Although in that example, helping the suicidal man is not compulsory to proceeding on and the man does not help in the later part of the game, it adds to the narrative and character building of the brothers. Using the same mechanic, the game designers can recontextualise it by adding short-term objectives which then turn the mini event into a narrative event. These mini-stages allow for memorable events which not only function as part of the overall narrative of the brothers' journey, but also create purposeful narrative events to enhance the larger narrative and the characterisation of the brothers. As such, the gameplay not only complements the narrative objectives by letting the game mechanics enact the narrative, it also enhances the narrative by recontextualising game mechanics into mini narrative events, achieving ludonarrative harmony.

Manipulating Player Controls for Narrative Effect. The difficulty of controlling both brothers at once also allows the players to experience the difficulty of good team-work. The different characteristics of each brother shows how important the brothers are to each other, as both brothers must fulfil their own parts to overcome obstacles. The game fully utilises the unique characteristic of each brother. For instance, at one point the players must lure an ogre into a cage, requiring players to have the older brother pull a lever to open the cage. The player must keep the cage open while moving the younger brother to lead the ogre into cage, and then shut the door while the younger brother slips through the bars. Here, the roles of the brothers are not interchangeable, as only the older brother is strong enough to move levers and the younger one small enough to slip through the bars, showing the importance of having the brothers work together.

The game enables players to better understand this by removing one of the brothers whom the player has become accustomed to controlling throughout the game. Near the end of the game, the older brother was fatally wounded in a fight against a spider creature right before obtaining the cure for their father. The younger brother then had to bury the brother and return home alone with the cure. The scene was heart-breaking, as the younger brother wept throughout when burying his older brother. The change in controls adds to the emotional impact, as with only one brother to control, the player only needs to use one hand on the controller instead of using both hands, making the loss of the older brother feel greater. In particular, in the final parts of the game, the younger brother comes across a platform that only the older brother is strong enough to pull, and is seemingly unable to do it himself. That is, until the player realises that even though the older brother is no longer around, they can still use the controls on the left hand and by doing so, the younger brother hears the voice of the older one encouraging him and summons enough strength to pull the lever. The fact that the player was controlling and carrying out the narrative makes taking away the controls upon the death of the older brother that much more powerful and emotional.

We have identified how *Brothers: A Tale of Two Sons* uses game mechanics to convey the narrative by perfectly matching the narrative and ludic objectives such that the player enacts the narrative by playing and advancing through the game, achieving ludonarrative harmony. In addition, by manipulating the player's control over the characters, the game can evoke strong emotional responses to the narrative.

5.2   Close Reading: Journey

We will now proceed with the analysis of *Journey*. *Journey* is an adventure puzzle game that takes the player through a world of deserted ruins, where the player plays as a robed character. As the title suggests, the player embarks on a journey, going through different trials and obstacles to travel to the top of the mountain. On the way, they may meet other travellers, or befriend carpet creatures that will help them on their journey. The player will eventually realise the journey is a prophecy and that they will ultimately meet their demise, only to be resurrected. Once the player reaches the top of the mountain, the game ends and restarts. The game uses no written text or dialogue. While the game can be played online with other players, the only form of communication between players is through "ringing", where a single musical note will be played and a symbol appear above the player's character. In *Journey*, the player actions are a way for players to enact the narrative and serve to let the players explore the world of the narrative.

Gameplay as Enacting Narrative. The core mechanic of *Journey* involves collecting hieroglyphic symbols to lengthen the player's scarf, and using the scarf to fly for a short period of time. Carpet creatures recharge the player's scarf and huge flying rock monsters will rip off parts of the scarf. The musical note the player makes is not only used as a way to communicate to other players, but also allows the player to "activate" hieroglyphs and "sleeping" carpets, and call carpet creatures to come to the player's aid.

Like *Brothers: A Tale of Two Sons*, the main narrative of *Journey* is conveyed through gameplay. By traversing the deserted ruins, freeing carpet creatures and climbing up the mountain, players enact the narrative of a traveller on a journey. Each game stage serves as part of the narrative arc. The obstacles and hostile creatures are the conflicts that the character faces in the story. The last stage where the player is resurrected and flies above the clouds to the top of the mountain resolves the narrative. As with *Brothers: A Tale of Two Sons*, *Journey* conveys the narrative by allowing the players to enact the narrative of the game. For example, there is a sequence in *Journey* where the player has to "ring" at multiple areas to released trapped carpet creatures. When all the creatures are released, they form a bridge allowing access to the next area. From this we can see that the game mechanic of "ringing" makes clear the causality in the game, as the player knows it was their actions that formed the bridge.

The mechanics also do a good job of conveying the character's state. Nearing the end of the game when the player is climbing up a snowy mountain, the cold causes the player's scarf to start to freeze, slowly losing the ability to fly. While the frost is visually represented, losing the ability to fly helps to indicate the severity of the cold. Similarly, at the last stage when flying above the clouds, the player's scarf remains almost constantly charged, allowing them to fly endlessly. This seems to represent a state of near immortality appropriate to the player character's resurrection at the end of the narrative.

In the case when the player is online, the narrative changes as players meet other players. They can choose to either accompany these other players, help them through each stage of the game, or leave them alone. When playing with other players, these players become companions to the player's character, a choice that is reflected in the game during the cut scene of the prophecy: it shows two robed figures instead of one, changing the game narrative to a story of companionship instead of a lone traveller.

Gameplay for Exploring Narrative Settings. While *Journey* allows players to enact the narrative through gameplay, the narrative is heavily supported by the many narrative devices and the narrative architecture [24] used in the game. A contextually rich environment can elicit pre-conceived ideas or narratives drawn from other forms of media, set up the narrative world of the game, embed narratives into the environmental objects, or allow for emergent narratives. *Journey* uses environmental storytelling extensively to evoke the setting and atmosphere of the game. The desolate ruins and hieroglyphs hint at a lost civilisation, with the red robes and carpets possibly pointing to a Tibetan or Middle Eastern influence [25], and the slow strings soundtrack giving a solemn, melancholy mood to the game. The game also uses a high level of realism of the visual graphics to let the players better establish a spatial presence within the game. With the narrative rich environment and the realistic visuals, it creates a simulative experience for the players when traversing through the game environment. The gameplay of *Journey* then not only enacts the narrative of the game. In addition, the narrative architecture adds upon the narrative derived from the game mechanics.

For example, as the game ends and the player is brought back to the start, it may seem as though the game simply restarted. However, with the Tibetan influences in the environment adding another layer of interpretation, the Eastern references may suggest the concept of reincarnation or rebirth. In the starting scene of the game, there are tall stones scattered across the desert that seem to be of no significance; however, knowing that the player dies and revives and comes back to the starting point, the stones then take on a different meaning as the players may interpret the stones to be tombstones. While the narrative architecture heavily informs the setting for the gameplay, conversely the gameplay can be used to let players see and explore the environment in a different light.

Even though the game relies heavily on visual cues, *Journey* also uses embedded storytelling [24] within the game such that new information about the narrative is uncovered through gameplay. The main narrative of *Journey* is mostly told through the gameplay. However, interspersed between each stage of the game are cut scenes in which the character appears in a bright white space with a larger robed figure dressed in white. During these cut scenes, the player is shown parts of a hieroglyphic mural that can be understood as the history of an ancient civilisation. The game not only embeds the history of the civilisation within the cut scenes, but also in the game environment. Throughout the game, players can search for hieroglyph murals at each stage of the game. The murals contain more history of the civilisation or hint at how the places of each stage were used in the past. Supplemented with the hieroglyphs shown in the cut scenes, players can understand the history of the civilisation better and add to their understanding of the game narrative by actively searching for the hieroglyph murals.

By using a combination of narrative devices and realistic visuals, *Journey* lets players feel present in and intrigued by the game environment, leading them to explore the game. Along with gameplay appropriate to the narrative, *Journey* is able to convey a complex narrative without the use of any words.

5.3   Close Reading: A Bird Story

We now move on to the close reading of *A Bird Story*. *A Bird Story* tells the story of a relationship between a boy and a bird. The player plays as a boy who has no friends in school and whose parents are constantly away. The boy rescues an injured bird from a badger and forms a heart-warming friendship with the bird. The boy tries to keep the bird a secret from his mother but is eventually found out and forbidden to keep the bird. In *A Bird Story*, gameplay is used as a means to progress time within the game.

Gameplay as Time Progression. Unlike the other two games, *A Bird Story* has very little in the way of game mechanics, and only has basic player interactions consisting of walking around the game world using arrow keys. Occasionally the game introduces mini-game events such as when the boy is competing with the bird in jumping into rain puddles, or navigating the paper airplane to find the bird's nest, but these events do not involve any difficulty or any need for skill on the part of the player. In addition, the outcomes of these mini games have no impact on the narrative or the game. The game also has many cut scenes, so much so that the player can easily forget that there is a need for any input. To overcome this, the game indicates with arrow keys when the player can control the boy. Despite the shortcomings of *A Bird Story* as a game and the heavy use of cut scenes to convey the narrative, the game is still able to use gameplay for storytelling by letting player actions turn time forwards or backwards.

The game uses very interesting and surrealistic ways of doing scene transitions. For example, when the boy heads home after school, instead of cutting the scene directly to the home or depicting the school and the way home realistically, the lockers in the school's corridors start to look like trees and the school building then slowly melts into the courtyard outside, so that the player doesn't have to go through a door when moving from inside the school building to the courtyard outdoors. Another example is a scene where the furniture of the living room appears in the middle of the forest. After the player steps into the "living room", the environment gradually changes from the forest to the boy's actual living room. In these moments, when the player controls the character and navigates the boy through surreal scene transitions, it feels as if time is being fast-forwarded as the blending of surroundings of different environments mimics the blur of the surroundings in peripheral vision when travelling at a high speed.

Another scene where *A Bird Story* uses player action to progress time is at the start of the game. The boy goes to bed and a scene that appears to be a dream sequence starts. The player can control the boy in that scene, but he walks backwards. The player walks past some shadows, hopping onto a paper plane that also flies backwards. The player will only realise at the end of the game that this sequence represents the boy moving backwards in time to the chronological start of the story, and the shadows that they pass by are future sequences of the boy with the bird in the game.

Even with the lack of game mechanics and player agency, *A Bird Story* makes use of surrealistic representations and player actions to represent the temporal progression and spatial movement of the narrative.

6 Discussion

From close readings of three wordless games, we have identified four techniques that the games use to convey a narrative through gameplay: gameplay as enacting narrative, manipulating player controls for narrative effect, gameplay for exploring narrative settings, and gameplay as time progression. We will now briefly discuss how the techniques relate to the literature.

Gameplay as enacting narrative involves having the player's actions convey the main narrative of the game. In the absence of words, both *Brothers: A Tale of Two Sons* and *Journey* manage to use the same technique with slight differences. *Brothers: A Tale of Two Sons* has short game stages that act as the narrative events of the game. This coincides with a technique that Dubbelman had identified: recontextualising the game mechanic for characterisation and narrative empathy. *Brothers: A Tale of Two Sons* does this by using the same mechanic that was introduced earlier in the game, recontextualised it by adding a short-term objective which then turns it into a narrative event. *Journey* changes the mechanic to match the development in the narrative as well as the player's emotions. Likewise, choosing to play with another player can change the narrative. This technique allows for ludonarrative harmony, as the game mechanics fully support and enhance the narrative experience of the game.

Gameplay as enacting narrative is also related to Jenkins' idea of spatial stories that are "held together by broadly defined goals and conflicts and pushed forward by the character's movement across the map" [24: p. 124]. Both games are dependent on being able to move from a starting point towards a main objective (heading to the top of the mountain or getting to the cure). Therefore, it is of no surprise that both games are of the same genre and have the same broad narrative structure of a hero's journey. Ryan [9] suggests that for interactive narratives to be on par with other mediums, they must be able to represent physical actions that have impact on the narrative world and verbal actions that have impact on the motivations of the characters. She points out that without using language, player actions are limited to physical ones which cannot affect other characters' relationships. However, *Journey* manages to allow players to develop a sense of camaraderie while travelling through the desert together, which players may interpret to be a connection between the characters. This is also represented through the change in the prophecy upon going through most of the stages with another player. The change in the prophecy, however, is only able to indicate the status of companionship and nothing more. Therefore, even though it is possible for relationships between characters to be represented in the narrative, this is still far from the ability to represent complex interpersonal relationships that Ryan is discussing. Hence, even though *Journey* shows promise in representing character relationships, it may be that for complex relationships to be supported, there is still a need for language.

Without the use of language, Journey had to make use of familiar conventions to set up the narrative world. In addition, the game embeds a higher-level narrative into the environmental objects. *Journey*'s use of realistic visuals also increases the narrative and game immersion. While most of the narrative content is communicated visually, the gameplay allows the player to explore the narrative-rich environment at their own pace. Although this may mean that the player's interpretation of the narrative does not match with the developer's authorial intentions, suggesting the old ludonarrative debate about the conflict between player's agency and narrative, this does not necessarily mean that the player-generated narrative is "wrong". Players may gain satisfaction and a sense of achievement from creating their own interpretation. Using their own experience to interpret the narrative, they can potentially create a more personally meaningful narrative.

Gameplay as time progression in *A Bird Story* serves to help the player move forward in time without impacting the events within the narrative. Of the four techniques, gameplay as time progression has the least narrative quality, with player actions having the least impact on the game narrative. However, even with very little impact on the game narrative, using the game actions to help progress the narrative can still serve to help the player feel agency. Tanenbaum and Tanenbaum [26] propose to think of agency as commitment to meaning for narrative rich games instead of agency as choice or freedom. Even when game actions do not allow for any decision making, the commitment to performing a meaningful game action helps to "facilitate meaningful expression". In this case, the gameplay of *A Bird Story* allows the player to feel agency by committing to the action of moving the character and at the same time progressing narrative time.

In the introduction, we discussed the relationship between language and narratives, and brought up Ryan's argument that only language can convey causality. Through our close readings, we have argued that gameplay can indicate causality by allowing players to carry out actions that affect and trigger subsequent events in the game. Enacting the scenes of the narrative in game time also gives the player a clear idea of causality and the progression of the narrative. However, while game mechanics may possibly help the player understand the causality of physical narrative events, the causality of events triggered by the thoughts and motives of characters may be difficult to convey, as complex thoughts may still require language for representation.

On the other hand, leaving the narrative and complex thought processes ambiguous is not necessarily a bad thing. Just as ambiguity is used in literature to allow for multiple interpretations [27] and to evoke emotional response [28], wordlessness in the game context can very likely do the same. We earlier discussed the possible differences in the narrative experience of wordless games as compared to games with words, suggesting that wordlessness possibly adds another level of difficulty to the gameplay. However, as the identified techniques help to convey the causality of player actions and time progression, this gives players a clear understanding of their actions while leaving the exact meaning of their actions open to interpretation by the players.

7   Conclusion

In this paper, we identified four different techniques by which gameplay is used to convey a narrative within wordless games: gameplay as enacting narrative, manipulating player controls for narrative effect, gameplay for exploring narrative settings, and gameplay as time progression. These techniques can empower game designers to design games wherein the game mechanics and player actions are used together to tell the game narrative. Future work will include conducting empirical studies of players playing existing wordless games to validate the techniques, and compiling the techniques in the form of design knowledge to better help designers in creating narrative games.

Acknowledgements. This research is partially supported by National University of Singapore, Faculty of Arts and Social Sciences.

References

1. Toh, W.: A multimodal discourse analysis of video games: a ludonarrative model In: Proceedings of DiGRA 2015 (2015)
2. Dubbelman, T.: Narrative game mechanics. In: Nack, F., Gordon, A.S. (eds.) ICIDS 2016. LNCS, vol. 10045, pp. 39–50. Springer, Cham (2016). https://doi.org/10.1007/978-3-319-48279-8_4
3. Larsen, B.A., Schoenau-Fog, H.: The narrative quality of game mechanics. In: Nack, F., Gordon, A.S. (eds.) ICIDS 2016. LNCS, vol. 10045, pp. 61–72. Springer, Cham (2016). https://doi.org/10.1007/978-3-319-48279-8_6
4. Toolan, M.: Narrative: linguistic and structural theories. In: Brown, K. (ed.) Encyclopedia of Language and Linguistics, 2nd edn., pp. 459–473. Elsevier, Oxford (2006)
5. Fludernik, M.: An Introduction to Narratology. Routledge, London (2009)
6. Ryan, M.-L.: Narrative Across Media: The Languages of Storytelling. University of Nebraska Press, Lincoln (2004)
7. Ryan, M.-L.: Toward a definition of narrative. In: Herman, D. (ed.) The Cambridge Companion to Narrative, pp. 22–36. Cambridge University Press, Cambridge (2007)
8. Borghi, A.M., Binkofski, F.: Words as Social Tools: An Embodied View Applied to Abstract Concepts. Springer, New York (2014). https://doi.org/10.1007/978-1-4614-9539-0
9. Ryan, M.-L.: Narration in various media. In: Hühn, P., et al. (eds.) The Living Handbook of Narratology. Hamburg University Press, Hamburg (2009)
10. Arizpe, E.: Meaning-making from wordless (or nearly wordless) picturebooks: what educational research expects and what readers have to say. Camb. J. Educ. J. **43**(2), 163–176 (2013)

11. Genette, G.: Paratexts: Thresholds of Interpretation. Cambridge University Press, Cambridge (1997). Trans. J.E. Lewin
12. Frasca, G.: Ludologists love stories, too: notes from a debate that never took place. In: Copier, M., Raessens, J. (eds.) Level-up: Digital Games Research Conference, pp. 92–99. Utrecht University, Utrecht (2003)
13. Juul, J.: Are games telling stories? A brief note on games and narratives. Game Stud. 1(1) (2001)
14. Murray, J.: The last word on ludology v narratology in game studies. In: International DiGRA Conference, June 2005
15. Hocking, C.: Ludonarrative Dissonance in Bioshock (2007). http://clicknothing.typepad.com/click_nothing/2007/10/ludonarrative-d.html. Accessed 23 June 2017
16. Brice, M.: Ludonarrative Resonance (2011). http://www.mattiebrice.com/ludonarrative-resonance/. Accessed 23 June 2017
17. Brice, M.: Narrative is a game mechanic (2012). http://www.popmatters.com/post/153895-narrative-is-a-game-mechanic/. Accessed 23 June 2017
18. Pynenburg, T.: Games worth a thousand words: critical approaches and ludonarrative harmony in interactive narratives. Honors Theses (2012)
19. Fabricatore, C.: Gameplay and game mechanics design: a key to quality in videogames. In: Proceedings of OECD-CERI Expert Meeting on Videogames and Education (2007)
20. Journey, thatgamecompany (2012)
21. Brothers: A Tale of Two Sons, Starbreeze Studios (2013)
22. A Bird Story, Freebird Studios (2014)
23. Bizzocchi, J., Tanenbaum, J.: Well read: applying close reading techniques to gameplay experiences. In: Drew, D. (ed.) Well Played 3.0, pp. 262–290. ETC Press (2011)
24. Jenkins, H.: Game design as narrative architecture. In: Wardrip-Fruin, N., Harrigan, P. (eds.) First Person: New Media as Story, Performance, and Game, pp. 118–130. MIT Press, Cambridge (2004)
25. Ohannessian, K.: Game designer Jenova Chen on the art behind his "Journey" (2012). https://www.fastcompany.com/1680062/game-designer-jenova-chen-on-the-art-behind-his-journey. Accessed 23 June 2017
26. Tanenbaum, K., Tanenbaum, J.: Commitment to meaning: a reframing of agency in games. In: Digital Arts and Culture Conference (2009)
27. Abrams, M.H., Harpham, G.: A Glossary of Literary Terms, 10th edn. Cengage Learning, Boston (2011)
28. Muzzillo, J.S.: Positive effects of ambiguity when created by rhetorical devices: to be or not to be. ETC Rev. Gen. Semant. 67(4), 452–468 (2010)

A Framework for Multi-participant Narratives Based on Multiplayer Game Interactions

Callum Spawforth$^{(\boxtimes)}$ and David E. Millard

University of Southampton, Southampton, UK
cs14g13@soton.ac.uk

Abstract. Multi-participant Interactive Narratives have the potential for novel types of story and experiences, but there is no framework to show what is possible, and therefore no description of what types of multi-participant narrative could exist. In this paper, we attempt to build such a framework by first considering the core characteristics of interactions in multiplayer games, and then considering how those might be used to define different types of multi-participant narrative. Our framework is based on a systematic analysis of 56 interactions across 17 multiplayer games, resulting in 9 distinguishing characteristics. We then validate this framework by applying it to 3 novel multiplayer games, showing that it successfully captures the player interactions, although some higher level design decisions are missed. Finally, we demonstrate that novel premises for multi-participant narratives can be constructed from these characteristics. Our work provides a foundation for considering the types of multi-participant narrative that are possible.

Keywords: Multi-participant narrative · Multiplayer games · Interactions

1 Introduction

The Interactive Digital Narrative (IDN) space has traditionally been focused on single-participant experiences [1–4], where a single reader interacts with a story system and has some agency over their experience of the story.

Narratives with multiple participants have the potential for interesting and novel types of story, but no clear approach to creating them exists, despite previous work in the area [5–7]. However, multiplayer video games are both widely studied, and applicable to the narrative space [8]. They support inter-player agency, where all participants collectively have agency over the experience. In a narrative context this raises interesting questions, such as to what extent participants have agency over each other's narratives, and how they might see the agency of others. The problem with answering these questions is that we have no framework that describes what types of multi-participant narrative might exist.

© Springer International Publishing AG 2017
N. Nunes et al. (Eds.): ICIDS 2017, LNCS 10690, pp. 150–162, 2017.
https://doi.org/10.1007/978-3-319-71027-3_13

In this paper, we attempt to construct such a framework using a categorisation of the interactions between players in multiplayer games. We have undertaken our own categorisation because existing research in multiplayer game interactions takes a game design perspective, using concepts that are not necessarily applicable to narratives such as considering avatars or skills [9–11].

We seek to answer two key questions: what are the core characteristics of interactions in games, and how can we use those characteristics to describe possible novel multi-participant narratives?

The framework is developed through a systematic analysis of a sample of top-rated multiplayer games (n = 17) across a variety of genres, and is validated by applying it to three video games that contain novel types of multiplayer experience and were not in the original sample. Finally, we create three story premises using the framework to demonstrate that by varying the characteristics within it we can inspire fundamentally different multi-participant narratives.

To our knowledge our work is the first attempt to define the range of possibilities for multi-participant narratives. In Sect. 2 we present a brief overview of existing work on interactions in digital games. Section 3 outlines our methodology for creating and validating the framework. Section 4 presents a description of the framework and provides an example of classifying the interactions from one of the sample games. Section 5 then presents the results of validating the framework against three games with novel approaches to multiplayer. Finally, in Sect. 6 we present three story premises inspired by the different characteristics within the framework, before concluding the paper in Sect. 7.

2   Background: Analysing Multiplayer Games

A previous approach to categorising multiplayer games is to model properties of the game. A simple model of multiplayer games consisting of rules, goals, props and tools was proposed by Zagal [12]. He identified six characteristics including "Social Interaction", "Cooperation and Competition" and "Synchronicity". While these could influence the overarching design of a narrative, their low fidelity prevents more detailed constructions.

Rocha [9] used a higher-fidelity approach, identifying a number of design patterns for cooperative mechanics. For example, the pattern "Complementarity", in which the abilities of players complement each other. Seif [13] extended this with further patterns, such as "Shared puzzles". While the essence of these patterns may apply in the narrative space, they assume concepts such as character abilities and manipulatable objects, which may not be true for narratives.

Reuter [10] developed a more applicable set of design patterns for collaborative multiplayer games. These are abstract, allowing them to be realised through a variety of different interaction mechanics. While patterns such as "Gathering Gate" are easily visualised in narrative, their abstract nature still leaves the challenge of implementation. Manninen [14] analyses interactions in more detail, proposing that interaction forms are "perceivable actions that act as manifestations of the user-user and user-environment interaction". His taxonomy of these enumerates different types of interaction, but it heavily focused on communication and doesn't identify how the nature of those interactions differs [15].

Our work focuses on modelling the differences between interactions at a higher fidelity than the earlier works, in order to understand how interactions may exist in the narrative space.

3   Methodology

The Systematic Analysis was an iterative coding analysis over the most popular games from Metacritic[1]. Metacritic was used due to the high per-game user rating count, quantity of games, and wide range of genres.

An initial sample list was created from the top 150 games of each of the 18 Metacritic genres. Non-multiplayer games were then removed, as were games with fewer ratings than the median of 39. The top game (sorted by user rating) from each genre was then selected to be analysed. However, the 'Party' genre was later removed as it primarily consisted of compilations of smaller games. This resulted in a sample set of 17 games, spread across 17 different genres with publication dates ranging from 1998 to 2013.

For each selected game, a single gamemode was chosen for analysis. This decision was based on the mode with the most information available (a particular problem with older games), typically the main or default gamemode.

A type of iterative coding was then performed on the chosen games. Interactions were identified using available information on the game, primarily video footage, articles, and reviews. During this process, some games were eliminated due to a lack of available information. When this occurred, the next highest rated game with sufficient information replaced it in the sample.

For our analysis we used a definition of interaction grounded in the works of Reuter [10] and Manninen [14], which state that interactions are "perceivable actions" with "perceivable visualisations".

For us, an interaction consists of two participants: an initiator and a recipient, and two parts: an action and an effect. An action is the command the initiator gives the system, such as "fire a bullet in this direction". The effect is the impact that action has on the game state, such as "injure this person and make a noise". The effect must be perceived by another player, in order for this to be an interaction [10].

An initial framework was created based on this definition, focusing on action and effect. As each interaction was identified, we attempted to classify it using the current framework. If an interaction could not be adequately described by the current set of characteristics, these were refined using the problematic interaction and other hypothetical edge cases to guide discussion. The refined characteristics were then reapplied against all identified interactions. This process continued until all identified interactions could be described by the refined characteristics. The identification of new interactions was then resumed.

---

[1] metacritic.com.

This iterative process allowed for the creation of our framework and acted as a form of self-verification. However, we also wanted to test the framework against games that were not in the sample set, and which were known for their unusual multiplayer mechanics.

To this end we applied the framework to three games considered to offer players a novel multiplayer experience, with the aim of discovering whether the framework adequately described the novel elements. The three games selected were *Dark Souls, Journey* and *Dead by Daylight*.

Our methodology is not intended to give an overall picture of interactions in multiplayer games. Although our sample is varied, we would not claim that it is representative. Rather we are using our selection criteria to ensure that the framework is based on the interactions of popular and well-known games, and see our contribution as the framework, rather than the classification itself.

4   The Framework

The games analysed are shown in Table 1. In total 56 interactions were identified from 17 games. From these interactions, 9 characteristics were identified and added to the framework, shown as a summary in Table 2 alongside examples from the sample set. Three characteristics address the interaction as a whole, while three focus on the initiator and another three on the recipient.

General Characteristics

Likelihood. When a player takes an action, an interaction only occurs if the effect of that action is perceived by another player [10]. Likelihood is the chance that an interaction occurs. It is *guaranteed* if the recipient can notice the effect regardless of their current situation or state, such as a message that always appears when a given action occurs. An interaction is *possible* if the recipient must be in a particular situation or state to experience the effect, such as needing to be visit a box to see that an item has been taken.

Interaction type. An interaction can be Informational or Mechanical. Informational interactions only change the information available to the other player, or enable further interactions that are informational. One clear example from the unclassified game *Team Fortress 2*, is spraying a decal on a surface. Mechanical interactions make more concrete alterations to the other player or their game-world, directly impacting the other player's agency.

Synchronicity. Adapted for interactions from Zagal's game-wide definitions [12], a synchronous interaction requires that all interaction participants be participating in the game at the same time. For example, applying a medical kit to a player in *The Last of Us*. In contrast, in an asynchronous interaction at least one of the players may not be actively participating in the game. While no examples of this arose in the analysis, Multi-User Dungeons are known to have asynchronous elements [12].

Table 1. Games classified during Framework Construction

Name	Short code	Date	Gamemode	Num. found interactions
Ratchet & Clank: Up Your Arsenal	RC	2004	Siege	4
Dragon Ball Z: Budokai Tenkaichi 3	DBZ	2005	Versus	2
The Last of Us	LU	2013	Survivors	9
Counter-Strike	CS	2000	Bomb-defusal	7
IL2-Sturmovik	IL2	2001	Team-deathmatch	3
Super Mario Advance 4	IL2	2003	Cooperative	1
World of Goo	WG	2008	Cooperative	4
Midnight Club 3: DUB Edition	MC3	2005	Capture the flag	3
Starcraft	SC	1998	2v2 Siege	4
Mario and Luigi: Superstar Saga	ML	2003	Main game	1
Race 07: Official WTCC Game	R07	2007	Race	2
Greg Hastings Tournament Paintball	GHTP	2005	Elimination	2
Advance Wars 2: Black Hole Rising	AW2	2003	FFA skirmish	2
James Bond 007: Everything or Nothing	JB	2003	Cooperative	3
Fire Emblem	FE	2003	Versus	2
Toy Soldiers	TS	2010	Versus	5
WWE Day of Reckoning	WWE	2004	Exhibition	2

Recipient Characteristics

Explicit Awareness. If the game explicitly informs the recipient that an effect was caused by another player, they are explicitly aware. This must always be extradiegetic [16], as it refers to the concept of a player. If this information is always perceivable, the recipient is *always explicitly aware*, for example a notification stating "Player X has scored a point". If the player may not be able to perceive this information, they are *possibly explicitly aware*, such as a message that only appears to players in a certain location. They may also *never* be *explicitly aware*.

Deductive Awareness. The recipient is deductively aware if it is possible to deduce that an effect was caused by a player from the game's rules. It may

Table 2. A summary of the characteristics identified in the 17 games analysed

Characteristic	Value	Count	Example
General characteristics			
Likelihood	Guaranteed	35	LU: "Killing a player"
	Possible	21	LU: "Emptying a Box"
Type	Mechanical	52	CS: "Shooting and injuring a player"
	Informational	4	WG: "Moving the cursor"
Synchronicity	Synchronous	56	LU: "Killing a player"
	Asynchronous	0	No example classified
Recipient Characteristics			
Explicit Awareness	Always	10	LU: "Healing an ally"
	Possibly	12	TS: "Taking control of a unit"
	Never	34	AW2: "Capturing a base"
Deductive Awareness	Always	49	FE: "Attack an enemy unit"
	Possibly	7	TS: "Attacking using a unit"
	Never	0	No example classified
Initiator Identifiability	Always	36	CS: "Killing a player"
	Possibly	20	LU: "Emptying a box of items"
	Never	0	No example classified
Initiator Characteristics			
Explicit Feedback	Always	8	LU: "Shooting at and hitting a player"
	Possibly	8	LU: "Emptying a box of items"
	Never	40	TS: "Queuing up a unit for deployment"
Deductive Feedback	Always	34	WG: "Moving the shared view"
	Possibly	22	CS: "Dropping a weapon on the ground"
	Never	0	No example classified
Recipient Identifiability	Always	42	LU: "Healing an ally"
	Possibly	14	LU: "Emptying a box of items"
	Never	0	No example classified

always possible to deduce an effect was caused by a player. For example, if a territory is captured, and only players are able to capture territories. However, it may only be *possible* to deduce in some situations, such as if a game has both players and environmental factors that can injure the recipient, and the recipient only knows that they have been injured. It is also possible that it may *never* be possible to deduce the source of the effect was a player.

Initiator Identifiability. Identifiability describes whether the recipient knows the identity of the player that has affected them. The initiator is *always* identifiable if the recipient always knows the player that caused the effect, for example if "[Initiator Name] has killed [Recipient Name]" always appears on the recipient's death. They are *possibly* identifiable if their ability to do depends upon their current situation or game state, e.g. they can observe who it is but are not guaranteed to. They may also *never* be able to identify the initiator.

Initiator Characteristics

Explicit Feedback. The counterpart to *Explicit Awareness*, the initiator receives explicit feedback if the game makes it explicit that they have affected a player with their action. Explicit feedback can either *always*, *possibly* or *never* occur in the same manner as *Explicit Awareness*.

Deductive Feedback. The counterpart to *Deductive Awareness*, the initiator receives deductive feedback if they can deduce from the rules and information available that they've affected a player. Deductive Feedback can either *always*, *possibly* or *never* occur in the same manner as *Deductive Awareness*.

Recipient Identifiability. The counterpart to *Initiator Identifiability*, this characteristic addresses whether the initiator can identify the affected recipient, but otherwise functions identically.

4.1   Communication, Bots, and Indirect Effects

A number of aspects were removed from consideration during classification, as they added significant ambiguity when assigning values to the framework.

The presence of free-form communication, such as voice and text based chat channels, obfuscates *Feedback*, *Awareness*, *Visibility* and *Identifiability*. The information available purely within an interaction is overridden by allowing the player to inform others of their participation.

Similarly, many games contain game-playing agents ("bots") that attempt to imitate humans. These can make it hard to determine the value for a particular characteristic, due to the difficulty of differentiating between bots and players. An initiator may believe they have affected a player, when they have instead affected a bot.

Finally, secondary effects arising from the context of an interaction were not considered within the framework. For example, a player may defeat another player, in turn saving the life of a third player.

4.2   Example Classification

Due to size limitations we cannot show the full classification, but as an example consider the interactions for *Ratchet & Clank* shown in Table 3.

In Capturing Territory, the initiator is the player taking the capture action. The recipient can be considered as any other player in the game. Capturing the area enables the initiator's team to revive at that location, making it a mechanical interaction. It is a *guaranteed* interaction, as it updates a persistent user-interface element. The recipient is always *deductively aware*, as only players

Table 3. Example interactions from "Ratchet & Clank: Up Your Arsenal", Siege Mode

Interaction name	Shooting and hitting a named player	Shooting and missing a named player	Killing a player	Capturing territory
Likelihood	Guaranteed	Possible	Guaranteed	Guaranteed
Type	Mechanical	Informational	Mechanical	Mechanical
Synchronicity	Sync.	Sync.	Sync.	Sync.
Explicit awareness	Possibly	Never	Always	Possibly
Deductive awareness	Possibly	Possibly	Possibly	Always
Initiator identifiability	Possibly	Possibly	Always	Possibly
Explicit feedback	Possibly	Possibly	Always	Possibly
Deductive feedback	Possibly	Possibly	Possibly	Always
Recipient identifiability	Always	Possibly	Always	Always

can capture control points. The *initiator identifiability* is possible as it requires the recipient to be in the vicinity and to observe the capture. For the initiator, they can *deduce* that they've affected every player, as every player either gains or loses access to a control point. The initiator can *identify* every recipient, as everyone in the game is affected.

It can be seen from Table 3 that the collection of interactions that make up this game mode have different profiles. This demonstrates why it is important to classify individual interactions rather than the game as a whole, as the aggregate of the interactions fails to capture these interesting differences, and would tend to converge on a value of 'possibly' for most of the characteristics. Modelling the interactions increases complexity but maintains the fidelity of the analysis, and allows for more meaningful comparisons.

5   Framework Validation

Having produced the framework and classified our sample set of games, we wanted to validate it by applying it to games that were outside the sample, but are known for their interesting approach to multiplayer. Each forms a small case study, that helps reveal the value and limitations of the framework.

5.1   Case Study 1: Dark Souls

Dark Souls is an action RPG, developed by FromSoftware and published by Namco in 2011 on a variety of 7th generation platforms. Dark Souls has a novel multiplayer system in which each player plays the game within their own version of the game's world. Various interactions exist that allow players to interact with the worlds of others, with "Signs" being one of the most prevalent.

"Signs" are runic symbols placed on the ground by players that have a chance to appear in other players' worlds. Signs allow the player to summon another player to their world, view a message, or invade the other player's world. The Gravelord Soul Sign, a type of invasion sign, also creates powerful opponents in the other player's world. The interesting interactions associated with these signs is when the initiator places the sign, which then appears in the recipient's world. Placing a sign has unusual characteristics according to our framework. Two types of sign (Message and Gravelord) are *asynchronous*. When placing all of these signs, *feedback* never occurs nor is the *recipient identifiable*.

Many interactions within Dark Souls are either a secondary result of the player's actions or are unintentionally triggered. For example, each death has a chance of leaving a "bloodstain" in the worlds of other players, which they can use to glean information about potentially dangerous areas. These passive interactions were also unusual in our original sample; the initiator in these cases is not *identifiable* nor is the recipient, and no *feedback* occurs. These characteristic values are unique to Dark Souls out of the twenty games classified in total, demonstrating a certain novelty in the games approach to multiplayer.

5.2   Case Study 2: Journey

Journey is an exploratory adventure game, developed by thatgamecompany and published by Sony Computer Entertainment in 2012 on 7th generation platforms. Its multiplayer system is notable in that it connects strangers, and limits their ability to communicate to in-game actions.

In Journey, players communicate in a limited sense by briefly creating a variable-size sphere above their avatar. Energy is restored to the other player if they touch the sphere. We categorised this as two interactions, one when the sphere is only seen and another when energy is restored. Both are *synchronous* with recipient and initiator *identifiable*. However, while the first is *informational*, *possible interaction* with *possibly deducible awareness* and *feedback*, the energy interaction is *mechanical* and *guaranteed* with *always deducible awareness* and *feedback*. However, in practice both interactions are frequently used to provide information to the other player. This suggests that in the second interaction the mechanical function is hiding the equally significant informational one.

A novel mechanic within Journey is that each player's energy is recharged when players are in very close proximity. Triggering this was categorised as a *guaranteed, mechanical, synchronous, always identifiable* interaction with *always deductive awareness* and *feedback*, this is an identical classification to interactions in both *IL-2 Sturmovik* and *World of Goo*. The novelty stems from Journey's design, which uses this subtle interaction to encourage a collaborative experience.

The most novel element of Journey is the way in which players are matched without explicit effort. As a player progresses, another player will simply appear, and many players fail to realise the newcomer is another player. Despite the significance of this matchmaking it cannot be considered an interaction (no triggering action) and therefore does not appear in our framework. This suggests that further study of the way in which players are matched in games is needed.

5.3 Case Study 3: Dead by Daylight

Dead by Daylight is a survival horror game, developed by Behavior Interactive and published by Starbreeze Studios in 2016 for 8th generation platforms. It is notable as it assigns different roles to players (survivors and killers).

The asymmetry between the roles results in interactions where a single action can have different effects on different players. For example, when a survivor fails a skill check. Other survivors perceive this as a loud noise and bright flash when nearby. However, the killer receives an extradiegetic indicator of the direction and distance. To classify this within the framework, the interaction was divided into two, survivor to survivor (S to S) and survivor to killer (S to K).

The S to S is a *possible interaction* that is *mechanical* and *synchronous* with *always deducible awareness, always deducible feedback, possible initiator identification* and an *always identifiable recipient*.

The S to K interaction differs in that it is *guaranteed* to be perceived by the killer. Thus the survivor can *always deduce* they've affected the killer. While the framework captured this asymmetry of perception by splitting the interaction, the relationship between the interactions is lost.

Asymmetry of agency is also a key aspect. The killer has the ability to significantly impact survivors, while survivors have little power against the killer. This is not reflected in our framework, in part due to the absence of roles, but also as there is no measurement of the impact of each interaction.

6 Using the Framework for Multi-participant Narratives

To demonstrate the applicability of our framework to multi-participant narrative, we can consider a number of different narrative premises inspired by the different characteristics identified in the framework.

Premise 1. A spree of killings has recently occurred in London. Two detectives are working the case - one from the local police station, another a private investigator, hired by a relative of the victims. Each character is played by a different participant. The two will never meet, but their interactions with the crime scene and victims will change the course of the other's investigation.

This narrative is inspired by an interaction using possible *deductive awareness* and no *feedback*, with *guaranteed* interactions and no ability to *identify* initiator or recipient. The participants may deduce someone is interfering with their investigation, but will be unaware of the effect their actions have on the other. This creates two intertwined narratives but with notably different experiences.

Premise 2. The Research and Development department of a large corporation is on the verge of a new technological breakthrough. Participant one follows the head of this department who must oversee the final stages of the research. Participant two follows one of their employees, who unbeknownst to the head is a corporate spy whose job it is to steal and then sabotage the research.

This premise has clear asymmetry. The spy is *always aware* and always receives *feedback* on their attempts to undermine the department, while the head has only *possible deductive awareness* and *possible deductive feedback*, and will never *identify* the spy.

Premise 3. The first participant listens to the conversation of two women sitting in a bar. The older woman reminisces on the critical decisions and mistakes she has made in her life, interspersed with revelations about the younger women's life that are directed by the first participant, perhaps in reaction to the experiences of the older women. The younger women's story culminates in her having aged, finding herself back at the bar explaining her life story to a different younger woman. This telling of the life story is then used for the next participant.

This cyclic premise is inspired by an *asynchronous* interaction in which the initiator possibly receives *deductive feedback*, but as a recipient only has *deductive awareness*, as they are never told how their experience has been affected by the decisions of another participant, but might figure this out by reflecting on the decisions that they themselves have made. The other player is *never* identified. The time aspect element of asynchronous storytelling in this case facilitate time advancing at different rates for different participants, and means they can interact independently much as they would with a single participant narrative.

7   Conclusion

In this paper, we sought to describe the potential of multiplayer narratives by creating a framework of multiplayer game interactions, and looking at what narratives constructed using this framework might be like.

We did this by performing an iterative analysis of popular multiplayer video games in order to classify their different interactions and create a framework. We then validated the framework by applying it to three games notable for their novel multiplayer experiences. We then constructed a set of story premises based on these characteristics to demonstrate how the framework might inspire significantly differing types of multi-participant narrative.

The first of the questions we set out to answer was what are the core characteristics of interactions in games? In total our framework contains nine characteristics: Interaction Likelihood, Type, Synchronicity, Explicit Awareness, Deductive Awareness, Explicit Feedback, Deductive Feedback, Initiator Identifiability, and Recipient Identifiability. The prevalence of perception within the framework leaves open the question of whether providing the illusion of other players' agency on your story would be sufficient. Similar to how the illusion of agency can prove equally engaging to the real thing [17].

During validation, we found that the characteristics were capable of classifying all of the identified interactions within the selected games. However, the distinction between *mechanical* and *informational* interactions was less clear in *Journey* and *Dead by Daylight*. This suggests that Interaction Type is not binary, but rather more of a spectrum, making it harder to classify.

Similarly, we found that the framework missed something important when describing games where interactions varied between participants playing different roles, particularly in cases where the relative power of participants was noticeably different. Novel aspects of players' roles, goals and relationships may have been missed. These elements may be better studied at a game-wide level.

The second question we wanted to address was how we can use those characteristics to describe possible novel multi-participant narratives. In particular moving to a more concrete definition of the different sorts of experience that could be created. We have shown that the framework can describe a variety of different multi-participant narratives, and the characteristics derived from games can be equally applied to narratives. In particular the different combinations of Awareness, Feedback, and Identity, could result in subtly different experiences.

The work described here only starts to explore the potential of multi-participant narratives. With the framework giving a clear idea of the sorts of stories that are possible, we now intend to explore how they might be implemented and authored. For our future work, we intend to create a multi-participant narrative system based on a sculptural hypertext model [7,18], we have already begun to explore how this might work [8] and how it could support the wide range of interactions identified within the framework.

Our hope is that this framework will act as a foundation for future work in this area, allowing developers and researchers to understand the types of multi-participant narratives that are possible, and build systems to support a variety of different multi-participant narrative experiences.

References

1. Cavazza, M., Charles, F., Mead, S.J.: Character-based interactive storytelling. IEEE Intell. Syst. **17**(4), 17–24 (2002)
2. Ciarlini, A.E.M., Pozzer, C.T., Furtado, A.L., Feijó, B.: A logic-based tool for interactive generation and dramatization of stories. In: ACE 2005, pp. 133–140. ACM, New York (2005)
3. Mateas, M., Stern, A.: Facade: an experiment in building a fully-realized interactive drama. In: Game Developers Conference, vol. 2 (2003)
4. Riedl, M.O., Young, R.M.: An intent-driven planner for multi-agent story generation. In: AAMAS 2004, pp. 186–193. IEEE Computer Society, Washington D.C. (2004)
5. Fairclough, C., Cunningham, P.: A multiplayer case based story engine. Technical report, Department of Computer Science, Trinity College Dublin (2003)
6. Peinado, F., Gervás, P.: Transferring game mastering laws to interactive digital storytelling. In: Göbel, S., Spierling, U., Hoffmann, A., Iurgel, I., Schneider, O., Dechau, J., Feix, A. (eds.) TIDSE 2004. LNCS, vol. 3105, pp. 48–54. Springer, Heidelberg (2004). https://doi.org/10.1007/978-3-540-27797-2_7
7. Bernstein, M.: Card shark and thespis: exotic tools for hypertext narrative. In: ACM HYPERTEXT 2001, pp. 41–50. ACM, New York (2001)
8. Spawforth, C., Millard, D.E.: Multiplayer games as a template for multiplayer narratives: a case study with dark souls. In: ACM Hypertext (2017)

9. Rocha, J.B., Mascarenhas, S., Prada, R.: Game mechanics for cooperative games. ZON Digital Games 2008, pp. 72–80 (2008)

10. Reuter, C., Wendel, V., Göbel, S., Steinmetz, R.: Game design patterns for collaborative player interactions. In: Proceedings of DiGRA (2014)

11. Cook, D.: What I've learned about designing multiplayer games so far. http://www.gamasutra.com/blogs/DanielCook/20140104/208021/What_Ive_learned_about_designing_multiplayer_games_so_far.php

12. Zagal, J.P., Nussbaum, M., Rosas, R.: A model to support the design of multiplayer games. Presence Teleoper. Virtual Environ. **9**(5), 448–462 (2000)

13. Seif El-Nasr, M., Aghabeigi, B., Milam, D., Erfani, M., Lameman, B., Maygoli, H., Mah, S.: Understanding and evaluating cooperative games. In: CHI 2010, pp. 253–262. ACM, New York (2010)

14. Manninen, T.: Interaction forms in multiplayer desktop virtual reality games. In: VRIC 2002 Conference, vol. 223, p. 232 (2002)

15. Manninen, T.: Rich interaction in the context of networked virtual environments – experiences gained from the multi-player games domain. In: Blandford, A., Vanderdonckt, J., Gray, P. (eds.) People and Computers XV – Interaction without Frontiers, pp. 383–398. Springer, London (2001). https://doi.org/10.1007/978-1-4471-0353-0_23

16. Genette, G.: Narrative Discourse: An Essay in Method. Cornell University Press, Ithaca (1983)

17. Fendt, M.W., Harrison, B., Ware, S.G., Cardona-Rivera, R.E., Roberts, D.L.: Achieving the illusion of agency. In: Oyarzun, D., Peinado, F., Young, R.M., Elizalde, A., Méndez, G. (eds.) ICIDS 2012. LNCS, vol. 7648, pp. 114–125. Springer, Heidelberg (2012). https://doi.org/10.1007/978-3-642-34851-8_11

18. Millard, D.E., Hargood, C., Jewell, M.O., Weal, M.J.: Canyons, deltas and plains. In: ACM Hypertext 2013, pp. 109–118 (2013)

Gaming Versus Storytelling: Understanding Children's Interactive Experiences in a Museum Setting

Marko Radeta[✉], Vanessa Cesario, Sónia Matos, and Valentina Nisi

Madeira Interactive Technologies Institute (M-ITI), 9029-105 Funchal, Portugal
{marko.radeta,vanessa.cesario,sonia.matos,
valentina.nisi}@m-iti.org

Abstract. While gaming and storytelling are considered to be common approaches to engage audiences with a museum's collections, a formal comparison of the two has not been found in literature. While gaming and storytelling are considered to be common approaches to engage audiences with a museum's collections, a formal comparison of the two has not been found in literature. In this paper, we present the design and comparative study of two distinct interventions, namely a mobile game and a mobile story that were designed to engage a young audience with the exhibit of the local natural history museum. Focusing on the same scientific content derived from the museum's collection, we compare the effects of both interactive experiences on a group of children. When comparing engagement, enjoyment and learning outcomes, we correlate results with data derived from observations and skin conductance biofeedback. The data collected so far suggest that children are 27% more excited when using the game application compared with the story driven one. Moreover, we find that children's excitement peaks when encountering selected artefacts presented in the museum exhibit. Finally, children's learning nearly doubled (44%) when using the game based experience versus the story. We conclude the paper by discussing the implications of our findings and by proposing potential future improvements.

Keywords: Interactive experiences · Gaming · Storytelling · Skin conductance · Proximity sensing

1 Introduction

Museums are gradually moving from a passive display of artifacts towards more interactive presentations, engaging visitors and augmenting their knowledge in new and compelling ways [17, 19]. Nevertheless, they find themselves competing for attention with the entertainment industry. Museums therefore need to make their "product" more appealing and attractive to a variety of audiences, while combining educational and entertainment aspects [22]. Gamification, storytelling and playful interaction [6, 13, 26, 37, 43] afforded by the ubiquity of mobile personal devices (in museum settings) offer opportunities to attract young visitors [5] enabling a closer relationship with the museum's stories and exhibits, and creating a "new and more powerful way to learn" [41].

© Springer International Publishing AG 2017
N. Nunes et al. (Eds.): ICIDS 2017, LNCS 10690, pp. 163–178, 2017.
https://doi.org/10.1007/978-3-319-71027-3_14

Previous research demonstrates that storytelling and game-based approaches bene-fits museums by promoting joyful and exciting experiences, which have the potential to support meaningful learning [16, 22]. Moreover, games [33, 48] and storytelling [12, 25] are two of the most used techniques to engage young and adult audiences as museum visitors. Mystery and treasure-hunting [8, 15] as well as problem solving tasks have the potential to engage, entertain and scaffold visitors' learning through museum contexts [3, 10, 34, 37, 44].

While on one hand, the use of mobile devices to enhance and enrich museum visits has a long history [4, 9, 18, 21, 27, 30, 31, 40], the idea that interactive playful mobile experiences can play an equal role alongside the learning mission of most museums is a more recent approach. Stories and games can boost the learning goals of the museum, while enhancing the playful aspects of the visit. The advantages and disadvantages of mobile gaming and storytelling in museum contexts have been extensively investigated, but the two approaches have not been compared at a practical level. What are the most appreciated features from both kinds of interventions? What works best in terms of learning, engagement and enjoyment with the museum and with which audiences? To answer these questions, we designed and compared two mobile interventions, a story driven (Ocean Story, hereafter OS) and game driven one (Ocean Game, hereafter OG). Aware of the long conversation between ludologists and narratologists, in defining driving strategies and building blocks in games versus narratives [1, 2, 7, 23, 24, 28, 32, 39, 49], we did not draw a straight line between the game and the story approach, however we did design two different approaches for the two interventions (OS and OG) that would make predominant use of game mechanics versus dramatic arc and narrative focus to motivate the audience. The two applications make use of the same scientific content and exhibits in the same museum settings. Our study aims at comparing engage-ment, enjoyment and learning outcomes of both of our applications, in order to better understand and hence design mixed gaming/storytelling interventions for young audi-ences.

Museums are therefore becoming hubs where children can experience various kind of entertainment while they enrich their knowledge and solve challenges by themselves [17]. Mobile gaming and storytelling experiences in museums have been an active arena of research. We report on several inspiring research projects that helped us design our interventions. Most of these interventions do not make a clear-cut distinction between game elements and story, hence rather fuse the two approaches into a single application. Research by Sánchez et al. [40] presents "Touch & Share", a Near Field Communication (NFC) and Tangible User Interface (TUI) game for children interacting with the taxi-dermied species of a local zoological museum. Cabrera et al. [8] reports on the design of an interactive museum game which allowed students to play and perform tasks related to certain artifacts. As shortcomings of their approach, the authors alert us about the danger of children losing interest in the interactive guide due to the complexity of the tasks, while others switched the focus from the displayed artifacts to the handheld computers. "Ghost Detector" [33], a story driven museum game for children, makes ghosts of various museums' artifacts appear on the screen of the young visitors' mobile device and challenges children to find the artifacts that the ghosts are representing. The study highlights that level of excitement and engagement within the museum premises that were raised by the ubiquitous story/game. "Intrigue at the museum" [48] is a plot driven mobile game for children structured around exploration and task performance. Its plot invites visitors to search for a thief in the museum among a set of virtual characters. By scanning tags deployed in the building the audience is given clues to help them solve the riddles. Following a constructivist approach, the game allows children to freely explore the museum environment, according to their own interests and agenda. Evaluation of this work shows that story driven mobile games represent a relevant learning resource in a museum setting while promoting engagement and entertainment.

Despite the abundant set of studies and recommendations from researchers, curators and content makers [22, 47], a comparison between a game versus a story approach and the difference between the effects these approaches have on users' enjoyment, engagement and learning outcomes, seems to be missing. This motivated our comparative study between a game and a story driven approach, thus designing the two different applications, conveying the same scientific information, however making the use of different engagement techniques (gaming-driven versus story-driven) as well as aesthetics and interaction mechanics. We aim to understand the best features of both techniques and to share the findings with the community of researchers and developers of mobile stories and games for museums.

1.1 Research Motivation and Questions

Motivated by understanding best practices in gaming versus narrative techniques utilized in a museum setting, we were guided by the following questions:

- **[Q1]** - Which interactions, in both approaches, cause more excitement in the users? By collecting children's ratings of the applications as well as field observations, complemented by the physiological data obtained through the use of the bio-sensing wristbands, we highlight the most exciting interactions for both the OG and the OS.
- **[Q2]** - Which of the two mediated experiences best supports learning? This is determined through pre and post tests on the children's knowledge.
- **[Q3]** - Which experience do children rate more motivational, engaging and enjoyable? In this instance, we make use of validated scales measuring enjoyment, engagement and intrinsic motivation.

1.2 Design of Two Interactive Experiences

Setup. In order to investigate which mode (gaming or storytelling) engages, amuses and teaches children the most, we created two interactive mobile experiences, the Ocean Game and the Ocean Story. The two mobile interventions, based on the same scientific information, were expressly tailored for the Museum of Natural History of Funchal, Madeira, Portugal (MNHF). As our main audience, we choose to target 10- to 12-year-old children, as according to the museum statistics, they are the most numerous visitors. With the help of the museum's staff, we selected 13 species that are relevant to the local marine fauna of the island, and paired them with 13 RFID proximity sensors (hereafter, beacons, Fig. 1, left) which acted as transmitters of media content. We opted for this technology as: (i) it is a low-cost solution that is already available on the market; (ii) it can be easily attached to most surfaces (glass, wood, concrete); (iii) it is capable of providing interactive experiences as well as contextually-aware interactions [45]. In addition to OG, we designed image icons that represented each one of the marine species. Such icons were placed on the beacons and appeared on the mobile screen upon encountering the specific marine species. Scientific content was presented to the children in form of written text appearing on the mobile screen. In the OS on the other hand, the information was triggered by the beacons, however without any image icon. There, the content was presented to the children through narration and several short and hand-drawn animations. Also, if a child would leave the proximity area of a beacon (while accessing content), all the other beacons were muted to reduce the interference.

Fig. 1. Estimote (http://www.estimote.com/) proximity beacons (left), representation of digital icon detected with phone when nearby the specie (middle) and image icon attached to the beacon on specie glass container (right) designed to attract attention to the selected museums' taxidermied marine species

The Ocean Game (OG). Designed as a point driven treasure-hunt, (Fig. 2, left), where children were prompted to search around the museum for each one of the 13-marine species signaled by visual images and in order to collect the points and digital icons. Children were invited to find and read 3 curious scientific facts about each specie. Once in proximity area of a beacon, a digital icon of the selected specie and a small animation was displayed on the device's screen. Using gestures such as taps and swipes, the children would browse 3 scientific facts related to that specific specie presented as short texts (Fig. 2, left). Each accomplished task would grant them points and several icons to collect on their mobile screen. At the end of the game, once all species are collected, children are asked to answer a quiz, which would give them points and rewards. The goal of the OG was to invite children to collect as many visual images as possible, as well as the points related to the correctness of their answers. A visual image of the species could only be collected once the user had read the three curiosities and photographed him or herself with the species. The collection of these selfie snapshots was, in our understanding, important to bridge the real-life surrounding with the mechanics of the game. At the end of the game, a special ranking was established, paring the children with certain marine species based on their quiz results (Fig. 2, left).

Fig. 2. Ocean Game (OG, on the left) and user Interface for treasure-hunting and marine species collection. Ocean Story (OS, on the right) depicting screenshots of diverse animations (intro, curiosities, outro)

The Ocean Story (OS). The story driven experience (Fig. 2, right) featured the same 13 marine species as short animations (4 image frames per second, in a loop). Hand drawn animations of all marine species were coupled with voiceover narration that described the animal's physical characteristics. The story features Madalena, a young fictional character, fond of the sea, who loses her precious notebook, full of scientific notes, during a storm. As a result, she is now asking our young audience to help her recover some of the notebook pages that are actually scattered around the museum. Madalena's story is conveyed by the voice of a young female actress. In addition to the narrated story, characteristic sounds of some exhibited species are added as background sounds (e.g.: the sound of the sea lion). The aesthetic quality of the animation as well as the aural qualities of the narration were intended to function as engaging mechanisms, payoff for the children's engagement. Once near the beacon, the animated content of the missing notebook page would pop up on the mobile screen. The content would narrate three scientific curiosities regarding a specific specie situated very close to the child. Before proceeding in the quest for more notebook pages, children had to view and listen to the three narrated scientific facts in their entirety. The OS participants were also given a headset for the purpose of immersing themselves in the story. Selfie images were omitted as we wanted to immerse children in the story. The story ends with the collection of 13 pages of Madalena's notebook, each one focused on a particular taxidermied species of the museum collection. At the end of the journey Madalena' thanks her young helpers and encourages to visit the museum again.

2   Methodology

We tested the OG and the OS with two distinct groups of children, with the same age and demographics. Our participants were between 9 and 10 years of age, 16 children participated in the gamified experience (OG) while 12 children participated in the story-driven experience (OS). In order to compare and contrast the outcomes generated by the gamified (OG) and the story driven (OS) approach to the museum exhibits, three distinct measurements were performed:

- **[M1]** - In both the OG and the OS, we measured skin conductance (hereafter SC) in order to measure children's physiological arousal during their use of each application. The collected data corresponds to 15 s before, and 15 s after specified key moments of each experience, namely the timestamps when the species or notebook pages have discovered.
- **[M2]** - We used pre and post test quizzes to evaluate what the children had learned from each experience. These tests included 13 short questions regarding each one of the 13 taxidermied marine species that were compiled based on our experience (e.g. "Which species use echolocation?"). For each question, multiple-choice answers with three species as examples were provided. For the OG, post test questions were presented on the mobile screen of the application, whereas for the OS, questions were presented on paper, to coincide with the metaphor of the Madalena's notebook.
- **[M3]** - Finally, we used the post test experience scales for (i) enjoyment (Smiley-ometer) and (ii) engagement (Again-Again Table) from the User Evaluation Toolkit, and (iii) surveys on intrinsic motivation [14, 38], by asking children to rate their own enjoyment, engagement, and intrinsic motivation. In the case of enjoyment, we asked children whether they were happy to participate. Regarding engagement, we asked children to rate whether they would be willing to undergo the experience a second time. Finally, for motivation we asked them to rate questions such as: 'I liked to explore the museum'; 'This activity was fun'; etc. M1 and M3 were further complemented with qualitative observations, that were collected during the children's experiences for both the OG and the OS.

Our study leverages the potential of unobtrusive sensing technologies to collect data regarding users' interactions in the museum context. Recent research shows an increased interest in unobtrusive sensing of interactive experiences [29, 42]. While research on technology driven experiences and gaming is very well established, physiological analysis and unobtrusive sensing in-the-wild is a growing area of interest in affective computing and interaction design [11, 35, 36]. However, there is still a scarcity of emotional understanding of the usage of interactive applications used by younger audiences in-situ. In order to obtain the emotional insight of the children during interactive experiences inside museums, we used the Empatica E4[1], a comfortable wireless wristband, which collect emotional arousal through skin conductance (SC) which is relevant to depicting stress, excitement and empathy [20, 46]. We collected the SC for each and whole participants' experience.

3   Results

In this section, we report on our obtained measurements, in-situ observations while mapping them to our three main research questions:

- **[R1]** - **Skin Conductance Responses.** In the case of OG, we analyzed and compared skin conductance responses of participants whilst standing in front of the same marine specie for 30 s (Fig. 3, left).

---

[1] https://www.empatica.com/e4-wristband.

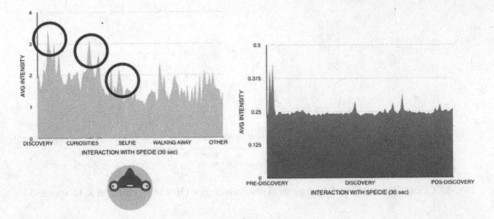

Fig. 3. Ocean Game (OG, left, 30 s × 16 children × 1 marine specie) and Ocean Story (OS, right, 30 s × 12 children × 1 marine specie) - Skin Conductance average during the discovery of a single marine specie (30 s of interactions). **OG Case:** Circles distinguishing the peaks (from left to right): (i) marine species discovered; (ii) curiosities explored; (iii) selfie image taken. **OS Case:** moments include: (i) pre-discovery; (ii) discovery; and (iii) post-discovery.

We have identified three occurring peak patterns (from left to right) and classified them according to the following categories: (i) DISCOVERY (obtained from collected timestamp from the application and synchronized with the wristband) - the moment when marine species and the corresponding beacon has been detected by the phone, and when the visual image of the species performs a subtle animation; (ii) CURIOSITIES (time difference between SELFIE and DISCOVERY) - the moment when participants browse or listen to each one of the three scientific curiosities and explore the characteristics of each marine specie; and (iii) SELFIE (timestamp obtained similarly as in DISCOVERY) - in here, when participants take a selfie snapshot with a single taxidermied marine species. We used these categories to reflect on the diverse moments of arousal paired with the action the child was performing. After analyzing the data, we identified presence of more arousal peaks during the interaction with OG rather than with OS. In fact, in the case of OS, there has been no significant differences between the moments of before, during and after discovering the species (Fig. 3). When analyzing the grand average of SC during the OG, we can observe a declining trend line where the DISCOVERY moment is dominant, followed by the CURIOSITIES and the SELFIE (Fig. 4). In the case of the OS, we did not find any significant differences when comparing the moments before and after discovering each notebook page, and while watching each one of the animations. Children were equally aroused during the animation watching and discovery actions. This suggests that the discovery of the image icon on the beacon (used in OG) or the appearance of it on the screen of the device might cause children to react with excitement to the interaction. Finally, by comparing the grand averages of SC's of all children, for both the OG and the OS (Fig. 5), we find that children are aroused 27% more during the OG.

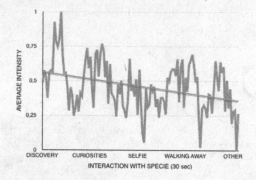

Fig. 4. Ocean Game – Grand average of skin conductance (30 s × 16 children × 13 species)

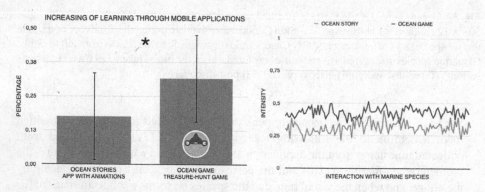

Fig. 5. Comparison of increasing of learning (on the left, with statistical significance) and comparison of grand average of skin conductance (on the right) across the Ocean Story (OS) and the Ocean Game (OG)

- **[R2] - Pre and Post Learning Tests.** Regarding the Q2, we performed the independent Samples T-Test analysis on the pre and post tests from OS (M = 0.18, SD = 0.16, rated by 12 children) and OG (M = 0.32, SD = 0.16, rated by 16 children). Percentage score gain showed significant statistical difference (t = −2.263, p = 0.038) with 95% CI (0.105, 0.175) and large effect size (d = −0.864) for OG. In fact, OS group learning was not significant at all (t = 2.2, p = 0.812) while OG clearly was (t = 2.13, p < 0.00001) with 95% CI (−925.448, 919.322) and large effect size (d = −1,769). Moreover, OS group forgot the knowledge (pre test 91 vs post test 89 correct answers) while OG group increased their ocean literacy knowledge for 44% (from 109 correct answers to 158) as seen in Fig. 5, on the left.
- **[R3] - Experience Scales.** In referring to Q3, at the end of children's exploration of the museum, we asked them to rate their own experiences. Enjoyment and engagement scales in both OG and OS were rated by all 28 children with highest possible scores (M = 5.00/5.00 for enjoyment, and M = 3.00/3.00 for engagement). Moreover, intrinsic motivation scales in the OG (M = 4.73/5.00, SD = 0.65, rated by 16 children) and in the OS (M = 4.69/5.00, SD = 0.64, rated by 12 children) show the data not to

be statistically significant ($t = -1.564$, $p = 0.14$). This suggest that both the OG and the OS have the potential of providing similar levels of enjoyment, engagement and intrinsic motivation. Moreover, while observing the children in museum, each group seemed to like both the experiences and the mobile applications.

Timeline Observations. We compared the starting and ending times of all participants for both interactive experiences. Start was identified as a moment when pressing the tag button on Empatica E4 wristband, located on the child's wrist. The end time was identified as a moment when all of the species were collected and quiz responded (OG) or final video watched (OS). In this case, the Ocean Game (OG) timeline showed that all 16 children managed to collect the marine species as well as answer the quiz in an average time of 13 min. For the Ocean Story (OS) the average time of the experiences was 14′22″ (excluding the written test) while the sum of timings of all animations is 13′44″. This shows that children had in average only 38″ to explore the museum and might suggest that children were speeding up the videos. We also observed that in the Ocean Story when children found one notebook page, they would soon move away from the spot where they encountered the content, to explore the rest of museum looking for more pages. When observing the OS participants, children's body language revealed signs of impatience (e.g. constant and rapid movements with one leg) while watching the animations. Moreover, 5 out of 10 children also had a negative time, meaning that they completed the experience before all animations had been completely watched (even below the total time of 13′44″).

In-Situ Observations. During both experiments, we observed children in action and notes were taken in response to our own direct observations. In the end of both experiences, participants were asked for a verbal evaluation of each experience. Regarding the OS, the participants were focused on finding the notebook pages, and rarely stopped to watch the animations. Since the OS content was not signaled by any colored sticker or marker, the children seemed confused or restless and they could not properly identify where to look for it. Our initial choice for not using image stickers was intended to make the task of finding each page more enticing and less obvious. On the other hand, according to our observations, we noted that it did negatively impact the children's exploration of the exhibit. Without visible markers, we often had to help the children find content within the various museum exhibits. Children's verbal feedback about the OS pointed out both positive and negative aspects of the experiences. Regarding the positive ones, the children stated that they liked searching and discovering the pages around the museum, having 7 of them mentioning things like "I like everything! There isn't anything I disliked," but only one of them explicitly reported that he liked to listen to the narrative. Regarding the less positive aspects, 5 of the children reported that they did not like the fact that it was mandatory to listen to all of the narrated scientific curiosities. In fact, we observed that when children would discover a page, they would soon move away to explore the rest of exhibit looking for more. This meant not fully watching some of the animations. Despite the fact that the other beacons were muted while content was running, the children found a way out, and speeded up the animations in order to complete the OS experience without listening to the narrations in full. Moreover, listening to audio in pairs was not something that the children were willing to do, thus when in pairs they always skipped content and moved to the next phase of the experience. Furthermore, it is interesting to notice that none of the children referred to the animations in a positive nor a negative way. In fact, they only talked about the narrated story. On the other hand, we did not ask specific questions regarding the visual qualities of the animations.

In the case of OG, most obvious observation revolved around the fact that most of the children's attention was spent on the task of taking a self-portrait with each one of the 13-marine species (this was also one of the peak arousal patters detected through the SC data). We also noticed that most of the children were concerned with their physical presentation in the self-portraits. Only few of the participants were interested in observing the taxidermied artifacts, and most children spent their time running around the museum in search for the image icons (which coincided with a peak arousal moment according to the SC data). However, the children that were focused on the museum artifacts were often thinking out loud with expressions such as: "I did not know that the seahorses were such small creatures. I thought they were bigger than this". These observations show that the children were connecting the digital visual images of the game with the artifacts that were presented in the museum. We were also able to conclude that most children were highly interested in collecting the image icons and points. Moreover, the children who focused on the museum artifacts were the only ones who actually took self-portraits with the taxidermied species as opposed to the rest of the children who were taking self-portraits with the image icon that was covering the proximity beacon. Also, only a few children spent time reading the scientific information presented in short texts on the screen, after capturing each marine specie's image icon. From the insights from post tests, it was evident that not all of them took the time or read or even understand the information. Overall, most children were reading or looking through the text quite rapidly and rushing through the game with the aim of finishing it on time. Regarding the quiz, at the end of the game, we noted one child worrying about their performance: "Ouch, I might not be able to get it right." Another child went back to the exhibit and as way of verifying their answers. Similarly to OS, all the children when asked reported feeling of excitement and enjoyment regarding the experience.

4   Discussion

In this section, we discuss the obtained results, report our insights, outline several research limitations as well as potential future studies.

Children and Scientific Information Delivery.   In both applications, while both interventions were met with high excitement by all children, we detected difficulties in engaging children with the scientific information proposed. Reflecting on the users' timelines we noted that the story-driven experience (OS) was sometimes completed before the total time that it would take to watch all of the animations in a sequence. While observing, we noted signs of impatience in children's body posture while listening to the narrations. We envisage that audio narrations, even if enhanced by special marine and underwater sounds, were not enough to hold the children's attention. We can attribute this to the unfinished qualities of some of the animations. More nuanced plot and character development as well as longer and more detailed animations accompanying the narrations might yield different results. Also, listening to audio in pairs was not an easy task for the children, who would excite each other and want to move on to more action together. For the Ocean Game (OG) similarly, children often just skimmed through the scientific curiosities reported in text, they often would not read but just pretend to, in order to be able to get the points and collect image icons. The results then were evident in the learning evaluation where they were not able to recall the correct answers to the post test questions.

Ocean Game Versus Ocean Story Excitement. Regarding Q1, and according to the collected data, the game experience resulted more exciting than the story experience. Data from biofeedback reveal that children were nearly one third more aroused during the OG rather than the OS (Fig. 5, right). Despite that it is arduous enough to derive exact explanations form the biofeedback alone, we can attempt some reasoning of the why's. Children experiencing the OS lost focus due to the visually repetitive nature of some of the animations and lack of visual signals in the museum to help them look for the content. In fact, the encounters with the marine species' digital icons in OG portrayed the highest arousal moment (overall for both experiences). However, we should take into account that it is entirely possible that the children were just excited to be at the museum, regardless of the technology employed.

Treasure-Hunting and Collecting Mechanisms. Through both studies we detected the highly motivating and exciting results from the treasure hunt (OG and OS) and collecting (OG) mechanisms generated by the applications. From our observations of the OG, we noted that children's excitement would raise when digital icons would appear on their mobile screen, as the children were producing sounds of excitement. On the other hand, in order to give prominence and flow to the story in OS, we did not place any visual cues to help children find content. The treasure hunt feeling in the OS was weakened instead of strengthened. Children were still motivated to look around the museum for content but less excitement was detected in the task. Moreover, we observe that children in OG were willing to find the species incentivized by the task of collecting the digital icons corresponding to each marine specie. As observed by O'Hara et al. [34], collection goals help children motivate their task when using playful mobile learning tools. This was not the case in OS.

Learning Outcomes. The OG reported double learning outcomes compared to the OS, despite the fact that engaging children with the learning content proved challenging in both applications. Regarding Q2, findings showed from the pre and post tests that children learned twice as much when engaged with the gamified experience when compared to the story-driven one. We would assume that, with the OG experience, the learning of the scientific information was reinforced by being presented as a short text and animated icons, compared to the long animations and narrations of the OS. In line with this, we can infer that the story-driven experience was asking for a higher and longer-term concentration. We can summarize that information is best presented as short nuggets of facts instead of longer scientific narrations. Long-term retention seems limited, so strategies for improving it are interesting areas for future work.

Games and Stories in Relation to Engagement and Motivation During Museum Visits. Finally, in relation to Q3, the children expressed themselves positively regarding engagement and intrinsic motivation for both the OG and the OS interactive experiences. Conversely, most of the children showed interest when searching and discovering the exhibition artifacts in novel ways. Nonetheless, we need to be also aware that their feedback could be a consequence of children acquiesce bias, as children are notoriously willing to please the adults and teachers. Therefore, we are aware of the limitations of using these scales as sole measurements of enjoyment and engagement to demonstrate how our young audience genuinely responded to both experiences.

5   Concluding Remarks

In summary, we learned that children are easy to engage in treasure hunt tasks and enjoy the use of both mobile games and mobile stories. The gamifications aspect of collecting digital icons, points and achievements worked well as a motivation to search around the museum. Nevertheless, this needs to be balanced with a more careful interface design so that the exploration does not take over from the learning objectives. Audio narration is not enough of a channel to involve young children with scientific content, even if coupled with simple animations, while short text seemed more effective. We envisage that with more appealing animations supporting the narrative, these results could be revisited and eventually we want to extend our testing to check the children's emotional connections with the story and its characters, or the digital icons of the marine species collected during the game. Finally, for these analyses we should take into the consideration that the age of children might have played an important role and how easily they engage in gaming practices rather than more reflective story experiences. Also, skin conductance data lack baselines per each child which are omitted with the purpose of avoiding the in-vitru setting and focusing on experience. Conversely, interference of wristbands with the clothes or activities of children might affect the data. Also, recruiting at least 20 participants per treatment would alleviate statistical issues with sample size. The story component was also focused on audio over visuals, however the oral narration could be much more compelling if accompanied by other sounds, which we tend to improve in future versions. Future work will also focus on improving several aspects of both applications, balancing learning with playful aspects of both, and on multimodal analysis of the differences of other collected physiological data (heart-rate variability inferred from blood-volume pulse, temperature, and movement from accelerometer) in comparison with our skin conductance results.

Acknowledgements. We wish to express our gratitude to the director and staff from the Museum of Natural History of Funchal (MNHF). We are very thankful to Dina Dionisio from M-ITI for helping us during the user-testing sessions with the children. Also, a special thank you goes to actress Sophie Gouveia from Teatro Metaphora in Câmara de Lobos. We would also like to acknowledge the work of animation students Tyler Carrigan, Pamela Gray and Amy Bruning from

Edinburgh College of Art. The sound recording of a pilot whale that was used in the Ocean Stories application was provided by the Whale Museum of Madeira while sounds of a monk seal were provided by the Madeiran Institute for Nature Conservation (IP-RAM). The work reported in this contribution was developed with the support of ARDITI (Project Number M14-20-09-5369-FSE-000001), the University of Edinburgh (CAHSS Knowledge Exchange and Impact grant) and the MITIExcell - EXCELENCIA INTERNACIONAL DE IDT&I NAS TIC funding (Project Number M1420-01-01450FEDER0000002), provided by the Regional Government of Madeira.

References

1. Aarseth, E.: Cybertext: Perspectives on Ergodic Literature. The Johns Hopkins University Press, Baltimore and London (1997)
2. Aarseth, E.: Genre trouble: narrativism and the art of simulation. In: Wardrip-Fruin, N., Harrigan, P. (eds.) First Person: New Media as Story, Performance, and Game. The MIT Press, Cambridge (2004)
3. Bakken, S.M., Pierroux, P.: Framing a topic: mobile video tasks in museum learning. Learn. Cult. Soc. Interact. **5**, 54–65 (2015)
4. Barton, J., Kindberg, T.: The Cooltown User Experience. HP Hewlett Packard, Palo Alto (2001)
5. Beale, K.: Museums at Play: Games, Interaction and Learning. Museums Etc, Edinburgh (2011)
6. Bedford, L.: Storytelling: the real work of museums. Curator Mus. J. **44**(1), 27–34 (2001)
7. Bogost, I.: Persuasive Games: The Expressive Power of Videogames. The MIT Press, Cambridge (2007)
8. Cabrera, J.S., Frutos, H.M., Stoica, A.G., et al.: Mystery in the museum: collaborative learning activities using handheld devices. In: Proceedings of the 7th International Conference on Human Computer Interaction with Mobile Devices and Services, pp. 315–318. ACM (2005)
9. Cahill, C., Kuhn, A., Schmoll, S., Lo, W.-T., McNally, B., Quintana, C.: Mobile learning in museums: how mobile supports for learning influence student behavior. In: Proceedings of the 10th International Conference on Interaction Design and Children, pp. 21–28. ACM (2011)
10. Charitonos, K., Blake, C., Scanlon, E., Jones, A.: Museum learning via social and mobile technologies: (how) can online interactions enhance the visitor experience? Br. J. Educ. Technol. **43**(5), 802–819 (2012)
11. Clegg, T., Norooz, L., Kang, S., Byrne, V., Katzen, M., Valez, R., Bonsignore, E.: Live physiological sensing and visualization ecosystems: an activity theory analysis. In: Proceedings of the 2017 CHI Conference on Human Factors in Computing Systems, pp. 2029–2041. ACM (2017)
12. Damala, A., van der Vaart, M., Clarke, L., et al.: Evaluating tangible and multisensory museum visiting experiences: lessons learned from the meSch project. In: Museums and the Web 2016, MW 2016 (2016)
13. Deterding, S., Björk, S.L., Nacke, L.E., Dixon, D., Lawley, E.: Designing gamification: creating gameful and playful experiences. In: CHI 2013 Extended Abstracts on Human Factors in Computing Systems, pp. 3263–3266. ACM (2013)
14. Dijk, E., Lingnau, A., Kockelkorn, H.: Measuring enjoyment of an interactive museum experience. In: Proceedings of the 14th ACM International Conference on Multimodal Interaction (ICMI 2012), pp. 249–256 (2012). https://doi.org/10.1145/2388676.2388728

15. Dini, R., Paternò, F., Santoro, C.: An environment to support multi-user interaction and cooperation for improving museum visits through games. In: Proceedings of the 9th International Conference on Human Computer Interaction with Mobile Devices and Services, pp. 515–521. ACM (2007)

16. Edwards, S., Schaller, D.: The name of the game: museums and digital learning elements. In: Din, H., Hecht, P. (eds.) The Digital Museum: A Think Guide. American Association of Museums, Washington, DC (2007)

17. Falk, J.H., Dierking, L.D.: Learning from Museums: Visitor Experiences and the Making of Meaning. AltaMira Press, Walnut Creek (2000)

18. Fleck, M., Frid, M., Kindberg, T., O'Brien-Strain, E., Rajani, R., Spasojevic, M.: From informing to remembering: ubiquitous systems in interactive museums. IEEE Pervasive Comput. 1(2), 13–21 (2012)

19. Hawkey, R.: Learning with Digital Technologies in Museums, Science Centres and Galleries. NESTA Futurelab Research (2004)

20. Hernandez, J., McDuff, D., Benavides, X., Amores, J., Maes, P., Picard, R.W.: AutoEmotive: bringing empathy to the driving experience to manage stress. In: Proceedings of the Companion Publication on Designing Interactive Systems, (DIS 2014), Vancouver, BC, Canada, 21–25 June 2014. https://doi.org/10.1145/2598784.2602780

21. Hsi, S., Fait, H.: RFID enhances visitors' museum experience at the exploratorium. Commun. ACM 48(9), 60–65 (2005)

22. Ioannidis, Y., El Raheb, K., Toli, E., Katifori, A., Boile, M., Mazura, M.: One object many stories: Introducing ICT in museums and collections through digital storytelling. In: Digital Heritage International Congress (DigitalHeritage), vol. 1, pp. 421–424. IEEE (2013)

23. Jenkins, H.: Game design as narrative architecture. In: Wardrip-Fruin, N., Harrigan, P. (eds.) First Person: New Media as Story, Performance, and Game. The MIT Press, Cambridge (2004)

24. Juul, J.: Games telling stories? - a brief note on games and narratives. Game Stud. 1(1) (2001). http://www.gamestudies.org

25. Katifori, A., et al.: CHESS: personalized storytelling experiences in museums. In: Mitchell, A., Fernández-Vara, C., Thue, D. (eds.) ICIDS 2014. LNCS, vol. 8832, pp. 232–235. Springer, Cham (2014). https://doi.org/10.1007/978-3-319-12337-0_28

26. Kelly, L.: The interrelationships between adult museum visitors' learning and their museum experiences (2007). http://australianmuseum.net.au/uploads/documents/6663/final%20thesis%20for%20graduation_kelly.pdf

27. Koushik, M., Lee, E.J., Pieroni, L., Sun, E., Yeh, C.-W.: Re-envisioning the museum experience: combining new technology with social-networking. In: Yang, H.S., Malaka, R., Hoshino, J., Han, J.H. (eds.) ICEC 2010. LNCS, vol. 6243, pp. 248–253. Springer, Heidelberg (2010). https://doi.org/10.1007/978-3-642-15399-0_24

28. Laurel, B.: Computers as Theatre. Addison-Wesley Longman Publishing Co., Inc., Boston (1991)

29. Liang, F., Nakatani, M., Kunze, K., Minamizawa, K.: Personalized record of the city Wander with a wearable device: a pilot study. In: Proceedings of the 2016 ACM International Joint Conference on Pervasive and Ubiquitous Computing: Adjunct, pp. 141–144. ACM, New York (2016)

30. Martin, J., Trummer, C.: Personalized multimedia information system for museums and exhibitions. In: Maybury, M., Stock, O., Wahlster, W. (eds.) INTETAIN 2005. LNCS, vol. 3814, pp. 332–335. Springer, Heidelberg (2005). https://doi.org/10.1007/11590323_46

31. Marty, P.F., Mendenhall, A., Douglas, I., et al.: The iterative design of a mobile learning application to support scientific inquiry. J. Learn. Des. 6(2), 41–66 (2013)

32. Murray, J.: From game-story to cyberdrama. In: Wardrip-Fruin, N., Harrigan, P. (eds.) First Person: New Media as Story, Performance, and Game. The MIT Press, Cambridge (2004)
33. Nilsson, T., Blackwell, A., Hogsden, C., Scruton, D.: Ghosts! a location-based Bluetooth LE mobile game for museum exploration. arXiv:1607.05654 [cs] (2016). Accessed 14 Jan 2017
34. O'Hara, K., Kindberg, T., Glancy, M., Baptista, L., Sukumaran, B., Kahana, G., Rowbotham, J.: Collecting and sharing location-based content on mobile phones in a zoo visitor experience. Comput. Support. Coop. Work (CSCW) **16**(1–2), 11–44 (2007)
35. Onorati, F., Regalia, G., Caborni, C., Picard, R.: Improvement of a convulsive seizure detector relying on accelerometer and electrodermal activity collected continuously by a wristband. Presented at the 2016 Epilepsy Pipeline Conference, San Francisco, California (2016)
36. Picard, R.W.: Measuring affect in the wild. In: D'Mello, S., Graesser, A., Schuller, B., Martin, J.-C. (eds.) ACII 2011. LNCS, vol. 6974, p. 3. Springer, Heidelberg (2011). https://doi.org/10.1007/978-3-642-24600-5_3
37. Pierroux, P., Bannon, L., Walker, K., Hall, T., Kaptelinin, V., Stuedahl, D.: MUSTEL: framing the design of technology-enhanced learning activities for museum visitors. Archives & Museum Informatics (2007)
38. Read, J., Macfarlane, S.: Endurability, engagement and expectations: measuring children's fun. In: Interaction Design and Children, pp. 1–23. Shaker Publishing (2002)
39. Ryan, M.: From narrative games to playable stories: toward a poetics of interactive narrative. Storyworlds J. Narrat. Stud. **1**, 43–59 (2009)
40. Sánchez, I., Cortés, M., Riekki, J., Oja, M.: NFC-based interactive learning environments for children. In: Proceedings of the 10th International Conference on Interaction Design and Children, pp. 205–208. ACM (2011). https://doi.org/10.1145/1999030.1999062
41. Shaffer, D.W., Squire, K.R., Halverson, R., Gee, J.P.: Video games and the future of learning. Phi Delta Kappan **87**(2), 105–111 (2005)
42. Sparrow, L.: Variations in visual exploration and physiological reactions during art perception when children visit the museum with a mobile electronic guide. In: Kapoula, Z., Vernet, M. (eds.) Aesthetics and Neuroscience, pp. 131–137. Springer, Cham (2016). https://doi.org/10.1007/978-3-319-46233-2_9
43. Springer, J., Borst Brazas, J., Kajder, S.: Digital storytelling at the national gallery of art. In: Bearman, D., Trant, J. (eds.) Museums and the Web. Archives & Museums Informatics, Arlington (2004)
44. Sung, Y.-T., Chang, K.-E., Hou, H.-T., Chen, P.-F.: Designing an electronic guidebook for learning engagement in a museum of history. Comput. Hum. Behav. **26**(1), 74–83 (2010)
45. Sykes, E.R., Pentland, S., Nardi, S.: Context-aware mobile apps using iBeacons: towards smarter interactions. In: Proceedings of the 25th Annual International Conference on Computer Science and Software Engineering, pp. 120–129. IBM Corp. (2015)
46. Westerink, J.H., Van Den Broek, E.L., Schut, M.H., Van Herk, J., Tuinenbreijer, K.: Computing emotion awareness through galvanic skin response and facial electromyography. In: Westerink, J.H.D.M., Ouwerkerk, M., Overbeek, T.J.M., Pasveer, W.F., de Ruyter, B. (eds.) Probing Experience, pp. 149–162. Springer, Dordrecht (2008). https://doi.org/10.1007/978-1-4020-6593-4_14
47. Wyman, B., Smith, S., Meyers, D., Godfrey, M.: Digital Storytelling in museums: observations and best practices. Curator Mus. J. **54**(4), 461–468 (2011)
48. Xhembulla, J.R.: Intrigue at the museum: facilitating engagement and learning through a location-based mobile game. International Association for the Development of the Information Society (2014). https://eric.ed.gov/?id=ED557238. Accessed 15 Jan 2017

49. Zimmerman, E.: Narrative, interactivity, play, and games: four naughty concepts in need of discipline. In: Wardrip-Fruin, N., Harrigan, P. (eds.) First Person: New Media as Story, Performance, and Game. The MIT Press, Cambridge (2004)

Emotion and Personality

Using Interactive Storytelling to Identify Personality Traits

Raul Paradeda[1,2]([✉]), Maria José Ferreira[1,3], Carlos Martinho[1], and Ana Paiva[1]

[1] INESC-ID and Instituto Superior Técnico, University of Lisbon, Lisbon, Portugal
{raul.paradeda,maria.jose.ferreira}@tecnico.ulisboa.pt,
{carlos.martinho,ana.paiva}@gaips.inesc-id.pt
[2] Rio Grande do Norte State University, Natal, Brazil
[3] Madeira Interactive Technologies Institute, Madeira, Portugal

Abstract. Each person feels and understands stories in a unique way. Stories have different meanings to people, and those depend on their personal experiences and personality. Each one of us is unique, with unique personality traits, classifiable through personality trait theories, such as the Myers-Briggs theory. In this paper, we describe how we have created a database of 155 individuals to extract their personality classifications based on Myers-Briggs Type Indicator and then used the fact that each person's individual traits impact the interpretation of interactive storytelling. With this work, we intend to perceive transparently (i.e. without questionnaire and using the language of the interactive experience itself) the person's personality in order to create through the use of persuasion a personalised narrative experience. Through a concrete study, we show how an Interactive Storytelling scenario can be used to identify users personality traits. In particular, by extracting the decisions taken by a user in an interactive storytelling scenario, we are able to predict the user's MBTI personality traits.

Keywords: Interactive storytelling · Personality traits · Myers-briggs type indicator · Decision points · Preferences

1 Introduction

Interactive Storytelling (IS) emerges from the overlap of narrative theory and computing [11]. Fundamental to IS is the role of the user who can perform activities that will significantly affect the story delivery or the story world [2]. In fact, IS has been used widely in different areas, such as to aid children to expand their imagination, improve their understanding of sensations and situations and to assist in the literacy learning [7,14]. Furthermore, a storytelling focused approach to education can be applied to learning literacy, both in primary and secondary school [16].

Yet, all of us are understand, interpret and feel stories in different ways. The personality traits of the students influence the way they approach education and

© Springer International Publishing AG 2017
N. Nunes et al. (Eds.): ICIDS 2017, LNCS 10690, pp. 181–192, 2017.
https://doi.org/10.1007/978-3-319-71027-3_15

how they learn. A good example is the work of [10] that claim that students are more likely to perform well and to trust their efficacy if they are interested in a topic. Student's preferences and personality affect their effort and persistence affecting their performance. That is, a person's personality has a vast influence on their way of life, their preferences, and how to take decisions.

Additionally, even in the games industry [6], the strategies of IS are used to lead the player through a path inside a story depending on the decisions made by that player. Famous games such as GTA^1, $Assassin's\ Creed^2$ and $Diablo^3$ use features of IS. Yet, in such games where there are different paths to take, which path the player should choose to enjoy more the game? Or, more specifically, which path can be better given his/her personality traits?

In some games, the choice of the path or even the game to be played depends on how the player think, feel and behave, which is dependent on the players' personality traits. For example, it seems more likely that a sportive person would enjoy soccer games, or a pacifist person would choose the more peaceful path in a war game.

Having the aforementioned in mind, this work describes the use of an IS scenario to identify the personality traits of the players according to the Myers-Briggs Type Indicator (MBTI) theory. The idea is that, as a user navigates through an interactive story she/he will have several Decisions Points (DP's), and those decisions are made according to the user's personality. Thus, as these DP's are shown during the story and are the trigger to activate a particular path, depending on the decision made, we can, in fact, determine the personality of the person. In other words, without applying questionnaire and using the language of the interactive experience itself, we will be able to perceive the person's personality in a transparent way. On the other hand, if we know the personality traits of the user, we can predict the path the user is going to take. Besides, with the correct identification of the person's personality and applying a persuasion technique, it will be possible to create a more individualised narrative experience that might be more attractive for different individuals.

In the research here presented we describe this dual influence. To do that, first, we applied an MBTI questionnaire to classify the person's personality traits and at the same time create a dataset to future comparisons. Secondly, with one small group of users that answered the MBTI questionnaire, we asked them to play our carefully designed interactive story. Finally, we compared the results obtained in the game and the questionnaire for this small group. The results show that we can identify (based on their decisions) in which MBTI personality, the player's personality traits can be associated. We were also able to establish

---

[1] Grand Theft Auto. Developers: DMA Design and Tarantula Studios. Publisher for Windows: Rockstar Games. Release: October 1997.

[2] Assassin's Creed. Developers: Ubisoft, Gameloft, Griptonite Games and Blue Byte. Publisher: Ubisoft. Release: November 2007.

[3] Diablo. Developers: Blizzard Entertainment, Synergistic Software (Hellfire expansion) and Climax Group. Publishers: Blizzard Entertainment and Sierra Entertainment. Release: December 1996.

some patterns related to the personality traits, in particular, whether players with the same personality will choose the same paths.

2   Personality Traits

Personality traits are essential characteristics of the human being, and they are factors that can influence our preferences and decision making. In the work of [17], the author describes a study aimed to find out how the personality affects ratio preference. The methodology used was, firstly was classified the personality traits according to a personality theory and, then, asked the participants to estimate the preferences to 15 horizontal and 15 vertical rectangles with different ratios, respectively. As results, the authors describe that there is a tendency of preference for the ratio of a square, the average degree of preference for golden ratios and a gradual declining dislike for ratios after golden ratios; and the personality impact the ratio of preference.

The research previously mentioned is just an example of how our personality may define what we enjoy or not. In this way, our main research tries to understand *the potential of IS to determine personality traits*.

The term personality trait was created to relate to enduring personal characteristics that are revealed in a particular pattern of behaviour in a variety of situations. In the literature, it is possible to find several instruments that can be used to categorise the person's personality traits, in particular, the Myers-Briggs Type Indicator (MBTI). MBTI is an introspective self-report questionnaire designed to indicate psychological preferences in how people perceive the world and make decisions [8]. It was constructed by Katharine Cook Briggs and her daughter Isabel Briggs Myers, and it is based on the typological theory proposed by Carl Jung [3]. *"The underlying assumption of the MBTI is that we all have specific preferences in the way we construe our experiences, and these preferences underlie our interests, needs, values and motivation"* [4]. This theory considers 16 personality types, resulting from the combination of four opposite pairs, representing preferences or dichotomies. The four possible pairs are Extraversion (E) - Introversion (I); Sensing (S) - iNtuition (N); Thinking (T) - Feeling (F) and Judging (J) or Perceiving (P). None of these types is "better" or "worse"; however, Briggs and Myers theorised that people innately "prefer" one overall the combination of type differences [8]. These types are typically referred to acronyms of four letters, the initial letters of each of the four type of preferences (except in the case of intuition, which uses the abbreviation 'N' to distinguish it from introversion). For instance, *ESTJ* stand for Extraversion, Sensing, Thinking and Judgement.

In this work, it was adopted the MBTI [15] as an instrument to evaluate and measure the decisions and preferences made by the player. Because, it has the characteristics of allowing to relate the scores obtained in the questionnaire with a context, for example, the scores in *'EI'* and *'JP'* dichotomies are regarding attitudes (or orientations) that reflect the ways in which the person is energized and how is the structure, or live the life; and the dichotomies *'SN'* and *'TF'* are regarding the mental functions. The *'SN'* is related on how the person gathering the information and are used for perception; and the dichotomy *'TF'* is regarding on how the information are organised and the decision-making and are used for judgment. With these characteristics, the use of this theory shows as a promising strategy to use in an Interactive Storytelling scenario. As the player must deal with decision making during the story.

3   Personality Traits in Interactive Storytelling: Methodology

In an IS scenario, the listener can be considered as a player since he can be an active element of the story, which performs activities that will significantly affect the story outcomes or the story world and its characters [2]. In the book [13][p. 106], the authors present seven types of players, a description of how important this distinction is when it is intended to know and define some players characteristics. Having the aforementioned in mind, the person's personality has been a recurring choice in player modelling. The work of Birk et al. [1] show that several player characteristics have an impact on motivation, expressed in terms of enjoyment and effort. They also argue that player enjoyment and effort, impact players in-game behaviours. In this sense, the MBTI theory makes sense by focusing on how the player perceives information in the world and makes decisions based on that. For example, in [9] the authors describe a model that have seven different archetypes of players, how they can be related to the typology of MBTI and how each archetype characterises a particular playing style.

To investigate the link between IS and personality, we framed our problem around the following two research questions:

- **RQ1** *"The decisions taken during a Storytelling Experience can identify the player's personality traits?"*
- **RQ2** *"Do people play Interactive Stories according to their real personality?"*

In order to answer our research questions, we have built a model capable of identifying the player's personality trait in real-time using an IS. In this sense, our methodology was divided in four: (1) the MBTI questionnaire; (2) the story design; (3) the system development; and the (4) final study to assess the validity of the approach.

3.1   MBTI Questionnaire

The MBTI test has many versions with different numbers of questions and in this work, was used a questionnaire with 70 questions[4]. The 16 distinctive personalities are typically referred to as an abbreviation of four letters, as already mentioned. In this questionnaire, each question has two choices *'a'* and *'b'* that

---

[4] http://tracymanford.typepad.com/test.pdf.

identify a pair of dichotomies. For example, the first question measure whether the person can be classified as '*E*' or '*I*', the second measure whether the person can be classified as '*S*' or '*N*', and so. From the 70 questions that composed the questionnaire used, 10 classify the '*EI*' dichotomies, while the '*SM*', '*TF*' and '*JP*' are distinguish from 20 questions respectively. In this questionnaire, the personality traits classification is the sum of answers '*a*' and '*b*' for each dichotomy. This means that whenever the person has more '*b*' answers for questions that measure the dichotomies 'JP', she/he tend to be more *Perceiving* than *Judging*. The use of this specific questionnaire is regarding the number of questions, allowing person to answer it in a short period of time (less than 20 min) and the fact that has been used in previous works such as [12,17].

In this way, we intend to apply this questionnaire to as many participants as possible to create a database that contains their MBTI personalities. Besides, we intend to identify which questions are more relevant' and discriminating for each dichotomy. Suppose that in the first question all the participants that were classified as '*E*' had chosen the letter '*a*' as the answer and all the participants that were classified as '*I*' had chosen the letter '*b*', then this question could be considered a discriminant question. We decided to follow this approach because it is not interesting to create and apply an IS with 70 DP's (one for each MBTI question). Although, we intend to identify and use just the most relevant questions to make a relation between each DP and the MBTI questions (see the next sections for a better explanation). In order to identify those relevant questions for each dichotomy, it was used the Cohen's Kappa coefficient, Eq. (1), between questions. In our analyses, it was used the dichotomy regarding the answer made in the question as relative observed agreement and the dichotomy given by the result of the MBTI questionnaire as the hypothetical probability of chance agreement. For example, a person was classified as having the preference '*E*' by the MBTI test result (hypothetical probability of chance agreement) and her/his answer to a specific question that measures the dichotomies '*E – I*' it will be the relative observed agreement.

$$k = [Pr(a) - Pr(e)]/[1 - Pr(e)] \qquad (1)$$

In Eq. (1), *Pr(a)* is the relative observed agreement, *Pr(e)* is the hypothetical probability of chance agreement and k is the Cohen's kappa index value.

Since some questions stand out more than the others (see results in Sect. 4.1) we decided to calculate weights for each option ('*a*' and '*b*') of those relevant questions. This was considered to be appropriate once we were using only a set of questions from the MBTI questionnaire. The weights of each option will be given to each option of the DP's in the IS, according to the Eq. (2).

$$W(q) = Np(Opx)/[Np(Opx) + Np(Opy)] \qquad (2)$$

In Eq. (2), *W(q)* is the weight to be assumed by the question '*q*'; *Np(Opx)* is the total number of participants which answered the first option, '*x*' and *Np(Opy)* is the total number of participants which answered the second option, '*y*'.

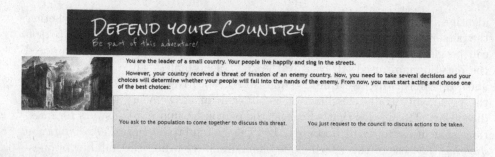

Fig. 1. Screen layout with the first scene of the IS.

3.2 Story Design

As mentioned earlier, an IS has DP's that work as triggers, to change the story flow. Using this feature, we intend to create a story with different paths that have DP's related to the MBTI questions. Particularly, as far the decisions are taken during the story, we intend to determine in which dichotomies of MBTI theory the players' personality trait can be related. For example, in a particular DP is measured whether the players have the predisposition to 'E' or 'I'.

During the story creation, that was written with the guidance of a professional with expertise in education, we tried to ensure that the participant is not influenced by any personality trait of the main character, after all, the protagonist will be the participant itself. To reinforce the previous idea, before the participants initiate the IS interaction, they were given the suggestion to act as if they were living this particular situation in reality. In addition, to reduce the possibility of incorporating a character very different from the participant it was introduced a character without background, own motivations, etc.

The story happens in the Middle Ages (or Medieval Period), and the user will perform the role of a country leader that received a threat from another country. The main goal of the story is to prevent her/his country from falling into the enemy hands. Furthermore, to captivate the player and increase her/his immersion during the story flow, in each scene a representative image of what is happening in the story is presented.

Figure 1 shows the beginning of the adventure and how the story is displayed to the player. At the top, is presented a banner with the name of the IS; on the left side, an image representative of the scene described in the middle, and in the bottom, it is presented two buttons with the possible decisions to be made. In this first scene, the dichotomies 'EI' is measured, with the follow decisions: *"You ask the population to come together to discuss this threat"* or *"You just request the council to discuss actions to be taken"*. In this DP, the first choice represents the extrovert dichotomy, 'E' and the second option to the introvert dichotomy, 'I' (both options are related to questions of the MBTI questionnaire).

The IS has a total of 30 DP's, but to finish it, the participant can go through a maximum of 21 DP's or a minimum of 16 DP's it all depends on the decisions taken. As mentioned before, each DP measures a specific dichotomy, so we tried to have the same amount of DP's for each dichotomy at each player interaction. For example, in the path where the player can reach the end of the story with 16 DP's, we ensure that he/she has chosen 4 DP's for each MBTI pair of dichotomy. The story should have an average duration of 20 min, and through the decisions made in each DP, we intend to find a pattern among people with the same personality traits regarding the decisions made.

At the end of the IS, we asked participants to fill in a questionnaire that was based on the work of [5] with some adaptations. Our goal with the survey is to measure: (a) what the participants thought about the decisions made and (b) what was their immersion level in the story.

3.3 System Development

For the implementation of the IS scenario, we used a multi-platform language, *C#*. This language allows us to use this scenario either as web and desktop platform. The goal is to use the desktop platform in the future, integrated with the frameworks that had been developed in our research group.

Figure 2 presents the model created for the IS scenario with the modules: Interactive Story Module (ISM) and Personality Module (PM). The Interactive Story module is responsible for showing to the user the text, the decisions to be made and an image. The Scene component gives the scene text, the Decision Points component provides the corresponding decisions, and the image that represents the scene is selected through the Immersion Component, see Fig. 1 for an example of the screen layout. After the user selects a decision, the Choices component saves it and send the proper preference and the weight of that decision to the PM. This module updates the correspondent preference value. In future, the PM will use the updated value to influence the ISM. At the end of the game, the

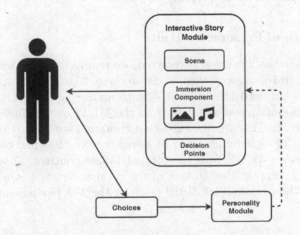

Fig. 2. Model created for the scenario used.

PM calculates the values received for each dichotomy and save the final MBTI classification according to our methodology. The calculation is done using the following equation:

$$D(x|y) = \begin{cases} x, \, if \sum_{(w(x))} > \sum_{(w(y))} \\ y, \, otherwise \end{cases} \qquad (3)$$

In Eq. (3), $D(x|y)$ is the dichotomy to be given to the participant, $w(x)$ is the weights of the dichotomy 'x' and $w(y)$ is the weights of the dichotomy 'y'.

3.4   Study

Our approach involves two steps: the first is gathering the information from the personality traits and the second is to play the IS. Regarding the first step, we had 200 people answering the on-line MBTI questionnaire[5] and as a motivation factor to them (according to participants' statements, this was motivating) it was sent a report about their personality traits related to a character of a series. To that matter, before filling the MBTI questionnaire participants we asked to choose a series of the following options: *Game of Thrones, Marvel Super Heroes, Harry Potter, Star Wars* and *Disney Princess*. For the second step, we randomly choose from the 155 (after removing duplicates data from the 200) participants 23 (18 female and 5 males) to play our on-line scenario[6] and in the end of the story they were asked to fill an on-line questionnaire[7] about the immersion and the decisions that they had made.

4   Results

Regarding our results, they can be divided in two: the Collection of Personality Traits and the Interactive Storytelling Experience.

4.1   Collection of Personality Traits

In this stage, from the 200 answers received, we removed duplicates and missing values, resulting in 155 answers cleaned. From these, 45 are males with an average age of 30.6 (7.44 std) and 110 are females with an average age of 34 (11.32 std).

Regarding the analysis of the data from the MBTI questionnaire, it was calculated the individual's statistics for each dichotomy, see Table 1. For example, for the first pair of dichotomies '*EI*', 68 persons were classified as Extroverted '*E*' which represents 43.87% from the total of 155, in contrast, 87 were classified as Introverted '*I*' representing 56.13% of the total population. On Table 2, it is possible to see the personalities distribution of the 155 participants. The most

---

[5] https://goo.gl/dm2KgQ.
[6] https://goo.gl/mizWCk.
[7] https://goo.gl/SsCgSP.

Table 1. Dichotomy statistics group by pairs of preferences.

EI		SN		TF		JP	
E	I	S	N	T	F	J	P
68	87	109	46	72	83	119	36
43.87%	56.13%	70.32%	29.68%	46.45%	53.55%	76.77%	23.23%

popular MBTI personality collected was the *"ISTJ"* with 33 persons, representing 21.29% from the total of participants. Making a brief comparison between our results with the results obtained by the Center for Applications of Psychological Type[8] (CAPT) ours follow the same pattern.

The CAPT results describe the estimated frequencies of the type of personality in the United States population, and our results were almost the same regarding the dichotomy with higher classification. For instance, in the *'EI'* pair the *'I'* stands out from the *'E'*, in the *'SN'* the *'S'* stands out from *'N'*, in the *'TF'* the *'F'* stands out from the *'T'* and finally in the pair *'JP'* the *'J'* stands out from the *'P'*. In addition, the six most popular MBTI personalities in the CAPT were also the same found by us (see Table 2).

Table 2. MBTI personalities classification group by total percentage.

ISTJ	ESTJ	ESFJ	ENFP	ENFJ	ISFJ	ESFP	INFJ
33	25	23	14	12	11	8	8
21.29%	16.13%	14.84%	9.03%	7.74%	7.10%	5.16%	5.16%
INTJ	ISFP	ISTP	INFP	ESTP	ENTJ	ENTP	INTP
5	4	3	3	2	2	1	1
3.23%	2.58%	1.94%	1.94%	1.29%	1.29%	0.65%	0.65%

With the results obtained from the MBTI questionnaires, it was applied the Cohen's Kappa coefficient, Eq. (1), to obtain the discriminant questions. Thus, it was found moderate agreement in 7 questions representing the dichotomies *'E'* and *'I'* and *'S'* and *'N'*, and 8 questions for each *'T'* and *'F'* and *'J'* and *'P'* dichotomies. In this sense, for the questions: of *'EI'* dichotomies we obtain minimum and maximum values of k [0.467; 0.705]; to *'SN'* k was [0.447; 0.618]; to *'TF'* k was [0.383; 0.515] and to *'JP'* k was [0.387; 0.443]; for all dichotomies $p < 0.0005$.

4.2   Interactive Storytelling Experience

To answer our first research question, we compared the final classification obtained with our model with the final classification of the MBTI questionnaires.

---

[8] https://www.capt.org/mbti-assessment/estimated-frequencies.htm?bhcp=1.

In this sense, our model correctly identified always 1 dichotomy from the four needed to obtain a personality. But, our results also reveal that: in 96% (22 out of 23 participants) it hits two dichotomies; in 61% (14 out of 23) reaches three dichotomies and in 17% (4 out of 23) achieve all four dichotomies.

Although our population did not have the ideal size, it helps by providing some good information to use for the future improvements. A good example is regarding the DP's chosen, it was found patterns of choice, in other words, once specific personalities have chosen the same options on the same DP's.

In addition, a statistical analysis was performed, comparing the decisions made in each DP with the answers made in the respective question from the MBTI questionnaire. The data was split into two groups for each pair of preferences. For example, regarding the dichotomy 'E–I', the first group has the answers collected from the questionnaire MBTI and the second group the correspondent answers in the IS scenario. Based on this, a normality test was performed and the results obtained a $p < .05$ for all groups, reporting that the data significantly deviated from a normal distribution. Next, to verify whether the person makes decisions according to the answers made in the personality test a correlation test (Chi-square test) was applied and it was observed the contingency coefficient value. As seen in Table 3, the p value was higher (close to 1) for the pairs 'S–N' and 'J–P', showing a high degree of association between these pairs of preferences.

Table 3. Results of Contingency-Coefficient.

E–I		S–N		T–F		J–P	
v = .098	p = .365	v = .014	p = .904	v = .062	p = .487	v = .015	p = .857

As mentioned before, it was applied a questionnaire after the IS to measure the immersion felt by the player and the decisions made. The questions were answered through a Likert scale of 1 to 5, ranging from 1- "strongly disagree" to 5- "strongly agree". The questions related with immersions were: *"I was able to imagine and visualise the environments of the story.", "I felt like I was the leader of the country."* and *"During the game, the time passed very fast.".* The answers collected for all the above questions had an average response higher than 3.5 (4.4, 4.5, and 3.9 respectively). Regarding the decisions taken by the participants, we asked them whether *"My decisions influenced the events of the story.";* *"I have been able to recognise the consequences of my decisions in the story."* and *"The end of the story was according to my decisions."* The results show that the average answer per question was equal or higher than 4.0 (4.6; 4.4 and 4.0 respectively).

According to the global results of this questionnaire, it is possible to say that most of the participants felt immerse in the story and that they also notice how their decisions influenced the flow of the story. Furthermore, players were asked for suggestions about the IS, some of those were: adding more related images to the scenes, increase the scene immersion with sounds (e.g. door opening, battle screams, etc.), medieval music and more description of scenes.

5   Conclusions and Future Work

This work describes an initial model that allows the classification of the person's personality traits using an IS scenario. Although the success rate was not the desired one, 80% for the four pairs of dichotomies. We believe that it is possible to classify the personality traits according to the MBTI theory using an IS approach instead of the traditional one (through a questionnaire). To accomplish this, we need to do some adjustments in the current model.

For the pair 'SN' and 'JP' there was found a proximity relationship between the MBTI questionnaire and the IS scenario, this could mean that people follow more their personality during the IS for these preferences. Regarding the pairs 'EI' and 'TF' the data collected can be interpreted in two ways. First, people do not follow their personality in the game (some follow their emotions others follow the strategy). Secondly, the DP's for these dichotomies might need some refinement regarding the design follow. Does this means, that some personalities feel more confident to play interactive games with preferences different from theirs than the others?

Despite the good results for the immersion level of the story, in future, we intend to implement the aforementioned improvements on the Immersion component, as well some modifications in the scenes and the DP's. In light of the presented results, we expected that a growth in the population that play the IS after the necessary refinements will provide better results to our future findings. We are also planning on moving from the on-line version for a desktop platform with the introduction of a social robot with the role of storyteller. Finally, we intend to use the person's personality to create a more individualised narrative experience that will be more enjoyable for the person by applying persuasion techniques in a storyteller robot.

Acknowledgments. We would like to thank Professor Isabel Benites who aided in the story creation, the National Council for Scientific and Technological Development (CNPq) program Science without Border: 201833/2014-0 - Brazil and Agência Regional para o Desenvolvimento e Tecnologia (ARDITI) - M1420-09-5369-000001, for PhD grants to first and second authors respectively. This work was also supported by Fundação para a Ciência e a Tecnologia: (FCT) - UID/CEC/50021/2013 and the project AMIGOS:PTDC/EEISII/7174/2014.

References

1. Birk, M.V., Toker, D., Mandryk, R.L., Conati, C.: Modeling motivation in a social network game using player-centric traits and personality traits. In: Ricci, F., Bontcheva, K., Conlan, O., Lawless, S. (eds.) UMAP 2015. LNCS, vol. 9146, pp. 18–30. Springer, Cham (2015). https://doi.org/10.1007/978-3-319-20267-9_2
2. Figueiredo, R., Paiva, A.: Affecting choices in interactive storytelling. In: AAAI Fall Symposium: Computational Models of Narrative (2010)
3. Jung, C., Adler, G., Hull, R.: Collected Works of C.G. Jung, Volume 6: Psychological Types. Princeton University Press, Princeton (2014)
4. Kaplan, R., Saccuzzo, D.: Psychological Testing: Principles, Applications, and Issues. Cengage Learning, Boston (2012)
5. Klimmt, C., Roth, C., Vermeulen, I., Vorderer, P.: The empirical assessment of the user experience in interactive storytelling: construct validation of candidate evaluation measures. Technical report. Integrating Research in Interactive Storytelling-IRIS (2010)
6. McDonald, E.: The Global Games Market 2017 — Per Region & Segment — Newzoo (2017). https://newzoo.com/insights/articles/the-global-games-market-will-reach-108-9-billion-in-2017-with-mobile-taking-42/
7. Miller, S., Pennycuff, L.: The power of story: Using storytelling to improve literacy learning. J. Cross-Discipl. Perspect. Educ. 1(1), 8 (2008)
8. Myers, I., Myers, P.: Gifts Differing: Understanding Personality Type. Davies-Black Publication, Palo Alto, California (1980)
9. Nacke, L.E., Bateman, C., Mandryk, R.L.: BrainHex: preliminary results from a neurobiological gamer typology survey. In: Anacleto, J.C., Fels, S., Graham, N., Kapralos, B., Saif El-Nasr, M., Stanley, K. (eds.) ICEC 2011. LNCS, vol. 6972, pp. 288–293. Springer, Heidelberg (2011). https://doi.org/10.1007/978-3-642-24500-8_31
10. OECD: Student Learning Attitudes, Engagement and Strategies. In: Learning for Tomorrow's World: First Results from PISA 2003, pp. 109–158. Organisation for Economic Cooperation and Development (OECD), Paris (2004)
11. Paiva, A.: The role of tangibles in interactive storytelling. In: Subsol, G. (ed.) ICVS 2005. LNCS, vol. 3805, pp. 225–228. Springer, Heidelberg (2005). https://doi.org/10.1007/11590361_26
12. Paradeda, R.B., Martinho, C., Paiva, A.: Persuasion based on personality traits: Using a social robot as storyteller. In: Proceedings of the Companion of the 2017 ACM/IEEE International Conference on Human-Robot Interaction, HRI 2017, NY, USA. pp. 367–368. ACM, New York (2017). https://doi.org/10.1145/3029798.3034824
13. Prada, R., Santos, P., Martinho, C.: Design E Desenvolvimento De Jogos. FCA (BRASIL)
14. Ryokai, K., Vaucelle, C., Cassell, J.: Virtual peers as partners in storytelling and literacy learning. J. Comput. Assist. Learn. 19(2), 195–208 (2003)
15. The Myers & Briggs Foundation: The Myers & Briggs Foundation - MBTI® Basics (2014). http://www.myersbriggs.org/my-mbti-personality-type/mbti-basics/
16. Van, G.: Potential applications of digital storytelling in education. In: Paper presented at the 3rd Twente Student Conference on IT, Department of Electrical Engineering, Mathematics and Computer Science (2005)
17. Wang, C.Y.: Preference measures of rectangle ratio on MBTI personality types. Art Des. Rev. 3(03), 69 (2015)

How Knowledge of the Player Character's Alignment Affect Decision Making in an Interactive Narrative

Mette Jakobsen[(✉)], Daniel Svejstrup Christensen, and Luis Emilio Bruni

Department of Architecture, Design and Media Technology, Section of Medialogy,
Aalborg University, Aalborg, Denmark
{mette,daniel}@galdrastudios.com, leb@create.aau.dk

Abstract. In game narrative the central role of the protagonist becomes a challenge as the protagonist often conflates with the player character, which the author and the player share control over. This paper investigates whether knowledge of the player character's alignment, i.e. the inner thoughts of the character, can influence how they decide to progress in a game. The player character's alignment will present an internal conflict, which will sometimes conflict with the external goal of a game. It is investigated whether players are more likely to abandon their external goal, and ultimately change their in-game behaviour, when exposed to the internal conflict of their character. A test was conducted in which participants played through one of two similar versions of the same game; one in which they were exposed to the player character's internal conflict, and another in which they were not. The test was conducted online and ended with 467 participants. The data shows that a significant ratio of players changed their behaviour in the game, when exposed to the inner conflict of the player character.

Keywords: Video games · Narrative · Protagonist · Player character · Character alignment · Internal conflict

1 Introduction

As the name points out, the player character (PC) is the specific point of view from which the subject interacts with an interactive storyworld. Such player character can be abstract or complex, depending on its role in the game's narrative [9,13]. However, in action-based video games, the PC is often also the protagonist of a story, which revolves around solving an external problem, e.g. a mission or a quest. The player's engagement with their character can be divided into goal-related and empathic engagement [10]. This means that there is a difference between the player being engaged in the goal for which the PC is just a mean, and the player being engaged with the PC by some sort of empathic emotional immersion. For instance, in a game like Super Mario Bros. [12], the player does not rescue the princess because they have developed any (pseudo)

© Springer International Publishing AG 2017
N. Nunes et al. (Eds.): ICIDS 2017, LNCS 10690, pp. 193–205, 2017.
https://doi.org/10.1007/978-3-319-71027-3_16

feelings for her (as in role-playing), but because the goal of the game correlates with the goal of the character (Mario) of rescuing his girlfriend. In this paper we investigate what happens in the opposite case: If the protagonist's values are in conflict with the goals of the game, will the player prioritize to be consistent with these values over achieving the goals of the game?

In [11] internal problems are defined as problems that occur in the mind (e.g. conflicts, dilemmas), as opposed to external problems that are found in the environment (e.g. challenges, obstacles). Empowering the player to choose how the protagonist reacts to internal problems poses an interesting problem; can players get invested in internal problems that are not their own? The interactivity of games does not easily combine with emotional immersion, because it requires players to feel empathy towards a computer-controlled character. According to Lankoski, the player's empathic engagement with the PC is dependent on three different factors; recognition, alignment, and allegiance [10]. Recognition refers to how the character is presented and interpreted, alignment relates to the player's access to the character's knowledge and affects, and allegiance is how the character can elicit sympathy by means of its moral appeal.

Internal problems are handled differently between games. [13] analysed two story-rich games, Dragon Age: Origins [5] and Mass Effect 2 [1], differentiating two types of PCs. In Mass Effect 2, the player has agency over their character's actions, but has no access to their voice or feelings, while in Dragon Age: Origins, the player has complete control over what their character says and does. The result is that in Mass Effect 2 the PC, Commander Shepard, is clearly the protagonist of the story, while in Dragon Age: Origins, the PC's protagonism is somewhat diminished. In Dragon Age: Origins, the interesting internal problems were instead found in the non-player character (NPC) cast, whom [13] argues to be the true protagonists of the story. The reason why developers might want to move the protagonist role of the narrative to a player independent NPC could be that it may be challenging to give the player power over the central character of the plot and still avoiding the character being flat [18], i.e., a character that does not change throughout the course of the work [7]. Another example comes from Undertale [8], a game that challenges the player's engagement in what would be both the goal of the game and the external problem: escape the kingdom of monsters. In their quest to escape, the player will encounter likeable characters, who serve the purpose as hinders of that goal. The player, who at this point is the protagonist of the story, thereby develops an internal conflict: not wanting to kill the monsters standing in their way. If the player changes their behaviour and spares the monsters, and thereby work directly against the given external goal, the game will adapt, producing an alternative ending.

We devised a test where subjects were presented with a series of choices. Every choice had one option that would help them reach their external goal, and another option that would work against it. In this condition we expected that players would prefer to advance the external goal. Another version of the same game was made, where subjects would be given information about their character's inner-world prior to making a choices, i.e., what Lankoski's refers to as alignment, the access players have to the character's actions, knowledge, and affects [10]. This information is conveyed as an internal monologue describing the PC's personal thoughts and concerns about the choice. At times, this inner-world would work against the option that leads to the external goal, and at other times the inner-world and the external goal would be congruent. The test was conducted online targeting a test- and control group, each group playing different versions of the game. We predicted that the test group, which was allowed entrance into the inner thoughts of the PC, would change their behaviour and become more inclined to refuse the option conflicting with their character's alignment, because their engagement would shift from goal-related towards emphatic. We therefore hypothesised that participants in the test group would abandon their external goal in congruence with the PC's concerns. The choices the players made were logged to a database, and when analysing the data it was found that the test- and control group made significantly different decisions. The test group was significantly more likely to follow their character's wishes and concerns, and abandon the goal of the game. Furthermore, in some control choices, i.e. choices where the PC's wishes correlated with the goal, the test group was also significantly more likely to follow the goal.

2   Experimental Design

We designed an online interactive story in which all subjects got similar experiences and levels of agency, the only difference between the test- and control group being the access or lack of access to the PC's inner-world. The application was preceded by a short demographic questionnaire. The bulk of the data was collected by tracking and recording the subjects' interaction and choices throughout the story.

2.1   The Prototype

In order to address the question of whether the subject aligns with the PC's inner-world in detriment of achieving the external goal, two versions of the same game were implemented. The game was decided to be designed as a visual novel, a genre that allows for a binary form of interaction that can be logged to evaluate players' behaviour. Visual novels consist of text and mostly static 2D graphics, resembling mixed-media novels. This genre was chosen because it utilizes option lists as the main form of interaction. Players must select their path from these lists, in order to progress, similar to hypertext games. This kind of purpose-selective form of interaction [15] mitigates the influence of gameplay on the narrative, when exploring the subjects' choices. Figure 1 shows how options and conversations are displayed in the prototype.

External Problem. It was a requirement to devise an external problem that was not emotionally laden in order to have a clear contrast between the external- and internal problem. Therefore we chose not to use a plot of an epical nature,

Fig. 1. The image on the left shows Crit Choice #1, where the player has to pick one of the two options to progress with the game. The image on the right shows a conversation between characters. Dialogue is displayed beneath the speaking actor.

e.g. to save the princess or bring peace to the world, but instead a simple plot which could still be engaging, provoke curiosity, and include a clear goal in its development. In our case it became a plot related to a treasure hunt, following the tradition in games of gathering collectable rewards. For this purpose we decided to use an epistemic mystery plot, over a dramatic plot, to dampen the baseline of the possible emotional engagement. An epistemic plot focuses on the subject's satisfaction of solving a puzzle rather than on increasing the emotional immersion [14]. The game's narrative was kept as didascalic [2] as possible (i.e. very figurative), with a very short Author-Audience Distance. The reason for this being that although a more abstract narrative might produce a sense of narrative closure, it may also produce a diverging understanding in the subjects, and thereby introducing potential noise in the data.

Crit Choices. Ten crucial moments (Crit Choices) were planned out in a linear story arch, where players had to choose whether to advance towards the goal of the game, i.e. getting treasure or not. The test group received information about the PC's alignment, in the form of a short text that was written as an inner monologue ascribed to the PC. The text described the character's thoughts about the choice the subject was about to enact. For six of the Crit Choices, the inner voice was opposed to advancing the external goal, while in four control Crit Choices they were congruent to advancing the external goal. The choices remained the same between test- and control group, however the control group was not given the inner monologue that informed them about the PC's internal dilemmas.

The following list contains the final ten Crit Choices, denoted as "conflicted" whenever the PC is opposed to taking the treasure:

1. Take a generic piece of treasure.
2. Break down a door, in order to possibly find more treasure (conflicted).

3. Take an emotional piece of treasure; a wedding ring (conflicted).
4. Your brother goes missing: Ignore this to search for treasure (conflicted).
5. Take a plot relevant treasure; a figurine.
6. Approach a crying ghost child, potential dangerous, to gain treasure.
7. Inquire the ghost child about treasure, instead of her crying (conflicted).
8. Your brother has been possessed by a ghost. Focus on stopping him from destroying treasures, instead of helping him (conflicted).
9. You pacify the ghosts and they turn into a valuable figurine. Bring it with you to keep it safe.
10. Leave your brother behind to get the treasure for yourself (conflicted).

Narrative. When the Crit Choices had been planned, the rest of the game was built around them in a flowchart structure. This gave the players an illusion of agency [6], because they were able to make choices which lead to different feedbacks according to their actions, but it was ensured that all participants would traverse the ten Crit Choices in the same order. Furthermore, it was ensured that all paths in the flowchart would yield the knowledge that the subjects needed to feel like they were uncovering the mystery plot, that they felt like they made the right choice, and that they were "winning" the game, in order to promote their sense of agency [17].

Player Character. For the PC to have inner thoughts with which the player can align (or not), it cannot be a cipher as defined by [9]. Opposed to a cipher the PC should have a discernible personality. The subjects had to have power over their character's actions though, and they should be able to make decisions that conflicted with the wishes of their character. This is the rationale for having a fixed background customizable character [9]. The subjects could customize the character by; deciding on their name, gender, and appearance. In addition they could make decisions for their character, most often related to the utterances they would express. There were, however, parts of the character they could not control or change, as for example that the character is a treasure hunter by profession, that they have a brother, and that they have a certain moral code which is represented in the inner monologue.

2.2   Data Collection

The test was implemented online in order to reach a large and diverse sample of test subjects. The game needed to be of a certain length, for it to have a proper dramatic arch and to fit in all ten Crit Choices. Having an online test allowed for multiple tests to be run simultaneously without supervision, thereby saving time and ultimately gathering more data than would have been feasible within a lab test setting. In addition, having the participants play the game on their own devices, and at their own leisure, made for a better representation of how they would play a game normally. Data was logged to an online MySQL database using PHP scripts, and all interactions with the game were logged asynchronously to the database, with each entry holding the data necessary for any play session to be recreated from the database.

Quality of Data. Several measures were taken to ensure the quality of the collected data. A demographic questionnaire was included which had to be submitted before participants were presented to the game. The purpose of the questionnaire was to distribute participants evenly between test groups. The sorting algorithm considered three features between test groups starting with gender balance, then size balance, and finally the amount of hours they reported spending on playing video games for an average day, as a representation of their gaming experience, in order to assure that each group would be similar in gender representation, size, and mean gaming experience. Gaming experience was included as an important criterion because it has been shown that players' gaming experience may have an important influence on the results [17]. Participants were also allowed to choose other as a possible gender option, and on a 5-point Likert scale they were also asked to report how willing they were to read in games. Because the database would be accessible online, some security measures needed to be implemented, in order to prevent data from being lost or altered, whether deliberately by an attacker, or due to unforeseen errors in the system. Measures were also taken to mitigate the possibility of false data being allowed into the data sample from outside the system.

3   Local Tests

Before the prototype was distributed online for testing, two local tests were conducted to assess the quality of the prototype, starting with a pilot test of the prototype while it was still being developed.

3.1   Pilot Test

The purpose of the pilot test was to assess the functionality of the prototype, players understanding of the graphical user interface (GUI), the quality of the narrative, and to develop and practice the test procedure for the preliminary test. The pilot test consisted of half the game content and the demographic questionnaire.

To test the quality of the prototype, a post-test questionnaire was added for participants to evaluate the narrative, containing the following items:

1. I felt curious about the story.
2. I felt the story was inconsistent.
3. I felt that the actions I took were meaningful within the context of the story.
4. I was able to see the results of my actions.
5. I felt that the story would have been different if I had selected different choices.
6. I felt like I had control over aspects of the story that I wanted control over.

7. At points, I had a hard time making sense of what was going on in the story.
8. My understanding of the characters is unclear.
9. I had a hard time recognizing the thread of the story.

All items in the questionnaire used a 5-point Likert scale. The first two items were questions related to the quality of the game, and the player's understanding of the narrative. Items 3–6 were drawn from a study about the illusion of agency [6]. Items 7–9 were about Narrative Understanding, which is considered a part of Narrative Engagement [3]. For the prototype to be of a proper quality, participants had to agree with item 1, 3, 4, 5, and 6, and disagree with item 2, 7, 8, and 9.

In addition, there was a two-item moral choice questionnaire used for evaluating each Crit Choice. One item was used to rate the difficulty of the choice, and the other for rating how emotional the choice had been, both using a 5-point Likert scale. The items in the moral choice questionnaires were taken from a study that investigated the influence of stress on moral decision making [16], and participants rated Crit Choices immediately after performing the choice. A semi-structured interview was conducted after each test session. This was mainly used to find issues with the GUI and the narrative, and allowed participants to share any thoughts they might have had about the test and the prototype.

The pilot test had 10 participants, 8 male and 2 female. The results revealed some shortcomings with both the GUI and in the test design, which were then acted upon. The results from the moral choice and post-test questionnaires seemed to be working, so these items were kept for the preliminary test.

3.2 Preliminary Test

As opposed to the final online version, the preliminary test was conducted in a local control setting, where it was possible to observe participants and perform interviews. The goal of the preliminary test was to assess the quality of the prototype and locate errors in the system before final testing. When looking at the database after the preliminary test, there seemed to be no missing data or flaws in the data stored. Two errors were observed in the game during the test, and were corrected before the prototype went online. The interviews revealed a good understanding of the GUI elements and the narrative.

The preliminary test had 10 participants, 6 male and 4 female, all first-year university students. The participants' field of study included Interaction Design, Media Technology, Robotics, Electrical Engineering, and Civil Engineering. The results from the post-test questionnaire all leaned towards the ends of the scales that were required for the prototype to be of a proper quality, however less so than seen with the pilot test, see Fig. 2. The reason behind this was investigated and when looking at the demographic questionnaire, for how willing participants were to read text in games, the median value was 4 (Agree) for the pilot test and 3 (Neutral) for the preliminary test. It is possible this could have caused the results from the post-test questionnaire to centre more around Neutral for the preliminary test, as the lack of willingness to read may have caused the participants to be less engaged with the prototype. The participants in the preliminary test did play through the whole game, while the participants in the pilot test only played half of the game, something which could have influenced the difference in the results. The participants of the preliminary test did, however, not mention anything during the interview when asked about the quality of the narrative that could lead to believe the latter part of the game was somehow inferior to the early half.

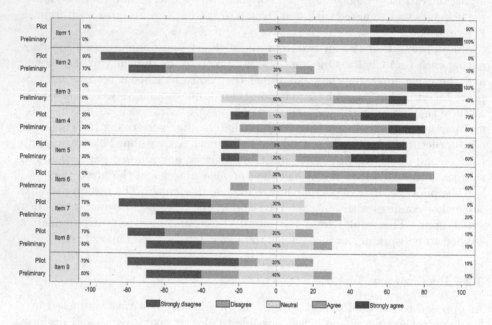

Fig. 2. Diverging stacked bar charts of the post-test questionnaire results from the pilot and preliminary tests.

The results of the moral choice questionnaires showed no difference in the median value for difficulty or emotional impact for Crit Choices between test groups. All Likert scales have a median of 2 (1: Not at all, 5: Extremely) which suggested that the average choice was not particularly difficult or emotional. The results for individual participants and individual choices ranged between 1 and 5 for both level of difficulty and emotional impact, and there were cases of choices being ranked on opposite ends of the scale and choices being ranked similarly on either end of the scale. These results suggested that participants experienced a diverse level of difficulty and emotional impact in the Crit Choices, both between participants for the same choice, and between choices for the same participant, but not between test groups.

Therefore the demographic questionnaire and the Crit Choices were not changed for the online test. The game and narrative also remained unaltered, aside from a few grammar and system corrections.

4   Results

The test was online from 12th of April to 2nd of May 2017, for a total of approx. 19 full days. By then the test had accumulated 467 completed play sessions. During this time, the game was distributed through social media, and promoted at local game related events; a game jam and a board game event.

Target Group. Distributing the test online resulted in a fairly diverse target group. However, it must be recognized that approaching people through social media sets some limitations to who might be reached and that different groups may not be equally represented in the data.

4.1   Noise Reduction

After the test had been concluded, several measures were taken to reduce possible sources of noise in the data, by removing participants with improper data entries from the sample. Only complete sessions, that were also the first session by any given IP, were considered, starting with a sample size of 434.

Participants who had reported an unwillingness to read in games were excluded from the sample because it was found during the preliminary test that this could cause participants to be less invested with the prototype and influence their experience. 18 sessions were removed from the sample for this reason.

In the preliminary test a participant was observed to have reported an unfeasible amount of hours spent playing games on an average day (24 h). Therefore John Tukey's outlier filter, with an IQR of 1.5, was performed to find outliers for that item. With this criterion 9 sessions were removed consisting of participants who reported they spend more than 8.5 h a day playing video games. Using the Model Human Processor [4], the minimum required time for reading text and making a choice could be estimated. By recreating play sessions from the database, the minimum required time for each action were estimated and compared to the time spent by the player.

Using this criterion, 38 sessions were removed from the sample consisting on players who were found have spent less time on completing the game than was estimated to be physiologically feasible, if assessing the content of the game properly. After noise reduction the test sample size became 369 subjects.

4.2   Analysis

Before noise reduction, the number of subjects of each gender was equally distributed between test groups, with 162 male participants and 69 female participants in each (thanks to the sorting algorithm). After sessions were removed the demographic distribution became a bit skewed between test groups because more male participants were removed from the test group, while more female participants were removed from the control group. The size of both test groups remained similar. A summary of the demographics can be seen in Table 1.

Table 1. The demographics of the remaining entries after noise reduction.

	Test group	Control group
Gender Male/Female/Other	120M/60F/2O	133M/54F/0O
Mean Age ± SD	25.01 ± 4.80	24.65 ± 4.17
Mean game experience ± SD	2.65 ± 1.48	2.58 ± 1.41
Total participants	182	187

Table 2. A list consisting of the p-values when running a two-sample t-test on each individual Crit Choice, across test groups.

Crit Choice	p-value	Crit Choice	p-value
#1	0.0031	#6	0.5722
#2	0.0238	#7	0.1204
#3	2.9992e − 06	#8	1.2890e − 08
#4	0.4723	#9	0.0002
#5	8.0789e − 13	#10	0.7406

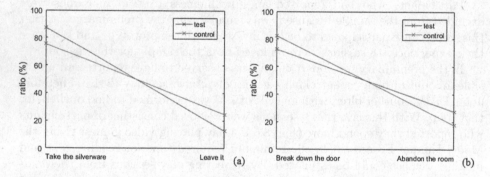

Fig. 3. (a) Crit Choice #1: The PC wants to pick up some abandoned silverware. (b) Crit Choice #2: The PC is reluctant about break down a door in search of treasure.

Crit Choices. The ten Crit Choices were analysed across test groups, using a two-sample t-test. The test yielded Crit Choice #1, #2, #3, #5, #8, and #9 to be significantly different across test groups, see Table 2. When considering the Bonferroni correction for 10 hypotheses, all except Crit Choice #2 remained significant. When looking at the ratio for each choice across test groups, it could be seen that for Crit Choice #2, #3, and #8, participants in the test group pursued the goal of the game to a lesser degree, see Figs. 3b, 4a, and 5a, respectively. For Crit Choice #1, #5, and #9, participants in the test group pursued the goal of the game to a higher degree, see Figs. 3a, 4b, and 5b, respectively. For all six Crit Choices, participants in the test group aligned their decision with the inner thoughts of the PC to a higher degree.

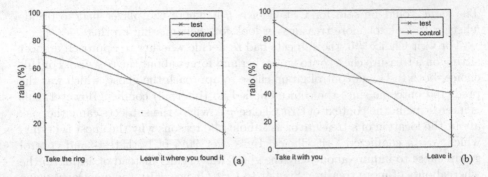

Fig. 4. (a) Crit Choice #3: The PC is reluctant about taking wedding ring. (b) Crit Choice #5: The PC wants to pick up a dusty figurine.

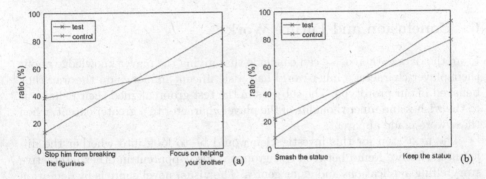

Fig. 5. (a) Crit Choice #8: The PC wants to help their brother, instead of securing the figurines their brother is breaking. (b) Crit Choice #9: The PC wants to bring the statue of the two ghost children with them.

5   Discussion

From the results it can be seen that giving the player knowledge about the player character's inner-world (alignment) significantly impacted some of the choices they made while playing. In these instances, the players are significantly inclined to make choices based on what their character thought, to the extent of being reassured to take a treasure when the control group was hesitant.

There were some instances in which there was no significant difference. Crit Choice #10, in which the player had to choose between finding more treasures or helping the PCs brother, the vast majority, over 95% in both test groups, chose to help the brother. The reason for this could be because interaction with the brother character had caused players to already be emotionally attached, or that the innate sibling relationship between the player character and the brother character lead the player to be unwilling to abandon the brother character at any case, and thus the inner monologue had little effect on this outcome.

The same could be said for Crit Choice #4, where the player had to decide whether to look for more treasures or look for their missing brother.

For Crit Choice #6, the subjects had to decide whether to approach a ghost sitting on a treasure chest, or to ignore her and forget about the treasure. For this choice, both test- and control group chose to approach the ghost, which was the predicted outcome since the choice implied no (internal) conflict. However, this is interesting in the context of Crit Choice #7, where the subjects can either ask about the location of a treasure or ask about the reasons why the ghost is crying, which was a conflicted Crit Choice. Here over 90% of both test- and control group chose to inquire about why the ghost was crying, instead of asking to the whereabouts of more treasure. Similar to Crit Choice #10, the emotional value of a crying child (the ghost) might be what provoked the subjects to abandon their goal and the effect of the inner monologue was therefore not apparent.

6   Conclusion and Future Work

From the data gathered, we can conclude that giving the player knowledge about their player character's inner-world had a significant influence on the way they behaved in our prototype. The subjects in the test group aligned their behaviour to the wishes and inner thoughts of the player character to a greater extent, when these were made apparent.

The next step for this investigation would be to look into whether the differences that we found between test groups is also apparent in other interactive storytelling applications and game genres. The visual novel genre is by definition a genre that weights story highly, and it would therefore be interesting to make a similar test in a genre like platformer or puzzle games, where there is usually less focus on story, and see if those players are willing to abandon their goal for the sake of the story. Another important aspect would be to look into other methods for revealing and representing the player character's inner-world, and see if they foster the same change in behaviour. Since different types of player characters might reveal their alignment in different ways, it is not necessarily attractive to use inner monologues in all types of interactive applications and games. Our implementation did not include auditive feedback, but it would be interesting to see if e.g. the sound of an increased heartbeat would make players reluctant to take a given treasure. We saw that players in both test groups were willing to abandon their goal for the sake of a crying child, and it could therefore be interesting to investigate the emotional influence of moral dilemmas.

With these insights designers can modulate knowledge of the player character's inner-world, to make players more likely to abandon certain goals of the game and pursue their character's wishes and congruency, and thereby provoke certain behaviours in an interactive storytelling application with different entertaining or normative educational purposes.

References

1. BioWare: Mass effect 2. Electronic Arts (2010)
2. Bruni, L.E.: Cognitive sustainability in the age of digital culture. tripleC **9**, 473–482 (2011)
3. Busselle, R., Bilandzic, H.: Measuring narrative engagement. Media Psychol. **12**(4), 321–347 (2009)
4. Card, S.K., Moran, T.P., Newell, A.: The model human processor. In: Handbook of Perception and Human Performance (1986)
5. BioWare Edmonton and Edge of Reality. Dragon age: Origins. Electronic Arts (2009)
6. Fendt, M.W., Harrison, B., Ware, S.G., Cardona-Rivera, R.E., Roberts, D.L.: Achieving the illusion of agency. In: Oyarzun, D., Peinado, F., Young, R.M., Elizalde, A., Méndez, G. (eds.) ICIDS 2012. LNCS, vol. 7648, pp. 114–125. Springer, Heidelberg (2012). https://doi.org/10.1007/978-3-642-34851-8_11
7. Forster, E.M.: Aspects of the Novel. Hartcourt Brace, San Diego (1995)
8. Fox, T.: Undertale (2015)
9. Heussner, T., Finley, T.K., Hepler, J.B.: The Game Narrative Toolbox. Focal Press, Waltham (2015)
10. Lankoski, P.: Player character engagement in computer games. Games Cult. **6**(4), 291–311 (2011)
11. Phillips, M.A., Huntley, C.: Dramatica, 10 edn. Write Brothers (2004)
12. Nintendo R&D4: Super Mario Bros. Nintendo Entertainment System (1985)
13. Jørgensen, K.: Game characters as narrative devices. A comparative analysis of dragon age: Origins and mass effect 2. J. Comput. Game Cult. **4**(2), 315–331 (2010)
14. Ryan, M.-L.: Interactive narrative, plot types, and interpersonal relations. In: ICIDS, pp. 6–13 (2008)
15. Ryan, M.-L.: Narrative as Virtual Reality 2: Revisiting Immersion and Interactivity in Literature and Electronic Media. Johns Hopkins University Press, Baltimore (2015)
16. Starcke, K., Polzer, C., Wolf, O.T., Brand, M.: Does stress alter everyday moral decision-making? Psychoneuroendocrinology **36**(2), 210–219 (2011)
17. Thue, D., Bulitko, V., Spetch, M., Romanuik, T.: A computational model of perceived agency in video games. In: Proceedings of the Seventh AAAI Conference on Artificial Intelligence and Interactive Digital Entertainment (2011)
18. Vella, D.: Modeling the semiotic structure of game characters. In: DiGRA, pp. 3–6, August 2014

Thinning the Fourth Wall
with Intelligent Prompt

Rossana Damiano[1,3], Vincenzo Lombardo[1,3(✉)], and Antonio Pizzo[2,3]

[1] Dipartimento di Informatica, Università di Torino, Turin, Italy
vincenzo.lombardo@unito.it
[2] Dipartimento di Studi Umanistici, Università di Torino, Turin, Italy
[3] CIRMA, Università di Torino, Turin, Italy

Abstract. This paper presents a digitally enhanced model of performer–audience communion in an interactive storytelling setting, based on an intelligent prompt system. The audience response is taken into account through emotion detection; the performer decides about her/his attitude towards the audience. The intelligent prompt advises the performer about how to continue the story. The model, named DoPPio-Gioco ("DoublePlay"), has been implemented as a prototype system, a virtual environment that realizes a feedback loop between the performer and audience.

Keywords: Intelligent prompt · Story editing · Emotion models

1 Introduction

This paper describes a model, called DoPPioGioco ("DoublePlay"), for permeating the fourth wall, "the age-old dream" of interactive storytelling [8, p. 1]. The model assumes a performer–audience relationship mediated by a system, the "intelligent prompt", which automatically prompts the next story chunk to be acted out by the performer in order to properly reacts to the audience's emotional engagement. DoppioGioco assumes a core emotional model that is employed for tagging the story chunks and classifying the audience reaction, and a real time engine that prompts the next chunk to be delivered as a consequence of the audience's response and the performer's current attitude. In this paper, we describe the model and a prototype system built for teaching interactive storytelling to a class of media and drama, eventually reflecting on the results of the workshop.

The inspiration for DoPPioGioco draws from two main sources. On the one hand, the line of research in studying and designing the experience of the audience, situated at the junction of HCI and media studies, surveyed by Brooker [6]. In particular, Tanenbaum reconsiders the notion of "subversive player" [19], developed in game studies to describe the user's attempts at breaking the boundaries of the interactivity allowed for by games, with the goal of making this

© Springer International Publishing AG 2017
N. Nunes et al. (Eds.): ICIDS 2017, LNCS 10690, pp. 206–218, 2017.
https://doi.org/10.1007/978-3-319-71027-3_17

behavior an intrinsic propellant of the game. On the other hand, the paradigm of improvisational theatre, which has opened the way to a computational approach for dominating the complexity of emergent storytelling [2,18]. The dynamics of improvisational theater have been described by Baumer and Magerko [5] in the perspective of interactive storytelling, using the Decision Cycle from Newell's Unified Theory of Cognition (*receive* new inputs, *elaborate* new knowledge, *propose* actions to take, *select* one of those actions, *execute* the action) as a conceptual framework for analyzing the way each performer takes advantage of the scene advancing moves of the others.

Drawing inspiration from the performers' ability to interpret the script in response to the audience reaction [1], DoPPioGioco acknowledges the traditional distinction between the roles of the author and the performer in story design and delivery. The narrative component is mostly handled offline, at the story editing time, as a combinatorial explosion of the possibilities arising from the storyline and emotional tagging system. DoPPioGioco is implemented as an interactive storytelling platform that offers the author an environment for crafting the story as a graph of story chunks and a function that prompts the performer by interpreting her/his task with an emotional rather than narrative matrix. The core of the intelligent prompt is the emotional model: emotions tag the story chunks, emotions are detected from the audience reactions, emotions are employed to prompt the next chunk.

2 Emotional Systems in Interactive Storytelling

Emotions have received much attention in interactive storytelling, both as a component of artificial character models, and as a feature of the story plot. While in synthetic characters emotions have become part of the processes that generate the character's behavior [7], thanks to the adoption of specialized models of emotional appraisal and coping issued by psychology [3], the role of emotions in the interactive generation of the plot has focussed on the engagement curves of Façade [11] and the emotional trajectories of emergent narrative (see the historical perspective in [10]). In the interactive drama Façade, the generation of the story was driven by a function that kept the emotional engagement of the user close to a target curve; in the Distributed Dramatic Management of the Emergent Narrative [20], predetermined emotional trajectories were employed as a metric for dramatic impact in the selection of characters' actions. With the exception of the systems mentioned above (see also [21]), most interactive storytelling systems do not directly address the emotional engagement of the audience. Rather, the research in interactive story generation tends to focus on the consistency of the plot in terms of characters' intentions and actions (see for example [13]). A notable exception is given by the use of player modeling to affect the emotional response of the users in [14].

Given the requirement of appraisal with respect to story chunks delivered through some audiovisual medium by the intelligent prompt, DoPPioGioco relies on the GEMEP model [4]: originally designed to support the creation of a corpus of clips displaying the perfomance of emotions by human actors, the GEMEP model is based on an extensive survey of the existing theories and models of emotions, including cognitive and dimensional models. GEMEP, GEneva Multimodal Emotion Portrayals, is a collection of audio and video recordings featuring actors portraying affective states, with different verbal contents and different modes of expression. Thanks to its syncretic and methodologically robust design, geared on performance, this model is especially suitable to annotate the affective content of media. In GEMEP, emotions are grouped along two axes: the *polarity* (positive/negative) and the *intensity* (high/low). The combination of these two axes provides four emotion families, each including three emotion types; within each family, the emotion categories are mainly characterized by different arousal levels:

- **Positive, high intensity:** amusement, pride, joy;
- **Positive, low intensity:** relief, interest, pleasure;
- **Negative, high intensity:** hot anger, panic fear, despair;
- **Negative, low intensity:** irritation, anxiety, sadness.

In the following, we introduce the DoPPioGioco model and the implemented system. Then, we describe the case study and the lesson learned from the experimental usage of the prototype as part of the teaching methodology.

3   Model DoPPioGioco

Basically, the DoPPioGioco system consists of an intelligent prompt, which navigates a story chunk graph annotated with emotions, and handles the performer's attitude towards the detected emotional response of the audience. The design of the graph of pre-authored story chunks follows a model of exhaustive combinatorics with respect to the four emotion families, with each story chunk annotated with a set of emotions. The performer can choose her/his attitude over two behavioral axes, the pleasant/opponent axis, and the low/high arousal axis, respectively (notice that both axes address the polarities of the GEMEP model). At each step, the audience responds to the last played story chunk; then, the initiative goes to the performer: she/he decides whether to empathize with the audience (*pleasant*) or to antagonize it (*opponent*), and whether to respond with a *low* or *high* arousal. Then, the intelligent prompt selects the next chunk among the suitable ones, depending on the interplay of the audience's emotional reaction and the selected attitude (one out of four combinations: *pleasant/low, pleasant/high, opponent/low, opponent/high*).

DoPPioGioco can be described through its two main functions, exemplified by the two system interfaces: the offline Story Manager editor, which organizes the story chunks in a story graph and supports the tagging of the story chunks (*units* in DoppioGioco terms); the online Stage Manager, which implements the intelligent prompt function by managing the story advancement in response to the audience's reactions.

Fig. 1. DoPPioGioco. The interface of the Story Manager.

The Story Manager (Fig. 1) allows the author to create and organize the units offline. Each unit consists of an audiovisual clip and a set of metadata elements describing it, such as title and textual. For each unit, the author has to provide the information needed to the story engine to create a consistent story at runtime: the precedence relations with the other units, needed to generate a causally motivated story, and the emotions attached to the unit, needed to account for the response of the audience. Each unit must be tagged with a set of emotions to ensure that the story engine can drive the story advancement consistently based on the combination of the emotional response of the audience and the attitude chosen by the user, thus enabling the intelligent prompt to break, metaphorically, the "fourth wall" (technology enhances the connection between the performer and the audience). Figure 1 shows the interface for the editing of the units. The interface is divided into four areas: the top left area contains the unit metadata; the top right area allows uploading and viewing the media asset that realizes the unit (typically, an audiovisual clip); the bottom left area contains the emotion tags: for example, the unit displayed in the figure is tagged with the emotion "sadness"; finally, the bottom right area allows specifying the units that precede and follow the unit. The story chart editing tool (see Fig. 3 in the next section) allows the author to manipulate the position of the units in the story chart.

When the system is run in the online mode (the intelligent prompt "on stage"), the Stage Manager enters into play (Fig. 2). After each unit, the audience responds by displaying a set of emotions: the individuals react in different ways, so the system computes the most frequent emotion, possibly raising to the family level (in case of wide variety). At this point, the performer can decide to *please* or *oppose* the audience, and set the intensity to *high* or *low*. After setting the

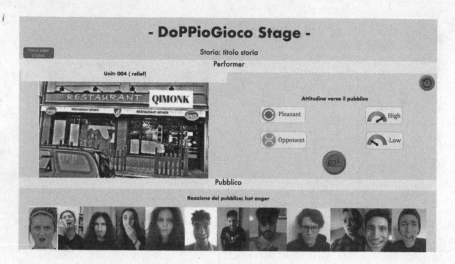

Fig. 2. DoPPioGioco. The interface of the Stage Manager. (Color figure online)

reaction type, the system picks up the next unit among the continuations allowed by the story graph. If several continuations are compatible with the current story unit and the response of the audience, the system selects one randomly. Figure 2 shows the interface for managing the stage. The interface is horizontally divided into two areas which represent, respectively, the performer's actions (top area) and the audience's response (bottom area). The top area contains, on the left, the last played unit; the right area is occupied by the performer's console for managing her/his attitude in the reaction to the audience: the four buttons refer to the global parameters of the emotional control of the continuation, namely polarity (negative or positive, i.e. "pleasant" or "opponent") and intensity ("low" or "high") – remember from Sect. 4.2 that each combination corresponds to an emotion family. The lower part of the interface contains a button for getting the emotional response of the audience ("Get response", not visible in the figure): when pressed, this button reveals the reaction of the audience and the button becomes invisible until the next unit is selected. For attaining a more realistic impression, the facial expressions of the audience members are displayed (in the figure, the by-a-majority emotion of "hot anger" has been computed by the system for the audience). The "go!" button posited below the console (in green, see Fig. 2) triggers the selection of the next unit: the new unit is loaded, the console is reset and the faces of the audience are replaced by the button "Get response".

4   The DoPPioGioco Implemented System

In this section, we illustrate the architecture of the system, describing the role played by the emotion model from the annotation of the units to the intelligent prompt.

4.1   Narrative-Emotional Model

Following an established practice in interactive storytelling, the story is formally structured as a directed graph (see an example from the case study in Fig. 3). The interaction with the audience determines the transition to the next node: in DoPPioGioco, the transitions that are not compatible with the response of the audience are filtered out by the emotion model superimposed to the story graph, and the decision about the continuation is carried out by the intelligent prompt described above.

This approach requires that the story units are annotated offline, by encoding not only their position in the story graph, but also the affective information brought by each story unit according to the author. So, each unit is labeled with a set of emotion tags (see Fig. 1), which represent the emotions that the author expects the audience to feel when the unit is delivered – based on its narrative content. The tags correspond to the emotion types encompassed in the GEMEP model (see Sect. 2). Finally, each unit must be associated with a video clip, that provides indications on what and how to perform 'on stage', when the unit is selected.

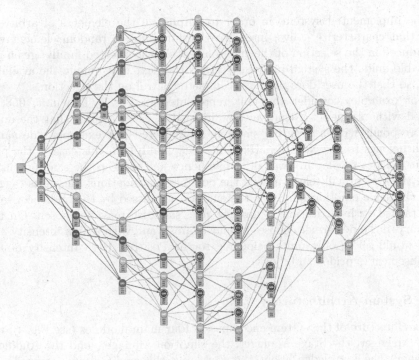

Fig. 3. The visualization of the story plot.

4.2 Annotating Emotions

In DoPPioGioco, the story units are annotated with the 12 emotion categories of the GEMEP model.[1] Issued from a compromise between the dimensional [12,15] and the cognitive models of emotions [17], the polarity–based account of emotions incorporated in GEMEP is suitable to deal with the polarity of the reaction to the audience's response implied by DoPPioGioco: as anticipated in Sect. 4.2, the the decision to play against (or pro) the audience can be directly mapped onto the negative/positive dimension of emotions in GEMEP, with "against" corresponding to the "opposite polarity" and "pro" to "same polarity" (see the definition of the emotion families in the previous section). The following *Reaction rules*, applied in a cascading way, determine the continuation of the story after collecting the audience's response and the performer's subsequent reaction:

– **R1:** *If* the selected choice is **pleasant**, *then* select the emotion families with the *same polarity*; *else* (the storyteller decides to be **opponent**), select the families with *opposite polarity*.
– **R2:** Given the *polarity* established by R1, tune the intensity level of the reaction to the selected *intensity* (low or high).

In the implemented system, in order to emphasize the elements of arbitrariness that characterize a live, interactive performance, a random element was introduced in the selection of the emotions within the selected family: given the available units, the system randomly selects the next unit among the available ones, so that the user does not have complete control on the selection.

For example, consider the unit represented in Fig. 1. The unit, 058, is tagged with "sadness" (Negative, Low intensity). Let's assume that the audience responds with a negative emotion, as expected (for example, "despair", which belongs to the Negative, High Intensity family). In this case, if the performer decides to play in favor of the audience and to keep the same intensity level, the system will select, among the possible continuations, the units tagged with the same emotion family as the emotion expressed by the audience; so, a unit tagged with "irritation", "anxiety" or "sadness" may be chosen. On the contrary, if the performer chooses to play against, and with a high intensity, the rules would select only units belonging to the Positive, High Intensity family ("amusement","pride" and "joy").

4.3 System Architecture

The architecture of the system encompasses four main modules (see Fig. 4): the Story Manager, the Stage Manager, the Emotion Manager, and the Audience Manager. The knowledge about the story and the media assets, created and

---

[1] The GEMEP model also encompasses 5 extra emotion types that don't fit in the categorial classification (Admiration, Tenderness, Disgust, Contempt, Surprise); they have been omitted from the emotion annotation in DoPPioGioco.

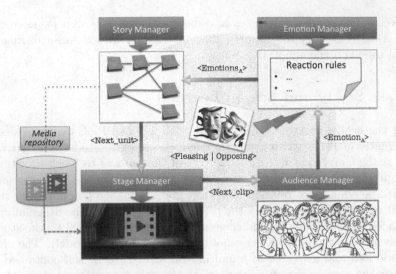

Fig. 4. The architecture of DoPPioGioco. Red lines represent the control flow of the system. (Color figure online)

uploaded offline through the interface displayed in Fig. 1, are embedded, respectively, into the Story Manager and into the Stage Manager (where they are stored in the Media Repository). The system loop orchestrates the interaction of the four modules in the following way:

1. The Audience Manager accounts for the reaction of the audience. The system relies on a face expression recognition API.[2] However, in the two case studies below, we have simulated the audience reaction through a random selection of emotions, displayed as pictures taken from a preloaded set provided by the participants.
2. The Emotion Manager takes as input the audience's response and the attitude selected by the performer for the reaction, and applies the Reaction Rules to compute the candidate emotion family, which becomes the input to the Story Manager.
3. The Story Manager selects the next unit based on the story graph and the emotion family selected by the Emotion Manager.
4. The Stage Manager takes as input the unit selected by the Story Manager and sends it to the player. The Stage Manager provides the properly called intelligent prompt: by consulting the story graph to select the possible continuations, it filters out the units that are not emotionally consistent with the attitude toward the audience's emotional response selected by the performer (and thus, with the emotion family determined by the Reaction rules).

Each module of the system is implemented as a web service (written in PHP and mySql), so as to allow the portability of the system across different devices

---

[2] https://azure.microsoft.com/en-us/services/cognitive-services/emotion/.

and media. The current interfaces have been developed as web pages and rely on the Ajax technology to support a fluid interaction with the user during both the real time and the annotation phases.

5   Case Study and Lesson Learned

During the academic years 2015–16 and 2016–17, DoPPioGioco provided the online platform for a writing lab targeted at graduate students in Arts and Media at the University of Turin. The goal of the lab was to teach the students to design and produce an interactive story by accounting for the emotions in the performer/audience relation. The actual performance has not been staged live, but each student could play the performer role through the Stage interface, being faced with a simulated audience (audience faces generated by the students themselves, 12 pictures, one per emotion in the GEMEP model). The chunks were produced and delivered in a multimedia format, to be self-contained with respect to the narrative content, and not as a simple suggestion to the performer in remembering the chunk addressed.

This lab was a test-bed for assessing the potentials of the platform for training goals. The staff consisted of a writing supervisor, a media producer, and a developer. The writing coordinator was in charge of coordinating the conception of the story, the design of the characters and the editing of the story in textual form. The producer coordinated the production of the audiovisual clips that realize the story units. The developer was engaged in debugging the software system and implementing small design modifications during the conduction of the laboratory. The first edition included 18 students. In this edition the story was created from scratch leveraging on the students' ideas. One main idea was selected through a contest held among the participants. After agreeing on one specific story plot, the class collaboratively designed the story graph. That means that each student was given a branch of story to be developed in a sequence of single story units. Finally, the students were divided into small teams and were assigned the editing, annotation and production of the story units. The final product was delivered online. In this edition of the lab, the story, titled "Clark", was a spooky thriller set in a hospital haunted by a ghostly presence. The main character of the story is a hospital worker, Clark, who comes across some apparently paranormal events. With the help of a mysterious and poised young girl, Magdalene, Clark investigates the origin of the events in a climax of horror. But the tale is nothing but a dream made by Clark before his first day in the new job: the alarm clock rings, and he wakes up. The story could evolve in different narrative ways, according to the audience reactions; however, after running several interactive sessions – where the students alternated between the roles of the performer and the audience, we realized that the story was sometimes perceived as sparse and lacking unity of action.

In the second edition of the lab, with 17 students, we leveraged on the experience of the previous year. First, we decide to use a looser type of narration, because the system is designed to help the performer to manage the emotional response of the audience, rather than guiding the narrative cause-effect chain. Second, we switched the students' focus on the emotions delivered rather than on the creation of the narrative sequence. Thus, we decided to provide a ready-made storyworld in the form of a repository that describes the life in a small American town in the Sixties, by employing the software developed by James Ryan for the performance/installation "Bad News" [16]. Using this software, we produced a specific setting that can be visualized as an exhaustive list of characters, occupations, relations, conflicts, family trees, etc. for a fictional smalltown. Moreover, yet beforehand, the writing coordinator designed and fixed the story plot structure in a form of a graph (Fig. 3) in which every story unit belongs to a specific set of emotions (see GEMEP model above) and linked to the others units accordingly. Once in the lab, we asked the participants to select a genre according the main conflicts listed. The choice was a mix between "romance" and "business competition". Thus, after a preliminary discussion, we came out with a story, titled "Hot bread", centered around two bakeries (an old established one and a new rampant one) mixed with a romance between the two main characters. Therefore, we divided the participants into authoring teams, after having experienced the unit connections in a physical performance simulation (see Fig. 5). Each group was assigned to write a specific set of units, according the following constrains: (1) being loosely consistent with the antecedent units; (2) being consistent with one of the emotions of the given set. This solution was successful in helping in the process of a collaborative writing (i.e. to produce story unit that were consistent one another) and to devise a multi-plot that was nevertheless aimed toward a closure. Indeed, the characters go through changes in their personal lives as a result of their professional and relational crossroads and the story emerged as inspired to serial formats (such as TV fiction).

The experience with DoPPioGioco was crucial to transmit to the students the notion that writing has to take into account the architecture of the interactive storytelling system (in our case, the suggestions issued by the intelligent prompt). In particular, how the writing methodology can take full advantage of the potential of the platform and how to identify the most suitable narrative type for it. In general, the students appreciated the approach underlying the system and correctly grasped the relation between the annotation of the units with the emotion tags and the generation of the story in the interplay with the audience, which allow the system to trespass the invisible "fourth wall" posited between performer and audience. The story graph proven to be successful in securing the connection among units and the branching for each type of emotion defined by our set. As a result of the changes in the design and genre of the story, the number of units dropped in the second edition (156 to 105); also, due to the more thorough design of the story, in the second edition the duration of the story was a function of the intensity of the emotions: more intense audience responses (remember from Sect. 4.3 that intensity was one of the two axes of the emotion system) led to shorter stories, i.e., stories composed of lower number of units. The tension between the creation of well crafted, consistent story line and the emotional response of the audience was both a challenge and an opportunity for the trainees. In particular, the factorization of the emotions in story

Fig. 5. Students as authors that physically simulate the graph of story units, also identifying responsibilities for unit–unit connections and improvising the story continuations before actually creating them. Notice the print graph of Fig. 3 on the upper left part of the image.

editing, and the dualism between the roles of story editor and producer, were suitable to promote a change of paradigm in their design and editing practices. The writing labs conducted with the system provided some useful insights for the redesign of the system. Putting forth emotions in the design of the story actually went against the standard practices previously learned by the students, mostly based on causal connections: as a result, designing the story in terms of emotions tended to put at risk the logical consistency of the incidents, requiring a careful control on the story graph. To alleviate this problem, a tool for checking their consistency, similarly to [9], may be added to the system in the future.

In order to train the students to cope with unexpected cases of audience responses, in both editions of the writing lab the recognition of the audience's emotions was replaced with a simulation of the audience. The random generation of the emotions of the audience, even if sometimes frustrating, turned out to be effective for teaching purposes, since it led the students to face the extreme consequences of the interaction with the audience. However, in order to reduce the gap between the author's expectations and the reactions of the audience, the set of emotions may be reduced to a more basic set. As future work, we plan to extend the use of the system to other storytelling forms, such as teaching and presentation, and in mixed forms, such as edutainment and infotainment.

6   Conclusion

In this paper, we described a model of performer–audience relationship mediated by an intelligent prompt, in an interactive storytelling setting. The DoPPioGioco model, implemented as a web–based system, provides the author with a story authoring interface, where story chunks are annotated with emotion tags; on stage, the performer receives from the system an intelligent prompt, computed by taking into account the audience's response and the performer's attitude towards the audience. The system has been employed in a class of interactive storytelling authoring, with the goal of training students to shift from a narrative perspective to an emotion–based perspective in interactive story editing. The focus was mostly on writing the story chunks, accounting for the exhaustive combinatorics of the system and simulating the performance through a stage manager provided via web. The experience was very stimulating for the students, with an improvement of the results attained along two editions.

We are planning to realize real live performances in the next editions, employing devices for capturing the facial reactions of the audience and providing a suitable haptic interface to the performer on stage.

Acknowledgments. The authors acknowledge James Ryan for having provided the software for the city simulation.

References

1. Alrutz, M., Listengarten, J., Wood, M.V.D.: Playing With Theory in Theatre Practice. Palgrave Macmillan, New York (2011)
2. Aylett, R., Louchart, S.: I contain multitudes: creativity and emergent narrative. In: Proceedings of the 9th ACM Conference on Creativity & Cognition, pp. 337–340. ACM (2013)
3. Aylett, R.S., Louchart, S., Dias, J., Paiva, A., Vala, M.: FearNot! – an experiment in emergent narrative. In: Panayiotopoulos, T., Gratch, J., Aylett, R., Ballin, D., Olivier, P., Rist, T. (eds.) IVA 2005. LNCS (LNAI), vol. 3661, pp. 305–316. Springer, Heidelberg (2005). https://doi.org/10.1007/11550617_26
4. Bänziger, T., Scherer, K.R.: Introducing the geneva multimodal emotion portrayal (GEMEP) corpus. Blueprint for affective computing, pp. 271–294 (2010)
5. Baumer, A., Magerko, B.: Narrative development in improvisational theatre. In: Iurgel, I.A., Zagalo, N., Petta, P. (eds.) ICIDS 2009. LNCS, vol. 5915, pp. 140–151. Springer, Heidelberg (2009). https://doi.org/10.1007/978-3-642-10643-9_19
6. Brooker, W.: The Audience Studies Reader. Psychology Press, Hove (2003)
7. Gratch, J., Marsella, S.: Tears and fears: Modeling emotions and emotional behaviors in synthetic agents. In: Proceedings of the Fifth International Conference on Autonomous Agents, pp. 278–285. ACM (2001)
8. Koenitz, H., Ferri, G., Haahr, M., Sezen, D., Sezen, T.Í. (eds.): Interactive Digital Narrative. History, theory and practice. Routledge, New York (2015)
9. Lombardo, V., Damiano, R.: Semantic annotation of narrative media objects. Multimed. Tools Appl. **59**(2), 407–439 (2012)

10. Louchart, S., Truesdale, J., Suttie, N., Aylett, R.: Emergent narrative: Past, present and future of an interactive storytelling approach. Interactive Digital Narrative. History, Theory and Practice, pp. 185–199. Routledge, New York (2015)
11. Mateas, M., Stern, A.: Façade: An experiment in building a fully-realized interactive drama. In: Game Developers Conference, vol. 2 (2003)
12. Plutchik, R.: Emotion: A psychoevolutionary Synthesis. Harpercollins College Division, New York (1980)
13. Riedl, M.O., Young, R.M.: Narrative planning: balancing plot and character. J. Artif. Intell. Res. **39**(1), 217–268 (2010)
14. Roberts, D.L., Narayanan, H., Isbell, C.L.: Learning to influence emotional responses for interactive storytelling. In: AAAI Spring Symposium: Intelligent Narrative Technologies, vol. II, pp. 95–102 (2009)
15. Russell, J.A.: Core affect and the psychological construction of emotion. Psychol. Rev. **110**(1), 145 (2003)
16. Samuel, B., Ryan, J., Summerville, A.J., Mateas, M., Wardrip-Fruin, N.: *Bad News*: An experiment in computationally assisted performance. In: Nack, F., Gordon, A.S. (eds.) ICIDS 2016. LNCS, vol. 10045, pp. 108–120. Springer, Cham (2016). https://doi.org/10.1007/978-3-319-48279-8_10
17. Scherer, K.R.: Appraisal theory. In: Dalgleish, T., Power, M. (eds.) Handbook of Cognition and Emotion, pp. 637–663. Wiley, Chichester (1999)
18. Swartjes, I., Theune, M.: An experiment in improvised interactive drama. In: Nijholt, A., Reidsma, D., Hondorp, H. (eds.) INTETAIN 2009. LNICSSITE, vol. 9, pp. 234–239. Springer, Heidelberg (2009). https://doi.org/10.1007/978-3-642-02315-6_25
19. Tanenbaum, J.: How i learned to stop worrying and love the gamer: reframing subversive play in story-based games. In: Proceedings of DiGRA (2013)
20. Weallans, A., Louchart, S., Aylett, R.: Distributed drama management: beyond double appraisal in emergent narrative. In: Oyarzun, D., Peinado, F., Young, R.M., Elizalde, A., Méndez, G. (eds.) ICIDS 2012. LNCS, vol. 7648, pp. 132–143. Springer, Heidelberg (2012). https://doi.org/10.1007/978-3-642-34851-8_13
21. Zagalo, N., Göbel, S., Torres, A., Malkewitz, R., Branco, V.: INSCAPE: Emotion expression and experience in an authoring environment. In: Göbel, S., Malkewitz, R., Iurgel, I. (eds.) TIDSE 2006. LNCS, vol. 4326, pp. 219–230. Springer, Heidelberg (2006). https://doi.org/10.1007/11944577_23

Virtual, Mixed and Augmented Reality

Who Are You? Voice-Over Perspective in Surround Video

Mirjam Vosmeer[1]([✉]), Christian Roth[2], and Hartmut Koenitz[2]

[1] Amsterdam University of Applied Sciences, Postbus 1025, 1000 Amsterdam, The Netherlands
m.s.vosmeer@hva.nl
[2] HKU University of the Arts, Postbox 1520, 3500 Utrecht, The Netherlands
{christian.roth,hartmut.koenitz}@hku.nl

Abstract. With the renewed interest in VR, new questions arise for content creators, as existing cinematic practices cannot simply be transferred. In this paper, we describe two experiments investigating which voice-over perspective elicits the best sense of presence for viewers of cinematic VR content. For the first experiment different voice-over narrations in first, second and third person perspectives were added to a VR video. This test showed that viewers preferred the voice-over in second person perspective, as this provided them with the strongest sense of presence and a feeling of 'being in the story'. In the second experiment, we used a short 360° documentary with a first person voice-over perspective, and compared it to a version of the same documentary with a second person voice-over, using a quantitative survey. In this experiment, however, no significant difference was found between the two groups of respondents. In our discussion, we explore several possible reasons that may have contributed to this outcome.

Keywords: User perspective · Presence · Cinematic VR · Oculus rift · Virtual reality · Interactive narrative design · Voice over

1 Introduction

As the loud marketing-driven headlines of the VR renaissance slowly disappear from magazines like Wired [1] and Forbes [2], a different challenge takes center stage: how can we produce compelling content, which keeps viewers entertained and intrigued, after the initial 'wow-effect' that VR tends to elicit, has worn off? Or, to be more exact: what do we need to do, in order to distinguish VR from film and other forms of entertainment media and thus establish VR as a viable new form? The answer, to be sure, lies with artistic choices. But while making the first steps towards developing an 'aesthetic language' of virtual reality, producers have come to realize that many questions concerning the production and user experience of VR still remain unanswered. Indeed, we argue that concrete, transferable knowledge of interactive narrative design methods is still scarce and thus this topic demands continuing attention from scholars and practitioners. [3, 4] Especially creators who explore the possibilities of 360° video content (in contrast to rendered VR content), find themselves probing a new field of media production that offers some of the characteristics of video games on one hand, while also possessing some cinematic qualities. Yet, many existing cinematic practices seem

N. Nunes et al. (Eds.): ICIDS 2017, LNCS 10690, pp. 221–232, 2017.
https://doi.org/10.1007/978-3-319-71027-3_18

to be no longer applicable, and therefore researchers from both academic and industrial backgrounds are busy exploring the basic demands of VR production. When it comes to user experience, we have only just begun to study the ways in which users (or patients, or clients, or customers) may indeed be affected by a message they encounter in an engrossing environment, instead of observing it through the established fourth wall of movie watching [5–9]. It is becoming clear that there are many fundamental knowledge gaps that still need to be filled in this domain, not only about the production of surround video content, but also about the way how the resulting products may be enjoyed by various audiences. After all, only appreciation amongst the general public will eventually lead to market success. It is therefore useful to start experimenting with specific characteristics of this new kind of media entertainment, and evaluate the impact on audiences.

For the two studies that are presented in this paper, we have explored a specific topic, the narrative perspective of video footage experienced with a head-mounted display such as Oculus Rift. Because the footage has been recorded in 360°, the viewer has a strong sense of being present in the movie, in contrast to traditional movie or TV consumption. This relates directly to the theoretical concept of 'presence', that is defined as 'being in the story world' [10]. In the context of interactive narrative, we relate presence to immersion (cf. Murray's affordances [11]), especially narrative immersion as described by Ryan [12]. She sees narrative immersion as an important aesthetic goal for interactive narratives. According to Ryan, this immersion can take at least three forms: spatial, temporal and emotional. While most traditional media are linked to emotional presence (for instance being immersion in a book, or a movie) that builds up over time, a VR experience immediately offers a sense of spatial presence. From the perspective of traditional film production, the problem is how to adjust to this condition, or more concretely, how to present stories for surround video content that suit the sense of presence that users experience. One solution to this problem is by adding voice-over narration: the voice of someone talking who is not visible in the video [13]. In order to use voice-over narration effectively, however, the first question that needs to be answered is about the perspective in which this voice-over should be talking: first person, second person, or third? In the next sections, we first give a short overview of voice-over in films, perspective in interactive experiences like video games and presence in virtual reality before we present the results of our experimental study on this topic.

2   Voice-Over and Perspective

Movie critics and storytelling experts have usually been suspicious, if not downright disapproving, of using voice-over in movies. McKee is quite explicit in his aversion to it: the trend toward using telling narration throughout a film threatens the future of our art [14]. He admits that someone like Woody Allen may have the gift to use counterpoint narration in a delightful way, but dismisses the efforts of most other scriptwriters: "it takes little talent and less effort to fill a soundtrack with explanation" [14]. After all, in a métier where 'Show, don't tell' is the basic rule, adding an extra voice to a scene is seen as a cheap shortcut and almost equals to admitting one's own woeful incompetence.

However, two particular advantages of using voice-over can be identified [15]: the first is the unique opportunity for intimacy that it provides, by offering insight into the character's mind. The second is the possibility to create irony through the clash of verbal comments with the visual track. Tabarraee defines the voice-over simply as: "[…] the voices in fiction film, whose sources are absent from the image frame" [16], but one specific kind of voice-over that immediately defies the previous definition, is the one in which the protagonist speaks straight to the camera, as is for instance the case in *High Fidelity* [16].

Here the source of the voice is clearly present within the frame, but by directly addressing the viewer, the protagonist steps out of the frame of the narrative. Another recent example of this type is seen in the popular HBO series *House of Cards*, in which politician Frank Underwood also addresses the camera directly, adding both insights into his actions and motivations, as well as irony to the story as it unfolds.

When looking at the position in time that a voice-over can address, Laamanen [17] makes the distinction between a voice that reflects back on the films' events from any point in the future, and a voice-over that speaks from a 'timeless present'. In her analysis of the use of voice-over narration, Kozloff [13] makes the distinction between first person narrators and third person narrators. A first person narrator can be either a character within the film that addresses the viewer from his or her particular point of view, but it can also be a nameless, omniscient narrator [13]. The third person is often also omniscient, and both can add new insights, intimacy and irony to the scene. It is remarkable that the second person perspective has hardly been the topic of scholarly analysis. One notable exception within recent history has been the by interactive fiction (IF) offline text adventure games like *Adventure* [18] and *Zork* [19]. Second person was also used in text-based online MUDs and MOOs. In the latter virtual worlds, that by now have gained a somewhat obscure legendary status, the user was often addressed from an second person perspective. In these examples, the text on the screen did not only describe the position of the avatar in the textual world and the characteristics of the specific location, but often also added insights into motives or the inner state of mind that the character was to experience. *LambdaMOO* [20], has in the past been a popular object for the examination of virtual-world social issues, for instance by [21]. Here, the player 'woke up' in a dark closet, gently encouraged to explore the adjoining spaces with the following text:

> You open the door and leave the darkness for the living room, closing the door behind you so as not to wake the sleeping people inside [20].

For our current explorations into VR narrative perspectives, we intend to reconsider this specific focalization, to find out whether it may have a new relevance in current media environments.

3   Presence and Immersion in VR

An important concept that comes up in both academic and industrial debates around the use and creation of VR is *presence* and, in relation to that, *immersion* [11, 12]. The term presence is usually defined as the 'sense of being there' [12]. Roth differentiates immersion from presence by defining immersion as an objective criterion which depends on hardware and software [22]. Presence is subsequently defined as the psychological more subjective sense of being in the environment, and mainly influenced by the content of the mediated world. Immersion could be seen as a quality of the medium, in this case a VR movie, while presence is a characteristic of the user experience. North and North [23] have pointed out the importance of evaluating the user experience within the design and development of VR systems. Specifically, they identify an increased need to conduct empirical studies in which the factors that create a higher sense of presence are investigated. When a producer of VR content wants to evaluate the immersive quality of a specific experience, or compare two or more different solutions for problems that occur during production, one of the possible ways to accomplish that is to measure the amount of presence that the user experiences. In the standardized assessment toolkit that Roth developed [24] to measure user responses to interactive stories, presence is accounted for with the following items (short scale version):

1. I felt like I was a part of the environment in the presentation.
2. I felt like I was actually there in the environment of the presentation.
3. I felt as though I was physically present in the environment of the presentation [24].

An important online source on the development of knowledge about production and reception of virtual reality experiences is the website of the Oculus Story Studio. In their blog, the members of the VR team write about their latest projects, and specifically about the challenges they encountered while creating them and the lessons they learned from it. Many of these insights are focused on the links between presence, narrative and interactivity and how they sometimes seem to exclude or overrule each other in VR. In November 2015, an article was posted on what author Matt Burdette named the "Swayze effect" [25]. This term refers to the way that a user may feel like a ghost when he or she is immersed in a virtual reality experience, and feels related to the characters that inhabit it, but at the same time is ignored by them. It seems that the absence of viewer agency creates an invisible wall between the viewer and the virtual environment. Or, as Burdette states: "The actors ignore you, the world remains indifferent to your presence, and yet you are so undeniably there" [25].

In the next section, we will describe our first study in which this sense of presence was used as a qualitative measurement to compare different versions of a VR video. In the second study, we will then proceed to investigate the possibility of overcoming the *Swayze effect* by adding an appropriate voice-over to a 360° documentary.

4   First Study

Taking into account that voice-over can add an important element to a movie, that is intimacy, we want to compare how different perspectives can add to the immersive experience that 360° video can provide. We compare the first and third person perspective, but we also want to explore the position of a narrator that is common in gaming but has thus far hardly been used in film, that is, the second person narrator. We choose to present all three voices in the 'timeless present', that is, speaking in the here and now, and we want to find out which narrator position would best suit the particular point of view that cinematic VR offers, and adds to the viewers experience presence, that is: of being 'in the middle of the movie'.

4.1 Method

For this experiment, we wanted to explore the impact of different voice-over perspectives, experienced while watching a movie in a surround video system such as Oculus Rift. We therefore recorded three different audio tracks of the same story: one was told in the first person, one in second person and one voice-over in third person. The video footage we used remained exactly the same in all three versions. It consisted of a boat ride through the Amsterdam canals. The viewer can look around and see the streets, the water and other boats. In the back of the boat is a man, who does not talk and does not react to the camera, but quietly guides the boat through the canal. The story we used was written by a professional screenwriter, and inspired by Greek mythology. In the text, the protagonist is a famous skater who realizes that he has just broken his neck and died while doing a trick, and is now carried to the hereafter by a ferryman. For the three recordings of the three different perspectives, the following scripts were used:

Table 1. The first lines of the scripts that were recorded to experiment with voice-over perspectives

First person	Second person	Third person
I opened my eyes and to my amazement I was not at the skate park anymore. Instead I was on this strange boat and I had no idea what I was doing here. When I looked down, I noticed that my body was gone. When I looked behind me, I saw a guy. He seemed friendly, smiling and all, but he was completely silent	You open your eyes and to your amazement you're not at the skate park anymore. Instead you're on this strange boat and you have no idea what you're doing here. When you look down, you notice that your body is gone. When you look behind you, you see a guy. He seems friendly, smiling and all, but he is completely silent	Fredric opened his eyes and to his amazement he was not at the skate park anymore. Instead he sat on this strange boat and he had no idea what he was doing there. When he looked down, he noticed that his body was gone. When he looked behind him, he saw a guy. The guy seemed friendly, smiling and all, but he was completely silent

The experiment was conducted with 21 respondents, who volunteered to take part in this study. The sample consisted of eleven male and ten female respondents, between the ages of 20 and 34. The experiment was conducted in a room at the Medialab at the Amsterdam University of Applied Sciences. The respondents first received a short instruction on the use of Oculus Rift, and then were shown the same video twice, but with two different audio tracks. The versions were randomly assigned, which meant that respondents watched either first perspective voice-over and second perspective voice-over, second and third, or first and third person, in a random order. Afterwards, the sense of presence that the users had experienced was examined by asking them to compare the two versions. They were confronted with the three items from assessment toolkit by Roth [24] and asked to rate these statements for both the videos they had seen. After that, they were asked to determine which of the two versions had given them the strongest sense of being physically a part of the environment, and of being *in the story*?

4.2 Results

Our experiment showed that of the respondents that were given a choice between second and first person perspective, and second and third person perspective, a large majority (75%) preferred the second person perspective. After the test, the respondents were asked to reflect on their experiences and to discuss the differences they had perceived when watching the two variations of the test scene. Many respondents stated that the third person narrative felt more like listening to an audio book, and that this perspective gave them the sense of just having to sit back and listen. Apparently the third person perspective did not stimulate them to engage or to look around, and they did not feel actively involved in the movie. With the first person perspective, on the other hand, many respondents indicated that they had a hard time identifying with the voice that was telling the story. It remained difficult for them to accept that this 'I' that was talking, was referring to the viewer himself or herself, instead of to an anonymous narrator that was talking from a position outside of the screen. With the second person perspective, however, a majority of the respondents experienced a strong sense of presence. They indicated that in this version, the visual perspective that was provided by the surround video content seemed to relate closely to the perspective that was given by the voice-over narration. This version also triggered them to look around and actively engage with the surround video content. In short, the second person perspective provided the strongest sense of actually being part of the story.

5 Engagement in Documentary VR

In the previous sections, the focus has been on VR experiences that lean towards drama and fiction. However, amongst the producers of traditional news media there is also a strong interest for the use of VR for documentary purposes. De la Pena et al. have introduced the concept and discussed the implications of immersive journalism, which they describe as the production of news in a form in which people can gain first person experiences of the events or situation described [26]. The ability of current VR technology has lead filmmaker and digital artist Chris Milk to state that VR can be considered as an 'empathy machine' [27]. However, this perspective has gained considerable criticism, for example from Janet Murray, who notes that empathy comes from the experience of carefully crafted works and not as an automatism from a particular platform [28].

Earlier in this paper, we introduced the so-called *Swayze effect*, that may occur when a user feels immersed in story world, but at the same time left out, as the story world itself and the characters inhibiting it seem completely indifferent to his or her presence. To overcome this perceived clash between presence and engagement, producers of VR experiences need to develop strategies that give the viewer a sense of urgency within the story world, even if they are not directly addressed by the characters within that world. In dramatic productions, this feature may be incorporated within the narrative, that may contain a plausible explanation for why the viewer is not made part of the action. However, with documentary VR, other means may be needed to prevent the user from feeling neglected in a world that he or she is actually expected to connect to and empathize with.

Elaborating on the experiment on voice-over perspective, we proposed to explore the possibility of overcoming the clash between engagement and presence in documentary VR by adding an experimental voice-over that addresses the user from a second person perspective. In the next section, we will describe our second study.

6   Second Study

Our second study was set up in cooperation with VPRO, a Dutch national television broadcast company, and IDFA, the International Documentary Festival in Amsterdam, in November 2016. For this experiment, 360° footage was used that had been shot on location amongst an Amish community in the US, by VPRO television. In the fragment, that lasts about 5 min, the viewer is introduced to Norman Yoder, who talks about his life in the countryside and the way the Amish community handles the pressures of modern communication technologies. In the original version, Yoder addresses the viewer from his own first person perspective. For the experiment version, a new voice-over was written and recorded that contains the same information, but addresses the viewer directly in a second person perspective (Table 2).

During three days of the IDFA festival, the experiment was conducted in the IDFA DocLab, a space within the festival that is devoted to explorations into new media and VR. The two versions of the Amish video were installed on two Samsung Gear VR Headsets. Visitors of the festival were invited to take part in the experiment, and were randomly assigned to watch the original or the experimental version. Afterwards, they were asked to fill in our questionnaire.

Elaborating on our insights into the use of voice-over perspective in VR, as described in the first part of this paper, we expected that the experimental version may give users a higher sense of presence, and may thus help in overcoming the *Swayze effect*, as was discussed in the previous paragraph. Thus, we reached the following two hypotheses:

H1: Participants feel more addressed in the 360° documentary using second person voice-over compared to the first person version.
H2: Participants experiencing the second person voice-over have a higher sense of presence in comparison to participants experiencing the first person version.

6.1   Method

A total of 119 participants (62 males, 57 females; average age $M = 36.24$ years, $SD = 14.34$ years) attending the IDFA festival event were randomly assigned to one of the two voice-over conditions, watched the documentary for 5 min. Subsequently, they completed a questionnaire on user experiences, which includes short scales on the following dimensions: usability, enjoyment, personal meaning (eudaimonic appraisal), attention, spatial presence, social presence, perception of being addressed. These dimensions were measured with a 5-point-Likert scale ranging from 1 (totally disagree) to 5 (totally agree), using between four and six items each. Reliability scores for all scales were satisfying (see Table 3). Participants had a moderate degree of computer game literacy (M = 2.38, SD = 1.09) and VR literacy (M = 2.32, SD = 1.00, both on a scale from 1, no experience, to 4, a lot of experience).

6.2   Results

Between-subject comparison by means of independent samples t-tests revealed that the voice-over manipulation had no effect on the perception of being addressed (see Table 1). Therefore, our first hypothesis is rejected. As a possible result of not feeling addressed, neither social nor spatial presence was significantly higher for the second person voice-over condition. Thus, H2 has also been rejected. Albeit not significant, we see a tendency of better ratings for the second perspective voice-over condition in regard to the level of attention and spatial presence.

Table 2. The first lines of the original **voice**-over as spoken by Norman Yoder, and the experimental version that was written in a second person perspective

First person	Second person
I'm Norman Yoder, and my wife Annie. We have three children And I don't understand all that media, Facebook, Twitter and all that	Your companion introduces himself as Norman Yoder. He and his is wife Annie have three children. Norman informs to you that he doesn't understand all that media such as Facebook and Twitter

Table 3. Group comparison with mean values (M), standard deviations (SD), significance level (p), and reliability of the scales (α).

Exp. dimension	Control group		Voice-over			
	M	SD	M	SD	p	Rel. a
Enjoyment	3.91	.58	3.93	.63	.860	.78
Attention	3.86	.64	4.11	.73	.063	.84
Meaning	3.04	.63	3.01	.74	.835	.84
Spatial presence	3.12	.90	3.45	.82	.079	.89
Social presence	2.75	.77	2.75	.68	1.00	.78
Feeling addressed	2.82	.54	2.97	.49	.121	.67
Usability	4.05	.47	4.09	.56	.630	.69

A general assessment of the experience based on all participants revealed that overall enjoyment, attention and usability were rated positively (around 4 on the 5-point Likert scale). We conclude that participants liked the experience, had no usability issues and were paying attention to the content (festival events can be loud and distracting, which was apparently not influencing the experience and results). However, perceived spatial and social presence and the perception of being addressed were all around the neutral mark (score of 3).

Independent-samples t-tests show that participants with VR experience (N = 81, M = 2.97, SD = .50) felt significantly more addressed than people without previous VR experience (N = 27, M = 2.65, SD = .48; p = .002), regardless of the voice-over manipulation. Furthermore, participants without VR experience (M = 4.20, SD = .46) rated their enjoyment significantly higher compared to those with previous VR experience (M = 3.82, SD = .59; p = .001).

7 Conclusion, Discussion and Future Research

Reflecting on our previous discussion of voice-over in movies, and how users were addressed in early video games, we may conclude that the use of voice-over narration seems a good solution to connect the viewers visual experience of a 360° video to the story that is told. While the use of voice-over has been frowned upon in movie-making circles, the new kind of 'presence' that 360° video content provides indeed seems to overrule previous 'laws' of cinematic storytelling. When looking back at the use of narrator perspectives in different media, it seems remarkable that the second person perspective that was already used in early text adventure games, but is not very common in films, now seems to provide a good way of engaging the user in the narrative that is being presented. This means that in the new domain of interactive storytelling that has opened up with the use of surround video content, principles of video gaming and movie watching can be productively combined, creating new kinds of media experiences for new audiences.

Our qualitative study indicated that viewers of 360° documentaries prefer the second-person perspective, as the first-person perspective creates a mismatch between the need for identification and the attributed voice of a stranger. In the quantitative study, one condition featured a second perspective voice-over instead of the original audio, which was presented to a control group. Results showed that this manipulation had no effect on the perception of being directly addressed by the voice-over and did not affect presence as hypothesized. However, we found that participants' general VR literacy plays a crucial role for their user experience. Participants with previous VR experiences felt significantly more addressed (independent from the voice-over manipulation) than those without any VR literacy. Participants that experienced VR for the first time were most likely focusing on experiencing different aspects of the system without paying much attention to the voice-over perspective. We therefore hypothesize that, once this group gets more familiar with VR systems, the novelty effect fades and nuances in the content, in our case the voice-over, should become more relevant. Nevertheless, the majority of our participants had prior VR experiences and still were not significantly influenced by our voice-over manipulation. Based on the results of our current experiment, we can therefore not claim that the so-called *Swayze effect* may be overruled by adding a voice-over to create an extra layer of intimacy that connects the viewer to the virtual world.

Another possible explanation for our results is a negative effect on the impression of authenticity of the interview material caused by replacing the original audio with a voice-over. In a study on the use of voice-over in television shows, Semmler et al. [29] showed that narration by the title character was significantly associated with increased parasocial relationship experience. This could indicate that in the experimental condition of our study, in which users were not directly addressed by the main character, they may have experienced a considerable reduced parasocial connection. Our results, however, do not indicate a loss of enjoyment and perceived meaningfulness due to the exposure to the second perspective voice-over.

The specific characteristics of the group of respondents that were involved in the second experiment may have also had impact on the results. After all, this study was conducted during an international documentary festival, and many of the respondents who watched our experimental footage and filled in our questionnaire, may have been looking at the presented material with a much more professional and critical eye, focusing more on the aesthetics of the documentary material itself than on characteristics of the VR 'carrier' that the material was presented through.

Another explanation for the lack of clear results from our second study may have had to do with the survey itself, and especially with the items of the scale that measured presence. After all, the items that we used to measure the amount of presence that viewers experienced were not specifically developed for use with virtual reality. For instance, it might be that the scales that were used focus more on emotional presence, than on spatial presence. Further investigations will be needed to reconsider the relative value of these scales within a VR context.

Addressing the user directly is a promising way to start as our first study shows. However, a third-person perspective might work as well and create a different experi-ence. This might be beneficial for documentary productions, which might want the audience to remain in some distance to a given character. In our next experiment, we aim to implement the findings of the current study, and use a voice-over from a second person perspective to guide the viewer through the narrative. In this project, however, we will add interactive elements to create an experience that is one step closer to fully-immersive interactive narrative. In this project, so-called interactive hotspots will be implemented in the video, that are triggered when the user looks at them for some time. The next research question we will explore is to find out how voice-over narration may guide the user towards the points in the video that he or she needs to look at in order for the story to proceed, without disrupting the sense of 'presence' that is induced by the surround video experience. Within this study we also aim to explore differences between respondents in their reactions depending on previous experience with VR, or video games. Future studies should also examine possible effects on character believability and perceived authenticity. Mixed audio, combining scenes with second perspective voice-over (e.g. to directly address the audience and to provide extra information) and original audio (to preserve the authenticity of the material) might be a fruitful design approach.

Acknowledgements. This research project is funded by SiA RAAK – Nationaal Regieorgaan Praktijkgericht Onderzoek. Special thanks to the students at Medialab Amsterdam for creating the source material and conducting the experiments for our first study. We also want to thank IDFA DocLab and VPRO television for their kind cooperation in the second study.

References

1. Watercutter, A.: Oculus is awesome for games, but it's the future of movies. Wired (2014). http://www.wired.com/2014/01/oculus-movies/. Accessed June 2017
2. Solomon, B.: Facebook buys Oculus virtual reality gaming startup for 2 billion. Forbes (2014). http://www.forbes.com/sites/briansolomon/2014/03/25/facebook-buys-oculus-virtual-reality-gaming-startup-for-2-billion/. Accessed June 2017
3. Koenitz, H.: Design approaches for interactive digital narrative. In: Schoenau-Fog, H., Bruni, L.E., Louchart, S., Baceviciute, S. (eds.) ICIDS 2015. LNCS, vol. 9445, pp. 50–57. Springer, Cham (2015). https://doi.org/10.1007/978-3-319-27036-4_5
4. Roth, C., Koenitz, H.: Towards creating a body of evidence-based interactive digital narrative design knowledge: approaches and challenges. In: AltMM 2017, Mountain View, CA (2017). http://doi.org/10.1145/3132361.3133942
5. Vosmeer, M., Schouten, B.: Interactive cinema: engagement and interaction. In: Mitchell, A., Fernández-Vara, C., Thue, D. (eds.) ICIDS 2014. LNCS, vol. 8832, pp. 140–147. Springer, Cham (2014). https://doi.org/10.1007/978-3-319-12337-0_14
6. Vosmeer, M., Roth, C., Schouten, B.: Interaction in surround video: the effect of auditory feedback on enjoyment. In: Schoenau-Fog, H., Bruni, L.E., Louchart, S., Baceviciute, S. (eds.) ICIDS 2015. LNCS, vol. 9445, pp. 202–210. Springer, Cham (2015). https://doi.org/10.1007/978-3-319-27036-4_19
7. Cho, J., Lee, T.-H., Ogden, J., Stewart, A., Tsai, T.-Y., Chen, J., Vituccio, R.: Imago: presence and emotion in virtual reality. In: ACM SIGGRAPH 2016 VR Village (ACM), p. 6 (2016)
8. Hodgkinson, G.: Lock up your stories - here comes Virtual Reality. TECHART: J. Arts Imaging Sci. 3(4), 10–14 (2016)
9. Kors, M., Ferri, G., Van der Spek, E., Ketel, C., Schouten, B.: A breathtaking journey: on the design of an empathy-arousing mixed-reality game. In: Proceedings of the 2016 Annual Symposium on Computer-Human Interaction in Play (ACM), pp. 91–104 (2016)
10. Riva, G., Mantovani, F., Capideville, C.-S., Preziosa, A., Morganti, F., Villani, D., Gaggioli, A., Botella, C., Mariano, A.M.: Affective interactions using virtual reality: the link between presence and emotions. CyberPsychol. Behav. 10(1), 45–56 (2007)
11. Murray, J.: Hamlet on the Holodeck: The Future of Narrative in Cyberspace. The MIT Press, Cambridge (1998)
12. Ryan, M.-L.: Narrative as Virtual Reality 2: Revisiting Immersion and Interactivity in Literature and Electronic Media. JHU Press, Baltimore (2015)
13. Kozloff, S.: Invisible Storytellers. University of California Press, Berkely (1988)
14. McKee, R.: Story: Substance, Structure, Style, and the Principles of Screenwriting. Harper-Collins Publishers, New York (1997)
15. Kozloff, S.: About a clueless boy and girl: Voice-over in romantic comedy today. Cinephile Voice-Over 8(1), 5–14 (2012)
16. Tabarraee, B.: Editor's note. Cinephile Voice-Over 8(1), 2 (2012)
17. Laamanen, C.: What does God hear? terrence malick, voice-over, and the tree of life. Cinephile Voice-Over 8(1), 15–20 (2012)
18. Crowther, W.: Adventure [Video Game] (1976)
19. Lebling: Zork [Video Game]. Infocom, Cambridge (1980)
20. Curtis, P.: LambdaMOO [online game] Xerox PARC. Washington USA: Played 1995 (1990)
21. Dibbell, J.: My Tiny Life. Fourth Estate Limited, London (1999)
22. Roth, C.: Experiencing Interactive Storytelling. Ph.D. thesis (2016). http://dare.ubvu.vu.nl/handle/1871/53840. Accessed June 2017

23. North, M.-M., North, S.-M.: A comparative study of sense of presence of traditional virtual reality and immersive environments. Austr. J. Inf. Syst. **20** (2016)

24. Roth, C., Koenitz, H.: Evaluating the user experience of interactive digital narrative. In: AltMM 2016, pp. 31–36. ACM Press, New York (2016). http://doi.org/10.1145/2983298.2983302

25. Burdette, M.: The Swayze effect (2016). https://storystudio.oculus.com/en-us/blog/the-swayze-effect/. Accessed June 2017

26. De la Pena, N., Weil, P., Llobera, J., et al.: Immersive journalism: Immersive virtual reality for the first-person experience of news. Presence: Teleoper. Virtual Exp. **19**(4), 291–301 (2010)

27. Milk, C.: How virtual reality can create the ultimate empathy machine (2015). https://www.ted.com/talks/chris_milk_how_virtual_reality_can_create_the_ultimate_empathy_machine?language=en. Accessed June 2017

28. Murray, J.H.: Not a Film and Not an Empathy Machine, 6 October 2016. https://immerse.news/not-a-film-and-not-an-empathy-machine-48b63b0eda93#.5n2m7lfnq. Accessed 20 Mar 2017

29. Semmler, S.-M., Loof, T., Berke, C.: The influence of audio-only character narration on character and narrative engagement. Commun. Res. Rep. **32**(1), 63–72 (2015)

Empathic Actualities: Toward a Taxonomy of Empathy in Virtual Reality

Joshua A. Fisher[(✉)]

Department of Digital Media, Georgia Institute of Technology, Tech Square Research Building,
85 5th St NW, Atlanta, GA, USA
jadlerfisher@gatech.edu

Abstract. This paper seeks to formalize the language of empathy surrounding Virtual Reality (VR). The immediacy of VR documentaries has been claimed to be so vivid that users are more capable of empathizing than through previous media. This is a laudable but ambiguous claim. Empathy's multiple definitions complicate how designers use the term. Further, the relationship between users, designers, and subjects in reality needs clarification if claims of empathy are to be made. This paper proposes that VR does not facilitate a direct relationship between a user and an experience's subject in reality to achieve empathy. Instead, VR designers establish role-plays to achieve an empathic actuality—an emotionally charged interpretation of life—which may result in compassion or sympathy. Users end up empathizing directly with a VR designer and their presented representations, not their subjects in lived reality. A review of existing experiences is discussed to clarify claims of empathy and put forward a foundational taxonomy.

Keywords: Virtual reality · Design · Empathy · Documentary theory

1 Introduction

The concept that became Star Trek's Holodeck was introduced by Gene Dolgoff, the holography researcher, who described holograms as, "the ultimate way of reproducing reality" [19]. This has become virtual reality's maxim. Faced with the vividness of these reproduced realities, practitioners claim that users feel a powerful sense of empathy for characters with whom they share a digital setting. Further, they claim that this empathy exceeds that of previous media [20]. It is a laudable assertion, but one that appears ambiguous.

Empathy's plurality of definitions complicates the way practitioners use the term, necessitating a formalized design language to sketch the borders of what empathy in virtual reality (VR) is and what it is meant to accomplish. Secondly, the relationships between VR practitioners, viewers, and subjects need to be clarified if claims of empathy are to be legitimized. Lastly, the tactics and strategies implemented to achieve empathy are varied and unsystematic, which casts doubt on their efficacy. In an effort to clarify the language, this paper seeks to formalize what is meant by empathy in VR.

© Springer International Publishing AG 2017
N. Nunes et al. (Eds.): ICIDS 2017, LNCS 10690, pp. 233–244, 2017.
https://doi.org/10.1007/978-3-319-71027-3_19

2 Empathy Machine or Empathic Actuality?

The claim of empathy was made famous by Chris Milk. In his 2015 Ted Talk, *How Virtual Reality Can Create the Ultimate Empathy Machine*, Milk describes VR:

> It's a machine but inside of it, it feels like real life. It feels like truth. And you feel present with the world … and with the people that you are inside of it with. …. And when you are sitting there in [Syrian child refugee Sidra's] room, you're not watching it through a television screen, you're not watching it through a window. You're sitting there with her. […] And because of that you feel her humanity in a deeper way. You empathize with her in a deeper way. And I think we can change minds with this machine.

By 2017, the phrase "empathy machine" has become a cliché. Even Academy Award winning director Kathryn Bigelow, when asked by an interviewer why she was drawn to make the VR documentary, The Protectors: Walk in the Ranger's Shoes, responded, "I think the simple reason was empathy" [27]. The rhetoric surrounding VR's affordance for empathy can be overwhelming and facile, but some artists are not completely buying into the hype.

Nonny de la Peña believes that one has to move within a VR space for empathy to occur [7]. Unlike Milk, de la Peña's experiences enable the user to walk around a virtual environment (VE) and view the action as an active witness:

> I pretty quickly these days can hear material and get the vérité moment that would work for an embodied experience […] Imagine you are walking around inside a story, now you are really engaging your body in the story […] And I think that is one of the reasons why people connect so deeply to these pieces and why they offer an entrée into a more empathic connection.

De la Peña refers to her work as Immersive Journalism [9]. Whereas Milk's work is primarily 360° VR cinema, de la Peña recreates events that have taken place in reality using VR, photogrammetry, and volumetric video. At the core of her work, de la Peña seeks to achieve a Response-as-if-Real effect on the part of users with the content of her documentaries [9]. She proposes that this helps users achieve a sense of empathy with her subjects in reality.

Both de la Peña and Milk seek to document and then design representations of a unique aspect of reality for their audiences. The rhetoric around these VR experiences presents them as reality, but this is problematic. If the documentary is meant to be in the performative mode, an audience is meant to have an emotional reaction with little reflection [23]. This hardly appears to be the goal and diminishes the work of Milk and de la Peña. However, similar rhetoric surrounding emerging media is common.

It was Roger Ebert who coined the phrase when he praised cinema as "a machine that generates empathy," allowing us to step outside of our own lived experiences [5]. However, these claims of delusional presence and counter-factual identification have been made for many other forms of representation, particularly for new story-telling media. Using only the printed word, Charles Dickens induced whole nations to weep over the death of Little Nell, to rejoice in the conversion of Ebenezer Scrooge, and to demand happy endings for his protagonists. He worked to expand class sympathies through his sentimental but sympathetic portrayals of the poor. The desire to create empathy on the part of writers and filmmakers, and the experiential enjoyment of empathy on the part of audiences, makes clear that VR is not necessarily doing anything new.

2.1 Issues with Portraying Reality and Claims of Empathy

Questions regarding media's ability to actually capture or record, faithfully, the reality of another and broadcast it to an audience is extensive [24]. Take another form of documentary, the memoir. James B. Mitchell questions their authenticity and "true" history [21]. He observes that they achieve Roland Barthes' effect of reality, making a problematic claim of authority upon history [3]. Such constructed histories, when popularized, have a palpable effect on how a society perceives its reality [24].

The manner in which a narrative may shift from being simply descriptive, observational even, to what's traditionally conceived of as a novel, has been discussed by David Herman. He positions a gradient of narrative in which its component qualities are configured into new forms that reflect society's predilections. Of these factors that make up a narrative, Herman puts forward qualia, the sense of what it's like for someone or something to have a particular experience. For Herman, this is critical for an effective narrative. Consider at one end of the spectrum, for example, memoir deconstructed to only its plot events upon a timeline. This would be almost observational: a run down of events and tantamount to zero-narrativity [14]. On the other end, a memoir in which a reader senses that they have an understanding of what it is like to be the memoirist has achieved a greater degree of narrativity. Succeeding in imparting qualia in the narrative may result in degrees of empathy on the part of the reader. However, as discussed by Mitchell, what may be imparted as qualia could be constructed, cobbled together with verisimilitudes, and this is problematic.

Consider those ramifications in tandem with Suzann Keen's theory of narrative empathy. Keen states that empathy in narratives requires the minimal elements of identity, situation, and feeling. Fealty to reality does not make the list. Keen cautions that achieving empathy requires a shared perspective by both the reader and author [17]. The reader may naturally empathize with the author's stance because it is similar to their own. Importantly, Keen recognizes that empathy can be used for rhetorical purposes to influence audiences and enforce pre-existing emotions [17]. The latter is what is at stake when practitioners intentionally use empathy to achieve rhetorical goals, whether related to the narrative itself or for commercial success. This same tension has been a point of extensive discourse in documentary studies, especially in relation to performative forms [23]. De la Peña's earlier invocation of cinéma vérité underscores this issue. Indeed, documentary studies provide clarification for issues regarding the rhetoric of popular media that claim to represent reality and encourage empathy [26].

2.2 Empathic Actualities

VR asserts its mediations as true representations of lived reality, even though it really transforms bodies into mutable wire frames, textures, and animations. These experiences are what John Grierson, father of British and Canadian documentary film, referred to as a "creative treatment of actuality" [1]. It is not that these experiences and the subjects within them do not exist, but that they are constructed and dramatically compressed. They are, in Grierson's language, "truth made beautiful" [1]. They are an interpretation of reality and therefore suspect. This complicates claims of empathy made by VR practitioners. In recognition of Keen's observation that empathy has a rhetoric, such problematic claims may have unintended and undue influence. This is due, in no small part, to the qualia of the actuality established by the documentarian. A user's perceived comprehension of an other's experience in their actuality has ramifications. After all, it is unsettling to consider that a user empathizes not with a subject in reality, but the designed qualia of a creatively treated representation. This may result in a user drawing conclusions that have a limited basis in lived reality. For this reason, empathy claims require a critical approach. After all, these representative VEs are designed to have a profound emotional impact on users. Following Grierson, these designed and emotionally charged experiences and their subjects are presented as empathic actualities. They are creatively treated aspects of reality that are actualized by the medium of VR with qualia designed to facilitate empathy.

3   Two Modes of Empathy

Empathy has its roots in both linguistics and philosophy, which have led to its dual meanings [29]. The word finds its etymological roots in empatheia, a combination of em, in or at; and pathos, passion or suffering [29]. It implies a traveling into someone else to understand their feelings. This meaning has resulted in our current conception of emotional empathy. Theodore Lipps, an early 20th century philosopher, established what is known as cognitive empathy. His contemporary, Robert Vischer, used the term Einfühlung, aesthetic sympathy, to describe the act of understanding an artist through their work. This term was promoted by Lipps, whose recognition of Einfühlung as a projection and recognition of the self into an object of perception became known as empathy in English [31]. The elevated concept describes cognitive work, an understanding of similarities between oneself and an artifact that results in a process of perspective taking with the artist.

3.1   Emotional Empathy as a Reflexive Mirror

Often understood through pathology, emotional empathy is the instantaneous and somatic reaction to a subject's emotions without the conscious intentionality of that subject. Emotion is seen as a contagion that colonizes the observer with feelings that are not their own [17]. This is empathy as a reflexive mirror. As an example, take a scene of supposed domestic bliss wherein someone is calmly reading a newspaper. Their partner returns home from errands fuming about traffic. In response, the calm reader begins to feel angry. The heightened emotional state gets both partners yelling and when the dust settles, no one is sure why a fight began in the first place. This is emotional empathy, a mirrored somatic response to another's emotional state.

3.2   Cognitive Empathy as Perspective-Taking

Theodore Lipps' first foray into cognitive empathy was not directed at understanding the minds of others, but the poetic soul of art pieces and beautiful objects. He believed that the appreciation of an artwork's beauty occurs because empathy allows us to see it, via analogy, as the artist [29]. An observer could empathize with an art piece to understand the emotional choices of the creator, and so come to understand that creator. Samuel Coleridge, speaking to these same assertions, believed empathy was the way in which a viewer's and creator's emotional states switch places via the artifact [4]. At the core of this exchange is the belief that empathy is a primary epistemic perceptive mode: A way of generating knowledge that uses gestures and expressions to infer an other. It posits that a representation could provide limitless access to another person's mind. This is perspective taking, a result of cognitive empathy.

4   Empathic Actualities in Virtual Reality

To some degree, both emotional and cognitive empathy are elicited by existing VR projects. The manner in which they are inspired within an audience is mediated through an empathic actuality. This complicates what the empathy machine, as shown in Fig. 1, claims to do when it places both the audience and the subject within a shared reality at the behest of the VR designer.

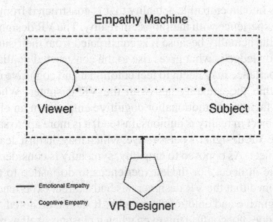

Fig. 1. The empathy machine magically places both the viewer and subject in a shared reality in which both emotional and cognitive empathy are supposed to occur.

The empathic actuality does not establish a direct relationship between the viewer and a subject. What a user experiences within this digital environment, how they may feel about a rendered character, does not establish a direct empathic relationship between themselves and who that character represents. Instead, a user empathizes with a VR designer's representation of their interpretation of that subject. For example, a user may empathize with a representation of a refugee child because they share a similar understanding of that child's plight with the VR practitioner. This creates a disjointed triangle as shown in Fig. 2 between the viewer, the VR designer, and the experience's subject in reality.

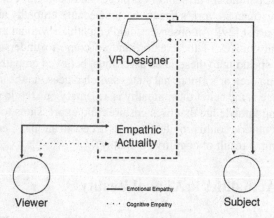

Fig. 2. A viewer's intention to empathize going into the VR experience is unmediated, but is influenced by the Empathic Actuality and may result in sympathy or compassion. The VR designer's empathy with the subject can neither be confirmed nor denied by the experience. The viewer empathizes with the designer and their representations of the subject in the experience.

A viewer enters into an empathic actuality that is constructed from a VR designer's knowledge of and experience with the subject in reality. The VR designer is intrinsically a part of the empathic actuality because it is constructed from their situated knowledge [12]. This same knowledge is what gives rise to the constructed qualia of the actuality. A viewer in the experience may begin to feel emotional and cognitive empathy with the representations within the actuality and with the VR designer. Whether or not this empathic actuality facilitates emotional or cognitive empathy in an effective way with the experience's subject in reality is dubious. Instead, it is more apt to say that the viewer empathizes with the VR designer's perspective, which may, in turn, lead to their sympathizing with the subject. As opposed to empathy, sympathy is considered to be a feeling of care for someone in need. For these experiences to do justice to the subjects they represent, it is assumed that the VR designer has had a direct experience with them that resulted in both cognitive and emotional empathy. It should be noted, however, that an experience in itself does not confirm this even when it presents itself as reality. Achieving accuracy within the empathic actuality and its efficacy is the onus of the VR designer. It is critically important for those working in the VR documentary space to do justice to those they represent in their experiences if claims of empathy are to be made with any legitimacy. The manner in which this might be appropriately accomplished is varied. However, the process partially relies upon the affordances of the documentarian's chosen VR technology, whether it be 360° VR cinema or a room-scale experience.

4.1   Strategies for Empathic Actualities

When a VR designer constructs an empathic actuality, they are establishing an opportunity for users to role play in an experience outside of their lived reality. Studies have shown that such role play experiences enhance active listening, social problem solving, and demonstrations of emotional empathy [25]. In VR, practitioners seek to achieve "Almost Real Live," a role play technique that seeks to get as close to real life as possible [25]. Within these role plays, connecting decisions to embodied movement and actions has helped participants conceptualize perspectives and develop unique, synthesized value systems [18]. In short, role plays have been shown to effectively establish cognitive empathy. An effective empathic actuality is then one that is "Almost Real Live." It allows a user the greatest degree of embodied interactions in connection with choices that have moral consequences. The more the user feels that their behavior has a consequence in the empathic actuality, the more likely they are to form a cognitive empathic connection. This is a natural parallel to other Human Computer Interaction work related to presence in VR [28] and interactive storytelling [22]. This resonance is further explored in a selection of work that exemplifies specific design strategies to achieve an effective empathic actuality.

Each case study was chosen because it exemplifies a particular design strategy, a set of interactions based on the affordances of the documentarian's chosen medium. The discussion of these strategies is meant to inform the work of the burgeoning VR documentary community: not just in terms of discourse and critique, but also in terms of accountability to one's subject and the responsibility to do justice to the documented.

5   Case Studies for Empathy in VR

A viewer may be aware of the particular perspective of the VR designer and their empathy strategies in the actuality. In film, this is exemplified in Michael Moore's documentaries wherein he uses the tactic of faux naïf to trick his subjects into saying something in a manner that suits his documentary's priorities [11]. It all looks like reality to the viewer after post-production, and that's the point. VR designers employ similar tactics and strategies to motivate empathy in their actualities.

The experiences were chosen for their varied degrees of dramatic agency. This was based on the premise that the greater the affordance for dramatic agency, such as in the role play experience of "Almost Real Live," the greater the affordance for empathy. Henry is a VR cinema experience with interaction limited to proprioception of the head, whereas Gnomes and Goblins is a room-scale VR experience for the HTC Vive with a diverse range of interactions. The difference in dramatic agency is stark. It is not that each new interaction may result in a new VR tactic for generating empathy. Rather, the scale of interactions, from minimal to life-like, affects the affordances for empathy. The design strategies discussed should be considered inclusive of a range of interactions within a certain stratum, and not singular.

The VR experiences presented in Table 1 are ranked from least to most effective for establishing empathy in empathic actualities. While the paper has been focused on VR documentaries, two other storytelling experiences are included. In these instances, the practitioners seek to establish empathy for fictional characters. The strategies are similar, but the accountability to do justice to an individual or community in reality may not be present.

Table 1. Design strategies for empathy

Case study	Design strategy	Design strategy explanation
Henry [6]	Passive witness	Traditional cinematic grammars such as close-ups are remediated to achieve similar empathic aims in VR
The Displaced [15]	Active witness	A user is directed to look in different directions via visual and aural cues
Gitmo [10]	Embodied in space	A user is embodied in space and they can perceive themselves in that body
Daniel's story [8]	Embodied interaction	A user can move about the VE and can interact to a degree with the subjects
Gnomes & Goblins [30]	Locus of control	A user feels a sense of dramatic agency and the control to make choices with moral consequences in the experience

5.1 Henry

Filmmaker Saschka Unseld encountered a design issue in his Oculus Story Studio VR cinema experience, Henry. The hedgehog is all alone on his birthday and feeling sad, so to inspire empathy the filmmaker uses cinematic grammar and moves him closer to the viewer as if in a close-up. In VR, this fails for a few reasons. First, since it is VR cinema, there is a chance that the user will not be looking in the right direction to catch Henry, even though he is ready for his close-up. Second, in VR users expect to be able to reach out to someone, especially when they are in need. At the very least, users tend to want to investigate the conflict. In Henry, the user is standing still and unable to move about or interact with the space. Though Henry's big eyes may stir some degree of emotional empathy, the capacity for cognitive empathy is doubtful [13]. The experience does not approach "Almost Real Live" because the user is a passive witness. They cannot move, only turn in a circle. The remediation of cinematic grammars for achieving empathy in VR is not necessarily effective because they keep the user from maximizing the medium's inherent affordances. Since the user is unable to celebrate with Henry, they are afforded an opportunity for sympathy and compassion. The potential for emotional empathy is happenstance.

5.2 The Displaced

The New York Times, in partnership with Chris Milk, is exploring VR documentaries that make unfamiliar territories familiar. These slow-paced visits to places users might not otherwise have access to are spaces and moments woven together with non-diegetic voiceover and narration. When these empathic actualities work, it is usually through a momentary framing, a spark connection when a child refugee looks you in the eyes across the space of a small boat. Users yearn to interact, but the refugee child sitting across from us remains closed to questions and help. In these empathic actualities, the feeling of emotional empathy is afforded for the viewer. The VR cinematographer is assumed to have some cognitive empathy with the child refugee. After all, they filmed the space to put the user in the boat with the refugee to hopefully share a moment of perspective-taking. The VR designer or filmmaker who sat in that boat to take that shot, at that moment, may have had a moment of direct cognitive empathy with the child. What users see allows them to have cognitive empathy with the filmmaker and potentially emotional empathy with the representation of the refugee.

In The Displaced, a 360° VR film with no interaction except swiveling in a circle to change point of view, there is a moment when the viewer is positioned on the edge of field in which a relief aid helicopter is dropping large sacks of food. Chuol, a displaced child close to the user's position struggles to lift one of the sacks. The moment is meant to trigger a reflexive emotional empathic response. This includes the visceral impulse to reach into the virtual world and literally lend a hand. Because users can physically relate to the situation of a particular person they have the opportunity to recognize a shared experience of dependency and vulnerability. Further, since they are not able to immediately help, users may be left with a desire to follow through and help in another way [16]. The immediacy of this moment achieves a degree of cognitive empathy and marks a contrast with the distancing techniques of voice over or the generalized panning of a setting. Still, the inability to reach out and help means that while the user may be immersed in the scene, they are not truly present [28]. A claim of shared reality is not valid, for if it were, a user could reach out and help. Again, the user is left with sympathy or compassion for the subject. Emotional empathy occurs through the representation. A user experiences cognitive empathy with the VR practitioner—both are unable to help in that moment. For the user, it is because they are not there in the field; for the designer, it is because they are filming and cannot interrupt the shot. This inability to help encourages a perspective-taking but not with the refugee.

5.3 Gitmo

Gitmo, created by Nonny de la Peña, began as a Second Life installation of Guantanamo Bay [10]. The initial experience allowed individuals to walk around the detention camp while a video of a father of one of the inmates read letters aloud from his imprisoned son. In her VR iteration, de la Peña places the user into the body of a male prisoner. He is bound in a vulnerable position within a cell. Next door, the audio of U.S. military personnel torturing another inmate can be heard. When the user turns their head, they see the horrible cell, the bound body of the detainee, and his haunting face staring back at them in a mirror, as if it were their own. Here de la Peña's tactic of embodying the user in space attempts to achieve an emotional and cognitive empathic connection. Users may have an emotional empathic reaction of fear or anxiety as they are constrained while their neighbor is tortured. As for cognitive empathy, Gitmo attempts to achieve perspective-taking by constraining the user's body in the VE so that it mimics that of the prisoner. This empathic actuality makes use of recorded audio and hours of research to achieve its accuracy. It is truer to an "Almost Real Live" role play scenario than either Henry or The Displaced. Even though there is no embodied interaction, the user is embodied not just in the space but within the body of the detainee. This facilitates cognitive empathy.

5.4   Daniel's Story

Daniel's Story is exemplary of de la Peña's foundational work and research. She posits that a VR system that offers a place, presents a mimicry of reality, and gives the user a virtual body with which to explore will be effective for generating empathy. De la Peña achieves embodied interaction to afford cognitive empathy through "Almost Real Live" scenarios. In Daniel's Story, users are in the living room of a family in north Georgia. They have the freedom to move around and witness a dramatic coming out story. The empathic actuality is composed of recorded documentary audio and the avatars of actors are recreated through volumetric video, their movements through motion capture. The memories of the protagonist guided the production. Users watch as Daniel, a young gay man, is confronted by his disapproving parents and grandparents. The prolonged engagement between the characters encourages users to be more active in the scene. They can move all about the space to get a better read on the gestures and facial expressions of the people in the family living room. When Daniel's estranged mother lets out a painful shriek, users are encouraged to run toward the action, ostensibly to see what has happened but also, perhaps, out of an emotional empathic response to an other being hurt. The ability to move naturally through the space, to rush to someone's aid, can have a powerful emotional impact. In this empathic actuality, de la Peña enables a plurality of avenues for achieving emotional empathy with all present within the scene. At the same time, the ability to move naturally and freely about the VE enables users the opportunity to explore deeply enough to achieve a sense of cognitive empathy.

5.5   Gnomes and Goblins

If Henry is unsuccessful in arousing this kind of empathy because the character is completely unavailable for interaction, the goblin in Gnomes and Goblins is its opposite. He has transparent interaction patterns that make it easy for users to relate to him and to get immediate feedback on their actions by observing his very readable responses. If users get too close, he runs away. If they put out an acorn, he comes out of hiding to grab it. Little by little, users win his trust and form emotional and cognitive empathy. There is a clear dramatic motivation and clear set of interaction mechanics to achieve the desired end. This increases a user's concern for the character and their interest in understanding his point of view. To a certain extent, the empathic actuality lets users deepen their empathy by enacting nurture, as they would for someone they personally care about. In this manner, the choices users make are emotionally motivated and reflect their morality. When users are shrunken down to the size of the goblins, a moment of direct perspective-taking occurs. In Gnomes and Goblins, users have a locus of control, the feeling that they matter enough in the VE to make a difference. Given the experience is fictional, this design mechanic has proven to be effective at influencing behavior in reality [2]. As VR experiences mature, establishing a locus of control in empathic actuality that results in a behavior change in reality will be the ultimate goal. There is little doubt that dramatic agency and a locus of control can be designed in tandem.

Design tactics for empathic actualities emphasize embodied interactions, a locus of control, and accurate representations that do justice to individuals and communities. Different experiences call for aspects to be used or discarded, but it is hoped that these proposed design tactics clarify the work in empathic actualities and will guide future development.

6   Conclusion

Although empathy in VR is not directly established between a user and an experience's subject in reality, the medium's affordance of placing a body within a new space provides an opportunity for the heightened understanding of an other through empathic actualities. It is critical to remember that the represented other and setting are artifacts constructed through the situated knowledge of the VR practitioner. Users empathize directly with that VR designer's representation of their subject. However, the representation can be accurate enough to achieve an "Almost Real Live" kind of role play which has proven to lead to behavior change. Recent work by Nonny de la Peña is exemplary of VR empathic actualities that do justice to the communities and individuals they represent. Fictional works like Gnomes and Goblins speak to the potential that dramatic agency, when considered in terms of locus of control for events in reality, may have in future VR experiences. Empathy in VR documentaries is about empathizing with the perspectives of designers and having sympathy or compassion for their subjects.

Acknowledgements. This work and the taxonomy in this paper were heavily influenced by discussions with Professor Janet H. Murray at the Georgia Institute of Technology.

References

1. McLane, B.A.: New History of Documentary Film. Bloomsbury, New York (2016)
2. Ahn, S., et al.: Short- and long-term effects of embodied experiences in immersive virtual environments on environmental locus of control and behavior. Comput. Hum. Behav. **39**, 235–245 (2014)
3. Barthes, R., Howard, R.: The Rustle of Language. University of California Press, Berkeley (2010)
4. Coleridge, S.: Biographia Literaria. Oxford University Press, London (1979)
5. Collette, O.: Moving Through Empathy: On "Life Itself" | Balder and Dash | Roger Ebert. http://www.rogerebert.com/balder-and-dash/moving-through-empathy-on-life-itself
6. Dau, R.: Henry. Oculus Story Studio (2015)
7. de la Peña, N.: #298: Nonny de la Peña on Empathy in VR | Voices of VR Podcast. http://voicesofvr.com/298-nonny-de-la-pena-on-empathy-in-vr/
8. de la Peña, N.: Daniel's Story. Emblematic (2016)

9. de la Peña, N., et al.: Immersive journalism: immersive virtual reality for the first-person experience of news. Presence: Teleoperators Virtual Environ. **19**(4), 291–301 (2010)
10. de la Peña, N.: Gitmo. Emblematic (2015)
11. Galloway, D.: From Michael Moore to JFK reloaded: Towards a working model of interactive documentary. J. Med. Pract. **8**(3), 325–339 (2007)
12. Haraway, D.: Situated knowledges: The science question in feminism and the privilege of partial perspective. Feminist Stud. **14**(3), 575–599 (1988)
13. Harrison, N., et al.: Processing of observed pupil size modulates perception of sadness and predicts empathy. Emotion **7**(4), 724–729 (2007)
14. Herman, D.: Basic Elements of Narrative. Wiley, Hoboken (2011)
15. Ismail, I., Solomon, B.C.: https://with.in/watch/the-displaced/
16. Jamison, L.: The Empathy Exams. Graywolf, Minneapolis (2014)
17. Keen, S.: A theory of narrative empathy. Narrative **14**, 207–236 (2006)
18. Lean, J., et al.: Simulations and games: Use and barriers in higher education. Act. Learn. High Educ. **7**(3), 227–242 (2006)
19. Meet The Man Behind The Holodeck, Part 1. http://www.startrek.com/article/meet-the-man-behind-the-holodeck-part-1
20. Milk, C.: How virtual reality can create the ultimate empathy machine (2015)
21. Mitchell, J.B.: Popular autobiography as historiography: the reality effect of Frank Mccourts Angelas ashes. Biography **26**, 607–624 (2003)
22. Murray, J.: Hamlet on the Holodeck. MIT Press, Boston (2017)
23. Nichols, B.: Representing Reality: Issues and Concepts in Documentary. Indiana University Press, Bloomington (2010)
24. Porter, R.: Rewriting the Self: Histories From the Renaissance to the Present. Routledge, London (1997)
25. Rao, D., Stupans, I.: Exploring the potential of role play in higher education: development of a typology and teacher guidelines. Innov. Educ. Teach. Inter. **49**(4), 427–436 (2012)
26. Renov, M.: Theorizing Documentary, pp. 1–37. Routledge, New York (2017)
27. Robertson, A.: At Tribeca's VR showcase, artists are trying to move beyond empathy. https://www.theverge.com/2017/5/3/15524404/tribeca-film-festival-2017-vr-empathy-machine-backlash
28. Slater, M., Wilbur, S.: A framework for immersive virtual environments (FIVE): speculations on the role of presence in virtual environments. Presence: Teleoperators Virtual Environ. **6**(6), 603–616 (1997)
29. Stueber, K.: Empathy (Stanford Encyclopedia of Philosophy). https://plato.stanford.edu/entries/empathy/
30. WeVR.: Gnomes and Goblins (preview) on Steam. http://store.steampowered.com/app/490840/Gnomes__Goblins_preview/
31. Zahavi, D.: Empathy, Embodiment and Interpersonal Understanding: From Lipps to Schutz. Inquiry **53**(3), 285–306 (2010)

Design for Emerging Media: How MR Designers Think About Storytelling, Process, and Defining the Field

Rebecca Rouse[1(✉)] and Evan Barba[2]

[1] Rensselaer Polytechnic Institute, 110 8th St., Troy, NY 12180, USA
rouser@rpi.edu
[2] Georgetown University, 37th and 0 Streets, NW, Washington DC 20057, USA
evan.barba@georgetown.edu

Abstract. Given mixed reality's (MR) unique status as an emerging medium that incorporates both the physical and the virtual in hybrid space, it is a particularly interesting field in which to study the design process as a whole, and interactive narrative design in particular. How prominently does story figure in MR design? What kinds of stories are being told? As MR tools become more accessible, the field is opening up to a wider variety of practitioners. However, the full breadth of methods and techniques being brought to bear in design for MR has not yet been studied. This paper presents findings from an interview study with fifteen leading MR designers, and describes the multiplicity of approaches they use. These approaches are presented as a matrix, composed of a opportunistic—deterministic spectrum (based on designs planned in advance vs. improvisation), and a storytelling—sensationalizing spectrum (based on designs aimed at narrative creation vs. development of a sensory experience).

1 Introduction

Despite a wealth of scholarship on mixed reality (MR) from many disciplinary perspectives, a comprehensive account of design practices for MR remains elusive. The choice to focus on the MR design process sets this study apart from the majority of work in the field, which commonly analyzes these experiences as discrete artifacts and discusses the effects of design choices in summative evaluations that sometimes obscure the pathways that led to those final results. Scholarship available on MR sometimes analyzes artifacts from humanities viewpoints, offering theoretical (but not prescriptive) frameworks [1–3]; often conceptualizes MR through the lens of human-computer interaction (HCI) as 'blended space' and focuses on user interface design and design metaphors [4, 5]; or approaches MR from technical standpoints in terms of the computer science and engineering development of systems [6–8]. MR is rarely discussed from a narrative design perspective, and when it has been, the conclusions reached have emphasized the importance of technology development, and not designers' approaches to narrative [9].

To situate this study with respect to Design Studies, it is helpful to provide a brief overview of the field. Frequently, the end-results of design, the artifacts themselves,

© Springer International Publishing AG 2017
N. Nunes et al. (Eds.): ICIDS 2017, LNCS 10690, pp. 245–258, 2017.
https://doi.org/10.1007/978-3-319-71027-3_20

are closely analyzed for clues about the designer's process [10–12]. Just as often, these same artifacts are examined in terms of the kinds of thinking they encourage or "afford" [13] in users. Design researchers are also interested in using design methods as a means of exploring complex and contested spaces or ideas [14] with the goals of creating repeatable "design thinking" processes, opening dialogue about future possibilities, and supporting innovation. As one step toward a more comprehensive understanding of MR as a design space, and in the vein of Goodman, Stolterman and Wakkary's [15] call to closely examine interaction design practice, we offer this initial study as an account of how MR designers imagine, build, and reflect on the complex hybrid experiences they create, and what kinds of stories they choose to tell.

It can be revealing to examine what kinds of stories get told in a new medium, what kinds of stories are not explored, and how these pioneering designers think about the work they are creating. In the earliest stages of new media, artifacts are often not well archived or preserved, and the voices of early designers are even less often captured or perceived as worthy of study (something we work towards remedying in this project). In these earliest phases of a new medium, artifacts are often not initially designed to include fictional narrative, and instead primarily designed to showcase the novel wonder or spectacle of the new technology itself. Media at this early stage can be understood as **media of attraction** [16]. Several scholars have addressed tensions between narrative and spectacle in media of attraction, specifically with regard to film [17–20]. This tension is not necessarily negative, and can generate interesting examples, as discussed in the works referenced here from Gunning, Gaudreault, Musser, and McMahan.

Some media move through this media of attraction phase to become fully institutionalized, as in commercialized and standardized media (such as film, radio, television, and videogames.) Other media do not leave the attraction phase, such as panoramas and theme parks. Examining differences in the use and experience of narrative is one approach to understanding why some forms institutionalize and others do not. Film, for example, began in the 1890 s with 'actualities' or non-fiction subjects, but quickly moved on to story film experiments–by Alice Guy Blaché, Georges Méliès, Edwin S. Porter and others–and then to institutionalization, around 1907 [17–22]. The case of the panorama is particularly interesting in terms of narrative. While historical narratives dominated the form, fictional stories were never told through this medium, an absence which may have contributed to the medium's resistance to institutionalization, although it persisted as a popular medium of attraction from the late 1790s through the early 1900s [23–25].

To clarify the intention of this study, we do not seek to claim MR as generative of entirely new forms of narrative or storytelling. Instead, we are looking at the critical question of fit in terms of what kinds of narratives designers are drawn to articulate, given the capabilities (and challenges) provided by MR. Media narrative scholar Marie Laure Ryan has articulated this question of fit as the crucial factor in determining a medium's entertainment capacity, and cultural staying power [26]. This study is of MR designers is positioned at a pivotal moment in the development of MR technology, as access to these tools is no longer restricted to those who can collaborate directly with university or corporate labs developing the technology themselves. Instead, today the MR design community includes a wide range of engineers, computer scientists, artists, game and simulation designers, scholar-practitioners, museum and cultural heritage professionals, educators, and students. This interdisciplinary mix of practitioners means that MR design methods are being shaped by a wide variety of other design traditions, and may present an interesting fusion of approaches. In addition, this early stage of MR's development as a medium provides us with a unique opportunity to examine what kinds of stories are being told with this set of technologies, giving us an historical touch-point for later analysis and a glimpse at future possibilities.

2 Methods

To begin illuminating the MR design process, we chose an interview methodology. While we were not able to include direct observation of the design process itself, we found that asking designers to reflect on their projects and processes yielded interesting information as well. As in all design, reflection both during and after development is a crucial component of the process. To gain a glimpse into the early stages of the design process, we included a hypothetical design challenge, inviting the designers to share initial brainstorming with us. We conducted semi-structured interviews with fifteen designers who are accomplished leaders in the field, each with a minimum of ten years of experience creating interactive works. The designers were first approached based on an analysis of their portfolios, which we felt had a particularly inspiring or original approach to combining the virtual and the real. Our interviews included the following seven questions as prompts for conversation:

- *What is your disciplinary background, and how have you adapted those practices to MR? Do you consider yourself an MR designer specifically?*
- *What does MR mean to you, and are there certain hallmarks or conventions that mark it as MR?*
- *Does MR provide something that no other medium can?*
- *Tell us about an interesting failure working with MR, and what you learned from it?*
- *Can you describe your design process, and how you move a project from concept to reality?*
- *What would an MR design framework need to accomplish in your opinion?*
- *Prompt for a hypothetical design challenge (described below)*

Of twenty designers invited to participate, fifteen were able to join the study. The designers who were interviewed are listed in Table 1, along with their primary affiliations. Interviews lasted sixty to ninety minutes and all interviewees were asked the same questions. All interviews were audio and video recorded, and transcribed. Our analysis followed a grounded theory approach [27] in which we reviewed the recordings and transcripts and identified emergent themes, including both threads of commonality connecting interviewees, as well as diverging viewpoints. In the following sections, we present our results, including information about how designers are defining the field of MR, how their design processes are structured, ways in which they approach storytelling, and challenges they identify.

Table 1. List of the fifteen designers who participated in the interview study, along with their primary affiliations

Mark Billinghurst	Professor of Human Computing Interaction at the University of South Australia
Benjamin Chang & Silvia Ruzanka	Art and design team in the Department of the Arts at Rensselaer Polytechnic Institute; Ruzanka is a Lecturer and Chang is an Associate Professor and Director of the Games and Simulation Arts and Sciences Program
Maribeth Gandy Coleman	Director of the Interactive Media Technology Center and Wearable Computing Center at Georgia Institute of Technology
Maria Engberg	Senior Lecturer in the Department of Computer Science and Media Technology at Malmö University
Caitlin Fisher	Canada Research Chair in Digital Culture, Associate Professor of Cinema and Media Arts, Co-Founder of the Future Cinema Lab, and Director of the Augmented Reality Lab at York University
Lissa Holloway-Attaway	Associate Professor of Media Arts, Aesthetics and Narration; Director of the Media Technology and Culture MTEC Research Group at the University of Skövde
Susan Kozel	Professor of New Media at Malmö University
David Krum	Co-Director of the Mixed Reality Lab at the University of Southern California Institute for Creative Technologies
Shawn Lawson	Professor and Graduate Program Director, Department of the Arts, Rensselaer Polytechnic Institute
Scott Rettberg	Professor of Digital Culture in the Department of Linguistic, Literary and Aesthetic Studies at the University of Bergen
Scott Snibbe	Interactive media artist and entrepreneur; founder and CEO of social music video startup EyeGroove
Camille Utterback	Interactive installation artist; Assistant Professor in the Department of Art and Art History, Stanford University
Sander Veenhof	Independent AR and VR developer; Founder of ManifestAR
Teresa Wennberg	Painter and multimedia artist; Artist in residence at the Center for Parallel Computers (PDC) a the Royal Institute of Technology (KTH) Stockholm

3   Shifting Definitions of Mixed Reality

Although only one third of the interviewees self-identified as MR designers specifi-cally, all of them have produced multiple projects that fit along the Virtuality Con-tinuum [28], which describes experiences based on how prominently they incorporate virtual elements. The continuum includes both augmented reality and augmented vir-tuality, as well as purely physical and virtual realities. While the designers' portfolios share many similar characteristics, the way in which they each categorize their own works, and how they develop respective definitions of MR, varied across three disci-plinary groupings: designers with a technical background; designers from the humanities; and designers from art practice. This variety of ways of defining their own practice (including the variety of terms for describing their own roles, such as developer, designer, artist, interactive artist, media practitioner, etc.) reflects the status of MR as a medium of attraction. The earliest filmmakers, for example, were called everything from 'presenter of views' to 'kinematographer' before the term 'director' was settled upon. The more technically-oriented designers were the most likely to identify as MR designers specifically, and they were also the most familiar with the canonical definition of MR illustrated in the Virtuality Continuum. This perspective naturally reflects these designers' training in Computer Science and Engineering, and their current context in university or industry laboratories focusing explicitly on MR technologies.

Digital Humanists made up a second group of designers, with varied backgrounds including English, Media Studies, and Games. This second group was more likely to conceptualize MR as a broad category of emerging media. While designers in the Digital Humanities group were generally familiar with more technical definitions of MR, these designers were conscious in their attempt to expand the definition in ways reflective of their own background and approach centered on media history and theory.

A third set of designers identified primarily as artists, and were more likely to express that such distinctions between a technical definition of MR and more media-theoretical-historical definition of MR were not very useful or relevant to current practice in interaction design. Designers in this third group were the most likely to espouse the belief that "it's all MR," interpreting MR in the broadest sense.

Despite these differences, there were points of consensus between the three disciplinary groups on the definition of MR. All designers noted the connection between physical and digital realities as the important hallmark of their work, and MR as a category in general. They were also clear that, to qualify as MR, the level of interaction must go beyond simple input paradigms like the mouse and keyboard and extend to include the entire body and/or surrounding space. What's more, the designers overwhelmingly agreed that they seek to foster not just the simple combination of physical and digital elements, but rather the total synthesizing experience that results from a user's interaction. MR design, in their terms, is a type of experience design in which the designer attempts to create an emergent reality that cannot simply be accounted for by the mere connection of physical and virtual elements in a given configuration. This emergent mixed reality was described alternately as a cognitive state of mind, a point of reference for interpreting action and experience, and as an emotive or affective experience that exists within the user as a result of interacting with connected physical and virtual elements.

In summary, designers coalesced around an understanding of mixed reality works as embodied, connected with a location in integral ways, and transformed through user experience resulting in a sum greater than its constituent parts. While this understanding is at odds with the commonly referenced technical definition supplied by the Virtuality Continuum, it is more in line with what the field has come to understand about user experience in the intervening decades since that continuum was first outlined. In the following section we discuss the processes these designers utilize to create these emergent experiential states.

4   Design Process: Opportunistic—Deterministic Spectrum

The majority of designers did not follow a standardized design process, citing the varieties of different contexts, subjects, and aims of each project requiring unique and custom approaches and tools. A few others took highly structured approaches citing more formal software engineering and usability tools and techniques. While four designers acknowledged using sketching, they did not see this as a formal design methodology. By far the more important element of the design process was prototyping and user testing. This is likely due to the still-emerging uses of MR technologies, and– despite the many thousands of hours of MR design experience these experts collectively embody–all of them exhibited humility when regarding the complexities of working within the medium.

To clarify the range of design process types implemented by the designers, we imagine the designers as placed along a spectrum representing this variety. Those who identified with the arts and humanities cluster more closely to the side of our spectrum we call **Opportunistic Design**. This approach is characterized by a less structured design process, high flexibility when determining the outcomes of projects, and a general willingness to adapt to the emergent phenomena that occur when introducing an MR intervention at a site. Camille Utterback articulated this approach particularly well:

> "So I usually start when I'm working on a piece for myself, there's some kind of question, and often that question has to do with the opportunity that you have at that moment. [...] there's a scrappiness to being an artist, you're always thinking what can I use from what's at hand, or take advantage of, or what's the opportunity here from a materials point of view."

The designers working at this end of the spectrum also seemed to have a "grab bag" of technical tricks from partially completed projects that they were willing and able to adapt to current projects if they saw a good fit. These designers were inherently more playful in their approach, and appeared more willing or able to take risks in their outcomes. Interestingly, they also saw the need for, and utility of, more structured design approaches. As Shawn Lawson described:

> "[...] there's a lot of trial and error and I try to be smarter which is usually the harder part. I started to draw diagrams, making gameplay flow diagrams [...] which makes the development significantly easier because I understand the mechanics of it."

Those on the **Deterministic Design** end of the spectrum favored more scientific or traditionally research-oriented approaches. Mark Billinghurst explained this clearly as follows:

> "We typically follow a traditional design thinking or interaction design approach. We basically have in many cases a well identified client and user so the first step of the process would be doing a needs analysis with the client, and then also talking with potential end users, [...] and from those needs we basically do a design exercise of several very quick and dirty prototypes, just paper sketching or quick mockups, and then from that we go into a more robust prototyping phase, we would build real working systems. Robust enough that they could be tested with real users. And the next step would be user evaluation, get real people to try it out. Then we'll cycle back around and go back to the original client end uses and present the results, do some more needs analysis, and potentially do that whole interaction design cycle two or three times when we get to the point when the final AR [augmented reality] experience is really well honed and tested."

This is not to say that designers with a more deterministic approach are inflexible. As many pointed out, they often need to redesign at various stages in the process in order to accommodate new constraints and information. However, the unifying characteristic within this group was the desire to minimize these sorts of emergent contingencies, while the opportunistic designers seemed to almost plan on some level of serendipity. In contrast, the deterministic designers strove to understand exactly what is required and deliver precisely what is needed to meet the needs defined early in the project.

5 "The Hope Diamond" Design Challenge

The final interview question was posed as a hypothetical design challenge: *How would you design an MR experience for the Hope Diamond?* We chose the Hope Diamond, a famously large diamond with a checkered past held in the Smithsonian's collection in Washington, DC, as an ultimate artifact, the prototypical museum object. We intended this final question as an intriguing design challenge, given the diamond's constraints: a nearly priceless object in terms of cost (prohibiting visitors from handling it, for example), yet almost blank in appearance (it is basically clear with a blueish tint) and surprisingly small in dimension (about one inch across). We invited each designer to brainstorm aloud, sharing their initial ideas about how they would think through a design for the Hope Diamond. We provided no guidance in terms of design goals or real-world constraints, and did not prompt the designers to consider narrative or any other particular characteristics.

Of course, the choice of object frames creative thinking. The nature of the object itself suggests what is important about it—it is a diamond, with all the physical properties of a diamond, and it is a cultural artifact worthy of being displayed in a major museum. Picking up on these two predominant aspects of the Hope Diamond the designers we interviewed tended to approach the history and cultural importance of the diamond using storytelling, while approaching the physical object itself though a collection of techniques that we call sensationalizing. By sensationalizing we mean to invoke the concept of sensation, as appealing to a variety of the body's senses, including visual spectacle.

5.1 Storytelling

In response to the design challenge, many designers were quick to focus their brainstorming around story concepts:

Lissa Holloway-Attaway: *"I always think about it as a storytelling problem, it's a narrative issue, so what's the way to construct some narrative around it, or a kind of framing experience that would allow me some kind of access to elements that I wouldn't think of, or wouldn't see."*

Caitlin Fisher: *"The first thing I'd do is collect the stories."*

Scott Rettberg: *"I'd have to think about story first. It's a pivot between technology and story."*

Scott Snibbe: *"Well it's about the story; [...] the key is the story, the suspense, if you never show [the diamond], it might be a lot more interesting."*

Sander Veenhof: *"A diamond is also a reflection, a mirror, [so I would] look at the material and then think how to trigger the right stories."*

In addition to the group of designers who invoked story explicitly as the core of their designs, a few designers implicitly used story without saying the word, and these designers all honed in on a notion of using narrative to reveal the history of the Hope Diamond. Historical narratives necessitate a moving between "then" and "now" in order to demonstrate relevance. MR's ability to layer provides easy access to creating such juxtapositions, and the use of the virtual here provides a mechanism to re-create relationships that have long-since disappeared. Most of the designers picked up on this affordance of MR technology and sought to operationalize it in the service of revealing history:

Maria Engberg: *"I would probably do something about its history [...] how many times it has changed hands, how many people owned it, has anyone worn it."*

Lissa Holloway-Attaway: *"[I would] make evident the history or legacy of this diamond, back to the diamond mine."*

David Krum: *"You could do a history of the Hope Diamond, who has owned it, what does that mean for those people, and what it represents."*

Teresa Wennberg: *"Maybe you could go to a historical part and see India, I think it's from India [...] or display all of the beautiful ladies who have worn it."*

Scott Snibbe: *"I think I'd put the deathbeds of the people who were killed by the diamond, and then you could see the people, if you have special glasses or projection or something like that, maybe you'd be able to get the people's stories [...] their moment of discovering [the diamond], and the moment of their death."*

Mark Billinghurst: *"Connect with some of the stories around the diamond, who were the previous owners, where it was found [...]. Maybe you'd have some kind of AR popups appearing where [...] you'd see the diamond, you could touch or tag around it and see the diamond replaced with a video avatar of an actor playing one of the previous owners talking about their experience owning the diamond or finding the diamond. [...] Basically use the physical diamond as an entry point into stories about the diamond, and to discussion about the politics of diamond mining today and in the past [...]".*

For Billinghurst, as with the other designers who used this approach, MR provides a method for the object to be situated and contextualized within multiple historical time periods and narratives. The diamond is positioned as a constant in ever-changing social and cultural contexts, and provides a consistent point of entry into different times and places, which are the real content of these experiences.

Fictionalizing. Fictionalization was only mentioned as a possibility by two of the fifteen designers: Caitlin Fisher and Maria Engberg. Interestingly, both Engberg and Fisher saw historical research as the springboard for creating imagined narratives. Fisher mentions using MR to create a 'haunting' experience, in which the user is pursued by the story beyond the physical bounds of the gallery space, then perhaps 'chased' back to the gallery to confront the object once again:

Caitlin Fisher: *"[...] Thankfully I'm not an historian, so I'd probably stretch the truth quite a bit. [...] Maybe even write a character, or write a mystery around it, or write a curse story, or make the user be cursed. [...] I would probably have a combination of things that were just audio, just creepy hauntings, I would probably try to make it scary [...] like this long mystery taking people around, and maybe they're haunted, and maybe it continues after they leave the room, you have rushing things behind them and as they go through the rest of the Smithsonian they actually hear more and more of the stories, and they're compelled back, maybe chased back to the Hope Diamond. [...] I would chase them out of the museum to a different place and back, preferably some place that would have some kind of intertextuality with the museum."*

Engberg's thinking followed a similar thread, in that the historical narrative was not the thing that should be communicated, but would rather serve as research material for a new narrative which would convey more of the author's own feelings and intentions:

Maria Engberg: *"I would like to have a mixed reality experience were when you went to see this object you hear the voices of the people who have touched or handled this object in some way. [...] It would start as an archival project learning about the diamond's history but I think also fairly quickly I would use that research as a ground for fictionalizing the history."*

The fact that only two of the fifteen designers mentioned a fictional narrative as a possibility may be another reflection of MR's media of attraction status, as the earliest phases in media development often include less engagement with fiction. This leads us to conclude we cannot yet say what aspects of MR best support fiction vs. non-fiction storytelling, or if conventions such as those which distinguish fictional from non-fictional films, for example, are even sensible in this medium. However it must be emphasized MR is still in a very early phase — far from institutionalization — and we also cannot yet say what the dominant software, hardware, or design techniques may become.

5.2 Sensationalizing

Approaches focused on the materiality of the Hope Diamond aimed to create somatic, embodied impressions, giving users the experience of possessing the diamond and experiencing its unique physical properties. These approaches were anti-narrative in many ways, and they provided open-ended experiences, as is common in media of attraction. When these approaches most closely resembled narrative experiences they were primarily instructional. For example, Krum describes an experience in which the causal processes surrounding the creation of diamonds were central, telling the story of diamond formation:

David Krum: *"Maybe you could talk about where the Hope Diamond came from, and how diamonds are formed, [...] do a VR experience of what a volcano is like, what are the forces involved, why are there diamonds in some places and not in others."*

However, even when communicating the causal forces that lead to diamond formation the experience relies heavily on physicality and spectacle. The "experience of a volcano" and physical forces are visceral ways of communicating the cause-and-effect processes behind the formation of diamonds. The other responses that were centered on materiality all convey a similar sort of somatic focus, emphasizing the wonder and playfulness made possible through mixed reality. For example, some respondents saw potential in the ability of MR to change the scale of the diamond, either by shrinking it or making it as large as a room or building:

Marc Billinghurst: *"[...] maybe use the diamond to transition from an AR experience to a VR experience where you could effectively shrink yourself very small, go inside the diamond and learn about diamond structure, some of the physical properties of diamonds."*

Lissa Holloway-Attaway: *"How could I be inside the diamond?"*

Teresa Wennberg: *"I would make [the diamond] very big, and I would make people go into it, and I would make them discover other worlds [...]. Yes, well, I would make it enormous."*

Other responses also placed emphasis on sensation and creating unexpected experiences that would not be possible without MR:

Shawn Lawson: *"over-enhanced sunbeams and sparkling ridiculously."*

Teresa Wennberg: *"Sound for sure — you could make it sing. Press there, it sings one song, press there, it talks. You could ask it questions and it would answer with a deep voice."*

Maria Engberg: *"I'm thinking a lot about audio, I would like to have a mixed reality experience where when you went to see this object you hear the voices of the people who have touched or handled this object in some way."*

Several of the designers keyed into the feeling and weight of the diamond as critically important to the experience, as Maribeth Gandy Coleman notes:

Maribeth Gandy Coleman: *"I would want to know what it was like to hold the Hope Diamond. Maybe some virtual tactile experience, I put my hand in a glove, and it feels like I'm touching it, feeling its weight, tapping on it, feeling what the surface of it feels like."*

However, many designers expressed a desire to remove the object entirely or hide it to create a sense of absence or loss. While in the quote above Snibbe saw this as an opportunity to create tension and suspense around a mystery storyline, the majority of the responses which took this approach emphasizing the diamond's absence aimed to create a sense of longing, or in the case of Chang and Ruzanka, even paranoia:

Susan Kozel: "*I would pick up on affect, materiality, and the politics of colonialism. [...] you have something called a 'hope' diamond, so you're immediately plunged into a sort of affective quality. So that could be a starting point to pull out questions of hope and despair and what this might mean in terms of visual media [...] The second one is what about the material quality of the diamond? Could that actually be brought into the visuality or the sonification, [...] layers like scrims, or textures, or signification within the physical space as well as the space of media.*"

Camille Utterback: "*It would be about grasping, and I would try somehow to illustrate how we want to hold things, and own things, which is impossible, and they are always falling out of our grasp. [...] Maybe it's not that they actually have to hold it but it's that this gesture of letting go or grabbing becomes a visual metaphor.*"

Shawn Lawson: "*One approach might be to be cheeky, and take the [Jeffrey Shaw] golden calf approach. And the [exhibit] does not have it [the diamond] there, but have a window into seeing the thing that's there ——it exists—but it doesn't really exist. You can kind of see it, but you can't really see it. It's an ephemeral thing, you can't wait to see it, but it's just a clear rock.*"

Benjamin Chang and Silvia Ruzanka: "*Do an exhibit where you give everybody this box that contains the Hope Diamond — and it's really heavy, has a chunk of lead in it —and you go through the exhibit, and all these virtual people are trying to steal it from you all along the way. So we get the feeling of having this thing that's pretty heavy and bulky and valuable and desired. You create this feeling of paranoia — maybe not everyone gets one of the boxes — have it that some don't.*"

The sensationalizing approach displayed in these examples seems not only a hallmark of media of attraction, but also related to the conceptual art tradition, which often has an ambivalent relationship with narrative. Instead of creating experiences structured around storytelling, these types of works seek to communicate with users on more embodied and visceral levels. The works are often open-ended, allowing users to construct their own narrative interpretations if they choose to. In this case, the designers are leveraging MR's potential for creating a patchwork of modes of interaction and representation, to act on the user in the name of a larger concept, communicated through a mix of physical sensation, and visual and/or auditory metaphor, all the while showcasing MR's novel capabilities. Designers' approaches across both the Opportunistic—Deterministic spectrum and Storytelling—Sensationalizing spectrum are visualized in Fig. 1.

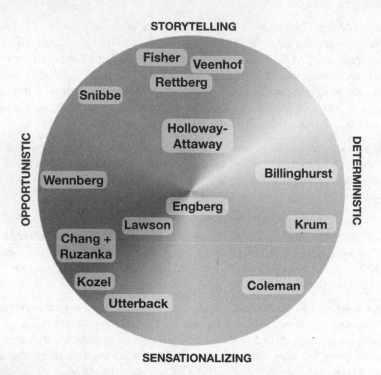

Fig. 1. Qualitative visualization of designers' approaches across both the Opportunistic—Deterministic spectrum and Storytelling—Sensationalizing spectrum reveals a wide range of blended techniques and aims. This breadth of creativity and experimentation in terms of range of design methods and goals is a hallmark quality of media of attraction, since designers operate in a medium in an early stage, prior to institutionalization.

6   Conclusions

The interviewees cited a number of major challenges for MR design, some of which were no different than those found in many other endeavors. Difficulty obtaining funding for large projects and difficulty forming coherent interdisciplinary teams were frequent issues. However, all respondents universally agreed that technical limitations were their largest frustration. Despite having many thousands of hours of project experience between them, none of the designers felt they could accurately predict the outcome of a project regardless of how familiar they were with the technology. Partly this is because they were often trying to conceive of new ways to deploy various technologies to create innovative experiences, sometimes it was because they were not completely sure what kind of mood or statement they wanted their project to create. Most often, though, it was unforeseen technical hurdles that had an outsize effect on the end result.

It is fascinating that despite recognizing how vital the cycle of discovering technical limits and developing workarounds to deal with these limits were to the formation of the end product, only one designer, Susan Kozel, explicitly welcomed these challenges as generative partners in the creative process: "I would have a horror of a perfectly glitch-free, constraint-free, fluid palette because I think it would point me more towards a predetermined aesthetic and a predetermined interface and sets of qualities that might come from the [technology] developers, for example, rather than from those of us who are composing the project."

Aside from Kozel, all designers interviewed were looking forward to a time when technological advancements would create tools for more accurate prototypes, less need for technical mastery of the various complex technologies needed, and a generally less onerous pathway from design conception to finished product. While the designers expressed that smoother pathways of moving their initial conceptions into realized experiences would be a great advancement for MR practice, it is also clear that this would fundamentally change the design process, and move the medium toward institutionalization. It is important that tool users and creators be conscious of the effects that introducing faster, less obtrusive, and more standardized tools might have on the overall design of MR experiences. Some designers did indeed express concern around large-scale corporate involvement in the field, as it represents a double-edged sword for designers. Corporate support of tool development could result in the type of advancement the majority of designers sought, but might also create restrictive distribution networks and overly codified aesthetics or audience expectation. A final challenge that was also mentioned by multiple designers is the difficulty in documenting and preserving MR works. While this issue is frustrating in and of itself, it may lead to much larger consequences. If works cannot be successfully documented, it means they are difficult to share, and therefore knowledge transfer is inhibited.

As MR develops at large, perhaps moving toward institutionalization, commercialization, and standardization, and away from a media of attraction phase, it will be interesting to see what approaches or processes solidify into convention and method, and what falls away. It will also be interesting to see how storytelling in MR will change as the field develops, and if designers reach consensus about which types of stories are the best fit for the capabilities MR offers. Our hope is this research provides valuable documentation of the MR field at this early stage, while possibilities are still fairly open, as we continue to navigate the frontier.

References

1. Barba, E.: Toward a language of mixed reality in the continuity style. Converg. Int. J. Res. New Media Technol. **20**, 41–54 (2013)
2. Farman, J.: Introduction to mobile interface theory. Mobile Interface Theory, 1–15 (2012)
3. Rouse, R., Engberg, M., JafariNaimi, N., Bolter, J.D.: MRx: an interdisciplinary framework for mixed reality experience design and criticism. Digit. Creativity **26**(3–4), 175–181 (2015)
4. Benyon, D.: Presence in Blended Spaces. Interact. Comput. **24**(4), 219–226 (2012)
5. Jetter, H., Zöllner, M., Gerken, J., Weiterer, H.: Design and Implementation of Post-WIMP Distributed User Interfaces with ZOIL. Int. J. Hum.-Comput. Interact. **28**(11), 737–747 (2012)
6. Billinghurst, M., Grasset, R.: Developing augmented reality applications. In: ACM SIGGRAPH ASIA, vol. 8(1) (2008)

7. Craig, A.B.: Understanding Augmented Reality. Morgan Kaufman, Waltham (2013)
8. Hill, A., Barba, E., MacIntyre, B., Gandy, M., Davidson, B.: Mirror worlds: experimenting with heterogeneous AR. In: International Symposium on Ubiquitous Virtual Reality, pp. 9–12 (2011)
9. Shilkrot, R., Montfort, N., Maes, P.: nARratives of augmented worlds. In: IEEE ISMAR International Symposium on Mixed and Augmented Reality (2014)
10. Cross, N.: Designerly Ways of Knowing. Birkhäuser Architecture (2007)
11. Schön, D.A.: The Reflective Practitioner: How Professionals Think in Action. Basic Books, New York (1984)
12. Seago, A., Dunne, A.: New methodologies in art and design research: the object as discourse. Des. Issues 15(2), 11–17 (1999)
13. Norman, D.: The Design of Everyday Things, Revised and Expanded Edition, pp. 1–36. Basic Books, New York (2013)
14. Dunne, A., Raby, F.: Speculative Everything: Design, Fiction, and Social Dreaming, pp. 1–5. MIT Press, Cambridge (2013)
15. Goodman, E., Stolterman, E., Wakkary, R.: Understanding interaction design practices. In: Proceedings of CHI 2011, pp. 1061–1070 (2011)
16. Rouse, R.: Media of attraction: a media archeology approach to panoramas, kinematography, mixed reality and beyond. In: Nack, F., Gordon, A.S. (eds.) ICIDS 2016. LNCS, vol. 10045, pp. 97–107. Springer, Cham (2016). https://doi.org/10.1007/978-3-319-48279-8_9
17. Gunning, T.: The cinema of attraction: early film, its spectator and the avant-garde. Wide Angle 8(3–4), 63–70 (1986)
18. Gaudreault, A.: Film and Attraction: From Kinematography to Cinema. University of Illinois Press, Chicago (2011)
19. Musser, C.: Rethinking early cinema: cinema of attractions and narrativity. Yale J. Criticism 7(2), 203–232 (1994)
20. McMahan, A., Blaché, A.G.: Lost Visionary of the Cinema. Continuum International Publishing Group, Inc., New York and London (2003)
21. Abel, R.: The Ciné Goes to Town: French Cinema, 1896–1914, Updated and Expanded Edition. University of California Press, Los Angeles and London (1998)
22. Musser, C.: The Emergence of Cinema: The American Screen to 1907. Scribners, New York (1990)
23. Oettermann, S.: The Panorama: A History of a Mass Medium. Zone Books, New York (1997)
24. Hyde, R.: Panoramania! The Art and Entertainment of the All-Embracing View. Trefoil Publications, London (1988)
25. Huhtamo, E.: Illusions in Motion: Media Archeology of the Moving Panorama and Related Spectacles. MIT Press, Cambridge (2013)
26. Ryan, M.: Will new media produce new narratives? In: Ryan, M. (ed.) Narrative Across Media. University of Nebraska Press, Lincoln (2004)
27. Strauss, A., Corbin, J.: Grounded theory research: procedures, canons, and evaluative criteria. Qual. Sociol. 13(1), 3–21 (1990)
28. Milgram, P., Kishino, F.: Taxonomy of mixed reality visual displays. IEICE Trans. Inf. Syst. E77-D(12), 1321–1329 (1994)

Posters

An Interactive Installation for Dynamic Visualization of Multi-author Narratives

Caterina Antonopoulou[✉]

University of the Aegean, Mytilene, Greece
caterina.antonopoulou@aegean.gr

Abstract. This paper introduces the interactive installation of Babel framework, developed to support dynamic composition and visualization of user generated narrative elements. Different versions of the same story are contributed by multiple authors through a web platform, they are annotated with metadata and stored in a database. The users of the installation retrieve the contributed content, explore it and recompose it in real time, thus articulating a unique trajectory in the narrative space. The interaction occurs through an intuitive computer vision interface that detects the light of a torch manipulated by the user.

Keywords: Interactive installation · Computer vision interface · Database · Multi-author narrative · User generated content · Digital storytelling

1 Structure and Content

Babel is a framework consisting of a web platform and an interactive installation, designed to support the creation and visualization of multi-author narratives. The narratives supported by Babel, follow a three-dimensional structure, as depicted in Fig. 1.

The first dimension represents the timeline consisting of discrete narrative units, the scenes. The second dimension represents the set of the alternative versions of each scene and the third one represents the characters of the story.

The set of the available versions of every scene is populated by multiple authors through a web platform designed for this purpose. The user interface of the platform allows users to upload multimedia content and annotate it with metatada, which facilitate future retrieval of the user generated content. The contributed versions varied in terms of the spatiotemporal context of the narrative, the featured characters, the spoken language, the aesthetics of the videos and the employed techniques and media.

N. Nunes et al. (Eds.): ICIDS 2017, LNCS 10690, pp. 261–264, 2017.
https://doi.org/10.1007/978-3-319-71027-3_21

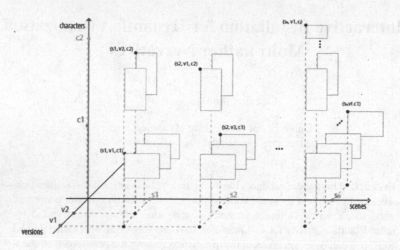

Fig. 1. The three dimensions of the narrative structure.

2   Installation Setup and User Interface

The project's infrastructure was designed in a modular way, that facilitates its extension and customization. The installation uses a local network of computers accessing a common database and filesystem. A set of a computer, a projection surface, a projector and a camera is used for every character of the story. The available versions of every scene/character pair are virtually placed on layers with augmenting depth, occupying a

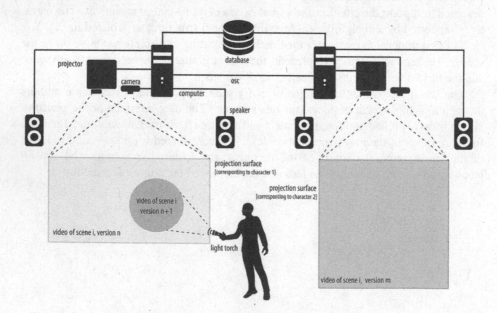

Fig. 2. The installation's setup.

virtual axis vertical to each projection surface. The projection surfaces are distributed around the installation space and the narrative follows an infinite loop.

The user explores and recomposes the available versions through an intuitive computer vision interface. By directing the light of a torch towards the screen, the user creates a virtual window (mask) to the next layer (Fig. 2). In a circular area around the target of the light, a part of the next version is revealed, while at the rest of the screen the current version is still projected. While the user keeps targeting the screen with the torch, the radius of the mask is gradually augmenting until it occupies the entire surface. The exploration and visualization of the alternative versions is independent for each character. However, the coherence of the narrative is preserved, as all versions follow the same fragmentation of the original story into scenes.

3   Software

Babel's installation (Fig. 3) was developed with opensource technologies (software, database and protocols). The custom software of the installation was developed with OpenFrameworks [1] and consists of four modules: the computer vision module, the video processing module, the database module and the network communication module.

Fig. 3. Babel's interactive installation.

The computer vision module is responsible for capturing the live video of the camera and detecting the light of the torch. The module processes every frame of the input video and extracts the coordinates of the brightest blob, using the OpenCV library [2].

The database module is responsible for querying the database and retrieving the adequate videos. The metadata of the videos are stored in a MySQL database [3] accessed by all computers. According to the user interaction, the software retrieves the videos that correspond to the current and the next version of a given scene/character pair.

The video processing module is responsible for the real-time processing of every frame of the current version and the next one. It replaces the pixels of the current version with the corresponding pixels of the next version within a circular area around the detected blob of the captured video. The radius of the circular area is proportional to the duration of the interaction.

The network communication module is responsible for the communication and the synchronization between the computers. The computers are connected through a switch and communicate via the Open Sound Control (OSC) protocol [4]. The computer in charge for the synchronization sends an OSC message to the rest of the computers at the end of every scene.

4 The Story

The selected script used as a case study during the various exhibitions of Babel is based on *Serially killed* [5], a story about an immortal man, obsessed with murder, but incapable of killing, who is repeatedly planning and experiencing his own murder. He chooses his murderers by chance, following a simple algorithm that he had invented. The story bares a latent resemblance to the structure of Babel's installation. Babel's narrative is looping infinitely, but each repetition is unique. It depends on the user interaction, the selected versions and the installation's algorithm. Similarly, the life of the main character follows an infinite loop. He experiences his death, returns to life, chooses his next murderer to re-experience his death. But every loop is unique as it depends on the chosen person, while some of his encounters hold surprises for him. His decisions are made through an algorithm resembling the algorithmic nature of the installation.

Acknowledgements. The author would like to thank all the authors that contributed their work to the project as well as the writer Kostas Kostakos (Old Boy) for his permission to use his story *Serially Killed*. The prototype version of Babel was tutorized by Ivan Marino and the project was awarded the visual arts grand *Golferich*s (Barcelona, 2010). The author would also like to acknowledge all the venues and festivals that hosted exhibitions of Babel.

References

1. OpenFrameworks Homepage. http://openframeworks.cc/. Last accessed 25 May 2017
2. OpenCV library. http://opencv.org/. Last accessed 25 May 2017
3. MySQL Homepage. https://www.mysql.com/. Last accessed 25 May 2017
4. Opensoundcontrol.org an Enabling Encoding for Media Applications. http://opensoundcontrol.org/. Last accessed 25 May 2017
5. Old Boy Homepage. http://old-boy.blogspot.gr/. Last accessed 25 May 2017

Factors of Immersion in Interactive Digital Storytelling

Sebastian Arndt$^{(\boxtimes)}$, Martin Ervik, and Andrew Perkis

Norwegian University of Science and Technology, Trondheim, Norway
sebastian.arndt@ntnu.no

Abstract. This paper describes the design and implementation of a system suitable for conducting an experiment investigating the level of immersion in Virtual Reality storytelling content. In the study, participants had to play through a digital story of high quality using the head mounted display of the HTC Vive and its controllers. The story consisted of five scenes with different content that assume a different level of immersion and interactivity. During the experiment, participants had their heart rate measured by a wearable health tracker. In addition, the participants needed to answer subjective questionnaires regarding their experience of that particular scene. We investigated what subjective factors are contributing to experienced immersion and whether the level of immersion is related to the measured heart rate. We can show that different subjective dimensions are contributing the level of immersion experienced and that heart rate is reflecting the level of interactivity of an interactive digital story.

Keywords: Interactive storytelling · Immersion · Experience · Physiology

1 Introduction

In traditional linear storytelling, the perceiver always follows a given and logical path through the story. Systems using Head-Mounted-Displays (HMD) in the fields of Virtual Reality (VR) allow for interactive storytelling. This brings new aspects of immersion [1] and engagement that need to be considered when producing content for new and interactive, digital narratives. Here, immersion may be defined as how our senses and emotions are deeply involved in an experience [2], making us feel as a part of what is happening in the story. This creates a link between emotions and immersion, which is of great interest when wanting to capture and measure the experience of a digital story, as emotions are closely related to physiological responses.

Recent work was performed on evaluating heart rate and electrodermal activity as immerse parameters for QoE in VR environments, while using HMD a passive system with no interactivity was presented [3]. Here, the participants had to sit still which limits the level of immersion and interactivity to some point. Adding the possibility to move around can increase the level of immersion, hence giving a better data basis.

© Springer International Publishing AG 2017
N. Nunes et al. (Eds.): ICIDS 2017, LNCS 10690, pp. 265–269, 2017.
https://doi.org/10.1007/978-3-319-71027-3_22

2 Experimental Setup

Our study used the Everest VR production as the high quality interactive storytelling content to be evaluated, played with the HTC VIVE VR. The user experiences how it is like to climb Mount Everest. To do so users are being exposed to a series of five iconic scenes in first person challenges. During which small challenges have to be performed by walking through the area and manipulating objects in the virtual world by using the handhold controllers. The different scenes will be used as the different type of content to be subjectively evaluated in terms of the level of immersion, as well as by measuring variations in heart rate from test participants. Due to the amount of interaction in each scene and the exposed content, different levels of immersion are being expected. Heart rate is measured by the Fitbit Charge 2. One of the objectives to investigate during this study was to identify which factors contribute to an immersive experience and whether physiological signals could be used as a parameter for the level of immersion when evaluating the Quality of Experience in digital storytelling by using head mounted displays in virtual reality. For this purpose, both subjective and physiological measurements are employed.

After each scene, the participant filled in a questionnaire targeting: (a) Quality aspects (audio, video and overall audiovisual quality), on a five-point absolute category rating scale (ACR). (b) Emotional responses: Self-assessment mannequin (SAM) questionnaire (level of valence, arousal and dominance). (c) Usability and Immersive aspects: The aim of these questions is to evaluate two of the key aspects in user QoE for an immersive environment. These questions have been compiled by evaluating different prior work on immersion, including the paper by [4, 5].

3 Results

23 participants conducted the experiment, whereby 20 of the participants are used for analysis (11 male, 9 female) with an average age of 24.9. Exclusion of participants' data is due to data from three of the participants being corrupted.

3.1 Subjective Data

A repeated measure ANOVA was used for statistical significance testing. In terms of quality ratings significant differences between the scenes could be identified for the perceived overall audiovisual ($F = 2.42$, $p \leq 0.1$) as well as for the video quality ($F = 2.32$, $p \leq 0.1$). With scene 1 receiving the lowest scores, and scene 4 and 5 receiving the highest score in both case. No significant differences was found for the audio quality ($F = 0.77$, n.s.).

The subjectively rated emotional response of the participants on the SAM scales for valence was rated similar among all scenes, with no significant difference ($F = 2.89$, n.s.). Arousal was rated highest for scene 2, and lowest for scene 1, with a significant overall effect ($F = 3.01$, $p \leq 0.01$). Dominance was rated highest for scenes 4 and 5 and lower for the other scenes (increasing in score from scene 1, 2 and 3) ($F = 2.79$, $p \leq 0.01$).

Analysis of the subjectively obtained measures for immersion reveal differences between scenes for some of the questions. Figure 1 shows a noticeable significance for question EXP1 and EXP2, such that scene 3 received lowest ratings. Clear statistical significance can be found for questions EXP6 and EXP9, such that scene 2 received the highest scores.

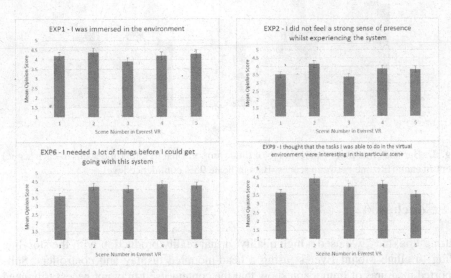

Fig. 1. Averages of self-reports on EXP1 (upper left), EXP2 (upper right), EXP6 (lower left), and EXP9 (lower right). Bars indicate 95% confidence level.

3.2 Physiological Data

For evaluation, the heart rate data from each participant is divided temporally into the five scene segments. Each of which is again divided into four heart rate zones which are derived on a participant's individual basis. Taking the participant's maximum and minimum measured heart rate, based on this the range in between was divided into four equally large zones. Using these zones, the average time spent by each participant in the different zones was calculated and analyzed in terms of the percentage of time spent in each of these. Such that differences between the different HR-zones in each scene can be analyzed and then identify highly arousing content in terms of increased HR. A pairwise T-test in Matlab was used to conduct the statistical analyzes of the different HRzones in each scene. The results of the analysis for the physiological data can be seen in Fig. 2. Here, it shows participants spent more time in the lower heart rate zones for scene 1 (in particular Zone 1). For the rest of the scenes participants spent of most of the time in Zone 2 and Zone 3. In scene 1, participants spent significantly less time in zone 4 than the rest of the HRzones. Scene 2 does not show statistical significance in terms of time spent within the different HR-zones. In scene 3 and 4, most of the time is spent in Zone 2 and Zone 3, resulting in statistical significance compared with Zone 1 and Zone 4.

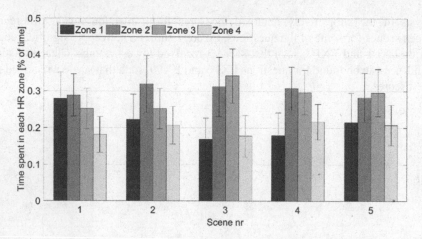

Fig. 2. Bar and error plot of percentage of time (proportional to total time spent in each scene) spent in each HR zone between scenes. Bars indicate 95% confidence level.

4 Conclusion

During this study, we used a high quality virtual reality production with the storyline being to climb Mount Everest using a head-mounted display and controllers. Self-reported measures of immersion show that the content itself may not necessarily need to be highly arousing in order to feel most immersed. It is therefore more important that the user of a VR has the impression of being in control of the experience and is therefore enjoying it more. When it comes to physiological measures of the VR-user, we can see that a more interactive scene leads to a higher level of heart rate. However, to better estimate the emotional state, measures such as heart-rate variability or skin conductance may be more appropriate, and need further investigations.

Acknowledgements. Thanks to Sólfar Studios for providing with Everest VR and technical support.

References

1. Grau, O.: Virtual Art: From Illusion to Immersion. MIT Press, Cambridge (2003)
2. McMahan, A.: Immersion, engagement and presence. In: Wolf, M., Perron, B. (eds.) The Video Game Theory Reader. Routledge, New York (2003)
3. Egan, D., Brennan, S., Barrett, J., Qiao, Y., Timmerer, C., Murray, N.: An evaluation of Heart Rate and ElectroDermal Activity as an objective QoE evaluation method for immersive virtual reality environments. In: 2016 Eighth International Conference on Quality of Multimedia Experience (QoMEX) (2016)

4. Lang, P.J, Bradley, M.M., Cuthbert, B.N.: International affective picture system (IAPS): technical manual and affective ratings. NIMH Center for the Study of Emotion and Attention (1997)
5. Chertoff, D.B., Goldiez, B., LaViola, J.J.: Virtual experience test: a virtual environment evaluation questionnaire. In: 2010 IEEE Virtual Reality Conference (VR) (2010)

Evaluating User Experience in 360º Storytelling Through Analytics

Paulo Bala[✉], Valentina Nisi, and Nuno Nunes

Madeira-ITI, University of Madeira, Campus da Penteada, 9020-105 Funchal, Portugal
paulo.bala@m-iti.org, {valentina,njn}@uma.pt

Abstract. A necessary component in the mass adoption of Virtual Reality (VR) is the creation of support tools to help creators develop and evaluate content. Emphasising the importance of User Experience (UX) in VR, analytics platforms are setup to understand participant's behaviour, therefore helping for a better understanding of the medium. This paper reviews evaluation methods for VR concerned with observation of user behaviour, and how these are structured in analytics platforms. By surveying existing platforms, we look at how these platforms support the creation and evaluation of VR experiences and apply this knowledge to design a platform for the specific context of VR Storytelling.

Keywords: Virtual Reality · VR analytics · Storytelling

1 Introduction

After decades of research and development, Virtual Reality (in which the user is immersed in virtual environments using a head mounted display) is on the cusp of mainstream adoption, yet it still dealing with barriers that affect User Experience (UX), shaping research and product development on the medium [1]. Evaluation platforms have risen to support development and help delineate best practices and guidelines for VR storytelling, therefore promoting higher quality content demanded by mass adoption. In this paper, we face the needs of UX research in VR to inform the tasks of creators, namely by: (i) looking at how VR content is evaluated; (ii) defining metrics that can be captured for the analysis of VR narratives; and (iii) exploring how this information can be visualized to provide usable insights into the structure of VR narratives. To achieve this, we reviewed works both in the academic and industry context (CognitiveVR[1], Retinad[2], Wistia[3], Facebook[4], Youtube[5], among others), applying this knowledge to the design of IVRUX, a novel platform for VR analytics, especially concerned with the narrative structure of the content.

---

[1] http://cognitivevr.co/.
[2] https://www.retinadvr.com/.
[3] https://wistia.com/.
[4] https://www.facebook.com/facebookmedia/get-started/discovery-tools-insights.
[5] https://youtube-creators.googleblog.com/2017/06/hot-and-cold-heatmaps-in-vr.html.

© Springer International Publishing AG 2017
N. Nunes et al. (Eds.): ICIDS 2017, LNCS 10690, pp. 270–273, 2017.
https://doi.org/10.1007/978-3-319-71027-3_23

2   Related Work

A common HCI method for evaluating interfaces is eye tracking to analyze visual attention in interfaces [2]. Gaze data can be visualized as aggregated plots that disregard
temporal information, in the form of statistical graphs (lines, bar charts, scatter/box
plots) and heatmaps (overlaid on the original media) or as visualization that does not
lose temporal information, such as timelines and scan path visualizations [3].These basic
concepts of eye tracking and gaze visualization have been applied in both academic and
industry settings to VR. Lowe et al. [4] mapped visual attention on stimuli from a 360°
video, recording gaze direction, and head orientation (viewing direction), to identify
attentional synchrony between users. Similarly, Bala et al. [5] recorded participants'
viewing direction in a 3D scene; user behaviour like following a conversation between
characters could still be observed even without using gaze tracking.

Based on the type of media used, VR analytics platforms can be separated in Model-
based VR (the virtual environment is entirely simulated by computer graphics render-
ings) or 360° Video (the virtual environment is 360° video footage captured in the real
setting) [6]. The first is geared for VR developers with coding experience, therefore
focusing on metrics for technical issues, rather than on user behaviour. The most
complete example of these is CognitiveVR that through a "drag&drop" SDK plugins,
collects data on the device (type, resolution, performance), user gaze and interaction
events, uniting it on an online dashboard ("Core Analytics"), where the researcher can
explore participant's profiles, insights based on usage metrics, identify optimization
possibilities and setup A/B tests. Through its "Scene Explorer", researchers can play-
back participants' sessions using event zones, gaze heatmaps, user paths and item
engagement, to identify error zones, low-performance assets, and player confusion.
"Scene Explorer" is focused on the development phase since the granularity of observing
each participant session is useful in determining situations that lead to unexpected user
behavior. "Core Analytics" is focused on the after development phase, since it takes
advantage of the aggregation of multiple participants to identify optimization opportunities that are not related to user behavior, but to devices and application attributes.

360° Video analytics platforms are mostly geared for creators without coding experience, therefore, rely on rigid workflows, incapable of expansion, and based on heatmaps visualizations, that require subjective visual analysis of data. For example,
Retinad, driven by marketing principles (like engagement, boredom, among others) to
understand its users and product placement, showcases gathered data on an online dashboard in the form of heatmaps on top of the equirectangular projection (unwrapped) of
videos. The online dashboard shows metrics such as number of viewers, impressions
(video fetched from its source), average time watched, and completion rate. Similarly,
some video hosting platform (Wistia, Facebook, and Youtube) offer custom 360° video
player capturing data anonymously. All platforms surveyed offer similar heatmaps visualizations, needing manual visual analysis to understand participants' attention. While
this might be acceptable for ads with a simple narrative structure (one ideal path) with
few points of interest and a short duration, there is a need for analytics platform to support
complex narrative structures.

3   IVRUX – Towards an Analytics Platform for VR Storytelling

Based on the need for evaluation of complex narrative structures in VR storytelling, we designed IVRUX, a VR analytics platform for 360° video. This tool, intended to be used in an academic context, offers a support system to facilitate communication of creators and/or researchers with participants. The system is composed of three components: an online dashboard for researchers (built using the Angular framework) and a mobile VR application for the participants (built using Unity), connected through a REST API backend (Node.js and MongoDB). The system is designed so that the researcher does not need to have any expert skills (e.g. coding) to evaluate content.

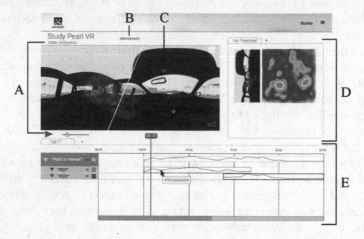

Fig. 1. High fidelity prototype for the visualization interface. (A) Media; (B) Participant selection; (C) Scanpaths; (D) Non-temporal visualizations; (E) Temporal visualizations.

On the online dashboard, researchers can create studies, selecting the media (video) to be tested and other relevant information. Through platform generated QR codes and/or emails, the researcher can invite participants or publicize the study. Participants, with the mobile VR application, can scan the QR codes to gain access to the study. As they join a study, they will be informed of the protocol and will be able to view the selected media (in VR), while the application gathers information on the viewing direction and device, among other metrics. After viewing (and uploading the recorded data to API backend), participants receive an email with a link to a post experience form. This separation between the form and the platform allows researchers to choose what type of questionnaires or interviews they prefer, and avoid the issue of simplifying the form for in-headset filling. After the study is over, the researcher uses the online dashboard to visualize data gathered (Fig. 1). This visualization interface is modular, so the researcher can choose the right metrics to best help him understand the study. In the analytics dashboard, the researcher can choose the scope of participants (segmentation of participants; B in Fig. 1), the media representation (first person view vs unwrapped video; A in Fig. 1), temporal visualizations (a heatmap overlaid on the video or the timeline; A and E in Fig. 1, respectively) and non-temporal visualizations (single heatmaps or graphs on core metrics; D in Fig. 1). This visualization respects time information through a scrubbable timeline (A in Fig. 1) and scan paths (C in Fig. 1). Outside this visualization, a video annotation interface allows the user to manually and/or automatically annotate the video according to their needs by using spatial and temporal points of interest (POI), grouped by layers, allowing for a more detailed and complex description of narrative structure in VR (e.g. a narrative with multiple branching and POIs). This annotation can be used in analytics to give more quantitative data to the process (E in Fig. 1). For example, the researcher can create a layer "Main POI" adding a POI to it, that changes in space and time along the video. In the analytics interface, he can then see more precise information such as the percentage of viewers following the main POI at a specific time. This process is equivalent to visually inspecting the whole video with heatmaps, but offers a quantitative score that can be used for A/B testing.

4   Conclusion and Future Work

In this paper, we surveyed evaluation methods for VR, focusing on analytics platforms, identifying a gap in the support of VR storytelling experiences. For this reason, we designed IVRUX to target VR storytellers collecting research data, gaining a better understanding of the underlying process. In this paper, we describe the motivation and design of IVRUX, while its implementation and evaluation is still ongoing. The medium itself and the modular structure of the platform is an interesting design space and a promising starting point for the exploration of visualization of VR data.

Acknowledgments.   We wish to acknowledge the support of LARSyS (UID/EEA/50009/2013). The project has been developed as part of MITIExcell (M1420-01-0145-FEDER-000002). The author Paulo Bala wishes to acknowledge Fundação para a Ciência e a Tecnologia for supporting his research through the Ph.D. Grant PD/BD/128330/2017.

References

1. 2016 AR and VR Survey Report: Perkins Coie & Upload (2016)
2. Nielsen, J., Pernice, K.: Eyetracking Web Usability. New Riders Publishing, Thousand Oaks (2009)
3. Blascheck, T., Kurzhals, K., Raschke, M., Burch, M., Weiskopf, D., Ertl, T.: State-of-the-Art of Visualization for Eye Tracking Data (2014)
4. Löwe, T., Stengel, M., Förster, E.-C., Grogorick, S., Magnor, M.: Visualization and analysis of head movement and gaze data for immersive video in head-mounted displays. In: Burch, M., Chuang, L., Fisher, B., Schmidt, A., Weiskopf, D. (eds.) ETVIS 2015. Springer, Heidelberg (2017)
5. Bala, P., Dionisio, M., Nisi, V., Nunes, N.: IVRUX: a tool for analyzing immersive narratives in virtual reality. In: Nack, F., Gordon, A.S. (eds.) ICIDS 2016. LNCS, vol. 10045, pp. 3–11. Springer, Cham (2016). https://doi.org/10.1007/978-3-319-48279-8_1
6. Slater, M., Sanchez-Vives, M.V.: Enhancing our lives with immersive virtual reality. Front. Robot. AI. **3**, 74 (2016)

Towards an Interaction Model for Interactive Narratives

Elin Carstensdottir[✉], Erica Kleinman, and Magy Seif El-Nasr

College of Computer and Information Science,
Northeastern University, Boston 02115, USA
elin@ccs.neu.edu, kleinman.e@husky.neu.edu,
m.seifel-nasr@northeastern.edu

Abstract. In the discussion of interactive narrative experiences and story-driven games, much of the current work has focused on analyzing and proposing models and frameworks based on narrative theory and ludology. However, the players' experience and interaction with such narrative structure and content is a topic that is currently understudied in the field. Specifically, questions regarding how the player interacts and perceives the impact of their interaction on the story are currently unanswered. This paper presents a step towards defining an interaction model that can be used to design and compare how a user participates in an interactive narrative.

Keywords: Interactive narrative · Interaction models · Close reading · Game analysis · Narrative interaction patterns · User experience

1 Introduction

One of the most challenging topics in video game design is the inclusion of narrative. While many games already incorporate narrative, how to embed narratives in games and how players can influence it is still being debated. Much of the research done in the field of interactive narrative focuses on several major themes, including narrative representation [1], user inclusion [2], and authoring [3]. Previous Work on computational models of narrative such as [4–6] has limited consideration for the players' experience, focusing instead on player modeling with an emphasis on how to account for player actions within an AI guided interactive narrative system. Unfortunately, this positions the player as a constraint to work around, rather than incorporating the interaction as part of the design. Two exemplary works that account for narrative presentation and/or user participation are IDtension [5] and the multimodal interactive narrative applications of Cavazza et al. such as [7]. Many researchers have argued for increased attention to the user experience in interactive narratives [5,8]. To the extent of our knowledge, however, there are no models or frameworks that describe user interaction in interactive narrative in a generalized way without being associated with a particular meaning or artifact. While examples of similar models

© Springer International Publishing AG 2017
N. Nunes et al. (Eds.): ICIDS 2017, LNCS 10690, pp. 274–277, 2017.
https://doi.org/10.1007/978-3-319-71027-3_24

	Façade	The Stanley Parable	The Wolf Among Us	Long Live the Queen	Oxenfree	Her Story	Gone Home	The Novelist	Final Fantasy XV	To the Moon	Undertale	Black Closet	Papers Please	ZE: Virtue's Last Reward	Prom Week	Persona 4	Dragon Age: Inquisition	Heavy Rain
Playtime	C	C	C	C	C	C	C	C	C	C	C	10 hr	C	10 hr	C	C	10 hr	C

Fig. 1. Each game selected for the study and the amount of time they were played for. 15 games were played to the end of the story, 3 were not completed due to time constraints. C = completed

exist for games [9], such works do not target interactive narratives. We propose that an interaction model can help address this because it can describe the way interactive narrative content is delivered and experienced.

Beudouin-Lafon defined an interaction model as: "a set of principles, rules and properties that guide the design of an interface. It describes how to combine interaction techniques in a meaningful and consistent way and defines the "look and feel" of the interaction from the user's perspective." [10] This work aims to realize the first part of this definition by describing consistent interaction patterns and design elements utilized by successful interactive narrative games.

To develop the model, a qualitative study was conducted using a close reading approach to identify a set of interaction patterns used in 18 commercial narrative games chosen for the study (see Fig. 1). We identified four distinct constructs of narrative interaction that make up the model: Structure, Narrative Mechanics, Interaction, and User Experience. Each construct consists of interaction design elements and patterns. This paper presents an overview of the model and its components.

2 Methodology

The games chosen for the sample were recognized for their narrative and varied in terms of product level and design features. Games that didn't include single-player modes and/or featured emergent narrative were excluded. The final sample consisted of 18 games (see Fig. 1). Close reading, a qualitative method originating in literary theory, was chosen to analyze the games. This method was chosen specifically to focus on user experience rather than how the narrative was structured and implemented. The data was analyzed using grounded theory approach and qualitative thematic analysis. A modified version of the "naïve reader" lens was used for the close reading [11]. The reading was performed by one researcher, as recommended by [12].

The researcher recorded herself describing her interaction with each game throughout each playthrough. The close reading was heavily driven by questions of how the player perceived her interaction, how the interaction was presented to her, and what means were provided to give the player both control over and feedback on her experience. Upon completing a playthrough of each game, the researcher transcribed the recordings. The data was then analyzed using a qualitative thematic analysis similar to [13] by two researchers.

3   The Model

The analysis resulted in patterns that can be grouped into four constructs or categories: Structure, Narrative Mechanics, Interaction, and User Experience. The first three constructs account for how the user can view the design and dynamics within the interactive narrative. The fourth constructs accounts for the result of this interaction and perception i.e. the user experience itself.

Structure is the computational layout of the story content, including graphics, text, and dialogue, represented as a graph. A player can experience story content by using mechanics to proceed from one node of story content to the next. Different structure types refer to how the content is arranged. When categorizing the story structures existing terminology was utilized or adapted. Where none existed in the literature, new terms were defined. Six different computational story structures were identified: Linear, Branching, Foldback, Broom, Hidden Story, and Opportunistic Story.

Narrative mechanics describes the rules and patterns through which the player interacts with the narrative. In this study we focus on story progression mechanics, a subset of narrative mechanics that consists of rules or patterns used to allow the player to progress through the story. Five distinct story progression themes were identified in the data: Progression through choice, progression through task completion, progression through scripted scenarios, progression through discovery, and progression through in-game systems.

Interaction includes elements that relate to interaction on a level similar to Game Feel [9] i.e. how a user is performing and perceiving their interaction. This includes input, input mapping, feedback, and presentation patterns. These themes influence the way the player interacts with and perceives the story. This construct focuses on how the game allows the player to interact with the narrative. It provides them with information regarding their abilities to perform interaction, in addition to the results of their interactions with the narrative.

User Experience refers to cognitive considerations relevant to the narrative experience including player reasoning and expectations, metaknowledge, and personal, player defined goals. These cognitive considerations are subject to individual differences as well as psychological and social factors.

4   Conclusion and Future Work

This paper presented a brief overview of a study to identify interaction patterns of 18 narrative driven video games (see Fig. 1). The results were used to construct an interaction model, serving as a step towards establishing a taxonomy for describing and comparing interaction in interactive narratives. We chose to focus the model on story progression, a central concern for an interactive narrative experience. In addition, it was chosen to focus on goal oriented interaction and target observable interaction patterns meant to guide the player through the story. The model is not a holistic one and does not include all the various elements needed to fully describe the player experience and other facets of interaction. This limitation will be addressed in future work.

Acknowledgments. Funding for this research was provided by the National Science Foundation Cyber-Human Systems under Grant No. 1526275.

References

1. Magerko, B.: Story representation and interactive drama. In: Proceedings of the First Annual Conference on Artificial Intelligence and Interactive Digital Entertainment (AIIDE 2005), pp. 87–92 (2005)
2. Mateas, M.: A neo-aristotelian theory of interactive drama. In: Working notes of the AI and Interactive Entertainment Symposium (2000)
3. McCoy, J., Treanor, M., Samuel, B., Tearse, B., Mateas, M., Wardrip-Fruin, N.: Authoring game-based interactive narrative using social games and comme il faut. In: Proceedings of the 4th International Conference & Festival of the Electronic Literature Organization (2010)
4. Seif El-Nasr, M.: A user-centric adaptive story architecture: borrowing from acting theories. In: Proceedings of the 2004 ACM SIGCHI International Conference on Advances in Computer Entertainment Technology - ACE 2004, pp. 109–116. ACM Press, New York (2004)
5. Szilas, N.: IDtension: a narrative engine for interactive drama. In: Stefan, G., et al. (ed.) Proceedings of the Technologies for Interactive Digital Storytelling and Entertainment (TIDSE) Conference, pp. 187–203. Frauenhofer IRB Verlag (2003)
6. Young, R.M., Riedl, M.: Towards an architecture for intelligent control of narrative in interactive virtual worlds. In: Proceedings of the 8th International Conference on Intelligent User Interfaces - IUI 2003, pp. 310–312. ACM Press, New York (2003)
7. Cavazza, M., Lugrin, J.L., Pizzi, D., Charles, F.: Madame Bovary on the holodeck: immersive interactive storytelling. In: Proceedings of the 15th International Conference on Multimedia, pp. 651–660 (2007)
8. Koenitz, H., Dubbelman, T., Knoller, N., Roth, C.: An integrated and iterative research direction for interactive digital narrative. In: Nack, F., Gordon, A.S. (eds.) ICIDS 2016. LNCS, vol. 10045, pp. 51–60. Springer, Cham (2016). https://doi.org/10.1007/978-3-319-48279-8_5
9. Swink, S.: Game Feel: A Game Designer's Guide to Virtual Sensation. Elsevier, Burlington, MA (2008)
10. Beaudouin-Lafon, M.: Instrumental interaction: an interaction model for designing post-WIMP user interfaces. In: Proceedings of the SIGCHI Conference on Human Factors in Computing Systems - CHI 2000, pp. 446–453. ACM Press, New York (2000)
11. Bizzocchi, J., Tanenbaum, J.: Well Read: Applying Close Reading Techniques to Gameplay Experiences, pp. 262–290. ETC Press, Pittsburgh (2011)
12. Aarseth, E.: Playing research: Methodological approaches to game analysis. In: Proceedings of the Digital Arts and Culture Conference (2003)
13. Moura, D., El-Nasr, M.S.: Design techniques for planning navigational systems in 3-D video games. Comput. Entertain. **12**(2), 1–25 (2015)

Using Interactive Fiction to Teach Pediatricians-in-Training About Child Abuse

Grant P. Christman[1(✉)], Sheree M. Schrager[1], and Kelly Callahan[2]

[1] Children's Hospital Los Angeles and University of Southern California, Los Angeles, USA
gchristman@chla.usc.edu
[2] Harbor-UCLA Medical Center, University of California Los Angeles, Los Angeles, USA

Abstract. Electronic learning is used extensively in medical education. Though some interventions have incorporated elements of gamification and narrative, interactive fiction is a novel approach to educating medical trainees. Diagnosis and management of child abuse requires competencies in patient care, systems-based practice, communication, and professionalism. This complexity, along with the emotional significance of caring for abused children, makes child abuse pediatrics an ideal topic for an initial implementation of an interactive-fiction-based learning module. This module will be compared to a standard e-learning module in the education of physicians training to become pediatricians.

Keywords: Interactive fiction · Serious games · Medical education

1 Introduction

Research has demonstrated that electronic learning methods (hereafter, e-learning) are as effective for medical education as traditional instruction methods such as in-person lectures [1]. Serious games have numerous applications in health care, both for patient education and medical provider education. Gamification of learning through point systems or leaderboards can be very successful in motivating medical trainees, who are often ambitious and competitive, though for the same reason can be discouraging to those who are not achieving as much as their peers [2]. Likewise, linear narratives have been used in a variety of ways in medical education, and are seen as memorable and useful for evaluating real patients with similar conditions [3]. Interactive, branching narratives have rarely been used in education, although virtual patients (a type of computer-based simulation) have been used to teach interprofessional education to psychiatric trainees and pharmacists [4] and narrative structuring exercises have been used to help first year-medical students understand patient experiences [5].

Despite the success of e-learning and narrative in other forms of medical education, we have found no examples of research on interactive fiction (IF) being used in this setting. Computer-based IF games have the potential to be a powerful tool for medical education because they capitalize on features of both narrative (e.g., immersion) and serious gaming (e.g., reward systems). Immersion in the narrative, with the learner becoming a character in a fictional story that supplies realistic consequences for medical decisions, has the potential to bring an emotional force to learning that is absent from

© Springer International Publishing AG 2017
N. Nunes et al. (Eds.): ICIDS 2017, LNCS 10690, pp. 278–281, 2017.
https://doi.org/10.1007/978-3-319-71027-3_25

other modalities. This may be particularly important for topics that carry special emotional heft, such as recognizing and responding to child abuse.

Education in child abuse diagnosis, management, and reporting is considered a standard part of pediatric residency training and accounts for 4% of the typical board certification exam issued by the American Board of Pediatrics [6]. Nevertheless, there are no national standards as to the quality and quantity of child abuse education in residency; physician comfort, knowledge, and skill in managing child abuse cases thus varies widely [7, 8]. Duty hour restrictions limit resident availability for in-person didactics, making e-learning interventions such as IF games logistically advantageous.

2 Study Methods

2.1 Participants and Procedures

Participants will be enrolled from three classes of pediatric residents at one university-affiliated children's hospital (n = 96). Participants will take a short survey of Likert-type items addressing their previous experience and perceived competence with several difficult situations commonly encountered in the medical setting, including recognizing and addressing child abuse, and a knowledge test with a subset of child abuse pediatric practice items validated by board-certified child abuse pediatricians.

Participants will then be randomized into one of two groups: control or experimental. Control participants will complete a traditional e-learning module on child abuse created in Articulate Storyline 2 and deployed as a SCORM package on a learning management system (LMS) running Moodle 2.6.5. This module is visual only due to the limited audio capabilities of some computers in the hospital environment. In addition to informational, text-based slides, it incorporates elements of interactivity, including short patient case vignettes with images of exam findings, multiple-choice questions addressing diagnostic and management decisions, and interactive diagrams with point-click or drag-and-drop functionality. The module is drawn from a series of modules that were validated by board-certified child abuse pediatricians and pilot tested on pediatric, emergency medicine, and family medicine residents.

The experimental group will complete an IF game covering the same learning objectives as the traditional module. The IF game will also be developed with Articulate Storyline 2 and deployed as a SCORM package on the LMS running Moodle 2.6.5, allowing for generation of comparable usage data in the two study arms. The IF game will be choice-based and have a branching narrative structure that responds to the choices of the user. Although the interface will be text-based, the player will have the option to reference the additional materials provided in the traditional module.

2.2 Evaluation

Data on usage patterns will be collected via the LMS, including amount of time spent interacting with the module. In the case of the IF module, additional information will be captured about specific choices made, internal game scores, number of attempts to play (or replay) the game, and number of branching paths explored. Two weeks after completing either the control or experimental learning session, all participants will repeat the attitude and competence items and knowledge test. Primary analyses will test the hypothesis that participants in the experimental (IF) group will report more comfort and perceived competence with addressing child abuse in the medical setting, and will score higher on the knowledge test, than participants in the control group. Secondary analyses on the IF group only will examine whether participants' choices during the game are associated with their attitudes and/or knowledge score. We hypothesize that participants who explored a greater number of plot branches, saw the "worst" ending, and replayed the game a greater number of times will have higher knowledge scores, and that participants with higher final scores will perceive themselves as more competent in recognizing and appropriately managing child abuse.

3   Interactive Fiction Narrative and Gameplay

The player character is introduced as a recently recruited attending pediatrician at a university-affiliated children's hospital. The story begins with the player receiving a call from an outside community hospital requesting to transfer a patient to the player's facility. The patient is a spirited 18-month-old girl named Caitlyn who presents with fussiness and an unusual skin finding. As is often the case in actual pediatric practice, it is not initially clear that the case involves child abuse – nor is it revealed to the player that this is an abuse-related learning experience. As the player makes choices in communication, diagnosis, and management, Caitlyn's story evolves over four acts beginning with the transfer request, followed by her evaluation at the player's hospital, the discovery of findings concerning for physical abuse, and an epilogue in which the player's choices in aggregate determine the outcomes for Caitlyn and her family.

The game will use internal flags to award points, initially hidden, for optimal behavior choices, including: asking for more information during the initial transfer call; not rejecting the transfer; correctly noting that the skin finding is a bruise; not incorrectly anchoring on the diagnosis of upper respiratory infection based on a red herring of a runny nose; ignoring the family's race and socioeconomic status (each associated with missed diagnoses of child abuse [9]); correctly ordering a head CT when the patient is persistently fussy; calling child protective services to make an abuse report (as mandated by law); being persistent with child protective services when they try to refuse the case; and pursuing the correct work-up for suspected abusive head trauma. The user may also click a "consult" button at critical choice points to access medical information pertinent to the case, which will be the information (images with exam findings, etc.) provided in the traditional e-learning module.

The choices will be scored out of a total of 10 points. Although ten minor branches will be possible, the story will progress along one of three major branching paths. The narrative includes barriers designed to encourage initial choices that lead to lower scores, to promote replaying and additional exploration. A score of 0–3 will correlate with a missed diagnosis with severe consequences for the patient, 4–6 with a delayed diagnosis, and 7–10 with a successful and timely diagnosis. The score will not be revealed until the module is completed, at which time the user may replay the game. A score of 11/10 may be obtained if extraordinary communication and persistence are demonstrated; in this case, the user will make a timely diagnosis of Caitlyn's abuse and discover that her 4-year-old brother Jacob is also a victim with serious injuries.

Overall, the IF game will cover the same medical knowledge and patient care objectives as the traditional module; however, the IF game may also convey skills in other competencies that are difficult to convey in other formats, such a communication. We also anticipate that having narrative consequences to management decisions, including the potential for harm to the patient, will increase the emotional significance of the learning experience when compared to the more sterile environment of brief vignettes and multiple choice questions. At the same time, the distance provided by the narrative structure—that is, the user acting through a character in the game rather than as "themselves"—may allow them the freedom to experiment with choices they might not make in an actual patient encounter.

4   Conclusion

IF has the potential to deliver engaging, memorable, and emotionally powerful learning experiences on serious topics like child abuse, in which decision-making is complex and choices can have life-changing consequences.

References

1. Cook, D.A., Levinson, A.J., Garside, S., Dupras, D.M., Erwin, P.J., Montori, V.M.: Internet-based learning in the health professions: a meta-analysis. JAMA **300**(10), 1181–1196 (2008). https://doi.org/10.1001/jama.300.10.1181
2. Rojas, D., Kapralos, B., Dubrowski, A.: The role of game elements in online learning within health professions education. Stud. Health Technol. Inform. **220**, 329–334 (2016)
3. D'Alessandro, D.M., Lewis, T.E., D'Alessandro, M.P.: A pediatric digital storytelling system for third year medical students: The virtual pediatric patients. BMC Med. Educ. **4**, 10 (2004). https://doi.org/10.1186/1472-6920-4-10
4. Wilkening, G.L., Gannon, J.M., Ross, C., Brennan, J.L., Fabian, T.J., Marcsisin, M.J., Benedict, N.J.: Evaluation of branched-narrative virtual patients for interprofessional education of psychiatry residents. Acad. Psychiatry **41**(1), 71–75 (2016). https://doi.org/10.1007/s40596-016-0531-1
5. Pullman, D., Bethune, C., Duke, P.: Narrative means to humanistic ends. Teach. Learn. Med. **17**(3), 279–284 (2005). https://doi.org/10.1207/s15328015tlm1703_14
6. The American Board of Pediatrics. General pediatrics content outline. https://www.abp.org/sites/abp/files/pdf/gp_contentoutline_2017.pdf
7. Starling, S.P., Heisler, K.W., Paulson, J.F., Youmans, E.: Child abuse training and knowledge: a national survey of emergency medicine, family medicine, and pediatric residents and program directors. Pediatrics **123**(4), e595–e602 (2009). https://doi.org/10.1542/peds.2008-2938
8. Anderst, J., Dowd, M.D.: Comparative needs in child abuse education and resources: perceptions from three medical specialties. Med. Educ. Online **15** (2010). https://doi.org/10.3402/meo.v15i0.5193
9. Jenny, C., Hymel, K.P., Ritzen, A., Reinert, S.E., Hay, T.C.: Analysis of missed cases of abusive head trauma. JAMA **281**(7), 621–626 (1999)

Interactive Imagining in Interactive Digital Narrative

Colette Daiute[✉] ⓘD and Robert O. Duncan ⓘD

The City University of New York, New York, NY, USA
`cdaiute@gc.cuny.edu`

Abstract. This poster presents cross-disciplinary theory to identify inter-dependent processes of digital and human systems involved in Interactive Digital Narrative (IDN). Extending previous research on IDN design affordances and Human Development (HD) capacities, the project explores theory with a method for understanding reciprocal person-program synergies. The poster defines this program-person synergy as "interactive imagining" and sketches a research approach for studying such shared processing. This illustrative research method involves the think-aloud protocol method adapted to foster IDN designer-player dialogue around problematic, surprising or otherwise interesting IDN episodes, indicated in previous pilot gameplay. The poster outlines a think-aloud study to examine the nature and impact of interactive imagining among student designer-players in an interdisciplinary college setting. The goal of this inquiry is to expand the definition of IDN as an inter-subjective process including the meta-reflections of designer and player, thereby advancing IDN theory and practice.

Keywords: IDN theory · Cross-disciplinary perspectives on IDN · Shared IDN design and player processes · IDN research · Interactive imagining

1 Toward Inter-subjective IDN Process

Interactive Digital Narrative (IDN) and Human Development (HD) theories have proceeded, for the most part, in parallel. IDN design and HD research have, of course, considered program and person, yet advancing IDN theory and practice must go further to identify inter-subjective processes. Pre- and post IDN testing can be used to infer the player's state of mind. If considered at all by users, the designer's intentions are assumed to be embedded in the IDN design. Evidence about the nature and consequence of recip-rocal designer-user reflection processes would suggest a meta-process of interaction. Consistent with other IDN scholars urging qualitative research into IDN process [1, 2], this poster proposes a specific inter-subjective IDN process and a method for studying it from the perspectives of computer science and psychology.

In addition to many technical advances, IDN scholars have achieved the current state of the art by analyzing rich varieties of IDN and by distinguishing itself from traditional narrative forms [3]. Concepts like world, events, characters, game mechanics, emergent narratives, and instantiations loosen IDN theory from the grip of assumptions about pre-determined linear narratives [4, 5]. In parallel, HD scholars are currently making

© Springer International Publishing AG 2017
N. Nunes et al. (Eds.): ICIDS 2017, LNCS 10690, pp. 282–285, 2017.
https://doi.org/10.1007/978-3-319-71027-3_26

progress on the user dimension, such as examining whether young people, in particular, benefit in their cognitive or emotional development [6, 7].

Recently, IDN design theory is increasing focus on the player, while the HD researcher is considering the unique affordances of the digital program. In the IDN field, users' processes are coming into clearer focus, such as with analyses of a recorded walk-though [1]. HD researchers have also recently begun to consider the program partner in videogames (including IDNs), by examining relationships of specific game mechanics with specific cognitive capacities [7]. Nevertheless, HD assessments of pre- and post-play user developments continue to rely on traditional measures of cognitive and emotional processes. Similarly, while IDN distinguishes itself from traditional narrative forms by highlighting the user as co-author, IDN research has done so primarily based on theory [8]. The challenge remaining is how to define and study interactions of consciousness as well as behavior – that is how to study *inter*-subjective IDN processes. Such a study would, for example, be guided by the questions "What meta-reflections do student designers and users express, and how might those expressions inform IDN theory, design, and practice?"

2   The Need to Identify Shared Processes

Identifying inter-subjective processes would allow computer science and psychology to create complementary behavioral assessments. Current behavioral measures may be sufficient for assessing player engagement and entertainment in IDN games. However, understanding the engagement process in psychological terms would further assessments of claims of serious games, such as fostering knowledge about historical periods, scientific concepts, intergroup conflict, or other social issues. Psychological constructs might interest IDN designers considering the potential impact of different game mechanics. Current HD behavioral measures may also suffice for assessing learning and development. Increasing understanding about potentially unique cognitive and emotional processes *in relation to* IDN requires advancing beyond extant methods, including pre- versus post-activity assessment. The designer of a game-like IDN involving tension between motivators like accumulating points versus acting empathetically toward a character as in certain serious games could be informed in surprising ways by users' expressions of their motivations. Users and those who work with them, such as in educational contexts, might likewise be informed by designer reflections, which could avoid frustrating needs for users to replay before being able to enjoy and benefit from complex game mechanics.

3   Interactive Imagining

Imagination has recently been defined as "The dynamic by which a person or a group of people temporarily 'leave' the here and now of a proximal experience to explore a distal experience (in the past, the future, or any alternative reality), before 'coming back' to the here and now" [9]. We posit "interactive imagining" as interdependent, not only in terms of sharing the IDN world, events, and objects but also of reflections *about* cognitive and affective dimensions involved in the potential and realized IDNs. Interactive imagining is thus the meta-dialogue created by designer and player. Like the multiple diverse narratives possible in any IDN, these meta-interactions are usually implicit, and, while they could interfere with play, making such interactions explicit could enhance IDN design and learning phases.

Examples of interactive imagining abound in *Papers Please*, an IDN involving a 'scenario from the point of view of the user acting as a border agent [10]. Episodes of potentially revealing interactive imagining during *Papers Please* occur around authorities' instructions to detain anyone caught with contraband, which is challenged by a character's bribes. Such a dilemma provokes a potential conflict between extrinsic motivations (following the authorities' rules to gain points, avoid citations, provide for the family, etc.) and players' intrinsic motivations (potentially worthwhile risks, such as accepting a contraband-carrying applicant to accumulate cash from a bribe, to advance the game toward a desired ending, etc.). With that example from a professionally designed game as a foundation, this inquiry sketches a method for exploring how student designer-user pairs bring interactive imagining out of the shadows of mind.

4   Studying Interactive Imagining

One way to examine interactive imagining in IDN is to adapt the think-aloud protocol used previously in cognitive science [11]. Think-aloud protocols involve verbalizing thoughts and feelings during a challenging activity. While such an approach is clearly not the same as unmonitored gameplay, it has provided useful insights, about cognitive and affective processing during education design [12]. Studying inter-subjective IDN processes like interactive imagining would involve making the virtual dialogue between designer and player explicit, even if interactions occur asynchronously. Typically, IDNs take longer to design than to play. It is still possible to study interactive imagining during several iterations of game development and testing using an asynchronous think-aloud protocol.

Undergraduate psychology students will develop and playtest IDN experiences in a project-based course. Development will occur in iterative stages that include conception, implementation, and playtesting. Evidence of interactive imagining will be documented using: (1) written summaries of the development process; (2) artifacts from the development process; and (3) video of think-aloud sessions. The think-aloud protocol progresses in five phases: (1) identification of episodes in a game prototype, (2) protocol set up and brief practice, (3) implementation of the think-aloud protocol with several IDN episodes, (4) analysis of the think-aloud protocols in relation to behavioral records of play (play traces), (5) interviews with the designer and user around transcripts of think-aloud protocol segments. The IDN episodes will be created and hosted on a website using Twine [13] with instructions to "express thoughts and feelings during development/play that are not just translations of your actions." Recordings of the think-aloud sessions will be analyzed for reflective categories, such as psychological states or expressions (e.g., "think," "wondered," "felt,") with overlapping points of reflection and overlapping categories indicating "inter-active imagining." For example, in an IDN that is designed to teach students about depression, designers and players might share similar language about characters that are depressed (e.g., "sad," "stressed," or "worried") compared to characters that are not depressed (e.g., "hopeful," "resilient," or "happy") [14].

Understanding the affordances and limitations of interactive imagining will inform stakeholders about the following foundational questions: (1) How do students form cognitive models when designing or experiencing IDNs? (2) How can IDNs foster interactive imagining? (3) How should IDNs be incorporated into classrooms to mediate learning? and (4) What data are needed to assess learning outcomes in pedagogies that use interactive imagining with IDNs?

References

1. Koenitz, H., Dubbelman, T., Knoller, N., Roth, C.: An integrated and iterative research direction for interactive digital narrative. In: Nack, F., Gordon, A.S. (eds.) ICIDS 2016. LNCS, vol. 10045, pp. 51–60. Springer, Cham (2016). https://doi.org/10.1007/978-3-319-48279-8_5
2. Dubbelman, T.: Narrative game mechanics. In: Nack, F., Gordon, Andrew S. (eds.) ICIDS 2016. LNCS, vol. 10045, pp. 39–50. Springer, Cham (2016). https://doi.org/10.1007/978-3-319-48279-8_4
3. Ryan, M.L.: Beyond myth and metaphor: narrative in digital media. Poetics Today **23**, 581–609 (2002)
4. Aarseth, E.: A narrative theory of games. In: FDG 2012 Proceedings of the International Conference on the Foundations of Digital Games, pp. 129–133. ACM, New York (2012)
5. Koenitz, H.: Towards a theoretical framework for interactive digital narrative. In: Aylett, R., Lim, M.Y., Louchart, S., Petta, P., Riedl, M. (eds.) ICIDS 2010. LNCS, vol. 6432, pp. 176–185. Springer, Heidelberg (2010). https://doi.org/10.1007/978-3-642-16638-9_22
6. Granic, I., Lobel, A., Engels, R.C.M.E.: The benefits of playing video games. Am. Psychol. **69**(1), 66–78 (2014)
7. Homer, B.D., Plass, J.L.: Level of interactivity and executive functions as predictors of learning in computer-based chemistry simulations. Comput. Hum. Behav. **36**, 365–375 (2014)
8. Murray, J.H.: Hamlet on the Holodeck: The Future of Narrative in Cyberspace Free Press, New York (1999)
9. Zittoun, T., Gillespie, A.: Internalization: how culture becomes mind. Cult. Psychol. **21**(4), 477–491 (2015)
10. Pope, L.: Papers Please, 3909 LLC (2013). http://papersplea.se/
11. Ericsson, K., Simon, H.: Protocol Analysis: Verbal Reports as Data, 2nd edn. MIT Press, Boston (1985)
12. Anderson, T., Shattuck, J.: Design-Based research: a decade of progress in education research? Educ. Res. **41**(1), 16–25 (2012)
13. Klimas, C.: Twinery: Twine Homepage (2009). https://twinery.org/
14. Daiute, C.: Narrative Inquiry: A Dynamic Approach. Sage Publications, Thousand Oaks (2014)

Repetition, Reward and Mastery: The Value of Game Design Patterns for the Analysis of Narrative Game Mechanics

Teun Dubbelman[✉]

HKU University of the Arts Utrecht, Utrecht, The Netherlands
teun.dubbelman@hku.nl

Abstract. This paper aims to expand existing knowledge on narrative game design. Specifically, the paper discusses the importance of game design patterns for the analysis of narrative game mechanics. By bringing together insights from cognitive narratology and game design theory, the paper creates a preliminary theoretical perspective for deconstructing the design of mechanic-driven narrative games. To support the theoretical argument, the paper discusses *Papers, Please* as case study.

Keywords: Narrative game design · Game analysis · Cognitive narratology · Ludology · Game studies · Interactive storytelling · Game development

1 Introduction

In recent years, narrative game design has emerged as an important discipline within the field of game development [1]. However, narrative game design is also relatively new and underdeveloped. In comparison to established narrative disciplines, it still needs to discover its own expressive language and shared practices. This paper aims to contribute to the development of narrative game design as a creative discipline by furthering our understanding of narrative game mechanics. The paper tries to expand our knowledge by introducing the notion of game design patterns to existing work on the topic of narrative game mechanics.

2 Narrative Game Mechanics

One of the most pressing challenges for the discipline of narrative game design is understanding how interaction can be used as an instrument for narrative expression. Within game studies, the complex relationship between the concepts of interaction and narrative has been fiercely debated [2, 3]. The acknowledgment of cognitive narratology as theoretical point of departure for the conceptualisation of game narratives, has helped the discourse to go beyond the well-known ludology versus narratology debate [4]. Games can be understood as narrative medium when narrativity is approached as a mental, sense-making activity, rather than the act of recounting events of the past in the present

© Springer International Publishing AG 2017
N. Nunes et al. (Eds.): ICIDS 2017, LNCS 10690, pp. 286–289, 2017.
https://doi.org/10.1007/978-3-319-71027-3_27

[5]. From a cognitive perspective, games can manifest narratives, even when there is no intention to express a predetermined story, since players create stories mentally through the real-time, dynamic interaction with the game system [6].

In previous work, I have proposed the concept of narrative game mechanics to discuss the narrative potential of the player's real-time interaction with game systems. Narrative game mechanics invite game agents, including the player, to perform actions that support the construction of engaging stories and fictional worlds in the embodied mind of the player [7]. By deciding what kind of mechanics a game employs, narrative designers control the potential actions of game agents, like player-characters and NPCs. These actions, subsequently, influence what kind of stories players mentally construct.

Game mechanics can be a powerful addition to the designer's creative palette for developing engaging narrative experiences, and can be used alongside similar devices, like on-screen choice prompts[1], and alternative devices, like environmental storytelling or cutscenes. To comprehend and further explore the narrative potential of game mechanics, a deeper understanding of the concept of narrative game mechanics is essential.

3 Game Design Patterns

The notion of game design patterns can assist in gaining a deeper understanding of narrative game mechanics. In their seminal publication *Patterns in Game Design*, Björk and Holopainen describe game design patterns as: 'descriptions of commonly reoccurring parts of the design of a game that concern gameplay' [8: p. 34]. Well-known examples of these reoccurring parts (i.e. patterns) are: enemies, boss monsters, obstacles, pick-ups and power-ups.

Some of the patterns described by Björk and Holopainen are applicable to game mechanics, and can assist in disclosing the conventions that many narrative game designers employ when incorporating a set of mechanics in the overall design of a game. For example, the pattern "limited set of actions" applies to the common practice of providing the player with a relatively limited set of mechanics for engaging with the game system. Players will be performing these core actions repetitively when playing. Similarly, the pattern "new abilities" concerns the prevailing practice of unlocking additional player-mechanics as a game progresses.

In the next section, I will explain how narrative game mechanics work in tandem with game design patterns to express narrative meaning. The case study of *Papers, Please* [9] will focus on the following design patterns: limited set of actions, new abilities, rewards and penalties, and mastery.

---

[1] An on-screen choice prompt presents the player with a small number of predefined choices in the form of an explicit cue (i.e. prompt) on the screen. Choices can be mundane, like choosing which item to pick or which sentence to speak, or they can be more dramatic, like determining which character perishes.

4 Case Study

In *Papers, Please* the player takes on the role of a border officer in the dystopian country of Arstotzka. The dictatorial regime of Arstotzka is under continuous threat from its neighboring countries. Smugglers are trying to sneak contraband in; banned revolutionaries are infiltrating, hoping to overthrow the government; and the poor living conditions of Arstotzka's citizens, makes an uprising an imminent possibility. At the border crossing, the player-character must check people and papers for law violations, using various guidelines and tools. The core mechanics of the game are: checking documents for inconsistencies, checking people for the presence of contraband and stamping papers, thereby allowing or denying access to Arstotzka.

Papers, Please makes the pattern "limited set of actions" narratively meaningful by connecting the pattern to the profession of the main character. The profession of the main character abides, or even demands, a continuous repetition of a limited set of actions. The border officer's task in Arstotzka is stamping papers and checking documents and people. By making the player perform this set of actions many times over, the player instantiates the narrative of the border officer, carrying out his routine job.

Papers, Please makes the pattern "new abilities" narratively meaningful by connecting the pattern to conflict and setting. Like many mechanic-driven games, the game introduces new abilities to players as they progress through the game. At the beginning of the game, the player can only check papers for standard information, like date of birth, sex and country of origin. When the regime starts to encounter more opposition, it reacts by making it harder for outsiders to enter the country. Every week, the player-character receives additional guidelines and tools for checking people and papers, like fingerprinting and body scanning. This way, the pattern of new abilities not only hands the player additional gameplay possibilities as they continue through the game, but the pattern also expresses the growing unrest, and the controlling and suppressive tendencies of Arstotzka's authoritarian regime.

Papers, Please makes the pattern "rewards and penalties" narratively meaningful by connecting the pattern to the main-character's income and his family's struggle to survive in an oppressed and poor country. In many mechanic-driven games, players receive rewards and penalties, according to their actions. These can be abstract, like points, but often, rewards and penalties are given additional, narrative meaning. In *Papers, Please*, the rewards and penalties are presented in the form of the main character's income. Every day, the player needs to process enough individuals to earn enough income, but also needs to be careful not to make too many mistakes, since this would result in a fine. The main character needs this income to support his family. If he fails to earn enough income, family members may die of undernourishment, sickness or hyperthermia. This way, the pattern of rewards and penalties imbues the player's performance with narrative meaning; it does not only determine how many gameplay points the player receives, but also how well the player-character's family is doing. Potentially, this additional narrative meaning strengthens the player's motivation to continue playing, since (s)he desires not only to receive a maximum number of gameplay points, but also strives to keep the player-character's family alive.

Finally, *Papers, Please* makes the pattern "mastery" narratively meaningful by connecting the pattern to the impossible conditions of living in a dictatorship such as Arstotzka. *Papers, Please* is difficult to master. Most players never get to complete the game. Because the player must take more guidelines into account as the game progresses, it becomes increasingly difficult not to make any mistakes. With every mistake made, the player receives another fine, endangering the family's wellbeing. This way, the game's increasing difficulty not only offers gameplay challenges, but also conveys the almost impossible living conditions of Arstotzka, and supports the instantiation of stories of survival and hardship. Moreover, the gameplay difficulty has the potential to create narrative tension. As the game becomes harder to master, players can start to feel more pressure. This pressure can strengthen the narrative experience, since it aligns with the rising sense of danger in the main character's life.

5   Conclusion

This paper has explored how game design patterns can assist in disclosing and describing the narrative function of game mechanics.

For a deeper understanding of the value of game design patterns for the analysis of narrative game mechanics, a more extensive study should be conducted. This study should include a broader range of game design patterns, and a wider variety of mechanic-driven narrative games. Additionally, the dynamic nature of meaning making in narrative games should be addressed in more depth. The meaning expressed by a single game design pattern in a specific game can differ from situation to situation, depending on variables such as player demographics, prior playthroughs and dynamic game states. A qualitative or quantitative user-study on narrative game mechanics could provide the necessary insights in this complex process of meaning construction.

References

1. Heussner, T., Finley, T.K., Hepler, J.B., Lemay, A.: The Game Narrative Toolbox. Focal Press, New York and London (2015)
2. Simons, J.: Narrative, games, and theory. Game Stud. Int. J. Comput. Game Res. **7** (2007). http://gamestudies.org/0701/articles/simons
3. Frasca, G.: Ludologists love stories, too: notes from a debate that never took place. In: Copier, M., Raessens, J. (eds.) Level-up, pp. 92–99. Utrecht University, Utrecht (2003)
4. Koenitz, H.: Towards a specific theory of interactive digital narrative. In: Koenitz, H., Ferri, G., Haahr, M., Sezen, D., Sezen, T.I. (eds.) Interactive Digital Narrative: History, Theory and Practice, pp. 91–105. Routledge, New York and London (2015)
5. Ryan, M.-L.: Narrative Across Media: The Languages of Storytelling. University of Nebraska Press, Lincoln (2004)
6. Ryan, M.-L.: Avatars of Story. University of Minnesota Press, Minneapolis (2006)
7. Dubbelman, T.: Narrative game mechanics. In: Nack, F., Gordon, Andrew S. (eds.) ICIDS 2016. LNCS, vol. 10045, pp. 39–50. Springer, Cham (2016). https://doi.org/10.1007/978-3-319-48279-8_4
8. Björk, S., Holopainen, J.: Patterns in Game Design. Charles River Media, Boston (2005)
9. 3909: Papers, Please. iOS, 8 August 2013

Towards a Narrative-Based Game Environment for Simulating Business Decisions

Stanley Yu Galan(✉), Michael Joshua Ramos, Aakov Dy, Yusin Kim,
and Ethel Ong(✉)

De La Salle University, 2401 Taft Avenue, Manila, Philippines
{stanley_yugalan,ethel.ong}@dlsu.edu.ph

Abstract. Case studies are narratives of a specific real-life or imagined situation. They are used as teaching tools to help students practice their critical decision-making skills. Interactive Storytelling has the potential to augment the case method for business education by allowing for the dynamic generation of new cases based on the player's actions. Decisions made in previous cases will affect future ones, providing the player with a deeper and more meaningful learning experience. In this paper, we present our approach in building an interactive storytelling environment with case studies as its central theme, to teach students about ethical business practices. Preliminary evaluation with business experts as well as students, corroborated the value of combining story generation within a game to teach ethical business management, and showed its potential for expansion into a wider domain.

Keywords: Interactive storytelling · Case studies · Story generation · Domain Knowledge Base

1 Introduction

In the classroom setup, educators make use of case studies to present students with a realistic look at specific real-life or imagined situations, and an opportunity to practice their decision-making skills in a low risk environment [1]. Students and educators analyze the prescribed cases and present their discussions or solutions, supported by the line of reasoning employed and assumptions made.

In this paper, we present our interactive storytelling system, Pizzeria Story. It is designed to teach students ethical business practices by presenting them with scenarios revolving around ethical issues. Ethical issues are problems that require one to choose from a number of alternative courses of action, some of which are ethically right while others are not [2]. Pizzeria Story is built around the common good principle which argues for how to organize the social economy to allow members of the community to realize common interest in the provision of certain basic goods [3]. The system covers ethical issues such as abusive behavior, employee misconduct, and misuse of company resources among others. What our research offers is an automated means of generating case narratives that are shaped by player actions in an interactive environment.

© Springer International Publishing AG 2017
N. Nunes et al. (Eds.): ICIDS 2017, LNCS 10690, pp. 290–294, 2017.
https://doi.org/10.1007/978-3-319-71027-3_28

We focus our discussion on (i) the computational model of storytelling knowledge derived from business cases deconstructed into Prolog assertions; and (ii) the game controller which integrates the game front end and story generation system. The latter dynamically generates stories that depict the desired theme to encourage critical and ethical thinking. The theme is the overarching message of the story and directs the narrative of the generative stories [4]. The player decides how he/she intends to resolve the issue raised in the narrative. These decisions update the dynamic game world in turn, allowing the decisions to alter the outcome of the story.

2 Domain Knowledge Base

The Domain Knowledge Base is comprised of business concepts, facts and rules represented as binary assertions, such as *desires(employee, high salary)*, *capableAction(waiter, serve)*, *receiveAction(customer, serve)*, *usedFor(tray, serve)* and *causeEvent(harass, quit)*. The representation is adapted from ConceptNet [5]. The use of Prolog facts to model the assertions enables the reuse of commonsense knowledge in generating stories of varying themes and genres [4, 5]. In the Pizzeria Story, these themes include workplace accident, sexual harassment, employee theft and angry customer. As shown in Listing 1, assertions in the form of Prolog facts are also used to characterize an employee in lines (1)–(3), and to describe an event in lines (4)–(5).

Listing 1. Sample assertions in the knowledge base of Pizzeria.

```
(1) hasGender(person('Mary'), gender('Female')).
(2) hasRole(person('Mary'), role('cashier')).
(3) worksAt(person('Mary'), organization('Pizzeria')).
(4) receiveAction(person('Mary'), action('sexually harass')).
(5) capableOf(person('Mary'), action('resign')).
```

3 The Game Environment

Adopting a 3D tycoon style game interface (shown in Fig. 1) designed using Unity, the setting places the player in charge of running a pizzeria. In order to keep the business afloat, the player must manage employees, product line (pizza) and supplies, as well as deal with workplace incidents depicted through interactive cases.

The game engine coordinates with the story generator to dynamically generate various business scenarios that the player encounters in the story world. The coordination proceeds in a cycle of story planning – surface text generation – story world update.

Fig. 1. Main interface of the game.

3.1 Generating a Story

Stories are comprised of logical sequences of events. An event is defined by a collection of assertions which can be the performance of an action by a character, such as *order taking* and *cooking*. An event may require certain constraints before it can be executed. These constraints are specified as pre-conditions.

Building the case involves selecting a story theme, instantiating a set of characters, then planning the sequence of events. Each story has a number of constraints to be followed such as number of characters and their associated traits. The contents of the stories are planned via Prolog queries. Templates are then used to convert the story plan (comprising of assertions) into surface text that is presented to the player. Consider the assertions in Listing 2 that comprise the plot unit for the story conflict, in this case, sexual harassment. Line (1) asserts that '*John*' is capable of performing the indicated action while line (2) asserts that '*Mary*' can be a recipient of that action.

Listing 2. Plot unit for the conflict.

```
(1) capableOf(person('John'), action('sexually harass')).
(2) receiveAction(person('Mary'), action('sexually harass')).
```

The next event is determined through causal relationships defined as *causeEvent* assertions in the knowledge base (KB), which returns the list of candidate outcomes for a given plot unit. The planner determines a set of candidate actions by querying the KB using the statement: **causeEvent (plot_class(_CAUSE), decision(_EFFECT))**. The results from the KB are then presented to the user as decision points in the game interface. Once the player makes a choice, it is used as parameter for the query that searches for the next event based on the *causeEvent* assertion. The series of events generated from this iterative process should eventually lead to the climax plot unit which contains assertions to narrate the pivotal moment of the story.

3.2 Updating the Story World

The update of the game interface and the story world state is achieved via an event's post-conditions. If event *Sexual Harassment* has the post-conditions **empMorale('Mary', -50)** and **empStatus('Mary', 'scared')** that assert the effect on the emotional state of '*Mary*', the corresponding statistics before and after the event are in Fig. 2.

Fig. 2. Statistics of Employee *Mary* before and after the Event *Sexual Harassment.*

4 Preliminary Results and Future Work

Cases help students in using their critical thinking and reasoning skills to make decisions about issues they may encounter in real-life situations. Results from preliminary testing with two business professors and 25 Applied Corporate Management undergraduate students at De La Salle University have shown the potential of using interactive story-telling in game-based environment to allow the computer and the learner to collaborate in simulating the outcomes of events in business management.

One of the expert evaluators remarked that the system was appropriate for teaching proper ethics to both undergraduate business students and school administrators alike. The student evaluators, added that they *"Loved the concept"* and felt that *"the idea of this game is good, and that it is timely"*. Overall feedback highlighted the value of combining story generation with a game, enabling the learners to become more invested in both the game and the generated stories. The evaluators particularly liked how player decisions in both the game and stories had a tangible effect on the story world. This aspect of the system encourages the learner to be more careful and deliberate with their decision making when dealing with ethical issues.

Recommendations for future work include adjusting the system to focus less on utilitarian ethics since it encouraged players to choose actions that lead to the most good even if it meant performing some unethical actions along the way. The scope of the system should also be expanded to encompass more of the overall business process instead of just ethical organizational management. These include marketing, supply chain, and dealing with competitions. Efforts should also be made to enable the story generator to produce more complex and ethically ambiguous stories that can make the game environment more challenging for the target audience. Finally, future research should explore the enhancement of the story world model to include an event history to track past events that have already been generated, especially in cases when the story event graph is cyclic.

References

1. Naumes, W., Naumes, J.R.: The Art & Craft of Case Writing, 3rd edn. M. E. Sharpe, Inc., Armonk (2012)
2. The Law Dictionary 2012: What is ETHICAL ISSUE? definition of ETHICAL ISSUE (Blacks Law Dictionary), October 2012. http://thelawdictionary.org/ethical-issue/. Accessed 30 Aug 2017
3. Lutz, M.: Economics for the Common Good: Two Centuries for Social Economic Thought in the Humanistic Tradition. Routledge, London (1999)
4. Ong, E.: A commonsense knowledge base for generating children's stories. In: Proceedings of the 2010 AAAI Fall Symposium Series on Common Sense Knowledge, pp. 82–87. AAAI Press (2010)
5. Liu, H., Singh, P.: ConceptNet - a practical commonsense reasoning tool-kit. BT Technol. J. **22**(4), 211–226 (2004)

What is a Convention in Interactive Narrative Design?

Hartmut Koenitz[✉], Christian Roth, Teun Dubbelman, and Noam Knoller

HKU University of the Arts Utrecht, Professorship Interactive Narrative Design, Nieuwekade 1,
3511 RV Utrecht, The Netherlands
{Hartmut.koenitz,christian.roth,teun.dubbelman,
noam.knoller}@hku.nl

Abstract. This paper reports on an aspect of a long-term project to create a body of evidence-based interactive narrative design methods. In this context, we discuss aspects of formal design descriptions as a basis for a quantitative approach to verify the effects of design choices on the experience of audiences. Specifically, we discuss the notion of 'design conventions' by acknowledging earlier usages of the term and the related discourse in video game studies.

Keywords: Interactive digital narrative · Interactive narrative design · User study · Design conventions

1 Introduction

In 2012, Janet Murray recognized the need for specific design conventions as one of the central challenges for digital interactive design [1]. More recently, one of the authors presented a range of design strategies for interactive digital narrative [2] and identified a lack of generalized design conventions. In this paper, we discuss the notion of 'design conventions' as an important aspect of our approach towards the identification and verification of such generalizable design methods.

2 Context

The aim of our longer-term project is to collect a body of empirically-based design methods for interactive narrative to be used by practitioners and in education [3]. In order for such an effort to be most useful, it should be contextualized in two dimensions: (1) existing vocabulary (2) existing knowledge. For the first dimension, this means to understand what terminology around 'design conventions' is already in use. For the second aspect, this means to contextualize our approach in the light of existing published design knowledge, most prominently in video game studies.

2.1 Design Conventions

What is a 'design convention'? Our initial understanding of the term is the following: A concrete design method that manifests the intention of a creator so that it transports

N. Nunes et al. (Eds.): ICIDS 2017, LNCS 10690, pp. 295–298, 2017.
https://doi.org/10.1007/978-3-319-71027-3_29

said intention and shapes the interactor's experience accordingly. Conventions are not shared equally between creator and audience. The creator designs her work in such a way that it evokes a conventional understanding in the audience. For example, the initial description and certain graphical hints on the screen can script the interactor to accept a certain role. This means the designer here uses text and graphics with a specific intention, while the interactor interprets these clues and uses them in a process of "active creation of belief" [4] Therefore, conventions are consciously used by creators to be nearly unconsciously received and applied by audiences. For example, Weizenbaum "scripts the interactor" [4] of his famous 'virtual therapist' *Eliza* [5] by starting with an on-screen question ("How are you today… What would you like to discuss?") and by providing a blinking insertion mark that prompts the user to reply. These concrete design choices (question and text input prompt) in connection with the contemporary cultural context (popularity of psychoanalysis in the US and a strong believe in the capabilities of artificial intelligence) compelled users to accept their role as patients in a therapy session and act accordingly.

Conventions also depend on a level of literacy in the specific mediated format – for example, we are used to the cinematic convention of 'continuity editing.' This practice of leaving out visual information (e.g. showing a person walking towards a door, then a door handle being pressed and then the same person outside a building, without showing the intermediate visuals) works on the knowledge that missing pieces of visual information will be supplied by the audience's imagination automatically. However, such "cultural conventions" [6] might only be shared by some members even in seemingly homogeneous western societies, e.g. the WASD keyboard convention for interactor movement in 3D games is only a convention for the group of people literate in 3D games. It might therefore be more appropriate to understand this aspect of conventions as group specific. As a result of this discussion, we can now clarify our usage of the term 'design convention' as short hand to mean 'concrete design methods to create conventional comprehension and effects in interactors.'

2.2 Design Conventions in Earlier Media

In *Inventing the Medium*, Janet Murray positions the invention and refinement of conventions as a central aspect in applying the potential of the digital medium for expression and meaning making:

> Designing any single artifact within this new medium is part of the broader collective effort of making meaning through the invention and refinement of digital media **conventions**. (our emphasis) [1]

Murray's usage of 'conventions' here extends the earlier usage of the term in cognitivist film studies and other disciplines. There, conventions cannot be 'invented' in the fullest sense of the word; rather, a certain technique (e.g. the jump cut) might be invented (or used for the first time) by a filmmaker. This technique becomes a convention only once it is routinely understood by audiences. However, even with regards to film, the process can be more immediate, as the famous 'Kuleshev effect' demonstrates: This early Soviet filmmaker created several versions of the same clip by intersecting it with emotionally charged images. By observing his audience he was able to demonstrate that the perception of the original clip changed depending on the intersected material. We may understand the result of his experimental setup as the discovery of a convention since Kuleshev's audiences shared a certain understanding of the different clips without being prompted.

2.3 Video Game Design Conventions

Before proceeding with our definition and vocabulary, we wish to consider the discourse in video game studies and design. This related field might already have established terminology which could be used in our effort. There is certainly no scarcity of publications on video game design. However, only a subset is concerned with the issue of establishing a descriptive and formal design vocabulary. When we find a development of terminology (as in [7, 8]), the focus is on formal descriptions for games. This leaves us with a much smaller group of publications focusing on the design process itself, for example Dough Church's *Formal Abstract Design Tools.* [9]

A popular approach towards a formal description of concrete design choices in video games is 'design patterns.' This kind of formalism is designed to provide a flexible, reusable solution towards solving specific problems [10]. Two collections of design patterns especially gained prominence: the *400 Project* [11] and Björk and Holopainen's book [12]. The latter authors describe game design patterns as "semiformal interdependent descriptions of commonly reoccurring parts of the design of a game" [12] While these collections provide valuable knowledge for game designers, there are considerable differences in their particular approaches. As Kreitmeier points out, quoting Gemma et al. [13]: "One person's pattern can be another person's primitive building block." The biggest drawback of game design patterns is therefore the lack of a precise (and shared) definition that would allow for direct comparison. Another drawback of this situation is that no collection can extend others without considerable work to bridge the gaps between different ontological categories. Yet, in a field with little consensus on terms and concepts, design patterns is still one of the most widely accepted concepts as Richard Rouse III reminds us more recently [14]. Yet, as Rouse concedes, for many designers, design rules are personal, written down only in their "own rule book."

3   Abstract Concepts vs. Design Conventions

A further aspect is the distinction between abstract concepts and concrete design conventions. For a first study [3], we selected "scripting the interactor" (StI) [4], a design concept originally identified by Janet Murray. StI casts an interactor into her role by providing context, managing expectations and exposing opportunities for action. Examples can include communicating roles and goals or informing the interactor of the experience to be expected. StI is therefore not a design convention by itself, but a conceptual abstraction which translates into a range of concrete designs conventions, for example a textual intro at the beginning of a game.

4   Conclusion

In this paper, we introduced our definition of 'design conventions' and discussed this concept in relation to fields like film studies and video game design. We align with Murray's definition and identify differences to earlier definitions. In video game studies we find a plethora of terms, but little shared vocabulary. Given this state of affairs, the term 'design convention' – while being a shorthand for a more complex relationship between the work of a creator and its audience – has the advantage of a clear lineage to earlier media forms via Murray's definition. Therefore, we will continue to use the term in our research effort.

References

1. Murray, J.H.: Inventing the Medium: Principles of Interaction Design as a Cultural Practice. MIT Press, Cambridge (2012)
2. Koenitz, H.: Design approaches for interactive digital narrative. In: Schoenau-Fog, H., Bruni, L.E., Louchart, S., Baceviciute, S. (eds.) ICIDS 2015. LNCS, vol. 9445, pp. 50–57. Springer, Cham (2015). https://doi.org/10.1007/978-3-319-27036-4_5
3. Roth, C., Koenitz, H.: Towards creating a body of evidence-based interactive digital narrative design knowledge: approaches and challenges. In: Proceedings of 2nd International Workshop on Multimedia Alternate Realities, AltMM 2017. ACM, New York (2017)
4. Murray, J.H.: Hamlet on the Holodeck: The Future of Narrative in Cyberspace. Free Press, New York (1997)
5. Weizenbaum, J.: Eliza — a computer program for the study of natural language communication between man and machine. Commun. ACM **9**, 36–45 (1966)
6. Norman, D.A.: Affordance, conventions, and design. Interactions **6**, 38–43 (1999)
7. Salen, K., Zimmerman, E.: Rules of Play. MIT Press, Cambridge (2004)
8. Costikyan, G.: I have no words & i must design: toward a critical vocabulary for games. In: Mäyrä, F. (ed.) Proceedings of Computer Games and Digital Cultures Conference, pp. 9–33. Tampere (2002)
9. Church, D.: Formal Abstract Design Tools (1999). https://www.gamasutra.com/view/feature/131764/formal_abstract_design_tools.php
10. Alexander, C., Ishikawa, S., Silverstein, M.: A Pattern Language. Oxford University Press, New York (1977)
11. Barwood, H., Falstein, N.: The 400 Project. http://www.theinspiracy.com/the-400-project.html
12. Björk, S., Holopainen, J.: Patterns in Game Design (Game Development Series). Charles River Media, Rockland (2004)
13. Gamma, E., Helm, R., Johnson, R., Vlissides, J.: Design patterns: abstraction and reuse of object-oriented design. In: Broy, M., Denert, E. (eds.) Software Pioneers. Springer, Heidelberg (2002). https://doi.org/10.1007/978-3-642-59412-0_40
14. Rouse III, R.: The Rise and Fall and Rise Again of Game Design Rules. http://www.gamasutra.com/blogs/RichardRouseIII/20150218/236699/The_Rise_and_Fall_and_Rise_Again_of_Game_Design_Rules.php

Interactive Storytelling for the Maintenance of Cultural Identity: The Potential of Affinity Spaces for the Exchange and Continuity of Intergenerational Cultural Knowledge

Juliana Monteiro[1(✉)] ⓘD, Carla Morais[2] ⓘD, and Miguel Carvalhais[3] ⓘD

[1] CIQUP/Faculty of Engineering, University of Porto, Porto, Portugal
juliana.monteiro@fe.up.pt
[2] CIQUP/Faculty of Sciences, University of Porto, Porto, Portugal
cmorais@fc.up.pt
[3] INESC TEC/Faculty of Fine Arts, University of Porto, Porto, Portugal
mcarvalhais@fba.up.pt

Abstract. In an increasingly aged society, with unmeasurable cultural richness kept by its elder elements for their vast life experience, it is urgent to preserve this cultural knowledge before it disappears. The capacity of the computational space to accommodate a virtualization of reality is evident, alongside with the possibility to preserve perspectives of reality with spontaneous and very easy to sort creations thanks to the web tools that now support content production by any common user. Despite all the relevant problematics brought by this context where the common user is simultaneously consumer and producer of information, the opportunities for the present and future of cultural identity maintenance are numerous. This paper approaches the idea of supporting the participatory maintenance of cultural identity through intergenerational storytelling and the dynamization of digital affinity spaces. Our contribution aims to grow the understanding of the role that interactive narratives can have in the real world and in the specific context of cultural identity maintenance, by developing new usage strategies to enhance cultural mediation with the tools we have available and with the help of social, ubiquitous and mobile storytelling strategies.

Keywords: Cultural identity · Storytelling · Affinity spaces · Intergenerational dynamics

1 Introduction

A series of technical innovations have marked the path from the birth of the Web to the present, reflecting a new perspective over knowledge and our urge to share it. Many theorists highlight the rise of a new intelligence that coordinates users in real time on the web, giving place to the birth of paradigms such as "Lovink's Mediactivism, Castells' Network affinities, Levy's Collective Intelligence and Barabarasi's model of Small Word aristocratic" [1]. In this context, we propose an approach of maintenance towards cultural identity through digital interactive storytelling, as an alternative to the traditional concept of preservation that by definition implies the absence of change [2].

© Springer International Publishing AG 2017
N. Nunes et al. (Eds.): ICIDS 2017, LNCS 10690, pp. 299–302, 2017.
https://doi.org/10.1007/978-3-319-71027-3_30

The term "maintenance" of cultural identity hence appears in our work as a result of the need we felt to express a combination of cultural identity safeguarding, appropriation and continuity that we expect to contribute to with our project.

2   A Participatory Approach on the Maintenance of Cultural Identity and the Opportunities of Interactive Storytelling Based on Affinity Spaces

The vision of connecting the concept of cultural legacy with storytelling has been approached by several works, some with an approach more related with digital story-telling and others that serve as pure memories archives. That is the case of *Archive*[1], *Europeana*[2] and *Arquivo de Memória*[3], that are projects that are more tuned with the scope of the archive. *Arquivo de Memória*, is particularly interesting for our work for being a project that aims to record and disseminate recent history, contributing to new social dynamics with the creation of a living archive. Other projects such as *New Dimensions in Testimony* [3] also highlight the potential of digital storytelling to continue the dialogue between generations for cultural knowledge, advancing the tradi-tion of passing down lessons through oral storytelling with the help of technology. In parallel, many authors have also identified the potential of synergies between storytelling and intergenerational dynamics [4–9]. For example, Davis highlights the participatory approach to intergenerational storytelling as key for "enabling untold but significant stories to emerge, and technical and storytelling skills to be transferred to participants through the process" [4].

In our study, the topic of cultural identity maintenance comes deeply connected to concepts of regional identity [10, 11], collective memory [12] and social memory [13]. The concept of regional identity affords us with a vision of identity as a "primordial nature of regions, accentuating their 'personality' and the harmony/unity between a region and its inhabitants" [10]. On another hand, the formation and survival of a collec-tive memory through different generations seems to be rather dependent of socialization and customs and not quite simply deriving from belonging to a distinct society and culture [12]. In parallel to this idea, Lundby approaches the potential for encouraging social participation by promoting the amateur production of digital stories, as he considers that "the kind of digital storytelling to be discussed here opens new ways of participation: in 'story circles' offline, as well as online peer contact on social networking sites" [14]. At the same time, social memory and a participatory approach on cultural identity maintenance experience new opportunities supported by web tools that allow any common user to simultaneously become producer and consumer of interactive stories, and are empowered by these opportunities. This takes our attention to the fact that the role of amateur cultural and media production has become a place for both enthusiasm and controversy regarding cultural studies. For example, Burgess arguments

---

[1]   www.archive.org.

[2]   www.europeana.eu.

[3]   www.arquivodememoria.pt.

on the new role of the "creative consumer" as a key to "a major potential disruption to the dominance of commercial media", but she also alerts to the "notion of a 'digital divide' based on hard access to information and communication technologies (ICTs)" [13], while Jenkins [15] brings up the concept of "participation gap" that stresses that the sole fact of having access to technology doesn't cover the important matter of knowing what to do with it and how. Nevertheless, the concept of affinity spaces [16] casts new ideas and opportunities for carrying with this participatory approach, as well as to enhance the capacity of maintaining cultural identity knowledge through interactive storytelling. The concept of affinity spaces appears as a response to the need to formulate alternative notions to the communities of practice, since the concept of "community" seems to carry the notion of membership, but the meaning of membership is not clear enough to define the many different degrees of being a member in some communities [16]. In this context, Gee defines the concept of affinity spaces with the following conditions: 1. Common endeavor, not race, class, gender or disability, is primary; 2. Newbies and masters and everyone else share common space; 3. Some portals are strong generators; 4. Internal grammar is transformed by external grammar; 5. Encourages intensive and extensive knowledge; 6. Encourages individual and distributed knowledge; 7. Encourages dispersed knowledge; 8. Uses and honors tacit knowledge; 9. Many different forms and routes to participation; 10. Lots of different routes to status; 11. Leadership is porous and leaders are resources [16]. Drawing on Jenkins et al. [17] eleven core media literacy skills for interacting with these new media affinity spaces, many unexplored opportunities for the specific context of cultural identity maintenance start to get shaped.

3   Final Considerations

This paper approaches the idea of developing intergenerational storytelling activities in affinity spaces in pervasive media, beyond the physical and geographical space, to understand their effects, challenges and opportunities for the maintenance of cultural identity. This idea is the base of our ongoing work regarding the study of cultural identity maintenance through intergenerational activities in affinity spaces.

The next steps for this research will consist on carrying with an ethnographic fieldwork to support a participatory approach to the maintenance of cultural identity through a set of workshops for intergenerational storytelling and through the dynamization of physical and digital affinity spaces. With this approach, we strive to contribute to the understanding of challenges and opportunities for the maintenance of cultural identity through interactive storytelling in affinity spaces.

Acknowledgments. The authors gratefully acknowledge the support of Fundação para a Ciência e Tecnologia (FCT–Portugal), through the Ph.D. Grant PD/BD/114139/2015.

References

1. Russo, V.: Urban mediactivism in web 3.0. Case analysis: the city of Chieti. In: Maturo, A., Hošková-Mayerová, Š., Soitu, D.-T., Kacprzyk, J. (eds.) Recent Trends in Social Systems: Quantitative Theories and Quantitative Models. SSDC, vol. 66, pp. 303–313. Springer, Cham (2017). https://doi.org/10.1007/978-3-319-40585-8_27
2. Severo, M.: Social Media as new Arenas for intangible cultural heritage. In: Proceedings of the European Conference on e-Learning, pp. 406–412 (2015)
3. Traum, D., et al.: New dimensions in testimony: digitally preserving a holocaust survivor's interactive storytelling. In: Schoenau-Fog, H., Bruni, L.E., Louchart, S., Baceviciute, S. (eds.) ICIDS 2015. LNCS, vol. 9445, pp. 269–281. Springer, Cham (2015). https://doi.org/10.1007/978-3-319-27036-4_26
4. Davis, D.: Intergenerational digital storytelling: A sustainable community initiative with inner-city residents. Vis. Commun. 10, 527–540 (2011)
5. Beltrán, R., Begun, S.: "It is medicine": narratives of healing from the aotearoa digital storytelling as indigenous media project (ADSIMP). Psychol. Dev. Soc. J. 26, 155–179 (2014)
6. Wexler, L., Eglinton, K., Gubrium, A.: Using digital stories to understand the lives of Alaska native young people. Youth Soc. 46, 478–504 (2014)
7. Couldry, N., Stephansen, H., Fotopoulou, A., MacDonald, R., Clark, W., Dickens, L.: Digital citizenship? Narrative exchange and the changing terms of civic culture. Citizensh. Stud. 18, 615–629 (2014)
8. Couldry, N., MacDonald, R., Stephansen, H., Clark, W., Dickens, L., Fotopoulou, A.: Constructing a digital storycircle: Digital infrastructure and mutual recognition. Int. J. Cult. Stud. 18, 501–517 (2015)
9. Clark, W., Couldry, N., MacDonald, R., Stephansen, H.C.: Digital platforms and narrative exchange: Hidden constraints, emerging agency. New Med. Soc. 17, 919–938 (2015)
10. Paasi, A.: Region and place: regional identity in question. Prog. Hum. Geogr. 27, 475–485 (2003)
11. Mutibwa, D.H.: Memory storytelling and the digital archive: revitalizing community and regional identities in the virtual age. J. Med. Cult. Polit. 12, 7–26 (2016)
12. Assmann, J., Czaplicka, J.: Collective memory and cultural identity. New Ger. Crit. 65, 125–133 (1995)
13. Burgess, J.: Hearing ordinary voices: Cultural studies, vernacular creativity and digital storytelling. Contin. J. Med. Cult. Stud. 20, 201–214 (2006)
14. Lundby, K.: Editorial: mediatized stories: mediation perspectives on digital storytelling. New Med. Soc. J. 10, 363–371 (2008)
15. Jenkins, H.: Convergence Culture: Where Old and New Media Collide. NYU press, New York (2006)
16. Gee, J.P.: Semiotic social spaces and affinity spaces. In: Barton, D., Tusting, K. (eds.) Beyond Communities Practice Language Power Social Context, pp. 214–232. Cambridge University Press, Cambridge (2005)
17. Jenkins, H., Purushotma, R., Weigel, M., Clinton, K., Robinson, A.J.: Confronting the Challenges of Participatory Culture. MIT Press, Cambridge (2009)

Applying Interactive Documentary as a Pedagogical Tool in High School Level

Valentina Moreno[1](✉) and Arnau Gifreu-Castells[2](✉)

[1] Universidad Complutense de Madrid, Madrid, Spain
valentmo@ucm.es
[2] ERAM – Universitat de Girona, Salt, Spain
agifreu@gmail.com

Abstract. This work explores the potential of interactive documentary as a teaching tool, both from a didactic perspective, in which the documentary is a viewing and learning tool. To do this, we analysed the characteristics of interactive documentary within the Educommunication framework.

Keywords: Interactive documentary · Education · Educommunication

1 Introduction

This work explores the potential of interactive documentary as a teaching tool, both from a didactic perspective, in which the documentary is a viewing and learning tool. To test our hypotheses, we carried out a quantitative exploratory study with a sample of 113 students from the 1st, 2nd and 4th years of secondary school in two high schools in Madrid. In this research, the students interacted with an interactive documentary and viewed its linear version. The study shows that the this interactive version of the documentary is more satisfyingly attractive, fun, easier to understand, immersive and holds the students' attention longer than its linear documentary version (Table 1).

N. Nunes et al. (Eds.): ICIDS 2017, LNCS 10690, pp. 303–307, 2017.
https://doi.org/10.1007/978-3-319-71027-3_31

Table 1. Distribution of the sample

Group	Total size	Methodological design
1st year	20	Students interacted only with the interactive documentary
2nd year	21	Student watched a linear version of the interactive documentary and after that interacted with the interactive documentary
4th year	72 (3 groups: A, B and D)	Group A, B and D watched a linear version of the interactive documentary. Group D interacted too with the interactive documentary

Source: elaborated by the authors

2 Theoretical Framework

2.1 Interactive Documentary

Interactive documentary has emerged from the convergence of several different disciplines, and thus its conceptualization is still in a process of development. Therefore, uses the mechanisms of the traditional documentary but incorporates modes of navigation and interaction [1] that allow the user to perform physical actions on the story and even collaborate in it.

2.2 Educommunication

In this research, we analyse the implementation of interactive documentary as an educational tool, including its use as a didactic platform and also as a constructivist learning tool. We take educommunication as a framework of educational theory, which proposes using the media as a tool for active learning. Educommunication has its roots in constructivism, an education theory inspired by Jean Piaget [2] and Lev Vygotsky [3], among others.

Educommunication is based on the pioneering studies of Célestin Freinet and Frank Raymond Leavis and Denys Thompson [4]. According to these perspectives, we learn to communicate to others what we know and to receive their feedback; therefore, the interaction to communication tools, such as radio, school newspapers or blogs, make a learning process possible in which it is not the medium that is relevant but rather the process of constructing the knowledge.

3 Methodology

The objective of this study is to analyse the elements of interactive documentary that can facilitate the teaching-learning processes from an educommunication perspective. To do this, we will study the application of interactive documentary as a didactic element. To delimit the research, we propose two specific objectives: to determine whether the interactive documentary analysed (*Pregoneros de Medellín*, Angela

Carabalí and Thibault Durand, 2015) is more attractive, fun, easy to understand and holds the students' attention better than its traditional documentary version (build with three sequences of the interactive documentary *Pregoneros de Medellín*). And, to determinate whether interactive documentary analysed increase the levels of empathy more than the linear edition. To achieve these objectives, we will carry out an exploratory study with a mixed research approach that works with qualitative and quantitative data [5, 6]. The data obtained will be compared with the analysis results of the previous literature and the results.

In this work, we also test the following hypotheses: H1: Interactive documentary enhances understanding and H2: The interactive documentary selected engages the student more in active learning and is more attractive than its classic documentary edition, which is a tool of passive knowledge. The study employed a sample of 113 high school students from the metropolitan area of Madrid, that evaluated the interactive documentary as a didactic tool. The students watched a linear version of interactive documentary and after, answered a questionnaire about it, or interacted with the interactive documentary and after, answered a questionnaire about it at the end of the interaction.

We designed post-viewing questionnaires for the linear documentary and other post-viewing questionnaires for the interactive documentary. Both questionnaires consisted of a Likert scale for evaluating the levels of: enjoyment, understanding, attraction, attention, willingness to work with videos in class, willingness to create videos in class, satisfaction with content, change in cultural viewpoint and levels of empathy.

4   Results

We compared the interactive viewing with the linear viewing of the 1st, 2nd and 4th year students by performing an Unpaired Student's t-Test to compare the levels of the different values (Table 2).

Comparison shows that all means of the interactive documentary variables are significantly higher those of the linear documentary variables. Therefore, it can be concluded that for this sample, interactive documentary is more fun, easier to understand, more attractive and better at holding their attention than linear documentary.

With respect to the research hypotheses, hypothesis H1 (Interactive documentary enhances understanding) was confirmed. The mean of the easy-to-understand variable is significantly higher for the interactive documentary (3.90) than for the linear documentary (2.77).

For H2 (Interactive documentary engages the student more in active learning, is more attractive and holds the student's attention better than the classic documentary, which is a tool of passive knowledge) the unpaired Student's t-test between the interactive and the linear documentaries with the sample of 113 students confirms that the mean of the attractiveness variable of the interactive documentary (3.41) was significantly higher than the mean of the same variable for the traditional documentary (2.52).

Table 2. Unpaired Student's t-test comparison of interactive version vs linear version.

	ID	N	Average	Standard deviation	Mean standard deviation	Sig
Fun?	Interaction	58	3.47	0.842	0.111	,002
	Screening	96	2.97	1.293	0.132	
Easy to understand?	Interaction	58	3.90	0.892	0.117	,000
	Screening	96	2.77	1.433	0.146	
Attractive?	Interaction	58	3.41	1.124	0.148	,000
	Screening	90	2.52	1.416	0.149	
Holds attention?	Interaction	57	3.63	1.159	0.154	,000
	Screening	92	3.08	1.578	0.164	
Work with video in class?	Interaction	57	4.18	1.136	0.150	,000
	Screening	92	3.38	1.436	0.150	
Did you like it?	Interaction	58	3.66	1.035	0.136	,000
	Screening	94	3.06	1.465	0.151	
Change cultural vision?	Interaction	58	3.43	1.244	0.163	,048
	Screening	93	2.88	1.390	0.144	
Generates empathy?	Interaction	58	3.79	1.072	0.141	,000
	Screening	92	3.16	1.507	0.157	

Source: Elaborated by the authors

5   Conclusion

Interactive documentary has grown and developed gradually and continually in recent years; however, we are still at a very early stage in the study of possible applications of this format. Throughout this work we have been able to verify the main objectives of the research. Although interactivity is an important element that students like about the format, it is evident that the story continues to be essential for attracting the public. To conclude, this study and previous works [7] indicate that interactive documentary can become a suitable educational tool; therefore, we consider it appropriate to promote designing interactive documentaries for teaching purposes and implementing them in schools.

References

1. Gifreu-Castells, A.: El documental interactiu com a nou gènere audiovisual. Estudi de l'aparició del nou gènere, aproximació a la seva definició i proposta de taxonomia i d'un model d'anàlisi a efectes d'avaluació, disseny i producció. [PhD]. Universitat Pompeu Fabra. Departament de Comunicació, Barcelona (2013)
2. Piaget, J.: Piaget's theory. In: Mussen, P.H. (ed.) Carmichael's Manual of Child Psychology, vol. 1. Wiley, New York (1970)
3. Vygotsky, L.S., Cole, M.: Mind in Society. Harvard University Press, Cambridge (1978)

4. Leavis, F.R., Thompson, D.: Culture and Environment: The Training of Critical Awareness. Chatto & Windus, London (1933)
5. Teddlie, C., Tashakkori, A.: Major issues and controversies in the use of mixed methods in the social and behavioral sciences. In: Handbook of mixed methods in social & behavioral research, pp. 3–50 (2003)
6. Creswell, J.W., Creswell, J.D.: Mixed methods research: developments, debates, and dilemmas. In: Swanson, R., Holton, E. (eds.) Research in organizations: foundations and methods of inquiry, pp. 315–326. Berret- Koehler Publishers Inc, San Francisco (2005)
7. Gifreu-Castells, A, Moreno, V.: Educational multimedia applied to the interactive nonfiction area. Using interactive documentary as a new model for learning. In: 2014 Proceedings of Edulearn Conference, pp. 1306–1315. IATED, Barcelona (2014)

Interactive Storytelling System for Enhancing Children's Creativity

Kaoru Sumi[✉] and Nozomu Yahata[✉]

Future University Hakodate, Hakodate, Japan
kaoru.sumi@acm.org, g2117049@fun.ac.jp

Abstract. We developed an interactive storytelling system that generates stories from hypothetical questions, called 'What-If' function. Specifically, the stories are expressed in a rule-based form 'If-Then'. The system allows users to create a story that has a synopsis different from the original story by changing the 'If' part. For example, if the user changes the appearance and personality of a character, the outline of the story also changes. We believe this process can help improve the creativity of users of the system. This system was also developed to help users visualize written stories as images and allow them to experience stories interactively. An evaluation experiment, conducted on 21 fifth graders in elementary school, showed an improvement in the children's creative ability.

Keywords: Story generation · Expanding storylines · 'What-If' function

1 Introduction

A story is like a rule-based system in which a storyline is expanded and one event triggers a latter event. A Japanese old proverb says, 'When the wind blows, pail-makers are profitable'. This metaphor means that the occurrence of an event may affect places and things that have no relation at first glance. Why? When the wind blows, pail-makers are profitable because the following phenomenon is developed. (1) A strong wind blows dust. (2) The dust enters people's eyes; the number of blind people increases. (3) Blind people buy a shamisen, a musical instrument made from cat skin (an occupation for the blind at that time). (4) Cats are killed to make the shamisen. (5) As the cat population decreases, the mice increase. (6) Mice bite pails. (7) The demand for pails increases, and pail-makers are profitable [1]. The story developed from common-sense knowledge of the living environment of the people in those days. Accordingly, we believe that a story will be developed by using common-sense knowledge when one event is triggered. As the development of each event changes, based on the hypothesis of what it would be like, a variety of stories will be developed.

In this study, we developed an interactive storytelling system that generates stories from hypothetical questions. An interactive storytelling system is defined as a system capable of developing stories in a non-linear order, and users can actively experience the stories [2]. In this system, a story is represented by expressing it in a knowledge base of an 'If-Then' format, according to common-sense knowledge. Users can create a story different from the original story simply by changing the 'If' part, called the 'What-If'

N. Nunes et al. (Eds.): ICIDS 2017, LNCS 10690, pp. 308–312, 2017.
https://doi.org/10.1007/978-3-319-71027-3_32

function. For example, if the user changes the appearances and personalities of a character, the outline of the story will change. It is therefore possible to generate different stories from the original story.

Scheherazade searches for answers to questions on the Internet and incorporates the answers into stories [3, 4]. In our proposed research, we do not use information on the Internet, but instead, we use common-sense knowledge as a prototype. With this 'What-If' function, users can try out the influence of various assumptions in their minds on things. We believe this will enhance the creativity of the user because the system can show that something will happen except what he/she was thinking.

We also believe this system can help users visually recognize the story by adding animations of the characters, 3D objects and scenes, as well as text information of the generated story. According to the research of Mayer [5], when the linguistic and image content are related, the image improves understanding; therefore, it is considered that the animation of this system helps understand the content. We adopted the method of previous studies [6–8] such as assigning animations from the text in-formation. Therefore, the subject of the text is linked to the character, the verb is linked to the action of the character, and the scene is linked to the visualized place.

In this research, we developed an interactive storytelling system with animations that generate stories from hypothetical questions based on the 'What-If' function that can change the If part of an If-Then formatted rule-based system and examine it as a system to improve children's creativity.

2   Interactive Storytelling System with "What-if" Function

In this system, a story is created by defining the state of characters and objects and applying rules linking personalities and appearances with behaviors of the characters on the rule-based system. Currently, the number of rules is 26. The rule-based system is defined by CLIPS, which is a rule-based engine, text, and animation. The 3D objects are displayed using Unity 5.0 of the game development environment. The 'defrule' in CLIPS defines rules of characters such as personalities or appearances. Using 'assert', the definition of characters can be changed.

We developed a system based on an existing story (Fig. 1). 'Snow White' is selected because it is a famous fairy tale from the first edition of the Grimm's Fairy Tales collection. Therefore, it is simple for users to imagine the story. Based on Snow White's original story, the system creates various stories by using the 'What-If' function. In this system, Snow White's final ending is represented in 17 styles. During the story generation session, a user has a chance to change the storyline. For example, when the user is confronted with the branch 'The queen visited the house of Snow White', and Snow White's definition was set to 'doubtful personality', the behavior will be the action of a doubtful personality based on the rules of common-sense knowledge such as 'If' part is 'doubtful personality' and 'Then' part is 'do not receive things from unknown people'. In the original story, if Snow White's definition is set to 'pure personality', then actions such as 'receives things from an unknown person', and finally 'gets into a coma' occur.

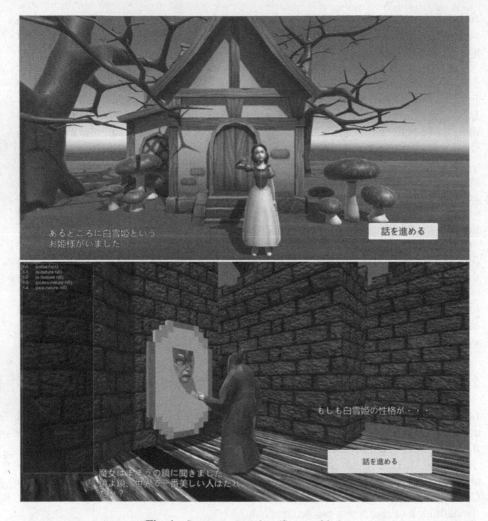

Fig. 1. System screenshot (Snow white).

By pressing the button on the screen, text information of the next storyline is read by a voice synthesizer and an animation appears. In addition, in the window on the left side of the screen, the user can operate it to confirm the definition of the characters currently selected by the user. The lower side of the screen shows the storyline. For example, when the user encounters the branch, 'The woman visits Snow White's house', the user sets the definition of Snow White with a 'doubtful character'. Then, based on the definition, it acts as 'do not receive apple from woman'. In addition, if Snow White's definition is 'pure personality', actions such as 'receive apple from woman' and consequently 'go into a coma' occur.

3 Conclusion

We conducted a workshop to evaluate the system for 21 fifth graders in elementary school and distributed a questionnaire to determine whether our system improves creativity and asked the users' impression of the system. We evaluated how creativity was enriched before and after the system was used via the creativity test [9]. The screen of the system was projected on a paper dome with a projector using a fisheye lens. The paper dome is shaped like half a sphere and is made of cardboard. The experiment took 45–50 min. In the creativity test, the experimenter showed the picture, asked children about continuation storyline of the picture, and then let them write it on the paper. The children were asked to write as many sentences as desired.

We compared the pre-test and post-test scores using an existing creativity test for children subjects in elementary school. Thus, since the children's post-test score significantly increased compared to the pre-test score, it could be concluded that the creativity of children improved. Observing the content written by the children on the post-test, there were many cases where they changed the personality of the characters. We observed cases where children created stories of how the story would look like if the characters were gentle, evil, and so on. It can be concluded that by using the 'What-If' function, children started imagining how the storyline would change if the personality of the character changed. According to the questionnaire, at least 90% of the children responded positively to questions such as: 'Is the story generated by the system more interesting than the existing story'? 'Is the system's operability good'? 'Is the system easy to understand'? They scored 4 or more in 5 grades. Thus, it could be concluded that the children are satisfied with the system. In the questionnaire, most comments noted that 'the system was fun because various stories could be created'. Therefore, we can conclude that it is interesting to generate various stories by using the 'What-If' function.

References

1. Jippensha, I.: Shanks Mare: Japan's Great Comic Novel of Travel & Ribaldry. Tuttle Publishing (2001)
2. Miller, C.H.: Digital Storytelling, Second Edition: A Creator's Guide to Interactive Entertainment. Focal Press, Oxford (2008)
3. Li, B., Lee-Urban, S., Johnston, G., Riedl, M.O.: Story generation with crowd-sourced plot graphs. In: Proceedings of the 27th AAAI Conference on Artificial Intelligence, Bellevue, Washington, July 2013
4. Li, B., Riedl, M.O.: Scheherazade: crowd-powered interactive narrative generation. In: The 29th AAAI Conference on Artificial Intelligence, Austin, Texas (2015)
5. Mayer, R.E.: Multimedia learning: Are we asking the right questions? Educ. Psychol. **32**, 1–19 (1997)
6. Sumi, K., Tanaka, K.: Automatic conversion from e-content into virtual storytelling. In: Subsol, G. (ed.) ICVS 2005. LNCS, vol. 3805, pp. 260–269. Springer, Heidelberg (2005). https://doi.org/10.1007/11590361_30
7. Sumi, K.: Interactive storytelling system using recycle-based story knowledge. In: Iurgel, I.A., Zagalo, N., Petta, P. (eds.) ICIDS 2009. LNCS, vol. 5915, pp. 74–85. Springer, Heidelberg (2009). https://doi.org/10.1007/978-3-642-10643-9_11

8. Sumi, K., Tanaka, K.: Facilitating understanding for children by translating web contents into a storybook. In: Bolc, L., Michalewicz, Z., Nishida, T. (eds.) IMTCI 2004. LNCS, vol. 3490, pp. 175–184. Springer, Heidelberg (2005). https://doi.org/10.1007/11558637_18

9. Yumino, K.: Sougoutekigakushu no gakuryoku sokutei to hyoukagihou nokaihatsu (Chap. 1), meijitosho (2001). http://www.dyumiken.com/LEFT/QandA/2-2.pdf. Last accessed 2 April 2017. (in Japanese)

Open World Story Generation for Increased Expressive Range

David Thue[✉], Stephan Schiffel, Tryggvi Þór Guðmundsson,
Guðni Fannar Kristjánsson, Kári Eiríksson, and Magnús Vilhelm Björnsson

School of Computer Science, Reykjavik University,
Menntavegur 1, Reykjavik 101, Iceland
{davidthue,stephans,tryggvi15,gudni14,kari14,magnusvb14}@ru.is

Abstract. To let authors shape the set of experiences that can occur when a generative Interactive Storytelling (IS) system is used, the process of authoring for the system must support specifying constraints over how different stories can progress. We present an extension to an existing IS system that both allows authors more flexibility in specifying the constraints and gives the generator more freedom in filling in the parts of the story that the authors leave unconstrained. Our approach is based on open-world planning using the IndiGolog action programming language and heuristic search for plan generation.

Keywords: Story generation · Open world planning · Heuristic search

1 Introduction

One of the primary goals of Interactive Storytelling (IS) is to create playable experiences that are both narratively rich and richly interactive. Given this ambition, it is essential to support a wide range of expression for the designers and authors of such experiences, since the systems and content they create will ultimately define the set of experiences that can occur [1]. To let authors shape the set of experiences that can occur when a generative IS system is used, the process of authoring for the system must support specifying constraints over how different stories can progress [1–4]. The way in which a generative IS system represents its constraints can create conflicts between expression and implementation. For example, while authors often give expressive freedom to the generator by *omission* (i.e., letting it determine any unconstrained aspects of the story's state), leaving the story's state unconstrained is at odds with a common assumption of AI Planning (that all unstated facts are necessarily false). Supporting this expressive freedom thus limits the kinds of planners that can be used. Prior work on "open world" story generation allowed authors to leave some story world facts undetermined [5], but true and false facts could only be asserted about the initial state of the story world. In a story world driven by a simulation, the initial state might represent only a small fraction of the circumstances under which an author might want one of their stories to start.

© Springer International Publishing AG 2017
N. Nunes et al. (Eds.): ICIDS 2017, LNCS 10690, pp. 313–316, 2017.
https://doi.org/10.1007/978-3-319-71027-3_33

In this paper, we describe new improvements to our previous work on this topic [6], in which authored constraints could be applied at any time in the story world (unlike [5]), but were limited to expressing only true or undetermined values. To address this limitation, we changed the planner in our existing system to support "open" worlds and improved its performance using a heuristic.

Illustrative Example. To illustrate the problem, we present a small example that uses terminology from our prior work [6]. An *outline* is a set of constraints that restrict both how and when a story should start (*initial conditions*) as well as how it should ultimately end (*final goals*). Authors create outlines in terms of *abstract entities*. Our generative IS system determines a story's *concrete entities* (which exist in the simulated world) at runtime; each abstract entity is automatically *mapped* to a concrete entity that satisfies the former's constraints. We add the notion of *intermediate goals*, which are similar to *landmarks* [2].

Given this terminology, consider a world with 3 concrete characters (*Sarah, John, Sam*), one article (*Necklace*), and 2 relations between them: *Has(Sarah, Necklace), ParentOf(Sarah, John)*. We can define an outline in which a villain somehow obtains an heirloom from the mother of the hero, but eventually the mother gets the heirloom back. It has 3 abstract characters (*Villain, Hero, Mother*), one abstract article (*Heirloom*), initial constraints (*Has(Mother, Heirloom), ParentOf(Mother, Hero)*, and ¬*Has(Villain, Heirloom)*), an intermediate goal (*Has(Villain, Heirloom)*), and a final goal (*Has(Mother, Heirloom)*).

The stories that can be generated from this outline and world state depend on the actions and entities that are defined in the world. One example could be: *map(Hero, John), map(Mother, Sarah), map(Heirloom, Necklace), map(Villain, Sam), steal(Villain, Mother, Heirloom), steal (Hero, Villain, Heirloom), give(Hero, Mother, Heirloom)*. The *map* actions in this example associate abstract entities from the story outline with concrete entities in the world.

We can use this example world to demonstrate how the closed world assumption in our previous planner [6] fails to support negative conditions in story outlines. With the closed world assumption, anything not mentioned in the initial state of the planner is considered false. Therefore, the initial state of the planner in our example would be represented simply as *Has(Sarah, Necklace)*. However, this initial state is the same as if we did not have the initial condition ¬*Has(Villain, Heirloom)* at all. That is, it does not distinguish between the two story outlines where (i) the villain must not have the heirloom at the beginning and (ii) the author does not care. Depending on the concrete implementation of the planner, there are two possible failure cases:

1. If the planner simply ignored negative preconditions, it could return mappings that violate these preconditions, e.g., *Villain* ↦ *Sarah, Heirloom* ↦ *Necklace*, because the condition ¬*Has(Villain, Heirloom)* is never checked.
2. If the planner treated all absent conditions as negative, it would fail to return valid mappings. For example, it would never return *Hero* ↦ *Sarah, Heirloom* ↦ *Necklace*, because the *Has(Hero, Heirloom)* is not an initial condition and thus must be false.

Since both cases are undesirable, we base our approach on IndiGolog [7], a planner that allows us to represent facts whose value is unknown.

2 Proposed Approach

Using IndiGolog, the initial state of our planning problem consists of all facts in the world as well as the initial conditions in the story outline, where each fact's value is explicitly represented. Thus, the initial conditions of our example in Sect. 1 become: *init(has(sam, necklace), true)*, *init(has(john, necklace), false)*, and *init(has(villain, heirloom), false)*. Our action definitions in IndiGolog are essentially unchanged from [6]; aside from the syntactic differences between IndiGolog and PDDL. The only addition is that negative preconditions are checked in the map actions. With these changes, our system achieves plan soundness and assignment soundness as defined in [6], while supporting more expressive story outlines by allowing negative initial conditions.

2.1 Planner Improvements and Heuristics

Our planner uses informed search with a heuristic function to estimate the cost of a plan. Common heuristics used in automated planning, such as delete relaxation heuristics [8], require perfect information and an explicit representation of the state (e.g., as a set of facts). However, due to the open-world assumption and the use of IndiGolog, we have neither. We implemented a number of simple heuristic features to improve the performance of the search by using two techniques for state space reduction, as we describe below.

State Space Reduction. The definition of our planning problem allows for plans that are equivalent in several ways. First, observe that once an abstract entity is mapped to a concrete one, actions that use the abstract or the concrete entity have the same effects due to the effect synchronizers defined in [6]. Second, actions involving different entities are independent of each other and can be reordered without changing the resulting state. For example, [*find(John, Necklace), find(Sarah, Ring)*] and [*find(Sarah, Ring), find(John, Necklace)*] result in the same state. To reduce the state space, we only consider actions with concrete entities and discard visited states whose partial plan only differs in terms of the order of mutually-independent actions.

Heuristic. Our heuristic estimates the cost of a plan as a linear combination of four features: the number of actions in the plan (L); the number of unfulfilled final goal conditions (F); the number of unfulfilled intermediate goal conditions (I); and the number of initial conditions that cannot be fulfilled with the mappings that are already in the plan (C).

We tested our heuristic features using six test worlds that we varied in terms of their numbers of concrete entities, abstract entities, initial conditions, intermediate goals, final goals, and steps for the shortest solution plan. All the features in the heuristic turned out to be necessary for finding plans for all six worlds in a reasonable amount of time (10 s). With the best weights that we found for the four features ($L = 1$, $F = 2$, $I = 3$, $C = 1$), the solution times for all six worlds ranged from 5 ms to 123 ms – nearly two orders of magnitude faster than when the features were ignored. More detailed data from our experiments has been reserved for the poster that will accompany this paper.

3   Discussion and Future Work

Our solution extends prior work to allow positive, negative, and undetermined conditions to be authored inside flexible story outlines, supporting the open world planning of interactive stories. We also introduced extensible heuristics for our new story planner, which achieve good performance for story generation tasks. Although the resulting computing times seem reasonable, there are edge cases of story outlines which cannot be completed in a reasonable amount of time. Specifically, the intermediate goal heuristic (I) can cause the planner to prefer mapping multiple abstract entities to the same concrete entity (when it simplifies meeting certain intermediate goals), but the resulting search path may never lead to a desired goal state in which those abstract entities satisfy mutually exclusive roles. In the future, these heuristics can potentially be modified to steer story generation towards stories of higher quality, such as those that are more interesting to each individual player.

References

1. Riedl, M.O., Young, R.M.: From linear story generation to branching story graphs. IEEE Comput. Graph. Appl. **26**(3), 23–31 (2006)
2. Porteous, J., Cavazza, M.: Controlling narrative generation with planning trajectories: the role of constraints. In: Iurgel, I.A., Zagalo, N., Petta, P. (eds.) ICIDS 2009. LNCS, vol. 5915, pp. 234–245. Springer, Heidelberg (2009). https://doi.org/10.1007/978-3-642-10643-9_28
3. Thue, D.: Generalized Experience Management. Ph.D. thesis, Department of Computing Science, University of Alberta, Canada (2015)
4. Weyhrauch, P.: Guiding Interactive Drama. Ph.D. thesis, School of Computer Science, Carnegie Mellon University, Pittsburgh, PA, USA (1997)
5. Riedl, M.O., Young, R.M.: Open-world planning for story generation. In: Proceedings of the 19th International Joint Conference on Artificial Intelligence, IJCAI 2005, pp. 1719–1720. Morgan Kaufmann Publishers Inc. (2005)
6. Thue, D., Schiffel, S., Árnason, R.A., Stefnisson, I.S., Steinarsson, B.: Delayed roles with authorable continuity in plan-based interactive storytelling. In: Nack, F., Gordon, A.S. (eds.) ICIDS 2016. LNCS, vol. 10045, pp. 258–269. Springer, Cham (2016). https://doi.org/10.1007/978-3-319-48279-8_23
7. De Giacomo, G., Lespérance, Y., Levesque, H.J., Sardina, S.: IndiGolog: a high-level programming language for embedded reasoning agents. In: El Fallah Seghrouchni, A., Dix, J., Dastani, M., Bordini, R.H. (eds.) Multi-Agent Programming: Languages, Tools and Applications, pp. 31–72. Springer, USA (2009)
8. Hoffmann, J., Nebel, B.: The FF planning system: fast plan generation through heuristic search. J. Artif. Intell. Res. **14**, 253–302 (2001)

Demos

Collisions and Constellations: On the Possible Intersection of Psychoethnography and Digital Storytelling

Justin Armstrong(✉) (iD)

Wellesley College, Wellesley, MA 02481, USA
jarmstro@wellesley.edu

Abstract. This proposal outlines the development of a collaborative model of ethnographic storytelling that utilizes readily available digital technology and ethnographic methodology to facilitate generative interactions toward the production of complex and evolving digital stories. Building on a methodology that I call *psychoethnography*, this project aims to create a fluid form of interactive digital storytelling that can be used in both academic and non-academic settings as a research and pedagogical tool.

Keywords: Ethnography · Digital storytelling · Visual anthropology · Situationism

1 Introduction

The stories of culture are not static, and therefore it seems only logical that the way we, as anthropologists and anthropologically-minded storytellers, convey them should be equally dynamic and fluid. The ways that we practice and teach anthropology and storytelling are primed for a new approach, one that foregrounds and embraces polyvocal, interactive, collaborative and unpredictable elements. In what follows, I outline the beginnings of a project that offers numerous possibilities for both research and pedagogy at the intersection of cultural anthropology, community development and digital storytelling. It is my hope that this project will offer an additional departure point for considering how, when, where and why we collect, translate and disseminate the stories of culture.

In the experimental theory and practice I have called psychoethnography, encounters with informants and fieldsites emerge from open-ended movements through place and the accompanying instances of participant-observation. For example, a would-be psychoethnographer might begin their 'drift' by simply taking an unknown bus or subway route and disembarking at either a randomly chosen stop or some predefined marker (the first stop containing the letter P, the 4th stop, wherever the man in the blue jacket gets off, etc.). This practice mirrors the Situationists' Psychogeographic Game of the Week, published in their journal, Potlatch throughout the mid-1950s. Here, I imagine extending this model to develop a series of Psychoethnographic Games of the Week, a series of prompts to encourage and guide psychoethnographers in their encounters with (and documentation of) the stories of everyday life. These prompts might be as simple

© Springer International Publishing AG 2017
N. Nunes et al. (Eds.): ICIDS 2017, LNCS 10690, pp. 319–322, 2017.
https://doi.org/10.1007/978-3-319-71027-3_34

as "visit the nearest/most distant ethnic restaurant/grocery in your city/town and ask customers and/or employees to tell you a brief story about their happiest memory", or as in-depth as "take the subway to every stop and ask for a story about riding the subway from one person at each station". These prompts could be delivered on a regular basis via email, text, or a more complex mobile application that allows participants to upload their 'responses' to the prompt using whatever media they choose. Here, the goal is to transpose what was first imagined by the Situationists of mid-century Paris as an anti-capitalist artistic practice into something to be undertaken as a form of collecting ethnographic and narrative 'data' in the field. This project aims to expand the original scope of what the Situationists called psychogeography (a sort of psycho-emotional response to random encounters as a result of 'drifting' through city streets) to include narrative and ethnographic practices that it was never intended to encompass.

While the Situationists initially imagined their project as a sort of artistic and political critique of capitalism [1], my transposition of these theories centers on an ethnographic foregrounding of chance occurrences, a re-imagining (and re-mapping) of the location of cultural anthropology, and on the process of storytelling-storyasking as a viable form of data collection. And while I understand that these practices are certainly not new to ethnography or storytelling, this project makes these elements of anthropological inquiry more explicit by essentially unplanning and reimagining many of the existing methodologies in contemporary anthropological fieldwork. More traditional modes of ethnographic fieldwork place significant methodological weight on developing relationships with key informants (often called 'gatekeepers'), language acquisition and extensive archival research ahead of any entry into the field. Psychoethnography, as I have envisioned it, does not seek to discredit current practices or refute their utility, it simply offers an additional (often parallel) avenue of cultural analysis that acts more like an overlay, or experimental tool. From my perspective, the more tools an anthropologist has in their tool-kit, the more well-rounded and dynamic their work will become. My intent is not to react against any prevailing issues in anthropology, rather it is to build on and add to existing modes of inquiry (for more insight into the process of researching and writing ethnography, see James Clifford and George Marcus' Writing Culture [1986] [2]). To better understand this proposed hybrid of psychogeography, narrative and ethnography, it is important to examine more carefully the Situationist concepts of psychogeography and dérive.

The beginnings of what would come to be known as psychogeography emerged in the mid-1950s with a small group of artists calling themselves the Letterist International, a collective of cultural producers and theorists whose goal was to enact a radical criticism of urban and capitalist power structures through artistic interventions. One of the first uses of the term psychogeography can be found in Guy Debord's 1955 essay "Introduction to a Critique of Urban Geography" in which he defines psychogeography as "the study of the precise laws and specific effects of the geographical environment, consciously organized or not, on the emotions and behavior of individuals" [1].

One of Debord's central tenets of psychogeography is the practice of dérive. This exercise explores the possibility of "rapid passage through varied ambiances" based on "playful-constructive behavior and awareness of psychological effects" that are "quite different from the classic notions of a journey or stroll" [1]. This reimagination of urban space questions the prevailing patterns of movement and civil engagement that dominate the post-industrial capitalist city. Here, the psychogeographer becomes something of a conduit through which the "varied ambiances" of the city are read and translated into a critique of the urban environment and its various forms of psychosocial affect and narrative. It is the reading and translation of the affect of marginal and secondary space that opens up the possibility for an engagement with alternative, coexistent views of the city. Moving this framework into the realms of cultural anthropology, the narratives that form the core of any ethnographic encounter emerge in a more generative and unpredictable manner. The story begins always-already unwritten with the anthropologist functioning more as a director than an author.

Using this psychoethnographic model for digital storytelling, one or more ethnographically motivated participant-observers head out into a given fieldsite to collect and collaborate with the people, places and things of a particular research setting. This setting might be a neighborhood, a small village, an institution, or some other sort of -scape [3] where the researcher-storytellers might encounter their subjects and their associated narratives. This data collection may take place over the course of an afternoon, a week, or even a year, offering either a snapshot of the narrative landscape of a given location or a multi-layered, in-depth ethnographic study. These forays might be themed (stories of first love), or completely open ("tell me a story"), allowing the people, places and things of a given site to dictate the form of its narrative. In this way, this project aims to maintain a rhizomatic [4] ethos, creating a work at is constantly in flux and open to revision. Non-hierarchy is key to the success of a project such as this in that it is important to avoid assigning a value to stories. All stories are equal and all data is valuable in building this 'storyscape'.

It is important to note that potential psychoethnographers should be keenly aware of the ethical concerns that may arise in the field (just as they would in any other ethnographic encounter). Among these must be the willingness to accept a refusal to share a story, the avoidance of mental, physical or emotional harm to your subjects, and the legal impact of collecting stories on sensitive topics. It is also important to explain to any participants what you will be doing with the data and how it will be distributed/ archived. And of course, permission to record/document the storyteller is always necessary. In general, common sense should prevail, but ethical considerations should always be at the forefront of an ethnographer's interactions in the field.

An example of a psychoethnographic endeavor might involve a group of psychoethnographers beginning a drift in a small rural village with the simple goal of collecting stories as told by locals, visitors and even other members of the group. With smartphones in hand, they might simply move through the location, accumulating impressions and encounters as still images, videos and/or audio recordings. This 'raw material' could then be archived on the Web in a way that allows both ethnographers and their subjects to assemble and reassemble their own narratives of the village and its environs, thereby creating a fluid, rhizomatic 'living' ethnography from a variety of perspectives. This type of approach to digital storytelling draws heavily on the work of visual anthropologists and filmakers. Films including Jean Rouch's 1967 Jaguar, Trịnh Thị Minh Hà's 1982 Reassemblage and Apichatpong Weerasethakul's 2000 Mysterious Object at Noon offer important touchstones for what collaborative visual ethnographic storytelling might look like. These films all present the subjects as collaborators where the filmmaker draws back as much as possible and allows the narrative to be guided by the people, places and things on the other side of the camera. Here, the ethnography becomes a collaborative, constantly evolving document of culture, a project that begins to blur the lines between author and audience.

This project is still in the development phase, but I believe that it offers a valuable jumping-off point for considering the rapidly evolving relationship between technology (using collaborative Web-based platforms, mobile devices, and digital image capture), anthropology and narrativity. Here, there are certainly a multiplicity of applications in both academic and non-academic settings, including community outreach, activism, education and policy making. Ideally, these psychoethnographies would be archived on the Web as open-access multimedia documents (photos, video, audio, interactive web design) wherein the collaborators would have editorial access over the content. Participants could receive an invitation and login to work as editor-collaborators on their particular storyscape. One example of a possible application of this form could involve the development of a psychoethnographic account of indigenous communities in northern Canada where the community members act as both contributors and collaborators in developing a storyscape of life in Canada's remote First Nations communities. A project such as this would hopefully help to foster a greater sense of community through shared experience across a vast geographic area. An approach such as this presents a democratic endeavor that sees storytelling and anthropological research as a collaborative, decentered pursuit. It is time to let the stories of everyday lives become moments of true critical insight.

References

1. Debord, G.: Introduction to a Critique of Urban Geography. Les Lèvres Nues #6, Paris (1955)
2. Clifford, J., Marcus, G. (eds.): Writing Culture: The Poetics and Politics of Ethnography. University of California Press, Oakland (1986)
3. Appadurai, A.: Disjuncture and difference in the global cultural economy. Theor. Cult. Soc. 7(2–3), 295–310 (1990). (Short Version)
4. Deleuze, G., Guattari, F.: A Thousand Plateaus: Capitalism and Schizophrenia. University of Minnesota Press, Minneapolis (1987)

Evaluating Visual Perceptive Media

Anna Frew[1] and Ian Forrester[2(✉)]

[1] Manchester Metropolitan University, Manchester M15 6BX, UK
[2] BBC R&D, Dockhouse, MediaCityUK, Salford Quays, Manchester M50 2LH, UK
ian.forrester@bbc.co.uk

Abstract. A contribution to Interactive Digital Storytelling is made through prototype *The Break Up* a film short for online TV and video using Object-Based Broadcasting. The prototype can change its music, video and color grade when informed by implicit interaction. This paper evaluates whether a music genre expected to suit the participant enhanced their experience. Half the participants saw *The Break Up* with music expected to suit them, half not, color grade and video were constant. They completed a form about their experience. Participants expected to not 'enjoy' the music scored their engagement somewhat higher (67/100) than those expected to like it (58/100). The prototype tested showed it was capable of automatically compositing media objects in response user context, combined with a positive reception to implicit personalization this indicates potential for further work.

Keywords: Perceptive media · Implicit interaction · Object-Based broadcasting

1 Introduction

Audiences feel empathy for characters when engaging with media [1] and are more likely to feel empathy for something familiar [2]. Therefore, we aim to create familiarity and in turn engagement via Perceptive Media. As described by Adrian Gradinar [3] Perceptive Media is broadcast content that has been informed by implicit interaction, in real-time using data from single or multiple sources, such as user profile or their context. There is a range of research that uses a similar concept to Object-Based Broadcasting in interactive digital narrative. Mei Si in 2015 [4] used structured information to personalize narrative. This differs from this prototype as it creates stories from information using explicit interaction. Jordan Rickman and Joshua Tanenbaum's [5] electronic literature is similar as it uses implicit interaction and real time delivery, based on location data, to generate dynamic soundtracks for road trips. This prototype differs in that it is both video and audio and is designed for online video rather than being geo-located. Marian Ursu [6] has conducted studies on how to deliver implicitly interactive personalized content for television. The prototype is dissimilar to this, as the technology powering it is not hand authored.

This paper describes the development of a Perceptive Media prototype that uses technology to deliver both visuals and audio. It considers whether the enjoyment of the film can be inferred from a viewer's music collection?

© Springer International Publishing AG 2017
N. Nunes et al. (Eds.): ICIDS 2017, LNCS 10690, pp. 323–326, 2017.
https://doi.org/10.1007/978-3-319-71027-3_35

2   Prototype Implicitly Personalized Short

The Break Up prototype is a romantic drama short that adapts according to data about the viewer. It uses Object-Based Broadcasting [7] where media objects (media and metadata) are assembled on the client-side using JavaScript in the user's browser, rather than being received as a complete file. The Break Up has 3 possible sets of 'media objects' set 1 the genre of the music, set 2 the color grading and set 3 the narrative content (through shot selection and length). When the user enters their email, data from their cloud profile is used to apply a color grade and select which music and videos to compile in real-time. The user views a reasoned combination of these selections. There are over 448 possible variations, therefore run time is between 4 min 15 secs and 5 min 20 secs.

Set 1 includes 14 genres of music that can be layered at the start and end. There is music to match the positive and negative endings available (28 tracks chosen by the director). The shot lengths define when the music begins and for how long. CSVs containing data on the key parts of the music and audio were converted into JSON format. The HTML5 compositor in the user's browser then uses the JSON values to drive the sequence. JSON describes the sequence to avoid layering music over dialogue. If a conflict is detected an appropriate real-time fade is applied using the AudioWebAPI.

Set 2, is 4 different color grades. All footage was initially color corrected. Further color grades are added in real-time through the browser's WebGL engine using lookup tables (LUT). The same video files are used in all sequences as the LUT is applied client side.

Set 3, the narrative content, is altered through the shots shown. There are two possible sets of starts, beginning with each character, and two sets of positive or negative endings. There are further small changes to the shot lengths to be consistent with the starts and endings. All the timelines created were converted from a Final Cut XML format to JSON files. The JSON includes which parts of the video need to be played at which time and time markers for the music. A full technical breakdown of the prototype is available at [8].

3   Methods

21 participants were included in this study. This was judged sufficient to answer the research question and determine areas for further exploration. 19 were recruited through a market research field agency and given an incentive, 2 were from within the BBC. There were 11 female and 10 male participants, aged 18 to 50 (a mean of 34). All participants had seen an online drama or visited the cinema in the past 6 months.

Participants installed and used mobile app Music + Personality [9] before visiting the BBC user testing lab. This app was selected as it indicates the genres of music on a user's mobile. On arrival, participants were given a consent form stating they would watch a short, followed by written and oral audio-recorded questions. All participants saw the same narrative and color grade, only the music genre was changed. Half the participants watched with a music genre expected to suit them and half did not. A participant was expected to like a genre of music if it was on their mobile. The narrative content was a woman arriving at a café, a conversation with her male abusive partner where their relationship ends, and her leaving him (the positive ending; in the negative ending she stays). A bronze color grade was selected, as is typical for romance. Variation in the music made the total run time between 5 min and 10–25 secs.

After watching, participants were asked "How much does the music fit the drama?" and "How engaging was the drama?" on a line based Likert scale. One end was 0, "not very much," the other 100, "very much." The scale the participants completed had no numerical value, the numbers were imposed in the analysis. After answering, participants were told the music they heard was personalized using data from the app. They were shown The Break Up with different music and the potential to change the narrative and color grading to demonstrate this. Participants completed the scale-based form again and were asked to orally elaborate on their answers. This aimed to capture any shift in opinion once they knew it was personalized. The recordings were transcribed and analyzed using grounded theory and thematic analysis.

4 Findings and Discussion

From "How much does the music fit the drama?" we expected similar ratings as all music was selected to match. As predicted, there was a small difference in medians: Liked: 51, Disliked: 56. 1 participant from the 'dislike' music group moved their score from 83 to 43 after knowing it was personalized stating, "given how much information about me you had, it should have been better." This highlights the danger of disappointment in implicit interaction, but in this case, supports the study's assumptions, as the participant was not expected to like the music.

From "How engaging was the drama?" we expected higher ratings from those who heard their preferred music genre. The half of the participants expected to like the music found their engagement with the drama to be somewhat above neutral with a median score of 58 before knowing it was personalized (64 afterwards). Those expected to dislike the music had a higher median of 67 before and 71 after knowing it was personalized. As the participants expected to dislike the music had a higher score, this indicates that there may not be a link between owning a genre of music and engagement in a personalized broadcast. This could be due to track choices, and the use of music score rather than songs. A comparison between songs and score in future work could answer this. After knowing it was personalized a third of the participants changed their score, all were improvements (+4 to +28 range). As all changes after knowing it was personalized were improvements, this may be the Forer effect [10], where participants feel vague personality descriptions that could be applicable to anyone are only for him or her. A prestige-laden setting such as our user-testing lab could increase the likelihood of this. For recognized broadcasters, this is potentially ethically problematic, as they could accidentally create a feeling of personalization beyond the reality.

5 Conclusion and Areas for Future Study

The prototype film short The Break Up uses Object Based Broadcasting informed by implicit interaction and can change its music, video and color grade. This paper evaluates whether a music genre expected to suit the participant enhanced their experience. The prototype tested showed it was capable of automatically compositing media objects in response user context. The findings show there was no strong indication that enjoyment of The Break Up can be inferred from a user's music collection. Participants expected to not enjoy the music scored their engagement higher (67 of 100) than those expected to like it (58 of 100). A successful prototype of implicit interactivity indicates this is an area for further research. As 21 participants are insufficient to test the variations beyond music and are not representative of the UK population as a whole a larger sample size would benefit further work. This could allow examination of color grade, narrative, and how participants talk about their experience of perceptive media with others. Additionally, a comparison of audience experience of a directed and an algorithmically generated short could be explored.

References

1. Freedberg, D., Gallese, V.: Motion, emotion and empathy in esthetic experience. Trends Cogn. Sci. **11**(5), 197–203 (2007)
2. Bernhardt, B.C., Singer, T.: The Neural Basis of Empathy. Annu. Rev. Neurosci. **35**(1), 1–23 (2012)
3. Gradinar, A., Burnett, D., Coulton, P.: Perceptive Media: adaptive storytelling for digital broadcast. In: 15th IFIP TC 13 International Conference on Human-Computer Interaction – INTERACT 2015 (2015)
4. Si, M.: Tell a Story About Anything. In: Schoenau-Fog, H., Bruni, L.E., Louchart, S., Baceviciute, S. (eds.) ICIDS 2015. LNCS, vol. 9445, pp. 361–365. Springer, Cham (2015). https://doi.org/10.1007/978-3-319-27036-4_37
5. Rickman, J., Tanenbaum, J.: GeoPoetry: designing location-based combinatorial electronic literature soundtracks for roadtrips. In: Nack, F., Gordon, A. (eds.) ICIDS 2016. LNCS, vol. 10045, pp. 85–96. Springer, Cham (2016). https://doi.org/10.1007/978-3-319-48279-8_8
6. Ursu, M.F., Kegel, I.C., Williams, D., Thomas, M., Mayer, H., Zsombori, V., Tuomola, M.L., Larsson, H., Wyver, J.: ShapeShifting TV: interactive screen media narratives. Multimed. Syst. **14**(2), 115–132 (2008)
7. Churnside, A., Melchior, M.E.F., Armstrong, M., Shotton, M., Brooks, M., Evans, M., Melchior, F.: Object-based broadcasting - curation, responsiveness and user experience. In: 2014 Conference on International Broadcasting Convention (IBC), p. 12.2 (2014)
8. Shorton, M.: BBC html5 Video Compositor, Github (2016). https://github.com/bbc/html5-video-compositor. Accessed 17 June 2017
9. Perceptiv, "Music + Personality." Preceptiv (2015)
10. Forer, B.: The fallacy of personal validation: a classroom demonstration of gullibility. J. Abnorm. Psychol. **44**, 118–121 (1949)

Biennale 4D – Exploring the Archives of the Swiss Pavilion at the «Biennale di Venezia» Art Exhibition

Kathrin Koebel[1]([✉]) [iD], Doris Agotai[1], Stefan Arisona[1] [iD], and Matthias Oberli[2] [iD]

[1] University of Applied Sciences and Arts Northwestern Switzerland FHNW, Bahnhofstrasse 6, 5210 Windisch, Switzerland
kathrin.koebel@students.fhnw.ch
[2] Swiss Institute for Art Research (SIK-ISEA), Zurich, Switzerland

Abstract. The Swiss pavilion at «Biennale di Venezia» offers a platform for national artists to expose their work. This well documented white cube displays the change of contemporary Swiss art from the early 50 s up to today. The project «Biennale 4D» pursues the goal to make the archives of these past art exhibitions more comprehensible by creating an interactive explorative environment through the use of innovative Virtual Reality technology. The project poses multiple challenges like visualization of historic content and its documentation, dealing with the heterogeneity and incompleteness of archives, interaction design and interaction mapping in VR space, integration of meta data as well as realizing a Virtual Reality experience for the public space with current VR technology.

Keywords: Virtual Reality · Interaction design · Interaction mapping · User experience · Cultural heritage · Virtual art exhibition · Interactive archive

1 Introduction

Since 1952, Switzerland is represented at the «Biennale di Venezia» with its own pavilion, designed by the Swiss architect Bruno Giacometti. At this bi-annual event the works of featured contemporary Swiss artists are displayed in this space. The exhibitions contain heterogeneous material of various disciplines of artistic work. They are well documented by the Swiss Institute for Art Research (SIK-ISEA) which has published two volumes titled «Biennale Venedig. Die Beteiligung der Schweiz 1920–2013» [1] containing detailed lists of the exposed works, photographs and articles. In addition, the material is published on a dedicated web archive at www.biennale-venezia.ch.

In order to make these archives more comprehensible, Biennale 4D pursues the goal of creating an explorative environment through the use of Virtual Reality technology. A pilot application was created by the Institute of 4D Technologies of FHNW and SIK-ISEA [2] to test the experience. The application allows users to explore the pavilion and displayed art works of different epochs with a VR headset. In this paper we highlight possible approaches using Virtual Reality in terms of user experience, interaction design and visualization, and the actual implementation of the Biennale 4D pilot application.

© Springer International Publishing AG 2017
N. Nunes et al. (Eds.): ICIDS 2017, LNCS 10690, pp. 327–331, 2017.
https://doi.org/10.1007/978-3-319-71027-3_36

2   Materials and Methods

We choose to use current Virtual Reality technology with a Head-Mounted Display (HMD) as hardware to create an interactive exploratory environment with the objective to make the content of the archives appealing to new audiences. Extensive research was conducted regarding the state of the art of technology in the given application domain. Although there are a number of web-based archives of art institutions [3, 4] available as well as some virtual museums [5, 6], Biennale 4D poses a unique challenge as it combines a virtual art exhibition experience enhanced with archive functionalities.

The research included visualization of exhibition reconstruction where learnings from the field of archaeology were taken into account. Various approaches regarding the degree of abstraction in the virtual representation of buildings and handling of incomplete data were considered. Research was conducted regarding standards for interaction patterns [7], navigation and user guidance in space as well as time dimension in VR applications. Particular focus was given to interaction design and interaction mapping, the degree of freedom in user movements and haptic feedback [8]. Technical possibilities as well as limits of VR technology were explored as well as methods of user experience (UX) testing in VR. Following the Lean UX method for agile development with its iterative «think», «make» and «check» phases, a strong emphasis was placed on rapid prototyping approach with ongoing user testing in the implementation of the prototype.

3   Results

The result of this research is a functional prototype of the Biennale 4D Virtual Reality application, which is implemented with Unity using the VRTK framework and optimized for the HTC Vive headset and hand controllers. It contains a 3D model of the pavilion's original design and a concept for visualization of the exhibition content of the selected years 1952, 1984, 2007 and 2013. Exhibition samples of various types of documentation levels are included, such as thoroughly documented, fragmentary documented, as well as experimental art works, e.g. video installations. The development of a consistent visual language for the heterogeneous work posed a challenge. Numerous

Fig. 1. Screenshots of the Biennale 4D prototype, displaying the chosen aesthetics for the visualization of the historical content. The original design of the pavilion was reduced and blur has been added to the wall textures in order to intuitively guide the user's focus to the documented art works. The time machine object (right) allows the user to interact with the time dimension.

experiments were made to discover a suitable visualization style (Fig. 1, left) that guides the user's focus away from the building to the artworks and their documentation.

The prototype allows the user to travel intuitively through time by means of inter-action with the time machine object (Fig. 1, right). This three-dimensional item offers affordances to the user about the exhibition content of the years he's passing by on his time journey navigating to the scene of the desired year. For spatial movement the application contains a navigation concept that allows the user to move within the virtual room either by position tracking of the user's movement in the physical space or via teleportation. It provides basic haptic feedback in case of collisions. Other forms of spatial navigation were considered (e.g. guided tour), however testing revealed a corre-lation between the user's degree of freedom regarding movement and the perceived user experience.

In addition, an information guide in the form of a virtual booklet offers meta data corresponding to the objects on display. This supplementary information can be accessed by pointing with a laser ray towards the desired item. And interactive hotspots have been added to the application to show additional material like archive photos.

Moreover, the prototype has been extensively tested in terms of user experience and usability. Through qualitative survey conducted using Hassenzahl's AttrakDiff method [9], the prototype received excellent results. Out of 28 dimensions only two were rated negative, both relating to the social aspect. While the app allows users to interact with art works, the current pilot doesn't support any form of interaction with other visitors.

4 Discussion

Virtual Reality technology allows new approaches of exhibition reconstruction. However, suitable processes for editing of exhibition content in this new medium need to be developed for a conclusive incorporation of historical material in this experimental virtual space. The nature of this application field requires thoughtful examination of aspects like substantiality, aesthetics as well as presence of time.

One of the major challenges is posed by the work with diverse materials. The appli-cation consists of three material layers (see Fig. 2): first the historical content (original artwork), second the dimension of its documentation (archive photos and other artefacts) and last the medium of the virtual room (mapping space). The handling of the second layer in particular leaves much room for interpretation and exploration.

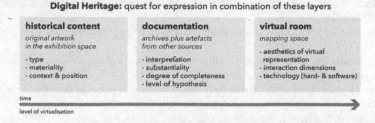

Fig. 2. Material layers of the Biennale 4D application.

Another challenge lies in the interaction mapping of three dimensions of interaction (time dimension, navigation with virtual space and interaction with meta data) which had to be reduced onto the two hand controllers of the user. In the initial prototype one hand was assigned with time travel whereas the other hand was designated for spatial movement and interaction with the objects (see Fig. 3). As the application is targeting an audience with little technical experience simplicity and intuitiveness are key.

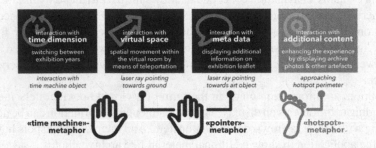

Fig. 3. Interaction dimensions with their corresponding actions, triggers and metaphors.

5   Conclusion

The initial research has provided a favorable proof of concept and is affirmed through user tests. The vision for the ongoing work consists in offering access to the full content of the Biennale archives in an even more interactive and immersive way and let a wider audience experience this valuable portion of Swiss art and cultural history. The work will be opening up new vistas for the exploration of image archives and exposition reconstruction and showing new prospects for the use of Virtual Reality in the realm of digital humanities.

Criterions for the success of the ongoing project include seamless embedding of this VR experience into the context of a larger exhibition, intuitiveness and simplicity of the application design, feasibility for usage in public space and lastly, attractiveness through keeping the right balance between knowledge transfer and entertainment.

References

1. Krähenbühl, R., Wyss, B.: Biennale Venedig. Die Beteiligung der Schweiz. Scheidegger & Spiess, Zürich (2013)
2. Biennale 4D. http://web.fhnw.ch/technik/projekte/i/bachelor16/kaufmann-koebel. Accessed 11 July 2017
3. William Kentridge: Five Themes. https://www.moma.org/interactives/exhibitions/2010/williamkentridge/flashCheck.html. Accessed 19 Apr 2016
4. Deutsche Digitale Bibliothek visualisiert. http://infovis.fh-potsdam.de/ddb. Accessed 19 Apr 2016
5. The Museum of Stolen Art. http://mosa.ziv.bz. Accessed 18 Apr 2016
6. Virtual Reality and the Museum of the Future. http://blog.europeana.eu/2013/12/virtual-reality-and-the-museum-of-the-future. Accessed 25 Mar 2016

7. Shedroff, N., Noessel, C.: Make It So, Interaction Design Lessons from Science Fiction. Rosenfeld Media, New York (2012)
8. Jerald, J.: The VR Book, Human-Centred Design for Virtual Reality. Association for Computing Machinery in collaboration with Morgan & Claypool, New York (2016)
9. Hassenzahl, M., Burmester, M., Koller, F.: AttrakDiff: Ein Fragebogen zur Messung wahrgenommener hedonischer und pragmatischer Qualität. In: Ziegler, J., Szwillus, G. (eds.) Mensch & Computer 2003. Interaktion in Bewegung, pp. 187–196. Vieweg + Teubner Verlag, Stuttgart, Leipzig (2003)

Subject and Subjectivity: A Conversational Game Using Possible Worlds

Ben Kybartas[1(✉)], Clark Verbrugge[1], and Jonathan Lessard[2]

[1] McGill University, Montreal, Canada
ben.kybartas@mail.mcgill.ca, clump@cs.mcgill.ca
[2] Concordia University, Montreal, Canada
jonathan.lessard@concordia.ca

Abstract. We present *Subject and Subjectivity*, an exploratory conversational game where players are tasked with matching their friends with the ideal bachelor. The system uses a modal logic approach to modeling the narrative, based upon Marie-Laure Ryan's possible worlds model for narrative [1]. The dialogue occurs in real-time and consists of navigating each character's multiple and often conflicting world views. The system allows flexible character authoring, demonstrated by having the demo be playable with either hand-authored or procedurally generated characters. The demo serves as an early experiment into the use of possible worlds logic for interactive storytelling and dialogue systems.

Keywords: Dialogue systems · Possible worlds

1 Introduction

Conversation poses a unique challenge and opportunity in the field of interactive storytelling. Conversation may serve multiple purposes, from conveying character personality and narrative meaning, to giving context about the underlying simulation and mechanics driving the narrative [2]. Most dialogue in games generally relies on branching and hand-authored dialogue, where players are presented with several choices of what to say or ask at each point in a dialogue [3]. This approach, however, is limited when dealing with systems where dialogue has to dynamically adapt to changes in context, such as when using procedurally generated content, or in heavily systems-driven games, where the authoring burden of traditional branching dialogue would be too great.

We present *Subject and Subjectivity*, a conversational game that uses character modeling to implement what Short calls an "exploration" conversation system [4]. In, exploration systems, the possible conversation topics are treated abstractly as a landscape, throughout which the player is able to traverse, often to make specific discoveries about the narrative. In the game, the conversation is used to explore the different characters' varying and conflicting perspectives of what makes an ideal bachelor, and attempts to match them with corresponding bachelor who most closely meets this ideal. Conversation occurs in real-time,

© Springer International Publishing AG 2017
N. Nunes et al. (Eds.): ICIDS 2017, LNCS 10690, pp. 332–335, 2017.
https://doi.org/10.1007/978-3-319-71027-3_37

and rather than picking literal lines of dialogue, the player picks directions in which to steer the conversation, e.g. changing the topic, or the bachelor being discussed.

2 Possible Worlds Model

In *Subject and Subjectivity*, the narrative and characters use a possible worlds model, based upon the model described by Marie-Laure Ryan [1]. Ryan's model consists of an *actual world*, that contains all truths about the narrative world, and a set of characters, who are each modeled with a set of *possible worlds*. Each possible world is a set of beliefs that the character wishes were true about the actual world. According to Ryan, the actual narrative consists of characters taking *actions* to make the actual world perfectly match each of their possible worlds. This is impossible, due to conflicts between a character's internal set of possible worlds, as well as conflicts between the possible worlds of different characters. The navigation and discovery of these conflicts forms the core of the narrative experience.

While a more formal model of Ryan's work remains a future goal, for the purpose of the demo we used a simplified and generalized form of the model, and based the content in part on the works of Jane Austen. In our model, a possible world is modeled as an array of boolean values. The boolean values map one-to-one onto a fixed array of propositions, and state the value of that proposition in this possible world. For the demo, there are three propositions: *the ideal bachelor is (not) wealthy, is (not) religious* and *is (not) ambitious*. So the possible world [*true, true, false*] would imply that the ideal bachelor is wealthy and religious, but not ambitious. We give each character three possible worlds, focused on different social perspectives, so each character considers their *personal* ideal bachelor, their *family*'s ideal bachelor, and what they think *society* considers an ideal bachelor. The bachelors themselves are also modeled as an array of the same three booleans, which in this case represents their truth-values, i.e. if they are wealthy, religious and/or ambitious. For this demo, the actual world consists only of the mapping between character and bachelor, as changing these mappings are the only action which may be taken. Given this minimal input, the system is still able to generate rich character interactions and exemplifies the potential of adapting the system to larger-scale interactive fiction scenarios.

3 Dialogue System

The dialogue system is specifically focused on discovering *conflicts*, which we define as points where the property of a given bachelor conflicts with a proposition from a character's possible world. For example, if a character's family thinks the ideal bachelor is wealthy, then a non-wealthy bachelor would be in *conflict* for that particular character, possible world, proposition combination. Since there are three propositions and three possible worlds, each character can have nine potential points of conflict with any given bachelor. We define *character satisfaction*, as the percentage of non-conflicts with a given bachelor. So if a character has 4 points of conflict with a bachelor, their overall satisfaction will be 5/9 or approximately 56%. The satisfaction is used at the endgame to provide players with feedback on whether the match went well or not. Since the satisfaction is hidden to the player, the conflicts must be discovered through conversation.

Conversation occurs in real-time, where the characters are able to talk among themselves, and even match/unmatch themselves with bachelors. The intention was to have a more natural feel to the dialogue, and avoid an interrogative conversation entirely controlled by the player. The dialogue maintains a notion of the *current position*, which is an array of four integers marking the index of the bachelor/character/possible world/proposition that are currently being discussed, and for simplicity we will call the four *topics*. There are two possible dialogue moves, asking and telling. A telling consists of the current character stating if the current bachelor is in a position of conflict or not. Asking, allows the current position of the dialogue to shift, but only in one topic at a time. This lends a flow to the dialogue and furthers the game-play goal of having the player feel like they are navigating through a dialogue rather than simply asking whatever question comes to mind.

In addition to dialogue, there are also two main actions, matching and unmatching bachelors. Players are only ever able to match characters with a bachelor, while the characters themselves can match or unmatch themselves as they see fit. Again, to keep the dialogue flowing smoothly, only the character and bachelor at the current point can be matched. While the player must make the matches based on what they have learned, characters determine potential matches by keeping a history of conflict/non-conflict points for each of the bachelors. Essentially, if the character has a majority of non-conflict points with the current bachelor, they will match themselves, and will unmatch if they are matched with a bachelor but have a majority of conflict points. The character memory is limited to the last five points of conflict/non-conflict, since full knowledge would theoretically allow them to converge on the ideal bachelor without any player input. Characters also have full knowledge of each other, and use this when they guide the conversation themselves. For example, if a character wants a particular bachelor who is matched to another character, then they will try to make that character discover points of conflict in order to get them to unmatch with that bachelor.

Actual lines of dialogue are realized using a context-free grammar (CFG), similar to Compton et al.'s *Tracery* [5], which the system queries by first converting the dialogue move into a symbol. The symbol then gets expanded by the grammar and is returned to the system as a line of dialogue which is then displayed to the player. The grammar approach allowed for custom and unique styles of speech for each character. For larger scale narratives, more scalable approaches to generating dialogue text would be required, for example using Ryan et al.'s *Expressionist* system, that allows the inclusion of metadata within a CFG [6].

Using this dialogue system and model also allowed for the use of procedural content. While it is possible to play an authored scenario that maximizes differences between characters, possible worlds and bachelors, there are also two additional scenarios, *random* and *balanced*. A random scenario assigns completely random true/false values to each bachelor and possible world, and allows for gameplay-breaking scenarios such as where no bachelor is ideal. Balanced generation generates characters and bachelors such that at least one bachelor is ideal for each character, which supports the gameplay goal of letting the player discover an ideal pairing for each character.

4   Conclusion

We presented *Subject and Subjectivity*, a conversational game that uses a possible worlds model of narrative and characters to support an exploratory dialogue system. The accompanying interactive demo shows that a dynamic and engaging dialogue system can be achieved, even with a small amount of content and a simple conflict model. Future work aims to more deeply explore the breadth of conflict that can be achieved with the possible worlds model, such as internal and inter-personal conflicts, as well as methods for scaling the system for large-scale interactive storytelling applications, where characters are deeply modeled and can be expected to take a number of actions. Similarly, extending the system to cover different forms of dialogue, such as non-verbal forms of communication, is also a goal. *Subject and Subjectivity* serves as a solid foundation and first step towards novel interactive storytelling systems based upon subjective characters and dialogue systems.

References

1. Ryan, M.L.: Possible Worlds, Artificial Intelligence, and Narrative Theory. Indiana University Press, Bloomington (1991)
2. Lessard, J., Arsenault, D.: The character as subjective interface. In: Nack, F., Gordon, A.S. (eds.) ICIDS 2016. LNCS, vol. 10045, pp. 317–324. Springer, Cham (2016). https://doi.org/10.1007/978-3-319-48279-8_28
3. Ryan, J., Mateas, M., Wardrip-Fruin, N.: A lightweight videogame dialogue manager. In: DiGRA/FDG - Proceedings of the First International Joint Conference of DiGRA and FDG, Dundee, Scotland. Digital Games Research Association and Society for the Advancement of the Science of Digital Games, August 2016
4. Short, E.: NPC Conversation Systems. In: IF Theory Reader, pp. 331–358. Transcript on Press, Boston (2011)
5. Compton, K., Kybartas, B., Mateas, M.: Tracery: an author-focused generative text tool. In: Schoenau-Fog, H., Bruni, L.E., Louchart, S., Baceviciute, S. (eds.) ICIDS 2015. LNCS, vol. 9445, pp. 154–161. Springer, Cham (2015). https://doi.org/10.1007/978-3-319-27036-4_14
6. Ryan, J., Seither, E., Mateas, M., Wardrip-Fruin, N.: Expressionist: an authoring tool for in-game text generation. In: Nack, F., Gordon, A.S. (eds.) ICIDS 2016. LNCS, vol. 10045, pp. 221–233. Springer, Cham (2016). https://doi.org/10.1007/978-3-319-48279-8_20

The *AntWriter* Improvisational Writing System: Visualizing and Coordinating Upcoming Actions

Alex Mitchell(✉), Jude Yew, Lonce Wyse, Dennis Ang, and Prashanth Thattai

Department of Communications and New Media,
National University of Singapore, Singapore, Singapore
{alexm,jude.yew,lonce.wyse}@nus.edu.sg,
{dennis,prashanth.thattai}@u.nus.edu

Abstract. Improvisational storytelling requires participants to be aware of collaborators' actions, and to anticipate each other's upcoming actions so as to create a coherent story. This paper describes the *AntWriter* improvisational writing system, a computer-based shared workspace for collaborative storytelling. Our system uses a "temporal window" to provide a visualization of a short slice of time where participants can coordinate their upcoming actions during real-time text-based storytelling performances. By providing a concrete, manipulable representation of upcoming actions, *AntWriter* aims to support anticipation of collaborators' upcoming actions as a means to encourage extremely short-term planning and coordination within real-time collaboration, without losing the immediacy and spontaneity of improvisational storytelling.

Keywords: Collaborative storytelling · Improvisation · Anticipation · Computer mediated communication

1 Introduction

When working together in a creative, real-time, improvisational situation, participants are simultaneously making sense of what the group is doing, and deciding what actions to take next. This requires that participants be able to anticipate their collaborators' upcoming actions, and coordinate their own actions so as to create a work that is both coherent and allows for individual expression and creativity. As this type of improvisation generally does not involve a script or score, and involves the creation of a work in real-time as the audience experiences it [1], there is typically no concrete representation of these upcoming actions.

Our research involves exploring the impact of providing a concrete, manipulable, shared representation of upcoming actions on the process of collaboration, coordination and communication in creative improvisations. To explore this question, we created *AntWriter*, a computer-based, shared workspace for real-time, collaborative, human-to-human storytelling that provides a 20-s "temporal window" in which participants can share their planned, upcoming actions. The

© Springer International Publishing AG 2017
N. Nunes et al. (Eds.): ICIDS 2017, LNCS 10690, pp. 336–340, 2017.
https://doi.org/10.1007/978-3-319-71027-3_38

idea is that the visualization of this small slice of time will encourage planning and afford coordination and communication while maintaining the spontaneity and immediacy of improvisational storytelling.

2   Related Work

Much work has been done to support synchronous collaborative writing [2,3], focusing on shared representations and tools for awareness and the use of shared workspace to support the writing process. Some of this work has focused specifically on collaborative storytelling, including the impact of the shared workspace on control and shared understanding [4], work on idea development and elaboration [5], and mobile storytelling by children [6]. Collaboration has also been explored in the context of networked theatre [7] and netprov [8].

There has also been work to support other forms of real-time creative collaboration, particularly improvisational music. The Mimi system [9] uses representation of future actions as a way for the AI system to communicate upcoming actions to a human collaborator during human-AI collaboration. Focusing instead on human-human collaboration, the *Anticipatory Score* [10] provides a scrolling "anticipatory" window into which participants can enter notation to indicate their intended actions, providing a short window in which participants can coordinate their actions before actually performing. A variation of the system was used for an observational study of improvisational music and storytelling [11]. Results suggested that while participants make use of the ability to share upcoming actions to coordinate their actions, there was a tension between the time needed to plan, and the immediate response needed during improvisation.

3   System Description

The *AntWriter* improvisational writing system is implemented in JavaScript and Node.js, and runs in the Chrome browser. Similar to the systems described in [10, 11], *AntWriter* provides a shared workspace consisting of a scrolling "temporal" window (see B in Fig. 1), in which users are able to create short text fragments or "offers". A key difference in our system is the inclusion of a "private", non-scrolling window (D), as described below.

When a user clicks in the temporal window, a blank text field is created. The user is able to type text into this text field, and is able to edit or delete this text at any time. All changes are immediately visible to all participants. The text field scrolls continually to the left, until it reaches the "now" line (A). When the text reaches the now line, the text is read out loud in the user's chosen voice. The text is then removed from the temporal window, and added to the end of the "script" (C). This script forms a record of the story.

The work by Mitchell et al. [11] suggests that encouraging participants to share upcoming actions may create a tension between the time needed to plan, and the immediacy of improvisation. In an attempt to recognize and potentially overcome this tension, we designed *AntWriter* to include a private, static

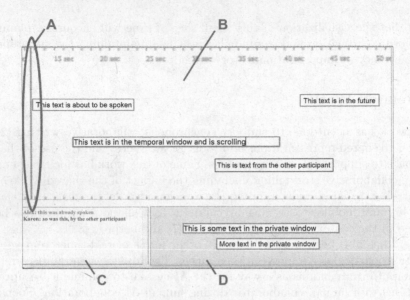

Fig. 1. The improvisational writing system, showing the "now" line (A), the temporal window (B), the script (C), and the private window (D).

window (D) in addition to the public, scrolling temporal window. As with the temporal window, users can create, edit, and delete text fragments within the private window. However, these text fragments do not move automatically, and are also not visible to the other users. Text fragments can be dragged between the private window and the temporal window. Once a text fragment is moved to the temporal window, it will be visible to all users, and will start scrolling towards the now line. Text fragments that are moved from the temporal window to the private window will no longer be visible to other users.

AntWriter is intended to be used in a performative setting. In a typical colocated performance, participants sit together on stage, each with a networked laptop computer running the software. The audience sees a variation of the system, showing only the script that results from the collaboration, projected on a large screen or TV monitor. Alternatively, the system can be used to support non-colocated performances, with a remote, online audience viewing the script on their own browsers, and hearing the story read out as it is being performed.

4   Current Status and Future Directions

The system as described in this paper is fully functional, and is currently available on GitHub.[1] Future work will involve exploring alternative representations of the "future", including experimenting with non-score-based visualizations. We will also explore other ways to mitigate the impact of the tension between

---

[1] https://github.com/narrativeandplay/AntWriter.

improvisation and planning, such as by allowing text fragments to be "pinned" in place in the temporal window, or providing a non-scrolling public window, similar to the private window but shared across users. We will be carrying out additional observational studies, both in the lab and in live performance settings, to better understand the impact of the temporal window on improvised creative performance, and to investigate the role of sensemaking, anticipation, expression of intent, and retrospection on creative collaboration. Finally, we are interested in exploring the role of AI participants in this type of creative collaboration.

5   Conclusion

In this paper we have described the *AntWriter* improvisational collaborative storytelling system. The system provides a concrete, shared representation of upcoming actions during real-time creative performance, as a means of exploring ways to integrate extremely short-term planning within improvisation. The goal of this work is to better support communication and coordination while maintaining the immediacy and spontaneity of improvised performance.

Acknowledgments. This research is funded under the National University of Singapore Humanities and Social Sciences Seed Fund grant "Communication Strategies in Real-time Computer-Mediated Creative Collaboration".

References

1. Dobrian, C.: Thoughts on composition and improvisation (1991). http://music. arts.uci.edu/dobrian/CD.comp.improv.htm
2. Baecker, R.M., Nastos, D., Posner, I.R., Mawby, K.L.: The user-centered iterative design of collaborative writing software. In: CHI 1993, pp. 399–405. ACM (1993)
3. Wang, D.: How people write together now: exploring and supporting today's computer-supported collaborative writing. In: CSCW 2016 Companion, pp. 175–179. ACM (2016)
4. Mitchell, A., Posner, I., Baecker, R.: Learning to write together using groupware. In: CHI 1995, New York, NY, USA, pp. 288–295. ACM Press/Addison-Wesley Publishing Co. (1995)
5. Cheng, J., Kang, L., Cosley, D.: Storeys: designing collaborative storytelling interfaces. In: CHI 2013 Extended Abstracts, pp. 3031–3034. ACM (2013)
6. Fails, J.A., Druin, A., Guha, M.L.: Interactive storytelling: interacting with people, environment, and technology. Int. J. Arts Technol. **7**(1), 112–124 (2014)
7. Jamieson, H.V.: Real Time, Virtual Space, Live Theatre. The Aotearoa Digital Arts Reader. Aotearoa Digital Arts and Clouds, Auckland (2008)
8. Marino, M., Wittig, R.: Netprov: Elements of an Emerging Form. Dichtung Digital 42 (2012)
9. Schankler, I., Chew, E., François, A.R.J.: Improvising with digital auto-scaffolding: how mimi changes and enhances the creative process. In: Lee, N. (ed.) Digital Da Vinci, pp. 99–125. Springer, New York (2014). https://doi.org/10.1007/978-1-4939-0536-2_5

10. Wyse, L., Yew, J.: A real-time score for collaborative just-in-time composition. Organised Sound **19**(3), 260 (2014)
11. Mitchell, A., Yew, J., Thattai, P., Loh, B., Ang, D., Wyse, L.: The temporal window: explicit representation of future actions in improvisational performances. In: Proceedings of C&C 2017, New York, NY, USA, pp. 28–38. ACM (2017)

Doctoral Consortium

How Interactivity Is Changing in Immersive Performances

An Approach of Understanding the Use of Interactive Technologies in Performance Art

Ágnes Karolina Bakk[(✉)] [iD]

Moholy-Nagy University of Art and Design, Bertalan Lajos Str. 2,
Budapest 1111, Hungary
bakk@mome.hu

Abstract. New, immersive or transmedia storytelling tools or game design elements can engage new audiences to watch performances. Companies which define themselves as performing art companies are creating immersive experiences that use various tactics in engaging their participants, including gamification mechanics and video game strategies, and also elements of interactive & transmedia storytelling, which increases the level of immersion as well. My research hypothesis is that new technology tools and immersive environments which incorporate video game mechanics used in performing arts context are changing the interactivity aspect of performances. To be able to scale or to define the level of interactivity in such productions it is necessary to perform an analysis using interactive storytelling, game studies and media archeology, but hermeneutical research and field studies (surveys and deep interviews) are also conducted. Phenomenological studies on the materiality of interaction design will also be used in defining the interactivity and the level of participation. In the current state of the work I'm focusing on "analogue" type of immersive performances (e.g. Danish company SIGNA) that can be analyzed with the help of a game studies approach, but I also focus on how these immersive performances create narrative environments. Parallel to this, I have conducted an audience survey which focused on whether the participants have the same interaction feeling as in video games or VR-environments.

Keywords: Performing arts · Immersive theatre · Games studies · Storytelling

1 Short Theoretical Introduction

1.1 Related Works

In my hermeneutical approach, my reference point is the work of Henry Jenkins and Marie-Laure Ryan on transmedia storytelling and how this work has influenced performing arts. Beside this I find Rebecca Rouse's notion "media of attraction" and her related theory highly relevant. I also find highly important to review new PhD or MA research such as Eva Baumgarten's Transmedia Storytelling im zeitgenössischen Theater (written at Universitat Wien) or Dr. Judith Ackermann's work on video games

© Springer International Publishing AG 2017
N. Nunes et al. (Eds.): ICIDS 2017, LNCS 10690, pp. 343–346, 2017.
https://doi.org/10.1007/978-3-319-71027-3_39

and performativity, that is also based on a groundbreaking research which helps further studies in this field.

1.2 Field Research

In the first year the focus of my research was more on performing arts&narrative design and new technology, with a special focus on pervasive games using locative media and their theatrical features. Among the performances and companies that I closely followed were the Germany-based machine eX, the UK-based Blast Theory and the Danish SIGNA. While focusing on these, one of the main aspects of my research is how the audience perceive immersive performances, whether they perceive them in a way similar to video games and what effect the use of new technologies have on this. According to my hypothesis, SIGNA's performances are totally immersive by using almost no technology, though they are creating a sense of a virtual game for the audience. Machina eX are creating live video game performances, where they are using many gadgets and tools in order to help the participants to tackle the next obstacle, also in order to win the game. Blast Theory's work is a more mixed media performance, and one of their latest productions, the application Karen is based on the concept how immersive and manipulative a mobile application can be. In June and July 2017 in cooperation with National Theatre of Mannheim, Germany, I conducted an audience survey with the participants of SIGNA's performance at Mannheim Schillertage Theater Festival.

1.3 Hermeneutical Research

Beside field research I'm also conducting hermeneutical research, but throughout various phenomenological readings I realized that my interest is more on how video game environment can be transposed in a performing arts context and how gamification can be introduced in a genuine way into theatre performances by using new technology tools and immersive environments. However, my initial research hypothesis is based on an idea of Henry Jenkins, who is defining the difference between interactivity and participation in the following way: "For me, interactivity is a property often designed and programmed into the technology and thus is much more likely to be under the control of media producers. Participation, on the other hand, is a property of the surrounding culture and is often something communities assert through their shared engagement with technologies, content and producers. An emphasis on interactivity pulls inevitably towards the idea of technology as itself liberatory (or constraining), whereas my own work is primarily focused on cultural practices that emerge around and often reshape the technological infrastructure" [1].

Based on Jenkins' idea my research was focusing on finding out whether new technology tools, which offer online or mixed-reality interactive platforms, are changing the sense of participation for the audience or not. It is also interesting to reflect on how different manners of using new technologies can have a "virtualizing" effect, how they are changing the concept of liveness. I will analyze how the different tools are tackling the reception aesthetics compared to traditional ways of watching theatre and how they are changing this behavior type into a participation-based performance. While researching these I have also been focusing on pervasive gaming strategies especially on the type of dramaturgy they are using.

Turning away from phenomenological approach and more towards these performances, I'm focusing on different game study approaches to differentiate performances that can belong more to the paidia type (like SIGNA's productions) and performances that belong more to ludus (like machina eX or Blast Theory's performances), using the conceptual framework of Gonzalo Frasca, based on his work "Simulation versus Narrative: Introduction to Ludology" [2], but also in analyzing the way how new technology tools are used, I'm taking different media archeology approaches like Rebecca Rouse's concept of "media of attraction" [3], which helps to draft a taxonomy for different uses. For analyzing the environments of the performing art production I rely on Gernot Böhme's "atmosphere" concept [4] but also Henry Jenkins' narrative architecture. Jesper Juul's concept about the narrative games [5] is also helping me draft one path from traditional performances through transmedia storytelling production and towards immersive video game-alike experience. To analyze more deeply the participants' behavior I'm going to use Dr. Judith Ackermann's concept of intra-ludic communication, that helps participant to create meaning in such genres that she defines 'Hybrid-Reality Theatre performances [6]. Graeme Kirkpatrick states that "the most important thing about computer games is not their content, if this is understood to mean a message that is transmitted and then interpreted by the audiences" [7]. My aim is to point out where performing arts can enter in creating a message or meaningfulness for their participants in these gamified situations in performing arts. However there are productions that seem to take an important turn towards using interactive storytelling mechanics, the contemporary performing arts is still in the process of change and it will soon re-position itself [8].

2 Future Plans

Conducting more audience research with the participants of Blast Theory and machina eX and comparing the outcomes of the analyses would be the next step in my dissertation's field research part. On hermeneutical side, with above mentioned theoretical tools, I'm planning to draft a theoretical path for theatre productions regarding what kind of methodology they can use to start incorporating tools for more immersive and engaging interactive performances.

By the end of my PhD-study I'll create a pervasive performance that is placed in a building with several rooms, and is connecting virtual performance characteristics with pervasive gaming. I'm also editing the blog zip-scene.com, where I'm publishing interviews with professionals from performing arts, gaming, and the hybrid theatre concept.

References

1. Jenkins, H.: Rethinking 'Rethinking Convergence/Culture'. Cult. Stud. **28**(2), 267–297 (2014). https://doi.org/10.1080/09502386.2013.801579
2. Gonzalo, F.: Simulation versus narrative. Introduction to ludology. In: Wolf, M.J.P., Perron, B. (eds.) The Video Game Theory Reader, pp. 221–258. Routledge, New York and London (2003)
3. Rouse, R.: Media of attraction: a media archeology approach to panoramas, kinematography, mixed reality and beyond. In: Nack, F., Gordon, A.S. (eds.) ICIDS 2016. LNCS, vol. 10045, pp. 97–107. Springer, Cham (2016). https://doi.org/10.1007/978-3-319-48279-8_9
4. Böhme, G.: Atmosphere as the fundamental concept of a new aesthetics. Thesis Eleven **36**, 113 (1993). https://doi.org/10.1177/072551369303600107
5. Juul, J.: Games telling stories? a brief note on games and narratives. GameStud. – Int. J. Comput. Game Res. Page. **1**(1), 1–12 (2001). http://gamestudies.org/0101/juul-gts/. Accessed 31 Aug 2017
6. Ackermann, J.: Meaning creation in digital gaming performance. The intraludic communication of hybrid reality theatre. In: Dichtung Digital, Content No. 44 (2014). http://www.dichtung-digital.de/journal/aktuelle-nummer/?postID=2437. Accessed 30 Sep 2017
7. Kirkpatrick, G.: Computer Games and the Social Imaginary, p. 160. Polity Press, Cambridge (2013)
8. Baumgartner, E.: Transmedia Storytelling im zeitgenössischen Theater, MA Diplomarbeit, p. 91. Universitat Wien, Vienna (2012)

Interactive Storytelling to Teach News Literacy to Children

Ioli Campos[1,2(✉)] (iD)

[1] University of Texas at Austin/Portugal Colab, Austin, TX 78712, USA
iolicampos.press@gmail.com
[2] Nova University of Lisbon, 1069-061 Lisbon, Portugal

Abstract. In this information saturated era, one might argue that learning how to better recognize fake news, misinformation and disinformation are important skills to master. Not only that, but in a participatory paradigm, it seems useful for the user to learn certain journalistic skills. This is called news literacy. Some scholars have been researching the use of digital media to teach news literacy to teenagers and college students, in particular interactive storytelling and gaming. However, less is known about platforms for younger children. And yet a few of those platforms exist. This paper summarizes an ongoing doctoral research and presents preliminary results about the analysis of eight platforms aimed at teaching news literacy to children. We examined the lessons delivered and how interactive storytelling elements were incorporated. We make recommendations for the design of future interactive platforms to teach news literacy. Ultimately our work extends knowledge of how news literacy is being approached in interactive digital platforms and of how interactive storytelling can better be used to foster news literacy.

Keywords: News literacy · Digital media · Storytelling · Games · Journalism education · Children

1 Improving News Literacy in Digital Media

Children are often around when the newscast is on and when adults discuss current events [1, 2]. However, one could argue that they lack the knowledge to contextualize the news around them. This includes not only contextualize the news' content (politics, science, education, and so on), but also its enthronement. By its enthronement we mean, for example, how journalists are not showing the reality in itself, but a perspective of that reality and how that perspective is built by them according to certain criteria.

There are a few digital platforms aimed at improving news literacy levels among children. However, most of the scholarly literature which analyzes news literacy education in digital platforms has mostly examined games for teenagers and college students. The goal of this research is to fill the gap in the literature by examining how digital platforms support news literacy for children at elementary level. To do that, we started by analyzing eight platforms. We were particularly interested in exploring how the use

© Springer International Publishing AG 2017
N. Nunes et al. (Eds.): ICIDS 2017, LNCS 10690, pp. 347–350, 2017.
https://doi.org/10.1007/978-3-319-71027-3_40

of interactive storytelling in simulations and games was supporting news literacy lessons. We also looked into learning platforms.

The term "news literacy" has been used specially by authors working in the fields of work of journalism and/or media literacy education. Its concept is often placed under the broader construct of media literacy [3]. Most authors define news literacy as the knowledge that allows individuals to become more critical news consumers, the skills that increase their independent thinking about their own news consumption experience [4, 5]. According to Rosenberg [6], there is urgency in teaching journalism tools to the general public because now these tools are essential for everybody [6].

The use of simulations to teach about journalism production isn't new, neither is it confined to the digital environment. Long before technology was being used to create games and educative platforms, games and role-playing were being used in the class-room to teach about journalism. Some of the strategies that were and continue to be used are, for example, mock media conferences and hypothetical reporting scenarios which may be particularly useful for the training coverage of dangerous situations [7]. Additionally, we believe this sort of pretend play may be very useful in the case of children who would be particularly vulnerable if thrown into real scenarios.

Role-playing games are a way to pretend play roles that differ from our real person. When we adopt that role, we are assuming a "projective identity", according to James Paul Gee. That role is in between who we really are and who we represent to be. Pretending to be that persona creates a learning experience for the user who can test this new role. This sort of simulation is often used in early childhood education [8].

The mix of games, reality and current events was coined as 'newsgames' by Gonzalo Frasca. Frasca [9] describes newsgames as a sort of simulation that resembles political cartoons. He describes them as a news genre and a tool to better understand the real world.

Ian Bogost, Simon Ferrari and Bobby Schweizer [10] further developed that concept in the book with the same name - "Newsgames". In that book, they propose a classifi-cation of newsgames that includes several categories. According to the authors' taxonomy, there are two kinds of games that aim at educating users about the news: newsgames about current events and literacy newsgames. However, the two educate users in two very different topics. While reportage newsgames seek to educate users about current issues; literacy newsgames seek to educate users about what it means to be a "good journalist" and the importance of journalism to the society.

Much has been written about game characteristics and elements. Indeed, in the case of the so called news literacy games we find that often they do not incorporate several of those elements. For that reason, we could argue if it is correct to call them games. In his study, Cameron demonstrates awareness of the weak borders between terms' choice. He says that the distinction between simulations, games and interactive fiction is "fuzzy" [7]. The examples of digital platforms which support news literacy are so few, that for the purpose of this study we considered that we should be receptive to several terms and approaches.

2   Research Work

In our research we ask how do digital simulations and games use interactive storytelling elements to improve news literacy among children from 7 to 9 years old? The study unpacks these questions in two stages through a triangulation of methods. First, the research does a formative evaluation of digital platforms in the field of news literacy and journalism for children, creating a selective list of the online best practices. Second, the research continues with the construction of an experiment and its testing through interviews.

3   Results

So far, our study has analyzed eight digital platforms which aim at improving news literacy among children. Six of them are available to the public at the Newseum, in Washington D.C.; one is an iPad app called NewsTutor and the other is available online at the News Literacy Project's website and it is called Checkology. Based on the analysis, there are some good examples in terms of interactive storytelling worth highlighting for the design of future digital platforms aimed at improving news literacy.

- The use of the first person simulation works well because it allows users to have an inside understanding of a craft that they usually only see from the outside.
- The use of a character like a news editor to pass along important news literacy lessons also works well because that way the message is incorporated in the playful activity and doesn't sound as much as actual lessons.
- The possibility of asking questions in an interactive way is another aspect that works well because grants users the feeling of control, even though if those possibilities are limited to only two or three options.
- The use of real life cases as a starting point for the game or digital interaction also seems to work very well. Additionally, several of the analyzed cases show that it is not necessary to always have the latest up-to-date stories. Interesting historical examples in journalism continue to be interesting to explore in this manner even if some time has gone by.

4   Status and Next Steps

The doctoral research is presently between stage one and two of the data gathering and analysis. The next steps are to test a prototype that gathers the assessed best practices and test that prototype through interviews with children. That empirical approach will allow a verification of the best methods to teach news literacy through interactive platforms.

In the end we argue that how well we tell the story about how journalists construct the news will have a greater impact in improving news literacy among children.

Acknowledgments. This doctoral research is being funded by Fundação para a Ciência e Tecnologia with the scholarship number SFRH/BD/52609/2014 and it is being advised by Professor António Granado.

References

1. Lemish, D.: Kindergartners' understandings of television: a cross cultural comparison. Commun. Stud. **48**, 109–126 (1997)
2. York, C., Scholl, R.M.: youth antecedents to news media consumption: parent and youth newspaper use, news discussion, and long-term news behavior. J. Mass Commun. Q. **92**, 681–699 (2015)
3. Mihailidis, P.: Introduction: news literacy in the dawn of a hypermedia age. In: Mihailidis, P. (ed.). News literacy: Global perspectives for the newsroom and the classroom. Nova Iorque, Washington DC, Berna, Frankfurt, Berlim, Viena e Oxford: Peter Lang (2012)
4. Loth, R.: What's Black and White and Re-Tweeted All Over? Teaching news literacy in a digital age. Joan Shorenstein Center on the Press, Politics and Public Policy. Discussion Paper Series. Harvard University. John F. Kennedy School of Government (2012)
5. Fleming, J.: "truthiness" and trust news media literacy strategies in the digital age. In: Tyner, K.R. (ed.) Media Literacy: New Agendas in Communication. Routledge, New York (2010)
6. Rosenberg, G.P.: Needle in a haystack: digital literacy in the age of infinite information. J. Digital Media Lit. **2** (2014)
7. Cameron, D.: Giving Games a Day Job: Developing a Digital Game-based Resource for Journalism Training. University of Wollongong, MA (2004)
8. Gee, J.P.: What Video Games Have to Teach Us about Learning and Literacy. Palgrave Macmillan, New York (2005)
9. Frasca, G.: Newsgaming. (n.d.)
10. Bogost, I., Ferrari, S., Schweizer, B.: Newsgames: Journalism at Play. MIT Press, Cambridge (2010)

Enhancing Museums' Experiences Through Games and Stories for Young Audiences

Vanessa Cesário[1,2(✉)], António Coelho[2,3], and Valentina Nisi[1]

[1] Madeira Interactive Technologies Institute, 9020-105 Funchal, Portugal
{vanessa.cesario,valentina.nisi}@m-iti.org
[2] Faculty of Engineering, University of Porto, 4200-465 Porto, Portugal
acoelho@fe.up.pt
[3] INESC TEC, University of Porto, 4200-465 Porto, Portugal

Abstract. Museums promote cultural experiences through the exhibits and the stories behind them. Nevertheless, museums are not always designed to engage and interest young audiences, particularly teenagers. This Ph.D. proposal in Digital Media explores how digital technologies can facilitate Natural History and Science Museums in fostering and creating immersive museum experiences for teenagers. Especially by using digital storytelling along with location-based gaming. The overall objectives of the work are to establish guidelines, design, develop and study interactive storytelling and gamification experiences in those type of museums focusing in particular on delivering pleasurable and engaging experiences for teens of 15–17 years old.

Keywords: Museums · Young audiences · Teenagers · Visitor user experience · Storytelling · Gamification · User-driven innovation · Cooperative inquiry

1 Introduction

Museums are described as places that materialize and visualize knowledge [1], and their goals are to collect, preserve and share their knowledge with the public. Museums are slowly but surely moving away from the metaphor of being just collections of artifacts to become centers where people can engage and empower their knowledge by discovering and challenging themselves [2, 3]; visitors are turning from passive to active participants [4, 5]. Storytelling has been known to be a very effective way to convey ideas and beliefs; museums not only tell us stories but also build those stories through the meaning-making process in which the visitors embark [6]. This allows museums' audience to indulge in narratives that aid the construction of meaningful memories as well as providing the fulfillment of a complete experience. Although the museums' spatially constructed narrative might be presented in a logical and consistent way, not all visitors choose to follow, learn and engage with it [7]. Still, it does not imply that all intended interactive experiences are delivered and perceived successfully, especially to suit all demographics. According to Falk [8], the so called "one size fits all experiences" does not apply for most of the museum visitors. The same can be said to the "net generation" which is seen as quite different from previous generations, particularly regarding

© Springer International Publishing AG 2017
N. Nunes et al. (Eds.): ICIDS 2017, LNCS 10690, pp. 351–354, 2017.
https://doi.org/10.1007/978-3-319-71027-3_41

beliefs and behaviors [9]. This generation is identified as an audience group that is often excluded from a museum's curatorial strategies [10]. In consequence, it is not only museums that seem to ignore a younger audience, this group itself seem to be generally disinterested in what museums might offer. Nevertheless, there could be other ways to engage teens in museums, and game-based approach could benefit museums by promoting positive attitudes around museum spaces morphing them into fun and exciting destinations in order to promote meaningful experiences [11]. The target audiences are the final users; hence, we agree that it is crucial to study their interests and desires, having them as "sources of innovation" [13] and "design partners" [14], in order · to deploy a high quality and enjoyable product.

2   Research Questions

With the present proposal, we envisage improving the message that the Natural History and Science Museums convey by incorporating novel technologies and introducing the fun factor to engage young visitors (15–17 years old).

The following research question will be addressed through this Ph.D.: *What are the guidelines for combining digital storytelling and gamification in order to enhance the museum experience of young visitors inside Natural History and Science Museums?* Having as hypothesis that *digital storytelling experiences empowered by game elements would engage the young museum audience (age: 15–17) inside Natural History and Science Museums, enhance their enjoyment of the visit and create awareness around the museum message.*

In order to test whether this hypothesis is true, the following questions aim to be answered: (1) *How can we gamify the current stories and knowledge of Natural History and Science Museums?*; (2) *How does a digital storytelling and game approach enhance the user experience of young visitors in a Natural History and Science Museum?*; (3) *Why do young visitors choose technologically mediated interactive experiences in Natural History and Science Museums?*

The contribution of this thesis would be a set of findings and guidelines that will aid in designing interactive experiences inside Natural History and Science Museums encompassing digital storytelling and gamification for the teenage audience.

3   Methodology

User-driven innovation sessions: how do teens would enhance their museum experience? At the first stage, we plan to lead user-driven innovation sessions with a sample of 200 teens in order to gather feedback and construct guidelines on how they perceive the museums as well to understand how they think interactive technologies could enhance their overall experience at a museum. We chose a user-driven innovation framework as it is mostly used by industry [12], we followed this approach to have the users as "sources of innovation" [13] alongside with a cooperative inquiry approach that positions teenagers as "design partners" [14]. The primary goal of this sessions is to embark teens in an experience jam for the selected museum. Once they have concrete ideas about the experience to be developed, they start to write about it and to design it on mockups of a smartphone.

We recently published the results of one of the co-design session with a group of 75 teens that was designed with the aim of rethinking a museum's interpretive exhibition through the use of mobile technology [16]. The design work of the students was analyzed in detail to extract design patterns/categories and potential insights. Most relevant categories that emerged from the study are (1) the need of diverse interactive experiences, (2) gaming, (3) location based technologies, and (4) social media. However, this publication only focused on the standards of young people in the creation and creativity of experiences, rather than the performance of a predetermined activity in the museum.

Perspective of the museum and its staff. To gamify the current museum storytelling of the selected museum – Natural History Museum of Funchal, and following a co-design approach as seen in [15], we will work closer to the curators of the selected museum and its staff to choose and iterate the stories they would like their teenage visitors to experience. The gamified interactive experiences that we will create would be used to guide and motivate the visitors aged 15–17 years old.

Moreover, other museums at the international context would be engaged in a set of interviews about their perspectives on how they engage teens in order to check what are the best and not so best practices that currently these museums are adopting.

Afterwards, we shift our focus towards quintessential core of the thesis by utilizing interactive technologies along with digital media with the aim of achieving an enjoyable museum experience for these young visitors via an iterative process of creation, testing and development.

Develop a museum experience. Following on the tracks of the previous studies and to test the guidelines that we are going to coming up, we will design 3 interactive mobile prototypes with different approaches: (1) story; (2) game; (3) mixed approach with story and game elements. Once the design prototype is finalized, we will start with user tests using Wizard of Oz methodology with 50 teens to further refine our design and evaluate the usability of the applications. The participants will be asked to complete typical tasks while the researcher watch, listen and take notes. The goal is to: (1) learn if participants are able to complete specified tasks; (2) identify how long it takes to complete specified tasks; (3) find out how satisfied participants are with the experience; (4) analyze the performance to verify if it meets our usability objectives.

Validating the guidelines found. After the usability iterations above mentioned, we will reach the technical development stage. We then will research about the user experience of teens with the three prototypes inside the museum's premises in order to test the proposed guidelines. During the tour with the mobile applications, the researcher will be taking notes about the visitors' behavior throughout the museum facilities. For this study, we are going to apply a *within subjects* experimental design study with 500 teenagers. The experiment will have three conditions: story-driven (S), game-driven (G), mixed of story and game driven (M). Moreover, in order to avoid order biases, the mobile applications developed will reach different species and paths within the museum. All the participants will be randomly assigned to perform conditions (S/G/M) or (G/S/M) or (M/S/G) or (S/G/M) or (G/M/S). At the end of the tours, the participants will be engaged in a structured interview and will be asked to answer validated surveys about engagement and visitor's user experience. These results would help us iterate the mobile applications and contents in order to make it accessible for all museum's audiences, focusing particularly on teenagers.

References

1. Fyfe, G.: Sociology and the social aspects of msuseums. In: Macdonald, S. (ed.) A Companion to Museums Studies, pp. 33–49. Blackwell Publishing, UK (2006)
2. Falk, J.H., Dierking, L.D.: Learning from Museums: Visitor Experiences and the Making of Meaning. AltaMira Press, Walnut Creek (2000)
3. Hawkey, R.: Learning with digital technologies in museums, science centres and galleries. NESTA Futurelab Research (2004)
4. Simon, N.: The Participatory Museum (2010). http://www.participatorymuseum.org/
5. Mancini, F., Carreras, C.: Techno-society at the service of memory institutions: Web 2.0 in museums. Catalan J. Commun. Cult. Stud. **2**, 59–76 (2010)
6. Kelly, L.: The Interrelationships between adult museum visitors' learning and their museum experiences (2007). http://australianmuseum.net.au/uploads/documents/6663/final%20thesis%20for%20graduation_kelly.pdf
7. Stenglin, M.K.: Packaging curiosities: towards a grammar of three-dimensional space (2004). https://ses.library.usyd.edu.au/handle/2123/635
8. Falk, J.H.: Identity and the Museum Visitor Experience. Routledge, Walnut Creek, California (2009)
9. Napoli, J., Ewing, M.T.: The net generation. J. Int. Consum. Mark. **13**, 21–34 (2000)
10. Tzibazi, V.: Participatory action research with young people in museums. Mus. Manag. Curatorship **28**, 153–171 (2013)
11. Edwards, S., Schaller, D.: The name of the game: museums and digital learning elements. In: Din, H., Hecht, P. (eds.) The Digital Museum: A Think Guide. American Association of Museums, Washington, DC (2007)
12. Buur, J., Matthews, B.: Participatory innovation: a research agenda. In: Proceedings of the Tenth Anniversary Conference on Participatory Design 2008, pp. 186–189. Indiana University, Indianapolis, IN, USA (2008)
13. Holmquist, L.E.: User-driven Innovation in the Future Applications Lab. In: CHI 2004 Extended Abstracts on Human Factors in Computing Systems, NY, USA, pp. 1091–1092. ACM, New York (2004)
14. Druin, A.: Cooperative inquiry: developing new technologies for children with children. In: Proceedings of the SIGCHI Conference on Human Factors in Computing Systems, NY, USA, pp. 592–599. ACM, New York (1999)
15. Ciolfi, L., Petrelli, D.: Studying a community of volunteers at a historic cemetery to inspire interaction concepts. In: Proceedings of the 7th International Conference on Communities and Technologies, NY, USA, pp. 139–148. ACM, New York (2015)
16. Cesário, V., Matos, S., Radeta, M., Nisi, V.: Designing interactive technologies for interpretive exhibitions: enabling teen participation through user-driven innovation. In: Bernhaupt, R., Dalvi, G., Joshi, A.K., Balkrishan, D., O'Neill, J., Winckler, M. (eds.) INTERACT 2017. LNCS, vol. 10513, pp. 232–241. Springer, Cham (2017)

That's not How It Should End: The Effect of Reader/Player Response on the Development of Narrative

Lynda Clark(✉) iD

Nottingham Trent University, Clifton Lane, Nottingham NG11 8NS, UK
lynda.clark2015@my.ntu.ac.uk

Abstract. My interactive novella, Writers Are Not Strangers, seeks to utilize the techniques suggested by studying Victorian serial stories and modern videogames alongside one another as interactive, fragmented, non-linear forms. Using the Choice-Script programming language, this apocalyptic game-story aims to challenge the fixity of boundaries between long-standing terms such as 'reader', 'writer' and 'text', and invite the reader-player to question the nature of their engagements with texts and their creators. The novella will be accompanied by a creative-critical thesis which interprets the Victorian serial as an interactive form and the modern videogame as a serialized text, thereby further destabilizing critical and creative assumptions about both forms. The thesis attempts to provide personal responses and critical study within a framing narrative which performatively engages with the ideas under discussion. For the purposes of this consortium, I will provide a work-in-progress version of the creative novella for feedback.

Keywords: Creative writing · Interactive fiction · Reader response

1 Research Context and Aims

The principal aims of this project are to:

(1) Produce a creative digital text using the ChoiceScript programming language and authoring tools
(2) Examine the ways in which techniques used in Victorian serial fiction may inform the creation of interactive texts, and, conversely, the ways in which interactive texts may inform critical readings of Victorian serials
(3) Question the fixity of boundaries between terms such as 'reader', 'writer' and 'text' via a detailed critical exploration of player/reader engagement with episodic texts

2 Critical Thesis Outline

This study begins by exploring the polarization in games criticism around narratological and ludological elements, (for example, Eskelinen versus Murray [1, 2]) and instead champions approaches which consider the interrelations between such elements. This chapter builds on the work of critics and scholars who reject traditional assumptions

© Springer International Publishing AG 2017
N. Nunes et al. (Eds.): ICIDS 2017, LNCS 10690, pp. 355–358, 2017.
https://doi.org/10.1007/978-3-319-71027-3_42

such as the indispensability of videogame visuals in relation to player engagement and enjoyment [3], or the diametric opposition of videogames and literature (for example, Mukherjee and Ensslin [4, 5]). Moving on from these ideas, the project draws on the findings of psychologists Heider and Simmel in their study of the human tendency to ascribe narrative motive to abstract shapes and their movements [6], considering these findings in relation to reader/player responses. For example, Thomas Was Alone [7] provides an alternative perspective on the characterization of Pip in Great Expectations [8], in that Pip, like Thomas, is an analogue for the reader/player, constructed largely in relation to other characters and his function within the story rather than through his own definitive characteristics. In revisiting the relationship between reader/player and player-character/protagonist in this way, this study aims to demonstrate the creative opportunities offered by emerging modes of interactivity and how they might be of particular use to writers.

The next chapter deepens this established link between Victorian serial fiction and videogames, using examples such as Great Expectations [8] and Thomas Was Alone [7] to explore the creative, structural, practical and thematic similarities between the two forms. The chapter argues that there is both critical and creative value in considering videogames as a serial medium, and Victorian serial fiction as an interactive form. Similarities such as the commercial factor in serial release [9] and the need for repetition of key details to cater to casual audiences provide pragmatic guidance for those writing in interactive forms. Other congruences help to situate videogames within a continuum of significant cultural artefacts, rather than as meaningless toys, as they are often presented. For example, contemporary concerns surrounding the harmful, 'addictive' qualities of the new medium leading to 'moral panic' (as in Hughes and Lund [10] or Young [11]); initial assertions from writers that plot coherence was impossible given the nature of the form (as in Butt and Tillotson [12] or Lewis [13]); and the gradual development of sensationalist elements away from shock value and towards something more measured, meaningful, and socially acceptable [14] all occurred (or are occurring) for both Victorian serials and videogames.

The thesis goes on to explore the complexity of the reader/player-protagonist relationship, building on the work outlined above and examining ways in which the protagonist/player-character may be considered both as an analogue for the reader/player and the writer/creator, and, at times, an antagonist of sorts, frustrating and circumventing the desires of the reader/player. For example, both Life is Strange [15] and 'The Hound of the Baskervilles' [16] encourage reader/players to take on the role of detective while simultaneously withholding information necessary to their 'investigation'. Drawing on ideas and techniques discussed in related creative-critical studies, such as Jasmine Donahaye's observations of the similarities and differences between the use of first person in fiction and criticism [17], or works which stress the impossibility of continuous, unbroken narratives [18] this section further interrogates the reader-character relationship.

The thesis proper will conclude with an examination of the endings of the study's key texts, and what such endings mean in the context of seriality, with a particular focus on character death as ending, and multiple endings. The chapter will consider the death and return of Sherlock Holmes [19, 20], and the death of Commander Shepard alongside the potential death of Chloe Price in Life is Strange [15] and the alternate ending of Great Expectations [8]. This will lead in to a critical reflection on the creative work, including how it has fulfilled the aims of the project and how it has been informed by the critical writing and associated research.

3   Creative Work Outline

The creative piece, Writers Are Not Strangers, will be available to play as a work-in-progress during the consortium via the following link: https://dashingdon.com/play/lclark10000/writers-are-not-strangers/mygame/. In brief, it follows the story of Alix, a young woman torn between her creative dreams, familial duties and career responsibilities, while a potentially world-ending meteorite looms overhead. The reader is encouraged to guide Alix's decisions, with some outcomes being a direct and clear result of those decisions and others arising from the combination or accumulation of previous choices. An initial player-inputted rating of Alix's creative work is only referred to in passing, but subsequent textual interventions will be referred to with increasing directness, until eventually the reader-player is forced to confront their impact on all areas of Alix's life, encouraging them to consider the effect of their responses to other creative works.

Although purely text-based, the novella utilizes various game-like mechanics as seen in visual novels and choice-based games. I am using various statistics to track reader-player actions. This includes the general playstyle and player interests, via stats such as 'positivity', 'career' and 'family', plus the attitude of certain characters towards both the reader-player and Alix based on the reader player's choices. This was based on the approval system seen in Dragon Age: Inquisition [21]. However, to maintain a more book-like appearance to the text, reader-players are not notified of the loss or acquisition of points applied to these stats.

Another source of inspiration is Hanon Ondricek's Fair [22], in which certain events happen in certain places at specific moments in real time, forcing the player to replay each section if they want to see the impact of events in each location. While real time generation of plotlines is not possible (or desirable) in my novella, the idea of certain occurrences being fixed points which the (re)player-reader can experience in different locations and circumstances was extremely interesting to me, and I have therefore attempted to incorporate this. This is achieved purely through composition, using a branch and bottle-neck structure [23] to allow the player freedom, but also constrain them to observing or experiencing certain events.

The critical thesis, like the creative novella aims to engage with the issues under discussion (authorship, fragmented narrative, audience-creator relationships, literary playfulness etc.) by embodying these ideas and principles.

References

1. Eskelinen, M.: Towards computer game studies. In: Wardrip-Fruin, N., Harrigan, P. (eds.) First Person: New Media as Story, Performance, and Game, pp. 36–44. The MIT Press, USA (2004)
2. Murray, J.: From game-story to cyberdrama. In: Wardrip-Fruin, N., Harrigan, P. (eds.) First Person: New Media as Story, Performance, and Game, pp. 2–11. The MIT Press, USA (2004)
3. Newman, J.: The myth of the ergodic videogame: some thoughts on player-character relationships in videogames, p. 2 (2002)
4. Mukherjee, S.: Video Games and Storytelling: Reading Games and Playing Books. Palgrave Macmillan, London (2015)
5. Ensslin, A.: Literary Gaming. MIT Press, Cambridge (2014)
6. Heider, F., Simmel, M.: An experimental study of apparent behavior. Am. J. Psychol. **57**, 243–259 (1944). https://doi.org/10.2307/1416950
7. Bithell, M.: Thomas Was Alone (2012)
8. Dickens, C.: Great Expectations. Vintage, London (2008)
9. Allen, R., Van den Berg, T.: Serialization in Popular Culture. Routledge, London (2014)
10. Hughes, L.K., Lund, M.: The Victorian Serial. University Press of Virginia, Charlottesville (1991)
11. Young, K.: Understanding online gaming addiction and treatment issues for adolescents. Am. J. Fam. Ther. **37**, 355–372 (2009)
12. Butt, J., Tillotson, K.: Dickens at Work. Methuen, London (1968)
13. Lewis H.: Why are we still so bad at talking about videogames? The New Statesman (2012). http://www.newstatesman.com/culture/2012/11/why-are-we-still-so-bad-talking-about-video-games. Accessed 7 Mar 2016
14. Wynne, D.: The Sensation Novel and the Victorian Family Magazine. Palgrave, UK (2001)
15. Dontnod Entertainment: Life is Strange (2015)
16. Conan, D.A.: The hound of the baskervilles. In: Trayler Ranson, H. (ed.) Sherlock Holmes: The Complete Stories, pp. 177–297. Wordsworth Editions, Ware (1902)
17. Donahaye, J.: Noisy, like a frog. In: Marggraf Turley, R. (ed.) The Writer in the Academy: Creative Interfrictions, pp. 199–219. D S Brewer, Cambridge (2011)
18. Benson, S., Connors, C.: Creative Criticism: An Anthology and Guide (2014)
19. Conan, D.A.: The final problem. In: Trayler Ranson, H. (ed.) Sherlock Holmes: The Complete Stories, pp. 830–846. Wordsworth Editions, Ware (1893)
20. Conan, D.A.: The empty house. In: Trayler Ranson, H. (ed.) Sherlock Holmes: The Complete Stories, pp. 849–865. Wordsworth Editions, Ware (1903)
21. Bioware: Dragon Age: Inquisition (2014)
22. Ondricek H.: Fair (2016)
23. Kabo Ashwell, S.: Standard patterns in choice-based games. These Heterogenous Tasks (2015). https://heterogenoustasks.wordpress.com/2015/01/26/standard-patterns-in-choice-based-games/. Accessed 31 Aug 2016

Leveraging on Transmedia Entertainment-Education to Offer Tourists a Meaningful Experience

Mara Dionisio[1,2(✉)], Valentina Nisi[1], and Nuno Correia[2]

[1] Madeira-ITI, University of Madeira, Campus da Penteada, 9020-105 Funchal, Portugal
{mara.dionisio,valentina.nisi}@m-iti.org
[2] Faculdade de Ciencias e Tecnologia da Universidade Nova de Lisboa,
Campus da Caparica, Lisbon, Portugal
nmc@fct.unl.pt

Abstract. Interactive technologies provide the tools to empower audiences to participate in new interactive storytelling experiences applied to tourism. We envisage studying how transmedia entertainment-education experiences can expose tourists towards local pressing issues and social good while providing them with a rich entertaining and educating experience. We describe the research approach that leads to design and implementation of a bespoke transmedia entertainment education experience, composed by two interconnected components: an online participatory portal ("Há-Vita") and a mobile context-aware story (Fragments of Laura). The experience was designed to encourage visitors to learn about Madeira's rich natural heritage and develop knowledge and awareness about its history and biodiversity.

Keywords: Transmedia storytelling · Entertainment education · Mobile technologies · Tourism experience · Research through design

1 Motivation and Objectives

Despite the economic crisis, the tourism industry is still growing and the design and staging of meaningful and satisfying experiences is a pressing need of tourist destinations [1]. We envisage that in this context transmedia entertainment-education experiences can play a role in sensitizing tourists towards local issues and social good while providing rich entertaining and educating experiences. Building our research on the state of the art of such novel entertainment experiences, we plan to study further how entertainment education theories, novel ubiquitous technologies and social marketing concepts can work together to create a valuable and cherished experience for tourists. Using a research by designing approach our objective is to create and evaluate the impact of a specific kind of projects that leverage from a transmedia entertainment education approach to raise tourist awareness towards pressing issues like for example environmental concerns, natural heritage or social challenges.

N. Nunes et al. (Eds.): ICIDS 2017, LNCS 10690, pp. 359–362, 2017.
https://doi.org/10.1007/978-3-319-71027-3_43

2 Building Blocks of the Theoretical Framework

2.1 Tourism Experience and Digital Tourism

The tourism market and the attitudes of people towards tourism as an experience and what to expect from it are continuously changing. For this reason it is crucial to understand the core of what is a tourist or traveler experience in order to meet these new expectations [1, 2]. These opportunities can only be created through a process of visiting, learning and enjoying activities in an environment away from home [3] and today's destinations need to be ready to deliver such experiences in order to keep their competitive advantage.

A large body of work has drawn attention to the impact, role and value of information and communication technologies (ICT) which support and can change existing and lead to new types of tourist experiences [4]. Our research interest lies in studying experiences that take advantage of the association of digital media to urban locations, with the intention of providing rich entertaining and educating experiences. Some of the most common types of such experiences crafted for tourists are location-based games/tours and augmented reality games [5] and more recently transmedia storytelling experiences [6]. This new era of entertainment give us a chance to mold the tourists perspectives and improve their knowledge on the local culture in order to contribute to a more consciously type of tourism that leads to a more authentic experiences.

2.2 Entertainment Education and Transmedia StoryTelling

Entertainment-Education (EE) is the process of purposely designing and implementing a media message to both entertain and educate in order to increase audience members' knowledge about an educational issue, create favorable attitude, shift social norms, and change over the behavior of individuals and communities [7]. An opportunity to enhance the ubiquitous nature of entertainment to educate people [8] can be found in the new technological advances in social media and in the use of immersive and ubiquitous technologies. A relatively new subject that may contribute to this cause is Transmedia Storytelling (TS), a subgenre of entertainment defined by Jenkins [9] as: "A story that unfolds across multiple media platforms with each new text making a distinctive and valuable contribution to the whole". Robert Pratten saw TS as a powerfull emerging tool for change, and to create a practical and theoretical defined space for this potential, he coined the term Transmedia for Change (T4C) [10]. He believes that stories told to the right people at the right time, can have an impact on their lives and on the lives of those around them. With similar origins to EE, T4C involves experiences that should lead to interpretation, education, personal and social growth. Later, Pratten coined the term: Pervasive Entertainment (PE) [11] as an evolution of transmedia storytelling. Soon after Pratten's notion of PE, Weinreich presented an interesting evolution of Pratten's concept, through the Immersive Engagement Model (IEM) [12] by adding a behavior change component to the Pervasive Entertainment model (Fig. 1). According to her, the ultimate goal of the IEM is to create an experience that leads the audience in taking some sort of action as a result of being engaged and motivated. She points out that awareness and education are necessary, but usually not sufficient by themselves to create real change.

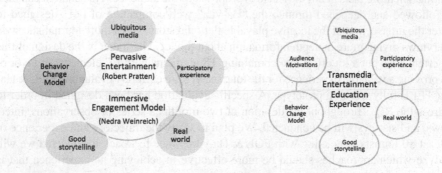

Fig. 1. (Left) Combination of Robert Pratten Pervasive Entertainment Model and Nedra Weinreich Immersive Engagement Model (IEM); (Right) transmedia entertainment education experience model

3 Research Questions

We propose to study Transmedia Entertainment Education Experiences (TEEE), inspired by Robert Pratten and Nedra Weindrech paradigms, we propose a further evolution based on their models, applied to a particular audience: *Tourists,* see Fig. 1. With this model we propose to take into account the principles from transmedia storytelling and entertainment education in a way that meet our target audience motivations and provides an enjoyable experience that in the end translates into a change. Based on this model and through this PHD thesis we plan to answer the following questions:

RQ1: Which findings and guidelines can support authors pursue successful TEEE for tourists?
RQ2: How can current entertainment technologies and media be used to better support the tourist experience in TEEE?
RQ3: Which evaluation strategies are suited to TEEE intended at tourists?

4 Proposed Research Approach

Our goal is to create experimental variability in the product prototype so as to formally test the underlying theoretical design questions at hand and in a real-world context. For this purpose we have developed "Fragments of Laura" & "Ha-vita" a combined transmedia experience aiming to create awareness among tourists about the importance of a unique UNESCO-protected ecosystem of the tourist island of Madeira. "Fragments of Laura" is a mobile experience mediated through a custom made mobile application that guides the audience to discover a story inspired by a combination of fictional drama, historical events and scientific information related to the island cultural and natural heritage. The story develops around seven plot points, each one instantiated at a different physical location in the city, content is delivered in form of audiovisual animation or interactive virtual reality scenes. At the end of each plot point, an interview fragment relating scientific facts about the island is proposed to the audience. This content can then be followed and deepened through the "Ha-vita" web companion of FoL, designed to foster the intersection of the locative playable fictional story with a more journalistic style interviews giving more in depth information about the local heritage. In the design of this experience we put a lot effort into combining TS elements with EE elements in favor of the proving a valuable experience for the tourists. We are currently evaluating FOL & Ha-vita TEEE fully working prototype. A specific evaluation has been designed in order to address the RQ. Throughout the duration of two months a series of observations, interviews, and surveys will be conducted. We plan to study the trajectory and experience of at least 30 tourists interacting with FOL & Ha-vita. Once feedback is collected we will analyze which approaches should be more effective in achieving an experience that is entertaining but that also provides a transformative experience to its users.

References

1. Pine, B.J., Gilmore, J.H.: The Experience Economy. Harvard Business Press, Boston (2011)
2. Cohen, E.: A phenomenology of tourist experiences. Sociology 13(2) (1979). http://journals.sagepub.com/doi/10.1177/003803857901300203#articleCitationDownloadContainer
3. Stamboulis, Y., Skayannis, P.: Innovation strategies and technology for experience-based tourism. Tour. Manage. 24, 35–43 (2003)
4. Neuhofer, B., Buhalis, D., Ladkin, Adele: Technology as a catalyst of change: enablers and barriers of the tourist experience and their consequences. In: Tussyadiah, I., Inversini, A. (eds.) Information and Communication Technologies in Tourism 2015, pp. 789–802. Springer, Cham (2015). https://doi.org/10.1007/978-3-319-14343-9_57
5. Avouris, N.M., Yiannoutsou, N.: A review of mobile location-based games for learning across physical and virtual spaces. J UCS. 18, 2120–2142 (2012)
6. Ferreiraa, S., Alvesa, A.P., Quicob, C.: Location Based Transmedia Storytelling in Social Media–Peter's TravelPlot Porto Case Study. In: E Rev. Tour. Res. ERTR ENTER 2014 Conference. (2014)
7. Singhal, A., Rogers, E.M.: The entertainment-education strategy in communication campaigns. Public Commun. Campaigns 3, 343–356 (2001)
8. Singhal, A., Rogers, E.: Entertainment-Education: A Communication Strategy for Social Change. Routledge Communication Series, p. 280. Routledge (2012)
9. Jenkins, H.: Convergence Culture: Where Old and New Media Collide. New York University Press, New York (2006)
10. Pratten, R.: Transmedia for Change. http://www.tstoryteller.com/transmedia-for-change
11. What is Pervasive Entertainment? – Transmedia Storyteller. http://www.tstoryteller.com/what-is-pervasive-entertainment
12. The Immersive Engagement Model: Transmedia Storytelling for Social Change. http://www.social-marketing.com/immersive-engagement.html

Embodied and Disembodied Voice: Characterizing Nonfiction Discourse in Cinematic-VR

Phillip Doyle[1,2](✉) iD

[1] Institute of Technology, Tralee, Kerry, Ireland
phillip.doyle@staff.ittralee.ie
[2] Dublin City University, Dublin, Ireland

Abstract. Here, *live-action* 'cinematic-VR, (also referred to as '360° video') is considered as a distinct *hybrid* technology, in that photographic image capture and processing methods are coupled with VR head mounted display (HMD) technologies.

This study examines cVR for its necessary reformulation of *embodiment* (and *disembodiment*) regarding both author and viewer, as they engage with pro-filmic reality via the respective technical apparatuses. For the author, the distinctive cVR production pipeline requires a shift in the treatment of the filmed scenario and their bodily relation to it; for the viewer, established structures of engagement with conventional (frame-bound) linear video are disrupted through the *cognitive insertion* of their body into the cVR scene.

With embodiment as its central thematic concern, this study will provide a theoretical grounding for nonfiction cVR in terms of its epistemological affordances and limitations as a technology. Following a critique of cVR as a yet unresolved *theoretical hybrid* (as engendering assumptions of both filmic and VR modes of representation), a mixed, primarily phenomenological study will be employed to gain insights into the nature of discourse in nonfiction cVR, and its reformulated dynamics between author and viewer.

Keywords: Nonfiction film · Media technology · Virtual reality · Cinematic VR

1 Background and Motivation

Virtual reality (VR) and its mixed-reality 'tech-sibling' *augmented reality* (AR) have recently seen significant investment: Google, Facebook and Samsung have staked speculative claims on VR as an emergent mode of communication and entertainment. High profile early adopters in the form of film producers deem VR a credible medium worthy of experimentation (Bigelow [1]; Jonze [2]) and publishers are willing to incorporate VR content on their platforms (VICE [3]; The New York Times [4]). As a discipline, VR is currently beset with taxonomical issues; its latest resurgence is taking place in a highly complex new media environment with many divergent modes of VR authoring, from linear video to fully programmed simulative environments, all ostensibly similar in their output as viewable on a singular type of 'VR' head mounted display. As modes of production diverge into fundamentally different domains, discussing 'VR' becomes

© Springer International Publishing AG 2017
N. Nunes et al. (Eds.): ICIDS 2017, LNCS 10690, pp. 363–366, 2017.
https://doi.org/10.1007/978-3-319-71027-3_44

increasingly problematic. As was stated in the MIT Open Documentary Lab's Virtually There conference proceedings, VR as a technology and as a mode of nonfiction representation "is in a state of interpretive flexibility" [5]. Narrow focus studies such as this are timely, considering the need for solid unambiguous research in the field: it is to this end that this study examines *nonfiction live-action cinematic VR* as a distinct form, in its *newness* (its existence a result of the leveraging of new camera and software technologies), while rooted in the past as a remediation of linear filmmaking.

2   Approach to the Study

The study thus far is organized thematically in the following fashion:

- cVR as hybrid technological artefact
- Analyses of the cVR remediated subcomponents
- cVR as embodied nonfiction discourse

2.1   CVR as Hybrid Technological Artefact

The aim here is to examine cVR and its hybrid nature from a technological standpoint, both in specific and general terms: this will inform subsequent discussion on the reflexively evolving relations between media technologies, authorship and ideologies pertaining to nonfiction representations[1].

cVR is discussed as a specific instance of hybridity with its own characteristics, determined by the sum of its component parts, incorporating a distinctly photographic production 'pipeline'. An objective here is to provide as close to an ontology of cVR as is possible by disambiguating it from ostensibly similar VR forms, and enumerating the various media technologies that converge within it for further analyses, namely: photography; film; video; panorama; stereoscopy and virtual reality.

General technological frameworks are used as a backdrop to studying the cVR artefact: the construct *remediation* [6] for example is apt as it offers a model for characterizing cVR as a reflexive interaction (both historically and contemporaneously) of technologies and their languages, while positing in its remediative 'logics' a *trajectory* on which media can be said to evolve towards perceived authenticity.

Further to the theme of *embodiment*, intrinsic concepts relating to technology and the body are explored through theorists such as Don Ihde who draws on the phenomenological traditions of embodied knowledge as response to the Cartesian-dualist paradigm [7]. Such paradigms describe in part the epistemological dichotomy of framed (traditional screen media) and frameless (VR HMD) representations.

---

[1] The portable 'sync-sound' camera in *cinema verité* is an historical example of such reflexivity in that it purported to afford the filmmaker (and viewer) a more *direct* relationship with reality, reflecting and informing broader ideologies relating to authorial authority.

2.2   Analyses of CVR's Constituent Parts

Here I disassemble cVR into its component parts for formal analyses as mediators of reality[2]. Proponents of nonfiction cVR make claims on its behalf of highly visceral experiences leading to more profound emotional connections with the viewed subjects. Here, such claims are contextualized in extant theories pertaining to ways in which the viewer is said to derive meaningful mediated experiences in film, VR etc. via the various interlinked phenomena contained in *viewing* (cognitive, affective, psychological and emotional). Broadly, cVR can be said to merge video content with VR: bound up in both however are shared legacies such as stereoscopic imagery and panoramic installations. There is necessary overlap between the forms but equally there is a wealth of literature devoted to the ontologies of each. My intention is to ascertain the following through extant studies: what impulses and drives does the viewer bring to the viewing experience and how do they *engage* with the form (and with what lasting effect)? Early writings on film provide theories of how the viewer is *immersed* in film (as opposed to theatre, for example [8]) and how our cognitive immersion in the framed moving image, coupled with evolved modes of cinematography allow us to *identify with* on-screen narratives (inevitably combined with *rhetorical* devices in nonfiction contexts). Comparative analyses will be made with similar phenomena in VR (immersion, presence etc.) with a view to deeper disambiguating and establishing the characteristics of cVR.

2.3   CVR as Embodied Nonfiction Discourse

Broadly, this aspect of the study brings the formal analyses of cVR and its constituent parts into a nonfiction context by drawing on extant theories relating to nonfiction discourse. In doing so, I will attempt to ascertain the nature and extent to which cVR informs debate over the embodied role of the author/camera (and by extension the viewer) in the representation of pro-filmic reality. Perennial issues of authorship, authority and the objective/subjective divide, are examined with regard to cVR and its related forms. Non-cVR artefacts that utilize similar production apparatuses such as highly portable and discreet cameras (the proprietary eponymic GoPro style of camera being a case in point) are used for comparison regarding embodied and disembodied authorship.

Nonfiction is in itself a complex label that requires characterization broadly and its subcategories and genres enumerated and explicated prior to detailed case studies: key genres currently examined are documentary, journalism (and their convergent forms) and ethnographic film. To borrow from Bill Nichols, each genre presents a particular 'organisational strategy' [9], containing variations of narrative and rhetorical devices to represent events in the historic world. Case studies currently marked for review are the cVR documentary *The Protectors* [1], the (non cVR) sensory-ethnographic film *Leviathan* [10] and the (non cVR) journalistic documentary *Sex: My British Job* [11]: each film resonates strongly with the themes of embodiment through the use of technology.

---

[2] The term 'reality' is rarely used in theoretical nonfiction discourse as it is bound up in metaphysical arguments of what constitutes the 'real' prior to representation. Here, for reasons of economy, I am using it to denote *nonfiction* representation.

3   Current Status and Next Steps

This study at present is at the literature review and early research methodologies stage.

More work is required to further resolve the technologically embodied nature of cVR in the context of existing production practices in nonfiction film and new media practices (mobile phones and web-docs for example). I am exploring potential methodologies for my original research which are beginning to emerge.

Content and genre analyses will be used to build a picture of the cVR form in the nonfiction context. Essentially the aim here is to locate the cVR artefact in the canon of nonfiction in order to establish an arena for further inquiry through interviewing of cVR producers: I intend to use phenomenological oriented methods to uncover attitudes to the craft of cVR production in terms of their embodied roles in production. It is likely that many of the cVR producers will work or have worked in 'traditional' film production which will make for interesting comparisons.

In addition, I intend to use both focus groups and interviews with cVR viewers to further ascertain the nature of the engagement with nonfiction discourse in cVR.

References

1. Bigelow, K.: The Protectors. Company 3 [us], USA (2017)
2. Milk, C., Jonze, S.: Vice News VR (2015)
3. VICE News: Chris Milk, Spike Jonze, and VICE News Bring the First-Ever Virtual Reality Newscast to Sundance. https://news.vice.com/article/chris-milk-spike-jonze-and-vice-news-bring-the-first-ever-virtual-reality-newscast-to-sundance
4. NYTVR. http://www.nytimes.com/marketing/nytvr/
5. Uricchio, W.: Virtually There: Documentary Meets Virtual Reality, p. 3. MIT, Cambridge (2016)
6. Bolter, J.D., Grusin, R.: Remediation: Understanding New Media. MIT Press, London, Cambridge (2000)
7. Ihde, D.: Bodies in Technology. University of Minnesota Press, Minneapolis (2002)
8. Metz, C.: On the impression of reality in the cinema. In: Film Language: A Semiotics of the Cinema, p. 268 (1974)
9. Nichols, B.: The voice of documentary. Film Q. **36**, 17–30 (1983). University of California Press
10. Castaing-Taylor, L., Paravel, V.: Leviathan. Dogwoof, France, UK, USA (2012)
11. Broomfield, N.: Sex: My British Job. Lafayette Films, London (2013)

Learning and Teaching Biodiversity Through a Storyteller Robot

Maria José Ferreira[1,2,3](✉), Valentina Nisi[3], Francisco Melo[1,2], and Ana Paiva[1,2]

[1] INESC-ID, University of Lisbon, Lisbon, Portugal
{fmelo,ana.paiva}@inesc-id.pt
[2] Instituto Superior Técnico, University of Lisbon, Lisbon, Portugal
maria.jose.ferreira@tecnico.ulisboa.pt
[3] Madeira Interactive Technologies Institute, Madeira, Portugal
valentina.nisi@m-iti.org

Abstract. This research project proposes the use of Child-Robot Interaction principles to boost the interest and engagement of young children in the biodiversity curriculum. We propose an architecture where a robot learns from children through an Interactive Story, while at the same time teaches them previous knowledge acquired in past interactions.

Keywords: Child-robot interaction · Interactive Storytelling · Learning · Teaching · Biodiversity

1 Introduction

People are used to seeing robots as machines that are programmed to perform precise instructions and/or tasks to help us, but in the last years, this role has been changing. More recently the new trend is to have robots receiving help from us to perform their tasks, to learn, and to become more autonomous. This concept is helpful since it can promote spontaneous "learning by teaching" outcomes, especially regarding children [5].

However, children can act in a very unpredictable way—especially young children. So how can we make robots maintain a social bond with them? The work of Belpaeme et al. [1] suggests that children respond better to robots that adapt their behaviour to them. The author also claim that physically embodied agents, such as robots, receive more attention than virtual agents, leading to promising results for education and social interaction.

Nowadays different approaches have been used in education to improve learning literacy and storytelling is a promising one [6]. The use of Interactive Storytelling (IS) has the benefit of supporting children in expanding their creativity, developing their perception of sensations and situations [3,4]. This is possible because, unlike a non-interactive story, IS allows them to be part of the narrative, inclusively influencing the children to make certain decisions at some

N. Nunes et al. (Eds.): ICIDS 2017, LNCS 10690, pp. 367–371, 2017.
https://doi.org/10.1007/978-3-319-71027-3_45

points. A good example is the work of Kory and Breazeal [2], where children interact with a social robot who is telling them a story. The companion robot used was designed to behave in one of two different ways. In one condition, the robot has a reduced vocabulary, while in the other condition the robot exhibits an increasing performance over time (evidenced through changes in its speech, behaviour and vocabulary). The authors state that children that interacted with the robot in the second condition maintained or increased the number of learned words and language diversity when compared with the children who interacted with the robot in the first condition.

The main goals of our research are multi-folded. On one hand, we aim to leverage Child-Robot Interaction (CRI) in order to increase children awareness and a basic understanding of basic Artificial Intelligence (AI) and Human-Robot Interaction (HRI) principles. On a different level, we aim to better understand how to improve children-robot interaction and build new relational models based on the learning by teaching paradigm, for both the child and the robot. Finally, as a specific output of this project, we evaluate the possibility of engaging young children with specific scientific subjects through HRI.

2 Methodology

As previously mentioned, in order to reach our research goals we propose exploring child-robot interaction in a storytelling context, where the robot plays a special part in the story. By maintaining a rich dialogue with the child, the robot will support the learning by teaching paradigm, on which the project rests. In this section, we describe a possible scenario of interaction and briefly discuss an architecture for the system, the interaction protocol, and possible deployment.

2.1 Integrating Storytelling with HRI

The interaction between child and robot will be driven by a narrative that will frame their encounters. In it, the robot acts as an alien recently arrived on Earth that is interested in learning about this new environment, for which it enrols the children's help. Children are asked to answer simple scientific questions (for example, "*Is this an endemic plant of the island or not?*"), interact with the robot both verbally and through an interactive display placed on the robot, and share local stories that the children may have gathered/know.

The interaction between child and robot in such a "child teaches robot" paradigm will facilitate the collection of local stories in a natural way. Such local stories can then enrich the narrative of the robot in future encounters. Eventually, the robot can re-tell the learned narrative artefacts by referring to the source of the information (for example, the robot can say "*I learned from Luísa that lives in Santana, that ...*"), giving context to the stories that are told.

2.2 Scenario

The teacher introduces *BioRobot* to the classroom, a special robotic guest from outer space who is curious about our nature. The interaction proceeds as the robot asks questions to the children about material previously covered in their school curriculum. The children provide answers as well as personal stories. These stories are conveyed to the robot through its touch screen panel or related to the teacher who, when needed, acts as a mediator between the guest and the children (for example, when the robot cannot understand the child's input). The robot incrementally learns about nature and biodiversity on an island, while the children consolidate their knowledge while engaging in HRI.

Architecture. Figure 1 presents a possible architecture for the system supporting the aforementioned interaction scenario. The IS module is responsible for guiding the learning process of *BioRobot* and the children through a story that relies on knowledge about the flora and fauna of an island. The child teaches *BioRobot* about what he/she knows about the island biodiversity,[1] and the robot teaches the child some past knowledge acquired from another child. Such information is stored in the Stories Database. The Computer Science module is responsible for conveying the child concepts about AI and Robotics through the guidance of a mediator (e.g., a teacher) along the story flow.

Child–Robot Interaction (CRI). We will promote the CRI experience through a specific story to be presented in the classroom environment. Classes of children's,

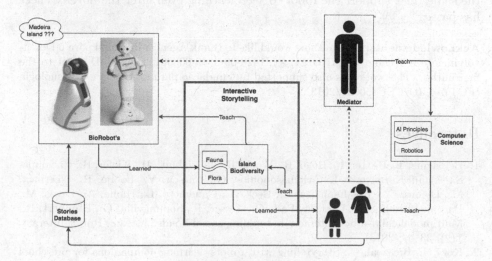

Fig. 1. System architecture.

---

[1] We note that the architecture can equally be used for similar interactions on other topics, simply replacing the subject of the interaction.

supported by their teacher and researchers will interact with *BioRobot*. By means of Q&A along a story, the robot asks and learns from the children about the scientific aspects of the natural patrimony of the island, while the children will grasp basic concepts of AI and Robotics.

Deployment. Finally, once enough learning has been acquired by the robot, *BioRobot* could be stationed at a local science park and will provide specialised tours for local children, supported by staff and teaching personnel. *BioRobot* will then interact with the public by providing information, stories, images projections as well as asking questions to children visiting the site. A help button and camera could guarantee remote parental or teachers control over the visits.

Ultimately, the *BioRobot* will maintain a web-based relationship with the children. The goal is for children continue to learn about biodiversity, engage with the robot (even if virtually), and also learn to form a social network among themselves. These will be done according to a protocol designed together with the schools involved in the project.

3   Conclusion

In this work, we present the first steps we intend to take in order to promote CRI using an IS scenario. Our main goals will allow us to investigate how can we improve CRI and at the same time build a relationship between the robot and the child that support the learning by teaching paradigm. In future, we intend that the approach followed will increase the young children engagement and at the same time, support the robot to keep learning even after the novelty effect has passed.

Acknowledgments. The authors would like to thank Agência Regional para o Desenvolvimento e Tecnologia (ARDITI) - M1420-09-5369-000001, for a PhD grant to the first author. This work was also supported by Fundação para a Ciência e a Tecnologia (FCT) - UID/CEC/50021/2013.

References

1. Belpaeme, T., Baxter, P., Read, R., Wood, R., Cuayáhuitl, H., Kiefer, B., Racioppa, S., Kruijff-Korbayová, I., Athanasopoulos, G., Enescu, V., Looije, R., Neerincx, M., Demiris, Y., Ros-Espinoza, R., Beck, A., Cañamero, L., Hiolle, A., Lewis, M., Baroni, I., Nalin, M., Cosi, P., Paci, G., Tesser, F., Sommavilla, G., Humbert, R.: Multimodal child-robot interaction: building social bonds. J. Hum. Robot Interact. **1**(2), 33–53 (2013)
2. Kory, J., Breazeal, C.: Storytelling with robots: learning companions for preschool children's language development. In: Proceedings of the 23rd IEEE International Symposium on Robot and Human Interactive Communication, pp. 643–648 (2014)
3. Miller, S., Pennycuff, L.: The power of story: using storytelling to improve literacy learning. J. Cross Discip. Perspect. Educ. **1**(1), 8 (2008)

4. Ryokai, K., Vaucelle, C., Cassell, J.: Virtual peers as partners in storytelling and literacy learning. J. Comput. Assist. Learn. **19**(2), 195–208 (2003)
5. Tanaka, F., Matsuzoe, S.: Children teach a care-receiving robot to promote their learning: field experiments in a classroom for vocabulary learning. J. Hum. Robot Interact. **1**(1), 78–95 (2012)
6. Van, G.: Potential applications of digital storytelling in education. In: 3rd Twente Student Conference on IT (2005)

Authoring Concepts and Tools for Interactive Digital Storytelling in the Field of Mobile Augmented Reality

Antonia Kampa[✉]

Hochschule RheinMain, Wiesbaden, Germany
antonia.kampa@hs-rm.de

Abstract. Producing systems for entertainment computing such as mobile augmented reality applications with interactive digital storytelling components is a complex and interdisciplinary task. It is producing a new form of media. Emerging new technologies will add to the complexity of authoring desired systems in the future, with the sort of conceptualizing and producing entertaining content suitable for those experiences. Today no publicly available authoring tool exists for producing such systems, but each is made from scratch by programmers and content authors from different fields. Providing authoring concepts and tools for an adjustable system allowing the use of various technologies can shift effort from developing entertaining applications towards producing entertaining content and therefore content quality and entertainment may rise.

Keywords: Authoring · Authoring tool · Interactive Digital Storytelling

1 Research Work

In the project SPIRIT, we designed entertaining experiences in cultural heritage sites through mobile location-based augmented reality (AR). The SPIRIT concept is based upon a strong storytelling metaphor. By using mobile devices (smart phones and tablets) as 'magic equipment', users can 'meet restless spirits of historical characters'. Creating this illusion (see left in Fig. 1) we originate a new media form, which we want to give structure, using the concept of Interactive Digital Storytelling (IDS). Content structures rely on specific interaction styles, unless only hyper-structures are involved. Often XML extensions are used as description languages [1, 2]. In SPIRIT, a Storytelling XML (STARML) dialect has been derived from ARML [3] by adding authoring-friendly XML-tags, with the focus on location-based content description for IDS. Further, a plot engine has been developed that interprets the STARML content structure, processes user interactions and triggers AR video and other media [4]. This engine uses conditions for planning. During development, a location-based experience with professionally produced media content has been authored by an interdisciplinary team and evaluated. Alongside, several authoring tools have been developed for assisting on-site authoring.

Next to system development, the research work described here pursues the extension of the state of the art of authoring concepts in this domain. Authoring AR content has been made accessible for programmers by systems like EDoS [5] and ComposAR [6]. For non-programmers, TaleBlazer [7] offers a visual script language like Scratch [8],

© Springer International Publishing AG 2017
N. Nunes et al. (Eds.): ICIDS 2017, LNCS 10690, pp. 372–375, 2017.
https://doi.org/10.1007/978-3-319-71027-3_46

with a graphical editor for creating location-based scavenger hunts. TaleBlazer has no open story structure and does not support transparent AR video. Aurasma [9] and Wikitude [10] offer AR content creation without the need of programming, but support no story-specific content structures. ARIS [11] and the Ingress Mission Creator [12] are authoring tools for location-based stories without supporting AR content or story-specific content structures. The SPIRIT application addresses further sensors such as the gyroscope.

An authoring concept is observing the authors [13] for authoring tool development. The SPIRIT authoring tool StoryPlaceAR was developed out of the need to author media content outdoors in an ad-hoc manner.

The system "immersive authoring for tangible AR" [14] transforms *'What You See Is What You Get'* authoring concept into *'What You Feel Is What You Get'*. VideoTestAR enables prototypical AR video production and automatically authors the STARML content structure for immediate experience testing.

In authoring for IDS, after content creation the story structure can be altered by filling in content into an existing story structure. For this, several working steps are performed on the same STARML file and folder system. This creates a bottleneck of collaboration and communication in an interdisciplinary team. In conclusion, this bottleneck exists for the authoring of XML structures for IDS systems. Authoring is considered a bottleneck in other domains [15]. Szilas [13] argues that the authoring bottleneck may not be solved by authoring tools, because they mainly serve specialized IDS experiences. Can an authoring tool ease this bottleneck problem? Enabling non-programmers to author IDS systems extends the authoring target group. STARML files may be worked on in a distributed manner, easing the bottleneck problem. Another problem of authoring complex IDS experiences is debugging existing, complex story structures [14]. We developed MockAR, which is an authoring tool for wire framing AR experiences and graphical user interfaces for non-programmers. It made debugging an easy task.

2   Results

Four authoring editors for non-programmers were developed with the focus on immediate testing, which enables on-site debugging. MockAR enables wire framing AR content. It also facilitated collaboration between programmers and designers. StoryPlaceAR (see middle in Fig. 1) enables fast and on-site authoring of location-based content. VideoTestAR (see right in Fig. 1) enables fast and prototypical AR video content creation for immediate testing. This saves the costly step of professional content production in the beginning and enables fast video testing and video debugging. StoryStructAR enables non-programmers creating a story structure by implicitly handling conditions for planning, instead of leaving that task to the author. It facilitates planning the plot of the authored story.

Fig. 1. Left: Storytelling Metaphor of meeting a spirit of the past; middle VideoTestAR and right StoryPlaceAR authoring tools for location based SPIRIT experiences.

Storytelling content structure elements and authoring friendly named XML-tags were contributed to the development of STARML. The plot engine for STARML was implemented communicating through a facade with the SPIRIT application following the facade pattern [16].

The authoring process of editing the STARML content structure by hand as well as using authoring tools for the same task has recently been evaluated with eight subjects. They were students without programming skills, who were trained by playing and watching the first complete SPIRIT experience in office circumstances, which means location-based data was faked. A practical workshop for experiencing location-dependent characteristics of the SPIRIT application was held with all subjects. Another practical workshop for editing a STARML template with an XML editor was held with the goal of creating their own story structures. In teams of two, they were given the task of developing SPIRIT experiences with linear and non-linear plots for users to explore their story. Their stories had to follow a valid storytelling structure [17]. Preliminary evaluation results show that the main obstacles the subjects mentioned in interviews were comprehension of complex storytelling and location-based structures, and programming angst. Only one of four groups produced a bug-free, playable SPIRIT experience edited by hand. Preliminary results show, that the developed authoring tools ease the stated obstacles. Seven of eight students claimed their work would be more efficient with the tools than without. They also appreciated the visualization of content wise separated aspects of the story structure, which the SPIRIT authoring tools offered.

MockAR was evaluated by three interviewed students with the result that IDS structures grow fast into confusing giants of finite state machines without abstraction. With growing number of states, the editing process becomes more difficult. Often students said they had no overview over the whole story, after creating a critical amount of data.

3   Next Steps

Evaluation results must be analyzed in the future and interpreted within a greater perspective of authoring IDS. Based on the evaluation results, an authoring model for an overall authoring concept for Interactive Digital Storytelling can be formulated. This authoring concept must define several methods and steps with the goal of story conceptualization and content production with the target group of interdisciplinary teams consisting of non-programmers. Early testing should be a part of the authoring concept.

Combined with the possibility of fast content creation, this facilitates content debugging. Authoring tasks are often focused on one aspect of a SPIRIT experience. The authoring concept therefore should be separated context-wise. Authoring tools must implement visualizations according to these separations. As creating a SPIRIT experience from scratch is complicated, authoring concepts for non-programmers should suggest templates for testing purposes as well as for learning possible applications of the underlying storytelling content structure.

References

1. Spierling, U., Weiß, S.A., Müller, W.: Towards accessible authoring tools for interactive storytelling. In: Göbel, S., Malkewitz, R., Iurgel, I. (eds.) TIDSE 2006. LNCS, vol. 4326, pp. 169–180. Springer, Heidelberg (2006). https://doi.org/10.1007/11944577_17
2. Szilas, N., Marty, O., Réty, J.-H.: Authoring highly generative interactive drama. In: Balet, O., Subsol, G., Torguet, P. (eds.) ICVS 2003. LNCS, vol. 2897, pp. 37–46. Springer, Heidelberg (2003). https://doi.org/10.1007/978-3-540-40014-1_5
3. Lechner, M. (ed.) OGC: OGC Augmented Reality Markup Language 2.0. Draft Candidate Standard (2013). https://portal.opengeospatial.org/files/?artifact_id=52739
4. Kampa, A.; Spierling, U.: Requirements and solutions for location-based augmented reality storytelling in an outdoor museum. In: Busch, C., Sieck, J. (eds.) Kultur und Informatik: Augmented Reality, pp. 105–117. Verlag Werner Huelsbusch, Glueckstadt, Berlin (2016)
5. Tran, C., George, S., Marfisi-Schottman, I.: EDoS: an authoring environment for serious games. Design based on three models. In: Proceedings of ECGBL 2010 The 4th European Conference on Games Based Learning, pp. 393–402 (2010)
6. Wang, Y., Langlotz, T., Billinghurst, M., Bell, T.: An authoring tool for mobile phone AR environments. In: Proceedings of New Zealand Computer Science Research Student Conference, vol. 9, pp. 1–4 (2009)
7. TaleBlazer: www.taleblazer.org. Accessed 01 Sep 2017
8. Scratch: https://scratch.mit.edu/. Accessed 01 Sep 2017
9. Aurasma Development Kit: https://www.aurasma.com/. Accessed 01 Sep 2017
10. Wikitude AR Application SDK: http://www.wikitude.com/. Accessed 01 Sep 2017
11. ARIS - Mobile Learning Experiences: http://arisgames.org/. Accessed 01 Sep 2017
12. Ingress Mission Creator: http://mission-author-dot-betaspike.appspot.com/. Accessed 01 Sep 2017
13. Spierling, U., Szilas, N.: Authoring issues beyond tools. In: Iurgel, I.A., Zagalo, N., Petta, P. (eds.) ICIDS 2009. LNCS, vol. 5915, pp. 50–61. Springer, Heidelberg (2009). https://doi.org/10.1007/978-3-642-10643-9_9
14. Lee, G.A., Nelles, C., Billinghurst, M., Kim, G.J.: Immersive authoring of tangible augmented reality applications. In: Proceedings of the 3rd IEEE/ACM International Symposium on Mixed and AR, pp. 172–181. IEEE Computer Society (2004)
15. Murray, T.: Authoring intelligent tutoring systems: an analysis of the state of the art. Int. J. Artif. Intell. Educ. (IJAIED) 10, 98–129 (1999)
16. Gamma, E.: Design Patterns: Elements of Reusable Object-Oriented Software. Pearson Education, Delhi (1995)
17. Chatman, S.: Story and Discourse. Narrative Structure in Fiction and Film. Cornell University Press, Ithaca (1978)

NOOA: Maintaining Cultural Identity Through Intergenerational Storytelling and Digital Affinity Spaces

Juliana Monteiro[1(✉)] , Carla Morais[2] , and Miguel Carvalhais[3]

[1] CIQUP, Faculty of Engineering of the University of Porto, Porto, Portugal
juliana.monteiro@fe.up.pt
[2] CIQUP, Faculty of Science of the University of Porto, Porto, Portugal
cmorais@fc.up.pt
[3] INESC/TEC, Faculty of Fine Arts of the University of Porto, Porto, Portugal
mcarvalhais@fba.up.pt

Abstract. The possibility to preserve perspectives of reality with spontaneous creations allowed by the web tools that now empower common users with content production skills highlights the numerous opportunities for the present and future of cultural identity maintenance. Our research approaches digital storytelling during intergenerational dynamics as a stage for a participatory contribution to the maintenance of cultural identity. With an ethnographic approach and with partnerships with existing senior movements, we seek to (a) understand the storytelling processes during intergenerational dynamics, (b) develop a framework for the participative creation of narratives in the context of intergenerational cultural identity maintenance, (c) support the participatory maintenance of cultural identity through a set of workshops for intergenerational storytelling, (d) understand the challenges and opportunities promoted by digital affinity spaces for the maintenance of cultural identity. Our contribution proposes to develop the understanding of the role that interactive narratives can have in the context of cultural identity maintenance, by developing new usage strategies to enhance cultural mediation through social and ubiquitous storytelling strategies.

Keywords: Cultural identity · Storytelling · Affinity spaces · Intergenerational dynamics

1 Introduction

We witness a whole breadth of new opportunities for cultural identity safeguarding, similar to those Gutenberg and the printing press presented in their time. The new media also brought new perspectives over knowledge and our urge to share it. Theorists refer the emergence of a new intelligence that mobilizes and coordinates users in real time on the web, in both virtual and physical realities, giving place to the birth of paradigms such as "Lovink's Mediactivism, Castells' Network affinities, Levy's Collective Intelligence and Barabarasi's model of Small Word aristocratic" [1]. The opportunities grow

© Springer International Publishing AG 2017
N. Nunes et al. (Eds.): ICIDS 2017, LNCS 10690, pp. 376–379, 2017.
https://doi.org/10.1007/978-3-319-71027-3_47

clear in this context for cultural identity maintenance involving intergenerational storytelling and digital affinity spaces, considering that nowadays we have the tools to record and maintain this knowledge in reach of any common user.

2 Core Topics

Our argument is supported by four theoretical concepts: cultural identity [2–6] storytelling [7, 8] intergenerational dynamics [9] and affinity spaces [10]. First of all, when we refer to cultural identity, we are referring to the "the practices, representations, expressions, knowledge, skills (…) that communities, groups and, in some cases, individuals recognize as part of their cultural heritage" [11], grasping the idea of intangible cultural heritage, regional identity and collective memory. Second, we refer to storytelling as "the effort to communicate events using words (prose or poetry), images, and sounds often including improvisation or embellishment" [8], and to intergenerational dynamics as "vehicles for the purposeful and ongoing exchange of resources and learning among older and younger generations" [9]. Finally, affinity spaces "focuses on the idea of a space in which people interact, rather than on membership in a community" and on the point that nowadays people, "young and old, are engaged in conversations within interest-driven groups" [10, 12].

In our study, the first two concepts identify the dimensions of potential for innovation that points to a need to study unexplored paths for cultural maintenance from intergenerational interactions, while the last two concepts are chosen as logical components for supporting our approach on these new paths of interaction. All together, we felt a need for a term broader than simple preservation to refer to cultural identity in the scope of our work. By clutching the possibilities allowed by affinity spaces and intergenerational storytelling to our work, and taking into account that both concepts implicate collaborative agency, we cannot expect to "preserve" in the sense of keeping knowledge without change [13]. Instead, we can anticipate a combination of cultural identity safeguarding, appropriation and continuity that we refer to as "maintenance".

The vision of connecting storytelling and intergenerational activities has been supported by many authors [14–17]. We believe that adding the purpose of cultural identity to this equation and highlighting the role of affinity spaces [10] dynamization may give a significant push on supporting the maintenance of cultural identity, pointing to the relevance of "a dimension of 'participatory culture' having implications not only for skill development but also involving the interest construct" [18]. We hence draw from Couldry's idea of digital storytelling as being "the whole range of personal stories now being told in potentially public form using digital media resources" [7], as well as from Lundby's idea of the potential for encouraging social participation by promoting the amateur production of digital stories "in 'story circles' offline, as well as online peer contact on social networking sites" [19]. The participatory potential is also stressed by Davis as it is able to allow "untold but significant stories to emerge, and technical and storytelling skills to be transferred to participants through the process" [14].

2.1   Literature Gap

We could understand from a preliminary state of the art review that often there has been made a connection between intergenerational dynamics and storytelling, or storytelling and cultural identity. Our contribution differs from the existing scientific production by identifying the potential synergies between our four core concepts, focusing on the intergenerational storytelling dynamics in affinity spaces in pervasive media to understand their challenges and opportunities for the maintenance of cultural identity.

3   Problem Statement and Research Goals

Our research explores digital storytelling approaches during intergenerational dynamics towards a participatory contribution to the maintenance of cultural identity in affinity spaces. To this effect, with an ethnographic approach and with partnerships with existing senior movements, the production of multimedia narrative artifacts will be carried during intergenerational dynamics, following the study of how these stories survive and evolve in affinity spaces, both physical and digital. Hence, this research aims to (a) understand the processes of storytelling during intergenerational dynamics; (b) develop a framework for the participative creation of narratives in the context of intergenerational cultural identity maintenance; (c) support a participatory approach to the maintenance of cultural identity through a set of workshops aimed at intergenerational storytelling and through the dynamization of digital affinity spaces; (d) understand the challenges and opportunities promoted by digital affinity spaces for the maintenance of cultural identity.

4   Final Remarks and Next Steps

We identified and pursued the opportunity for connecting intergenerational storytelling in affinity spaces with the maintenance of cultural identity from our preliminary state of the art review. Our next steps consist on preparing an ethnographic approach with partnership with a network of senior movements, for the production of multimedia narrative artifacts that will be carried during intergenerational dynamics and ultimately be part on our attempt for cultural identity maintenance through the dynamization of digital affinity spaces. The preparation phase of this approach strives to trace a path for keeping this cultural information available and in constant appropriation and development, as well as for consistently engaging both generations in the project.

Acknowledgments.   The authors acknowledge the support of Fundação para a Ciência e Tecnologia (FCT – Portugal), through the Ph.D. Grant PD/BD/114139/2015.

References

1. Russo, V.: Urban mediactivism in web 3.0. Case analysis: the city of Chieti. In: Maturo, A., Hošková-Mayerová, Š., Soitu, D.-T., Kacprzyk, J. (eds.) Recent Trends in Social Systems: Quantitative Theories and Quantitative Models. SSDC, vol. 66, pp. 303–313. Springer, Cham (2017). https://doi.org/10.1007/978-3-319-40585-8_27
2. Assmann, J., Czaplicka, J.: Collective memory and cultural identity. New Ger. Crit. **65**, 125–133 (1995)
3. Hall, S., Du Gay, P.: Questions of cultural identity. Br. J. Sociol. **48**, 153 (1997)
4. Paasi, A.: Region and place: regional identity in question. Prog. Hum. Geogr. **27**, 475–485 (2003)
5. Burgess, J.: Hearing ordinary voices: cultural studies, vernacular creativity and digital storytelling. Contin. J. Media Cult. Stud. **20**, 201–214 (2006)
6. Mutibwa, D.H.: Memory, storytelling and the digital archive: revitalizing community and regional identities in the virtual age. Int. J. Media Cult. Polit. **12**, 7–26 (2016)
7. Couldry, N.: Mediatization or mediation? Alternative understandings of the emergent space of digital storytelling. New Media Soc. **10**, 373–391 (2008)
8. Haigh, C., Hardy, P.: Tell me a story—a conceptual exploration of storytelling in healthcare education. Nurse Educ. Today **31**, 408–411 (2011)
9. Boström, A.: Intergenerational solidarity–and the need for lifelong and lifewide education to enhance community well-being. In: Intergenerational Solidarity and Older Adults' Education in Community, pp. 47–55 (2012)
10. Gee, J.P.: Semiotic social spaces and affinity spaces. In: Barton, D. (ed.) Beyond Communities of Practice. Language Power and Social Context, pp. 214–232. Cambridge University Press, Cambridge (2005)
11. Text of the convention for the safeguarding of the intangible cultural heritage - intangible heritage - culture sector – UNESCO. https://ich.unesco.org/en/convention
12. Gee, J.P.: Accountable Talk and Learning in Popular Culture: The Game/Affinity Paradigm. Socializing Intelligence Through Academic Talk and Dialogue. Routledge, AERA books, New York (2015)
13. Severo, M.: Social media as new arenas for intangible cultural heritage. In: Proceedings of the European Conference on e-Learning, pp. 406–412 (2015)
14. Davis, D.: Intergenerational digital storytelling: a sustainable community initiative with inner-city residents. Vis. Commun. **10**, 527–540 (2011)
15. Beltrán, R., Begun, S.: "It is Medicine": narratives of healing from the aotearoa digital storytelling as indigenous media project (ADSIMP). Psychol. Dev. Soc. J. **26**, 155–179 (2014)
16. Wexler, L., Eglinton, K., Gubrium, A.: Using digital stories to understand the lives of Alaska native young people. Youth Soc. **46**, 478–504 (2014)
17. Couldry, N., MacDonald, R., Stephansen, H., Clark, W., Dickens, L., Fotopoulou, A.: Constructing a digital storycircle: digital infrastructure and mutual recognition. Int. J. Cult. Stud. **18**, 501–517 (2015)
18. Arnone, M.P., Small, R.V., Chauncey, S.A., McKenna, H.P.: Curiosity, interest and engagement in technology-pervasive learning environments: a new research agenda. Educ. Technol. Res. Dev. **59**, 181–198 (2011)
19. Lundby, K.: Editorial: mediatized stories: mediation perspectives on digital storytelling. New Media Soc. **10**, 363–371 (2008)

An Epistemological Approach to the Creation of Interactive VR Fiction Films

María Cecilia Reyes[(✉)]

Università degli Studi di Genova, Genoa, Italy
maria.cecilia.reyes@edu.unige.it

Abstract. The PhD project presented in this paper introduces a proposal for an epistemological paradigm addressed to the creation of interactive immersive fiction films. In order to provide conceptual tools for the analysis and creation of a fluent and engaging interactive VR narrative, the study investigates the convergence of aesthetics, storytelling and interactivity. These theoretical foundations lead to the practical production of an interactive immersive film prototype. The main objective is to create a fluent interactive cinematographic experience in which the final feeling for the user is the sensation of having *lived* the story, with some degree of agency inside it.

Keywords: Interactive digital storytelling · Interactive immersive cinematography · Medium-conscious narratology · Virtual reality

1 Introduction

This research study is born inside the PhD program on Digital Humanities of the University of Genoa (Italy), as a project that merges the humanistic knowledge of narratology, literature, theater and arts history, with the technological components and possibilities of Virtual Reality (VR) as a medium for Interactive Digital Storytelling (IDS). The project was also accepted by Universidad del Norte (Colombia), in a joint degree agreement, in the PhD program on Communication Sciences. Communication studies enriches the project by adding the *medium study* point of view, i.e., by identifying how the medium shapes the narrative and, consequently, the user's experience.

In 2016 VR technologies for creation and reproduction opened to the big public. Different kinds of narratives for virtual environments (VE) start to emerge on a wide spectrum that moves along the level of interactivity: on one end there are videogames, simulations and 3D objects manipulations, and on the other end there are linear narratives with no interactive options given to the user. In this research study, the objective is the creation of Interactive VR Fiction Films, a narrative experience where the user follows the flow of a storyline but also has some degree of interactivity within the storyworld and decisional power upon the course of the story.

So far, in audiovisual history it is possible to find interactive films [1] and videos [2], narrative videogames, interactive narratives with synthetic agents [3] and linear VR films, made with animation or live action, that are gaining recognition in traditional film festivals [4], but interactive immersive films as an art form is not yet developed. From a

© Springer International Publishing AG 2017
N. Nunes et al. (Eds.): ICIDS 2017, LNCS 10690, pp. 380–383, 2017.
https://doi.org/10.1007/978-3-319-71027-3_48

cinematographic point of view, audiovisual language is still trying to figure out how to tell engaging linear stories in VEs, while the medium itself and its different user interaction forms are also under research and development, waiting for the common user feedback.

2   An Epistemological Approach

A VR narrative takes its first inspiration from the art that is naturally closer to it: cinema as an audiovisual medium for telling stories. But at the same time cinematographic narrative creates its language from theater and classical narratology. The nature of VR allows the addition of some degree of interaction through different kinds of Human Computer Interfaces (HCI), giving the users different levels of agency [5] and decisional power upon the flow of the story, and consequently upon their own experience. These possibilities add a level of depth on the related narratology.

The creation process of an interactive immersive narrative generates different questions, within the communication act, starting from the semiotic nature of VR: if the audiovisual sign is composed by the auditory and the visual signs [6], which is the sign of virtual reality, where sensorial perceptions of the world are being communicated rather than single messages/discourses [7]? From the storyteller/creator point of view: Which concepts from other art forms of storytelling can be applied in a VR narrative? How can the *creator* narrate a solid and coherent story inside an immersive environment, giving the user agency and power upon the flow of the story? On the other side, the receptor find his/herself at the center of the scene: How does the user "read/live" an interactive story in a VE?

In order to answer such questions, this dissertation is based on three theoretical axes:

Aesthetics. Change and evolution of the aesthetic paradigm being the user at the center of the audiovisual work.
Narratology. Concepts from literature, theater, cinema and IDS that can be applied in VR.
Interactivity. Types of interactions inside the VR storytelling.

The research methodology mixes literature review, case studies and the production of an interactive VR fiction film prototype in order to prove the presented narratological and interactive concepts. For the production of the prototype, I am adapting the cinematographic production process for filmmaking to the specificities of Live Action VR.

2.1   Objectives

Main Objective. Analyzing the convergence between narratology, interactive digital storytelling (IDS) and virtual reality, in order to create interactive immersive fiction films.

Specific Objectives

1. Describing the aesthetic change by putting the receptor at the center of the scene.
2. Identifying analogies and differences between elements of classic narratology in literature and cinema, and interactive digital storytelling.
3. Proposing guidelines for the creation of an interactive immersive fiction film.

3   Issues Related to the Creation of Interactive Immersive Films

The first stage on the creation of an interactive VR film is the writing of the interactive story. For this, I base my study on *hyperfiction* or interactive fiction, a form of narrative based on a bifurcated story, where users rearrange story fragments into different configurations [8]; the single interactions inside the experience are *reactive* [9], from a technological point of view, but challenging from the narratological/authorial side. In order to keep the narrative flow and the empathy of the user towards the story, I propose a screenwriting framework that combines the cinematographic classic structure with a way to *interactivize* the Hero's Journey [10]; in this way the dramatic tension of the experience is ensured while a well-known model for storytelling as Campbell's Hero's Journey offers a solid structure for story construction.

From the interactive design point of view different question emerge: What kind of interactions are going to be used and in which way will they affect the story? How to write a fluent and coherent story where a single narrative node is both source and destination of another one or possibly of multiple other nodes? Several narratological issues emerge from the fact of using 360° view, that haven't been completely defined by theory: Who tells the story? Who is the user inside the story? Is the user part of the story at all? Considering how fiction, creation and enjoyment change in a VE, on one side, and how interactivity shapes the flow of the story and the enjoyment of the user on the other side, leads to a *medium-conscious* narratology for VR [11].

4   Current Status and Further Steps

At the time, the aesthetics, narratological and interactive theoretical foundations have been studied in order to identify the main aspects to be considered on the creation of an interactive immersion fiction film: the change of the aesthetic paradigm in a 360° environments, the storytelling inside the sphere, the classical narratological concepts from literature, theater and cinema that can be applied in the VE, and, finally, the interactive possibilities inside the VR storytelling. These aspects guided the creation process of the interactive immersive short film "ZENA": from the screenwriting framework to the final product to be tested. The user testing will provide data about the flow of the interactive immersive narrative.

The work proposed can serve as a starting point to develop further research along different directions. For instance:

- In this project interactions have been designed as conscious choices for the user to make along the development of the story, but it is possible to design automatic choices based on user's biofeedback data while s/he is living the experience.
- The screenwriting framework can be used as a canvas for interactive pre scripted stories where any kind of Human Computer Interface (HCI) could make the choices; further research could be conducted to determine how the different HCI can be used in the purpose of achieve a look-like cinematographic experience.
- In this research the Hero's Journey, as storytelling model, has been *interactivized,* in order to ensure a well-structured pre scripted story that is able to create empathy in the spectator. Further research could use other storytelling structures as models to create interactive screenplays.

References

1. Kelomees, R., Hales, C.: Expanding Practices in Audiovisual Narrative. Cambridge Scholars Publishing, Newcastle upon Tyne (2014)
2. Hammoud, R.: Interactive Video. Springer, Heidelberg (2006)
3. Mateas, M., Stern, A.: Façade: An Experiment in Building a Fully-Realized Interactive Drama (2003)
4. Dipollina, A., Saviano, C., Assante, E.: Venezia, la realtà virtuale è in concorso alla Mostra. Spettacoli - La Repubblica (2017). http://www.repubblica.it/spettacoli/cinema/2017/03/29/news/venezia_per_la_prima_volta_una_sezone_di_cinema_virtuale-161709455/. Accessed 28 Jul 2017
5. Murray, J.H.: Hamlet on the Holodeck: The Future of Narrative in Cyberspace. MIT Press, Cambridge (1997)
6. Hall, S.: Codificar y decodificar. In: Culture, Media & Lenguaje, pp. 129–139. Hutchinson, London (1980)
7. Diodato, R.: Aesthetics of the Virtual: SUNY Series in Contemporary Italian Philosophy. State University of New York Press, Albany (2012)
8. Ryan, M.: From narrative games to playable stories: toward a poetics of interactive narrative. Storyworlds J. Narrative Stud. 1(1), 43–59 (2009). Project MUSE database. University of Nebraska Press. Accessed 17 Apr 2017
9. Crawford, C.: Chris Crawford on Interactive Storytelling. New Riders Games, Berkeley (2005)
10. Reyes, M.: Screenwriting framework for an interactive virtual reality film. In: Paper presented at the 3rd Immersive Research Network Conference iLRN, June 2017. http://castor.tugraz.at/doku/iLRN2017/iLRN2017OnlineProceedings.pdf
11. Ryan, M.: Story/worlds/media: tuning the instruments of a media- conscious narratology. In: Ryan, M., Thon, J. (eds.) Storyworlds across media: Toward a media-conscious narratology. University of Nebraska Press, Lincoln (2014)

User and Player Engagement in Local News and/as Interactive Narratives

Torbjörn Svensson[✉]

University of Skövde, 408, 541 28 Skövde, Sweden
torbjorn.svensson@his.se

Abstract. This paper presents a new approach to the understanding of gamification within the context of local news, foregrounding the varied ways that games and interactable narratives engage player/readers through increased interactability, relationship-building and dynamic storytelling. The research extends a model of Self Determination Theory in an approach for development of a new kind of local digital news-service where readers are given more possibilities to interact with the non-fiction narratives of news stories.

1 Introduction

The PhD research described in this paper is conducted within the Level Up project, funded by the Ann-Marie and Gustaf Anders media research foundation. The main goal of the Level Up project is to increase the reading and sharing of local news presented via a digital platform and targeted towards youth (16–39 years).

The field of Newsgames is fully outlined in the *Newsgames* book [1] and Foxmans TowCenter report Play the News [2]. However, my project is not about making games for local news, neither is it focusing "classic" gamification where for example, players gain points for reading news. Instead my research focuses on how games and interactive narratives engage players and if this engagement can be transferred to non-fiction interactive media.

In my research I will review the digitalization of the local news media in light of the transition of games and narratives to the digital realm. I focus on how digital (on-line, multiplayer) games engage users by facilitating autonomy, challenging competence and offering relatedness to other players. Could these mechanisms be transferred from on-line games to on-line news services and also there engage readers?

2 Gamification: A Problematic Term

The "gamification" of local news to many may seem a straightforward task to add traditional game functions (creating point systems, leaderboards and using player achievements) for readers of local news to engage them in the content. But if one avoids an overt and overly simplistic definition of the term ("the use of game elements in a non-game context") as many claim (Deterding, et al. 2011) one can provide a critique of the

© Springer International Publishing AG 2017
N. Nunes et al. (Eds.): ICIDS 2017, LNCS 10690, pp. 384–387, 2017.
https://doi.org/10.1007/978-3-319-71027-3_49

term that expands the understanding of player engagement through increased interactability of the news medium.

Ian Bogost's influential positional piece Gamification is Bullshit [4] followed up with an extended analysis in Why gamification is Bullshit [5] in the anthology The Gameful World has strongly influenced many game-scholars definitions and understanding of the word gamification. Deterding takes another approach than Bogost and offers a sociologically influenced reflection on gamification in his article The Ambiguity of Games: Histories and Discourses of a Gameful World [6]. Here Deterding offers the possibility to widen the term and deepen the discussion around the engaging mechanisms of games, without fully dismissing the impact that rewards for players can generate. I find this a fruitful foundation for further exploration.

2.1 Self Determination Theory and Breaking Out of Gamifications Black Box

Deci and Ryan have since their seminal book on the subject in 1985 [7] together, individually, and with other scholars published several papers and books [8, 9] presenting and showing the use of Self Determination Theory. Self Determination Theory (SDT) is a psychological needs fulfillment and motivation theory that is based around the three concepts Competence, Autonomy and Relatedness. "Competence or mastery is our fundamental need to feel effective and successful in the moment-to-moment activities of life... ... Autonomy is our fundamental need to feel volitional in what we do. We want to determine the path we are on and whenever possible have meaningful opportunities from which we can chose freely... ...Relatedness is our fundamental need to feel supported by others." [10, pp. 120–121]

SDT has lately been applied to computer-games by Deci and Rigby in both a journal article [11] and later the book Glued to games [12]. Scott Rigby has also deepened the description of motivation and SDT applied to gamification in the article Gamification and motivation in the anthology The Gameful World [10].

The idea to gamify actions and objects, from saving energy in a home setting [13], to social networking sites for employees [14] has often involved points, badges, achievements. The main problem of these kind of gamifications, besides the fact that the positive effects seem to be very dependent on situation and users [15], is that gamelike reward systems may be added to non-games or other gaming situations not easily identified as traditional games. Games are, of course, comprised of many elements, but at its base, a game may be defined as an activity in itself, a set of actions taken by a player to fulfill a task in a game world. The playing of the game by the rules is a means to the games end. This also holds for analog games. To gamify something that is not a game is splitting this relationship and the "gaming" then becomes the means to reach another end, outside of the game's end. Players get rewarded for striving towards a goal that lies outside of the game. In this case players are actually rewarded for an activity that they would hopefully have engaged in for other reasons than rewards.

According to SDT the above-mentioned forms of gamification is identified as extrinsic rewards/extrinsic motivation, to motivate by giving the user/player a reward that is not well connected to the activity. If we are to use any kind of reward systems or progression enticer for on-line news they should be well connected to the activity of engaging in local news.

Using SDT to Analyze and Change On-Line News? As research has shown, millennials are engaged by news but not from the same news sources as earlier generations [16]. Additionally they do not read the printed newspapers or newspaper web sites. If we study the newspaper or digital versions of today's newspapers compared to digital games from a SDT perspective, we find that there are some interesting differences. When it comes to autonomy, games give players real or illusory freedom to interact with the game world. The highest sense of autonomy is given in "sandbox" type games, like Minecraft [17]. The reading of news is also driven forward by the player/reader and is format dependent. There are differing degrees of interactability between print and digital news formats, where the printed newspaper actually can give a higher degree of interactability than a high number of equally sized linked headlines on 4–5 screens worth of scrolling in the digital format. Without a clear overview and higher degree of interactedness the possibilities for the reader to feel autonomy is limited.

Well-designed games are excellent at letting the player feel competent by introducing new mechanics, abilities or enemies in pedagogical ways, thereby increasing the challenges as players increase their skills. On-line news does not generally adapt to the readers' level of competence or take into account that the readers may become more competent and increase in knowledge with every article they read within a specific subject area. It is a given that on-line games are effective at allowing players to relate to each other and thereby help to forge relationships among players. This aspect of relatedness is, however, poorly developed in current online-news format, where often readers have no sense of whether or not other readers are reading the same article, and where they may, thus, be considered co-participants in the news content.

In all three primary areas of SDT (autonomy, competence and relatedness), games provide a means for fulfilling the needs of its users. The digitalization of news media has not, however, provided the users with the same possibilities. And it is here that-gamification models could be focused and extended. This change could provide a basis to acknowledge the differences and similarities between individual users, and it could provide game-like possibilities regarding choices and paths, challenging the readers competence for news subjects. Significantly, it could also provide a method through dynamic user content creation to support relationships among readers.

This view of gamification opens up for increased interactions where news readers can comment and draw deeper relationships to news-stories with the possibility to offer their personal insights and to create additional content.

3   Status and Next Steps: Case Studies and Halfway Seminar

The theoretical framework laid out in this paper will be used in two case studies to empirically study interaction and engagement with news. The first case to be studied is the ongoing work with the Level Up projects internal prototype for a local news social media platform with the working title nUs. Right now the core of nUs is a news-aggregating mechanic where the user/player acts as editor and promotes stories from regular news sites, but with added comments. The second case is Mobile Stories, a project where the basic idea is to teach schoolchildren (ages 13 and up) about journalism. The core of Mobile Stories is a mobile app that is a learning tool and an editor/publishing platform for news content. The Level Up project is coming up to its halfway point during the autumn 2017 and documentation of the research will be presented late this year taking into account the research I propose for the Doctoral Consortium at ICIDS.

References

1. Bogost, I., Ferrari, S., Schweizer, B.: Newsgames: Journalism at Play. MIT Press, Cambridge (2010). 235 p
2. Foxman, M.: Play the News, fun and games in digital journalism, in A Tow/Knight Report, p. 62. Columbia Journalism School, Tow Center for Digital Journalism (2015)
3. Deterding, S., et al.: Gamification. using game-design elements in non-gaming contexts. In: CHI 2011 Extended Abstracts on Human Factors in Computing Systems, pp. 2425–2428. ACM, Vancouver (2011)
4. Bogost, I.: Gamification is bullshit. The Atlantic (2011)
5. Bogost, I.: Why gamification is bullshit 2. In: The gameful World: Approaches, Issues, Applications, p. 65 (2015)
6. Deterding, S.: The Ambiguity of Games: Histories and Discourses of a Gameful World (2014)
7. Deci, E.L.: Intrinsic motivation and self-determination in human behavior/Edward L. Deci and Richard M. Ryan. In: Ryan, R.M. (ed.) Perspectives in social psychology. Plenum, New York (1985)
8. Ryan, R.M., Deci, E.L.: Intrinsic and extrinsic motivations: Classic definitions and new directions. Contemp. Educ. Psychol. 25(1), 54–67 (2000)
9. Deci, E.L., Ryan, R.M.: Self-determination. Wiley Online Library (2010)
10. Rigby, C.S.: Gamification and motivation 4. In: The gameful World: Approaches, Issues, Applications, p. 113 (2015)
11. Ryan, R.M., Rigby, C.S., Przybylski, A.: The motivational pull of video games: a self-determination theory approach. Motiv. Emot. 30(4), 344–360 (2006)
12. Rigby, S., Ryan, R.M.: Glued to Games: How video games draw us in and hold us spellbound. ABC-CLIO, Santa Barbara (2011)
13. Gustafsson, A., Bång, M., Svahn, M.: Power explorer: a casual game style for encouraging long term behavior change among teenagers. In: Proceedings of the International Conference on Advances in Computer Enterntainment Technology. ACM (2009)
14. Farzan, R., et al.: Results from deploying a participation incentive mechanism within the enterprise. In: Proceedings of the SIGCHI conference on Human factors in computing systems. ACM (2008)
15. Hamari, J., Koivisto, J., Sarsa, H.: Does gamification work? – a literature review of empirical studies on gamification. In: 2014 47th Hawaii International Conference on System Sciences (2014)
16. Poindexter, P.M.: Millennials, News, and Social Media: Is News Engagement a Thing of the Past?. Peter Lang, New York (2012)
17. Mojang: Minecraft. Mojang, Sweden (2009)

Grammar Stories: A Proposal for the Narrativization of Abstract Contents

Serena Zampolli[✉]

Università degli Studi di Genova, Genoa, Italy
serena.zampolli@edu.unige.it

Abstract. This research study revolves around the development of a process to transform abstract concepts into stories. Specifically, it works on the grammar rules of English which prove to be problematic for Italian learners of English as a foreign language. This study argues that content in story-form is better processed by the human brain compared to non-narrative content, and highlights how the discussion on narrativization of abstract content is still open. The proposed process could be the first step towards a new representation of abstract knowledge and possibly towards the automated creation of metaphorical stories.

Keywords: Narrativization · Language learning · Narrative learning · Storytelling

1 Introduction

This research study is being developed at the University of Genoa (Italy), within the PhD program on Digital Humanities. It intertwines storytelling and language teaching, exploring the possibilities offered by visual narratives of facilitating the memorization of English grammar rules.

The target learners are Italian teenagers and adults, who live in their home country and study or practice English as a foreign language [1], therefore relying mostly on explicit memory [2, 3].

Grammar rules are abstract concepts and difficult to be mentally visualized by learners. This might be the reason it seems often difficult for foreign learners to retrieve and apply these pieces of information while talking and even writing [4]. The present study investigates the outcomes of changing the way grammar rules are presented, in order to observe if this betters their retrieval and application.

Extensive study of the literature highlighted the necessity to find a way to help learners to visualize the grammar rules, and the benefit of doing so by means of narrative. Stories are the easiest form for our brain to process information and knowledge, and have always constituted a powerful ally in the delivery of content in education.

This PhD project aims to design a narrativization technique which could help learners retain and apply the rules, until the linguistic process is automatized in the brain and no longer needs memory aids. This study is intended to serve English teachers in their work, as well as adolescent and adult learners of English as a foreign language.

© Springer International Publishing AG 2017
N. Nunes et al. (Eds.): ICIDS 2017, LNCS 10690, pp. 388–391, 2017.
https://doi.org/10.1007/978-3-319-71027-3_50

Once accomplished and widely tested, this technique could also constitute the basis for the creation of automated procedures to narrativize abstract contents.

2   Towards a Meaningful Narrativization of Abstract Contents

Our brain is hardwired to deal with stories [5, 6]. In fact, storytelling has played a crucial role in the development of our species, [7] to the point studies have proved we understand the world around us [8, 9] and organize our memories [10] in story-form.

The grammar rules of a foreign language are abstract information. They are not framed into story-form, but embedded in a web of associations [11]. When a learner of a foreign language does not live in a country where that language is spoken or is not exposed to it consistently, the grammar rule can not be reinforced by usage and its retention in memory relies on the explicit memory. Being not framed into story form, their retention is weaker [12, 13], and without reinforcement is very likely to fade and disappear from memory with time. This might be the reason why learners of a foreign language often seem to not be able to apply rules they know.

Moreover, our brain relies strongly on visuals. A proof of this comes from the world of professional mnemonists, who enhance their memory by using techniques, like the method of *loci*, where they consciously convert information into images. This change of format allows the information to become concrete, and therefore memorable [14].

It seems very appropriate to consider presenting abstract information in story form: not only they become easier for the brain to process, they also have the power to create mental images through words, allowing the transfer of concepts from one mental domain to another. Moreover, sensory details create images that allow trans-domain neural mapping within the mind of the story receiver [7]. This result can be argued to be even more at hand if the story is told not only via words, but using multimedia artifacts, and current technology allows learners to be both viewers and creators of multimedia products such as videos.

For all these reasons, giving abstract information a visual and narrative form seems a profitable way to facilitate their retention. However, despite the consistent amount of research about the advantages of the narrative form, stories are still not used much in education when it comes to the teaching of abstract concepts and a process to narrativize abstract contents effectively is still to be defined.

This PhD dissertation is an attempt in this direction, with a particular interest for educational and cognitive outcomes of the designed process. The research intertwines four main theoretical domains. Each of them is related to all the others, as shown in Fig. 1, where all relations are characterized with their main theoretical reference:

The research methodology mixes literature review with experimentations in schools and in informal learning situations of a proposal to narrativize abstract grammatical contents.

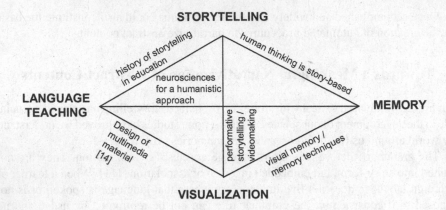

Fig. 1. Theoretical framework model

3   Current Status and Further Steps

At the present time, the theoretical framework has been widely explored and a narrativization procedure has been developed. This is the result of a series of development steps: firstly, a story narrativizing one grammar rule was created and presented in video form; this production was analyzed, schematized and then the process was reapplied to another rule, which highlighted the need to improve the narrativization procedure. Other attempts followed, supported by both experience and an extended study of storytelling techniques [15] and narratology [4], up to reach a form that could be successfully applied to a variety of different grammar rules.

During a first exploratory application in school, the procedure was taught to first year's high school students. They were all able to apply it to English grammar rules and produce visual stories delivering the requested linguistic information. The same laboratory will now be repeated in three other classes, in order to gather data on its replicability and effectivity as learning aid in different educational contexts.

At the same time, an experimentation on adults informally learning English as a foreign language is being conducted: volunteers are showed some videos narrativizing grammar rules, and their appreciation and possible learning gains will be investigated via self-evaluation questionnaires. This experimentation aims to investigate if receiving such stories, rather than creating them as in the school-based experimentations, can also be helpful to understand and memorize abstract concepts.

The narrativization procedure developed focuses on grammar rules, specifically the ones that prove to be difficult for Italian learners [16], but it can constitute a first step towards a meaningful narrativization of abstract contents of other kinds. To this end, it will be necessary to design a step-by-step procedure that can work on diverse types of abstract information. This is why the next step is to test the validity of the proposed procedure extensively and evaluate its impact on learning. Extensive texting, moreover, would offer the opportunity to build a corpus of visual components of different kinds, suitable to embodying linguistic elements. If the process will prove valid to work on grammar rules, its application could be possibly extended and adapted to other knowledge areas dealing with abstraction.

The outcomes of this study, therefore, are expected to constitute a useful starting point towards automating the creation of stories effectively representing abstract concepts.

References

1. Balboni, P.: Le sfide di Babele. Utet, Torino (2002)
2. Solomon, Y., O'Neill, J.: Mathematics and narrative. Lang. Educ. **12**(3), 210–221 (1998)
3. Foer, J.: Moonwalking with Einstein - The Art and Science of Remembering Everything. The Penguin Press, New York (2011)
4. Tornitore, T.: Della Narratologia. Genova University Press, Genova (2014)
5. Schumann, J., Crowell, S., Jones, N., Lee, N., Schucter, S.A., Wood, L.A.: The Neurobiology of Learning: Perspectives from Second Language Acquisition. Lawrence Erlbaum Associates, Mahwah (2004)
6. Plass, J., Kaplan, U.: Emotional design in digital media for learning. In: Tettegah, S., Gartmeier, M. (eds.) Emotions, Technology, Design, and Learning. Elsevier, London, San Diego, Waltham, Oxford (2016)
7. Mandler, J., Johnson, N.: Remembrance of things parsed: story structure and recall. Cogn. Psychol. **9**, 111–151 (1977)
8. Bruner, J.: Acts of Meaning. Harvard University Press, Cambridge (1990)
9. Bruner, J.: Making Stories - Law, Literature, Life. Harvard University Press, Cambridge (2003)
10. Schank, R.: Tell Me a Story - Narrative and Intelligence. Northwestern University Press, Evanston (1990)
11. Carey, B.: How We Learn - The Surprising Truth about When, Where and Why It Happens. Random House, New York (2015)
12. Mandler, J.: Stories, Scripts, and Senses: Aspects of Schema Theory. Lawrence Erlbaum, Hillsdale (1984)
13. Odangiu, F.: The actor in the storytelling school. In: Dramatica - Studia Universitatis Babes-Bolyai. Thematic issue: Narrative Structures in Contemporary Performing Arts, vol. 62, No. LXII, 1 March 2017, pp. 23–34 (2017). http://studia.ubbcluj.ro/download/pdf/1078.pdf
14. Haven, K.: Story Proof - The Science Behind the Startling Power of Story. Libraries Unlimited, Westport (2007)
15. Pinker, S.: How the Mind Works. W.W. Norton & Company Inc., New York (1997)
16. Swan, M., Smith, B. (eds.): Learner English: A Teacher's Guide to Interference and Other Problems. Cambridge Handbooks for Language Teachers. Cambridge University Press, Cambridge (2001)

Workshops

Bringing Together Interactive Digital Storytelling with Tangible Interaction: Challenges and Opportunities

Alejandro Catala[1(✉)], Mariët Theune[1], Cristina Sylla[2], and Pedro Ribeiro[3]

[1] Human Media Interaction, University of Twente, Enschede, The Netherlands
{a.catala,m.theune}@utwente.nl
[2] Center for Child Studies/engageLab, University of Minho, Braga, Portugal
sylla@engagelab.org
[3] Rhine-Waal University of Applied Sciences, Kamp-Lintfort, Germany
Pedro.Ribeiro@hochschule-rhein-waal.de

Abstract. This workshop aims to explore challenges and potential opportunities in bringing interactive digital storytelling into the realm of tangible and embodied interaction. To this end, experts from both fields are invited to present and discuss their ideas. Besides fostering discussion and potential collaborations, the goal is to come up with new and suitable computational storytelling models and define design guidelines/strategies.

Keywords: Storytelling · Tangible interaction · Intelligent systems · Computational models

1 Description of the Workshop

1.1 Background and Goals

The emergence of tangible interaction and physical interfaces as a new interaction paradigm provides rich interactive spaces that are close to our senses and our way to understand the real world. We expect that including tangible or physical affordances in interactive storytelling settings will be commonplace in the future, bringing potential opportunities to improve storytelling tools, as well as the quality of the related user experiences by going more physical. However, using tangible objects for storytelling can be demanding and bring additional research challenges, as such digital/physical tools expand the boundaries of the system beyond the digital space where computations typically take place. For example, while interactive storytelling systems in virtual environments are based on elaborated narrative models that build on artificial intelligence, therefore facilitating the development of more complex story plots, tangible and embodied storytelling systems rely less on computational story modeling, and instead focus primarily on free story creation and play (e.g. [2,4]). We envision that ideally, a system

© Springer International Publishing AG 2017
N. Nunes et al. (Eds.): ICIDS 2017, LNCS 10690, pp. 395–398, 2017.
https://doi.org/10.1007/978-3-319-71027-3_51

should combine the affordances of both modalities, this is, provide physical interaction and a good story. An example is the TOK interface [5], which combines physical elements with story creation. Here, the story world was designed using behaviour trees (BTs) and modelled to bring a certain degree of surprise in the unfolding of the narrative. Another significant research effort combining tangible interfaces with artificial intelligence for producing emergent narratives is shown in [1]. As well, there are examples of systems with pre-scripted narrative such as the work in [3]. However, the development of such systems is challenging, and there are many open questions, such as:

- How can we bring digital interactive storytelling and storytelling with tangible objects together?
- How can we effectively include autonomous and intelligent tangible characters (e.g. small robots or active tangibles) when designing storytelling settings?
- How can we embed computational models (typically working in virtual environments) into tangible interfaces?
- Which are the advantages and current limitations of existing systems?

In order to explore these issues, our community needs to reflect on the implications of embedding tangible elements in storytelling systems and discuss how to combine tangible interfaces with narrative models and computational intelligence. With this goal in mind, this workshop aims at getting deeper insights in the field by bringing together experienced researchers and practitioners from the tangible and embodied interaction fields, and digital interactive storytelling communities, to share experiences and foster discussion on these topics. Further, the expected outcome is that this workshop contributes to start possible research collaborations, which lead to new computational storytelling models specifically focusing on tangible and embodied interaction, and design guidelines and/or strategies. Joint publications reporting the cluster discussions will be sought and encouraged.

1.2 Call for Participation

Participants are encouraged to share their experiences and vision on bringing digital interactive storytelling and tangible storytelling together by submitting a short informal position paper (1–3 pages in the Springer LNCS format).

Topics of special interest that would positively feed the development of the workshop are, for example:

- Tangible interaction and interfaces for storytelling systems
- Storytelling with intelligent embodied characters (e.g. robots, hybrid agents, etc.)
- Tangible autonomous characters
- Computational intelligence applied to storytelling with physical interfaces
- Other forms of relevant and novel tangible expression for interactive storytelling

Prospective participants interested in presenting a contribution are expected to fill in a participation form and submit an abstract and a position paper.

IMPORTANT DATES:

- September, 20th: abstract submission (1/2 page; max. 500 words)
- September, 28th: notification of abstract acceptance
- October, 15th: submission of position papers (1–3 pages in the Springer LNCS format)

The submission process will be managed through the workshop's website (https://www.utwente.nl/ewi/hmi/cobotnity/icids2017tangibleworkshop/). Accepted papers will be made available internally to all the participants before the workshop in order to prepare the joint sessions effectively. Possibilities for a prospective publication as an outcome of the workshop contributions will be announced in the workshop. In particular, we plan to call for extended papers to be published in a special issue or a post-proceedings publication.

1.3   Format and Schedule

The contributions will be presented during the workshop, in the form of a short talk, an interactive demo, or a video showcasing some prototype. The participants can choose the format that best suits their contribution/material, although the last two types are encouraged. The aim of having the presentations is twofold: help to identify primary challenges, opportunities, constraints and limitations; and serve as input for a discussion and design session in which participants will collaborate in small groups or clusters. We expect to gather a maximum of 15 participants, which would lead to 3–4 design clusters groups. In the design session, the clusters are expected to pick a challenge and specific constraints (e.g. domain, target users, technology limitations...), identify limitations and opportunities, and work together to propose a design of a storytelling prototype that would allow to start exploring or addressing current limitations. Finally, the clusters will share their results and a joint discussion will be carried out in order to define design guidelines/strategies and decide on specific actions to consolidate future collaborations.

The workshop will (tentatively) be scheduled as follows:

13.30–15.00 Introduction, Talks/Demos
15.00–15.15 Break
15.15–16.10 Cluster work
16.10–17.00 Sharing, Joint Discussion and Conclusion

1.4   Equipment and Resources

The additional materials needed are a projector, a projection screen, tables that can be re-arranged according to the number of participants, and paper sheets and pens to boost design discussions. Depending on the nature of some demos, some wall power supplies may be needed to connect laptops or similar devices.

2   Organizers

The organizers have together a mixed background on diverse areas such as interactive storytelling, virtual actors/characters, virtual agents, tangible and embodied interaction, human computer-interaction, artificial intelligence and computational linguistics. Such combination is beneficial to ensure that different perspectives are present in the design sessions during the workshop.

Alejandro Catala (a.catala@utwente.nl), Human Media Interaction, University of Twente, The Netherlands

.   Mariët Theune (m.theune@utwente.nl), Human Media Interaction, University of Twente, The Netherlands

Cristina Sylla (sylla@engagelab.org), Center for Child Studies/engageLab, University of Minho, Portugal

Pedro   Ribeiro   (Pedro.Ribeiro@hochschule-rhein-waal.de),   Rhine-Waal University of Applied Sciences, Germany

You can address your questions and your interest in participating to Alejandro Catala by email.

Acknowledgments. Alejandro Catala has received funding support from the European Union's Horizon 2020 research and innovation programme under the Marie Sklodowska-Curie grant agreement No 701991. Cristina Sylla has been financed by the Human Potential Operating Programme (HPOP) of the European Social Fund, and the Portuguese Ministry for Science, Technology and Higher Education (MCTES) Postdoctoral Grant SFRH/BPD/111891/2015.

References

1. Alofs, T., Theune, M., Swartjes, I.: A tabletop interactive storytelling system: designing for social interaction. Int. J. Arts Technol. **8**(3), 188–211 (2015)
2. Catala, A., Theune, M., Reidsma, D., ter Stal, S., Heylen, D.: Exploring childrens use of a remotely controlled surfacebot character for storytelling. In: 9th International Conference on Intelligent Technologies for Interactive Entertainment, INTETAIN 2017, 10 pages (2017)
3. Leite, I., McCoy, M., Lohani, M., Ullman, D., Salomons, D., Stokes, C., Rivers, S., Scassellati, B.: Emotional storytelling in the classroom: individual versus group interaction between children and robots. In: Proceedings of the Tenth Annual ACM/IEEE International Conference on Human-Robot Interaction (HRI 2015), pp. 75–82 (2015)
4. Ribeiro, P., Iurgel, I., Ferreira, M.: Voodoo: a system that allows children to create animated stories with action figures as interface. In: Si, M., Thue, D., André, E., Lester, J.C., Tanenbaum, J., Zammitto, V. (eds.) ICIDS 2011. LNCS, vol. 7069, pp. 354–357. Springer, Heidelberg (2011). https://doi.org/10.1007/978-3-642-25289-1_47
5. Sylla, C., Coutinho, C., Branco, P.: A digital manipulative for embodied "stage-narrative" creation. Entertain. Comput. **5**(4), 495–507 (2014)

Film-Live

An Innovative Immersive and Interactive Cinema Experience

Mattia Costa[1], Chiara Ligi[1,2], and Francesca Piredda[3(✉)]

[1] Film-Live Association, Milan, Italy
mattiacosta@hotmail.it, chiara.ligi@gmail.com
[2] Design School, Politecnico di Milano, Milan, Italy
[3] Design Department, Politecnico di Milano, Milan, Italy
francesca.piredda@polimi.it

Abstract. This full-day workshop introduces to Film-Live, an innovative and immersive cinema experience, which transforms the act of watching films into a participatory, interactive and engaging event. Film-Live is a film shot and broadcasted live that ends out of the screen: spectators of Film-Live are able to personally interact with the story, entering and exploring the narration by breaking the fourth wall. Working with both professionals and academics, participants will be able to experiment with live cinematography experience and create a short Film-Live, a choral work, which will be filmed, streamed and projected live. The main goal of the workshop is the investigation and discussion of possible applications of the Film-Live format, enhancing expressive and narrative interactions between film and reality, in order to actively engage with the audience.

Keywords: Live cinema · Audience engagement · Film research · Media design

1 Introduction

Film-Live is a film shot and screened at the same time, realized with the sequence shot technique [1]. It is an immersive and engaging new kind of cinema experience: the audience has the outstanding chance to watch a film shot in real-time, in front of his eyes, and to enter the narration by physically breaking the fourth wall, eventually discovering that the detachment between reality and fiction is abolished. Due to the possibility of crossing the boundaries of the set, the spectator can personally interact with the elements of the story (the characters, the objects, and the location) and physically explore the imagery of the narration. In fact, as soon as the camera enters the same space where the screening of the Film-Live is in progress, the boundary between fiction and reality fades away, and the film itself becomes reality. The spectator can enter the real places, used as movie sets, which are still vibrant with the ongoing action out of the screen.

2   Description

The workshop aims to explore further Film-Live exploiting potentialities and limits of live filming, investigating and discussing on possible expressive and dramatic interactions between film and reality, in order to engage with the audience.

Film-Live is an inter-disciplinary language, which connects cinema, artistic research, theatre, live music, live recording, live streaming and happening. It strongly ties in with the surrounding space. Film-Live stresses the ambiguity of the spectator's perceptions and transforms him in an active participant. It generally consists of two moments: the projection of the film shot in real time and its continuation beyond the screen. The relationship between these two phases implies that the participant - no more simply a spectator - can experience first-hand the complexity of reality: operating a radical change of perspective, he can define the final meaning of the narration, living, interpreting and transforming the film into something "real".

On one hand, Film-Live represents an innovative format capable of generating a strong impact on the audience; on the other hand, a further value is added: as a language and trans-disciplinary method, Film-Live can in fact combine art worlds (Cinema, live music, live broadcast, theatre) with those of academic research, with significant impact on the education field.

In this perspective, Film-Live can be proposed as:

(1) a possible tool for research methodologies, in tune with contemporary experiences that include digital technology and "live", in particular. Media are often designed to explore issues of scientific relevance in a different way to the traditional methods of observing, collecting, reading and disseminating data. Film-Live can be included among the "inventive methods" described by Celia Lury and Nina Wakeford [2] as far as it can be used in multiple contexts and continuously introduced into new scenarios, expanding the "real" and grasping the "excess".

(2) A vehicle for communicating to both qualified and non-qualified audience the results of academic research, towards the democratization of knowledge, and the dissemination of academic and artistic practice, with obvious training potential.

In other words, Film-Live can become a tool for cultural participation, a dynamic product that can be used extensively outside the academic environment, useful in helping to understand the countless "stories" that happen in an complex era such as the one we are living in.

As a final remark, we can consider then Film-Live as a *media of attraction* [3] as far as it is at the same time *interdisciplinary*, as it combines together cinema, live music, live broadcast, theatre in a multichannel performance; *participatory*, as the audience has an active role especially in the second part of the experience; *seamed*, as Film-Live is based on improvisation both in terms of the acting performance and the music/sound live playing; *rough*, as it is filmed live all the special effects and the film's tricks or *truka* are made in a traditional cinematic way using the elements of the mise-en-scène; *unassimilated* by the cinema system and out of the distribution system.

The workshop is aimed at introducing to Film-Live format and experimenting live cinematography as a choral work filmed, projected and streamed live.

Participants will be able to experience this innovative cinematographic experience that provides to the audience the magic of cinema together with the emotions of the live streaming, enhancing the complexity of reality.

3   Goals and Expected Outcomes

We will work with both professionals and academics, in order to explore further the potentialities of Film-Live language and practice. We will develop live cinematic narratives where a unique point of view is guiding the narrative experience; we will stream live the narratives on web or social media, calling the online community to interact and guide the ongoing action. The specific goals are: offering a Film-Live experience to the international community and collecting feedbacks from participants about the Film-Live as language, as format, as practice; stressing the live dimension of the narratives; stressing the live interaction with both the audience in presence and the online community.

Expected outcomes of the workshop can be considered from three main perspectives: from the point of view of the content, the output is identified in a Film-Live streaming on social media (Film-Live Facebook fanpage plus participants' personal profiles). From the point of view of the method, we expect that we can implement and discuss a design process for the creation of Film-Live, as part of our research in the field of audiovisual storytelling and media design. Furthermore, an expected outcome is to develop a small network of people interested in this field of inquiry, providing feedbacks and exchanging skills and knowledge about new forms of interactive storytelling.

4   Program

Origins and codes of Film-Live (2 h) - Brief introduction to Film-Live language: definition and specificity, cinematographic and aesthetic references, expressive and production potentialities. Focus on its possible uses in the field of entertainment, promotion, research and training/education.

Topic/subject definition and experiment building (2 h) - Introduction to the topic chosen for the workshop and definition of the subject on which the Film-Live experiment will be developed.

Contents: Identification of the subject, definition of the narrative, subdivision of the participants into working groups.

Narration: Subject development and spatial narration development, definition of the climax (fiction/reality intersections).

Direction and cinematography: Study of the space and first approach to camera movements, brief introduction to photography, lights, and lighting atmosphere.

Live mise-en-scène and shooting (2/3 h) - Staging rehearsal and camera movements' tests. Shooting and live streaming. Participants in the workshop will be able to experience the live mise-en-scène, the sequence shot technique and the live direction.

Feedbacks and conclusions (1 h) - Sharing feedbacks about Film-Live and the workshop.

Participants are asked to use their own mobile devices.

References

1. Costa M.: Unicità spazio-temporale e risorgenza del reale nel Film-Live, bachelor degree thesis, supervisors: Longari, E., Rosa, P. Accademia di Belle Arti di Brera, Milan (2010). http://www.film-live.org
2. Lury, C., Wakeford, N. (eds.): Inventive Methods: The Happening of the Social. Routledge, New York (2012)
3. Rouse, R.: Media of attraction: a media archeology approach to panoramas, kinematography, mixed reality and beyond. In: Nack, F., Gordon, A.S. (eds.) ICIDS 2016. LNCS, vol. 10045, pp. 97–107. Springer, Cham (2016). https://doi.org/10.1007/978-3-319-48279-8_9

Workshop Transmedia Journalism and Interactive Documentary in Dialogue

Renira Rampazzo Gambarato[1](✉) [iD] and Alessandro Nani[2] [iD]

[1] National University Higher School of Economics, Moscow, Russia
rgambarato@hse.ru
[2] Tallinn University, Tallinn, Estonia
alessandro.nani@tlu.ee

Abstract. This half-day workshop promotes a hands-on approach to recent developments in transmedia storytelling and its application to journalism and interactive documentary (iDoc). Transmedia journalism, as well as any other application of transmedia storytelling in fictional and nonfictional realms, is characterized by the involvement of (a) multiple media platforms; (b) content expansion; and (c) audience engagement. The premise of iDocs is the active flow of information. With the support of digital technologies, iDocs presuppose that the user must be able to (physically) do something, which implies the audience can form its own storyline by choosing the path to experience the story, watching a video, seeing a photo, etc. The workshop starts with an introduction to the primordial role of transmedia audiences, the relationship between transmedia journalism and iDocs, and cases studies that illustrate the theory. The participants, organized in groups, work together to experience how to transform a single news story into a transmedia project.

Keywords: Audience engagement · Digital technologies · Interactive documentary · Transmedia journalism · Transmedia storytelling

1 Topic and Goal

This half-day workshop promotes a hands-on approach to recent developments in transmedia storytelling and its application to journalism and interactive documentary (iDoc). Transmedia journalism, as well as any other application of transmedia storytelling in fictional and nonfictional realms, is characterized by the involvement of (a) multiple media platforms; (b) content expansion; and (c) audience engagement. Transmedia journalism can take advantage of different media platforms such as television, radio, print media, and, above all, the Internet and mobile media to tell deeper stories. The content expansion, opposed to the repetition of the same message across multiple platforms, is the essence of transmedia storytelling and, therefore, should be the focal point of transmedia journalism as well. The enrichment of the narrative is facilitated by the extended content. Audience engagement involves mechanisms of interactivity, such as the selection of the elements to be explored, the option to read a text, watch a video, enlarge photographs, access maps, click in hyperlinks, and share information through social networks. Moreover, audience engagement deals with participation via, for instance, remixing content and creating original user-generated content. The premise of iDocs is the active flow of information. With the

© Springer International Publishing AG 2017
N. Nunes et al. (Eds.): ICIDS 2017, LNCS 10690, pp. 403–404, 2017.
https://doi.org/10.1007/978-3-319-71027-3_53

support of digital technologies, iDocs presuppose that the user must be able to (physically) do something, which implies the audience can form its own storyline by choosing the path to experience the story, watching a video, seeing a photo etc. The transmedial environment is ideal for developing iDocs in the sense that it integrates various levels of the storyworld, engage the audience, and takes advantage of digital tools to do so. The workshop starts with an introduction to the primordial role of transmedia audiences, the relationship between transmedia journalism and iDocs, and cases studies that illustrate the theory. The participants, organized in groups, work together to experience how to transform a single news story into a transmedia project. Therefore, the goal is to give the participants a hands-on opportunity to apply transmedia tools to transform a single news story into a transmedia experience.

2 Outcomes

(a) Theoretical knowledge regarding recent developments in transmedia storytelling and its application to journalism and interactive documentary (iDoc).
(b) Practical exercise applying transmedia tools to transform a single news story into a transmedia project.

3 Format

09:00–09:45 = Transmedia Storytelling: Audiences, Interaction and Participation
09:45–10:30 = Transmedia Journalism and its Relation to Interactive Documentary
10:30–10:45 = Coffee Break
10:45–12:00 = Practical exercise

4 Equipment

For organizers: Projector, loudspeaker, Internet access, white board, marker. For participants: Laptops or tablets.

5 Number of Participants

Maximum number of participants is 20.

6 Call for Participation

This half-day workshop promotes a hands-on approach to the emerging field of transmedia journalism and its relations to interactive documentary. We will discuss the conceptualization of transmedia journalism, interactive documentary, and transmedia audiences. Case studies will illustrate the discussion and pave the way to a practical exercise on how to transform a single news story into a transmedia project.

Authoring for Interactive Storytelling Workshop

Charlie Hargood[1]([✉]), Alex Mitchell[2], David E. Millard[3], and Ulrike Spierling[4]

[1] Bournemouth University, Poole, UK
chargood@bournemouth.ac.uk
[2] National University of Singapore, Singapore, Singapore
alexm@nus.edu.sg
[3] University of Southampton, Southampton, UK
dem@ecs.soton.ac.uk
[4] RheinMain University of Applied Sciences, Wiesbaden, Germany
ulrike.spierling@hs-rm.de

Abstract. One of the most significant challenges facing narrative systems research is the authoring of interactive storytelling, and the processes and technology to support it. In this workshop we propose to host a discussion and presented new work in this space from researchers in creative and technical domains from both the Hypertext and Interactive Storytelling communities.

1 Topic, Goals, and Expected Outcomes

The authoring of interactive storytelling, and the processes and technology to support it, remains one of the most significant challenges facing narrative systems research. This workshop aims to bring together creatives, technologists, and associated researchers in a collective meeting to share research and advances in this space. Relevant work includes authoring tools, methodologies for authorship, frameworks and technology for assisting writers, and experimental paradigms of interactive storytelling creation such as locative storytelling and AR narrative.

The workshop aims to:

- Create a meeting venue for active researchers in this area to come together and share their work
- Foster a community around this work, as a step towards future collaboration
- Identify substantial challenges in this area that may be collectively targeted going forward
- Provide a venue for publication of early work in this space

As well as the above aims, this workshop also aims to bridge the gap within the narrative systems research community between the interactive storytelling community (whose natural venue is ICIDS) and the Hypertext Narrative community (whose natural venue is ACM Hypertext). Both communities have been exploring interactive storytelling authorship in recent years, and it is our hope that a workshop organised by researchers from both communities can provide

© Springer International Publishing AG 2017
N. Nunes et al. (Eds.): ICIDS 2017, LNCS 10690, pp. 405–408, 2017.
https://doi.org/10.1007/978-3-319-71027-3_54

a focal point for dialogue and collaboration. Two of the organisers have run several workshops, both separately (Spierling at ICIDS 2008, 2009 and 2010) and together (Mitchell and Spierling at ICIDS 2014 and 2016) on similar topics. Similarly, the other two organizers (Hargood and Millard) have run a successful narrative systems workshop series at ACM Hypertext since 2011[1]. The proposed workshop aims to form the basis of a workshop series, following on from the earlier ICIDS workshops, acting as a sister workshop series to the NHT workshop series and potentially forming a connection between the two communities. This would be a notable outcome, and may in future lead to a special issue journal publication fed by contributions from both workshops.

2   Format and Proposed Schedule

Our proposal is for a **Half Day** workshop.

We propose a mixture of a structured paper session and a less structured "unconference" session. Paper sessions provide an opportunity for young researchers to publish their early work and for early position papers on new ideas from more established researchers for work that is not yet ready or mature enough for the main conference. The purpose of these works is to gather community feedback on early progress, and stimulate discussion with new ideas in the area. An "unconference" can be defined as: "a meeting for which the agenda is defined by the attendees at the start of the meeting". In this case a series of proposed discussions, activities, and meetings will be gathered over the day and this will be formed into plenary discussions and/or spin out meetings in the unconference session. This gives attendees an opportunity to have more specific meetings on targeted areas and to use the workshop as a platform to host collaborations and conversations inspired by the earlier part of the workshop. The organisers have been using this format of formal presentation followed by unconference in a similar workshop series (NHT) with repeated success.

A draft schedule for the workshop is as follows:

Time	Session
12.00–13.00	Lunch
13.00–13.15	Welcome
13.15–14.30	Presentation session
14.30–15.00	Coffee
15.00–17.00	Unconference
17.00–17.15	Conclusions and close

Other than seating, tables, projector, and white board, no special equipment or resources are needed for this workshop.

---

[1] http://nht.ecs.soton.ac.uk.

3   Call for Participation (Draft)

Authoring for Interactive Storytelling 2017 (AIS'17)

A Workshop @ ICIDS'17 in Madeira, 14th Nov 2017

This call for participation is seeking submitted papers and attendance at the Authoring for Interactive Storytelling workshop held at ICIDS 2017 in Madeira. This workshop seeks to provide a venue for researchers in the area of interactive digital narrative authoring and narrative systems to share early work, new ideas, and identify challenges facing the field, with a view to fostering collaboration and the formation of a coherent research community in this space.

This workshop will provide structured paper presentations and unstructured "unconference" sessions, the content of which will be dictated by the workshop attendees during the workshop session itself. Papers submitted to this workshop should be 3–6 pages long, and in Springer LNCS format. Papers will be peer reviewed, and successful submissions will presented at the workshop. There is also the potential that papers accepted to the workshop will be published as part of the workshop proceedings. Submissions should be sent to chargood@bournemouth.ac.uk by midnight on 15th September. Topics relevant to this workshop include:

- Authoring tools
- Frameworks for interactive digital narrative authoring
- Digital writing methodologies
- Co-Design of interactive digital narrative
- Locative and in-situ authoring
- Experimental digital writing paradigms
- New media creation and production
- Assisting technology for writers

Key Dates:

- Submissions due: 15th September
- Notification due: 29th September
- Workshop: 14th November 2017

Organisers:

- Charlie Hargood - chargood@bournemouth.ac.uk
- Alex Mitchell - alexm@nus.edu.sg
- David Millard - dem@ecs.soton.ac.uk
- Ulrike Spierling - ulrike.spierling@hs-rm.de

4   Participants

Our participants will most likely come from the following groups:

- PhD Students and Early Career Researchers presenting their work on inter-active digital narrative authoring
- Academics, Researchers, Writers, and members of the creative industries interested in interactive digital narrative authoring

We expect a maximum of 40 attendees, with a likely attendance of approximately 15–25. This is based on the organisers' experience of running similar workshops such as NHT and the earlier ICIDS workshops.

5   Organising Committee

5.1   Organisers

This workshop's organisers are academics from the wider interactive storytelling and narrative systems community. All have experience in running academic workshops (Hargood and Millard have run NHT since 2011, and Mitchell and Spierling have run previous versions of ICIDS authoring workshops in 2008, 2009, 2010, 2014 and 2016).

- Charlie Hargood - Bournemouth University - chargood@bournemouth.ac.uk
- Alex Mitchell - National University of Singapore - alexm@nus.edu.sg
- David Millard - University of Southampton - dem@ecs.soton.ac.uk
- Ulrike Spierling - Hochschule RheinMain, University of Applied Sciences - ulrike.spierling@hs-rm.de

5.2   Potential Programme Committee

The following represents a likely programme committee in addition to the organisers (though not yet confirmed/consulted).

- Mark Bernstein - Eastgate Systems
- Fred Charles - Bournemouth University
- Rosamund Davies - Greenwich University
- Mads Haahr - Trinity College Dublin
- Ido Iurgel - Rhine-Waal University of Applied Sciences
- Stacey Mason - UCSC
- Valentina Nisi - Madeira Interactive Technologies Institute
- Nicolas Szilas - TECFA, University of Geneva
- Mark Weal - University of Southampton

1st Workshop on the History of Expressive Systems

James Ryan[1](✉) and Mark J. Nelson[2](✉)

[1] Expressive Intelligence Studio, University of California, Santa Cruz, USA
jor@soe.ucsc.edu
[2] The MetaMakers Institute, Falmouth University, Falmouth, UK
mjn@anadrome.org

Abstract. The first meeting of a new workshop series on the History of Expressive Systems (HEX) is being held at ICIDS 2017. By 'expressive systems', we broadly mean computer systems (or predigital procedural methods) that were developed with expressive or creative aims. HEX is meant to illuminate and celebrate the history of systems in this area, especially the untold histories of projects that are today forgotten or relatively unknown.

1 Overview: Topic and Goals

The first meeting of a new workshop series on the History of Expressive Systems (HEX) is being held at ICIDS 2017. By 'expressive systems', we broadly mean computer systems (or predigital procedural methods) that were developed with expressive or creative aims; this is meant to be a superset of the areas called creative AI, expressive AI, videogame AI, computational creativity, interactive storytelling, computational narrative, procedural music, computer poetry, generative art, and more. While much of this purview intersects with projects in artificial intelligence, we are more broadly interested in procedural methods of all kinds (even predigital ones, as mentioned above).

HEX is meant to illuminate and celebrate the *history* of systems in this area, especially the untold histories of projects that are today forgotten or relatively unknown. Most historical overviews of expressive systems in the literature today are confined to short blurbs in related-works sections, and upon further investigation these brief histories are often at best incomplete. For example, most accounts of the history of story generation cite Sheldon Klein's automatic novel writer [2] as the earliest known system (*e.g.*, [1,6]), but in a recent paper undertaking the HEX initiative we have demonstrated that three other forgotten systems preceded Klein's [3].

Why should we care about old, forgotten work? If we view expressive systems as a vast design space, we can think of each implemented system as an exploratory vessel that ventures into a previously uncharted sector. If these exploratory missions are successful, they signal directions that future systems may move further into to find greater success. When success is not had, the failed projects tell us which

© Springer International Publishing AG 2017
N. Nunes et al. (Eds.): ICIDS 2017, LNCS 10690, pp. 409–412, 2017.
https://doi.org/10.1007/978-3-319-71027-3_55

areas to avoid. In this way, we learn about spaces that incrementalist research may push further into, dead sectors that we should not return to, and all the other still uncharted areas that we do not know much about at all. Thus, both good and bad systems generate new knowledge that is useful to contemporary and future practitioners. But when we forget about past systems—novel explorations in design space—we lose the knowledge that was generated by those systems: we forget what has been explored and what has not, and which areas are worth exploring further. In our own historical research, we have discovered systems whose forgotten methods were considered novel when later systems unknowingly reimplemented them decades later.

Beyond these fundamental practical reasons lies the more simple goal of recording an accurate historical record, which encompasses not just a series of names and dates, or a series of system architectures, but also intellectual through lines that trace our fields' histories. Expressive systems are often developed in applied technical areas, but all human endeavor, especially in the area of research, has intellectual underpinnings and emerges out of intellectual contexts. Even in technical areas, there is a history of ideas that undergirds the evolution of systems over time. Returning to practical concerns, good ideas for systems can lead to bad implementations of them, and so we should track ideas too so that we might have another stab at carrying them out well.

Since historical work on expressive systems is important, as we have argued, and since there is little work in this area being done, as we have indicated, we aim to introduce HEX as not just a workshop, but also a new community to provide a home for the first foundational work on the history of this area. In tandem with the first meeting of this workshop, we will also be launching a new repository for historically important expressive systems. This online resource will compile metadata, papers, media coverage, and code listings for historical expressive systems, with a call to action to contemporary researchers and practitioners to reimplement or rationally reconstruct the systems.

Moving forward, we plan to hold HEX at conferences in a variety of fields, with the particular kinds of expressive systems that are of primary interest corresponding to the purview of the host conference. As such, for the first HEX workshop we will emphasize systems related to interactive storytelling and adjacent areas, including story generation, computational narratology, expressive text generation, and so forth.

2 Format and Schedule

The first HEX meeting will be a half-day workshop consisting of talks based on submitted papers or abstracts. One of these talks may be an invited keynote presentation from an author of a historically important expressive system, who will give a personal/oral account of its development and intellectual/institutional context. We expect between 10 and 20 total participants.

3   Expected Outcomes

We will reiterate the following expected outcomes alluded to above:

- Bring together for the first time a community of researchers and practitioners who are interested in the history of expressive systems. Relatedly, we seek to establish a venue that solicits this kind of work and legitimizes it as a full-fledged research area in our larger field.
- Identify overlooked systems not currently included in the historical canon. A result of such identification could be an initial set of system entries in the forthcoming HEX repository (mentioned above) and an expansive list of promising research topics that could be presented at a future HEX meeting (or related venues).
- Present draft histories for feedback in advance of later publication (in a special issue of a journal, or in a workshop proceedings published on the forthcoming HEX website).
- Increase familiarity with historically used techniques and their successes/failures, with an eye towards updating implementations or reimplementing them, and using that historical knowledge to inform current designs (or analyses of current designs and/or their provenances).

4   Call for Papers

We invite researchers interested in the history of expressive systems to participate in the first Workshop on the History of Expressive Systems (HEX1), to be held at ICIDS 2017 in beautiful Funchal, Madeira, on November 14, 2017.[1] The purpose of this workshop is to improve the historical understanding of our field, both to ensure an accurate historical record for its own sake, but also to bring the history 'into the present' by understanding lines of research and their implications for current work in this rapidly expanding area.

By 'expressive systems', we broadly mean computer systems (or predigital procedural methods) that were developed with expressive or creative aims; this is meant to be a superset of the areas called creative AI, expressive AI, videogame AI, computational creativity, interactive storytelling, computational narrative, procedural music, computer poetry, generative art, and more.

4.1   Scope

For this first iteration of the workshop held at ICIDS, we prefer a focus on systems within the usual scope of ICIDS, i.e. historical computational narrative systems, videogame narrative, story generation, expressive natural language generation, text bots, e-literature, story understanding, computational narratology, etc. Additionally, histories of the field itself (or specific eras, approaches, etc.) would be a great fit for HEX.

---

[1] Here, we reproduce our call for papers, as distributed prior to the workshop.

Here are some examples of potential contributions:

- Portraits of forgotten or relatively unknown expressive systems.
- Histories of specific research labs, such as the Yale AI Project led by Roger Schank in the 1970s.
- Overviews of the careers of unheralded researchers or practitioners, especially those from groups not well represented in the standard histories of the field.
- Reimplementations of early expressive systems, such as Montfort's reimplementation of Strachey's 1952 love-letter generator.[2]
- Rational reconstructions of expressive systems, such as *Skald* [5] or *Wide Ruled* [4].
- Reappraisals of conventionally disregarded systems, such as Wardrip-Fruin's extensive overview of TALE-SPIN's underlying processes [6].
- Reframings of known historical systems as expressive systems, or specifically as narrative systems—for example, mainframe war simulations of the 1950s.
- Discussion of obscure computer games as early examples of interactive storytelling, such as Don Daglow's 1973 *Star Trek* game that extensively featured character dialogue.[3]
- Bringing history into the present: borrowing old techniques for new settings and architectures.
- Bringing the present into history: applying new techniques to old settings and architectures.
- Many more. Not sure if your project is a good fit? Reach out and ask us!

References

1. Gervas, P.: Computational approaches to storytelling and creativity. AI Mag. **30**(3), 49 (2009)
2. Klein, S., et al.: A program for generating reports on the status and history of stochastically modifiable semantic models of arbitrary universes. University of Wisconsin Technical report TR142 (1971)
3. Ryan, J.: Grimes' fairy tales: a 1960s story generator. In: Proceedings of the International Conference on Interactive Digital Storytelling (2017)
4. Skorupski, J., Jayapalan, L., Marquez, S., Mateas, M.: Wide ruled: a friendly interface to author-goal based story generation. In: Cavazza, M., Donikian, S. (eds.) ICVS 2007. LNCS, vol. 4871, pp. 26–37. Springer, Heidelberg (2007). https://doi.org/10.1007/978-3-540-77039-8_3
5. Tearse, B., Mawhorter, P., Mateas, M., Wardrip-Fruin, N.: Skald: minstrel reconstructed. IEEE Trans. Comput. Intell. AI Games **6**(2), 156–165 (2014)
6. Wardrip-Fruin, N.: Expressive Processing: Digital Fictions, Computer Games, and Software Studies. MIT Press, Cambridge (2009)

---

[2] https://nickm.com/memslam/love_letters.html.
[3] https://en.wikipedia.org/wiki/Star_Trek_(script_game).

Author Index

Agotai, Doris 327
Ang, Dennis 336
Antonopoulou, Caterina 261
Arisona, Stefan 327
Armstrong, Justin 319
Arndt, Sebastian 265

Bakk, Ágnes Karolina 343
Bakker, René 3
Bala, Paulo 270
Barba, Evan 245
Bellassai, Jenna 12
Björnsson, Magnús Vilhelm 313
Bruni, Luis Emilio 193

Callahan, Kelly 278
Campos, Ioli 347
Carstensdottir, Elin 274
Carvalhais, Miguel 299, 376
Catala, Alejandro 395
Cesário, Vanessa 163, 351
Christensen, Daniel Svejstrup 193
Christman, Grant P. 278
Clark, Lynda 355
Coelho, António 351
Connolly, Olivia 12
Correia, Nuno 359
Costa, Mattia 399
Cychosz, Margaret 12

Daiute, Colette 282
Damiano, Rossana 206
Dionisio, Mara 359
Doyle, Phillip 363
Dubbelman, Teun 286, 295
Duncan, Robert O. 282
Dy, Aakov 290

Eiríksson, Kári 313
Ervik, Martin 265

Ferreira, Maria José 181, 367
Fisher, Joshua A. 233

Flores, Luis 75
Forrester, Ian 323
Frew, Anna 323

Gambarato, Renira Rampazzo 403
Gifreu-Castells, Arnau 303
Gordon, Andrew S. 12
Guðmundsson, Tryggvi Þór 313

Hales, Chris 117
Hargood, Charlie 63, 405
Howard, Yvonne 63

Iurgel, Ido 3

Jakobsen, Mette 193

Kahl, Timo 3
Kampa, Antonia 372
Kim, Yusin 290
Kleinman, Erica 274
Knoller, Noam 295
Koebel, Kathrin 327
Koenitz, Hartmut 221, 295
Kristjánsson, Guðni Fannar 313
Kybartas, Ben 332

Lessard, Jonathan 332
Ligi, Chiara 399
Lombardo, Vincenzo 206
Lugthart, Sarah 38

Martinho, Carlos 181
Massarczyk, Erik 49
Matos, Sónia 163
Melo, Francisco 367
Millard, David E. 63, 150, 405
Mitchell, Alex 137, 336, 405
Monteiro, Juliana 299, 376
Morais, Carla 299, 376
Moreno, Valentina 303

Nanì, Alessandro 403
Nelson, Mark J. 104, 409

Nisi, Valentina   163, 270, 351, 359, 367
Nunes, Nuno   270

Oberli, Matthias   327
Odimegwu, Obiageli   12
Olsen, David   104
Ong, Ethel   290

Packer, Heather S.   63
Paiva, Ana   181, 367
Papadopoulos, Petros   63
Paradeda, Raul   181
Perkis, Andrew   265
Piredda, Francesca   399
Pizzo, Antonio   206

Quispel, Annemarie   38

Radeta, Marko   163
Ramos, Michael Joshua   290
Reyes, María Cecilia   380
Ribeiro, Pedro   395
Roemmele, Melissa   12
Roth, Christian   221, 295
Rouse, Rebecca   245
Ryan, James   89, 409

Schiffel, Stephan   313
Schrager, Sheree M.   278

Seif El-Nasr, Magy   274
Sim, Yuin Theng   137
Spawforth, Callum   150
Spierling, Ulrike   49, 405
Sumi, Kaoru   308
Svensson, Torbjörn   384
Sylla, Cristina   395

Thattai, Prashanth   336
Theune, Mariët   395
Thue, David   75, 313

van Dartel, Michel   38
van Turnhout, Koen   3
Verbrugge, Clark   332
Vosmeer, Mirjam   221

Winzer, Peter   49
Wood, Hannah   24
Wyse, Lonce   336

Yahata, Nozomu   308
Yew, Jude   336
Yu Galan, Stanley   290

Zampolli, Serena   126, 388
Zimmer, Frank   3

Printed in the United States
By Bookmasters